Economic Anthropology

Economic Anthropology

Edited, with an Introduction, by

STUART PLATTNER

STANFORD UNIVERSITY PRESS
Stanford, California

Stanford University Press
Stanford, California
© 1989 by the Board of Trustees of the
Leland Stanford Junior University
Printed in the United States of America
Original printing 1989
Last figure below indicates date of this printing:
06 05 04 03 02 01 00 99

Contents

Contributors

James M. Acheson is Professor, Department of Anthropology, University of Maine.

Peggy F. Barlett is Professor, Department of Anthropology, Emory University.

Frances F. Berdan is Professor and Chair, Department of Anthropology, California State University at San Bernardino.

Laurel Bossen is Canada Research Fellow, Department of Anthropology, McGill University.

Frank Cancian is Professor, Department of Anthropology, University of California at Irvine.

Elizabeth Cashdan is Associate Professor, Department of Anthropology, University of Utah.

Norbert Dannhaeuser is Associate Professor, Department of Anthropology, Texas A&M University.

Christina H. Gladwin is Associate Professor, Department of Food and Resource Economics, University of Florida at Gainesville.

Allen Johnson is Professor and Chair, Department of Anthropology, University of California at Los Angeles.

Stuart Plattner is Program Director for Cultural Anthropology, National Science Foundation.

William Roseberry is Associate Professor, Department of Anthropology, The New School.

M. Estellie Smith is Professor, Department of Anthropology, State University of New York College at Oswego.

*I once asked Jean Learned, an economist who studied these materials on Pana-
jachel, what she as an economist would have done differently. The considered
reply was unexpected to me, yet wholly obvious. As an economist she would
not have spent years in a community of 800 people without records of prices
and the like. Panajachel is a place for the skills of (say) an anthropologist, not
an economist. Conversely, an anthropologist is not trained to cope with the
problems of a nation in the world community.*

—Sol Tax, Preface to *Penny Capitalism*, 1953

*As the world becomes smaller, the division of labor between development econo-
mists and economic anthropologists becomes fuzzier; and it is now hard to
distinguish some economists from some economic anthropologists.*

—Christina Gladwin, Chapter 15, this volume

Preface

This is the first comprehensive text in economic anthropology since the 1970's. The book covers the traditional topics of economic behavior and institutions in foraging bands, horticultural tribes, precapitalist states, agrarian or peasant societies, and industrialized states, as well as newer issues such as sex roles, common-property resources, the informal sector, and mass marketing in developing urban areas. We also include more in-depth coverage of some subjects than does any other text in the field, subjects like the central place theory of markets and marketplaces and the fundamentals of economic behavior in markets.

The approach is empirical, and though not ignoring controversy, aims to tell the reader what we know about the world rather than recording how we came to know it or disputing alternative views of the finer points of what we know. The relation depicted here between economics and anthropology is contemporary. Although not denying the extraordinary differences between these two fields, the authors of this book see the fields as complementary. We have come a long way from the approach reflected in Sol Tax's preface (quoted above) to his seminal book *Penny Capitalism*. The economic anthropology presented here is designed to train the student to deal with "the problems of a nation in the world economy" in ways that traditionally trained economists are simply incapable of dealing with.

For years, teachers and students of economic anthropology have had to be content with using a variety of aging sources: LeClair and Schneider (1968), Dalton (1967), Belshaw (1965), Nash (1966), or less comprehensive efforts such as Wolf (1966), Sahlins (1968), and Service (1966)—usually supplemented by large collections of more recent articles copied and placed on library reserve lists. Marshall Sahlins's *Stone-Age Economics* (1972) and Harold Schneider's *Economic Man* (1974) filled relatively narrow niches in the field but are now out of date.

Like the rest of anthropology, economic anthropology began life as a predominantly descriptive field. The earliest texts (for example, Herskovits 1952) compiled "exotic" economic customs and lumped together societies at different levels of integration. Foraging bands, horticultural tribes, and agricultural peasants were all discussed as "primitives." An example from Australian aboriginal society would follow one from an Indian peasant village. The general effects of poverty, small scale, and primitive technology were not distinguished from the specific imperatives of corporate kinship groups and community management of resources. This confusion was compounded by an inattention to local historical context. The behavior of groups undergoing severe stress because of colonial governance was analyzed as if those groups were in some sort of timeless equilibrium. The principle of the psychic unity of humankind (the assumption that all humans use intelligence to solve problems under constraints) was subverted by discussions of "primitive rationality" that made the "natives" seem almost mystical. The early analyses of the potlatch, for example, portrayed the Indians as competing for a generalized "prestige" because they did not have to compete economically.

Economic anthropology grew rapidly in the 1960's and climaxed in an extended argument called the "substantivist-formalist" debate (the theoretical issues underlying that debate are discussed below in the Introduction). This wide-ranging, increasingly bitter polemic absorbed the energies of much of the field for several years, and most participants ceased publishing new arguments—more out of a disgust with polemic than from any conviction that the issues had been resolved. The contributors to this book can in fact identify with several of the issues on both sides of the debate. On the one hand, we analyze different social systems as operating by appropriately different organizing principles and institutions. For example, we see clearly that a capitalist market can discipline behavior only where private property exists and where labor is relatively free to contract with capital. The relevance of market theory to tribal society must be demonstrated, not assumed. On the other hand, we understand that all humans exercise economic choices, subject to their local institutional constraints. For example, hunters and gatherers consciously plan their excursions so as to return with "enough" food, just as market vendors hope to return from a day's selling with "enough" income. This book hopes to bury the old debate by seriously considering underlying concepts such as "embeddedness" and "rational choice" (to be defined below in the Introduction).

After the substantivist-formalist debate, some economic anthropologists shifted their interests toward historical analysis. The theories and concepts used were influenced by contemporary Marxism (the social science rather than the revolutionary dogma). This approach is more properly called "historical materialism," and this book offers the student an introduction to its basic issues and concepts. We also introduce the reader to basic material in the fields of gender roles and common-property resource management. Our goal is to cover the fundamental areas in economic anthropology thoroughly, even as we guide the student toward some of the field's fascinating extremities.

The work represented here is more analytic than descriptive. The historical context of the observed social reality is given due consideration, and important parameters (such as the development of social infrastructure or the degree of riskiness of a transaction) are distinguished from enduring institutional constraints such as kinship obligations. Individuals in any culture are seen as fully "rational," in the sense that their solutions to their economic problems make sense once the many constraints (social, cultural, cognitive, and political, as well as economic) that individuals must take into account are understood. This does not mean that the solutions are optimal—merely that our analysis will make the behavior, or for that matter the institutions, understandable as a reasoned human response to a complex situation. Readers will see what we mean in the following chapters.

The creation of this book began with my concern about the lack of a useful text that covered the exciting developments in economic anthropology. I sat down to write one in 1974 and got as far as an article on central place theory (1975) before other interests and concerns put the project in deep storage.

A few years later the creation of a new professional society provided a supportive setting that indirectly stimulated this book's development. In 1980 Harold Schneider invited some economic anthropologists to a meeting in Bloomington, Indiana, to discuss the possibility of creating a new professional society to address the needs of our subfield. That meeting produced the Society for Economic Anthropology (SEA), whose *Newsletter*, annual spring meeting, and annual *Proceedings* (Ortiz 1983; Maclachlan 1987; Plattner 1985; Greenfield and Strickon 1986; Bennett and Bowen 1988) have been very successful. The SEA's accomplishments helped establish a modern, professional subfield and finally cooled the embers of the substantivist-formalist controversy of the 1960's. The SEA was interested in empirically based positive (not negative) studies on *all* aspects of the study of human economic behavior and institutions. Substantivists, formalists, archaeologists, ethnohistorians, economists, economic historians, economic geographers, and all others interested in this study were welcome. This mixture produced a series of professional meetings that quickly became known for their intellectual liveliness.

Because one cannot always concentrate purely on intellectual matters at a professional meeting, the conversation usually came around to teaching. After years of commiserating with colleagues about the lack of a solid, exciting text in our field, I finally approached a few teachers in late 1984 and asked if they were interested in collaborating on a new text. The enthusiastic response resulted in this volume.

I asked the participants to imagine a bright senior undergraduate who had come into their office, looked them in the eye, and asked them to tell what their field of study knew about the world. We want to teach that student what economic anthropology knows, more than how we found it out or what the philosophical and historical implications of our knowledge may be. This book is suitable for high-level undergraduate as well as introductory graduate courses. We recommend that students go over the issues in this book chapter by chapter and that each student select a book-length ethnographic study (such as Cancian's 1965 *Economics and Prestige in a Maya Community*) or a series of articles on an economic institution (on tribal long-distance trade, gender roles in agriculture, and so on) as the basis for a term paper.

The participants were selected to cover all of the more significant areas of modern economic anthropology, broadly conceived. I circulated a list of topics and participants to a small group of people, asking them for comments, additions, and modifications. Most of the original participants then wrote papers for this volume. We discussed the content of each chapter with its author, who produced a second draft. Finally, the other authors and I commented on this draft, and the author completed the necessary revisions.

I would like to acknowledge Frank Cancian's helpful critical comments on this Preface and the support for the project of William W. Carver, Editor at Stanford University Press.

S.P.

Economic Anthropology

1

Introduction

Stuart Plattner

Economic anthropology studies diverse things: a Bushman hunting wild game in the South African desert, how the nutrition of Mexican peasants changes when the international price of oil changes, or how a vendor in a big-city public marketplace selects vegetables for resale. The subject matter of the field is old as well as broad, for scientists, travelers, and colonial administrators have written about the economic institutions of exotic and non-Western peoples for hundreds of years. Economic anthropology as a formal discipline became popular in the 1950's and 1960's, when anthropology grew along with other scientific disciplines, and it has developed a rich literature since then. This book presents contemporary issues as well as the solid core of knowledge that has developed since the 1950's. In this Introduction I will define the discipline and some of its fundamental concepts and then give an overview of the chapters that follow.

Economic anthropology is the study of *economic* institutions and behavior done in *anthropological* places and in *ethnographic* style. The combination of these three elements gives economic anthropology its character as a discipline. What do *economic*, *anthropological*, and *ethnographic* mean? We will start with anthropology.

Economic Anthropology as Anthropology

Anthropology is the cover term for the subdisciplines of archaeology (the study of human prehistory and history), physical anthropology (the study of human biological adaptation over the span of human evolution), cultural anthropology (the comparative study of human culture and society), and anthropological linguistics (the study of the cultural functions of language). The task of anthropology in the scientific division of labor is often said to be the description and explanation of the human condition across all cultures and times. This is quite a tall order and an intellectually imperialist point of view, since it implies that all other social sciences are mere branches of anthropological knowledge. Many disciplines dream of grandeur in this way when they define their field of study. In fact, anthropologists have tended to study exotic, often primitive or underdeveloped places with an approach that is relatively *holistic*, meaning that behavior in one domain is related to several others. Anthropologists are usually sensitive to context, or to the wider setting and the local history of the particular behavior under scrutiny, and can invariably be counted on to understand, and often represent, the indigenous or "native" point of view.[1]

Beyond that, anthropology varies enormously in its style of research. Some studies are akin to history, some to sociology, political science, or economics. Some research is purely descriptive, some analytic; some researchers focus on one case study, others on a comparative problem; some take a Marxist point of view and study inequalities, others take a neoclassical approach and study individual decision making under constraints. This diversity is both a strength and a weakness. It is a strength, because so many sources of knowledge come together in the field that it continually sparkles with new ideas; a weakness, because such diverse efforts make focused advances in theory and empirical studies difficult. As the philosophers say, there are many paths to the truth. The fields with a thousand flowers blooming are most beautiful.

Economic Anthropology as Ethnography

An *ethnography* is a study of a single society (*ethnology* is the comparative study of all known societies). Economic anthropologists usually observe the people they study or their artifacts for extended periods of time through fieldwork. The usual study technique for living cultures is "participant observation," where the field-worker lives in the local community and involves him- or herself in as many activities as possible in the normal round of activities.[2] This gives deep insight into the local culture's point of view and value system, which is the hallmark of the anthropological method. This method evolved through a field-worker observing face-to-face interactions between residents in local communities. Ethnographers have also studied larger regions (such as systems

[1] This is true even for studies in the ethnographer's own society and is one way an anthropological study differs from a sociological study. See such classic ethnographies of U.S. society as LaBarre (1962), Myerhoff (1978), or Stack (1974).

[2] Field-workers usually try to study at least a full year. The normal procedure is to add three or six months to the annual cycle to allow time to learn how to study the local situation, so the typical anthropological fieldwork lasts fifteen to eighteen months. Bernard (1988) gives a sophisticated introduction to research methods in cultural anthropology.

of marketplaces), sectors of societies (such as occupational groups, like traders), or specific institutions (for example, marketplaces).

The traditional community field-worker's goal is to learn enough of the rules of behavior for daily life to become unobtrusive. The insiders will then forget the outsider is there and will act normally.[3] Most of the data are generated by conversations, interviews, and direct observations by the ethnographer (often supplemented with information produced by trained local research assistants). This contrasts with economists and sociologists, who usually work with data produced by public agencies or professional survey organizations.

Ethnographers are thus more involved with the people in the social systems they study than are social scientists, who study statistics collected by bureaucratic offices. The benefit of this is that anthropologists often bring a commitment, sometimes a passion, to their studies that other social scientists do not; but the cost is often a lack of objectivity about the particular case and the committing of the cardinal anthropological sin—generalizing from small samples.

Holism

Ethnographic method is usually *holistic*, meaning that people's lives are studied in the context of their many activities, statuses, and roles. This is a result of the ordinary subject matter of the field. Anthropologists originally specialized in "primitive" cultures, where they were the only Western scientists present. They dabbled in fields like agronomy, economics, geography, history, political science, psychology, and sociology since there were no expert studies they could turn to for background information. The local scale of community life (in any small community) usually allows the live-in field-worker to become intimately involved with the people. It is hard to limit your focus to agriculture, for example, when you live with the farmer and see his economic activities embedded in his other roles as father, church-member, community political actor, and so on. The household and the local community have thus been important foci of study, even when the subject matter is advanced industrial society.

Embeddedness

This means that economic activity is often explained relative to the social or political constraints of the social system. Economic anthro-

[3] Insiders never really forget that an outsider is among them. The challenge of ethnographic method is to distinguish normal behavior from reactions to the ethnographer's presence. Some ethnographers abandon this challenge by focusing on the insider-outsider interaction itself. They trade social science for a kind of journalism as they celebrate the unique trans-cultural encounter.

pologists interpret the economy as *"embedded* in society." For example, one of the functions of tribal long-distance trade (which occurs in a region with no superordinate government) is intercommunity political integration. The "purely economic" exchange of goods cannot exist and would be meaningless to the local participants without the political relationships.

All economies are embedded in societies, and the economic anthropological approach to economic analysis sensitizes us to the same issues in large-scale industrialized societies. People sometimes think that the economy of a developed country like the United States is "totally rationalized." They see the economic sphere of behavior as separate from the social, religious, and political spheres, free to follow its own purely economic logic. But this is false. For example, the reason that the United States stopped buying sugar from Cuba in the 1960's is political, not economic; retail activity peaks in late December for religious, not economic, reasons; and the fact that marijuana is one of the larger cash crops in California is of social as much as economic importance. This is an important point: Economic behavior and institutions can be analyzed in terms of purely economic parameters, but this merely ignores the relevant noneconomic parameters.[4]

The History of Anthropology and the Anthropology of History

Academic anthropology is a creation of nineteenth-century Western culture. The earlier ethnographers were concerned to record the primitive lifeways they saw vanishing from the landscape in the face of the juggernaut of Western industrial capitalism (usually referred to as "civilization"). Many cultural anthropologists felt that the purest styles of human life (most similar to our prehistoric ancestors) were represented by "noble savages." They wanted to record these rare cultural types in what became known as "salvage ethnography." In the field of American Indian studies, some well-known ethnographies were done by anthropologists interviewing aged Indians sitting in a hotel room, the Indian culture as a behavioral system having effectively disappeared from the face of earth.

Others had a real concern to serve as cultural "brokers," interpreting the conquered, often brutalized culture to the outside colonial world

---

[4] We will see later, in a discussion of the substantivist-formalist controversy, that the opposite is also true: An analysis of economic behavior "purely" in cultural and institutional terms merely closes its eyes to the relevant economic parameters.

and vice versa. And some studied indigenous culture with an eye toward achieving the superior political control that comes from better understanding.

Out of these studies came a unique set of ethnographic values: that native cultures are best interpreted as integrated wholes (not the "tattered remnants" that were often visible), and that native rationality is sensible and intelligent once the local context is understood.[5] These values represent *cultural relativism*, which is the position that different life-styles deserve respect as adaptive solutions to common human, existential problems.[6]

Along with these values a point of view developed about non-Western cultures. One aspect of this, now discredited, was a concept called the "ethnographic present." This was a fiction that the primitive or peasant culture could be described in a timeless, precolonial state, innocent of capitalist or colonial sin. The ethnographers *saw* societies involved in violent upheaval and change as a result of the penetration of capitalist forms of exchange into their previously kinship-based economies; what they often *recorded* were the parts of this reality that were somehow sanitized of the most overt Western influences. This produced a vision of the world beyond the pale of Western capitalism —untouched, isolated, and pristine. The task of Western development was usually seen as introducing capitalism and economic growth to these primitive cultures.

Some exceptional works of regional and global history of newer vintage have corrected this vision. They show how the development of modern capitalism from the fifteenth century onward was a process of significant interaction between the European core and the African, Asian, and American peripheries. Many tribal and peasant peoples in the hinterland were reacting to European influences far earlier than their first direct contact. Massive population movements and cultural changes occurred because of trade and warfare directly stimulated by Europeans. Some of the most well-known primitive cultures, like the Indian horseback raiders of the American West, had changed dramatically in the recent past. The availability of a new form of transportation

---

[5] This is the hypothesis of "the psychic unity of humankind," which proposes that the cognitive and reasoning abilities of human populations everywhere are within the same range of variation, and that differences are therefore explainable by different adaptations to local circumstances.

[6] This simple definition of relativism is sufficient for the purposes of this introduction. The reader should know that the subject of cultural relativism is hotly debated in anthropology. Some deny the relevance of scientific method because of relativism; others claim that relativism begs for a stronger scientific method in anthropology. Interested readers can enter this literature through Geertz (1984) and Spiro (1986).

(the horse) and new resources to fight over (European trade goods) formed this Indian culture in the eighteenth and nineteenth centuries. Similar analyses have been done for other supposedly "pristine" groups like the Maya Indians of Mexico and some African tribal societies (Wolf 1982). The fiction of the primitive as untouched by Western influences until direct colonial penetration has been shown to be false. The primitive, tribal, peasant world is shaped as it is because of many years of economic interactions with Western capitalism.[7]

Economic Anthropology as Economics

The textbook definition of economics usually includes diverse elements such as the study of exchange transactions; the study of the use of scarce resources to produce commodities and distribute them for consumption; the study of how people earn their living; and the study of wealth. The leading text offers the following general definition of the field:

Economics is the study of how men and society end up *choosing*, with or without the use of money, to employ *scarce* productive resources which could have alternative uses, to produce various commodities and distribute them for consumption, now or in the future, among various people and groups in society. [Samuelson and Nordhaus 1985: 4]

Economics in the capitalist world is conventionally divided into micro- and macroeconomics, pertaining to theories of individual actors and of social systems. The governing paradigm of capitalist economics is usually called "neoclassicism" and derives from many Western theorists, from Adam Smith to Keynes and Samuelson. In much of the developing world and in the socialist/communist countries, the discipline of economics draws from a different paradigm, usually traced to Karl Marx. Marx's impact as a social scientist is considerable but is usually overshadowed by his fame as a political reformer. A "Marxist" economic theory denotes an approach that looks at the distribution of material wealth and political power across the socioeconomic classes of a society (Marxism in economic anthropology will be discussed below). Anthropologists are eclectic users of economic paradigms, taking concepts and interests from both neoclassicism and Marxist materialism. Most economists in the United States are firmly neoclassicist. Thus in capitalist or socialist countries, economic anthropology uses a broader range of economic ideas than does economics. In this section I will first

---

[7] Frank (1968), Wallerstein (1974), and Wolf (1982) are outstanding examples of this genre.

review some basic concepts in neoclassical economics and then discuss the difficulties that arise when we try to use them in economic anthropology.

Normative and Descriptive Theory

Microeconomics uses a well-developed body of theory to identify rational economic decisions for individuals or firms.[8] It is a *prescriptive* (sometimes called "normative") theory, meaning it specifies how people should act if they want to make efficient economic decisions. This is in stark contrast to most anthropological theory, which is *descriptive*, meaning it analyzes what people actually do. The fundamental assumption of microeconomic theory is that people know what they want. Their economic choices express their wants, which are defined by their culture and which are not necessarily the same as their biologically defined needs. We need food and shelter to survive biologically, but the hamburgers and central heating, or antelope meat and grass huts, are cultural artifacts.

Maximization of Utility

Technically, people are assumed to "maximize their utility," which means they choose the alternative that gives the most satisfaction, value, or benefit in a context of limited means ("scarce resources"). The chooser solves the problem of comparing disparate goods (should I eat lunch today? or skip lunch and buy that cassette?) by measuring the *value* of each in "utility" and by measuring the *cost* of each in standard units of money (or time or energy).[9]

Note that the definition of resources as the *means* available to people to achieve their goals is general. Money, energy, and time are limited for most of us, and even the rich face the inexorable constraints of the human body and the 24-hour day. Means are also multipurpose. There is no choice problem if means are useful in only one way. But money,

[8] Macroeconomics is concerned for the most part with the structure and function of the capitalist system in industrialized countries. It is not relevant for most anthropological concerns. There once was a thriving branch of economics called *institutional economics*, which studied things of great interest to anthropologists. This field is now quite reduced and focuses on economic history.

[9] Utility is a tricky concept. It has "face validity," since we actually do compare different things like food and musical entertainment. Because we compare them, there must be some single dimension on which we evaluate them, and we might as well call that dimension "utility." But unless we have an independent measure of utility, its use is merely tautological: Why did Joe buy the hamburger rather than the record? Because the hamburger obviously had more utility for him at that time. How do we know it had more utility? Because Joe preferred it.

energy, and time can be used in various creative activities. Time spent with Joe is not available to spend (alone) with Jean.

The loss in alternative value from using some means is known as the *opportunity cost*. The opportunity cost of time spent with Joe is the loss of the value of that time spent with Jean. This is the fundamental economic choice problem cited many years ago by Robbins: "Economics is the science which studies human behavior as a relationship between ends and scarce means which have alternative uses" (1932, reproduced in LeClair and Schneider 1968). This approach is commonly known as "neoclassical" economics.

The rational or *economizing* actor will select those opportunities that yield the maximal good (or a given level of good for the least cost). This assumption is called the *maximizing* assumption and has been the heart of microeconomics for many years. It assumes that people (1) are calculating beings who use forethought before acting and understand their own values; (2) have the necessary knowledge (which may be probabilistic) about costs, incomes, and yields with respect to all their options; and (3) have the necessary calculating ability to solve the maximization problems.

These are fairly strong, unrealistic assumptions to make about people in any society. If the theory were always used normatively, the unreality of the assumptions would present no problem. The economic analysis would start with constraints and resources and show the best feasible outcome. But many economists and most anthropologists would use the theory descriptively to explain observed behavior. Unrealistic assumptions in descriptive theories are real problems.[10] For this reason many anthropologists, in common with other social scientists, have been suspicious of the relevance of neoclassical economic theory.[11] In particular, one of the most distinctive facts about most everyday economic behavior is *aversion to risk*. Most people design their lives so that bad outcomes and surprises, which are usually caused by faulty information, are minimized. Some of the most exciting new work in economics and anthropology attempts to theorize about how rational choices are made *without* excellent forethought, knowledge, and calculations.

[10] There is a fascinating literature on the relevance of realism in economic assumptions. Some say that the only concern should be the final predictions of the theory; others say the theory must be grounded in intuitively reasonable assumptions to explain anything. Interested readers can get into the issues by reading Samuelson (1963) and Friedman (1953), both Nobel laureates in economics, who present opposite sides of the argument.

[11] Herbert Simon won the Nobel prize in economics for work that included an investigation of the limits of human rationality.

Marginal Analysis

The field of microeconomics studies what happens when rational decision makers with scarce resources must act in a world of *diminishing marginal value*. Value here can refer to an individual's utility, to the product of a productive process, or to the yield of some transaction. The margin is the edge, the last or most recent aspect of the phenomenon. For example, consider agricultural factors of production, meaning the things that create a product like corn: water, fertilizer, labor, seed, and the like. The marginal product of a factor such as fertilizer is the increase in the total product, corn, caused by the addition of another unit of fertilizer, *holding constant the effects of other factors like water, labor, seed, and sunlight.*

When the marginal value (output) is plotted against the quantity of the resource used (input), it produces a curve like that in Fig. 1.1. The curve traces the change in the value of the last unit of the factor as a function of the total quantity of the good that is created. Of most things that cause benefits in our lives, the curve says that a little is good but that a lot is bad. For example, a little water makes the corn grow, a lot drowns the field. A little food allows a body to function, a lot poisons it. A few sales give the business some profits, too many stress it so that it chokes on its own activity and fails. This is a fact of life. We could conceive of a world where marginal values stayed constant, or increased, but here on earth they decrease. This seems to be true for all good things, even love. Do you value time spent with your loved one?

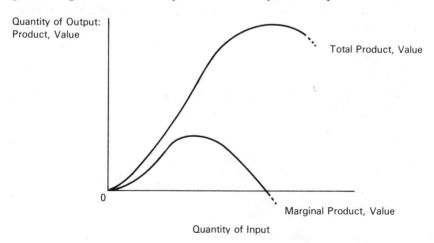

Fig. 1.1. Marginal product or value.

Do you want more time with him or her? Every minute of every day, with no privacy? All day, all night?

Rational Choice

The marginal value curve assumes that the value peaks at a certain point. Microeconomics defines the rational decision as the choice of that level of production, exchange, consumption, or activity in general that will produce the most *net* utility for any given level of resource input (or a given utility for the least amount of input). This means the decision maker will use factors or inputs to the point where their net marginal return (marginal value minus marginal cost) is at a maximum, and no more. The farmer will use so much water, at a given cost, to attain the maximum level of corn production possible given that farmer's constraints of money, land, time, energy, and opportunity costs of the factors of production. The consumer will purchase so many goods, and no more, to maximize his or her overall net level of satisfaction, given constraints and opportunity costs of money, time, energy, social resources, and limitations.[12]

If marginal value simply increased, or if means were not scarce or multipurpose, we would have no economic choice problem. But humans (and other animals) have such problems—whether we are a South African Bushman deciding whether to hunt to the north or the south, a Melanesian tribesman choosing between planting a large or small yam garden, a Mexican peasant farmer deciding whether to decrease his subsistence crop area in order to plant a cash crop,[13] or an industrialist deciding whether to build a new factory or to contract with suppliers.[14] Although all the examples of economic choice just mentioned deal with production, the same issues apply to distribution and consumption.

Transferring Concepts from Economics to Anthropology

Economics grew up as a field of study in rapidly developing capitalist societies. Although the basic terms of economics are defined abstractly, they fit best the capitalist, industrialized economy in which they were

---

[12] Note that this definition of *rational* has the virtue of being clearly objective.

[13] A subsistence crop is used directly by the producer. A cash crop is sold to get cash that is used to buy subsistence items.

[14] The implications of economic choice without exchange, for example, for animals choosing which foods to seek, are explored by the field of study in ecology known as optimal foraging theory. Cashdan's chapter, below, covers issues in this field.

developed. The attempt to transfer them to the analysis of noncapitalist societies has created problems. Trying to comprehend the economic activity of an economy organized on the basis of corporate kinship groups, for example, is as difficult as it is for a speaker of English to understand the importance of tones in Chinese or Zapotec (a Mexican Indian language).

The main problem is the "embeddedness" of economic activities mentioned above.[15] The social and cultural matrix of our own economic behavior is transparent to us so that, for example, heightened retail sales at Christmas seems "just" economic, not religious. But the cultural context of economic behavior in exotic societies is blatantly obvious. For example, *production* implies a discrete activity, a creation of economic value by changing the characteristics of a good. This activity is conceptually separate from *religion*, because in Western society, religious actors do not create economic production while they are doing religious acts. The closest we get occurs when religious leaders bless or certify the tools of production (for example, the priest blessing the fishing boats or the rabbi certifying that the food factory is kosher).

This separation of spheres of behavior creates a problem for the economic anthropologist, who analyzes something that looks like "economic" production but that is also clearly "religious." Consider the Mayan Indian farmer who carefully budgets money to have the appropriate prayers said in his cornfield, because he believes that the corn won't grow without the prayers. The cost of the prayers is a real cost of production *to the farmer*, but not to the agricultural engineer who visits the area to advise how to grow corn better. To say that the farmer would be more productive if he didn't "waste his time" in prayers to the Earth Gods is about as useful as saying that productivity in the United States would increase if all manufacturing plants stopped "wasting" weekend production time by closing. Sure, it is true by definition, but lots of manufacturers and their workers do not consider working on weekends. After all (they may respond), they are working to live, not living to work.

In an industrialized society, the division of labor is complex, and the scale of the social units often quite large. This means that relationships between people are easily analyzed as single-stranded roles, such as that between the ticket seller and the movie patron. This is purely and simply a short-run, discrete economic relationship, because

---

[15] Sociologist Mark Granovetter gives an excellent statement of the issues in characterizing what he calls "undersocialized" (pure rational choice) as opposed to "oversocialized" actors (who behave according to social norms). He analyzes economic acts as embedded in a matrix of social relations (1985).

the attributes of the individuals (such as residence, religion, ethnicity, personality, and so on) are simply not relevant to the transaction of cash for ticket. Economists also indulge in the fiction that an employer-employee relationship is "purely" economic. When the duration of the transaction over time creates more complexity, economists ruefully describe it as "introducing" noneconomic issues into what "should be" a simple economic relation.

The facts of life in nonindustrialized societies are that relationships are rarely single stranded. One's economic collaborators (or competitors) are also one's kinsmen, political allies (or enemies), neighbors, and so on. The careless use of a technical economic concept that is formally defined in terms of economic function, but that implies a particular sociocultural context in Western society, can confuse labeling with explanation.[16] The challenge for economic anthropology is to convert the formal concepts of economics to free them of hidden cultural bias. The corresponding challenge for economics is to redefine basic theory to make visible its Western cultural biases. For example, kinship is not normally considered part of the employment relation in economic analyses of industrialized societies. However, the role of kinship in securing livelihood is obvious. For proof, just speak to someone who tried to get a job through a skilled crafts union without kinship ties.

As we shall see, the concern that economic concepts are not easily transferable to non-Western societies has played a large part in the development of the discipline of economic anthropology.

Contentious Issues: Formalists and Substantivists

Hunter-gatherers, capitalists, peasants, and nonmonetized tribal people all face the choice problem caused by scarce means with alternative uses. The context of choice may differ from culture to culture, including the particular means and their uses, the ends, and the constraints and opportunities. Yet a Bushman setting out on a hunt for meat or for buried tubers has to choose a direction and distance to travel that have direct and opportunity costs in terms of energy and time. A tribalist exchanging ceremonial valuables with a traditional trading partner for fame, glory, and political influence must choose which valuable to exchange with which partner at which time.

[16] For example, an analysis of bride price in Africa used a statistical analysis based on a competitive market. The analysis implied that there was a market for wives. Plattner (1974) criticized the author for not demonstrating the existence of such a market, or any functional equivalent, for brides. Without such a demonstration, the analysis was more tautology than explanation.

Economic anthropologists who have analyzed choice as the product of rational decisions that involve marginal values were called "formalists" in an academic debate in the 1960's about the proper theories for economic anthropology. The crux of the approach is the assumption that individuals in every culture exercise rational choice in a means-ends, constraints, and opportunities framework.

Critics of this approach, calling themselves "substantivists," described it as lumping together features of different cultures.[17] The critique has two parts: a descriptive or historicist bias that is antigeneralizing, and a concern that the terms of neoclassical theory can have meaning only in a capitalist society.

Substantivists argued that the differences between cultures like bands, tribes, colonized tribalists, peasants, and capitalists are so crucial as to render analyses based on a single "theory" (the rational choice paradigm) either dead wrong or so abstract as to be simplistic or irrelevant. The use of such models seemed presumptuous and ethnocentric to the substantivists because they believed that "primitive economy is different from market industrialism not in degree but in kind" (Dalton 1968: 164). I think this is a matter of definition and of analytical preference. *All* generalizations across different societies cannot be invalid; rather, the value of any generalization must be decided on a case-by-case basis. Some anthropologists prefer more historical and particularistic work while others prefer more social scientific and generalizing work. There is certainly a need for good work of both kinds.

Critics of the formalist type of economic anthropology had a stronger argument than a distaste for generalization: They did not believe that scarcity was part of the human condition. They defined the scarcity of *means* in primitive society as a scarcity of *wealth*, a particular historical condition caused by the "penetration" of Western capitalism into native societies. They argued that aboriginal economies were kinship based and fully embedded in social, moral, and political interaction. Therefore, the individual choice calculus was based not on economic profit and loss but on social, political, and moral concerns. Precolonial economies had no market for labor and often no multipurpose money, so the very context of economic choice lacked the most important attributes of capitalist society, where the theory of economizing choice was created. Few individuals in band or tribal societies were poor in material goods, since the noncapitalist ethos was for powerful Big Men to *give* more than they received. The organizing principles of non-Western econo-

---

[17] The terms *formalist* and *substantivist* come from the work of Polanyi (1957), as interpreted by Dalton (1961, 1968).

mies were based not on market exchange but on different principles such as *reciprocity* and *redistribution*.[18] The former was a pattern of exchange through gifts in the context of long-term relationships, the latter a pattern of exchange based on kinship-based leaders receiving and redistributing subsistence goods.

As for agrarian or peasant society, the main productive strategy, argued the substantivists, was "production for use" (meaning subsistence) rather than "production for exchange."[19] Because the producers did not enter the market in order to exchange things, the market value of goods and services was irrelevant. Thus, they concluded, a model of choice based on scarce means was ethnocentric and inappropriate for the analysis of non-Western behavior. They attacked the use of terms defined in the economic literature with reference to capitalist financial markets—terms like "interest," "credit," and "capital"—to describe analogous institutions in band and tribal societies.[20]

The argument was hot and heavy, and generated a good bit of heat in proportion to the light.[21] The substantivists felt they were carrying the cultural relativist flag of modern anthropology, because their approach did not impose a Western, capitalist set of assumptions on a foreign reality. The formalists felt they were carrying the social scientific flag, because their approach was nomothetic and generalizing. Many scholars could not resist the urge to publish their opinions, definitions, and conclusions, but too few put their approach to empirical test. Careers were made by people criticizing each other's opinions, with strong and often bitterly felt arguments. After a number of years, most anthropologists who followed the discussion became disillusioned with theoretical pronouncements and polemics. They did not stop doing empirical research but stopped arguing about how to go about it.

At this point, some years after, the issues seem clearer. We take the substantivist truth for granted that all economies are "embedded," which means that the economy is an *aspect* of social life rather than a segment of society (Gudeman 1986). Scarcity of resources (defined broadly to include time and energy) *is* an obvious fact of life, and analyses of tribal behavior have demonstrated the appropriateness of a rational choice point of view. For example, Healey (1984) analyzed barter among New Guinea tribesmen and showed that risk was a factor in

[18] These terms are from Polanyi (1957).

[19] The terms come from Marx (1976).

[20] The works of Polanyi (1957), Dalton (1961), and Sahlins (1972) cover the full range of issues.

[21] Interested readers can consult the original sources in LeClair and Schneider (1968) and in Dalton (1961) and Sahlins (1972). My personal opinion is that this is a nonissue for the reasons given. Both approaches can yield valuable understanding.

an individual's choice of trading partners. The case described in the chapter on Marxism, below, shows tribalists enjoying a monopoly over production. Research on peasants who may sell much or little of their products on the open market shows them making complex economizing decisions.[22]

Certainly we must analyze economic behavior (in any society) in terms of social, political, or religious functions, but this does not negate the importance of the analysis of the economic functions. So long as the microeconomic approach to primitive economy looks for rational choice behavior (as opposed to assuming its existence), then the substantivist criticism is misapplied. The "rational choice theory of economic behavior" in this case becomes a paradigm or point of view, not a descriptive generalization. If we assume that people everywhere are rational and can verbalize their choice procedures, then our microeconomic scientific task is to find and analyze economic behavior.[23]

Neither side won the argument. As with so many social science controversies, they fade away rather than die. The substantivist concern with the integrity and logic of local institutions has been an important force in cultural anthropology. It is all too easy for formalists to label an exotic institution with an impressive technical, familiar term, and pretend that the thing has been explained.[24] The substantivist introduction of models of non-Western economic institutions, redistribution, and reciprocity was (and is) a healthy stimulus to analyze indigenous systems as they function.

After the substantivist-formalist polemic quieted down, some anthropologists shifted their interest to a more historical and regional approach. These anthropologists developed their interest in the unique features of non-Western institutions into the study of how these societies developed under Western domination. They found the concepts and theories of "historical materialism" or Marxism useful.

Marxist Perspectives in Economic Anthropology

Marxism is a lively part of modern social science, apart from Marxism's status as a political ideology or call for social and economic change.

---

[22] The book edited by Barlett (1980) contains several excellent studies.

[23] Cancian made this point in a dispassionate, intelligent comment on the issues in the formalist-substantivist debate in 1966.

[24] I call this the "Ghidra" principle, after a Japanese monster movie of the 1960's. The movie showed the monster rampaging around a city when a newscaster announced that "the crisis was over, the monster has been identified, his name is Ghidra!" Naming the monster doesn't solve the rampaging problem, and naming our scientific ignorance with a word of jargon doesn't explain the real world.

Here I will briefly introduce some issues and concepts in order to answer the question of whether there is a "Marxist" economic anthropology.

Students who attempt to read the rapidly growing body of writings known as contemporary Marxism (also called historical materialism or political economy) often complain that the arguments in this literature seem more interpretive than scientific. Many Marxist writers delight in tracing arcane bits of definition to an original publication by Marx or Engels, and feel that a "correct" definition (according to how close one can trace a definition to one of Marx or Engels) is sufficient analysis. This is fine for those interested in the history of ideas but is not appropriate for an empirical social science.

Scientifically valuable empirical analyses in Marxist traditions certainly exist and have a well-defined point of view. Donham (forthcoming) summarizes this as a clear focus on *history* and *ideology* as they constrain the analysis of inequalities of social power and wealth. The first step in a Marxist analysis is to describe the inequalities in the distribution of wealth and power in the society. Wealth and power here are defined so as to include the usual things (money, possessions, influence, and so on) but without fail must include the sources of productive wealth. Thus the well-known phrase "control over the means of production" implies the study of who has control over the tools, money, knowledge, or people who create the products that the society values. Contemporary Marxism finds this ownership to be unequally distributed in most societies, but the worst inequalities are found in capitalist societies.

Such inequalities are usually structured along socially defined lines (such as kinship, social background, and residence) and define socioeconomic classes. Capitalists and wage workers are the basic classes Marxists study in capitalist industrial societies, but analysts of noncapitalist (that is, tribal- or kinship-based) societies sometimes use related ideas to study men vs. women, or elders vs. juniors as social classes subject to inequalities. The boundaries of these classes constitute "contradictions" in Marxist thought, in the sense that the inequalities contradict the social pretense that people are "equal." In industrial societies the contradictions represent lines of potential opposition where class-based revolutionary change can realign the distribution of power and wealth.

An ideal Marxist analysis would first study the distribution and functions of power by studying how the products valued by that society are produced and converted into wealth, and how that wealth is distributed among segments of society. The historical context and development of the observed distribution would be intensively examined for patterns of change over time. The historical study would show how the patterns of inequalities in control over productive assets are reproduced over time. And the ideological means by which the poor accept their low positions and the rich justify their high status would be studied. These systems of belief are called hegemonies because they "uphold special interests while appearing to express general concerns" (Donham forthcoming).

Is there a place for a Marxist perspective in economic anthropology? Certainly the issues just mentioned are clearly in the realm of economic anthropology. The use of special concepts like contradiction, reproduction, or hegemony, as defined above, would mark the study as Marxist. If all the study did was to label features in a society with terms derived from Marxist theory, its wider interest would be limited. But in so far as the study analyzed an empirical situation using these concepts, and showed how the society worked, then the substance of the study could just as well be labeled economic anthropology. Thus there is a Marxist economic anthropology in the same way that there is a neoclassical economic anthropology, since there are people doing empirical studies with concepts and scientific problems inspired by the respective paradigms. The neoclassical approach is reflected in the basic concepts summarized earlier in this chapter. The basic concepts and issues of the Marxist approach are summarized in a separate chapter of this book.

An Overview of the Book

The book is organized into several groupings of chapters, although each chapter can also stand alone. Chapters 2, 3, and 4 cover bands, tribes, and primitive states and so replicate the traditional evolutionary schema. The material covered is not all traditional, however, because more recent issues such as evolutionary ecology are also introduced. Chapters 5, 6, and 7 cover peasant societies and range from a global perspective to a community level, as well as to one sector of society-regional marketing systems. Chapters 8, 9, and 10 cover aspects of capitalism and industrialized states, ranging from models of individual economic behavior in market contexts, to the role of mass-produced and distributed consumer goods in economic development, to an analysis of agriculture in the United States. Chapters 11, 12, 13, and 14 introduce themes and issues that crosscut the rest—including the "informal sector" of capitalist economies, gender roles, common-property resources, and the social science perspective known as historical materialism, or Marxism. The final chapter (Chapter 15) is an appreciation of the differing perspectives of economics and anthropology as disciplines and is written by a professional economist. All the other chapters are written by anthropologists.

The simplest economic organization we know of exists in band societies. Elizabeth Cashdan (Chapter 2, "Hunters and Gatherers: Economic Behavior in Bands") describes how foraging bands function as societies in intimate contact with their environments. She discusses work and leisure, diet, seasonal variation (both predictable and nonpredictable), land ownership and tenure, and the relation of foragers to the wider contemporary world.

Much of classical economic anthropology was devoted to the study of tribal societies. Allen Johnson (Chapter 3, "Horticulturalists: Economic Behavior in Tribes") contrasts horticulturists with foragers and peasants, and illustrates his points about horticulturists with case material on the Machiguenga (Peru) and the Enga (New Guinea). Warfare and the prestige economy are also discussed. Many of the most famous noncapitalist economic institutions, such as the Kula ring of Melanesia and the potlatch are described and analyzed here.

The economic analysis of early state economies has been an important part of economic anthropology. Frances Berdan (Chapter 4, "Trade and Markets in Precapitalist States") shows that markets and trade have extensive precapitalist histories. She focuses on specialization and urbanization, as well as on taxes and tribute. She analyzes the role and influence of professional merchants, specialized trading locales such as ports of trade, and the nature of exchanges (including the use of currencies). Although some generalizations about trade and markets in precapitalist states can be made, this chapter recognizes that there was considerable regional variation. A case study of trade and markets in the Aztec empire is presented to illustrate, in concrete terms, one cultural expression of this variation.

Most of the people of the world today live in agrarian societies based on peasant agriculture rather than on mechanized farming and industry. William Roseberry (Chapter 5, "Peasants and the World") discusses the development of the modern world economic system. He gives the macrolevel perspective on the study of peasant economic institutions. The material covered includes world-system theory, the importance of the historical perspective, the closing and opening of peasant communities, and the value of regional and macrolevel context in understanding the local case. Material about a Venezuelan coffee-producing region is included for illustration.

The general treatment of peasant economy continues in Chapter 6 ("Economic Behavior in Peasant Communities"). Frank Cancian presents a community-level analysis of agrarian economic behavior. The main issues discussed include socioeconomic homogeneity in peasant communities, the model of the closed corporate community, the model of "the image of limited good," and issues of Chayanov's theory. Socioeconomic heterogeneity in peasant communities is analyzed with case material from Zinacantan, Mexico, and Paso, Costa Rica. Strategies of agricultural production and local-level development are also discussed.

Patterns of marketplaces, including central place systems of markets, are discussed by Stuart Plattner (Chapter 7, "Markets and Marketplaces"). Elements of central place theory and the development of demand for goods in a developing agrarian region are discussed with reference to the well-known studies by G. William Skinner for China and Carol Smith for Guatemala. Case material on Mexican itinerant peddlers is also presented for illustration.

In Chapter 8, Plattner discusses "Economic Behavior in Markets" (that is, the micro level) by analyzing the conditions fostering personal, or equilibrating, economic relationships. People who must make economic exchanges are seen as facing risks of loss due to insufficiencies of information about goods, transactions, and actors. The causes of problems in information are analyzed as poor infrastructure in communications, political integration, and transport and storage, which in turn are caused by excessively cheap labor and scarce capital.

The most "traditional" societies in today's world consume Coca-Cola, cigarettes, and other industrial goods. Norbert Dannhaeuser (Chapter 9, "Marketing in Developing Urban Areas") introduces the student to changes in market arrangements of consumer products that have taken place in major Third World societies during the past 35 years. He describes the development and spread of a mass market for industrial consumer goods in urban and rural areas of these societies, and illustrates the role played by multinational corporations and large indigenous concerns in exploiting the expanded consumer base. Much of the chapter discusses new channel institutions and marketing strategies, as well as the manner in which traditional trade has been affected by these innovations. Case material from Dagupan, Philippines, and Nasik, India, is presented.

Peggy Barlett (Chapter 10, "Industrial Agriculture") shows the relevance of economic anthropology to the analysis of production in the developed world. She analyzes the nature of the family farm, as contrasted with corporate farms and part-time farms. The chapter discusses the contraction of the farmers' realm of control; the role of agribusiness and of government in the supply and regulation of inputs, credit, marketing, and conservation; and issues of efficiency. The crisis in U.S. agriculture of the 1980's is set in historical context.

The issue of an informal sector or informal economy within a larger economy grew out of the massive urbanization of the developing world in recent years. This cash- and family-based sector of the economy is best known through studies of urban hawkers or peddlers. M. Estellie Smith (Chapter 11, "The Informal Economy") discusses how anthropologists followed their rural villagers to the cities and observed their involvement in work that at first seemed peripheral, but then was shown to be critical for the ongoing function of the urban and national economies.

Chapter 12 analyzes the sexual division of labor in terms of broad patterns of foraging, horticultural, and agricultural economies. Laurel Bossen (in her chapter "Women and Economic Institutions") analyzes the economics of marriage systems (bride wealth, dowry, bride service) and their relation to systems of labor and property, reproduction, and inheritance. She also discusses the impact of economic development and capitalism on indigenous sex roles, using case material from a Mayan Indian community.

James Acheson (Chapter 13, "Management of Common-Property Resources") outlines the theory of how societies control productive resources that are publicly owned. Taking off from the well-known "tragedy of the commons" model, Acheson shows how many communities develop rules to limit access, control conflict, and otherwise manage the problems of common property.

Stuart Plattner (Chapter 14, "Marxism") gives the basic elements of historical materialism or neo-Marxism. After defining the approach as holistic, historical, and production oriented, he discusses three basic modes of production: capitalist, tributary (usually called peasant), and kinship (tribal). The material is discussed in terms of case studies of New Guinea tribal salt production and Hindu (Indian) sacred cows. Finally, the concept of petty commodity production is discussed with reference to a case study of a Guatemalan Indian weaving industry.

Christina Gladwin (Chapter 15, "On the Division of Labor Between Economics and Economic Anthropology") compares the disciplines of economic anthropology and economics as ways to study economic behavior. Using case material from studies of the decision making of farmers in Mexico, Guatemala, and Florida, she discusses the exceptions that prove the conventional wisdom of the differences between the two fields: that anthropology is microlevel in scope, qualitative in method, and flexible (or vague) in its paradigm, while economics is macrolevel, quantitative, and rigidly neoclassicist.

2

Hunters and Gatherers: Economic Behavior in Bands

Elizabeth Cashdan

Hunters and gatherers—people who live primarily on wild plant and animal foods—are found today as small, politically marginal remnant populations in only a few parts of the world. From the perspective of the human species, however, this is a very recent phenomenon. It is sometimes difficult to remember that fully modern human beings lived successfully as hunter-gatherers for tens of thousands of years before anyone began to domesticate plants and animals. Indeed, it has been estimated (Lee and DeVore 1968) that over 90 percent of the people who have ever lived on earth were hunter-gatherers. For this reason, and because hunting and gathering played an important role in human evolution, it is appropriate to begin the comparative study of economic behavior with a look at this highly successful and resilient way of life.

An understanding of the principles governing economic behavior among hunters and gatherers can shed a great deal of light on our evolutionary past, and many of the anthropologists who study such people do so with this aim in mind. It is important to realize, however, that all hunter-gatherers in the world today are in contact, directly or indirectly, with the world economy. This fact should caution us against viewing today's hunter-gatherers as "snapshots" of the past. The relationship of today's foragers to the wider economic world will be considered at the end of this chapter.

All hunter-gatherers in the world today live in what anthropologists call "bands." Bands are small social groups of related individuals, usually consisting of fewer than 100 people. They are typically egalitarian, lacking chiefs and other formal authority structures. Relationships among bands are also informal; individuals maintain social and kinship

I am grateful to Eric Smith, Stu Plattner, and Peggy Barlett for their helpful comments on an earlier version of this paper. My perspective on hunter-gatherer economics was shaped by many people, but I am particularly indebted to Lewis Binford for his insights and inspiration.

ties with members of other bands, but the bands themselves are not organized collectively through formal economic or political institutions.

There is a tendency to think of "hunter-gatherers" and "bands" as synonymous, but that is because most of the hunter-gatherers known ethnographically live in marginal habitats where a band-level social system is most adaptive. Historically and archaeologically, we know of a number of foraging societies whose social systems resemble the agricultural tribes and chiefdoms described in the next chapter. All of these nonband hunter-gatherers are found in productive environments with abundant natural resources. Among the best documented are the traditional (precontact) hunting-gathering-fishing chiefdoms of the northwest coast of North America. The rich coastal resources of that area made it possible for nonagricultural peoples to live in comparatively dense, settled communities, and it is not surprising that their economic organization resembled agriculturalists in some important respects. Prehistorically, it appears that foragers with a similar type of social and economic organization may have lived along many of the major rivers of Europe.

By the time anthropologists arrived on the scene, all the hunter-gatherers in these productive environments had long since disappeared, out-competed economically and militarily by more powerful food-producing groups. Our knowledge of hunter-gatherers is therefore biased toward the few band-level hunter-gatherers who still survive, in places such as the Arctic, the southern African deserts, and the African and South American tropical forests. These groups provide the bulk of our data on hunter-gatherers and will be the focus of the discussion to follow.

Work and Leisure

Time Allocation in the "Original Affluent Society"

How hard or easy is it for hunter-gatherers to earn a living? How much time do men and women spend working, and how productive is their labor? At a conference held in 1966, a number of field-workers presented data that attested to a surprising conclusion: Hunter-gatherers, even those living in seemingly harsh environments such as the Kalahari and Australian deserts, are able to live very well indeed by devoting only some 20 or 30 hours per week to the food quest. These findings led one participant to dub hunter-gatherers the "original affluent society," affluent not because they are wealthy in material things, but because they are able to satisfy their needs and wants with comparative ease. Although later research has shown this to be an overstatement, it remains true that among many hunter-gatherers subsistence work is

TABLE 2.1
Work Hours Per Week Among the !Kung

	Subsistence work	Tool making and fixing	Subtotal	Housework	Total work week
Men	21.6	7.5	29.1	15.4	44.5
Women	12.6	5.1	17.7	22.4	40.1
Average, both sexes	17.1	6.3	23.4	18.9	42.3

SOURCE: Lee (1979: 278).

intermittent, leisure time is abundant, and nutritional status is excellent.

The !Kung San (or Bushmen), who live in southern Africa's Kalahari Desert, are the most compelling example of a leisured band society. In order to determine how hard the !Kung were working, Richard Lee (1968, 1979) made a "work diary" of the residents and visitors at Dobe, one of the main water holes in the !Kung area. Each day during a four-week period in 1964 he recorded each person's primary activity (gathering, hunting, staying in camp, visiting), as well as the weight of all meat and vegetable foods brought into camp. Lee found that "subsistence work" (hunting or gathering) occupied adults for only 2.4 days per week on the average. Yet this leisured work schedule supplied the camp with an abundant and well-balanced diet consisting of 258 g (9.1 oz) of meat per person per day and a varied assortment of vegetable foods. Most of the protein and calories in the !Kung diet, in fact, come from vegetable sources (chiefly mongongo nuts) rather than meat. Taking all food sources together, Lee found that the !Kung were getting 96.3 g of protein per person per day, a large amount even by Western standards.[1] Medical studies bear out the nutritional data; though the !Kung are lean, there is no evidence of nutritional deficiencies, and their general health is good (Truswell and Hansen 1976).

What are the !Kung doing when they are not out gathering vegetable foods and hunting game? A lot of the time is taken up with visiting and socializing, but other types of work are also important. Table 2.1 compares the hours spent hunting and gathering ("subsistence work") with estimates of the hours devoted to "maintenance work" (manufacture, maintenance, and repair of tools and other items) and "housework"

[1] Their caloric intake (2,355 calories per person per day) is lower by U.S. standards, but the !Kung are small in stature (157 cm for adult males, 147 cm for adult females), and their caloric intake is probably appropriate for individuals of their height and weight (Lee 1979). There is, however, some dispute about this; although no one argues that the !Kung are malnourished, it has been suggested that their caloric intake may be marginal (Truswell and Hansen 1976), especially at certain seasons of the year (Wilmsen 1979).

(which includes processing mongongo nuts and other foods, collecting firewood, tending the fire, serving food, and so on). When these tasks are added to the hours spent in subsistence work, the !Kung workweek averages 42.3 hours. This is still somewhat less than our own, if we consider the time we spend on housework and maintenance tasks in addition to time spent "at work" away from home.

An interesting sex difference is apparent in the !Kung work data; men are spending considerably more time in both subsistence and mainte- nance tasks and have a somewhat longer workweek overall (44.5 hours as compared with 40.1), while women spend more time doing "house- work," as defined above. The difference in time devoted to subsistence work by women and men does not, however, mean that men are the main breadwinners of !Kung society. Because more calories can be ob- tained per hour by gathering than by hunting in this area, women, who do most of the gathering, actually contribute most of the calories to the !Kung diet.

Lee's study of time allocation among the !Kung was a major improve- ment over the subjective statements that had typified the earlier litera- ture, and it remains one of the few quantitative studies of work effort among a hunting and gathering society. However, the limited duration of his study (four weeks in July) means that seasonal variation in work effort could not be considered. Resources are comparatively abundant during these months, and data collected by Draper (forthcoming) on another !Kung group indicates that the time devoted by the !Kung to subsistence work may be lowest at this time of year (see Fig. 2.1).

How typical are the !Kung? Recent data on other foraging societies indicate that there is considerable variation in hunter-gatherer work effort and that some foragers work as much as (or more than) most hor- ticulturalists. Among the G/wi, a San group living in a somewhat more arid region of the Kalahari, men and women spend an average of 32.5 hours per week in subsistence work (Tanaka 1980), compared with the 17.1 hours spent by the Dobe !Kung.

The Aché, a group of foragers who live in the tropical forests of Para- guay, are another case in point. The Aché today live primarily at a Catholic mission, but they continue to make frequent foraging trips in the forest nearby. Their behavior on these trips has been the focus of an exceptionally thorough study by a group of scholars from the Univer- sity of Utah. In their time-allocation studies (Hill et al. 1985; Hurtado et al. 1985), these researchers used two main techniques: First, they followed randomly selected men and women throughout an entire day and recorded how much time each individual devoted to each of sev- eral activities. Second, they recorded the activities of as many adults as

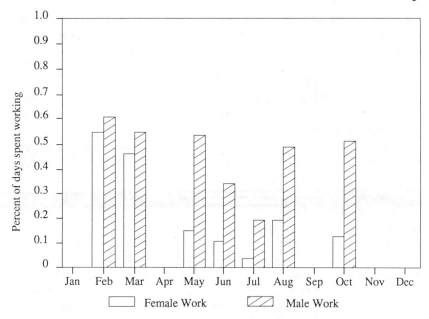

Fig. 2.1. Male and Female Work at /Du/da. Source: Draper, forthcoming.

possible at ten-minute intervals throughout the day. Their data show that Aché men spend an average of 43.5 hours per week procuring food (equivalent to Lee's "subsistence work"), which means they are working about twice as hard as the Dobe !Kung men. Other work (food processing, maintenance work) occupied the men for an additional 1.5 hours per day.

The pattern of work for Aché women is quite different (Hurtado et al. 1985). Whereas Aché men hunt more or less continuously when out of camp, the work of the women is more varied and discontinuous. Unlike !Kung bands, which typically remain at the same campsite for several weeks, the Aché move camp every day or two, and the responsibility for moving the belongings (utensils, bedding, and so on) falls to the women. Much of their work, consequently, involves carrying the family belongings from one location to another. They stop frequently as they walk, either to gather vegetable foods, to process game, or just to rest. They stop walking in early afternoon to set up the camp, after which they may spend their time gathering food nearby or doing other chores. Unlike the men, only 14 percent of their time (1.85 hours per day) was devoted to food-related activities (procuring and processing food), while 46 percent (5.5 hours per day) was spent in leisure.

Before we conclude that women in foraging camps have an easier life than men, we should note that childcare, which is primarily women's work among the !Kung and the Aché, was not included in any of the time-allocation studies mentioned above. It is very difficult to quantify time devoted to childcare, since women care for children while they do other things, but it does limit and affect the other kinds of work they do. The role of childcare in women's work will be discussed further below and in more detail in Chapter 12.

Clearly, there is no simple answer to the question of how hard foragers work. The data suggest considerable variation, probably within the same range as nonforaging societies. We can, however, demolish with confidence the old stereotype that hunter-gatherers had to work all the time simply to get enough food to eat. A corollary of this mistaken view was that agriculture, being more productive, freed hunter-gatherers from their burdensome life and gave them the leisure time to "build culture" and enjoy the finer things of life. The data summarized above indicate that this is not the case. Although the origin of agriculture is a complex problem, the prevailing view among anthropologists is that hunter-gatherers did not begin cultivating crops until decreased returns from hunting and gathering—perhaps resulting from increased population density—forced them into it. As one !Kung man said to Richard Lee, "Why should we plant when there are so many mongongo nuts in the world?"

Childcare and the Division of Labor

The division of labor in foraging bands is the simplest known anywhere, being based chiefly on sex and, to a lesser extent, age. The sexual division of labor appears to be a human universal, one that sets us apart from other species. Unlike nearly all animal species, where adults forage for themselves, human foragers divide up the economic tasks according to sex and share the fruits of their labor with each other.

The patterning in the types of tasks allocated to females and males in hunting-gathering bands shows a surprising amount of consistency. As a broad generalization, men are usually the hunters, especially of large and mobile game, while women gather the plants. Why? The chief reason is probably that the types of tasks performed by women are those most compatible with childcare (Brown 1970). The mobility of the resource is one important factor in determining this. Jochim (1981) has pointed out that big game, which are highly mobile, are procured by men; sedentary resources such as plants, shellfish, and insects are typically collected by women; and small game and fish, which are intermediate in mobility, may be collected by either. The danger of the work and the degree to which it requires concentrated attention are also factors determining its compatibility with childcare. Hence it is not surprising that in the collection of nuts and fruits from trees, men often have the job of climbing the trees and knocking down the fruits, while in cooperative game drives women are more likely to act as drivers and men as capturers. These constraints may also affect productivity. Hurtado et al. (1985) suggest that because the work of Aché women must be compatible with childcare, their productivity is probably lower than it would be if they were free to choose foods on the basis of caloric return alone.

The amount of time each sex devotes to food collection depends in part on the relative importance of game and vegetable foods in the diet, since women and men differ in the types of foods they collect. Some of this is conditioned by the resources available in the environment. Meat is especially important in the Eskimo (Inuit) diet because of the paucity of vegetable foods in the Arctic. Because of this, Eskimo men bring in virtually all the food, while other tasks, such as food processing, are done by the women. Vegetable foods are much more important among the !Kung, but even here local environmental variation can be important. !Kung men work harder at /Du/da than at Dobe, some 95 km to the north, apparently because /Du/da has fewer mongongo nut trees and more game, so that hunting plays a more important role (Draper forthcoming).

Why do individual hunter-gatherers work as much (or as little) as they do? Data bearing on this are scanty, but there is evidence that Aché women and !Kung men work harder if they have more dependent offspring to support (Draper forthcoming; Hurtado et al. 1985). There is widespread sharing of food within hunter-gatherer bands, however, which mitigates differences in consumption to a large extent. The effects of food sharing on individual productivity have not yet been adequately explored. One might expect that food sharing would discourage production, since the more productive individual would not keep the extra food. Something like this probably does take place among the !Kung, where hunters who have been successful may take a rest for a few weeks so that they can eat the meat obtained by others (Lee 1979; Wiessner 1982). Among the Aché, however, this is not the case, and good hunters work even longer hours than poor ones (Kaplan and Hill 1985). Benefits that accrue to these hardworking Aché hunters are not directly economic, since they do not keep the meat, but may involve preferential treatment from fellow band-members. In support of this, Kaplan and Hill have shown that above-average hunters have more children and that their children are more likely to survive. More research of this sort on the reasons for intragroup differences is needed before we can fully understand the patterns of work and leisure in foraging society.

What Foragers Eat, and Why

The image of "man the hunter" has long fired the imagination of theorists interested in our evolutionary past, in part because humans are the only primate that regularly hunts, and in part because the remains of hunting (bones, teeth) have been well preserved in the archaeological record, whereas those of gathering have not. Nonetheless, many hunter-gatherers depend more heavily on plant than on animal foods, and dietary data on extant foragers are provoking a long-overdue interest in the role of "woman the gatherer." Estimates of the proportion of societies that depend more heavily on gathering than hunting vary, depending on the sample of societies chosen and on how the activities are defined. On the basis of a world sample of 58 foraging societies, Lee (1968) found the primary subsistence activity to be gathering in 50 percent of societies, hunting in only 19 percent, and fishing in 31 percent. The proportions calculated by Martin and Voorhies (1975) and by Ember (1978) are quite different but still show gathering to predominate over hunting as the primary subsistence activity. Not surprisingly, hunting is most important primarily in higher latitudes, where growing seasons are short and vegetable foods are scarce, and gathering is more important in temperate areas.

In all foraging societies, however, people are very selective about which foods in the environment they will eat. Their decisions are influenced by economic considerations, namely, the efficiency with which certain foods can be procured. Anthropologists interested in hunter-gatherer diet choice have found models drawn from evolutionary ecology (especially those known as "optimal foraging theory") to be very helpful in understanding this aspect of human behavior. Although the theory was developed by biologists to explain the behavior of non-human animals, it is based on many of the economic assumptions that underlie models in microeconomics (see Chapter 1). Some of the models, in fact, were borrowed directly from economics, so it is not surprising that they have been successful in explaining the behavior of human foragers as well.

Optimal foraging theorists assume that natural selection will favor animals that harvest their food efficiently. "Efficiency" is usually taken to mean getting the most calories in the shortest period of time, but calories per hour is not the only thing that could be maximized. Calo-

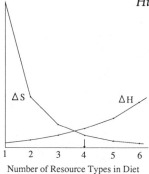

Number of Resource Types in Diet

Fig. 2.2. Optimal diet breadth model. Resource types are added to the diet in decreasing order of profitability. ΔH, change in average handling time, shows how the average handling time increases as lower-ranked resources are added. ΔS, change in average search time, shows how the average search time decreases as resources are added to the diet. Lines intersect at the optimal number of resource types. Source: MacArthur and Pianka 1966: 605. Reproduced courtesy of the University of Chicago Press.

ries produced per unit land area might be more important if land is scarce, and protein produced per unit time might be more important if protein is more limiting than calories. Energetic efficiency is the optimization goal assumed in most optimal foraging models, and there are good reasons for this choice (Smith 1979), but it should be realized that it is an assumption that need not apply in all cases.

Optimal foraging models have been developed for many aspects of economic behavior, but we will consider only one in detail here, the model of optimal diet choice. The optimal diet model (initially developed by MacArthur and Pianka 1966) assumes a homogeneous environment, where resources are encountered randomly. Each food type has a cost (the time taken to procure and process it, often called "handling" time) and a benefit (the net caloric value of the food). The profitability of a food type, then, can be measured by the ratio of benefit to cost, and an optimal forager should prefer the most profitable food items.

But how many different food types should he take? This decision depends on the trade-off between "handling" time, the time it takes to get the item once it is encountered, and "search" time. If a forager chooses only the most profitable items, he will have a high rate of return for each item once he encounters it, but he will have to spend a lot of time "searching" for the food item. If he is willing to be less selective, he will spend less time searching, but he will have a lower rate of return when actually procuring and processing the prey. Fig. 2.2 shows how search time and handling (or "pursuit") time change as resources are added

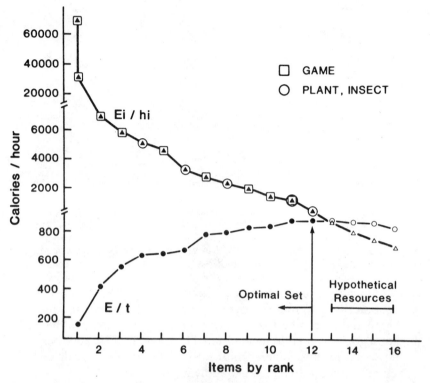

Fig. 2.3. An optimal diet breadth model of Aché resources. The leftmost point on the lower curve was obtained by adding the caloric returns obtained from the top-ranked resources (see Table 2.2), and dividing by the total time spent acquiring them (total search time plus handling time for these two resources). The next point was obtained by adding the caloric returns from the second-ranked resources to the numerator and the handling time for these resources to the denominator. Source: Hawkes, Hill, and O'Connell 1982: 390. Reproduced by permission of the American Anthropological Association. Not for further reproduction.

E = total calories acquired while foraging
E_i = calories available in a unit of resource i
h_i = handling time per unit of resource i
$t = \sum h_i$ plus search time
Hence:
E_i/h_i = calories per handling hour for each resource, after being encountered (search time not considered)
E/t = average returns from foraging that result from the addition of each resource.

TABLE 2.2
Food Types in the Aché Diet

Resource	E/h	Rank
Collared peccary	65,000	1
Deer	27,300	1
Paca	6,964	2
Coati	6,964	2
Armadillo	5,909	3
Snake	5,882	3
Oranges	5,071	4
Bird	4,769	5
Honey	3,266	6
White-lipped peccary	2,746	7
Palm larvae	2,367	8
Fish	2,120	9
Palm heart	1,526	10
Monkey	1,215	11
Palm fiber	1,200	11
Palm fruit	946	12

SOURCE: Hawkes, Hill, and O'Connell 1982. Reproduced by permission of the American Anthropological Association. Not for further reproduction.

to the diet. The optimal diet breadth occurs where these two curves intersect, that is, when the decrease in search time gained by adding food types just equals the increased handling time of procuring them.

In later formulations of this model, the optimal number of food types is determined by comparing the profitability of each food type, once encountered, with the average return rate for all food types of higher rank. Fig. 2.3 shows how Hawkes et al. (1982) have applied this model to the Aché diet. The upper curve shows the profitability—calories obtained per handling hour—of each resource type in the Aché diet (see Table 2.2). The lower curve shows the average returns that accrue from the addition of each resource (calories/handling time + search time). It can be seen from the graph that the addition of item 12, palm fruit, produces marginally more calories per hour than a diet limited to the higher-ranked resources, and so palm fruit is included in the optimal diet set. Any resource less profitable than this (the "hypothetical resources" in the graph) would reduce average foraging returns and so is not taken. The Aché data fit the model extremely well. It is interesting that while the highest ranked resources were taken by the Aché whenever they were encountered, monkeys (ranked 11) and palm fruit (ranked 12) were occasionally not pursued. This ambivalence may reflect their comparatively low return rates, and possibly variation from place to place in average returns.

The model can also be used to predict how changes in technology and resource abundance will affect optimal diet breadth. It is clear from Fig. 2.2 that a decrease in search costs will result in a reduction in the number of food types in the optimal diet. Because search costs (the time it takes to find prey) decrease as prey become more abundant, greater abundance of highly ranked resources should be associated with a more specialized diet. This relationship was suggested for the Alyawara, aboriginal hunter-gatherers of Australia. O'Connell and Hawkes (1981) were puzzled that none of the Alyawara they observed collected seeds, although seeds are plentiful in the area and are reported to be a traditional Alyawara food item. Seeds, however, are comparatively inefficient to collect and process. O'Connell and Hawkes suggest that the recent inclusion of "highly ranked" (in the sense discussed previously) European foods in the Alyawara diet has therefore been associated with the deletion of seeds from the diet. Although the decision to adopt European foods probably involves many factors in addition to economic efficiency, the low efficiency of seed collecting does seem to be the reason why seeds, rather than other traditional foods, are no longer taken by the Alyawara.

A decrease in search time might also come about because of changing technology. Winterhalder (1981) has argued that there were two stages in the adoption of new technology by the Cree Indians and that these stages had different effects on Cree diet breadth. The first technological improvements obtained by the Cree were muskets, repeating rifles, and other devices that improved the pursuit (hence, "handling time") of game. More recently, the Cree have obtained snowmobiles and outboard motors, the chief effect of which is to decrease search time. The optimal diet breadth model predicts that efficiency in searching should result in a constriction of diet breadth, and Winterhalder presents evidence that this new technology has, indeed, been associated with a more specialized diet.

The studies of O'Connell and Hawkes (1981) and Winterhalder (1981) demonstrate that exposure to European foods and technology does not necessarily make optimal foraging theory inapplicable to human foragers, but rather can be used as a natural experiment in which new foraging options may lead to changes in optimal behavior. This is an important lesson for those interested in human prehistory. Although we cannot simply extrapolate from the present to the past, theory can help us to understand the principles of foraging behavior and hence to make meaningful inferences about the economic behavior of foragers in a wide range of circumstances.

Food choice is a complex topic, and optimal foraging theory should be viewed as one new way—not the only way—of explaining it. One limitation of most optimal foraging models is their assumption that people will act so as to maximize energetic efficiency. This is reasonable in many cases, but there are circumstances where other goals may be more appropriate. The need for other nutrients is a case in point. Keene (1981) and Reidhead (1980) have analyzed the diets of prehistoric foragers using linear programming models, which make it possible to consider a variety of resource needs. They have shown that noncaloric nutrients and resources (such as calcium, ascorbic acid, and hides) may have been harder to obtain than calories during some months of the year, and that optimal foraging decisions must be altered accordingly. More generally, a desire for dietary diversity may itself be an important consideration in what foragers collect, and where they go to collect it (Harpending and Davis 1977).

The security afforded by certain resources may also be important. Lee (1979) has pointed out that meat, although desirable, is less predictable than plant foods, because the success of hunters is uncertain and variable. The !Kung, he argues, rely heavily on vegetable foods because they are a secure source of food, not just because they are efficient to collect. There is no doubt that a concern for security underlies many aspects of hunter-gatherer economics, and this issue will be treated in more detail below.

Coping with Seasonal Variation: Mobility, Group Size, and Storage

Agricultural and industrial societies have many ways of buffering environmental variation. At the simplest level, storage evens out temporal variation in resource abundance, and trade does the same for spatial variation. The individual consumer in our society does not have to worry about being where the resources are, when they are available. The resources are virtually always locally available, although the price may reflect the effort involved in making them so. The situation for hunter-gatherer bands is completely different. Rather than being insulated from environmental variation in this way, they "track" the variation, adjusting to it through changes in location and local group size.

Hunter-gatherers often adjust to predictable seasonal variation by living in relatively large "macroband" camps during part of the year and dispersing into smaller, "microband" family-sized groups during the remaining months. The macroband phase, which takes place when important resources are abundant enough to support a large group, is often a time for ceremonies, trade, and other activities that are best performed in large groups. Meggitt (1962) refers to this time as the "ceremonial season" for the Walbiri of Australia, who gather together temporarily in large groups (occasionally as large as several hundred) to perform initiation and other rituals. People typically enjoy the macro-band season, which facilitates visiting and courting as well as more formal rituals and ceremonial events.

For the !Kung, who live in an arid area with few permanent sources of water, rainfall and the distribution of water sources determine the seasonal patterns of mobility and group size. In the area around Dobe there are only five permanent water holes that hold water through-out the year. In the wet season there are many more sources of water, ranging from seasonal pans that hold water for a few days or months to trees that hold a small amount of water in reservoirs in their trunks. In a pinch, the !Kung can also obtain moisture from succulent roots. The more transient water sources can support only a small number of people, and access to the water is often difficult. The !Kung use them when they can, however, since they are often located near valuable plant foods, and the resources near the permanent water holes could not support a large number of people year-round. During the rainy season, therefore, the !Kung disperse into small family groups, where they use the plant foods near the seasonal water sources. In the dry season, they aggregate into larger groups at the water holes. In tradi-tional times, from three to as many as seven bands (approximately 60 to 140 people) would converge at a single water hole during the dry season (Lee 1968, 1979).

Seasonal changes in group size can be expected wherever important resources (water, game, and so on) change in availability and abun-dance throughout the year. The particular details, however, depend on the characteristics of the local environment. The G/wi San inhabit a more arid part of the Kalahari than the !Kung, with no permanent water holes to form a basis for aggregation. Consequently, they aggre-gate during the rainy season (the opposite pattern of the !Kung), when they can use water from the best of the seasonal pools. During the dry season, when these pools have dried up, the G/wi split up into family groups and use the moisture from scattered water-bearing melons and roots (Tanaka 1980; Silberbauer 1981).

Mobility is critical in allowing hunter-gatherer bands to adjust to changes in the distribution and abundance of resources. Binford (1980) has clarified the diversity of such patterns by distinguishing the settle-ment systems of two types of hunter-gatherers, whom he terms "for-agers" and "collectors." Foragers typically range out from a residential camp to hunt and gather and return to the camp at the end of the day. Food is not stored but is collected each day and used as it is procured. Foragers are usually found in tropical regions where resources are comparatively homogeneous; the Aché and the San are examples of hunter-gatherers with this type of mobility strategy. Such groups change the location of their residential camps fairly frequently. The most mobile foragers are those in the tropical forests; the Aché are an extreme case in point, moving camp an average of 50 times per year, about 7 km each time (Binford 1980). The Dobe !Kung, "tethered" to their water holes, move camp less frequently (five times per year, on the average), but travel farther with each move (about 22 km).

Collectors differ from foragers in that they obtain specific resources through specially organized task groups. They are found in areas where critical resources are located very far apart and hence cannot be obtained from a single camp. The collector solution is to locate the residential camp near one resource and send out a specialized task group to procure another resource in a different area. The task group often moves a considerable distance away, forming a temporary camp at the resource site, and usually procures a large volume of food while at the temporary camp. The food may then be cached, temporarily, before being transported to the rest of the group. The Eskimo are a good example of hunter-gatherers with a "collector" strategy, and the Dogrib Indians of northwest Canada are another. During the fall, Dogrib hunters, traveling with canoes, leave the main camp and journey long distances (some 300 km, all upstream) to meet the caribou as they migrate south from the tundra. The hunters remain at the kill site for three or four weeks, and when enough caribou have been killed, they process and dry the meat for transport home to their families (Helm 1972). This pattern is typical of groups in northern latitudes but can be found wherever key resources cannot be obtained at the same general location (Binford 1980). These different mobility strategies are the key means by which hunter-gatherers adapt to spatial variation in the distribution of resources.

Storage is not widely practiced by hunter-gatherers, but it does play an important role among collectors such as the Eskimo, because it enables them to cope with highly seasonal environments. Resources in the tropics change throughout the year, but there are always food sources available. There is no need, consequently, to gather a large amount at one time and store it for later use. In more northern regions, on the other hand, many resources are available in superabundances for limited times and are then unavailable for the rest of the year. In such circumstances, time efficiency is especially important so that sufficient

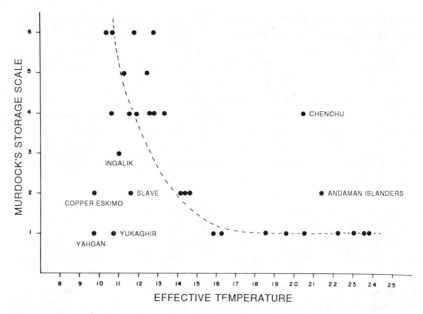

Fig. 2.4. The relationship between storage dependence and effective temperature. Source: Binford 1980: 16. Reproduced by permission of the Society for American Archaeology.

food can be obtained to last the group throughout the rest of the year. Storage, primarily the storage of meat by freezing, enables the Eskimo to survive over the winter. As a general rule, dependence on storage increases as the length of the growing season decreases (Binford 1980). This can be seen in the graph in Fig. 2.4, which shows the relationship between effective temperature (an indicator of the length and intensity of the growing season) and dependence on storage for 31 hunting and gathering societies.

Unpredictable Variation: Distribution in Hunter-Gatherer Bands

Much of hunter-gatherer culture can be interpreted as a means of adjustment to variation in the distribution and abundance of resources. In the preceding section, we considered how hunter-gatherers cope with predictable seasonal variation. Food supplies can also vary unpredictably, due to the vagaries of weather, animal movements, and just plain luck. How do hunter-gatherers cope with such risks? The most important way is through the widespread sharing of food.

Game is an especially unpredictable food source. During any given hunt, the hunters may or may not find game, and they may or may not be successful in bringing down what game they find. Even the best hunters may have runs of bad luck, during which they bring no game back to camp. One way of reducing the resulting variance in meat intake is through sharing. This works because the variance in success for a group of hunters (hunting independently) is less than the variance in success for the individual hunters themselves. In this respect, food sharing resembles commercial insurance, where losses are shared among many different individuals in order to reduce the risk to each. It is a good way of coping with risk, provided that each hunter's chance of success on a given day is uncorrelated with that of the others.

Why should a successful hunter be willing to share his hard-won gains? At an analytical level, it can be argued that such a strategy makes good economic sense. If a hunter can be confident that others will share with him when he is unsuccessful, the security of sharing will probably be more important than a temporary excess of meat. The confidence that others will reciprocate is not automatic but is achieved through a strong ethic of sharing and "generalized reciprocity" (see Chapter 1). Among the !Kung, there are strong socialization pressures against hoarding, and if a person is not generous, the norms of sharing are reinforced by continual badgering and dunning for gifts. Stinginess and selfishness are widely deplored among hunter-gatherers. It is virtually impossible for hoarding and stinginess to take place unnoticed in a hunter-gatherer band, since people are in close and constant contact and private storage places do not usually exist. The risk of ruining one's good name and of being slighted in future exchanges is usually enough to keep people playing by the rules.

Cultural rules concerning meat distribution reinforce these values. The !Kung share arrows widely with men of neighboring bands, and it is customary for the owner of the arrow that first penetrates the animal to be in charge of distributing the meat. Portions are distributed first to the hunters, then to other families in the band, and they in turn distribute meat to their relatives, friends, and visitors (Marshall 1961). Meat sharing is equally widespread among the Mbuti Pygmies and is governed by precise rules. The borrowing of hunting nets is common, and the rule is that the borrower of the net gets one leg and the owner gets the rest. If a second arrow was needed to kill an animal, the hunter who shot it gets the loins and haunches; and if a dog was used to track the prey, its owner gets other designated portions. The person who makes the morning fire before a hunt gets the heads of all animals killed that day. These primary owners then redistribute portions to other band members until all have received a share (Harako 1981). Similar formal rules guide the distribution of large game among the desert aborigines of Western Australia (Gould 1981). These rules serve to dissipate any feelings of ownership by the man who actually makes the kill, and he often receives a comparatively small share in the final distribution.

It is significant that the hunter-gatherer literature abounds with descriptions of meat sharing but says little about the sharing of plant foods. Although some of this may reflect the fact that plant foods are shared less formally, it probably also reflects a real difference in the degree to which the two types of resources are shared. Large game is typically shared very widely, often with individuals in other bands, whereas plant foods and small game may be shared with only the individual family and close relatives. This is probably a consequence both of differences in "food package" size and of differences in predictability, since the returns from hunting are more variable than those from gathering.

In a formal test of these arguments, Kaplan and Hill (1985) analyzed how widely the Aché share 17 different resources. They show that the degree to which food is shared is highly correlated both with the variance among families in the amount procured (a measure of the "riskiness" of the resource) and with the food package size. They also demonstrate that the Aché benefit nutritionally from band-level sharing, although some individuals benefit more than others.

Storage is another way of coping with unpredictable variation in food supplies, but hunter-gatherers rarely use storage for these purposes. When food is stored as a means of coping with seasonal variation, however, it appears to make food sharing less necessary. The Nunamiut Eskimo procure large quantities of caribou meat during the spring and fall caribou migrations, and much of the food obtained during these periods is stored for later use. It is expected that each household will obtain enough meat for its own needs, and sharing does not normally take place outside the family unit. The only time that caribou meat is regularly shared by the Nunamiut is in late summer, when caribou are taken infrequently and in small numbers (Binford 1978).

Storage is probably a high-cost activity for most mobile hunter-gatherers. It can be difficult and time-consuming to prepare food and facilities for storage, and a mobile group would have to spend a lot of time transporting the stored food from the cache to the camp. Storage is more economical for less mobile groups, because of the decrease in travel and transport time. The Tolowa, Tututni, and Coast Yurok of California's northwest coast, who lived in permanent coastal villages for nine to ten months of the year, are a case in point. These settled

foragers regularly stored dried meat, fish, and acorns, and did not normally share food between families (Gould 1981).

Band-level sharing is a good way of coping with variance in hunting success and other local sources of risk. More regional sources of
risk, such as variation in rainfall from place to place, require food
sharing on a more regional level. This is most easily accomplished by
"visiting" relatives in a band that is camped in a temporarily more
well-favored area. Interband mobility of this sort is widespread among
hunter-gatherers, especially those living in unpredictable environments. The !Kung and G/wi San inhabit an environment with great
spatial and temporal variation in rainfall, such that one area can be in-
undated with rain while an area a few miles away is parched. The San
cope with this unpredictable regional variation by visiting friends and
relatives in other areas, knowing that the visit will be returned when
fortunes are reversed. As with food sharing, reciprocity is not automatic. Maintaining close ties with people in other areas, therefore, is
crucial. One way in which this is accomplished is by marrying people
in other bands so that there will be kinsmen in other areas whom one
can visit. Among the !Kung, for example, the average distance between
the birthplaces of mates is 70 km (Yellen and Harpending 1972).

The !Kung reinforce these kinship ties through a system of delayed
reciprocity known as "hxaro." To hxaro someone is to give that person
a gift with the understanding that at some point in the future the recipient will make a return gift to the donor. Blankets, necklaces, and other
material items are appropriate hxaro gifts. Hxaro partners attempt to
make their return gifts of approximately equivalent value, but the most
important aspect of hxaro is the social relationship that it maintains between the partners. Wiessner (1982) has shown that the !Kung choose
their hxaro partners carefully and systematically. Because one function
of hxaro is to give a person an alternative residence in another area,
partners are selected for their location as well as for their abilities and
personal qualities. People strive for a set of partners that allows them
access to a wide range of areas and to areas of high quality (ibid.).

Just as storage can substitute for food sharing as a means of coping
with risk, it can also substitute, to some extent, for interregional visiting. The G//ana are a group of Kalahari foragers who supplement their
diet of wild foods with some cultivation and goat husbandry. This
affords them some protection against fluctuations in resources, since
melons (a water source), grain, and beans are stored, and goats are
stored meat on the hoof. The greater sedentism of the G//ana also enables them to store a variety of other items at the field site, including

wild foods, drums for water storage, and skins, which can be traded for cash or other goods. These are all sources of security that enable the G//ana to cope with temporary shortages of food or water. Like other Kalahari foragers, the G//ana have widespread marriage ties that enable them to visit other bands when necessary, and such visiting is common. In recent times, however, as they accumulate more property, there has been a trend toward marrying people from the same place. Only 14 percent of older G//ana women, but 41 percent of younger women, were born in the same place as their husbands. The distance between birthplaces of mates has shrunk from an average of 56 km to 38 km (Cashdan 1984). Part of the reason for this trend is probably their greater dependence on storage as a source of security, which makes interband visiting (and the widespread marriage ties on which it is based) less necessary.

The sharing of food and the recirculation of material items typical of foraging societies result in an extreme leveling of "wealth." This economic egalitarianism is often mirrored by political egalitarianism as well. The !Kung are intolerant of arrogance, and they are very skilled at verbal put-downs that enforce humility. Usually people direct these put-downs at themselves before others have to do so; the proper behavior of a !Kung hunter who has made a big kill is to mention it in passing and in a deprecating fashion (Lee 1979). Harako (1981) has observed the same behavior among the Mbuti. The G//ana, who rely to a greater extent on food production and stored wealth, have neither the economic leveling nor the admiration for humility typical of these other groups (Cashdan 1980).

Ownership and Land Tenure

Marx and Engels theorized that a stage of primitive communism existed before the rise of the state and the division of society into classes, and the egalitarianism and sharing typical of hunter-gatherers support this position. It should not be supposed, however, that foragers do not understand personal property and land tenure. Material items such as tools, clothing, and ornaments are owned by individuals for their own use, and virtually all foragers have systems of land tenure (usually communal) that control access to the land and its resources.

Discussions of land ownership among hunter-gatherers are often phrased in terms of "territoriality" (an ecological concept) rather than "land tenure" (an economic one), but both concepts are appropriate for hunter-gatherers, and both will be used here. The diversity of systems of land ownership is great. Among the Vedda of Ceylon, to take a "territorial" extreme, the band territory was subdivided for individual band members, who could pass their property on to their children. Territory boundaries not clearly defined by natural features were marked by pictures, cut into tree trunks, of a man with a drawn bow. Territories were guarded and intruders might be shot, although the borders were so well known that quarrels over trespass were rare (Seligmann and Seligmann 1911). At the other extreme, the Hadza of Tanzania reportedly have a very fluid system of land use, such that any individual may camp wherever he wishes without asking permission (Woodburn 1968).

A far more common pattern is that of the !Kung San. Each !Kung territory ("n!ore") is associated with a core group of long-standing residents who are spoken of as the "owners" of the n!ore, and whom outsiders approach when seeking permission to visit. They act as spokespersons for the wishes of the band in this regard and should not be thought of as "owners" in the Western sense. A !Kung child inherits access rights to the n!ore of each parent and has primary rights to the n!ore in which he chooses to settle. N!ore boundaries are recognized by natural landmarks and are neither marked nor defended. Permission to use the resources of another n!ore is always asked but is rarely refused. Bands who do not want visitors to remain do not usually refuse permission outright but rather make them feel unwelcome so that they will leave of their own accord (Lee 1979; Wiessner 1980).

Models from ecology have proven to be useful in understanding variation in territoriality among human foragers. One predictable area of variation is territory size. Because an animal in a poor territory must cover more land to obtain the same amount of resources as one in a richer territory, there is typically an inverse relationship between territory size and resource abundance. This relationship has also been documented for some human foragers, such as the Cree-Ojibwa Indians of eastern Canada (Rogers 1969) and the foragers of aboriginal Australia (Birdsell 1953; Peterson 1972). In both of these regions, band territories are smaller where resources are more abundant.

The degree of territoriality—that is, the degree to which foragers are concerned about defending boundaries and excluding outsiders—is also predictable. Because defending territorial boundaries takes time and energy, ecologists argue that animals engage in territorial defense only when it is economical to do so, that is, when the benefits of exclusive access exceed the costs of defense. No benefits accrue from territorial defense unless there is some competition for resources, so we should not expect to find territoriality where resources are so abundant that there is no basis for competition. This applies to many human foragers. For example, Heinz (1972: 410) says of the !Ko San that "an overabundance of any one of the important resources may cause territoriality to become insignificant during the period of such abundance."

Assuming that there is competition for resources, what other factors affect the costs and benefits of territorial defense? Two important variables cited by ecologists are the abundance and predictability of resources. Scarce resources are less defensible because they are associated with large territories, which are more costly to monitor and defend. Resources that are unpredictable, transient, or highly mobile should also be less economical to defend, since it does not pay to defend a territory unless one can be confident that the resources will be there when they are wanted.

As Dyson-Hudson and Smith (1978) have shown, these predictions can explain much of the variation in hunter-gatherer land tenure. The Western Shoshone of the North American Great Basin inhabit a very arid area, where most resources are both sparse and unpredictable. As we would expect, "The Shoshoni lacked any form of ownership of land or resources on it. . . . The sparse and erratic occurrence of vegetable foods required that territories exploited by different families and villages not only should vary from year to year but should greatly overlap. . . . Under such conditions, ownership of vegetable food resources would have been a disadvantage to everyone" (Steward 1938: 254). The Owens Valley Paiute, at the edge of the Great Basin, present a sharp contrast to the Western Shoshone. Their land, which lay between the Sierra Nevada and the White Mountains, was a comparatively fertile zone fed by mountain streams. Resources were abundant and varied, enabling them to obtain all essential food resources within 32 km of their villages. The natural abundance and predictability were increased still further by the irrigation of wild seed patches. Because of the local abundance, the Owens Valley Paiute lived in permanent villages and had clearly demarcated and defended territories. The territories were owned by bands (villages or groups of villages), and plots of pine nut trees within band territories were owned by individual families. Trespass on pine nut areas led to fights, although not to bloodshed, and fear of evil magic reinforced these sanctions (Steward 1938).

Foragers and the Wider World

All hunter-gatherers today have been affected by the world economy, and this section will consider the effects of this relationship. It should not be supposed, however, that economic ties to the wider world began with the modern era. Though it is impossible to reconstruct the regional economies of hunters who lived "in a world of hunters," evidence from early ethnographies and oral histories suggests that regional trade of durable goods was important and widespread. This section will begin, therefore, with a discussion of this interband exchange. Next, we will consider the social and economic ties that exist between hunter-gatherers and their agropastoral neighbors. The section will conclude with a discussion of development problems and prospects facing hunter-gatherers today.

It is often difficult, both empirically and theoretically, to make a clear distinction between gift exchange (such as the !Kung system of hxaro) and trade. In most cases, the exchange is valued both because of the goods themselves and because of the social relationships maintained between exchange partners. The relative importance of these factors varies from case to case. Hxaro today is primarily important because it reinforces social ties that can be called upon during times of local scarcity. The economic value of the goods themselves, while appreciated, is clearly secondary. It is possible, however, that hxaro functioned differently in the past, before the !Kung began obtaining metal and metal tools from outsiders. Wiessner (1982) has speculated that hxaro may have been the vehicle for distributing important natural resources, such as flint, that are not widely available but that were needed for arrowheads and other tools. She points out that hxaro partners are not simply isolated dyads but are connected as links in a chain over a wide area. This would have permitted the movement of goods over long distances.

Trade in aboriginal Australia was also based, in part, on environmental variation in the source of raw materials and was clearly of economic importance. The exchange network in Queensland (northeast Australia) was similar to hxaro in that it consisted of gift exchanges between partners from nearby bands, the partnerships being linked in a chain that ran 620 km from the coast to the interior. Unlike hxaro, however, the exchange was based on economic specialization, and the rates of exchange appear to reflect variation in supply and demand. At the coast (the source of sting ray spears), twelve spears were customarily exchanged for one ax. But 240 km south, closer to the quarry source for the stone axes and further from the source of spears, spears and axes were traded one for one. Still farther south, one spear was "presumably" exchanged for several axes (Sharp 1952).

Exchange relationships between foragers and their agricultural and pastoral neighbors are also a phenomenon of great antiquity. Archaeological evidence from southern Africa (Denbow 1984) and southern central Africa (Miller 1969) indicates that Iron Age agriculturalists and pastoralists lived side by side with Late Stone Age foraging peoples, both groups maintaining their separate economies and probably trading goods such as pottery and metal objects for beads and stone tools. Wild animal bones found in the Iron Age sites may also be evidence for the exchange of food products, a type of trade that exists today. This proximity and contact between foragers and food producers has existed for nearly 2,000 years in these areas. Foragers and food producers have typically exploited different niches within the same general area, and this has allowed them to persist as separate, independent groups, interacting through symbiotic trade relationships.

Traditional trading relationships between foragers and farmers (that is, where foragers are not producing large amounts for commodity sale on the world market) tend to be egalitarian and symbiotic. I will illustrate the nature of these relationships through two examples, the Mbuti Pygmies of the Congo (Turnbull 1961; Hart 1978) and the Agta of the Philippines (Peterson 1978, 1984). In both cases, the recent intensification of production for trade in external markets has had destabilizing and potentially damaging effects.

Among both Mbuti and Agta foragers, trade with their agricultural neighbors consists primarily of the exchange of meat and other forest products for cultivated crops. The exchange benefits both parties. For the Agta, whose production is focused on hunting and fishing, obtaining corn from Palanan farmers is an easier way to obtain needed carbohydrates than either gathering or cultivating their own crops. The Agta do engage in some limited cultivation, but the mobility required by hunting prevents their remaining by their fields to tend them. The cultivation is, therefore, necessarily small scale. Increasing their dependence on cultivation would make hunting difficult and would also create friction with their Palanan neighbors because of competition over agricultural land. The exchange also benefits the Palanan agriculturalists. The Palanan are limited in sources of protein, because livestock require land for pasturage that is better used for cultivation. The alternative strategy, feeding stock, is also uneconomical; Peterson suggests that the Palanan do better by trading extra grain to Agta hunters than by feeding it directly to chickens and pigs. Probably similar economic incentives exist in the Mbuti case, although documentation is lacking.

The trade between Agta and Mbuti foragers and farmers is sporadic and casual and is conducted largely between trading partners. The hunters are expected to bring game to the villages of their agricultural trading partners, and they are given grain in return. There is no bargaining, nor are there fixed exchange rates. But if the hunters are displeased with the amount they are given, they will simply begin trading with another farmer. They may even take the farmer's food if it is not freely offered (Peterson 1978; Turnbull 1965). On the other hand, some rights and obligations are expected in these relationships. The Palanan farmers plant 10 to 30 percent in excess of their own needs in anticipation of Agta requests for trade, and the Agta, correspondingly, give high priority to the protein needs of their trading partners when they distribute game meat. Either may call on the other for help with game or carbohydrate foods, even when they have nothing to trade at the time. Agta and Mbuti foragers also occasionally work for the farmers as field laborers for a few days at a time, in exchange for food or wages.

The relationships between Agta and Mbuti foragers and their agricultural neighbors have traditionally been rather egalitarian, with both parties having the freedom to break off the exchange when desired. Turnbull (1965) emphasizes that the Mbuti always have the option of simply returning to full-time hunting and gathering in the forest, and both Mbuti and Agta occasionally do this. It is less obvious, however, that this is a long-term option that all Mbuti and Agta could enjoy. Because of the encroachment of agriculturalists on the surrounding forest, Peterson (1978) doubts that the forest could for long support the entire Agta population without the Palanan trade. This may also be the case for the Mbuti, at least in certain areas (Hart 1978: 331). Hart and Hart (1986) have argued that even where population density is low, primary forest in the Mbuti area is so poor in usable wild plant foods as to be uninhabitable by hunter-gatherers who do not have some access to agricultural crops.

The Mbuti and Agta, like foragers elsewhere, are now becoming incorporated into commercial trade with outside markets. Among the Mbuti, this has taken the form of entrepreneurs from the nearby towns and cities coming into Mbuti camps to buy meat, which they then sell at local markets outside the forest. In return, these traders give the Mbuti cassava flour and rice. These professional middlemen differ from their traditional exchange partners in the scale at which they want to trade. They are not satisfied with the small quantities and wide variety of forest products given to the villagers but want to buy as much meat as they can carry away with them. The casual and irregular nature of the traditional trade, which depends on the Mbuti going to the villagers when they wish to do so, is also unsatisfactory for these traders. To monopolize the meat trade and make it more regular and intensive, the traders now come into the Mbuti forest camps. Their attempts to maximize their profits have met with only limited success, because the

Mbuti take food on credit when they have no meat to sell, and the traders frequently are forced to leave with large outstanding debts. The Mbuti ultimately control the trade, since they have other sources of agricultural crops, and they know the traders must eventually leave whether their credit is paid or not (Hart 1978).

The Mbuti have maintained a considerable amount of autonomy in spite of the traders, and their traditional way of life has in many respects remained much the same. Meat (that portion not sold to the traders) is shared in the traditional manner, and cassava flour bought from the traders is shared in a similar fashion. Thus far, therefore, the Mbuti have simply incorporated the commercial trade foods into the traditional communal system of food exchange.

There is no question, however, that the traders have had a large impact on the intensity of hunting among the Mbuti, causing increases in the time spent hunting, the number of nets used in the hunt, and the amount of meat procured. When traders are not in the camp, the Mbuti have a leisurely schedule of hunting about four times a week, with each hunt lasting a little over five hours. With traders in camp, they hunt nearly six times a week, with each hunt lasting almost seven hours. Hunting with this intensity has the potential for seriously depleting the antelope population and has already been accompanied by an increase in band movements and size of hunting ranges (Hart 1978).

There has also been a trend toward payment for meat in cash, which could cause major changes for the Mbuti. Food and material goods have always been widely shared among the Mbuti, as is typical among hunter-gatherers. Money, however, is not being shared in this way (Hart 1978). The storage of wealth and the incorporation into a market economy, therefore, may make fundamental changes in the Mbuti's egalitarian way of life.

Sharing networks and stored wealth (money or livestock) are both ways of coping with the risk of temporary scarcity, but the transition from one to the other is not an easy one for foragers to make. Storage depends upon the accumulation of larger amounts than can be used at any one time, but such accumulation is difficult where people are expected to share whenever they have a surplus. "Upwardly mobile" foragers who wish to rely on their own accumulation of livestock, crops, or money are faced with the choice of cutting off relationships with their importuning kinsmen (whom they need for social and emotional as well as economic security) or giving in with a good grace. Typically, they do the latter. The growing importance of wage labor and large-scale trade, however, has begun to change this. A common pattern, exemplified by the Mbuti, is for traditional goods to be shared but key wealth items, like cash, to be taken out of the sharing network. The same thing has been happening among the !Kung. As Wiessner (1982) has explained, "In the recent past when the !Kung first acquired some livestock, they would slaughter them so that the meat could be distributed. Today, livestock has moved out of the system of reciprocity and become an asset like the land." So long as the milk is shared and donkeys are lent to others when asked, such accumulation is tolerated by other !Kung.

Whereas trade between foragers and food producers is a practice of some antiquity, the use of hunter-gatherers as a source of labor is a more recent development. It is a practice more likely to lead to dependency relationships between hunter-gatherers and their employers. The Kalahari San are a case in point. Early explorers of a century ago noted that the San provided neighboring pastoralists with game and trophies such as ivory, sometimes in trade and sometimes as tribute to the local chiefs. In spite of some animosity between the groups, the San's foraging way of life seems to have remained much the same throughout this period. Today, however, their lives have been drastically affected by their large-scale involvement in the pastoral economy. Large numbers of cattle, together with commercial hunting, have reduced game populations and induced many San to abandon hunting and settle down on the cattle posts of wealthy cattle owners. The form of the relationship has changed over the years, but the San have remained in a position of dependency because of their lack of cattle and the difficulty of hunting and gathering where cattle are abundant. During the nineteenth century and part of the twentieth century, many San were "hereditary servants" who worked without pay for wealthy cattle owners in exchange for food. The San today have more autonomy, in that they are free to leave an employer when they wish to do so, and most are recompensed for their labor with the occasional gift of a calf, as well as milk, some meat, and the draft power of the animals. Few San have cattle of their own, however, and without this source of wealth they remain Botswana's "underclass" (Hitchcock 1982; Cashdan 1986).

A similar pattern is described by Bahuchet and Guillaume (1982) for the Aka Pygmies of the Congo. Early relationships between the Aka and their farming neighbors involved only small-scale exchange of meat for cultivated crops and other items. The Aka became more heavily involved in trade as external demand for nontraditional products (rubber, ivory, pelts, palm nuts) grew in importance, but they retained their basic hunting and gathering economy throughout most of this time. With the commercial production of coffee in the 1960's, however, the Aka were used less as suppliers of their traditional forest products than as an agricultural labor force, in exchange for food, manufactured goods, and money. As with the San, the use of Aka labor in commercial agriculture meant decreased mobility, poorer hunting around the settled camps, and a switch to farming without independent production.

There are some bright spots in this discouraging picture, and they stem from the recent political successes and growing autonomy of hunter-gatherers in the developed capitalist countries of Canada and Australia. It was long assumed by the governments of these countries that the hunter-gatherers would inevitably become assimilated into the larger economy. Hunter-gatherers in both countries, however, have shown a surprisingly strong commitment to political self-determination and to hunting and gathering. The indigenous peoples of Australia, Canada, and Alaska are now a force to be reckoned with, because their marginal and remote lands have recently become immensely valuable to companies wishing to exploit the lands for oil and minerals. In spite of much pressure by wealthy corporations, the aborigines of Australia's Northern Territory have had an impressive measure of success in pressing for legislation that will grant them control of at least some of their traditional lands (Peterson 1982). The interest in land rights in Australia has been accompanied by a "back to the land" outstation movement, where aboriginal peoples are returning to their native lands to depend, at least partially, on hunting and gathering (Coombs et al. 1982). Although this move may seem regressive, people on the outstations have better health and higher morale, and it may best be seen as part of a movement to claim greater control over their lands and the uses to which they will be put. The Cree of northern Canada, similarly, have been provoked by recent mining activity into pressing for land and hunting rights. With the aid of legislative protection, many Cree are now depending more heavily on subsistence hunting than they were doing ten years ago (Feit 1982). There is now reason to hope that through the skillful use of the tools of the dominant society—pushing for legal land rights through legislation and court claims and using the media to influence public opinion—hunter-gatherers in today's capitalist countries can make an effective transition toward being equal partners in the larger economy.

3

Horticulturalists:
Economic Behavior in Tribes

Allen Johnson

The term "horticulturalist" covers a large and diverse array of economic and social systems. As an anthropological type, it serves to fill the gap between "simple" forager societies on the one hand and "complex" agrarian states on the other. For the evolutionist, the rise of civilization depended on the great technological transition from "harvesting energy" (foraging wild foods) to "harnessing energy" (domestication of plant and animal foods; White 1959). Yet the agrarian state and civilization did not arise immediately from plant domestication: In most known instances, a period of slowly increasing dependence on domesticated plants among small groups of horticulturalists preceded the rise of "civilized" states. Hence, our own ancestors were at one time probably horticulturalists.

Horticulture remains important in the study of modern populations because it is the economic basis of most of what are referred to as "tribal societies." With their lineages and clans, elaborate intergroup ceremonies, endemic warfare, and intricate competition between leaders for political control, they have provided stark contrasts—and some provoking similarities—to our own economy and society.

When first observed by Westerners, horticultural societies were regarded as backward in all respects, from the supposed inefficiency of their means of production to their seeming lack of respect for the individual, as inferred, for example, from the control of land and marriage by the elder males of the lineage. Their comparatively disorganized warfare—which depended on ambush, sneak attack, and episodic homicide even of women and children of the enemy group—also seemed more savage than the professionalized battles of modern armies.

With time, we have come to modify these ethnocentric views, recog-

I am grateful to Timothy Earle for his analyses of the Enga, Trobriand, and Tsembaga cases cited herein. For further detail on all cases see Johnson and Earle (1987).

nizing that the economic, social, and political characteristics of horticulturalists are adaptive responses to specific environmental and historical circumstances. In this chapter we will review the main economic features of horticultural societies and of some of the central debates concerning them. We will first identify the core features that distinguish horticulturalists from foragers and peasants, and the main dimension along which types of horticulturalists differ from one another. We will then examine two very different horticultural economies, with briefer looks at a number of other important ethnographic cases of horticulturalists. This chapter will also address crucial debates concerning the economic efficiency of horticulturalists, the "environmental potential" of the tropics, the causes of war among horticulturalists, and the reasons for the grandiose displays of wealth characteristic of the "prestige economy."

Horticulturalists as an Economic Type: Theme and Variations

"Horticulturalist" is one of those categories, common enough in our field, whose meaning seems clear until we attempt to define its boundaries exactly—that is, provide rules for deciding who is a horticulturalist and who is not. Only then is it apparent that the boundaries are fuzzy and littered with variants.

Common Features

It is simplest to begin by listing the features most widely shared by contemporary horticultural peoples around the world:

1. Distribution throughout the humid tropics;
2. Dependence on slash and burn or shifting cultivation of root crops for the vast bulk of food energy in the diet;
3. Production for subsistence;
4. Provision of labor and technology by the nuclear or extended family of the producer;
5. Control of land by multifamily corporate kin groups;
6. Settlement in villages or in well-defined clan territories, with populations of several hundred members;
7. Endemic warfare (before modern pacification);
8. Political leaders of either the headman or the Big Man varieties, with important roles in production, exchange, and resource allocation.[1]

---

[1] The term *headman* refers to leaders of villages (groups of up to several hundred individuals living close together), who generally lack power beyond their ability to lead by

In addition to these general features, two others may be mentioned that, although not universal, have caught the imagination of anthropologists and economists:

9. Overproduction of staple foods so that substantial amounts of food energy are "lost," either when producing gardens are abandoned to forest regrowth or as crops in storage bins rot (to the delight of their owners, who gain prestige as a consequence); and,

10. An intergroup "prestige economy" characterized by the use of primitive valuables and money, the existence of separate "spheres of exchange," and competitive feasting and gift giving in which the greatest prestige accrues to the most generous givers.

Horticulturalists vs. Foragers

Having located some central tendencies of the horticultural economy, we may now chart some of its debatable boundaries. Horticulturalists are distinct from foragers in their dependence on domesticated plants for the bulk of their food energy. This distinction becomes difficult to apply in unusual cases where domesticated plants provide only a small portion of a diet that is still largely obtained by foraging. For example, the Siriono Indians of the Bolivian rain forest (Holmberg 1969) forage for wild foods in an extensive territory but also scatter tiny horticultural plots throughout the region. They visit these plots while on trek, depending on them as secure sources of food energy to supplement their diet of wild foods.

Though supplementary, garden produce is essential to the Siriono's ability to survive periods when wild foods are scarce, particularly in the wet season, when travel is difficult. We could classify the Siriono either as foragers or as horticulturalists, therefore, depending on which aspect of their economy we regard as most important. Such cases raise the interesting theoretical issue of why an evolutionarily more "advanced" technology like horticulture has failed to replace foraging. It may be that domestication is not really a more efficient technology than foraging, but is rather a kind of economic intensification made necessary by population growth and pressure on resources. Accordingly, peoples living at low population densities do not have to intensify using horticulture and are free to remain mobile foragers (cf. Cohen 1977).

---

example and to make motivational speeches. Big Men lead groups of similar size, but in more complex political systems where they are kinbased (clans) and the Big Men are "men of renown" who play key roles in "intergroup collectivities" as discussed below. Big Men have more power than headmen and to some degree can bully followers into line.

Horticulturalists vs. Peasants

The boundary between horticulturalists and peasant agriculturalists is, if anything, more difficult to define. In general:

1. Peasant agriculturalists are found in more advanced political systems, such as complex chiefdoms and agrarian states;

2. They practice very intensive land use involving crop rotation, permanent annual cropping, or even multiple cropping within the same year; fallows are short or nonexistent in contrast to the long fallows characteristic of horticulturalists;

3. Their agricultural methods are also more *labor* intensive, as in hand transplanting from seedbed to field, manuring, mulching and mounding, and terracing;

4. They use technological inputs purchased in the market, such as farm implements and fertilizer, and they sell part of their production in the market;

5. They often depend on technologically difficult, state-controlled facilities—irrigation or drainage systems, storehouses, seagoing craft, roads, and the like—to complete their economic tasks;

6. Since they do not themselves own or control these essential capital improvements, they must pay some form of rent, tax, or tribute to a controlling elite; and,

7. They are specialized producers in a complex economic system that includes such other production specialists as fishers and herders, processing specialists (such as millers, bakers, and brewers), and craft specialists.

Again, the differences are quantitative rather than qualitative, and it is often a matter of emphasis whether a group is labeled "horticultural" or "peasant." For example, the Trobriand Islanders (Malinowski 1935) live on a Melanesian island that has been completely transformed by human activity. They depend for a living on carefully cultivated plots under the management of the chief and his garden magicians, and must participate in a multi-island trade network (the famous "kula ring") in order to obtain such essential items as green stone for axes, traded in exchange for yams from their own gardens. The only wild foods they consume are those they obtain from full-time fishing communities along the coast, and they must pay a kind of rent in the form of "gifts" of yams to the chief, who is owner of all the lands of the chiefdom.

Hence, whereas the Siriono appear to be almost foragers, with tiny gardens acting as a kind of insurance against random or seasonal scarcity of wild foods, the Trobrianders appear to be almost peasants, with elite-controlled access to intensively farmed land and dependence on a kind of regional market for necessities they cannot themselves provision. Additional possibilities for mixing horticulture with other economic strategies have probably been common in history: The tiny millet gardens planted by the Turkana herders of Kenya in unusually wet years (Gulliver 1951), or the small plots of cotton, gourds, and perhaps maize among the prehistoric fishers of coastal Peru (Mosely and Day 1982) come to mind.

Two Cases

We need not delve further into such boundary questions. Instead, we will treat horticulturalists as a continuum along which cases vary according to levels of population pressure on resources and the consequent intensification of production. At one end are tropical horticulturalists living at low population densities, with a relative abundance of land for horticulture and an extent of forest in which they may forage for fish, game, insects, and wild nuts, fruits, roots, and other vegetable foods. Such people are only mildly territorial and are comparatively free to move their settlements; leadership is minimal and, apart from the need for defensive alliances where warfare is common, households are autonomous and self-sufficient. At the other end are horticulturalists living under high population densities, where wild foods are virtually nonexistent, and even good agricultural land is scarce. Domesticated supplements to wild foods, to provide protein, fats, and other essential or highly desirable nutrients, are necessary and time-consuming aspects of the economy. Access to land is tightly controlled through kin groups, and relations between landholding groups are coordinated through a system of debt, credit, and exchange in which all families participate, but some hold more power than others. We turn now to examine in more detail these two endpoints of a continuum, viewing first the low-density Machiguenga Indians of the Peruvian Amazon, and then the high-density Mae Enga of the New Guinea highlands.

The Machiguenga: Extensive Horticulturalists of the Peruvian Rain Forest

The Machiguenga speak an Arawakan Indian language and inhabit the upper Amazon rain forest of southeastern Peru. Although they are in the foothills of the Andes, virtually in the shadow of the great Inca fortification at Machu Picchu, the Machiguenga live in small family groups scattered widely throughout the forest. Indeed, in their familistic independence and mobile pattern of settlement, they are very similar to small-group foragers such as the !Kung San (Lee 1979) or the

Nunamiut Eskimos (Gubser 1965; Spencer 1959). Despite their dependence on domesticated plants for the bulk of their food energy, the Machiguenga have little in common with the Andean peasant farmers a few score kilometers to the west, who provisioned the Inca Empire in the past and who remain vital to the economies of the Andean nations.

The Machiguenga economy is well suited to their environment. For a tropical region, the soils are of above-average fertility (Johnson 1983: 33). In the forests and streams surrounding their settlements, the Machiguenga encounter a wide diversity of fish, game, fruits, vegetables, and nuts. Between the rich production of food energy from their gardens, and the great diversity of nutrients obtained from the wild foods they forage, they enjoy an ample and balanced diet. Physically, this dietary sufficiency is reflected in overall good health, including appropriate body weights for height, good teeth and gums, skin unblemished except for insect bites, and shiny black hair. Although the Machiguenga do suffer a number of health problems from infections, snakebites, and injuries, these are a consequence of their way of life in a wild environment, not of their lack of food.

This overall dietary well-being raises a crucial issue for horticultural economies, especially those from the Amazon: If resources are abundant and diet is fully adequate, why have population densities remained so low and political development so minimal? The original answer offered for this dilemma was the doctrine of "Limited Environmental Potential" (Meggers 1954). According to this argument, the capacity of the tropics to support agricultural populations is very low. Topsoils are shallow and easily degraded; clearing the forest exposes these thin soils to the powerful tropical sun and the pounding of heavy tropical rains, both of which contribute to the breakdown of the soil's "crumb structure," which is vital to plant life; weeds grow in such luxurience that they outstrip the crops and, over time, require greater and greater amounts of labor to keep a field in production; and virulent plant diseases and pests can destroy a single crop before it matures to harvest.

The consequence of these environmental "limiting factors" was taken to be that, in order to adapt to their environment, tropical populations had to remain small and widely scattered, farming their plots for a few years and then abandoning them to the healing process of forest regeneration. Only with such "shifting cultivation," the argument went, could the tropical soils be protected from degradation and eventual sterility.

This is a plausible argument with some supporting evidence in its favor. In the Machiguenga case, soils do lose fertility with horticulture and over a few years become quite impoverished; weeds, meanwhile, become increasingly dense and, as their roots entrench, difficult to remove. There comes the point, after a few years of cultivation, when clearing a new garden is preferable to cultivating an old one, despite the high cost of clearing a garden from virgin forest. Thus it appears reasonable that the Machiguenga should live at a population density well below one person per square kilometer, scattered in groups of from 5 to 35 members dwarfed by the vast forest surrounding them.

The difficulty with this as an explanation for low population densities and small community sizes in Amazonia, however, was recognized early by Carneiro (1960). Even given the limited "environmental potential" of tropical soils (and, we are learning, not all tropical soils are so poor), the communities of Amazonia are often so small and scattered that there is abundant farmland in their vicinities, ample to meet the needs for food energy of much larger communities indefinitely, without having to move or scatter. This is essentially true for the Machiguenga, and thus a shortage of good garden land cannot in itself be the only explanation for the small scale of Machiguenga economy and society. As we now examine the Machiguenga system of production and distribution, we will be alert for other signs of scarcity that might limit the size and density of their population.

The basis of the Machiguenga economy is the production of staple crops in horticultural gardens. After a plot of land, selected for its good soils, gentle slope, and convenient location, has been cleared and its tangle of vegetation allowed to dry, it is burned. Once believed to result in uncontrollable fires that laid the forest waste, such fire agriculture is now recognized to be an efficient means of clearing vegetation and of leaving a fertilizing layer of ash on the surface.

Of all crops, manioc (cassava) accounts for about 65 percent of production. Next in importance is maize, a crop that grows only in newly cleared gardens. Although maize accounts for only some 20 percent of production, it is so important to the Machiguenga that it is the primary reason why every household or cluster of households (hamlet) attempts to clear at least one new garden each year. A possible reason for this is that whereas manioc is a rich source of carbohydrate food energy, maize is also a source of vegetable protein and oil, both of which are scarce in manioc and the other root crops in the Machiguenga diet (Baksh 1985; Johnson and Baksh 1987).

Beyond these basic staples, which are seen as the primary responsibility of the men, a wide range of other crops are planted (cf. Conklin 1957), usually by the women, who seek out unused pockets of soil within the manioc-maize grid and plant cocoyam, yam, sweet potato, pineapple, squash, gourds, and a number of other crops that add variety and spice to the staple diet; many useful nonfood crops, such as cotton, palm, and balsa, are also planted. Once growth is under way, the soil is quickly overgrown with a tangle of vines, medium-height foliage like manioc, and some tree crops such as banana, guava, and avocado. It has been observed that, both in the diversity of plants and in the protection they give the soil, the slash-and-burn garden of extensive horticulturalists like the Machiguenga imitates the jungle and helps reduce soil erosion and infestations of insects and diseases (Anderson 1954: 120–125; Geertz 1963).

Machiguenga horticulture is highly productive. An average family of about seven members, with several gardens totaling about 1 hectare in area, invests some 2,600 hours per year, or about eight hours per person per week. The result is an overabundance of food energy (more than twice as many calories will be produced as will be consumed) and a sufficiency of the other major nutrients recommended for a good diet (Johnson and Behrens 1982). Thus, with a few hours of work per day, Machiguenga horticulturalists produce a more than ample food supply. This is typical of native Amazonian communities still living under traditional horticultural regimes (Berlin and Markell 1977).

We need to moderate this picture of abundance only slightly at this point. The Machiguenga themselves do not regard good garden land as abundant, but rather as quite scarce. This is so because their favorite soils, black in color and full of bits of shale that make the soil soft and easy to work, are rare. The more common soils are red and black clays that, although they produce decent crops, particularly of manioc, are hard to plant and hard to weed. Furthermore, if one wishes to place one's house near good garden land, as well as near a clean mountain stream for drinking water, yet not too far from a river where fish are available, then the number of ideal settlement sites is actually very scarce. Thus, even with regard to garden land, the Machiguenga would not share our view that land is abundant and that there is no need to shift settlement frequently in order to obtain good land.

Despite their heavy dependence on horticulture for sustenance, the Machiguenga place inordinate emphasis on wild foods. That is, whereas their labor in gardens is very productive (1 calorie of energy invested in garden work produces about 17 calories of food energy in return), their labor in wild food is barely rewarded: 1 calorie invested in fishing produces only 1.4 calories of food energy, and a calorie of work invested in forest foods yields only 0.8 of a calorie. Why should such meager returns motivate the Machiguenga, who are not impractical people, to

expend nearly as much labor time procuring wild food as they do in
garden work?

The answer is that, in the streams and large areas of forest that surround their isolated homesteads and gardens lies a great diversity of
foods and raw materials that are essential for the self-sufficient life the
Machiguenga value. In the forest they hunt a large number of game
birds and mammals. They also forage among more than 40 varieties of
edible grubs and caterpillars, and collect many wild nuts, fruits, and
vegetables. In the rivers they catch a similar diversity of fish, as well as
crustaceans and other water creatures. These foods become available at
different times throughout the year, providing a continuously varying
and much prized diversity of tastes and nutrients to their bland diet
of garden staples. Indeed, the Machiguenga are very disappointed in,
and can hardly bring themselves to eat, a meal that consists solely of
manioc or other root crops (Baksh 1985).

Beyond this, the forest is a rich storehouse of raw materials. All
housing materials, from hardwood posts to palm leaf roofs and palm
wood walls and floors, come from the forest. Fibers for tying and for
manufacturing coarse twine, bamboo and cana brava for knives and
combs, and materials for constructing baskets, boxes, mats, and even
toys for children all originate in wild forest plants. Knowledge of the
whereabouts and abundance of these materials is so important that
late afternoon and evening hours are often consumed by detailed and
vivid accounts of forays into the forest, with eager audiences partici-
pating and asking for information to be repeated and elaborated. These
conversations have much the same flavor as among ourselves when
shoppers get together to discuss bargains and the availability of scarce
commodities.

Hence we may characterize Machiguenga gardens as providing the
subsistence security of the Machiguenga diet in the form of calorie-rich
carbohydrate root crops, and the forest and streams as providing the
nutritional balance and taste excitement. In addition, the forest provides the raw materials that allow the Machiguenga to manufacture all
their material needs and thus avoid dependence on markets or neighboring societies.

We should keep in mind, therefore, that when such low-density
horticultural areas are described by outsiders as "underpopulated" or
"underdeveloped," the Machiguenga would not agree. In their view,
large areas of forest reserves are necessary to supply them with the full
complement of resources they require. In fact, most of these resources
are rather scarce even at the low Machiguenga population density. A
hamlet of five houses can use up all the roofing leaves available within

an hour's walk of the settlement and can exhaust local supplies of game and fish, requiring several hours' travel before supplies are found. At such times the Machiguenga are apt to look askance when their neighbors, who live perhaps an hour distant, appear in their vicinity on foraging trips: From their standpoint, the environment is becoming too crowded!

For the Machiguenga, a high quality of life is synonymous with family self-sufficiency and independence. They can achieve this under normal conditions by producing a surplus of inexpensive garden foods, by foraging a sufficient amount of wild foods and raw materials in the forest (possible only with low population density and scattered settlements), and by mastering the skills necessary to produce the manufactures on which they depend: house, clothing, bow and arrows, digging sticks, carrying bags, storage baskets, and numerous secondary items like combs, necklaces, and wooden spoons.

In fact, the social and political organization of the Machiguenga reflects this basic adaptation. The primary residence unit is the family household or extended family hamlet. Depending on the season or the availability of good land and hunting and fishing areas, individuals will settle alone or with a few close kinsmen for several years. Each year they will clear at least one new garden to grow maize and will cultivate older gardens, where maize will not grow but where manioc and the wide diversity of women's crops will grow for two or three more years before the garden is abandoned. Meanwhile, the nearby forest is exploited for its bounty. As the best local garden lands are used up, and as the wild resources become depleted locally, families will think of moving and may select a site and clear a new garden even while living at the old site. As the new garden comes into production, they will begin a new house and enter a period of dual residence until they finally settle in the new location, returning periodically to harvest tree crops and other useful cultigens from the old gardens. When these moves take place, not all the families from the old location may move: Each family is independent and assesses its own self-interest before deciding whether to stay with its present group, join another, or live alone as a single nuclear family household for a period of time.

This family-level society is characterized by the absence of many traits that have come to be associated with horticulturalists. Their kinship system does not greatly emphasize unilineal reckoning of descent, nor does it include lineages, clans, or other corporate (property-holding) groups. Territoriality is weak, restricted to the courtesy of not foraging too close to another settlement without some prior agreement. Marriages are matters of personal preference of the individuals involved, in consultation with their immediate families. There are no village or village-level polities, no headmen or other multihousehold leaders, nor is there warfare (although sporadic individual violence occurs). Finally, ceremonial life is little developed: Apart from the curing rituals undertaken by family members, and the occasional beer feast hosted by a local family, people do not meet in groups and do not engage in group political or religious events.

Lest we perpetuate a frequent error with regard to such groups, we should not end on the theme of what they lack. What they enjoy is a great deal of personal freedom to choose where and with whom to live, a low level of interpersonal violence, control of the main factors of production within the household and extended family hamlet, and a nutritious and diverse diet. Their shifting horticulture allows them to farm the best available soils at the peak of their productivity and to forage locally for wild foods. Because of the low population densities, people are free to move when the best soils have given out and when local wild foods have become scarce. Since soils do lose fertility rapidly under cultivation, and since wild foods are widely scattered and easily depleted, shifting settlement and a mixture of horticulture and foraging provide them a cost-efficient and nutritious diet. What they "lack" mostly are the costly consequences of dense human settlement and pressure on natural resources.

In sum, the Machiguenga represent an extreme case of horticulturalists living at low population density with a comparative abundance of life-sustaining resources. The central points to note from this example are the following:

1. Horticulture mixed with foraging wild foods is an efficient use of labor and provides a nutritious diet to tropical populations.

2. This system works well at low population densities, where people scatter to avoid competition over good agricultural land and wild resources, because tropical soils deplete easily, weeds get out of hand easily, the best, easiest-to-work soils are scarce, and wild foods are easily depleted.

3. Under such ideal conditions, there is little warfare, settlement is in households and extended-family hamlets, and ceremonial life and political structures are little elaborated, because they are not needed.

Is there any evidence to suggest that serious economic problems would arise for the Machiguenga if they were to increase the size and local density of their populations? Baksh (1985) studied a recently settled Machiguenga village of 250 members, artifically created by the efforts of government and missionary agencies. Although the village was settled in a previously uninhabited area that was rich in land and wild resources, after only a few years the game were largely hunted out, and people were dependent on abundant fish in many nearby streams for fat and protein in their diet.

It was at this point that Baksh began his study. Over the next year and a half, he was able to document the depletion of fish from the region's streams. As nearby streams were emptied of fish, people traveled ever greater distances to maintain an adequate level of fish in their diet. Travel time to fish increased four times over the study period, from 0.6 hours per trip to 2.4 hours. Primarily for this reason, the output/input ratio (labor efficiency) of fishing declined, and total work effort increased as people attempted to maintain the diet to which they had become accustomed. Population began to disperse more as the village emptied out while foraging families traveled to fishing areas. Fish eventually became more scarce in the diet, and the number of disputes (such as verbal fights and fist fights) increased dramatically. The quality of the diet became more erratic, and overall quality declined.

Finally, the community was on the verge of fissioning when the village leader managed to salvage it by moving the whole community a day's travel downstream, where wild foods were still abundant. This involved an enormous cost in new housing, but it was the only way to hold the community together. From his study, Baksh concluded that the vulnerability of faunal resources to quick depletion by concentrated human settlements is the main reason why Amazon communities have remained small, living at low densities, with high settlement mobility and limited political elaboration.

The Central Enga: Intensive Horticulturalists of the New Guinea Highlands

As we turn now to the opposite end of the spectrum, we will see that families come to be integrated in a widespread political economy with which they must interact. They are bound through military alliances, property relations, and economic exchanges with comparatively large numbers of other family groups. This binding of families into highly interdependent groups is required by the increasing scarcity of resources that accompanies population growth and drives families, that would probably prefer greater independence if they had the choice, to seek the protection and security of larger groups for their very survival.

The Central Enga occupy a mountainous region in the highlands of Papua New Guinea and include both the Mae Enga (Meggitt 1977) and the Raiapu Enga (Waddell 1972). The Central Enga are representative of the core populations of highland New Guinea, where dense populations practice intensive horticulture in high, open intermontane valleys. The climate is tropical and moist, although the altitude can cause low temperatures to fall below 10°C in the cool season. Below about 1,400 m lie malarial rain forests that are virtually uninhabited. In the preferred zone, between 1,400 m and 2,200 m, where midmountain and valley forest once dominated, now lie rich valleys filled with garden plots and fallow areas. Above 2,200 m lie forests that shelter some game and provide foraging areas for pigs. Of the land available to Enga clans, however, less than 10 percent remains as forest, the rest being heavily cultivated. This reflects the Enga population densities of from 33 to 97 persons per square kilometer, from 100 to 300 times the density of the Machiguenga.

Such high population densities are sustained by an intensive horticulture based on sweet potatoes, some slash-and-burn gardens, and pig husbandry. Foraging wild foods is an insignificant part of the economy. The Enga diet concentrates on sweet potatoes for food energy, pigs for protein and fats, and the slash-and-burn gardens for a diversity of other nutrients.

Intensive horticulture centers on permanent monocropping of sweet potatoes.[2] Garden plots are made up of small mounds, each about 9 feet in diameter, which are constructed after each harvest by folding green manure—composed of old sweet potato vines, leaves, and other mulch—into soft earth and allowing it to decompose. Into these fertilized mounds the new sweet potatoes are planted and cared for. This intensive horticulture is concentrated on the rich soils of the valley floors and in the alluvial fans that border the valleys, and it is there that the greatest concentrations of Enga population are found. In a sample Raiapu community, Waddell (1972) found that 62.5 percent of garden land was in permanent sweet potato cultivation. This highly productive cultivation of a root crop that, like manioc, is rich in food energy but poor in other nutrients, is the basis for some of the greatest population densities known among horticulturalists.

Along the steeper slopes of the valley, a variety of crops, such as yams, bananas, and many other species, are cultivated in slash-and-burn gardens with fallow periods of from ten to fourteen years, half the length of Machiguenga fallows. These shorter fallows are almost certainly the result of population pressure, for such short fallows do not allow complete regeneration of tropical soils under most conditions. In fact, as a result of the deforestation of the region, a number of for-

[2] Monocropping refers to agricultural fields where only one crop is planted. The usual pattern for tropical horticulturalists like the Machiguenga is often termed "multicropping," or planting several crops intermixed in the same field.

merly wild trees are now grown in gardens for use in building, fencing, lashing, and other manufacturing purposes, and for firewood.

Aside from the astonishing productivity of sweet potatoes, the most dramatic aspect of the Central Enga economy is pig husbandry. The pig population generally exceeds that of the humans, and, since uncultivated areas are relatively scarce, the pigs have nowhere to forage and must be fed the same sweet potatoes that humans eat. Essential for protein and fat in the diet, pigs consume more agricultural produce than humans do (Waddell 1972: Table 28) and require about 440 hours per person per year. Yet pigs provide only about 2 percent of the Enga diet, and return only about 40 calories of food energy per hour of labor invested. Because such an hour of labor probably costs 200 or more calories of energy in work, it is clear that pigs do not pay for themselves in energy terms and can be justified only as sources of scarce nutrients of the kind that the Machiguenga are used to finding wild in forests and streams.

Nevertheless, the Central Enga do not enjoy an abundant diet. With the loss of wild foods, their diet depends heavily on sweet potato tubers alone. In some areas of the highlands, protein-calorie malnutrition is common among infants, and the diet is generally deficient. Among the Enga—because of the availability of slash-and-burn gardens (and the growing availability of purchased foods such as tinned meat)—the diet at present appears adequate (Waddell 1972: 122–25). But the consequences of intensified horticulture on the social and political organization of the Central Enga have been far-reaching and profound.

Primary among these is warfare. In such crowded landscapes, with all the best land in short supply and carefully controlled, there are many immediate or proximal causes of warfare: rape or infidelity, theft of pigs or wealth objects, witchcraft accusations, and even verbal insults. But Meggitt's (1977) careful study of Mae Enga warfare convincingly demonstrates that the predominant underlying cause of warfare is competition over scarce agricultural land. Mae Enga communities deliberately pick on smaller neighboring groups for warfare, driving them off and annexing their land. Over half of Enga wars are over land in this very direct sense.

Before modern pacification, such warfare was endemic in the highlands. It was a major cause of death among men and a chronic source of insecurity. All movement outside one's own clan territory was hazardous and undertaken only in armed groups (Meggitt 1977: 44). Men had to be ready to defend their territories when threatened with attack, and this in turn placed a great emphasis on building and maintaining military alliances. It also put a premium on reproducing many offspring, for attrition was high, and groups had to maintain a high population growth rate to remain politically and militarily viable. It is from the twin circumstances of scarce sweet potato land and chronic warfare that the main elaborations of the Enga political economy—in contrast to that of the Machiguenga—arose.

The differences between the Machiguenga and the Enga are not so apparent at the level of the family and the domestic economy. The basic Enga unit of production is also the nuclear family household, and most work is performed individually. One important distinction is found: Enga women do most of the agricultural work, in addition to cooking and caring for children. Enga men are responsible for clearing and fencing gardens but thereafter are most likely to be found engaged in numerous public, political activities. Individual men own the lands they farm, having received them at marriage from the lands controlled by their families and kin groups, and each household controls the labor and technology on which it relies for subsistence. To this degree, the Enga are like horticulturalists everywhere in being economically self-sufficient household subsistence producers.

Crucial limits on the autonomy of the household, however, distinguish the Enga from the Machiguenga. For one, Enga households are generally found in extended family hamlets composed of the members of a single patrilineage; in some cases the men of the patrilineage eat and sleep in a men's house, surrounded by separate houses for their wives and children. The activities of clearing gardens, fencing (to protect them from marauding pigs), and building houses are done by the men of this patrilineal group, working cooperatively. The main economic advantage to these groups is that, by fencing a garden communally, they save greatly on the labor and materials that would otherwise be needed to fence off separate plots within the communal clearing. Beyond this strictly economic advantage, the men of the patrilineage, being close biological kin, are strong and welcome supporters of one another in marriages, feasts, and other politically important matters.

Still, the Enga households and hamlets are quite similar to those of the Machiguenga. Where the Machiguenga pool wild foods in their hamlets, the Enga pool labor. It is also noteworthy that, like the Machiguenga hamlet, there is very little ceremonial or symbolic elaboration within the Enga hamlet. Only at the higher levels of political integration are the symbolic developments of the prestige economy encountered.

The average Enga patrilineage group numbers about 33 and is the same scale of close-knit extended family as the Machiguenga hamlet. At the next level, however, is the Enga subclan, a group numbering about 90 members that owns a sacred dance ground and a sacred grove of trees. Members of a subclan are required to pool wealth for bride payments whenever any of their members marries and in support of one of their members who is striving to become a Big Man. A subclan is in competition with other subclans for prestige, which affects its members' ability to obtain wives and their desirability as partners in regional alliances. An individual householder is motivated to contribute to his subclan's political and economic activities, therefore, because his immediate family's self-interest is intimately bound with that of the subclan.

The Enga subclan is a unit approximately the size of the largest corporate kin groups in societies occupying the less densely populated highland fringe of New Guinea, such as the Tsembaga (see below). But the Enga are organized into a still higher level grouping, the clan, which averages about 350 members and is the ultimate owner and defender of the territory of the clan, from which all clan members ultimately derive their subsistence. Clans own carefully defined territories and defend them both in battle and on ceremonial occasions. They are led by Big Men who speak for their clans in interclan relations and who work within their clans to mobilize the separate households for military, political, and ceremonial action.

Like the subclan, the clan is an arena for dramatic public activities. The clan owns a main dance ground and an ancestral cult house. At these ceremonial centers, public gatherings take place that emphasize the unity of the group as against other clans. Sackschewsky (1970: 52) sees this as an essential tactic to overcome the fierce independence of Enga households, where "each man makes his own decisions." Such familistic independence creates problems for Big Men, who encourage interfamily unity in the effort to enhance the strength of their own clans in a fiercely competitive and dangerous social environment.

Let us imagine the problems faced by the members of an Enga clan. They are trying to make an adequate subsistence from small amounts of intensely utilized land. Surrounding them is a world of enemies ready to drive them from their land and seize it at the first sign of weakness. They must attempt to neutralize this external threat by several means: (1) by maintaining a large, unified group, they show strength in numbers, making others afraid to attack them; (2) by collaborating in the accumulation of food and wealth to be generously given away at ceremonies, they make themselves attractive as feasting partners; and (3) by being strong and wealthy, they become attractive as allies for defensive purposes, turning their neighbors either into friends or into outnumbered enemies. These three goals can be achieved only if each member of a clan is willing to fight on behalf of other members, to avoid fighting within the clan (even though it is with his clan members that a man is most directly in competition for land, since they are his most immediate neighbors), and to give up a share of his precious household accumulation of food and wealth objects in order that his Big Man may host an impressive feast.

This dependence of the household on the economic and political success of the clan is the basis of the Big Man's power. A Big Man is a local leader who motivates his followers to act in concert. He does not hold office and has no ultimate institutional power, so he must lead by pleading and bullyragging. His personal characteristics make him a leader (Keesing 1983): He is usually a good speaker, convincing to his listeners; he has an excellent memory for kinship relations and for past transactions in societies where there is no writing; he is a peacemaker whenever possible, arranging compensatory payments and fines in order to avoid direct violent retribution from groups who feel they have been injured; and, when all else fails, he leads his followers into battle.

Of great importance in this system is the exchange of brides between patrilineal groups, for which payments of food, especially pigs, and wealth objects are required. An individual's political position—which affects his access to land, pigs, and other necessities—depends on alliances formed via his own marriage and those of his close kin. A Big Man, skilled as a negotiator and extremely knowledgeable about the delicate web of alliances created across the generations by a myriad of previous marriages and wealth payments, can help a group to marry well and maintain its competitive edge. By arranging his own marriages, of course, the Big Man cannot only increase the number of alliances in which he is personally involved, but he can also bring more women, which is to say, more production of sweet potatoes and pigs, under his control. Hence, as he strengthens his group, he does not neglect his own personal power, as measured by his control of women, pigs, and wealth objects. His efforts both public and personal come together most visibly when he succeeds in hosting a feast.

Among the most dramatic economic institutions on earth, the Melanesian feasts have fascinated economic anthropologists. The Big Man works for months, painfully acquiring food and wealth from his reluctant followers, only to present them in spectacular accumulations—as *gifts* to his allies. But the generosity has an edge, as the Kawelka Big Man Ongka put it: "I have won. I have knocked you down by giving so much" (Ongka 1974). And the Big Man expects that his turn will come to be hosted by his allies, when they will be morally bound to return his gift with an equivalent or larger one. The "conspicuous consumption" and underlying competitiveness of these displays of generosity have been regarded as so similar to philanthropy in our own economy as to seem to close the gap between "primitive" and "modern" economies.

But the Big Man feast must be understood in context. Similar to the famous potlatch of the northwest coast of North America, these feasts do not exist merely as arenas for grandiose men to flaunt their ambition. As analyzed for the northwest coast, the competitive feast is the most dramatic event in a complex of interactions that maintain what Newman (1957) calls "the intergroup collectivity." We must remember that, beyond the Enga clan, there is no group that can guarantee the rights of the individual, in the sense that the modern state does for us. Beyond the clan are only allies, strangers, and enemies. Many of them covet the desirable lands of other clans, and, if they sense weakness, they will strike. Small groups—weak in numbers and vulnerable to attack—must seek to swell their numbers and to attract allies in other clans. Thus an individual family's access to the means of subsistence depends on the success of its clan in the political arena, ultimately in the size of fighting force that can be mounted from within the clan and recruited from allied clans.

In the absence of courts and constitutions regulating intergroup relations, the Big Men assume central importance. It is they who maintain and advertise their group's attractiveness as allies (hence the bragging and showmanship that accompany Big Man feasts), who mediate disputes to avoid the dangerous extremity of homicidal violence, who remember old alliances and initiate new ones. Despite the public competitiveness between Big Men as they attempt to humiliate one another with generosity, over time they develop relationships of a predictable, even trustworthy, nature with other Big Men, lending intergroup stability in an unstable world.

A good example of this stabilizing effect is seen in the *Te* cycle, a series of competitive exchanges that link many Central Enga clans. Starting at one end of the chain, initiatory gifts of pigs, salt, and other valuables are given as individual exchanges from one partner to the next down the chain of clans. Big Men do not have to be directly involved, since such individual exchanges follow personal lines of alliance. But because the gifts are flowing in one direction down the chain of clans, after a time the giving clans begin to demand repayment. As this signal passes through the system, individuals amass pigs for larger feasts at the opposite, or receiving end, of the chain. These larger interclan ceremonies are full of oratory and display that serve to advertise the size and wealth of individual clans. Over a period of months a series of large gifting ceremonies move back up the chain of clans toward the beginning. The emphasis on prestige in these ceremonies is certainly gratifying to the participants, but it serves larger purposes: to maintain peace by substituting competitive feasting for open warfare, to establish and reinforce alliances, and to advertise a clan's attractiveness as an ally and fearsomeness as an enemy.

The central points to note from this example are the following:

1. The high population density of the Enga, hundreds of times that of the Machiguenga, implies two related developments: First, there is little wild forest left and virtually no supply of wild foods for the diet; and, second, the best horticultural land is fully occupied and in permanent use. These two primary consequences of population growth have further implications.

2. One is an intensive mode of food production that does not rely so much on regeneration of natural soil fertility through fallowing as upon mounding and the addition of green manure to soils. Because of the Enga's reliance on pigs, these fields must support not only the human population but also that of the pigs, who consume as much garden produce as humans do. The labor costs of pigs therefore include both producing their food and building fences to control their predation of gardens. Although the Enga populations are able to provide their basic nutritional needs in this manner, other highland groups with similar economies do show some signs of malnutrition, suggesting that overall production is not much more than adequate.

3. Furthermore, with land scarce, warfare shows a clear emphasis on territorial expansion and displacement. In response to this basic threat to their livelihood, families participate, albeit somewhat reluctantly, in the political activities of the lineage and clan. Although these activities often appear belligerent and can lead to warfare by deflecting hostilities outside the clan or local alliance of clans, it remains true that they have the primary function of preventing violence and stabilizing access to land.

The three major paths for creating alliances are marriage exchanges, sharing of food at feasts (commensality), and an intricate web of debt and credit established through exchanges of food and wealth objects. All of these together constitute the prestige economies for which such groups are famous. Crucial junctures in the prestige economy are occupied by Big Men, who earn their status by personally managing the complex alliances that provide a degree of security to otherwise vulnerable groups of closely related kin.

Specific Issues in Horticultural Economics

With the Machiguenga and Enga cases, we have reviewed a central theme relating differences between horticultural societies to population density and the intensification of production. We now step back from the ethnographic level to examine some specific issues that pertain to many horticultural societies. For convenience, I have grouped them into two subsets: those issues having to do with warfare among horticulturalists, and those having to do with the complex of features known as the prestige economy. After examining the several issues, I will argue that all are closely related to each other and to the main theme of population density and intensification of production.

Warfare

Most horticultural societies, unless pacified by colonizing powers, experience frequent, endemic warfare. But the variation is great. Scattered, low-density groups like the Machiguenga do not experience organized warfare, although occasional incidents of homicide are reported. Other Amazon groups, like the Yanomamo (Chagnon 1983), are more or less continuously exposed to attacks ranging from single homicides to organized raids intended to kill all the men of a village. In the Solomon Islands (Keesing 1983), wars and raids are uncommon, but there is a high, steady incidence of homicides between members of enemy groups. And in highland New Guinea, actual wars between enemy warriors are fought in organized battles on designated battlefields.

As various as the styles of warfare are the causes that have been identified by anthropologists. Most commonly mentioned as causes of single episodes of violence are fights over women, especially over issues affecting reproduction, such as premarital affairs, infidelity, rape, and abrogation of marriage agreements; revenge for previous killings; theft; displacement of an enemy group and seizure of its land; witchcraft; and anger stemming from verbal abuse and insults.

Despite the diversity of forms and reasons for warfare among horticulturalists, a number of general points can be made. First, there seems little doubt that a major cause of such warfare is the competition between men for reproductive access to women. Chagnon (1983) has developed this argument most fully for the Yanomamo of Venezuela, but reports of war from other horticultural societies confirm that fights over women are among the most frequently cited reasons for violence. The logic of this explanation is sociobiological: Men's reproductive success depends on their access to fertile women and is threatened when other men seek access to their women either by seduction or by force.

As an explanation, however, this sociobiological one is limited because it explains a variable by a constant; that is, in sociobiological terms, men everywhere seek reproductive success through controlled access to fertile women, but only in some places does this lead to the raids and homicides characteristic of horticultural warfare. The Machiguenga, as is common in family-level societies, manage aggression by prohibiting its open expression and by killing or driving off individuals who are unable to control their violence. In complex societies, peasants and others must control their expressions of violence or face punishment by empowered officials. Thus, although a desire to obtain fertile mates may be a motive for violence, it tells us little about the form the violence may take in specific situations.

An explanation that avoids this difficulty sees warfare among horticulturalists as reflecting competition over scarce natural resources, such as game or agricultural land. As we have seen, this explanation is supported by data from the densely settled highlands of New Guinea, where prime agricultural land is scarce and where histories of warfare clearly show that victors take over the lands of their defeated enemies. Can such an explanation apply, however, where population densities are lower than in the extreme Enga case?

Let us briefly examine a famous case, that of the Tsembaga of the fringe of the central highlands of New Guinea, as first described by Rappaport (1967) in *Pigs for the Ancestors*. In a rugged mountain landscape, uninhabited at lower elevations because of the prevalent danger of malaria and lacking the broad valleys and alluvial fans of the Enga, the Tsembaga population density is only about 14 persons per square kilometer. They practice slash-and-burn cultivation with somewhat longer fallows than the Enga do, and lack the permanent fields where the Enga grow sweet potatoes. But like the Enga, the Tsembaga obtain little wild food from their forests and depend on pigs for dietary fat and protein.

Warfare is a familiar part of Tsembaga life. Homicide is common, and open battles, though sporadic, are very violent. They explain warfare as revenge for previous killings, but here also evidence suggests that warfare ultimately results from competition between groups for prime agricultural land. Tsembaga battles are generally between neighboring groups, reflecting tensions that accumulate over years. Such battles, though deadly, are often tests of strength that do not resolve anything. When one group senses, however, that it has clear superiority over the other, it does not hesitate but strikes massively to kill as many opponents as possible and drive them from their land. Then, the victors destroy the crops of the defeated group, including the trees that bear an oil-rich edible fruit (*komba*). The defeated group flees, scattering to temporary shelter in the homes of kin and allies in other groups.

The defeated group's lands are not immediately occupied. Because of the ceremonial system, a defeated group has a chance to reoccupy its lands. Organized in clans much like the Enga clans, the Tsembaga inherit rights to the land that is owned and defended by their clan. Land rights are sanctified in ritual, especially in ancestor worship. Each clan has its own fighting-magic house, its own set of fighting stones, and a dance ground; through common rituals, its identity and unity are reinforced.

A major ritual sequence regulates the disposal of land after a defeat. When one group is clearly defeated, a truce can be instituted. Thereafter, war between the two groups is not possible for many years. During the peace that follows, great emphasis is placed on raising quantities of pigs. When a concensus emerges that enough pigs are available, clans plant stakes marking their territorial boundaries. Preparations for the *kaiko* feast are then undertaken, lasting many months. The *kaiko* ceremony signals the end of the truce, and war is once again possible. If by this time the defeated group has not reoccupied its lands, the victorious clan pulls out the ceremonial stakes and incorporates the lands into its own clan territory. If the defeated clan has reoccupied its lands, its members must be prepared once again to defend them.

Rappaport viewed the *kaiko* and related rituals as mechanisms for regulating crucial variables—such as the distribution of the human population, the size of the pig population, and the occurrence of warfare—in Tsembaga human ecology. Accordingly, in the absence of centralized authority, the ceremonial system channels information, providing decision rules, and "sanctifying" the ecologically adaptive strategies. Although later writers questioned whether the system worked as efficiently to maintain population balance as Rappaport had envisioned (Lowman 1980; Clarke 1982), there can be no doubt that the variables of land, population, and warfare are intimately connected to one another and to the ceremonial system. As analysed by Peoples (1982), the *kaiko* and related ceremonies serve primarily to create and maintain alliances. Each group finds itself in a competition to be strong in order to fend off enemy attack. Individual clan members are motivated to join the ceremonial system because the strength of their clan affects their own secure access to land, their ability to attract mates, and their success in exchanges of food and wealth.

Hence, the Tsembaga prestige economy is similar to that of the Enga:

Warfare, ultimately resulting in the competitive exclusion of a population from its lands, instigates pervasive social and cultural structures to establish regions of peace and stability in an inherently dangerous and unstable world. The prestige economy, with its emphasis on creating linkages between individuals and groups through exchange of food, mates, and other necessities, accomplishes this goal to a remarkable degree, even though the continued existence of war reveals the upper limits beyond which such integrative efforts fail.

If this argument applies to both the high-density Enga and the lower-density Tsembaga, can it apply also to the much lower density populations of native Amazonia, such as the Yanomamo? Chagnon (1980) has argued that it cannot and calls for two separate explanations, one for the Amazon and another for New Guinea. As we saw, Chagnon prefers the male competition for mates as an explanation of Amazon warfare. Harris (1977), however, has argued that, although agricultural land does appear to be abundant among the Yanomamo, wild resources are scarce and thus it is hunting territories they are fighting over. We saw that Baksh's study of depletion of faunal resources among the Machiguenga showed a resulting increase in conflict and the near fissioning of the village. But Chagnon has pointed out that behaviors that should accompany warfare over land are absent; the Yanomamo are only weakly territorial at best and do not ordinarily displace one another via warfare. He also finds that there is abundant horticultural land and vast areas of forest for hunting available to the Yanomamo he studied along the Orinoco lowlands.

Other ethnographic data on the Yanomamo (cf. Smole 1976; Biocca 1971), however, reveals that their primary habitat, the Guiana Highlands, is a region of poor soils and game, a habitat quite unlike the rich riverine lowlands where Chagnon studied a recent immigrant group. In the highlands, Yanomamo tend to be more territorial and experience difficulty in finding good land for horticulture. Once located near good land, they tend to stay there, clearing new plots adjacent to the old ones. In some areas, widespread destruction of forest into economically useless savannas has occurred, apparently through human overuse of the land (Smole 1976). Furthermore, two important tree crops, plantains and oil-rich peach palms, are cultivated continuously for up to fifteen years so that, over time, the territory surrounding a Yanomamo settlement comes to be filled with old gardens still producing crucial garden foods. It is not surprising, therefore, that in these highlands we have some reports of displacement of groups by violent attacks in order to seize land, including the existing agricultural improvements (Biocca 1971). For the highlands where the Yanomamo traditionally lived, then, the argument that resource scarcity provokes warfare between groups, New Guinea style, is not so unlikely as it seems for the lowland areas recently colonized by the Yanomamo.

Although it is the seemingly uncontrolled violent aggression that has attracted much interest in horticultural warfare, what is actually more impressive is the great lengths to which horticultural peoples go to avoid war. Among the Yanomamo, the *reaho* feast is an effort to build alliances and diffuse angry feelings. Hosts are expected to be generous with food and other useful items. Guests accept this generosity and with it the obligation to repay the generosity at a later feast at which they become hosts. In rituals like endocannibalism, where the crushed bones of the dead are consumed by their living relatives, group loyalties are strengthened by focusing anger outside onto the enemies believed to have caused the death.

If there should be angry disputes between guests and hosts—and usually there are unresolved issues—members of each group air their grievances in the community clearing, under controlled circumstances. If words do not suffice, men square off and duel with fist blows, each taking turns delivering and standing to receive. A still higher level of violence is the club fight, also carefully controlled by leaders, where men trade blows on the head with hardwood clubs. The object of these orchestrated battles is "to fight so we may become friends again." These battles are, writes Chagnon (1983: 170), "the antithesis of war."

In horticultural societies, households, as we have seen, are largely autonomous economic units. Why then do they so frequently join large villages—where disputes and competitive feelings are inevitable—or other large corporate groups such as subclans and clans? The main reason is warfare. Larger groups are necessary for defense, and it is the leaders of such groups, headmen or Big Men, who take the main responsibility for adjudicating disputes and seeking peaceful solutions. Because their leadership powers are limited by the inevitable divisions within their own groups, the leaders do not always succeed, and then they must prepare defensive and offensive moves. It is for this reason that Chagnon refers to the Yanomamo leaders as masters of the politics of brinkmanship.

The Prestige Economy

In most horticultural groups, the public ceremonial—characterized by feasting, competitive events like races and wrestling, displays of finery and wealth objects, and competitive gift giving geared to enhance the giver's prestige while humiliating the recipient—is as endemic as warfare. Again, various causes have been identified. Most dramatically obvious is the self-aggrandizement of political leaders, who parade themselves boastfully before the assembled throng, claiming superior prestige for themselves and their followings: hence, the label prestige economy (Herskovits 1952: 461–83). Participants are seen as motivated to seek prestige (a cultural value) in the same opportunistic way that people in our culture yearn to acquire and display wealth through expensive cars, furs, jewelry, and homes.

Among the best-known horticultural examples of a prestige economy is the "kula ring" in which the Trobriand Islanders participated (Malinowski 1922). Malinowski argued that these horticulturalists and fishers off the coast of New Guinea could not be understood in terms of a simplistic model of "Economic Man"—that is, as motivated purely by materialistic self-interest. Trobrianders do many things that cannot be explained so simply: They perform elaborate garden-magic rituals, expend much energy on garden aesthetics such as carved fence posts, raise yams not for themselves but for their sister's husbands, accumulate so many yams that they may rot in storehouses and stimulate the envy of rivals, and participate in an interisland trade ring primarily to obtain the armshells and necklaces that they covet as the most valuable objects they can own. Malinowski's argument is an example of the substantivist position (see the Introduction to this volume) that "economy is embedded in society" and that economic behavior is determined by the values of the particular cultural tradition of that society.

As with the sociobiological explanation for warfare, however, this explanation does not take us very far. Either everyone desires prestige (that is, it is human nature), in which case a variable is again being explained by a constant, or else some cultures "value" prestige more than others (compare the modesty and self-effacement required of such diverse peoples as the forager !Kung San [Lee 1984] and the Mexican peasantry [Lewis 1951]). If the latter is the case, then we must ask why prestige is so central to the economic motivation of horticulturalists?

In the case of the kula ring, later research and analyses (Austen 1945; Burton 1975; Powell 1960, 1969; Uberoi 1962; Weiner 1976, 1983) have located adaptive aspects of the Trobriand prestige economy overlooked by Malinowski. The Trobriand Islands were heavily populated by horticulturalists practicing intensive yam cultivation. Because of droughts, Trobrianders did experience years of food scarcity, unpredictably though not chronically. Land was controlled by chiefs who, with the help of so-called garden magicians, coordinated agricultural production to maximize yields. Garden magic, therefore, was not merely a matter of spiritual significance but a means to organize production in an effort to guarantee yields under circumstances of risk.

In addition, chiefs accumulated large stores of yams in public, open-sided yam houses next to the chief's house in the village center. It is significant that the storehouses of individual commoner houses were closed and private, and that it was primarily the chief who commanded gifts of yams from his wives' brothers. Because not every man gave his harvest to his sister's husband, not every man publicly displayed excesses of yams in order to gain prestige. It was the chiefs, acting in the political economy as storage and redistribution centers for yams during periods of food scarcity, who did so. When their yams rotted, it was not simply prestige but a welcome abundance of food that was signified.

Chiefs also had functions in interisland trade. They organized the construction of seaworthy boats and controlled their use, paying for the labor with their "excess" yams. They initiated and coordinated trading expeditions in which the kula valuables were a symbolically major, but otherwise minor, aspect of the voyage. Boats, laden with yams, traveled to other islands, where yams could be traded for other essential raw materials and artifacts that the other, agriculturally impoverished, islands produced. Thus the chief was at the center of a kind of multi-island trade network or market. The kula valuables, by sanctifying trading partnerships, stabilized the regional economy. Because warfare was also common between groups, the leaders and the prestige economy of the Trobriands also had the same functions of alliance and defense as we saw for the Enga, Tsembaga, and Yanomamo.

Cross-culturally there are several economic problems that encourage the rise of prominent individuals because of the need for leadership and centralized control (Johnson and Earle 1987). Most common among these are risk management, where the food supply is unpredictable or seasonally scarce; warfare, where leaders coordinate offense and defense but also seek alliances in order to surround their communities in buffer zones of peace; capital investments, especially the construction and maintenance of large-scale technology beyond the capacity of single, independent households; and trade in nonmarket economies, where leaders arrange trading opportunities, keep accounts by remembering past transactions, negotiate present deals, and help maintain a peaceful framework for trade.

It is no coincidence, therefore, that the Trobrianders, with the most centralized leadership of the horticultural societies we have considered here, met all four of these conditions. Among other horticulturalists, however, most of these occasions for leadership do not occur frequently. The tropical lack of seasons and the general reliability of horticulture mean that the risks of food production are comparatively low. Food storage and the movement of food from one zone to another are of relatively minor importance. Instances that do occur include the Yanomamo feast, which distributes a temporary overabundance of plantains and peach palm fruits to allied groups, and the large yam storage structures maintained by Trobriand chiefs, from which "surpluses" of yams may be distributed to needy families during the droughts and seasonal shortages that plague this intensive horticultural system. In good years, the chief's yams rot, enhancing his prestige and leading Western observers to decry the wastefulness of primitive horticulture. But in poor years, the chief's stores are the difference between life and death to his following. This is a good example of Leibig's Law of the Minimum (Hardesty 1977: 196–99), which asserts that any population adapting to its environment must not adapt to the "average productivity," but rather to the bad years, in which a minimum of food will be available; inevitably, in good years, some of the available food supply will not be consumed.

Capital investments in technology are also rare in horticultural economies. The great bulk of food production is managed at the household level or at the hamlet level. Group technology—such as boats, wells, irrigation systems, fishing weirs, and so forth—are uncommon. The boats of the Pacific islanders are the clearest exception to this rule, and such craft, used in fishing, warfare, and trade, are controlled by chiefs or by "boat owners" who are de facto chiefs.

Trade is likewise of secondary importance in horticultural economies. It is rarely absent, however. The Yanomamo, for example, were involved in trade networks that integrated many tribal groups in Venezuela before the disruptions of European contact (Arvelo-Jimenez 1984). In general, the feasts that occur with regularity between horticultural groups are occasions on which individuals can bring wealth, pigs, agricultural produce, and crafts to a marketlike setting, where they may be bartered for desired items.

Wealth items are eagerly sought by men at such feasts. In unusual cases, some wealth items may be exchanged only for other items of comparable value. That is, separate "spheres of exchange" (Bohannan 1955) exist so that special valuables like shell necklaces cannot be exchanged for ordinary goods like yams. But more commonly, primitive valuables are somewhat like money, in that they can be used to buy and sell a variety of goods and services, including food, pigs, weapons, manufactures, and, of course, brides (cf. Keesing 1983).

So it is primarily warfare that brings about the prestige economy in horticultural societies. Warfare drives families into villages and clans for defense. Feasting, marriage, and exchange are all means for maintaining peace within and between villages and clans. In such intergroup relations, a group needs a leader capable of mental bookkeeping, exhortatory speeches, negotiation and bluff, and, when all efforts fail, military strategy. The Big Man who hosts a feast demonstrates not only his own eminence but also the productive power and numbers of his following. He dresses larger than life and parades before the assembly on behalf of his following. The piles of food, pigs, and wealth objects he gives away are all distributed by the guest Big Men among their followings so that a quantity of gifts originating from individual households in group A are received by individual households in group B. Later these will be reciprocated, reinforcing a sense of trust and interdependence between groups. Marriage exchanges between groups are especially powerful ties that make violence between the groups much less likely. The symbolism of the feast, with food sharing at the heart of it, but also the ceremonial songs, dances, and contests, all serve to announce groupings and alliances that strengthen linkages and override divisions (cf. Maybury-Lewis 1974).

In sum, horticulturalists are an intermediate stage in the evolution of social and economic systems, between familistic foragers and peasant farmers. Within this large category are many variations, depending largely on the environment and population density. Typically, they occupy defined territories, within which access to land is controlled by corporate kin groups that are also charged with the responsibility to defend these life-sustaining lands from outsiders. In a threatening social environment, great efforts are expended in building alliances in order to guarantee undisturbed pursuit of horticulture in the home territory. Hence a major investment of economic activity becomes bound up with such alliance-building strategies as arranged marriages with bride wealth payments, reciprocal gift exchanges, and public feasts that help create, symbolize, reinforce, and advertise mutuality and trust between potentially hostile groups.

Horticulturalists provide many excellent examples of how essential it is that we examine economic processes as aspects of political economy (Johnson and Earle 1987). At the family level of the Machiguenga, it is true, we can provide a fairly complete economic analysis simply by referring to the self-interest of individuals and their immediate families. Economic behavior is opportunistic as determined by the costs and benefits of the procurement strategies available in that environment at that level of technology. But as soon as violent competition reaches the point where families must group together into villages and clans to defend the integrity of their families and their access to basic resources, all economic behavior is embedded in social rules concerning who may marry, who may farm what lands, to whom one owes credit or from whom one deserves payment, and so on. It is not, as the substantivist position once held, that individual rationality ceases to apply. Rather, the entire context of individual rationality has shifted, with a greater emphasis being placed on the social environment as compared to the natural environment. Indeed, it may be said that the evolution of economic behavior is primarily the evolution of the political economy, as more and more individuals with their families become integrated into ever larger, mutually responsive economic communities.

4

Trade and Markets in Precapitalist States

Frances F. Berdan

The study of the economic systems of early states and empires has always been a part of economic anthropology. These economies were characterized by nascent forms of many modern economic institutions and activities, such as specialized production, markets, money, taxes, foreign trade, and professional merchants. Although in a broad sense these ancient economic systems may remind us of modern economies, they nonetheless carry an aura of the exotic: Money forms ranged from animals to cloth to cacao beans; bustling outdoor marketplaces teemed with unfamiliar sounds, smells, and products; priests administering temples of the gods were at times active political forces in owning land and collecting taxes; international trading ventures carried different risks and employed some different strategies than their modern counterparts.

In this chapter, both the familiar and the exotic are presented. We will first glimpse the general features of the early states and empires and consider the special problems of studying such ancient states and economies. Then we will delve into their more specific forms of economic organization. Throughout, stress will be placed on antiquity and variation: Economic features such as markets, taxes, and foreign trade have their roots deep in antiquity, and the forms these took varied considerably from state to state, empire to empire.

By 3000 B.C. the stage was set for the advent of full-blown states in the Old World; by 2200 B.C. several states and even empires were in full sway. The Sumerians were ensconced in Mesopotamia; Egypt was in the throes of the Old Kingdom; Knossos, the Minoan capital on Crete, had been founded and was flourishing; civilization was thriving in the

I would like to express my gratitude to Stuart Plattner for helpful comments on an earlier draft of this chapter. I also greatly appreciate the assistance of the Graphic Arts Department at California State University San Bernardino in drafting the maps and figures.

Indus Valley; and China was experiencing the rise and fall of powerful dynastic kingdoms. However, more than 2,000 years remained before states and empires would develop in the New World, notably Mexico and Peru, and they would flourish there for only some 1,500 years. During this time innumerable states rose and fell in both the Old and New worlds.

The earliest states, and those that followed them in succession,[1] were extensive political entities characterized by large populations, a centralized government enjoying a monopoly of force and supported by a system of legal codes, and a social hierarchy dividing the populace into classes or castes. The population tended to be concentrated in dense (often urban) settlements. States may also be defined structurally as multilevel regional political systems containing at least three hierarchically arranged administrative levels (Wright and Johnson 1975; Brumfiel 1983; Hodge 1984).[2] This "systemic" view of states allows us to include a wide range of political entities, from small city-states (with fewer levels) to large territorial empires (with more levels).[3]

[1] Scholars typically distinguish between "primary states" and "secondary states." The former represent incipient or original state development from nonstate forms of organization. Such developments probably took place in relatively few parts of the world, notably Mesopotamia, Egypt, China, the Indus Valley, Mesoamerica, and Peru. "Secondary states" were built upon already-existing states. Wright (1977: 393) sees little difference in form between the earlier and later types, while Service (1975: 303–4), calling them "archaic civilizations" and "modern primitive states," does. Because I am focusing more on the structures of early states than on their origins and development, and see few qualitative differences in the basic features of the two types of states, I will follow Wright's conclusions and include both types in this chapter.

[2] Wenke (1980: 431) provides an illustration of this notion of administrative levels: "For example, in a simple agricultural village . . . there are many decisions to be made about what crops to plant, how much of the harvest is to be stored, who gets what share of the land, who marries whom, and so forth. Many of these decisions are made by individuals, but some of those which directly affect the whole community are made by a village headman. We might say, then, that this village headman represents the first level of the decision-making hierarchy—he directs the activities of others who do the work. A second level of administrative hierarchy would exist if there were people charged with coordinating the activities of these village headmen and correcting or approving their decisions —perhaps government agents charged with taxing and administering local affairs. Such agents would be under a third administrative level, and additional levels may exist above this."

[3] The early states varied considerably in scale. They ranged from relatively small, autonomous city-states to the great expansionist empires. City-states essentially focused around a single major center or city, with a supporting hinterland of towns and villages. The city was the administrative, social, religious, economic, and intellectual heart of the city-state. An empire is a political entity that has expanded beyond its own city-state bounds to encompass other political entities (often city-states themselves), frequently of quite varied cultural and linguistic backgrounds. Typically such expansion was accomplished by military conquest, although other means were also employed (see Luttwak 1976). Following conquest or other form of subjugation, the very presence of new overlords created a more complex set of bureaucratic arrangements by adding a new administrative level atop that of the subjugated city-state.

Early states were supported by relatively productive and multifaceted economies. They were based on intensive agricultural production that yielded considerable and fairly reliable surpluses. These surpluses supported large concentrated populations, often in cities, and allowed a segment of the population to pursue nonagricultural specializations such as religious offices, political positions, craft production, and trading enterprises. Specializations were complemented by elaborate exchange mechanisms. Market and marketplace exchange arose early; marketplaces or bazaars provided the arenas to facilitate movements of goods from producers to consumers. It eased exchanges based on specialization and variations in regional production. Specialized trading centers developed, especially serving the needs of long-distance merchants, and the trade in these centers often carried strong political overtones. Ancient states also imposed taxes on their citizenry. Some more aggressive states, the military empires, also exacted tribute from their conquered subjects. Markets, long-distance trade, and taxes/tribute were woven together in intricate and sometimes unstable arrangements.

These facets of the ancient economies—agricultural production, specialization, marketplace exchange, long-distance trade, and political involvement in economic arrangements—were patterned differently in each state. So some states, such as the Minoan on Crete, were heavily reliant on long-distance trading enterprises; others, such as the Roman Empire, derived extensive resources from tribute demands. Some empires, like the Inca, seem to have controlled production and distribution of goods more through state-regulated tribute than through trade or marketplaces. Other empires, like the Aztec, relied more heavily on marketplace exchange than tribute to move goods across regions.

Antiquity and variation: These are the themes that are pursued in this chapter on early state economies. As background, the chapter includes a brief discussion of the nature of information available on early states and empires and also covers theories and models that have been presented to better understand those states. This is followed by a case study of the Aztec Empire, which provides a concrete example of an early state economy. The major economic features presented in the case study are then discussed in broader terms as they apply to ancient state economies generally. The most significant of these features are specialization, taxation/tribute, the meaning of trade and the roles of professional merchants, and the importance and functions of markets and marketplaces.[4] Each economic feature will be discussed with

[4] There are additional aspects to these economies that are both interesting and controversial, such as the nature and scale of agricultural production, and the organization of

reference to its most notable context: specialization with urbanization, tribute with the polity, professional merchants with trading entrepôts, and markets with regional integration.

Reconstructing Ancient States and Their Economies

Peoples in the early civilizations left behind monuments, artifacts, and histories that are enigmatic and frequently mysterious to the twentieth-century researcher. It is perhaps inevitable that scientific and humanistic questions would be raised about these ancient societies. The questions raised revolve, in a general sense, around two dimensions: dynamics and functions.

In the area of dynamics, one of the most long-standing and hotly debated questions concerns the origins and evolution of the early states. How and why did the ancient states arise? What were the forces behind their development?[5] Questions of evolutionary dynamics have also been applied to already-formed states: What sorts of changes do states go through? Do they have a predictable life cycle? What circumstances or forces are involved in the transformation of states and empires? And, finally, what causes can be linked to the demise of state after state, empire after empire? These questions pertain to the realm of ancient economies because many explanations and answers to these questions are economic in nature, particularly those that deal with technological and organizational control over natural resources (for example, Wittfogel 1957).

This chapter will focus on questions of function, which address the operation of the early states regardless of their origins or potential for growth, decline, or collapse. In the economic arena, a prominent question has been: To what extent, and in what ways, was the economy embedded in the political and social institutions of the state? Much recent research has been leaning away from a focus on heavy state involvement in the economy to viewing the ancient economies in terms of freer market arrangements. The question of market vs. state control of the economy is significant, and there may be a compromise alternative (see below). Related to this are the nature and extent of long-distance trade: What stimulated it? What sustained it? What inhibited it? What was the role of professional merchants? What, again, was the role of

---

labor. References for this chapter should lead the interested reader to more information on these topics.

[5] See especially Cohen and Service 1978; Wittfogel 1957; Carneiro 1970; Claessen and Skalnik 1978; Wright and Johnson 1975; Wright 1977.

the state? Answering these questions requires the systematic collection and careful analysis of data on a variety of early empires.

Data and Evidence

Schliemann's uncovering of Troy in the 1870's was a revelation. It ushered in a new era, an era where archaeology (relying on data from excavations) and history (based on written and oral accounts, sometimes seen as fact, sometimes as myth) became tentative partners in unraveling the past. It is a critical partnership, since the information from neither history nor archaeology is complete. In other words, the data on the early states and their economies are fragmentary. The people who left behind oral or written accounts did not do so with the twentieth-century historian in mind; they normally wrote their accounts at the time, for their own times. Because their writings or oral expressions reflect their own cultural and personal biases, the resulting accounts are sometimes vague, often incomplete, and virtually always subject to interpretation by today's historian.

The archaeologist's task is no easier. The archaeologist reconstructs past lifeways on the basis of material remains. But people do not conveniently leave behind everything of their lives, generation after generation, in thoughtful consideration of a future archaeologist. Time eats away at perishable remains, reducing the range of materials available for archaeological study. Subsequent human occupations often disturb the arrangement of earlier remains, complicating the archaeologist's task. Consequently, the archaeologist pieces together ancient lifeways from partial remains of buildings, often looted burials and offerings, and broken bits of material discards. Only rarely, as at Pompeii or Herculaneum, are relatively complete and intact sites available for study.

Like the historian, the archaeologist asks, How well or completely do these remains reflect the actual lives and cultures of the people of the early states and empires? To reconstruct those lifeways, researchers of ancient states sift through mounds of data for evidence relevant to questions of early state formation, functioning, and change. They must carefully evaluate the available information, always recognizing its fragmentary and sometimes contradictory nature. Working under these constraints, they rely on logical, scientific interpretations to provide patterned descriptions and logical explanations. This is the realm of theory and models.

Theory and Models

Much of the early conceptual work on ancient state economies was developed by the economic historian Karl Polanyi and his associates.

The thrust of the Polanyi approach is to analyze economic features (most notably, forms of distribution) in relation to their social and political context. In *Trade and Market in the Early Empires*, the economies of several early states were presented with this in mind. Polanyi interpreted economic activity, especially distribution, as embedded in societal institutions (see Chapter 1, this volume). The importance of this point of view is that economic institutions are analyzed with reference to the rest of the society. Polanyi suggests three generalized forms of economic integration through which exchange systems in economies may be instituted: reciprocity, redistribution, and market exchange. Reciprocity refers, in his terms, to nonmarket exchange between social equals, as in gift giving. Redistribution involves the accumulation of surpluses at a local level, their collection at a center (such as by a chief or the Internal Revenue Service), and their subsequent distribution (hence, redistribution). Market exchange refers to transactions of goods or services governed by the market principle, and often in the context of a marketplace. Symmetrical groupings are therefore the context for reciprocity, centricity is necessary for redistribution, and a price-regulated market system provides the framework for market exchange.

This approach turns our attention to the social, political, and religious institutions with which economies articulate. In the early states, redistribution in the form of tribute and taxation would be embedded in centralized authority and allocative centers, whether secular or sacred. Reciprocity would involve the relatively symmetrical relationships found between kin, villagers, rulers of city-states, and so on. Market exchange would take place primarily in marketplaces, frequently conducted on a rotating basis and sometimes following a calendar of religious events. Marketplace exchange served to facilitate distribution of a wide range of specialized goods on local, regional, and interregional levels. Marketplaces frequently attracted professional long-distance merchants as well as more regionally based merchants. But the long-distance entrepreneurs also often carried the flag of state, and in such service they conducted political and economic business in relatively neutral trading entrepôts.

The Polanyi model recognizes that all of these distribution arrangements may be present in any given early state or empire (as they usually were), yet the underlying goal is to discover which of these arrangements dominated the economy overall. Thus, for example, the notion of "temple economies" and "palace economies" in the ancient Near East has been a prominent one, focusing on the redistributive sphere as dominant (for example, Adams 1966: 125–28; Postgate 1972; Oppenheim 1977: 89, 95–109). This orientation has enjoyed some popularity also among Mesoamerican scholars in arguments favoring political control over the economy (such as Carrasco 1978). And, as another example, ports of trade in Mesoamerica and other parts of the ancient world have been portrayed as neutral locales where trade was conducted in the absence of markets (see Polanyi et al. 1957; Chapman 1957). Yet these various reconstructions have generally been shown to have been quite overstated, in that normally a variety of economic mechanisms combined to stimulate and facilitate movements of goods (see Lamberg-Karlovsky 1975: 350; Berdan 1983; Silver 1983, 1985).

One neglected aspect of studies of the ancient economies has been the importance and role of markets. Current research, however, has placed more emphasis on both the presence of marketplaces in the early states and empires and on the operation of a market economy, with its attendant assumptions of scarcity, supply and demand, maximization, hierarchically ordered centers, and so on (see Chapter 7 on markets, this volume). Thus, for example, the marketless nature of Mesoamerican ports of trade has been challenged (Berdan 1978), and the "moneyless" characterization of early Assyrian markets has been criticized:

[T]he proposals put forth by Polanyi . . . about Old Assyrian moneyless markets must be rejected. Markets most certainly existed, even within a wholesale-retail format, and merchants were specialized and capitalistic. Individual profit was a prime motivation; even smuggling existed to increase profits through evading taxes and tolls. [Lamberg-Karlovsky 1975: 350].

To aid in reconstructing market aspects of the ancient state economies, certain locational models have become especially popular and have served as useful tools for interpretation. Particularly significant in current research is the central place model, which has enjoyed a long and fruitful history in geography and a more recent flourishing in anthropology. The basic assumptions and uses of this model are summarized in Chapter 7 in this volume. In applying the central place model to ancient state economies, anthropologists have sought to facilitate reconstructions of settlement hierarchies and to improve predictions of market behavior. But caution should be exercised in applying this "ideal model" to real situations. Geographic, religious, social, and political factors often set central place settlement patterns askew.

The case study that follows describes the economy of one ancient state, the Aztecs of Mexico. Some researchers have seen the Aztec economy as overwhelmingly controlled by the polity; others have concluded that the economy was essentially governed by the market principle and by activities in marketplaces. This section presents a concrete case where political involvement in the economy and the operation of marketplaces and the market principle were woven together in a workable system. In addition, the Aztec economy exemplifies the most usual characteristics of the early state economies: intense agricultural production; specialization; and well-developed taxation/tribute, foreign trade, and market exchange systems.

Case Study: The Aztecs of Mexico

At the time of the Spanish arrival in 1519, the Aztecs had amassed an extensive empire that encompassed most of central and southern Mexico (see Map 4.1). The "Aztec Empire" was in reality a coalition among three ethnic groups occupying important city-states in the Valley of Mexico: the Mexica of Tenochtitlan, the Acolhua of Texcoco, and the Tepaneca of Tlacopan. It was the Mexica who came to dominate the confederation and whose city rose to prominence in the valley (to become, after the Spanish conquest, Mexico City). This Triple Alliance had been in force for only some 90 years before the arrival of Cortés and his soldiers, during which time it had embarked on a persistent course of military conquest and regional economic control.

The empire was administered from cities in the Valley of Mexico, a

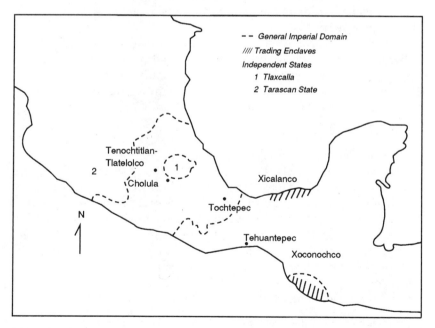

Map 4.1. The Aztec empire in 1519.

basin almost entirely circumscribed by mountains and dominated by an enormous lake (see Map 4.2). The greatest of these cities just before the Spanish arrival was Tenochtitlan, an island city with a population estimated at between 150,000 and 200,000. This city was the seat of the Mexica ruler (*tlatoani*), who, along with his military and civil advisers, judges, stewards and other officials, saw to the business of government.

The *tlatoani* sat at the apex of an intense system of social stratification. There were basically two main divisions: nobles and commoners. But the nobility were further graded into different levels based on birthright and achievement in warfare. Noble status, of whatever grade, brought with it special perquisites, such as rights to own land privately, construct houses of two stories (where houses were customarily of one story only), and conspicuously display special clothing and fancy accoutrements. Their energies were directed toward the affairs of state, as high-level administrators, tribute collectors, governors of distant provinces, military officers, priests, or scribes.

Commoners (*macehualtin*) were less colorful as they walked the streets or canoed the canals: Their jobs mainly involved agricultural work, fishing, trading, or craft production. They also served as the rank and file in the military and could be called upon to serve the state in distant wars. If valiant, a commoner might gain considerable esteem and some special perquisites.[6]

In a vague area between nobles and commoners were the artisans of luxury wares (*tolteca*) and the professional merchants (*pochteca*, or *oztomeca*). Although of general commoner status, people in these professions frequently became extremely wealthy and at times even felt the need to conceal their wealth from the traditional nobles.

Production and Specialization

Intensive agriculture provided the foundation for this complex and highly urbanized society. Large surpluses in food (particularly maize, beans, squash, and chile) were produced throughout the valley and beyond. The most intensive form of agriculture was practiced on the lakeshore *chinampas* (misnamed "floating gardens"), where several crops a year could be produced through judicious use of seedbeds and selection of crops. But there was considerable geographic diversity throughout the area controlled by the empire, and some crops were geographically contained within specific ecological zones, such as cotton and cacao in the "hot lands" and maguey in the cooler, drier regions.

[6] This is highly simplified. For a more extensive treatment, see Berdan 1982.

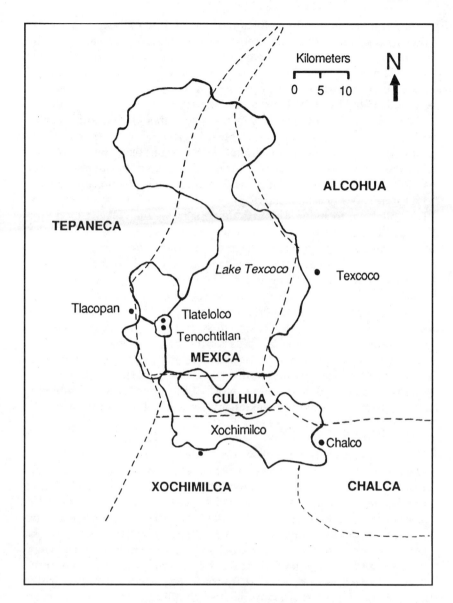

Map 4.2. Major cultural areas of the Valley of Mexico, 1519. Source: Gibson 1964: 14.

Many nonagricultural products were also found in restricted zones. Precious feathers, stones, and metals were all found in areas throughout the empire, but none of them in close proximity to the Aztec capital cities. Nonetheless, these precious products worked their way into the valley cities, where they were formed into objects of high social and economic value by skilled specialized artisans.

Artisans specializing in fancy, expensive wares tended to cluster in their own districts (*calpulli*) of the cities. They were, by all appearances, grouped into guildlike organizations, with the craft being handed down from parent to child. There was an internal system of quality control as well as social differentiation within the "guild" (from apprentices to masters). The artisans also displayed a cohesiveness represented by their collective focus on a patron deity, such as the "Flayed God" for the metalworkers and the god "Coyote's Spirit Companion" for the featherworkers. These were full-time specialists whose craft required long years of training. Apparently their work could be commissioned by the royal palace, but they also produced for a broader market.

Intense specialization also occurred in other, less fancy crafts. Work in less-than-precious stones, in making mats, and in producing pottery all required a substantial investment in training and time and some investment in capital (such as kilns for the potter). Some of these artisans may have worked on a part-time basis, and although some of their work may have been commissioned directly by the palace (such as that of stonemasons and carpenters), most of their products undoubtedly were distributed through the extensive network of marketplaces.

Taxes and Tribute

Whether administrator, cultivator, featherworker, or mat maker, all individuals in the empire were subject to tax or tribute obligations imposed by the state. This took many forms: Commoners in the local area (say, Tenochtitlan or Texcoco) would be taxed in the form of corvée labor (on, for example, irrigation works, causeways, or temples) and be required to provide daily provisions for the royal palaces. They might also be required to pay in goods such as maize or cloth. Artisans were taxed in kind. Nobles paid their dues by serving the state in administrative capacities and, at least by the time of the last Mexica ruler Motecuhzoma II (r. 1502–1520), by attending the ruler in his palace. In the provinces, tribute payment was a condition of conquest, and it was usually payable at regular intervals: quarterly, semiannually, or annually. This tribute took the form of foodstuffs and cloth (some 280,000 pieces annually) and various items such as bowls, wooden beams, elaborate warrior costumes, shells, jade beads, gold disks, and bunches of valuable tropical feathers. Some conquered districts, situated close to enemy borders, were required to render war matériel or enemy captives to the Mexica as tribute. The fate of these captives was undoubtedly the same as for others captured in battle: human sacrifice in extravagant religious ceremonies.

Local and conquered people alike had additional obligations when special events arose, such as the dedication of a temple, the installation of a new ruler, or the death of an old one. The goods and services rendered at such occasions, as well as the regularly scheduled tributes, were put to a variety of uses by the polity: to support administrative and military activities, to underwrite the standard of living in the royal palaces, to provide gifts and commissions to deserving people (particularly those who had excelled on the battlefield), to maintain emergency stores in the event of famine, and to finance foreign trading expeditions.

Professional Merchants and Foreign Trade

Some foreign trade thus carried the flag of state. The merchants who conducted this long-distance foreign trade were organized into guilds much as were the luxury artisans, residing in separate city districts, controlling membership, providing training for the neophyte, collectively worshiping a patron deity, and exhibiting a complex system of ranking within the organization, with the head merchants acting on behalf of the guild in accepting commissions from the ruler. The merchants were extremely achievement oriented: When a merchant became successful (that is, wealthy) enough, he sponsored a feast and might even purchase a slave for sacrifice in the celebration. This ostentatious display of feast and sacrifice was costly but morally approved, because the expense was applied toward heightened social status within the guild.[7]

These professional merchants acted both as state agents and as private entrepreneurs. They traded actively in marketplaces within the imperial domain, but they also traveled to trading enclaves in areas beyond direct Aztec control. On these expeditions they carried expensive goods belonging to the Mexica ruler. These were exchanged with the ruler of the trading center, who in turn assured the merchants' safety, even providing them escorts through hostile territory. The merchants also carried luxury and ordinary goods belonging to themselves or to

---

[7] Detailed descriptions of the merchant feasts, as well as other aspects of Aztec life, are found in the sixteenth-century works of Bernardino de Sahagún (1950–1982).

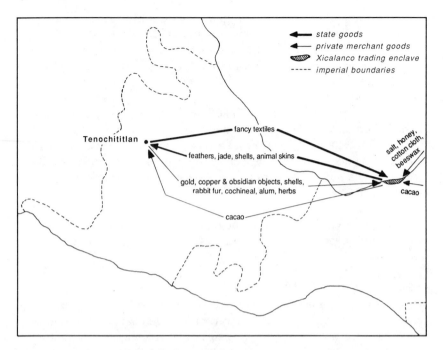

Map 4.3. Long-distance Aztec trade.

members of the guild who stayed home. These goods were traded in the local marketplaces with the local populace or with merchants from other faraway lands (see Map 4.3).

Markets and Marketplaces

Marketplaces were found not only in the trading enclaves but also in towns and cities throughout the empire. These marketplaces varied considerably in terms of the frequency with which they met, the range of goods available, and the types of traders offering their wares for sale. Most markets were held on a five-day rotating schedule, although some of the larger ones (in the major cities) were also active daily. The grandest marketplace in the empire was at Tlatelolco (sister city of Tenochtitlan), and here could be found every product of the land, from local maize and tomatoes to distantly grown cotton and cacao. Manufactured goods could be found in abundance: everyday wares such as pottery and mats, expensive goods such as polished gold and elaborately decorated cloth. Other marketplaces in the empire were less well stocked: Small marketplaces would have mainly served as distribution points for staples and everyday necessities, whereas larger regional ones would have a selection of exotic wares available. Some market-places became renowned for specializations such as slaves, pottery, or turkeys. Marketplaces on hostile borders often displayed a wide range of luxury goods as well as more generally consumable commodities. These borderland markets also attracted professional merchants and may have provided an arena for the exchange of goods from bordering states, goods otherwise unavailable because of military antagonisms (Berdan 1985).

Marketplaces, especially the larger ones, attracted a wide range of traders: long-distance professional merchants dealing in items of high value and low bulk, regional traders (traveling mainly between highlands and lowlands) carrying goods of medium value but high bulk (such as cacao and cotton), and local persons selling small lots of their own production, usually of relatively low value and high bulk. Specialized producers could therefore provision themselves through the wide range of goods available in the marketplaces. The process of market-place exchange was facilitated by the diversity of traders engaged in moving and exchanging these goods and by the use of certain commodities as money forms. Lengths of cotton cloth seemed to have provided the most important measure of value, and cacao beans, individually of very low value, may have been used as an acceptable way of evening out exchanges (perhaps as a widely accepted medium of exchange).

How were these different aspects of the Aztec economy interrelated? Intense specialization in the production of goods, coupled with large surpluses, was dependent on the availability of efficient exchange mechanisms as outlets for the specialized products and as a means for the specialist to obtain other necessary goods. The extensive market-place network provided the essential arena for these exchanges: A wide variety of goods was available on a reasonably predictable basis, and everyone in the empire, from small-scale cultivator to royal adviser, could provision a household by a visit to the appropriate marketplace. But tribute must also be paid, and householders met those requirements through their own production efforts and through purchasing goods in the marketplaces. Some of these goods were made available by regional merchants, others by long-distance merchants. Aside from their own privately owned goods, the professional long-distance merchants were also entrusted with some of the extensive tribute stores of the state; they traded these state goods with rulers of distant trading enclaves, at the same time fulfilling their own entrepreneurial goals in marketplaces in these outlying districts. An intricate web was formed among tribute, trade, and markets.

Ancient State Economies

In broad outline, the Aztec case is not so different from many other early states. Yet the Aztecs are only one cultural expression of the early state economies. Others, like the Inca, emphasized redistribution more than markets. Some, like the Phoenicians, built more on a foundation of trade than of agriculture. Yet all were highly specialized, and all exhibited some blend of exchange through trade, markets, and taxation/tribute. The presence of these forms is ancient, and they demonstrate the diverse and ingenious ways people in the early states met their economic needs.

Specialization and Urbanization

Even in the smallest-scale societies, some people may become specialized, normally on a part-time basis. For example, people with inclinations toward shamanism or who are particularly talented as toolmakers may find their skills in demand, sufficiently so that others are willing to relinquish part of their excess food production to obtain the products or services of these specialists. Such specialization usually remains "part time" because of the lack of adequate surplus production to support these people full time or a lack of sufficient demand for the special products or services to keep the specialists employed full time. Specialization can also develop from direct political intervention, which may leave an individual with little choice as to productive activities; conquest resulting in tribute demands or slavery is an example.

So specialization, as idea or as fact, was not novel with the early states and cities. But the scale on which it developed was new. Early state economies, typically based on intensive agriculture, were sufficiently productive to allow (and encourage or force) many people to devote their time, energy, and talents full time to enterprises other than food production.[8] This high degree of specialization was related, at least in a general sense, to the production of surpluses: The food-producing arm of the economy was intense and reliable enough to release some people from food-production activities altogether.[9] Their

[8] Food production itself tended to be specialized in the early state economies. In Mesopotamia, for example, the seemingly uniform riverine zones were in fact highly differentiated into areas of wheat and barley farming, garden and orchard cultivation, herding, and reed and fish procurement (Adams 1966: 48). Similarly, central Mexico has been described as a "symbiotic region" because of the great variation in productive potential throughout the region (Sanders 1956).

[9] This is oversimplified. For a review of problems associated with the relationships between surplus and the growth of the state, see Adams 1966: 45–48. Similarly, the notion of "urbanism" is problematical, so much so that some authors have hesitated to use the term "urban" at all. For good overviews, see Blanton 1976 and Wheatley 1972.

productive energies could therefore be channeled elsewhere: to the political arena, to military service, to religious affairs, or to other aspects of the economy, notably craft production and trade.

These specializations tended to be concentrated in nucleated settlements, most notably urban centers or cities (see note 9). The reason is that concentration improves efficiency because of economies of transportation (Trigger 1972: 578–79). One would expect, therefore, to find concentrations of political, religious, and economic specialists, with their associated structures and activities, in cities rather than in the cities' hinterlands. So rulers with their palaces, judges with their courts, priests with their temples and festivals, and artisans and merchants with their markets would tend to be found in close proximity for efficiency's sake. But early cities differed markedly in their degree of centralization. Some, like Teotihuacan in central Mexico (flourished ca. A.D. 100 to A.D. 700) incorporated neighboring populations and served as the focus of all major functions over a broad territory. Other centers, such as the Classic Mayan ones in southern Mexico and Guatemala (which flourished ca. A.D. 300 to A.D. 900), tended to be more decentralized in population and function (Blanton et al. 1981).

The complexity and variation of specializations in the urban setting are especially revealed through a closer look at craft production. When crafts are concentrated in cities, the advantages of specialization and economies of scale apply. The production of tools and preparation of raw materials can be left to other specialists, whereas if each craft is separate, workmen normally prepare their own tools and materials (Trigger 1972). Some early cities, like Teotihuacan in Mexico, seem to exemplify the above principle. It is estimated that 25 percent of the city's households were involved in some sort of craft production (Millon 1976: 233).[10] Much of this production seems to have been organized in workshop arrangements in urban apartment compounds, with a preponderance of obsidian working (over 300 workshops), supplemented by some 200 workshops for the production of ceramics, shell, and stones other than obsidian (Marcus 1983: 216). Such a scale of production is suggestive of production for commercial (export) purposes with possible monopolistic control (ibid.; Blanton et al. 1981: 241).

Yet there were other early cities that deviated from the above rule. Joyce Marcus (1983) points this out by contrasting the craft production strategy of Teotihuacan with that of Monte Alban, also in Mexico, and Cheng-chou, a Shang Chinese city (1523–1027 B.C.). In Monte Alban, artisans constituted only 10–13 percent of the total urban population

[10] A considerable proportion of the early urban population was probably made up of agricultural producers (Sjoberg 1960; Millon 1981: 220; Trigger 1972: 579–80).

(Blanton 1978: 96). Yet this does not mean that there was proportionately less craft production overall, for Monte Alban's hinterland was dotted with numerous specialized villages. Similarly, Cheng-chou housed craft specialists outside the city walls and exhibited the same sort of village specialization characteristic of the Monte Alban region. Archaeologists have associated each village in the countryside with a different occupational specialty, which must have promoted a high degree of economic interdependence among villages and between city and village. In these cases, specialization flourished in a dispersed fashion, quite unlike the urban concentrations of artisans that characterized Teotihuacan (Marcus 1983: 217–18). Such dispersed craft production may have been geared more for local consumption than for commercial purposes (Blanton 1978) and was probably produced on more of a domestic scale than in a workshop format.

What is obvious through Marcus's examples is that there were alternatives in the distribution of artisans in early states; the artisans need not have been huddled closely in urban settings.

The locations of crafts may have been linked to other factors. In ancient Rome, for example, some crafts were considered bothersome because of the irritating noise they created; one Roman city ordered that noisy crafts be carried on outside the city (Burford 1972: 77). Similarly, some crafts notorious for the smell they created, particularly tanneries, were excluded from the Roman cities because "the tannery annoys everybody, for the tanner has to deal with dead animals; he has to live far from town, and the stench reveals his presence, even when he is hiding" (ibid.: 78).[11]

Whether in city or countryside, the artisan produced for a socially stratified society. Some products—such as utilitarian pottery, cloth, and basic household tools—were consumed broadly throughout the society. Other products, such as extra-fine cloth or precious stone jewelry, were often restricted to those on the upper rungs of the society, whether by sumptuary laws or by the ability to pay for them.[12] Craftsmen producing utilitarian wares could be housed in city or village and might work full time or part time. And although there would be many consumers of such products, there were undoubtedly many producers as well. Considerable numbers of these artisans were either permanently or periodically in the employ of palace and temple. For example,

[11] Tanneries may have been singled out in Roman times for such exclusion, for this apparently was not the case in the earlier Athens; nor was it the case with other "smelly crafts" in Rome, such as the dyeing and fulling of cloth (Burford 1972: 78, 80).

[12] The categorizing of an object as "utilitarian" or "luxury" is of course an artifact of culture, and cultures differ considerably in this regard.

Robert Adams analyzed personnel lists kept by the Shuruppak palace (Early Dynastic III city of Ur, ca. 2700–2400 B.C.). There were considerable numbers of craftsmen in the palace's employ: "Separately grouped under their respective foremen were masons, potters, reed-weavers, clothworkers, leatherworkers, carpenters, stonecutters, millers, brewers, and perhaps others" (Adams 1966: 143).

Luxury artisans normally resided in the cities, where they were often attached to palace or temple, producing their fine wares for a restricted set of consumers. Typically, the production of elite goods, such as intricate work in precious metals and stones, entailed complicated procedures requiring training and some capital outlay. This could be provided by wealthy institutions or individuals. In ancient Egypt, for example, temples often received raw materials as part of their "income" and could serve as "patrons of manufacture," either using the finished products themselves or exporting them. A study of sculptors' workshops in an ancient Egyptian city revealed that several workshops were situated in residential neighborhoods (Kemp 1972: 673). Although some of this luxury production may have been geared directly for palace or temple consumption, much of it must have been oriented to private consumers who could afford statues of themselves or of their especially revered deities (ibid.).

Both luxury and utilitarian artisans exhibited certain distinctive features of social organization. In the Egyptian example cited above, some of the sculptors' workshops were focused on courtyards, while some of the work seemed to be undertaken in a normal household context. And aside from substantial "factories" in the town center, sculptors and glass manufacturers alike had workshops in the suburbs, in a manner suggesting neighborhood specialization in craft production. The multitudinous workshops in Teotihuacan, described earlier, were grouped in apartment compounds, and the Aztec cities had clear-cut residential districts where plyers of the different crafts lived and worked. This grouping into quarters or districts was in some cases based on ethnicity. In other instances, such as Shang China, kinship may have provided the organizational cement. In this case, it is likely that some crafts were in the hands of specific kin groups and that certain aspects of production of a particular craft were controlled by specific lineages (Wheatley 1971: 66). Whatever the grouping, artisans—luxury artisans in particular—tended to restrict access to craft work. In some cases, this took the form of guilds that restricted membership, assured quality workmanship, assumed responsibility for training, and provided social and economic rewards for successful members.

Protected and supported by these or other similar groups, artisans could produce for private consumers (in the context of a market or marketplace) or be commissioned by the state. In this latter context, the artisan became enmeshed in the redistributive sphere of the early state economies, that of tribute and taxation.

Taxes, Tribute, and Polity

The administrative, religious, and military structures of early states required financing, and the primary means was through the imposition of taxes on the citizenry or tribute on its conquered subjects. In many instances, the primary functions of state focused on palaces of kings or temples of priests who controlled extensive resources and maintained considerable stores.

Taxation by king or priest could take many forms. Head taxes yielded notable incomes in Pharaonic Egypt and much of southwest Asia. One such tax, payable partly in kind and partly in money, is said to have been the foremost source of income for Alexander the Great's Persian empire (Heichelheim 1958: 172). Other taxes levied in Persia, beginning at an early date, included land taxes, herd taxes, trade taxes, market taxes, and harbor taxes (ibid.; Simkin 1968: 6). Taxes like these seem to have derived from the concept that the king owned everything in the land: Every transaction to acquire wealth or produce goods had to be bought, by a tax, from the royal house (Heichelheim 1958: 174–75).

Easily as important as taxes in kind or money were taxes in labor. For example, in the ancient Near Eastern monarchies,

Each inhabitant had to work for the king a certain number of days annually, unless he paid a certain amount in money instead into the royal treasury or belonged to a privileged group. The masses of the people which were under such an obligation were employed on public works, the digging and maintenance of canals and drainage works, agricultural work on state domains, the building of roads, city walls, palace and temple buildings, pyramids, and other royal graves and state cemeteries, fishing and seafaring for the royal service . . . and so on. [Heichelheim 1958: 176]

This was a fairly typical set of labor demands imposed on a state's populace, from Mesoamerica to Mesopotamia.

Tribute—as unpopular payments in kind, money, or labor to a conqueror—served as a major source of wealth for imperial palaces. Typically the specifics of tribute demands were set at the time of conquest, with the ever present threat that any rebellion would be met with military reprisals and increased tribute demands. In the ancient Near East, Mesoamerica, and elsewhere, tribute requirements varied considerably depending on the circumstances of conquest: in some instances they appear as strictly fixed demands, in others merely as occasional gifts (ibid.: 175; Berdan 1982: 36–38). Whatever the conditions and amounts, tribute symbolized the political and economic control of one group over another and brought in enormous amounts of wealth to further solidify that control, both at home and abroad.

Much of the income collected from taxes and tribute was stored directly within or beside palaces and temples. Reportedly the royal Urartian cellars (in Turkey) had storage space for 55,000 gallons of wine, and "when the Assyrians under Sargon II invaded Urartu in 714 B.C., a problem faced by the invaders was the irresistible appeal the local wine had for the Assyrian troops" (Ozguc 1973: 51). Temple storehouses were common in Mesopotamia; in times of war, sacking of a temple's storehouses was amazingly lucrative for the conquerors and devastating for the conquered (Postgate 1972: 815).

These stores, of palace or temple, symbolized the economic control over the land held by king or priest. They served to underwrite an exaggerated standard of living for those fortunates, supported administrative and religious functions, financed wars and trading expeditions, provided gifts for the worthy or privileged, and served as a bastion against years of famine. The early temples and palaces managed these resources on varying scales and in somewhat differing ways.

For example, the operation of the temple of Ta Prohm, near Angkor in Cambodia (dedicated in 1186), was on a particularly grand scale. The recorded property of the temple included gold and silver dishes, 35 diamonds, 40,620 pearls, 4,540 precious stones, 876 Chinese veils, 512 sets of silk bedding, 523 parasols, 2,387 sets of ceremonial garb for the holy images, and unstated quantities of rice, molasses, oil, cereals, wax, sandalwood, and camphor (Wheatley 1971: 265). Aside from material wealth, the temple also had people attached to it in a sort of feifdom: as many as 3,140 settlements with a population of 79,365 persons (ibid.). This sort of control over the populace and its economic productivity was not unusual nor even especially extravagant for that time and region. The same ruler who erected this temple insisted on dedicating his kingdom to Buddhism, and at the time of his death "there were more than 20,000 statues in gold, silver, bronze, and stone distributed in shrines throughout the realm, and 306,372 persons, living in 13,500 villages and consuming 38,000 tons of rice annually, were employed in [the shrines'] service" (ibid.: 265–66). In this system, economic production was managed in a centralized redistributive fashion, with people producing for the temples and receiving support in return.

Somewhat less unilateral control was exercised by the temples of early Mesopotamia. Postgate (1972: 815) describes the temple as the community's "wealthy neighbor." It was supported by gifts and offerings from the residents of the community; occasionally these gifts took the form of extensive grants of people (slaves or virtual slaves) or lands by wealthy individuals, most notably kings. The offerings donated by community members generally were considered to be necessary duties, and as such may be labeled as taxes. Aside from their movable wealth, the temples also controlled lands, which served as their bases for wealth and power (ibid.: 816). Some temples could become powerful beyond their own home base, like one in northern Babylonia that not only had granaries in its home city but also owned grain depots in villages and towns elsewhere.

In some aspects the temple could become a self-contained economic entity: While it managed herds and flocks of animals, it could also administer workshops for the processing of pastoral products, particularly hides and wool. In the agricultural arena, its fields produced grains that could be stored in great quantities; in Babylonia and Assyria, temples made loans of this stored grain to peasants to sustain them until their next harvest (Postgate 1972: 814).

But the temple personnel, especially those in large cities, also looked beyond their own immediate realm for economic opportunities. Some supplied capital for trading expeditions, whether by land or sea, thus applying their accumulated wealth to commercial ventures (ibid.). A similar pattern developed in ancient Egypt, where temples owned their own merchant ships to travel to more distant markets in Egypt and abroad (Kemp 1972: 660).

These temples, whether in Egypt, Babylonia, or Cambodia, served as redistributive focal points in the local and regional economic systems. Although temples and palaces exercised considerable control over land and labor and maintained large stores of movable wealth, they did not monopolize the economy. In early Sumeria, for example, Curtin (1984: 64) points out that most of the land really belonged to private individuals and that markets and fluctuating prices could be found in Mesopotamia as early as the end of the fourth millennium B.C. Furthermore, in Egypt and the Near East at least, temples did not confine themselves to redistributive forms of exchange but linked into trading activities that required them to relinquish some political control to the more strictly economic forces guiding trading enterprises.

Professional Merchants and Trading Enclaves

Although tribute and taxation were, essentially, associated with political and religious institutions, professional merchants and their trading activities displayed an interesting mix of political involvement and entrepreneurship. On the one hand, the early merchants' need for capital in their risky enterprises tied them at times to palace and temple; on the other, the transactions marking their dealings were not always political in nature but responded to economic forces and had economic goals and consequences.

In the earliest states, long-distance trade may have been especially aimed at satisfying the special status-related needs of elites. Prestige goods of high value and low bulk, such as precious stones, rare metals, shimmering feathers, or finely worked shell, were transported over great distances and reserved for the use of the high ranking. Later, as trade routes and trading relationships became more firmly established, everyday goods were added to the merchants' repertoire, and merchants of different grades and types came to supply not only valuable items for elites but also food staples and utilitarian wares for people in the society generally.

Merchants, especially full-time professional merchants, frequently had an uncertain and ambivalent social status. In some cases, such as the Mayan *ppolom*, it appears that they were members of the elite themselves (Blom 1932). However, in many other cases, they appear as lower-class individuals socially but sometimes with great wealth economically. And they were not necessarily always popular. In ancient Greece, for example, trade for profit was considered a dishonorable profession; the god Hermes presided over both merchants and thieves (Curtin 1984: 75–76). Similarly, the Aztec word for trader, *tlanecuilo*, was also the word for "swindler." Merchants came under further suspicion as travelers, and sometimes residents, in foreign lands. They were strangers.

Additional ambivalence derived from their political and patron affiliations. In some instances, such as in the Third Dynasty of Ur in Mesopotamia (ca. 2125–2000 B.C.), merchants were seemingly attached to temples directly as servants. In later times, however, the temples lost their monopoly over capital, and these merchants (called *tamkaru*) became more independent and rose to dominate trade, brokerage, and moneylending in Ur. But intricate economic relationships still existed between sponsor and merchant. For example, credit was available to traders, who sometimes split their risk among a number of investors. Another way of reducing the lender's risk was to hold the merchant responsible for repayment of a loan, even if the voyage was unsuccessful.

Hammurabi's code shows the *tamkarum* sometimes traveling with his goods, sometimes staying in one place and sending his goods out with a traveling agent, sometimes financing the trade of others. . . . The government still participated directly in the trade in food, though it used the independent *tamkaru* as its agent. It also taxed trade and maintained some forms of commercial control, but most trade was carried out as private enterprise. [Curtin 1984: 67]

In Athens of the fifth and fourth centuries B.C., traders had no single sources of wealthy banks or moneylenders to subsidize them and thus turned to a variety of individuals and institutions for investments. For this time and place, lenders took the risks, which included ship and cargo loss from storms, piracy, or poor navigation; or cargo devaluation from unexpectedly low exchange rates. Even the security put up by the trader consisted of his precarious ship or cargo. Therefore, lenders charged the traders high rates of interest—67.5 percent and even as high as 100 percent (Casson 1984: 28). However high the risk, investors were tempted by the correspondingly high return from trading ventures: One could, if one's ship came in, double one's money in just a few months during the sailing season.

Whether the patron was a wealthy individual or a temple, or whether the merchant risked his own capital or someone else's, the goal of trade was to "maximize return without jeopardizing future relationships" (Kohl 1978: 468). To attain that goal, guildlike organizations of merchants, some resembling "family firms" (Silver 1985: 39–41), developed in many early states. Such organizations may have begun as early as the third millennium B.C. in the Near East and were designed to protect merchants and their interests in both domestic and foreign commercial arenas (Heichelheim 1958: 126). Merchant guilds exercised some control over their membership and the comportment of members (through courts). The guilds were also internally stratified with leaders and other functionaries and tended to reside in special quarters of cities and towns. In trading centers far from home, they eased the process of doing business. For example, Assyrian merchants trading in Anatolia (present day Turkey) maintained their own organizations in the Anatolian trading centers. The officials of these locally based organizations would accompany a caravan on its arrival to the palace of the prince or king, who had first priority in selecting goods. There the merchant officials would bargain with the palace officials for the purchase of some of the caravan's cargo. The price set for these purchases had a number of hidden costs, for the palace provided some storage space for merchants' goods, policed the roads, and helped the merchants collect outstanding debts (Ozguc 1969: 250–51; Curtin 1984: 69). These negotiations, however, applied only to a small percentage of the entire cargo; the remainder was carried by the merchants to their own district in the city and sold in the marketplace.

In the above example, long-distance professional merchants conducted trade in both political and market contexts. This was characteristic of the numerous trading centers in the early state economies. Trading centers arose in the early states to provide a relatively neutral setting for trade among merchants offering very different products and from very different states (who may even have been warring with one another). Typically the polity of the entrepôt assured the safety of foreign merchants, and princely palaces normally purchased some of the merchant's wares. In the view of Polanyi and his associates (1957), these were politically and militarily neutral ports of trade where exchanges were exclusively between foreign merchants and local port of trade rulers. It has become abundantly clear, however, that this model of administered foreign trade does not mirror reality: Marketplaces operating on market principles were a normal fixture of these trading centers, and access to these markets was probably a major stimulus to long-distance trading ventures.

Such entrepôts, noted for their ability to attract a colorful and desirable mosaic of merchants and goods, arose perhaps as early as 3500 B.C. in the Middle East. Probably in their early forms, trading centers served merchants dealing in a limited range of goods, particularly goods of high value and low bulk that could be transported over long distances with hopes of high economic returns. Given the costs of acquiring these goods and the value attached to them, they were most likely geared toward elite consumption. However, as trading activities became more customary and well entrenched in the early states, the merchants carried a broader range of goods and expanded into products with a broader range of value. For example, early Phoenician trade brought Iberian metals (especially silver) to the Levant; later, slaves, pottery, and foods such as wine and olive oil were added to the mercantile imports. In exchange, the Phoenicians exported products such as timber, dyes, and textiles (Curtin 1984: 76).[13]

In many cases, professional merchants would actually reside more or less permanently in a foreign commercial center. They would then serve as "cross-cultural brokers," encouraging and facilitating trade between their own people and their hosts. Relationships between foreign merchant and host community could take a variety of forms:

In some circumstances, rulers of the host society treated the traders as a pariah caste, to be exploited or robbed at will, whose presence was tolerated only be-

---

[13] Examples of the goods traded over long distances in ancient times are too abundant to present here. A descriptive summary is available in Heichelheim (1958: 116–25), and a discussion and analysis is provided by Curtin (1984). Both sources include a large number of relevant references.

cause it was useful. . . . Other merchants sought successfully to establish themselves as autonomous, self-governing communities, often by a self-conscious pacifism and neutrality toward all political struggles. [Curtin 1984: 5]

Strategies in ancient Greece for dealing with foreign merchants fell somewhere between these extremes. Foreign merchants were labeled *metics*, and as such were levied a special tax, could not own land, and needed a citizen to represent them in the courts. But the restrictions do not seem to have been any more extensive than this, and the *metic* merchants must have found their own solutions, for many Greek cities did gain commercial importance (ibid.: 77–78).

It has become increasingly clear that, instead of ports of trade administered along strictly political lines, these trading centers were a mix of political involvement and economic motivations. Critics of the earlier (Polanyi) approach point out that the commercial centers were places where rapidly fluctuating prices were important to merchants, where political authorities interfered in trade "but never to the extent of successfully suppressing the underlying play of supply and demand, though here as elsewhere in the history of commerce, protection costs were an inescapable cost of doing business" (ibid.: 70). Thus we enter the realm of early markets.

Markets, Marketplaces, and Regional Integration

Markets and marketplaces are not precisely the same thing: "In economics a market is not a place, but a situation in which a good is supplied by some ('sellers'), demanded by others ('buyers'), and the value ('price') of that good is determined by the decisions of all the buyers and sellers" (La Lone 1982: 300). These decisions reflect the interplay between supply and demand, and prices can fluctuate according to their changing relationships. A marketplace is the actual physical meeting place for supply and demand crowds. The distinction between markets and marketplaces is important because conditions may exist where markets are in force without actual contact between suppliers and demanders, and marketplaces may exist without the support of market principles.

Both markets and marketplaces existed in the early states. In contrast to Polanyi's estimate of fourth century B.C. Greece for the beginnings of a free exchange market, recent evidence argues strongly for the appearance of markets and marketplaces far back into antiquity. The presence of a market network[14] is suggested for Mesopotamia for as early as the

[14] By market network, Lamberg-Karlovsky means "the processes of institutionalized transactions of commodities and services channeled from an area of high supply to one of high demand." The emphasis is more on market than marketplace.

fourth millennium B.C. (Lamberg-Karlovsky 1975: 345). By 2000 B.C., trade was conducted by private merchants in Anatolia for purposes of economic gain (Adams 1974: 246–47; Kohl 1978: 468).

Trade in a market or marketplace context involved more than just the long-distance professional merchants exchanging their exotic wares with one another. It involved traders whose range (of goods and of territory) was less expansive, and small-scale local producers of food or crafts. It could, if extensive, involve virtually everyone in the society, if not as producers, then as consumers.

This wide range of marketplace participants, from professional merchants dealing in luxury wares to local householders selling small lots of their own production, operated in a variety of marketplace types. Early Anatolia, for example, had nine major marketplaces, but there were also a number of smaller, less important marketplaces. Professional merchants traveling great distances were more interested in the larger marketplaces, but they apparently also had dealings in the smaller ones, since they maintained representatives there (Ozguc 1969: 250). This suggests a hierarchy of marketplaces as analyzed in the chapter on markets in this volume.

In a hierarchy of marketplace types, the important concepts are the demand threshold of the supplier ("the area containing sufficient consumer demand to enable the supplier to earn normal profits") and the range of a good ("the circumscribed area beyond which buyers would not be willing to travel to purchase the good in question") (Skinner 1977: 277). The demand threshold for precious metals, for example, would necessarily be great since few people overall would be able to afford (or be allowed to flaunt) such luxuries. People would be willing to travel long distances to obtain such goods. On the other hand, grains, being widely available and consumed by everyone, would have a more limited threshold and range. It follows, then, that there would be many more marketplaces, relatively close to one another and rather small in their range of offerings, selling grain and other everyday necessities. There would be fewer marketplaces, at a greater distance from one another, selling precious items; these would be the marketplaces most popular with the merchant who has traveled great distances in search of a profit. Therefore, everyday consumer goods would be in heavy demand and available in all marketplaces, from the smallest to the largest; highly specialized (and normally more highly "priced") wares would have a more limited demand and be available only in the larger, more widely spaced marketplaces.

This does not mean, however, that the smaller marketplaces would never see the awesome merchant caravans or not have specialized

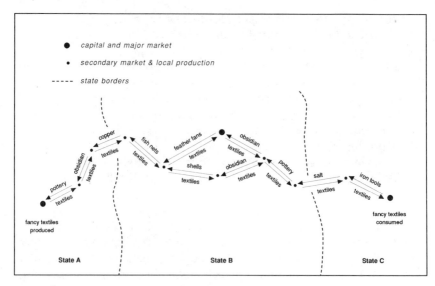

Fig. 4.1. Hypothetical movement of textiles through relay trade.

goods available. Specialized merchants and wares undoubtedly passed through all levels of the marketplace system, often through a process of "relay trade." In relay trade, people bought and resold goods in marketplaces without having to travel far from home; goods moved across the countryside in short hops but ultimately traveled long distances (see Fig. 4.1). Curtin (1984: 17) sees this happening in Africa with the movements of copper, iron, and certain shells; Adams (1974: 246) suggests a similar pattern with specialized textiles in trade between southern Mesopotamia and Anatolia. It may have been quite common. For example, it did not necessarily require long-distance merchants to supply the people of the Indus civilization with their exotic wares. Shells from the Indian Ocean; tin from Iran, south India, and Malaysia; precious and semiprecious stones from Iran, India, and Indochina; and silver, copper, and lead from eastern Iran and India—all these could have been relayed from marketplace to marketplace through the hands of local traders and regional merchants.

Exchanges in marketplaces were facilitated from an early date by the use of various forms of money. Although the use of coin as a form of money with legal status did not develop until around the late seventh century B.C. in Asia Minor (Grierson 1977: 33), other objects served at least one money function in the earlier states. Today, money is considered to serve four major functions: as a medium of exchange, a standard of value, for payment, and as a storage of wealth. In the early states, the primary and perhaps only function of money may have been as a standard or measure of value, as argued by Grierson (1977). Although various commodities may have been valued in terms of grain measures, number of oxen, or weights of metals, the actual exchanges involving the commodities did not necessarily involve these measures. One example follows:

In the 15th year of Rameses II (c. 1275 B.C.) a merchant offered the Egyptian lady Erenofre a Syrian slave girl whose price, no doubt after bargaining, was fixed at 4 deben 1 kite (about 373 g) of silver. Erenofre made up a selection of clothes and blankets to the value of 2 deben 2⅓ kite—the details are set out in the record—and then borrowed a miscellany of objects from her neighbors— bronze vessels, a pot of honey, ten shirts, ten deben of copper ingots—till the price was made up. [Ibid.: 17]

A second example from the same time and place "deals with the purchase of an ox valued at 120 deben of copper, the payment being made up by two pots of fat (60 deben), five good shirts (25 deben), one dress (20 deben), and one hide (15 deben)" (ibid.). These measures of value took the form of commodities such as uncoined metals (copper, silver, and gold were especially popular), cloth, grain, or animals. In Homeric Greece, for example, the standard of value was the ox, and gifts were exchanged not using the oxen themselves, but rather precious objects valued in terms of so many oxen (ibid.: 16). In Pharaonic Egypt, it was weights of copper, and for Assyrian traders it was silver (Adams 1974: 246). The values of these monies fluctuated over time and space in response to market forces. Although the presence of money is not essential for specialized production or administered long-distance trade, it is generally associated with the development of markets (Grierson 1977), and it has been argued that "its introduction transformed the scale and complexity of ancient economic systems" (Kohl 1978: 468).

Market and marketplace systems developed with varying intensity throughout the ancient world. Particularly noteworthy is the case of the Inca, who developed marketplaces in a rather minimal way. Distribution of goods and services was apparently managed primarily through the redistributive efforts of the state (La Lone 1982; Earle 1982). In striking contrast was the Aztec empire, which, as seen above, boasted an intricate network of marketplaces throughout the imperial domain.

Regularities and Variation in Ancient State Economies

It is clear that the early state economies used a variety of strategies, in different combinations and with different emphases, to move essential and preferred goods from hand to hand. All exhibited a high degree of full-time specialization in political, religious, and economic arenas, and all blended trade, markets, and taxation/tribute to provision the state and individual consumers. The Polanyi approach of characterizing certain economies as "redistributive" or "market" is therefore less fruitful than an approach that accepts the presence of a variety of exchange strategies and seeks to unravel the relationships among them.

We have seen that, although specialization is a regular characteristic of early states and empires, its geographic patterning varied considerably. Some states displayed urban concentrations of craft specialists; others had such specialists decentralized into villages of a city's hinterland. "Efficiency" is an argument presented in favor of concentrating artisans in urban settings; yet where raw materials (such as clays, quarry stones, or woods) are dispersed in the countryside, such efficiency may be less compelling, especially in the early states, where transport was not developed on a large scale. In any case, either pattern of specialization was dependent on available networks for exchanging surpluses and for obtaining goods and products not directly produced by the household or other consuming unit.

All early states were financed by some imposition of taxes or tribute on their populace. Small states (such as city-states with few administrative levels) could command fewer overall resources in this manner than could the geographically extensive empires. The latter, encompassing a variety of ecological zones and diverse ethnic peoples, normally imposed taxes on their own citizenry and tribute on conquered groups (which usually included city-states, themselves demanding taxes). Thus sometimes households were double-taxed, or even triple-taxed, depending on the number of imposed political levels. At whatever level, tax and tribute impositions symbolized the control of the state over the populace and its means of production (most notably, land). They also underwrote the state's activities and its functionaries' standards of living. These demands varied therefore depending on the needs of the state, on the state's ability to enforce its demands, and on the availability of resources or desired goods within the state's domain.

When important resources lay beyond the area controlled by a state, state-commissioned trading activities provided an alternative strategy for obtaining such resources, products, or goods. It is not clear whether, historically, large-scale trading ventures developed from private or political initiative. Whatever their origins, large-scale trading enterprises in the early states required considerable capital, which was provided variably by private individuals, temples, palaces, or the backing of the merchant's guild or family firm organization. A merchant (or merchants, for given the high risks of long-distance travel in the ancient world, large cadres often traveled together) was then obligated to his sponsor to trade successfully on his behalf.[15] This did not preclude the merchant from engaging in his own entrepreneurial doings at the same time. The usual case was that such merchant ventures were entrepreneurial, with economic gain in mind, but these ventures frequently were undertaken on behalf of, or with some connection to, the state, the gods, or an overriding organization of merchants. Thus it was common in the early states that long-distance trade combined entrepreneurial goals and political involvement. Likewise, the primary meeting place for long-distance merchants, the trading center, was also a combination of political relationships (the host polity often providing security, storage, and an assured trading partnership) and market exchange.

Markets and marketplaces were a usual part of the landscape of early states and empires. Although in a few cases (such as the Inca) markets appear to have been of relatively small importance in moving goods, in most early states markets played a significant role in moving goods of all kinds and at all levels. Marketplaces were not limited to the major urban centers; instead, states usually had a range of small-, medium-, and large-scale marketplaces, which allowed participation by all and allowed the regular provisioning of all households, from small cottages to elegant palaces. In this hierarchy of marketplaces, the most widely demanded goods, such as staple foodstuffs and cloth, were available at all marketplaces, whereas the more restricted luxuries were found with regularity only in the major marketplaces. Marketplaces were frequented by local specialists selling small surpluses, by regional traders, and by long-distance professional merchants. The workings of the market principle with price fluctuations allowed for these people to gain economically from their transactions in these marketplaces. States (and especially empires) with extensive market and marketplace systems had the facility to move small and large lots of goods across regions, linking different ecological zones and cultural regions.

These patterns of specialization and exchange are ancient in origin and exhibit the ingenuity with which people in the early states and empires satisfied their economic needs. Through varying combinations of markets, foreign trade, and taxation/tribute, state and religious endeavors were financed, specialized production enhanced, and individual households provisioned.

---

[15] This is not to exclude women from entrepreneurial roles.

5

Peasants and the World

William Roseberry

As anthropologists began to study people they were later to call "peasants," they encountered some difficult, troubling problems. Standard ethnographic practice called for a lone anthropologist to live in a settlement or set of settlements for an extended period and describe the activities, patterns of life, values, beliefs, and rituals of the people who lived there. The stated goal was to reconstruct the culture of those people; to engage in such an exercise, the anthropologist generally assumed that the community in which he or she had lived could be treated as a whole, as a discrete—or at least discernible—society.

The Problem of the "Bounded" Village

In peasant villages, however, it gradually became apparent that a holistic approach that drew boundaries around the village itself was inadequate. The word "gradually" deserves some emphasis here: It is always embarrassing for anthropologists to admit that when they go to exotic places they see exotica, but they also see something of what they expect to see, what their theoretical models and personal dispositions tell them should be there. One of the earliest anthropological studies of peasants produced a classic debate related to this very problem. Robert Redfield went to Tepoztlán in Mexico during the 1920's. His classic monograph described a folk society that was in many ways idyllic, the opposite of the Chicago from which Redfield had come (Redfield 1930). Decades later, Oscar Lewis restudied Tepoztlán and found conflict where Redfield had found harmony, exploitation where Redfield had found homogeneity (Lewis 1951). Of more immediate note, however, is the fact that in Redfield's early work in Tepoztlán and Yuca-

I thank Stuart Plattner and Peggy Barlett for their comments on an early draft of this chapter.

tan, he developed his classic model of the folk society. Although he was working with people many anthropologists would today consider peasants, his early statements of the folk model did not adequately distinguish between the people he was studying and those studied by anthropologists working in more primitive settings. Of course, Redfield drew upon European literature in outlining his concept of the folk society—especially from late nineteenth-century writing on peasantries and on gemeinschaft-gesellschaft oppositions (see Silverman 1979).

It was not until after World War II that anthropologists began to notice, worry about, and conceptualize fundamental differences between primitives and peasants. In the 1948 edition of his text *Anthropology*, Alfred Kroeber wrote a brief commentary on peasantries, calling them "part societies and part cultures" (p. 284), a description that was repeated in subsequent conceptualizations. This definition only makes sense in opposition to a definition of primitive communities as whole societies and cultures—a view subsequent generations of anthropologists have questioned (see, for example, Lesser 1985; Wolf 1982). In what sense were peasant villages part societies and cultures? Economically, it was clear that peasant villages could not be described without reference to other localities. Peasants might farm land owned by a person who lived in a nearby or distant city, or by a corporation with headquarters in a different country. Their payment of rent established an ongoing relationship beyond the confines of the village. They might produce crops that would be sold in nearby market towns. If the crops included export products like coffee or tobacco, the market town would represent but one link in a chain that eventually led to the centers of the world economy. Likewise, peasants might purchase goods that had been produced in other cities, regions, or countries. Politically, peasant villages were part of larger, more inclusive administrative units. Representatives of those units—such as public registrars, teachers, tax collectors, extension agents, police, or national guard units and the like —might reside in or regularly visit the village. Culturally, what Redfield called the "little tradition" of the village came into regular contact with the "great tradition" of the city or of the wider civilization of which it was a part. Villagers might be Catholic, Moslem, or Hindu, and priests or other religious specialists from those traditions might reside in or regularly visit the village. The peasant was part of a wider world, and the anthropologist studying the peasant had to understand something about that wider world as well.

With the increasing awareness of this problem after World War II, anthropologists began to question old methods and assumptions and to experiment with new ones. Although several attempts were made, one deserves special mention: the Puerto Rico project led by Julian Steward and conducted by students who have since become major contributors to anthropological literature, including Robert Manners, Sidney Mintz, Elena Padilla, Raymond Scheele, and Eric Wolf. Based on fieldwork conducted in the late 1940's, the project was directly related to two major publications in the methodological rethinking of the period: Steward's *Area Research: Theory and Practice* (1950), a methodological handbook; and *The People of Puerto Rico* (Steward et al. 1956), which contains the substantive findings of the study.

World-System Theory

Although these and related studies contributed to a period of methodological ferment in the 1950's, the infusion of dependency literature and world-system perspectives in the 1960's and 1970's produced an even more serious crisis of anthropological confidence. Dependency literature (generally associated with its most popular—and extreme—spokesman, Andre Gunder Frank; see his 1967 and 1969 works) and the closely related world-system literature (generally associated with Immanuel Wallerstein; see especially his 1974 and 1979 works) came from outside anthropology but offered important implications for the anthropological study of peasants. Writers in this tradition did not start with the peasant village, and the understanding of village life was not their chosen problem. Rather, they were trying to account for the creation and persistence of economic backwardness or underdevelopment, and they argued that backwardness was a direct product of the development of capitalism.

The basic assumptions of a world-system perspective are these:

1. A social scientist should study social wholes. In the modern world, there is only one effective social whole, and that is the "world system."

2. The world system is integrated economically rather than politically. That is, it is a world economy composed of numerous politically independent but economically interdependent states.

3. The world system is economically differentiated, composed of (a) a core, consisting of the states at the developed center of the world economy (for example, the United States and northwestern Europe); (b) a periphery, consisting of the underdeveloped states in the so-called Third World (for example, Bolivia, Honduras, and Jamaica); and (c) a semiperiphery, composed of buffer states that have more opportunities for development than peripheral states, exercise some degree of eco-

nomic influence over their neighbors, but are nonetheless not "core" (for example, Mexico, Venezuela, South Africa, and various Mediterranean and East European countries).

4. This internationally structured inequality is a deeply rooted historical product, created with the formation of a capitalist world economy in the sixteenth century and shaped across four centuries of colonial and postcolonial change.

5. Social processes in particular regions can be understood only in terms of the place and function of those regions within the larger world system. Indeed, it is common for world-system theorists to explain problems in the periphery or semiperiphery in terms of two factors: (a) developments occurring in the core; or (b) the maintenance requirements of the system as a whole.

If this perspective is taken seriously, it seems to leave no space for the anthropology most anthropologists practice. Yet many anthropologists who do take this seriously have also questioned key provisions of the world-system perspective. The people we live with and write about generally live in the periphery and semiperiphery of Wallerstein's world system. As the price of their products collapses on world markets, as foreign corporations buy up their land, or as other foreign investors abandon what had once been a prosperous, lively region, the capitalist core profoundly influences peripheral regions and the people who live in them.

But we also see major aspects of their economic, social, and cultural life that cannot be explained in terms of the core. We see lively regional marketing systems, in which locally produced commodities are circulated. We see local merchants who follow entrepreneurial strategies that are at odds with the strategies of foreign investors. And on occasion and under conditions not of their choosing, we see local people adopting a variety of forms of resistance to the demands of local and foreign capital. Although we try to see peasants as part of the wider world, we also view an approach that attempts to explain everything in terms of the needs or dynamics of the capitalist core, or of the system as a whole, as profoundly functionalist and reductive. The attempt to maintain an anthropological perspective within a global frame presents enormous historical and methodological problems. This chapter focuses on these problems, but it discusses them in the context of an example from Venezuela. After presenting the example, we discuss a variety of issues that arise from it.

A Venezuelan Example

The Boconó District is the political designation for two high river valleys surrounded by mountain walls in the Venezuelan Andes.[1] It is relatively isolated, though hardly inaccessible. The major highways that connect western Venezuela with Caracas pass through lowlands to the north and south. From each, a single road—treacherous in the rainy season—crosses the cordillera to the mountain valley and town of Boconó. As one crosses the mountains and drives past peasant houses precariously perched on mountain slopes, the smell of cooking fires and the sight of coffee drying on small patios or on the edge of the pavement, of bananas or bunched black beans, or of the head of a freshly butchered hog hanging from the rafters near the house entrance is enough to convince the traveler that he or she is entering a different world.

If the traveler spends much time in Boconó, the first impression will be validated to a certain extent. The enclosed valley forms a discernible economic and social unit, with the town of Boconó serving as a bulking and distribution center for a number of satellite towns and villages. The town is also the capital of an administrative district within the state of Trujillo. And there is much in the town and country life of the residents that is culturally specific.

Yet even the first impression would be partial. Upon arrival, one notices that the town is hardly isolated from the wider world. Caracas newspapers and magazines are readily available. Teenagers wear sweatshirts from U.S. universities when they are not wearing their high school uniforms. Stores owned by Italian and Arab immigrants sell clothes, furniture, appliances, and hardware manufactured in other parts of Venezuela or in Colombia or the United States.

If one also investigates something of the history and social life of Boconó, one quickly encounters surprises. A nineteenth-century newspaper will offer expressions of praise and sorrow upon the death of Garibaldi. A visit to the countryside to participate in a funeral marking the first anniversary of the death of a family patriarch will produce images that confirm the impression of isolation and images that suggest wider connections and networks. Sitting outside the house drinking *miche* (a homemade rum) with a group of men while others say the rosary inside, the visitor has to explain where he has lived and what he is doing. And he learns to his surprise that all of the men have been to Caracas within the past year, some staying for several months to work.

[1] The description of this district is based on material found in Roseberry 1983.

He listens as they start to exchange suggestions about work opportunities and employers as some of their number begin to plan another trip to the city during the slack season.

These surface impressions give only a hint of the problems that confront the anthropologist who attempts to understand peasant economic and social life in terms of local and daily interactions and relationships and in terms of the wider economic relations and fields of power that affect those daily and local interactions.

The Importance of Coffee

The primary product of the Boconó District is coffee. In the second half of the nineteenth century, Boconó was one of a series of high valleys in the Venezuelan Andes that began to attract migrants from other parts of Venezuela and immigrants from southern Europe, especially Spain and Italy. The migrants settled on unclaimed national lands as well as on disputed indigenous reserve lands (*resguardos*) and started small-scale coffee farms. The European immigrants settled in towns like Boconó and combined petty commerce with the coffee trade. These traders would buy the coffee from scattered farmers, often extending credit to secure a set of coffee-providing clients. The traders would then organize mule trains that would carry the coffee over the mountains to a lowland city, where the coffee would be deposited in the branch warehouses of a Maracaibo trading company. From the warehouse, it would be carried to a port on Lake Maracaibo and then shipped by steamer to Maracaibo and eventually to Hamburg or New York.

The Maracaibo companies extended credit to local traders such as those in Boconó, following strategies similar to those followed by local traders in their dealings with local farmers. Since the nineteenth century, then, local farmers have been part of a complex web that eventually connected them to the centers of the world economy. When one remembers that coffee is subject to dramatic price fluctuations, the importance of these connections becomes even more apparent. Effects of a decline in prices would be multiple. Let us say that the price of coffee dropped by 50 percent during an international crisis. (This is a modest assumption: During the depression of the 1930's, prices in Venezuela dropped to one-fourth of their 1928 level.) With such a drop, the local trader must provide the Maracaibo company with twice as much coffee just to meet his previously contracted debts. To do this, he must press his local producers to provide him with more coffee for the same reason. Because coffee is a perennial and does not produce a yield for the first few years after planting, the farmer is not in a flexible position and cannot respond easily to the swings of market prices.

But let us say he gives in to the demands of the Boconó trader and plants more coffee, expanding into marginal lands that will be less productive or expanding into land that had previously been devoted to food crops. The immediate effects may be dramatic. Whatever efforts are undertaken, some of the farmers and some of the traders will be unable to provide enough coffee to meet their debt obligations. Even those who do will face difficulties in providing for their families. They will have less income to purchase food and other necessities, and the expansion of coffee will have left them with less homegrown food for the household. If prices recover in a few years, the decision to expand coffee acreage (extended many times over in other regions) may contribute to a situation of overproduction that will contribute to yet another market crisis. The expansion may also lead to an ecological crisis that may not become apparent for decades.

It is readily apparent, then, that the attempt to understand the coffee economy of Boconó must engage a variety of levels of analysis. One must take into account the various levels at which economic actors are operating and making decisions that affect Boconó—in New York, Hamburg, Maracaibo, Boconó. One must examine the strategies of local merchants and of local producers in order to understand the likely outcome of a crisis or the response to periods of economic boom. And one must consider the other areas from which people have come to Boconó, the practices, traditions, and values that migrants and immigrants bring with them to an expanding region.

Petroleum

Yet the involvement of Boconó with a wider world is not limited to the coffee economy. Two additional relations deserve mention. When people think of Venezuela, they think not of coffee but of petroleum. Although coffee was Venezuela's most important export in the late nineteenth and early twentieth centuries, petroleum has dominated Venezuela's economy and polity since the 1920's. The direct and indirect effects have been remarkable. The petroleum sector itself employs few people and produces enormous wealth. In the support services and industries that grew up around petroleum, and, more important, in the expansion of the state sector on the basis of royalties from petroleum companies, a nucleus was formed for the transformation of Venezuela. Growth of the state sector and of a population of middle-income bureaucrats stimulated the growth of a large tertiary sector of commerce and services, a sector located in a number of cities but most importantly in Caracas.

The petroleum expansion was occurring just as the coffee economy entered into a major collapse with the 1930's depression. The postulated negative consequences of a crisis described above were realized with even greater severity. To this day, "the fall of coffee" is an event of tremendous symbolic import in Venezuelan public memory. With the changes associated with the petroleum economy, however, residents from Boconó and other coffee areas could move to cities like Maracaibo or Caracas. This movement has been so important that it is difficult to limit one's study to Boconó without taking into account population movements between Boconó and Caracas and other cities. It is not uncommon to find an aged farmer who will tell you that all of his children live in Caracas and that he visits them there once a year.

The second, related, development concerns the impact of the petroleum transformation on those who have remained in Boconó. The growth of the Venezuelan state has resulted in increasing centralization of politics and economics. Over the past 30 years the government has created a number of credit and marketing programs that have displaced private merchants from their formerly dominant position in the coffee economy. At present, the government is the most important creditor and coffee buyer in Boconó. Credit decisions invariably require approval in a central office, meaning that local farmers are increasingly dependent upon the central government. Such decisions involve political favoritism as well, giving the party in power increased leverage over local farmers.

The Historical Dimension

The description of the Boconó District already suggests one of this chapter's most important points. Too often anthropologists have formulated their problems and conducted their studies with a shallow time frame. When functionalist perspectives were dominant, this synchronic focus was taken as a point of honor. On the one hand, it was argued that the history of the people we studied could not be recovered. On the other hand, it was suggested that even if historical processes could be known (and in many cases it became clear that documentary and oral historical sources were much richer than had been supposed), history itself could tell us very little. A "genetic" approach was rejected in favor of an "analytical" approach; the operation and functioning of a particular social feature could be explained in terms of the structure of the social relations of the present. Economic anthropologists were especially prone to such a synchronic bias, given the assumptions they were taking from economics and the nature of the data (input-output analyses, household budgets, price fluctuations, and the like) they were collecting. Thus the classic monograph might contain an introductory chapter that would include a section on history, but the historical sketch would not be integrated with the social and economic analysis in the book's core.

Yet a historical perspective is fundamental to all attempts to place local regions within a world system. Such a perspective has several dimensions, and the anthropologist who would use a world-system approach must be careful not to reduce his or her historical understanding to the simple statement that a particular region has long been part of a capitalist economy.

The Importance of Studying Patterns of Change over Time

It should be clear that the nature of the relationship between a local region and the world economy changes with time. During the colonial era, Boconó and the Venezuelan Andes in general were quite marginal to the colonial economy. Although one can come up with a list of imports and exports for the period that shows a relationship between the region and the emerging centers of the world economy, it would be inappropriate to suggest that one could understand the dynamics of local life or of the regional economy only in terms of the needs or dynamics of the world system or of the system's core. During the nineteenth century, the development of a coffee economy brought the region into a much more integral relationship with the centers of the world economy as the international division of labor intensified. Capital was invested in the region, Venezuelan and European immigrants settled in the region, and fundamental aspects of local life depended on coffee prices determined elsewhere. Even during this period, however, it would be inadequate to turn one's attention solely to international coffee markets.

Local merchants were indebted to larger trading houses, but they did not act as their agents. Rather, they pursued personal interests that were not necessarily identical with, and in many cases were contradictory to, the interests of foreign merchants or of the system as a whole. During the twentieth century, the region's close integration with the world market was loosened as coffee declined; yet local dynamics were drawn more tightly than before into the processes of the world system as Venezuela became an oil republic. As indicated above, this precipitated a national transformation that had profound local consequences. Furthermore, the importance of this question cannot be reduced to a homily that would tell us simply that the nature of the relationship between a local region and the world system is constantly changing. It is also important to recognize that the social relations that characterize one period or one type of relationship continue to carry social, economic, and political weight in a subsequent period. The development of a coffee economy introduced fundamental changes, but it was not created out of thin air. Structural features (for example, marketing systems, road networks, forms of property, settlement patterns, class relations) of the colonial economy served as the immediate context for the investment of capital in coffee production. Many of these features were transformed; some could be transformed only through a political struggle between liberals and conservatives during the last half of the nineteenth century.

The Importance of Understanding the Past in Order to Explain the Present

Another consequence of an historical approach is the fresh perspective it provides on the local actors themselves. Too often, anthropologists debate the relative weight of local, regional, national, and international factors on the activity of local peasants, artisans, or traders as if these actors were simply historical givens, ready to act within and be influenced by the present situation. This is particularly true when we consider peasantries, the structure of which may be projected into a dim past and whose formation may be seen as logically and historically prior to the influence of a world system. In Boconó, however, small-scale family farms began to appear only with the formation of a coffee economy in the nineteenth century, in association with a transformation of property relationships that broke up formerly impartible colonial properties and indigenous reserve lands.

In a fundamental sense, the very emergence of a peasantry was tied to the region's integration within an international division of labor. Furthermore, many of the small farmers who turned to coffee or who moved into the region to plant coffee were becoming more entrepreneurial, contracting debts and planting an export commodity on their best lands during a period of economic boom. Certain aspects of their strategy were bequeathed to their children and grandchildren as a boom economy entered into crisis. The response of small farmers to the mid-twentieth-century crisis would make little sense unless one understood these nineteenth-century legacies.

Closed and Open Peasant Communities

In one sense this point is hardly surprising. In a preliminary typology of Latin American peasantries made over three decades ago, Eric Wolf (1955) suggested an opposition between "closed" and "open" peasantries. The distinction was based in history. The closed type corresponded to former nuclear areas in Mesoamerica and Peru that had precolonial state systems and peasant agriculture. The corporate com-

munity was seen as a colonial product, fixing the indigenous population on the ground as a source of labor and tax revenue. The open type
was seen to emerge in frontier zones during the nineteenth-century expansion of export production. The Boconó peasantry was clearly open
in Wolf's sense (see Cancian's discussion in Chapter 6).

Too often, however, the historical nature of Wolf's distinction is lost,
especially when anthropologists study closed types. Field-workers may
have a bit to say about the early colonial period and the changes introduced by conquest, but they will then skip over four centuries to the
ethnographic present as if the intervening periods involved no fundamental changes. Recent reevaluations demonstrate, however, that the
development of export production in crops such as coffee introduced
important changes in closed zones just as it was creating peasantries in
open zones.

One recent study has reexamined the history of many of the communities in Chiapas, a region of some of the most extensive anthropological fieldwork in recent decades, and has found fundamental
transformations in those communities with the development of coffee
production, the migration of Indians to work on lowland plantations,
and the like (Wasserstrom 1983). Among the most interesting of the
new developments, both in this study and elsewhere, is the reinterpretation of the development of the civil-religious hierarchy. Fundamental
aspects of this system are now seen to have emerged during the nineteenth century (Rus and Wasserstrom 1980; Chance and Taylor 1985).

Anthropologists who try to place peasantries in a wider world, then,
cannot be content with a synchronic approach. They need to pay close
attention to the complex interplay of external pressure and internal response over time and need to be aware of the possibility that those
features of peasant life that seem most traditional or customary may be
the results of past impositions, responses, or accommodations. It may
be that the traditional peasant is part of a modern history, a history that
has placed the peasant in a wider world.

The Methodological Dimension

This historically oriented world-system perspective presents a number of methodological dilemmas for the anthropologist. The first concerns the appropriate level or unit of analysis. How does one talk about
local regions in terms of local, national, and international factors without losing methodological control? The Wallerstein solution—that one
studies social systems as wholes and therefore concentrates on the
world system itself—leaves no room for anthropology. Most anthro-

pologists who pay attention to such issues will want to start with a local region and attempt to say something about that region in terms of local and extralocal relationships and social forces. Yet they will be confronted by a constant methodological strain.

Unfortunately, most of the metaphors anthropologists use to talk about such a strain are either spatial or involve some conception of analytical layers or levels. The classic early conception was Julian Steward's "levels of sociocultural integration" (Steward 1955). Derived from his evolutionary studies, it argued that earlier levels of social organization (for example, family, band, and community) were incorporated but not fully subsumed within higher levels of organization. Thus the family, once a maximal unit of organization, was incorporated within states without losing its distinctive character. When this concept was applied to the study of complex societies, one could study the various sociocultural levels and their interrelations. Spatial metaphors result from anthropologists' field practice. We study in communities, and as we consider the effect of national and global phenomena, we ask what within the local situation is to be understood in terms of local relationships and what is to be understood in terms of larger forces. As we ask these questions, we often start with an implicit or explicit spatial model that moves from communities to regions to nations to the world.

The Problem with a Regional Approach

As anthropologists became dissatisfied with community studies, some of them moved toward regional studies. Although this alters one's definition of local and nonlocal relations, it does little to address the central methodological problem. It tends to remove anthropologists from the intimate daily interactions that have been the source of much ethnographic knowledge, yet it does not necessarily give them a bird's-eye view. Indeed, they may still have a "worm's-eye view" in that many of the forces and relations that affect a region are located elsewhere (cf. C. Smith 1976: 3). Recall the Venezuelan example. To understand Boconó, one has to talk about the formation of a coffee economy in the nineteenth century, the collapse of that economy in the context of a petroleum boom, the migration of residents to Caracas and other cities, and the centralization of the Venezuelan state and its increasing role in local life. Regardless of whether one started with a local community or the Boconó District as a whole, most of these developments would be seen as extralocal, and the view one gets of them from Boconó is necessarily partial.

The Importance of Understanding Macrolevel
Influences on Microlevel Behavior

To resolve the methodological dilemma, we need to move beyond the spatial and layer cake metaphors we use to describe it. Our earlier discussion showed that the very formation of many regions and communities is tied to transformations in the world economy. To ignore the world economy and study a local realm apart from a nonlocal realm may preserve analytical rigor, but at the expense of historical understanding. To avoid this, we need to concentrate on relationships that transcend spatial boundaries, that take the apparently external and make it internal to our model of a social situation. "Anthropologists don't study villages," wrote Clifford Geertz (1973: 22), "they study in villages." Although he was making a somewhat different point, this insight is relevant to the present discussion. As we study in communities, we need to be creative in our conceptualization and study of relationships, institutions, and networks that are apparently foreign to the community.

Let us consider recent attempts to do this, beginning with our Venezuelan example. The author's principal methodological decision in Boconó was to concentrate on coffee. Such a commodity orientation can be extremely useful because the investigator is dealing with a product that is produced locally but exchanged on world markets. In the case of Boconó, coffee was the principal means of integration between the region and the nation and world in the nineteenth and early twentieth centuries. An investigator could deal with local production arrangements, the transformation of forms of landed property and work organization, relations with local merchants, connections between local merchants and trading companies, and so on. Of course, certain kinds of information are necessarily lost in such a study. Although coffee dominates the local economy, it occupies a small percentage of cultivable surface area. And there is a lively regional marketing network completely separate from the coffee trade. Such choices, and the recognition that one's study is necessarily partial, are basic to anthropological fieldwork.

With a commodity orientation, however, one can shift the spatial focus at various points in the research. In the Venezuelan study, the author concentrated on the town of Boconó, the center of a coffee-producing region and the home of a group of coffee merchants. From that point, the study could shift its focus toward local producers by following the merchants' networks, or it could turn attention beyond Boconó toward the trading companies by following another set of networks. Given a related set of research problems, this study concentrated on relationships between merchants and small farmers within the region, combining archival research in the land registry (where it was possible to reconstruct changes in credit structures by examining old mortgages) and interviews with key figures. The study did not, however, move toward the wider world with the same detail. It did not explore the archives of the Maracaibo trading companies themselves or examine their relations with German or American markets.

Examples of Innovative New Macrolevel Research

Other studies have been equally sensitive to local processes while paying more attention to developments beyond local regions. Two recent works provide models for future work. Ann Stoler's recent study of the plantation belt in Sumatra (1985) was not limited to a single commodity but concentrated on the plantation belt of Sumatra's East Coast. The region produced rubber, tobacco, tea, and palm oil, among other goods. What most clearly made the region a unit was the conjunction of plantation production and Dutch colonialism. In undertaking her study, she conducted fieldwork in the region, interviewing workers, foremen, and managers and studying one of the quasi-peasant villages. But she also examined archives in Sumatra and the Netherlands, and while in the Netherlands she interviewed retired plantation managers. Because Javanese migrants constitute much of the labor force, she was able to incorporate insights from earlier fieldwork in Java as well, noting fundamental differences between Javanese village life and the attempt to reconstitute the semblance of peasant life in a plantation context.

Chris Gjording's (forthcoming) study of a proposed (but never realized) copper mining project in Panama is also innovative. Gjording was concerned about the potential impact of the project on the Guaymi Indians, and he was also interested in their developing resistance to the project. To assess impacts and gain insight into the formation of new social movements, he had to conduct local fieldwork. A full understanding of the impact of the project also required analysis of national and international developments. Gjording eschewed a spatial definition of his unit of analysis and concentrated on the mining project itself. This allowed him to explore the role of the project within the Panamanian state's plans for economic and political development, the plans of various multinational corporations that entered and withdrew from the project, fluctuations within the international copper market, decision-making processes at the World Bank, and the increasingly assertive, if conflictual, attempts by Guaymi Indians to find an appropriate response to a project they came to regard as a threat to their livelihood. Fieldwork involved residence among the Guaymi, but it also involved a period of time in Panama City interviewing government officials as well as time in New York interviewing multinational executives and World Bank officers.

Both of these studies offer models for future anthropological work. Like the Venezuela study, they conceive a local situation in a global context. Also like the Venezuela study, analysis of the relations of production and exchange involved with export commodities provides the means for a significant expansion of anthropological focus. Unlike the Venezuela study, they are less rooted in a particular locale; the fieldworkers conducted research at the centers of the world economy as well as the peripheries, and they made certain aspects of the dynamics of the center (colonial policies, market fluctuations, corporate investment strategies, lending agency requirements, and so on) internal to their analysis of particular regions in the periphery of the world system.

The Problem of Social Homogeneity in Peasant Communities

A second methodological issue, not restricted to world-system analyses, is simultaneously created and obscured by the style of presentation adopted in this chapter. We have talked about "peasants and the world" as if peasants were a simple, undifferentiated, and isolable group. This makes sense in terms of an anthropological history: Most of the issues discussed in this chapter came out of an anthropological move toward the study of peasant populations. The presentation makes less sense, however, in terms of the concrete social situation of actual peasantries.

In the first place, peasantries are generally characterized by marked social differentiation. A few households may be able, in most years, to provide for themselves without sending household members to work elsewhere for wages and without turning to the market except for those essentials that cannot be produced on the farm. Some households will be more favorably situated, hiring laborers and selling much of their produce. (With export commodity production such as that found in Boconó, market relations are more complicated for all of the types discussed here.) Many households will, however, be less favorably situated, and they may have to send some household members out to work on a regular basis. Indeed, some members of the household may work outside so frequently that it is more appropriate to consider them proletarians.

In the second place, anthropologists studying rural peoples have not dealt simply with peasantries. From quite early on they have also studied twentieth-century plantation zones with populations of rural proletarians. The Puerto Rico project coordinated by Julian Steward examined a range of rural types, from the peasants producing tobacco and coffee in the interior to the rural proletarians on corporate sugar plantations on the coast. Indeed, Sidney Mintz's study of a plantation community on Puerto Rico's south coast introduced the concept of rural proletarian to anthropological discourse (Steward et al. 1956; Mintz 1953, 1959, 1974a, 1974b). Since then, anthropologists have examined a range of productive enterprises and rural types.

Yet the problem is even more complex. Analytical distinctions are easy when we contrast a community of "peasants" with a community of "proletarians." But these distinctions become more difficult when the investigator is attempting to understand a population of small-scale landowners who farm their land but who also regularly engage in wage labor. In some cases, the mix of farm work and off-farm work is unevenly distributed within the household, with one member (say, the husband and father) maintaining the farm while other members (sons and daughters) work elsewhere (on other farms, in nearby towns, as laborers or as domestic servants), and while other members (the wife and daughters) take in laundry or make lace for sale to merchants. In such cases, a "proletariat" seems to be hidden within a "peasant" community (cf. Mintz 1974a).

The complexity of relationship is not restricted to the relationship of peasant to proletarian. Our image of peasants is often one that emphasizes an agricultural strategy, with the household unit farming a piece of land and working off the farm for wages to supplement farm produce. Recent research, however, shows that such households engage in a variety of reproduction and accumulation strategies, including weaving, sewing, brick making, cooking, petty trade, and the like. The classic image of the peasant may be the result of an agricultural bias in our models that blinds us to a large population of simple commodity producers with little access to land. It also precludes a more sophisticated understanding of the actual reproduction strategies of those people we call peasants (for good discussions of simple commodity producers, see Cook 1976, 1982, 1984a, 1984b, 1984c; C. Smith 1984a, 1984b, 1984c; G. Smith 1979, 1985; Chevalier 1983; Kahn 1980; Friedmann 1980; Bernstein 1979).

Such complexity has produced a theoretical debate about the appropriateness of a peasant concept (Ennew et al. 1977; Friedmann 1980; Roseberry 1983, 1985; C. Smith 1985; Littlejohn 1977). More important for current purposes is a discussion of methodological styles for understanding this complexity. Although the problem is hardly specific to world-system approaches, the form that complexity itself takes is one that often carries individuals beyond specific locales. For example, reproduction strategies may involve seasonal or permanent migration, and what looks like "permanent" migration may well be reversed after a number of years. Likewise, petty trade may involve regional and extraregional marketing systems that require attention.

The most obvious methodological tool for capturing differentiation is statistical. Based on extensive and detailed household surveys and inventories, numerous studies have produced rich profiles of the producing populations of particular communities and regions. Aside from the obvious benefits in terms of more accurate presentations, many of these studies have made important contributions to ongoing theoretical debates about the character and direction of differentiation among rural peoples (C. Smith 1984a; Cook 1984b, 1984c; Deere and de Janvry 1981).

The best of the recent studies include detailed information on activities within and beyond the household. It is only with such data that we can move from statistical portraiture to meaningful discussions of change over time. For example, in his large-scale study of craft production in the Oaxaca Valley, Scott Cook has gathered data on a large survey population, data that allow him to document the differentiation among household enterprises across and within various groups. He organizes the data according to broad occupational category (such as peasant cultivator, artisan) but also explores different patterns of differentiation among rural industries (brick making, embroidery, backstrap loom weaving, treadle loom weaving). In trying to understand the different patterns, he explores various marketing processes and production techniques within the context of the regional economy, but he also draws upon his examination of the reproduction and accumulation strategies of particular households. As a result, he is able to make informed suggestions about the future direction of the enterprises themselves as well as the process of class formation in the Oaxaca Valley (Cook 1984a, 1984b, 1984c).

Analysis of the complexity of relationship within and among households need not depend on statistics. One can also learn a great deal from the analysis of particular households and lives. An advantage of this sort of analysis is that it allows for greater time depth. Gavin Smith has explored changing strategies of household reproduction over 100 years in the central Peruvian community of Huasicancha, connecting the shifts with changing labor relations on a nearby hacienda and developing possibilities for migration to Lima, to the provincial city of Huancayo, or to the nearby copper mines. He also connects these transformations with the political and economic history of Peru. More recently, he has used a network analysis to explore the complex relations established between resident villagers and migrants to Lima. Migrants specialize in selling fruit and form multistranded exchange relations with particular households in Huasicancha. These result in complex social institutions that Smith calls "household confederations," by means of which labor, goods, and people can move back and forth between village and metropolis. Had Smith restricted his study to either the village or the urban barrio, he would have been in a poor position to examine this important institution. By concentrating on particular household enterprises and tracing their multistranded networks, and by placing those developing networks in time, he was able to produce a much more sophisticated study (G. Smith 1979).

Much can also be done with classic anthropological field techniques that might seem to have little to do with a world-system approach. A particularly useful method for moving beyond bounded spatial units and exploring change over time is life history. One of the best known and most creative uses of life history in anthropology is Sidney Mintz's *Worker in the Cane* (1974b), which should be read in conjunction with his chapter on "Cañamelar" in *The People of Puerto Rico* (Steward 1956). The latter work was an analysis of the formation and structure of a proletariat in the sugar-producing region of Puerto Rico's south coast, a study that paid close attention to the history of the region, the structure of the sugar industry, and the social relations and culture of the sugar workers themselves. *Worker in the Cane*, a subsequent work, presents one worker's account of his life. Mintz has divided Taso's account into periods that reflect important periods in Puerto Rico's history, and after each section Mintz presents a commentary that tries to link the personal life with the larger history. This is but one creative example of the ethnographic styles anthropologists can adopt as they attempt to illuminate real lives in real places while exploring the economic, political, and cultural effects of the world system on those lives.

A world-system perspective offers a fundamental challenge to traditional anthropological practice. It forces us to be more historical, to see that the apparently isolated peoples we study are not so removed from the larger social and economic and political forces of the modern world as they may seem to be. It provokes us to rethink privileged concepts and to recast favored methodological procedures. Such a perspective does not, however, undermine anthropology. Although anthropological subjects have been formed within a world historical context, the global processes in which they have sometimes been caught have been uneven, and the responses of local populations have been uneven and varied as well. If anthropologists must be innovative in their research methods, most anthropologists will continue to work and live in particular locales. Even as we place those locales in larger contexts, we will want to know how these larger contexts affected real people in real places: what was done to those people, what they thought about it, what they said about it, what they did about it.

6

Economic Behavior
in Peasant Communities

Frank Cancian

Peasants live in two worlds. On the one hand, they are poor, isolated, subsistence-oriented, rural people. They care most about what is going on in their fields and their villages, and their communities reflect this inward-looking orientation. On the other hand, as the preceding chapter has shown, peasants are very dependent on the world outside their communities. They are subject to political and economic forces that emanate from far beyond the area of their everyday concern, and their communities also reflect these important connections to the larger society. These two characteristics of peasant life led to Alfred Kroeber's famous definition: "Peasants are definitely rural—yet live in relation to market towns; they form a class segment of a larger population which usually contains also urban centers. . . . They constitute part-societies with part-cultures" (1948: 284).

Many things have changed since Kroeber made his statement, but the study of peasants still requires attention to both the local, more independent, aspects of their lives and the strong influence of the larger society on the way they live. Roseberry's chapter on "Peasants and the World" concentrated on the latter. This chapter will concentrate more on studies of economic and social relations inside peasant communities.

Peasants differ from the urban elite, who live in state societies, because of (1) their geographic separateness, (2) their economic and political subordination, and (3) their ability to produce their own food. The first two characteristics are shared by peasants and urban ethnic minorities in some industrial societies. Ethnic minorities often live apart, as peasants do; and, in one way or another, they transfer some of their product or labor to people who control the larger society. Both peasants and urban ethnic minorities are also subordinate in the sense that they are often treated as backward and not worthy of respect by others

Thanks to Peggy Barlett, Pete Brown, Carole Browner, Francesca Cancian, Stuart Plattner, Art Rubel, Alice Saltzman, and an anonymous reviewer for comments on drafts of this paper.

within their society. Peasants differ from urban ethnic minorities because they are rural and usually produce much of their own food. Thus they can withdraw more easily from the larger society when times are especially hard. This distinctive capacity to isolate themselves has inspired much of the analysis of peasant society that we will review in this chapter.

There are many peasants in the world—probably more than a billion people living in more than a million villages. They are an important part of many countries, including, to take only a few examples, China, Poland, Peru, Vietnam, Tanzania, Turkey, Italy, and Mexico. Thus peasant communities are important to economic anthropology for two reasons: They represent a distinctive kind of economic situation, and they include about one-fourth of the world's population.

The great numbers lead to great diversity. Peasant families have different contemporary living situations and different histories. They live in low, hot, flat, coastal areas and in high, cold, rugged mountains, in arid climates and rainy ones. Some work full-time on their own land, others rent, sharecrop, or work part-time as artisans, and still others spend much of their time working for wages in distant places. Many peasants have seen or participated in a national revolution in recent decades. Some are in close touch with the national government through political and economic development programs; others are isolated in the hinterlands. Some grow a commercial crop (like coffee) and are dependent on a world market beyond their control. Others grow a grain (like corn or rice) that ensures basic subsistence for their families without recourse to the market. Most peasants live in poor countries, and many live in countries that were once colonies of European nations.

The great diversity means that no generalization applies to all peasant communities at all times. General statements about peasants are usually limited or conditional generalizations. They apply under some conditions, and not under others. Thus, we have two tasks in this chapter. One is to review the most enlightening general statements made about economic relations inside modern and contemporary peasant communities. The other is to specify the conditions under which the generalizations are most apt to apply. We must always ask two questions: What is true about peasants? And when is it true? That is, what are the limits on its applicability?

I will lump students of peasant economic behavior into three groups: homogeneity theorists, heterogeneity theorists (DeWalt 1979), and differentiation theorists. Homogeneity theorists see peasants as having a special sociocultural system that makes them different from other people and makes them resistant to associations with nonpeasants and to economic change. Heterogeneity theorists see peasants as similar to other people and find them generally eager to change when genuine opportunities are available to them. The third group, differentiation theorists, is more concerned with the way relations with the larger economic system affect peasants and with the history of the transformation of peasants from relatively independent producers of their own subsistence to rural residents who must sell their products or their labor to survive. To some extent these three approaches to peasants are just like conditional generalizations—for example, the homogeneity view applies better at some places and times, and the heterogeneity view applies better at different places and times. In part, however, the different approaches reflect the fact that the different scholars ask different questions and look at different aspects of the same peasant communities.

Whatever the approach, it is useful to remember the distinction between closed and open peasant communities that Eric Wolf (1955) made more than 30 years ago. The closed communities are more inward-looking than the open communities. They tend to produce basic grains for food rather than commercial crops and often have cultural, historical, or political differences with the larger society. Open communities usually have many more economic, political, and cultural connections to the larger society. The influence of the outside world is a more direct and more important part of everyday life in open communities.

In recent decades the number of open communities has grown dramatically. The spread of markets, technology, and communications—of Coca-Cola, fertilizers, and transistor radios—has brought millions of peasants into the world system. Land shortages have led many rural people to migrate in search of work. We will see that, over the years, all these connections to the larger system have undermined peasants' ability to withdraw and have changed internal relations in their communities.

The chapter is divided into six parts. I will begin with background on a concrete example that will be useful throughout the chapter and then look at what each of the three approaches has to say about peasant economic behavior and the social and political behavior in which it is embedded. These reviews are followed by a summary of the varied economic activities that have given the term "peasant" new meanings, and by a discussion of ideas about long-term change in peasant communities.

Zinacantan, a Peasant Community

Zinacantan, a Maya Indian community in the mountains of southeastern Mexico, will serve as the main example in this chapter. Though

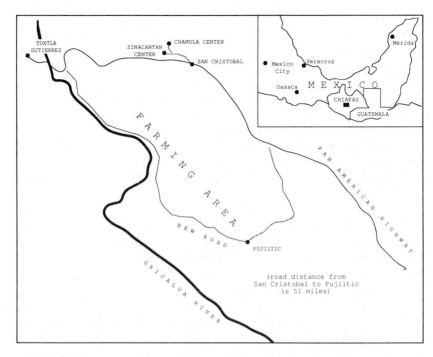

Map 6.1. Zinacantan and environs.

no single example can illustrate all the complexities of peasant life, it is important to have, wherever possible, a concrete referent for the general statements that follow. I chose Zinacantan for three reasons. First, it has features that clearly illustrate the generalizations made by homogeneity theorists, heterogeneity theorists, and differentiation theorists. Second, it has been studied extensively by many anthropologists, and much is known about it.[1] Finally, since I have done fieldwork there for more than 3 years over the last 25 years, I can provide richer illustrations than I could for a case known to me exclusively through the written work of others.

When I first went to Zinacantan in 1960, the population of about 7,500 lived in about a dozen hamlets clustered on hillsides and in valleys around the ceremonial and political center. Zinacantan Center, with its churches, sacred mountains, and town hall, served as the official point of contact with the outside world. A rocky, unpaved road connected it to San Cristóbal, the trading city (Map 6.1) that the Spanish estab-

[1] See especially Vogt 1969, 1978.

lished when they arrived in the sixteenth century, a few years after the conquest of central Mexico.

In the 1960's, Zinacantecos (the people of Zinacantan) went freque.'tly to San Cristóbal (pop. 25,000) to trade with the non-Indian resid 'nts of the city (who are called Ladinos) and with Indians from other communities in the highlands who also came to the San Cristóbal market (see Plattner, "Markets and Marketplaces," this volume). The internal affairs of Zinacantan were controlled by Zinacantecos within a structure set by the state (Chiapas) and Mexican national governments. Political relations with the outside world were handled through Zinacanteco brokers.

Yet Zinacantecos were isolated from the larger world represented by San Cristóbal. Few adult men and almost no adult women could speak Spanish, and their many relationships with Ladinos were confined to economic matters: selling corn and beans, buying yarn, cloth, and tools, renting farmland in the distant Grijalva River valley, delivering coffee brought by Zinacanteco muleteers from distant backcountry plantations controlled by Ladinos, or seeking unskilled wage work in agriculture or occasionally in construction. Though the building of the Pan American Highway through Zinacantan in the 1950's (see Map 6.1) provided work for many Zinacantecos, especially young men saving for their marriages, most Zinacantecos earned a living farming corn on rented land far from their community. In 1960 they were fairly independent producers who were able to both feed their families and sell parts of their crops in San Cristóbal.

This had not always been so. When the Spanish colonizers arrived in the early sixteenth century, Zinacantecos were traders as well as corn farmers. In fact, the road that connects Zinacantan Center to San Cristóbal runs along a trade route that had connected Guatemala with central Mexico before the Spanish conquest. So Zinacantecos were not strangers to contact with distant cultures. Nor had corn farming been their principal occupation for long. After the conquest, their principal means of livelihood shifted repeatedly with changing Spanish interests that depended on pressures from the world beyond their region. One of the blackest periods in Zinacantan's history was the late nineteenth century, when the "reform" laws of 1856, and later the policies of Mexican dictator Porfirio Díaz, deprived many Indian communities of their land and concentrated it in Ladino hands. At that time many Zinacantecos were reduced to debt peonage on the lowland plantations, where they presently rent land (Collier 1975; Wasserstrom 1983). The worst aspects of this system ended with the Mexican revolution of 1910, which resulted in the new constitution of 1917 and led to major land reform during the term of Lázaro Cárdenas (1934–1940), who was the first Mexican president to serve the full six-year term that is now standard.

Since the 1930's, land reform has coincided with increasing prosperity and many other changes that improved the lot of Zinacantecos and other Mexican peasants, but few peasants in and around Zinacantan received plots large enough to support a family. Zinacantecos were relatively fortunate because they lived within walking distance of the lowland fields near the Grijalva River that became available for rent as a result of land reform. Others, like those from the neighboring township of Chamula, had even smaller plots in their community and were too far from the lowlands to successfully farm corn there. Many of them survived by traveling to work as contract laborers on the distant coffee plantations along the Pacific coast. More recently they found wage work in cities that grew rapidly during Mexico's oil boom in the 1970's.

The two sides of peasant life show themselves in this brief sketch of Zinacantan. On the one hand, Zinacantecos were traders connected to distant places even before the Spanish conquest. Since the conquest, they have been subject to changing policies dictated by conquerors and the national state. So their connection to the world outside their community is old and important. On the other hand, they are independent producers of their own subsistence; they speak their own language and maintain their own cultural traditions. As we will see below, there are many ways in which they can and do close out the outside world.

As we look at the general statements that follow, it is important to remember that in Zinacantan, as in any peasant community, these different aspects of peasant life are usually present at the same time, and that the emphasis on contact or isolation changes over time. The powerful generalizations and models that help us think about peasants sometimes clarify by emphasizing some aspects of peasant life to the exclusion of others. Anyone who wants to understand peasant life must be ready to mix generalizations to approximate the complex world in which peasants live.

The Homogeneity Approach

It has often been observed that peasant communities are homogeneous. This generalization usually has two parts. First, it means that socioeconomic differences between households are small and that people are uniformly poor. "Small" and "poor" are relative to the "big" differences and "rich" people found in the larger society within which peasants live. Such comparison with nonpeasants is usually present in studies of peasants, though it is often implicit. Second, the generalization means there are local customs that generate and maintain a homogeneous population. Homogeneity theorists make both statements: those about socioeconomic conditions in peasant communities, and those about the processes that keep things that way.

In this section we will look at three versions of homogeneity theory. Anthropologists who see culture in institutions (like Eric Wolf, discussed below) emphasize institutions that resemble what we might call enforced philanthropy. These institutions involve strong social pressure to participate in community rituals and personal recognition and prestige for those who sponsor rituals at their own expense. The expenditures tend to "level" any individual who has gotten rich. Along with other customs regarding land tenure, they bound the community, making it hard for insiders to leave and outsiders to enter. These customs have important influences on economic relations inside the peasant community and on the way its members interact with the world outside.

Anthropologists who see culture in human cognition (like George Foster, discussed below) emphasize distinctive peasant ideas and images of reality. These ideas lead to communities where individuals interact so as to maintain "shared poverty" and where potentially upsetting innovations from outside are discouraged. Despite their different starting points and different interpretations, Wolf and Foster observe many similarities in peasant communities.

A. V. Chayanov is the third and last homogeneity theorist who will be considered below. Although Wolf and Foster are quite different from each other, they both argue for the central importance of the relation between the peasant and the larger system. In this they follow Kroeber's definition about part-societies and part-cultures, a definition formulated in the middle of this century. Chayanov, a Russian agricultural economist who wrote in the early part of the century, emphasized the isolation of peasants and the ways in which their independence from the larger system makes their economic behavior distinctive. Following translation of his writings from the original Russian in 1966, his ideas became important in current debates about socioeconomic differentiation in peasant societies.

All three of these theorists see peasant social and economic organization as different from modern, industrial, free-market (capitalistic) organization, which encourages individual accumulation of wealth and leads to socioeconomic differentiation or heterogeneity. Implicitly at least, each sees peasant communities as a cultural form that resists these trends and leads to socioeconomic homogeneity.

Eric Wolf: The Closed Corporate Community

Eric Wolf is the most influential homogeneity theorist. In a classic paper (Wolf 1957) he compared peasant communities in Mesoamerica (the ancient high culture area of Mexico and Guatemala) and Central Java, and found that they were similar in many of the ways just mentioned. He says:

The cultural configuration which I wish to discuss concerns the organization of peasant groups into closed, corporate communities. By peasant I mean an agricultural producer in effective control of land who carries on agriculture as a means of livelihood, not as a business for profit. In Mesoamerica, as in Central Java, we find such agricultural producers organized into communities with similar characteristics. They are similar in that they maintain a body of rights to possessions, such as land. They are similar because both put pressures on members to redistribute surpluses at their command, preferably in the operation of a religious system, and induce them to content themselves with the rewards of "shared poverty." They are similar in that they strive to prevent outsiders from becoming members of the community, and in placing limits on the ability of members to communicate with the larger society. That is to say, in both areas they are corporate organizations, maintaining a perpetuity of rights and membership; and they are closed corporations, because they limit these privileges to insiders, and discourage close participation of members in the social relations of the larger society (1957: 1–2).

Many anthropologists found these and similar patterns of behavior in culturally diverse peasant communities across the world. Wolf's statements emphasize the isolated, local aspect of many peasant communities—the inward-looking part of their two-sided nature.

These general features of peasant communities attracted the attention of people with very different practical interests. Some saw virtue in the tight-knit life of the local community and the emphasis on equality. They, like many urban-to-rural migrants in the United States today, sought to change their own communities in the direction of these characteristics. Others fought to break into the bounded, corporate community and to integrate peasant individuals into national life through programs of "economic modernization" and "community development." For both types of people, and for many others with intermediate views, Wolf's model of the closed corporate community differentiated peasant behavior from that expected in modern, urban settings.

Zinacantan illustrates many aspects of Wolf's closed corporate community, especially because its system of religious offices connected with the Catholic church is typical of the religious systems Wolf described.

In Zinacantan a man's community-wide reputation is established in large part through service in the religious cargo system. The cargos are year-long offices whose incumbents sponsor religious fiestas at great expense to themselves. Similar systems have been described for many Middle American communities. They have been called variously the ladder system, the civil-religious hierarchy, and the cofradia system.

In the Zinacantan cargo system there are four levels of offices arranged in a hierarchy. A man seeking honor or prestige in the community must serve one of about 35 first-level cargos to begin his career. After that, he is eligible to serve one of 12 second-level cargos, then one of six third-level cargos, and finally one of two fourth-level cargos. . . .

First service does not usually occur until the age of 35 or 40, and years of "rest" between service periods are required to earn the money necessary to sponsor fiestas. Thus, many men who hope to compete for the limited number of offices on higher levels die before reaching their goal. . . .

Both the authority invested in the particular office and the cost of performing the ritual associated with it contribute to the prestige. For example, the Mayordomo Rey is in charge of a chapel in the ceremonial center. A Mayordomo Rey must spend considerably more than 10,000 pesos (measured in 1960 pesos [equal to about $3,000 in 1988]) in the course of a year's service. The Mayordomo San Antonio must spend about 3,000 pesos. His principal duties involve ceremonial patterns directed by someone else. Thus a man who serves as Mayordomo Rey acquires much more prestige because he has more authority and spends more than one who serves as Mayordomo San Antonio. . . .

To maintain and enhance prestige established through service in a first-level cargo, a man must progress through higher levels of the system as he becomes older. The ultimate goal is completion of a fourth cargo. The rewards for completion come mostly in respect and deference, though the "elder" status is also recognized by exemption from local taxes (a small saving compared to the cost of service). [Cancian 1974: 164–66]

Since all of the effort put into cargo service is worthless outside of Zinacantan, the cargo system clearly distinguishes the community from its social environment. That is, it defines a social boundary around it. In other places as well, ritual service helps to maintain social solidarity and cultural isolation. It dominates internal economic relations (in which social and economic aspects are usually hard to separate) even while the people are economically dependent on the larger world. These ritual institutions typify the inward-looking aspect of peasant communities that is so well described by Wolf's generalizations about closed corporate communities.

Many peasant communities have no religious system of the kind described here. And, as we will see below (especially when we look at Paso toward the end of this chapter), not all peasant communities are closed corporations that divide people into insiders and outsiders. Thus the generalizations made about closed corporate peasant communities are not always true. We must ask, When are they true?

When and Why Do Closed Corporate Communities Appear?

According to Wolf, the closed corporate community developed in reaction to events in the larger society—it is conditional on the relation
of the local community to the larger society.

In some places, where the society was "dualized" into a "dominant
entrepreneurial sector and a dominated sector of peasants," the closed
corporate community formed as a part of this historical process. In
many of these places, the dualization occurred during conquest and
colonization of the area by Europeans.

Both in Mesoamerica and Central Java, the conquerors occupied the land and
proceeded to organize labor to produce crops and goods for sale in newly established markets. The native peasantry did not command the requisite culturally
developed skills and resources to participate in the development of large-scale
enterprises for profit. In both areas, therefore, the peasantry was forced to
supply labor to the new enterprises, but barred from direct participation in
the resultant returns. In both areas, moreover, the conquerors also seized control of large-scale trade, and deprived the native population of direct access to
sources of wealth acquired through trade, such as they had commanded in the
pre-conquest past.

Yet in both areas, the peasantry—forced to work on colonist enterprises—
did not become converted into a permanent labor force. The part-time laborer
continued to draw the larger share of his subsistence from his own efforts on
the land. From the point of view of the entrepreneurial sector, the peasant
sector remained primarily a labor reserve where labor could maintain itself at
no cost to the enterprises. This served to maintain the importance of land in
peasant life. At the same time, and in both areas, land in the hands of the peasantry had to be limited in amount, or the peasantry would not have possessed
sufficient incentive to offer its labor to the entrepreneurial sector. It is significant in this regard that the relation between peasant and entrepreneur was not
"feudal." No economic, political, or legal tie bound a particular peasant to a
particular colonist. . . . If access to land thus remained important to the peasantry, land itself became a scarce resource and subject to intense competition
especially when the peasant population began to grow in numbers. [Wolf 1957:
8–9]

In other places, Wolf sees the closed corporate community as the result of "internal colonization"—that is, as the result of a similar process
of polarization taking place within a society. In all cases, "dualization"
or polarization is crucial to the appearance of the closed corporate community.

Wolf observed that open rather than closed peasant communities developed in still other places as the result of different relations between
the countryside and the larger society.

In China, free buying and selling of land has been present from early times.
Communities are not endogamous and rarely closed to outsiders, even where a

single stratified "clan" or tsu held sway. Constant circulation of local landowners into the imperial bureaucracy and of officials into local communities where they acquired land prevented the formation of closed communities. Moreover, state controls maintained through control of large-scale water works heavily curtailed the autonomy of the local group. In such a society, relations between individual villagers and individual government officials offered more security and promise than relations among the villagers themselves. [Ibid.: 6–7]

There were also many open peasant communities in Latin America. There, according to Wolf, they "arose in response to the rising demand for cash crops which accompanied the development of capitalism in Europe" (1955: 462). On still another continent, Wolf observed that open peasant communities seemed to have developed in pre-British Uganda, where land was not scarce and people were able to change their alliances in order to better their life chances. We will return to open peasant communities below in the section on heterogeneity theorists.

In sum, according to Wolf, the closed corporate community is a distinctive sociocultural form that developed in many parts of the world in response to the dualization of society. Peasant communities are not inherently closed. Rather, closed corporate peasant communities developed in response to certain conditions in the larger society—specifically conditions under which the dominant nonpeasants found it useful to employ peasant labor part-time and limit peasant access to land, as they did near Zinacantan in the nineteenth century.

By now it is clear that we must be careful to distinguish between traditional and aboriginal aspects of peasant communities. Closed corporate communities have often been labeled traditional and contrasted with the modern sectors of the societies in which they exist. They have been characterized as repositories of aboriginal custom, and the reluctance of peasants to interact with the larger society has been seen as reluctance to part with these ancient customs. This has been the widespread conclusion of people in the modern sector. But, given Wolf's view, these "traditions" are better seen as the result of a historical process that polarized the larger society, creating a peasant culture that was inward looking precisely because of its relation with the outside world.

Wolf's historical/structural view of peasant institutions contrasts with Foster's cultural/cognitive view, which we will now review. Yet what follows simply describes another side of the same behavioral patterns. Foster also sees the peasant community as an adaptation made to ensure survival in very limited economic circumstances.

George Foster: The Image of Limited Good

George Foster sees "cognitive orientation" as the explanation for much human behavior. He says: "The members of every society share a common cognitive orientation which is, in effect, an unverbalized, implicit expression of their understanding of the 'rules of the game' of living" (1965: 293). Peasants have a distinctive cognitive orientation.

The model of cognitive orientation that seems to me best to account for peasant behavior is the "Image of Limited Good." By "Image of Limited Good" I mean that broad areas of peasant behavior are patterned in such fashion as to suggest that peasants view their social, economic, and natural universes—their total environment—as one in which all the desired things in life such as land, wealth, health, friendship and love, manliness and honor, respect and status, power and influence, security and safety, *exist in finite quantity and are always in short supply*, as far as the peasant is concerned. Not only do these and all other "good things" exist in finite and limited quantities, but in addition *there is no way directly within peasant power to increase the available quantities.* [1965: 296]

According to Foster, the Image of Limited Good explains much peasant behavior that helps to keep the community homogeneous. Peasants, he says, are fearful that they will upset the balance that includes their share of the dangerously small local "pie." No individual wants to stand out in any way. Thus peasants hesitate to accept leadership roles (ibid.: 303), they gossip and negatively sanction anyone who changes his relative economic standing in the community, and they maintain local institutions (like the cargo system) that restore balance when economic differentiation does occur (ibid.: 305).

Peasant culture includes other elements that Foster believes help peasants deal with differentiation. For example, in the community of Tzintzuntzan, Michoacán, Mexico, where Foster made repeated field studies over many decades (see especially Foster 1967), people who change their economic status are often said to have discovered buried treasure. Foster says this explanation makes it possible for their neighbors to recognize the wealth while maintaining the "Image of the Static Economy" (an earlier, more specific kind of Image of Limited Good) and approving of the person who changed economic status (Foster 1964). I have heard similar "treasure tales" in Zinacantan, where they were also used to explain differences in wealth.

The other possible explanation for new wealth, given the Image of the Static Economy, is that the person "has encroached upon the shares rightfully belonging to others" (ibid.: 1964: 40). In an early paper (1960–61), Foster emphasized the quality of interpersonal relations in peasant society that he sees as a result of these beliefs. He found that peasants live tense, atomistic (individualistic), interpersonal lives. They fear what their fellow villagers will do to them. Peasants are distrustful, suspicious, hostile gossips who depend on no one except close family members. They are competitive rather than cooperative, and often find themselves in conflict with their fellow villagers. Foster based this characterization on his own observations and on a wide range of descriptions by others. For example, he quotes S. C. Dube's description of a village in India (Foster 1960–61: 176): "People attaining conspicuous success are invariably the subject of malicious criticism [and] . . . people . . . indulge in malicious gossip and backbiting. Mutual suspicion characterizes the general nature of interpersonal relations."

These features of peasant behavior are closely reflected in economic life: Individualism and suspicion mean that peasants will not cooperate with each other for their mutual benefit, the Image of Limited Good means they do not think it is worth trying to improve their economic lot, and the envy and hostility mean that those who try and succeed will soon suffer negative sanctions from their neighbors. Clearly, insofar as Foster's characterization of peasant cognitive orientation is true, it provides a powerful explanation of the failure of peasants to participate in economic development programs supported by national governments and international agencies of various kinds.

Foster's ideas, like others that explain peasant "resistance" to economic development programs, are potentially of great practical importance. To take advantage of their practical implications, we must know under what conditions they provide an accurate model of peasant thought and behavior.

When Does the Image of Limited Good Apply?

Foster's explanation of when and why peasants have the Image of Limited Good and the interpersonal behavior patterns that accompany it has two distinct parts. First, Foster says that the Image of Limited Good originates as a realistic assessment of the world:

When the peasant views his economic world as one in which Limited Good prevails, and he can progress only at the expense of another, he is usually very near the truth. Peasant economies, as pointed out by many authors, are not productive. In the average village there is only a finite amount of wealth produced, and no amount of extra hard work will significantly change the figure. [1965: 297]

This explanation of the origin of the Image of Limited Good does not make the peasant different from other people. He[2] seems to be like

---

[2] Virtually all peasant literature is about the men in these societies. Bossen (1984) makes an illuminating comparison of peasant and nonpeasant women.

anyone else might be in the same situation. In fact, Foster noted in the early paper mentioned above that the interpersonal relations that go with the Image of Limited Good are not limited to peasants:

I do not suggest that this type of interpersonal relations is limited exclusively to peasant society; we know, in fact, that it exists under other conditions, and that it can be anticipated in many situations of limited and sharply competitive opportunity. It has been produced experimentally by depriving volunteers of adequate food to the point where they perceive starvation as a real threat. [1960–61: 178]

Thus the origins of the Image of Limited Good and its distribution make it, potentially, a universal human phenomenon. It occurs when it is a good assessment of economic reality in peasant communities and in other settings as well. Simply put, Foster argues that poor people whose prospects for improving their situations are very limited develop the Image of Limited Good.

Second, Foster says, the Image of Limited Good is important to the analysis of peasant economic behavior because it hangs on even when it is no longer a realistic assessment of the economic situation. It is a cognitive orientation, a part of culture that persists somewhat independently of the changing material world.

[A] peasant's cognitive view provides moral and other precepts that are guides to—in fact, may be said to produce—behavior that may not be appropriate to the changing conditions of life he has not yet grasped. For this reason when the cognitive orientation of large numbers of a nation's people is out of tune with reality, these people will behave in a way that will appear irrational to those who are more nearly attuned to reality. Such people will be seen as constituting a drag (as indeed they may be) on a nation's development, and they will be cutting themselves off from the opportunity to participate in the benefits that economic progress can bring. [1965: 295–96]

In sum, the Image of Limited Good applies when it is realistic, and it persists even when it has ceased to be realistic. Foster's clear prose dramatizes the importance of the persistence of the cognitive orientation he has labeled the Image of Limited Good.[3] His analysis suggests that the Image of Limited Good will not be found where it is not realistic and has not been realistic for some time. But a problem remains, for Foster does not tell us how long it takes for cultures to adjust to new realities.

---

[3] Those who read Foster carefully know that he writes as an apologist for peasants. He argues that peasant conservatism is appropriate behavior for people with peasants' beliefs and that economic development programs should try to change real conditions so that cognition will also change. Nonetheless, his position, as it is popularly interpreted, is subject to a number of criticisms related to the negative image of peasants it has created.

This problem is not unique to Foster's analysis. Any analysis that uses cultural persistence as an explanation is subject to the same difficulties. The difficulties are as great for institutional analyses like Wolf's as they are for cognitive analyses like Foster's, for both give specific cultural features an active role in explaining the persistence of peasant society. We will see later that the heterogeneity theorists who emphasize cross-cultural similarities rather than cultural explanations of differences avoid this problem, but they do not solve it.

We can also ask, Does their culture really distinguish peasants from other people? Are peasants uniquely nasty? Foster's original characterization of interpersonal relations in peasant society was subjected to two thought-provoking critiques that raise important questions about peasant behavior. Oscar Lewis agreed with Foster about the quality of interpersonal relations in peasant society. But, Lewis insisted, interpersonal relations are not necessarily better in urban society. He says, "In my own field work, I had a conception of a good society as an ideal type against which I could measure both the urban life of Chicago and the peasant life of Tepoztlan, and find them both wanting" (1960–61: 179). As this critique suggests, it is very hard to establish a solid basis for comparison, for the quality of interpersonal relations is hard to judge.

Julian Pitt-Rivers raises the problem in another way. He suggests that the qualities Foster ascribes to peasant interpersonal relations could be described differently:

Moreover, for each of the terms a contrary alternative can be found if one wishes to evaluate the same behavior favorably instead of unfavorably. *Individualism* in the sense of refusal to cooperate may be called noble independence. Refusal to cooperate with urban people, particularly representatives of the state, is, I believe, a common characteristic of peasant communities who do not regard this as in any way ignoble. Since urban people frequently deceive them and always patronize them this attitude might be called common sense. . . . *Distrust and suspicion* become prudence once one regards the distrust as justified. . . . *Gossip unrelenting and harsh* is straightforwardness to the person who wishes to hear it. [1960–61: 181]

Given these complex and contradictory arguments, what can we conclude about cognitive orientation, interpersonal behavior, and related economic behavior in peasant communities? At least the following, I think:

1. Many observers think peasants resist economic change and are nasty in their interpersonal relations outside the family.

2. Foster and many who follow his interpretation believe that these behaviors are produced by a cognitive orientation, The Image of Lim-

ited Good, and that this cognitive orientation (culture) persists even when it is not a realistic assessment of the situation.[4]

3. It is not clear that all peasants or only peasants have this cognitive orientation and the behavior patterns associated with it. And it can be very hard to identify the conditions under which Foster's analysis applies.

Foster and Wolf represent the two classic and distinct approaches to peasants in American anthropology (Silverman 1979). Although their views about culture differ greatly, both find peasant culture important to understanding peasant communities, and they see similar patterns of behavior in peasant communities. Chayanov, whose views we will look at next, is quite different from both of them.

A. V. Chayanov: The Peasant Economy as a Special Type

A. V. Chayanov saw peasants as independent from the larger society. He saw the peasant family as a producing unit not connected to the market economy. Thus the essential relation of peasants to the larger society expressed in Kroeber's definition and in virtually all anthropological work on peasants was left out of Chayanov's basic model. As we will see, it made its way back in when the model was applied to concrete situations.

Chayanov was an agricultural economist working in Russia in the early part of this century. As noted above, his writings became influential in economic anthropology after their publication in translation in 1966.[5] Two related ideas are most important in current discussions. The first is a model of peasant economic strategy—of the way peasant families approach earning a living. The second draws out the implications of this model for the structure of peasant communities and explains the origin of peasant homogeneity much differently from Wolf and Foster.

Peasants, according to Chayanov, are primarily concerned with providing for their own families. Their strategy is as follows. When the family has many small children, the peasant parents work very hard to support them all. They expand the size of their fields to meet the needs of the family. Later, when the children grow up and can contribute to their own support by work in the fields, the parents work less hard.

---

[4] Many people who study economic development believe that outside experts who have little direct stake in peasant survival often are less realistic than peasants about the likely results of their proposals for change.

[5] See Teodor Shanin (1972, 1973, 1987) for more on Chayanov's theory, modern research on Russian peasants, and discussion of contemporary social science ideas about peasant economy.

TABLE 6.1
Simplified Model of Chayanov's Family Cycle

Years married	People present*	Consumers	Workers	C/W Ratio
1	HW	2	2	1.0
5	HWC	3	2	1.5
10	HWCC	4	2	2.0
20	HWCC	4	3	1.3
25	HWC	3	3	1.0
30	HW	2	2	1.0

NOTE: Chayanov's original table is more complicated because he tried to be more realistic by weighting consumption and contributions to production differently for men, women, and children of different ages.
*H = Husband, W = Wife, C = Child

And, eventually, the children leave and the size of the family farm is again reduced.

In Chayanov's theory of peasant economy, this image of peasant family development is expressed in a consumer/worker ratio. Adults are workers (producers), and both children and adults are consumers. Thus the consumer/worker ratio goes up when there are many small children in a family. Table 6.1 displays my simplified version of this thinking and illustrates the essential elements of Chayanov's theory. The consumer/worker ratio is low when the newly married couple are both working on the farm. It goes up as children are born and later falls as the children become workers as well as consumers. The family cycle is finally completed when the children leave (or, alternatively, the aged parents live with one of their children). In this model, the consumer/worker ratio defines how hard the workers have to work to support the family, and it describes the variation in their level of effort that Chayanov saw as a distinctive feature of peasant society.

In other economies, according to the neoclassical logic that underlay Chayanov's thinking, people have infinite wants, wants that keep them working at a pretty constant level. If the needs of their children go down, they have other goals—in our society, for example, a new car or a new living-room rug—that will keep them from significantly lowering the level of production. In Chayanov's model, peasants are not connected to socially defined infinite needs that keep them working. In this sense they are isolated from the larger society in which they live. As we will see below, in Chayanov's time there was important disagreement about whether this theoretical picture of isolation truly characterized actual peasant societies.

Chayanov's thinking also relates to the structure of peasant communities. There were clear differences in landholding and other signs of wealth in the Russian peasant communities with which he was familiar, but Chayanov saw the communities as basically egalitarian. The relative wealth and poverty, he argued, were not part of long-term relations among families. He used his theory of the family cycle and the distinctive peasant economic strategy to explain away the economic differentiation that did exist. As he saw it, the family cycle accounted for much of the difference between peasants who had a lot of land and those who had little land at any given point in time. That is, families in their expanded state would have a lot of mouths to feed and therefore would have a lot of land under cultivation. At the beginning or the end of their child-growing years (see Table 6.1) they would have smaller amounts of land. Thus differences between families were not permanent. Rather, he argued, the apparent differences between rich and poor peasants were products of their temporary positions in the family cycle. Considered over time, all peasants went through the same expanded and contracted periods of farm production. Thus they were essentially homogeneous in socioeconomic terms.

When Does Chayanov's Model Apply?

Chayanov intended his model to apply best to "pure family farms." According to his definition, such farms never hire labor to supplement that of family members. They are isolated from the labor market. As noted above, their goal is simply to maintain the family at a socially acceptable level of living. Thus, he thought, they cannot be understood in terms of "profit." Like the peasants in Wolf's characterization of the closed corporate community quoted above, they carry on "agriculture as a means of livelihood, not a business for a profit."

Chayanov recognized that, in order for his model to apply reasonably well, peasant families would have to be able to increase and decrease their labor effort virtually at will. And, of course, that would be difficult to do in most places, for access to land is limited. Thus Chayanov (1966: 111–13) noted that the model would be most appropriate in places with low population density and in places where land could be easily bought, sold, and rented. He also noted that peasant families might adjust to their situation by working outside of agriculture when they had more labor than their land could absorb—or that they might increase utilization of labor by changing to crops that demand more labor input per unit of land (see, for example, the case of Paso below).

Despite these limitations, Chayanov claimed that his model applied to many peasants in many countries: "Especially in non-European countries like India, China, and Japan, this group of farms forms a very considerable social sector. Its total proportion in the world economy is such that it fully deserves special attention and study" (ibid.: 112). Not everybody agreed with Chayanov's estimate of how well his model of peasant farm organization applied to real situations. His claim that "in Russia 90 percent of the total mass of peasant farms are pure family farms" (ibid.), made in 1925, was especially important because it differed from Lenin's assessment published in 1899 (pp. 179–80). Lenin, who also analyzed extensive surveys of Russian farms, said that much peasant production in Russia had become capitalist production, in which labor was bought and sold like a commodity. As we will discuss in detail in the section on differentiation theory, Lenin saw a bifurcation of the countryside into a peasant bourgeoisie and a landless or almost landless rural proletariat. He emphasized the connection with the larger capitalist economy, and he did not see the isolated, equal, and independent farms Chayanov did.[6]

Chayanov's theory is a particularly useful addition to the homogeneity theories of Wolf and Foster because it contrasts with their anthropological understanding of peasants living in the context of a larger society. As is typical of microeconomic thinkers, Chayanov approaches social behavior by lumping together the behavior of isolated individuals (families)—rather than by explaining individual actions as conforming to cultural and social patterns. He sees peasant culture in family behavior rather than community behavior. Thus, though he seeks to explain similar patterns of peasant behavior, Chayanov's theory is radically different from those of Wolf and Foster. In the summary that follows, I emphasize the anthropological approaches. Many of the features listed have no place in Chayanov's theory of peasant economy.

Summary of the Homogeneity Theorists

Because peasants live in many different situations, it is not surprising that most of the general statements reviewed so far are conditional generalizations. Despite this variety, most observers and interpreters of peasants and peasant communities find that peasants who live in closed communities are relatively:

---

[6] Both Lenin and Chayanov made scholarly arguments that had important political implications. Lenin, the dominant leader of the Russian Revolution, died in 1924. Chayanov, an important scholar and agricultural planner, advocated cooperatives as the basis for organization of agriculture. He was jailed in the late 1920's—a few years after he published his major work—at about the time that it was decided to collectivize much of the Russian countryside.

1. *Poor*. Peasants are poor in two ways: in an absolute sense (that is, they have little reserve to sustain them in bad times), and in a relative sense (that is, many nonpeasants in their societies are richer than peasants).

2. *Subjugated*. Politically and economically, peasants are weaker than the urban sectors of their societies, and in many societies their cultural traditions are regarded as inferior to those of the city.

3. *Self-sufficient* (autonomous). Peasants produce a very high proportion of what they consume (especially food) and are thus able to withdraw from contact with the dominant sector and reduce their dependence on the market. Within communities, families tend to be independent production units.

4. *Isolated*. Peasants are isolated in two ways. First, in keeping with their subjugation, they are geographically separate and are often politically, culturally, and linguistically cut off from the dominant urban sector of the society. Second, in keeping with their self-sufficiency, their ties to the larger system are often weak—that is, these ties do not dictate the details of their everyday life.

The common characteristics of the peasant situation just listed seem to make peasant communities:

5. *Homogeneous*. They have cultural features that create pressures toward homogeneity, including ritual practices that redistribute wealth and prevent it from being invested in a manner that would accumulate capital, and a belief system that negatively sanctions those that flaunt wealth. These characteristics are often seen as an adaptation to poverty. They include a norm of "shared poverty."

6. *Corporate* (bounded). There are clear markers of membership, including joint responsibilities (like ritual) and joint resources (like land) that clarify the differences between insiders and outsiders.

7. *Resistant to change programs*. Economic plans promoted by nonpeasants are often rejected. This seems to result from the persistence of the cultural characteristics just listed and from peasant realism about the usefulness of the programs.

8. *Socially intense*. Social relations are intense within the community, but investigators disagree about the quality of interpersonal relations. Peasants are often characterized as competitive and nasty, sometimes as cooperative. It is hard to know whether the different characterizations result mostly from the investigators' different approaches or from differences in peasant behavior at different times and in different places.

We have seen how peasants are thought of as different from other people. For many years this approach provided the dominant view of social and economic behavior inside peasant communities.

The Heterogeneity Approach

More recently many observers have stressed the social and economic heterogeneity within peasant communities. They have argued that differences between people within peasant communities offer a key to understanding the internal dynamics of the communities and the responses peasants make to economic change programs (DeWalt 1979; Pelto and Pelto 1975).

For example, my research in Zinacantan shows that men who took expensive cargos early in their lives continued to do so later in life; they remained rich, while those from poor families tended to remain poor by local standards. Though the pressure brought by the cargo system and other customs stressed by the homogeneity theorists were important in everyday life in Zinacantan, they did not homogenize the population. We will see that heterogeneity in the form of socioeconomic stratification was also important in everyday life and that many Zinacantecos with the resources needed to pursue economic opportunities did so. They did not resist change.

Similar differences between the rich and poor within peasant communities are found in many other places as well. Thus the patterns of the closed corporate community, the Image of Limited Good, and the peasant economy as a special type do not dominate peasant behavior everywhere and at all times.

Heterogeneity theorists also assume that peasants are like other people (Ortiz 1973: 1; Barlett 1982: 8). They do not emphasize the distinctive features of peasant society and culture that are crucial to the views of homogeneity theorists like Wolf, Foster, and Chayanov. Nor do they have special theories to explain peasant economic behavior or peasant response to economic development programs. Because peasant behavior is seen as similar to that of other people, there is no specific heterogeneity theory of peasant culture as a distinctive mode of living.

To appreciate this different approach to peasant behavior, we will have to see the world as more complicated than the one presented by homogeneity theory alone. The heterogeneity approach expands understanding of peasant behavior, but the insights of the homogeneity approach remain valid in many places. We will see that institutions like the cargo system, and norms of shared poverty enforced by fear or envy, may exist without completely homogenizing the population.

The same cultural features may both display existing heterogeneity and create pressure for homogeneity.

In this section I will present two examples of analyses that illustrate this newer approach to peasant community structure and economic behavior. One of them, Zinacantan, involves a very close approximation to a closed corporate community in Wolf's terms. The other, Paso, involves an open peasant community. Despite the vastly different cultures, institutions, and local political and economic situations, each exhibits patterns of economic behavior that are best understood in terms of the differences among people in the community.

Zinacantan: Heterogeneity in a Closed Corporate Community

I will describe two aspects of Zinacanteco life that illustrate the importance of socioeconomic heterogeneity: the cargo system and the response to economic opportunities created by change in the regional economic system.

In 1960, when I arrived in Zinacantan for the first time, the cargo system was flourishing (Cancian 1965). Virtually every Zinacanteco man (and his family) participated in some way. Zinacantecos talked about the religious importance of all cargo service and were reluctant to say that one kind of cargo service was more important than another. They seemed to have the norm of shared poverty.

Yet it became obvious that participants were not equal. Some cargos were more expensive than others, and it seemed to me that men who took more expensive cargos received more respect in social situations. For example, if a group of men were gathered in a house and a young man arrived to join them, he should, according to Zinacanteco custom, greet each of those there individually, bowing to each man older than he. But if the group was so big that this would disrupt and delay its activity for too long, he might not rigidly follow the rules of etiquette. In actuality he might bow elaborately to those who had passed the most expensive and prestigious cargos and skimp a bit on the others, even if they were older than those he greeted more formally. This difference in respect was consistent with the idea of a closed corporate community, for those honored best exemplified the norms of community service. The observed heterogeneity confirmed the importance of the cargo system—the institution central to the maintenance of homogeneity. In important ways, Zinacantan was like a closed corporate community.

When I examined surveys and censuses of Zinacanteco families, more differences appeared. Men who served in expensive cargos had fathers who had done the same. Persistent differentiation also showed up in marriages: The spouses tended to come from families in which the fathers had similar records of cargo service. Zinacantecos clearly knew who was who, and behaved accordingly in important aspects of their lives. The community showed patterns of social stratification, despite spoken adherence to norms of equality. Though Zinacantecos were virtually all poor relative to rich people outside Zinacantan, they clearly distinguished rich and poor among themselves (Cancian 1965).

During the 1950's and 1960's, increasing prosperity in Mexico and Chiapas and increasing population in Zinacantan led to increased demand for cargos. The prosperity that gave Zinacantecos more disposable income to spend on cargos developed outside of Zinacantan. The population growth that increased the number of people wanting to serve cargos was an internal force for change. Because of both kinds of pressure, waiting lists were established, and many Zinacantecos put their names down for cargos twenty years or more in the future. In 1966 the lists recorded requests for cargos to be served in 1988. Zinacantecos seemed to be intensely competing with each other for positions within their community, and the cargo system seemed to be a way to legitimate economic success within the norms of the closed corporate community. The heterogeneity was clear and persistent, and it was confined to interaction among Zinacantecos—for cargos as markers of prestige were useless outside of Zinacantan. Although Zinacantecos were far from homogeneous, they were expressing their differences within the community and in a way that kept them isolated from the outside world. In short, they preferred local prestige symbols to ones (like watches and radios) current in the world around them.

Willingness to make contact with the outside world showed up a bit later when Mexican government programs brought many changes to the region. New roads were built in the area where Zinacantecos farmed, and new markets for their corn were created by government programs designed to supply urban consumers while helping the small farmer avoid sales at low prices to local middlemen. In studying responses to these programs (Cancian 1972), I focused on issues that distinguish the homogeneity and heterogeneity approaches. I wanted to see if I needed to characterize peasants (Zinacantecos) as a special kind of people in order to understand their economic behavior. Specifically, I asked two questions inspired by the homogeneity analysis of closed communities: First, were Zinacantecos resistant to change? And, second, did the social relations displayed in their responses show a distinctively peasant pattern?

The first question is hard to answer. As with Foster's question about the quality of interpersonal relations, it is difficult to establish a legitimate basis of comparison. Zinacantecos did not change the minute government officials made a new program available, nor did they change in exactly the way officials intended. Does this mean they were resistant to change? Hundreds of studies (Rogers 1983) have shown that there is always a delay between the introduction of a new technology and its utilization by farmers of all kinds, and that farmers often adapt the official design to their own purposes. Thus the standard of comparison must be the behavior of other agriculturalists, peasants, and nonpeasant farmers, not some ideal set by an outside bureaucrat or social scientist. Because (as in Foster's case) every situation is different, it is difficult to say what is a reasonably fast response and what is stubborn resistance to change.

What did Zinacantecos do in response to government programs? When new roads were built in and near the areas where they farmed, and when the government established a corn-buying system designed to help the small farmer, Zinacantecos seemed to change very fast. Almost immediately, some Zinacantecos took advantage of the new roads, abandoned mule transport of corn, and adopted truck transport, which enabled them to reach more productive land that had formerly been too far away from their homes. And soon many were braving a bureaucratic maze of regulations in order to sell corn for the favorable price the government was offering. Within a few more years, many other Zinacantecos had followed these leaders. As far as I could tell, earlier lack of dramatic change reflected lack of opportunity, not resistance to change. Zinacanteco culture, the same culture that persisted in the cargo system, did not seem to impede economic change.

Is Zinacanteco Economic Behavior Special?

Did the social relations displayed in economic change in Zinacantan show a distinctly peasant pattern, or did Zinacantecos respond like other agriculturalists? To answer this question, I set out to compare Zinacanteco behavior with that of agriculturalists in communities in other parts of the world. Rogers (1983) had found that richer farmers in many communities were usually among the first to change. His generalization is illustrated in Fig. 6.1.

When I recorded which farmers in Zinacantan responded first to the new opportunities to sell corn to the government in the early 1960's, I found a different pattern (see Fig. 6.2). I eventually labeled this pattern "upper middle class conservatism." As far as I could tell, rich Zinacantecos and the ones that might be labeled the "lower middle class" were more likely to change than the poor ones and the ones of upper middle rank within the community. I interpreted the "upper middle class

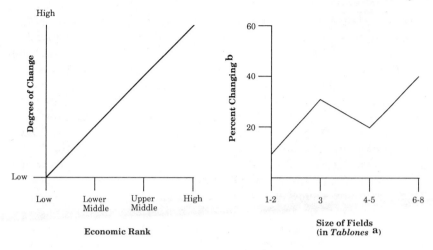

Fig. 6.1 (*above left*). Predicted relation of economic rank and new economic behavior.

Fig. 6.2 (*above right*). Actual relation of size of fields and new economic behavior in the hamlet of Nachig. Source: Cancian 1972: 152.
[a]A *tablon* is about 0.7 hectares of land. This much land usually produced about a ton of corn. About one-fourth of the farmers are in each size category.
[b]Percentage of people of this rank who were among the first to sell corn to the government.

conservatism" to be avoidance of the risks inherent in being among the first to change.

Does the difference between the pattern in Fig. 6.1 and the pattern in Fig. 6.2 mean that Zinacanteco behavior is special? I decided to look more closely at some of the studies behind Rogers's generalization to see if the communities were like Zinacantan in any way.

Using original data provided by many other field-workers, I looked for parallel patterns in comparable communities in other parts of the world—communities where most households depended on farming of the type that was dominant in their area. It turned out that the pattern of "upper middle class conservatism" appeared in rural communities in many places—including India, Kenya, Pakistan, and the Philippines. You might expect this pattern to be limited to peasants. But it also appeared among Japanese small farmers, and in a Missouri community and a county in Wisconsin (Cancian 1979). As far as I can tell, "upper middle class conservatism" is characteristic of Zinacantecos, and of people in general, when they work under the conditions I described. Zinacanteco behavior is not special.

There are conditions under which my theory about upper middle class conservatism will not apply. For example, agriculturalists in Pakistan are not usually concerned about their rank relative to agriculturalists in Wisconsin. They care most about their neighbors—just as Zinacantecos care most about other Zinacantecos and less about people in Pakistan, Wisconsin, or Missouri. My theory depends on a "community of reference"—a local social group within which the rank positions specified in the theory are important. Thus, although the theory holds in many different cultures in many different parts of the world, there are at least two conditions under which it would not work. In some cases a "community of reference" may exist, but it will be difficult to figure out who belongs to it and therefore difficult to tell who is in what rank (Cancian 1981). In other cases the people in a localized population may care more about their connections to people and institutions elsewhere. That is, geographical neighbors may have different "communities of reference." This second limit on the usefulness of the theory is probably getting more important in rural communities that house many labor migrants.

In sum, this look at the Zinacanteco response to economic change, and the comparison with agriculturalists in other places, leads me to two conclusions. First, the internal heterogeneity of peasant communities is an important key to understanding the economic behavior of the people who live in them—even when there are at the same time local customs that seem to promote socioeconomic homogeneity. Second, in economic behavior involving response to change, it is hard to distinguish peasants from other people.

Paso: Heterogeneity in an Open Community in Costa Rica

Open peasant communities differ from closed corporate communities in many ways. They usually depend on a cash crop like coffee, cocoa, or bananas, and are thus more connected to the market than closed corporate communities. When Wolf originally defined the type, he said it "comprises peasants who regularly sell a cash crop constituting probably between 50 and 75 percent of their total production" (1955: 461). In Latin America these communities tend to be in the humid lowlands rather than the highlands, and they are usually less ethnically distinct (Indian) than closed corporate communities, Wolf says:

The open community differs from the corporate peasant community in a number of ways. The corporate peasant community is composed primarily of one subculture, the peasantry. The open community comprises a number of subcultures of which the peasantry is only one, although the most important functional segment. The corporate community emphasizes resistance to influences from without which might threaten its integrity. The open community, on the other hand, emphasizes continuous interaction with the outside world and ties its fortunes to outside demands. The corporate community frowns on individual accumulation and display of wealth and strives to reduce the effects of such accumulation on the communal structure. It resists reshaping of relationships; it defends the traditional equilibrium. The open-ended community permits and expects individual accumulation and display of wealth during periods of rising outside demand and allows this new wealth much influence in the periodic reshaping of social ties. [Ibid.: 462]

In sum, the open community is more connected to and dependent on the larger system in a number of ways, and its internal socioeconomic relations are quite different from those in a closed corporate community.

Here we will look at a single open community, Paso, which was studied by Peggy Barlett from September 1972 to September 1973. Barlett interviewed each household head several times and reconstructed land use patterns in Paso for the twenty years before her fieldwork— so she is able to describe changes that took place during that period.

Paso is a community of seventy-five households that conforms closely to Wolf's "open peasant community" type (Wolf 1955). The houses in Paso are scattered in a dispersed settlement pattern to take advantage of small streams on the slopes of the mountain. There is a small center of the community, along the highway, that consists of a school, community center, two general stores, and a few houses. Almost all households are active agriculturalists and 91 percent of them are nuclear families.

The Paso area is mountainous and too steep for plowing, and thus the traditional method of corn and bean production was the predominant land use pattern twenty years ago. By this method, corn fields are cut and burned at the end of the dry season. When the rainy season begins, Pasanos plant corn using a machete and dibble stick. . . .

As the population of Paso has increased, most farmers can no longer rotate their grain fields with fallow and have adapted slash and burn methods to fields that are used every year. Predictably, soil fertility has declined, and traditional corn and beans now make up only 38 percent of the amount of land they once occupied. Along with the decline in traditional grains goes a sharp decline in the number of *manzanas* in fallow and in forest land (a *manzana* equals .69 hectares or 1.7 acres).

The most dramatic change in land use has been a shift to pasture—more than 50 percent of the land in Paso is now in pasture, an increase from 223 *manzanas* to 535 in the last twenty years. Pasture is used to raise cattle, which are sold mainly for export to the United States. This increase in pasture acreage has resulted from the rapidly rising price of beef in the United States and the removal of the quota on the United States' imports of foreign beef.

There has also been a dramatic increase in tobacco cultivation, from one *manzana* to forty-five, in the same twenty-year period. While the figures for tobacco are small, they represent an important ecological change because tobacco requires annual terracing of the soil. Using shovels, farmers pile the soil of the hillside into contour ridges. This exhausting work must be repeated every year and is the only agricultural work in Paso that is paid at a higher wage. After the tobacco is harvested from the terrace, corn and beans are planted together. Tobacco production is therefore a rotation of a cash crop with corn and beans, and the terraces produce three different harvests each year.

In addition to the major shifts of land into tobacco and pasture, there has also been an increase in coffee plantings. However, coffee is an auxiliary crop for most households. . . . Larger plantings have been facilitated by the new road, built ten years ago, which makes it easier to ship out the coffee harvest. [Barlett 1977: 286–87]

The cultural heritage of Paso also fits Wolf's type. Barlett says, "The cultural patterns I describe represent the adaptation of Spanish culture to the New World, separate from Aztec or Incan empires and African traditions. As such, this account provides an important contrast to the life of Guatemalan, Peruvian, or Brazilian peasants" (1982: 8).

Barlett found that differences in the amount of land owned by Paso residents were great and that these differences best explained the land use choices they made during her fieldwork. To assess the effects of internal heterogeneity on land use choices, Barlett divided the households in Paso into five categories: large, medium, and small landowners, heirs who had no land but could expect to inherit some, and landless households who had no prospects to inherit. Households in the last two categories depended exclusively on rented land. In Paso the 26 small landowners had up to 7 *manzanas*, the 17 medium landowners had up to 28 *manzanas*, and the 8 large landowners had between 49 and 167 *manzanas*. Differences between the landowners were substantial especially when compared with the differences in field size observed in Zinacantan (see Fig. 6.2; a *tablon* is about equal to a *manzana*). While differences in Zinacantan were limited to those possible within a fairly labor-intensive system for producing a single crop complex (corn and beans) on rented land, the changes in land distribution in Paso resulted in greater internal differentiation and led to the production of different crops by different farmers.

Barlett's findings include the following:

1. Land was scarce, and it was hard to find land for rent in Paso.

2. All Paso households had mixed land use strategies, and all grew some corn and beans.

3. Cattle raising (which produced low profits per unit of land but involved little labor) was concentrated among those with more land. All eight large landowners had cattle. They dedicated an average of 58.4 *manzanas* to cattle, while medium and small landowners averaged 8.3 and 0.4 *manzanas*, respectively, and the heirs and landless had no cattle.

4. Tobacco-raising families all included at least one male between the ages of 13 and 50.

5. Large landowners did not produce tobacco (which yielded great profits per unit of land but required intensive labor). The one exception was a family with three grown sons. This family had recently bought the land that made them large landowners and was using tobacco profits to pay for the land.

In sum, Barlett found that "land use choices in Paso depend primarily on access to land" (1977: 295). The large landowners substituted land for labor, and produced cattle for export. Families with able-bodied males and little land tended to choose the labor-intensive tobacco option, despite the drudgery of the work involved.[7]

Over the twenty-year period Barlett studied, residents responded to opportunities in cattle and tobacco production created by market forces emanating from distant lands, including the United States. In the process, both the dependence of Pasanos on the outside world and the socioeconomic differences between Pasanos have increased—just as they have in many communities that have adapted new technologies and become more connected to the market system.

Summary: Heterogeneity in Closed and Open Communities

In 1960 Zinacantan looked like a closed corporate community in many ways. Zinacanteco language and ethnic identity isolated the people from the national culture and identified them as culturally inferior in the eyes of their Ladino neighbors. The Mexican Revolution and the land reform that followed it had made Zinacantecos more self-sufficient than they had been a century before, and flourishing community ritual life emphasized separation from the Ladino world.

Nonetheless, Zinacantecos were not uniformly poor. In their ritual activities they displayed clear differences between individuals and families. This internal stratification was also reflected in their interaction with the economic world around them, especially in their responses to economic change.

Paso, an open peasant community, presents a more direct contrast with the characteristics homogeneity theorists have attributed to closed communities. Paso's residents are not isolated or self-sufficient. Though they grow some corn and beans for subsistence, they depend on com-

---

[7] When Barlett used Chayanov's ideas to predict who would grow tobacco, she did not find that families with the highest consumer/worker ratios chose the intensive tobacco work, because some of those families had enough land to choose cattle over tobacco. Paso, with its very unequal distribution of land, did not meet the conditions Chayanov set.

mercial production of tobacco, coffee, and beef. And though families in the community are independent production units, they cannot easily withdraw from dependence on national and international market trends.

Paso does not have the cultural distinctiveness characteristic of closed corporate communities. There are no important language or cultural barriers between Pasanos and the outside world, no local symbols of community membership. Pasanos are part of the national culture.

In Paso, poverty is a characteristic of individual families, and changes over the period studied by Barlett increased the differences between rich and poor. As Wolf said, "The open-ended community permits and expects individual accumulation and display of wealth during periods of rising outside demand and allows this new wealth much influence in the periodic reshaping of social ties" (1955: 462).

In sum, Zinacantan and Paso differed in the relation of their cultures to the national culture and in the degree of difference between the richest and poorest residents in the community. Despite these differences, focus on the socioeconomic inequality within each community is crucial to understanding how its people behaved. Neither case required the development of a special theory of peasant economic behavior. Thus heterogeneity theory proved useful under diverse circumstances.

Despite their substantial differences, Zinacantan and Paso are subject to similar pressures from the larger system. Next we will look at the political economy approach, which focuses on these pressures, and we will see that Zinacantan has also changed in the 1970's and 1980's.

The Political Economy Approach and Differentiation Theory

In the last few decades, connections to the larger economic system—like the sale of beef and coffee in world markets that brought changes to Paso—have affected the way many peasants live. Life inside peasant communities has also changed because more families now depend on income from members who migrate great distances to find wage work. Although they have always had some connections to the larger economy, peasants and peasant communities in recent decades have become less self-sufficient, less distinct from their environment, and more directly dependent on the larger system. They have lost much of their ability to withdraw from the larger system.

The way scholars study peasants has also changed in recent years. The political economy approach—which emphasizes historical processes and the relation of local events to events in the regional, national, and international systems—has become important in understanding the transformation of peasant societies. Because the political economy approach is much broader than anthropology, the discussion of it that follows is much more partial and incomplete than the characterizations of the homogeneity and heterogeneity approaches presented above. In keeping with the focus of this chapter, I will concentrate on what the study of political economy has to say about behavior inside peasant communities.

V. I. Lenin: The Differentiation of the Peasantry

The most important political economy interpretations of behavior in peasant communities involve differentiation theory. This theory asserts that connection to the larger system initiates a historical process through which peasants become either capitalists (that is, bourgeoisie, owners of the means of production who depend on the labor of others) or proletarians (that is, people who must sell their labor in order to survive). The classic statement of this idea that connections to the capitalist economy of the larger society will make peasants differentiate into two classes was made by Lenin in his *Development of Capitalism in Russia* (1899). After reviewing data from detailed studies of the Russian peasantry (some of the same studies Chayanov later used), Lenin concludes:

1. The social-economic situation in which the contemporary Russian peasantry find themselves is that of commodity economy. . . . the peasant is completely subordinated to the market, on which he is dependent as regards both his personal consumption and his farming, not to mention the payment of taxes.

2. The system of social-economic relations existing among the peasantry (agricultural and village-community) shows us the presence of all those contradictions which are inherent in every commodity economy and every order of capitalism: competition, the struggle for economic independence, the grabbing of land (purchasable and rentable), the concentration of production in the hands of a minority, the forcing of the majority into the ranks of the proletariat. . . .

3. The sum total of all the economic contradictions among the peasantry constitutes what we call the differentiation of the peasantry. The peasants themselves very aptly and strikingly characterize this process with the term 'depeasantising.' This process signifies the utter dissolution of the old, patriarchal peasantry and the creation of *new types* of rural inhabitants. . . .

Undoubtedly, the emergence of property inequality is the starting-point of the whole process, but the process is not at all confined to property 'differentiation.' The old peasantry is not only 'differentiating,' it is being completely dissolved, it is ceasing to exist, it is being ousted by absolutely new types of rural inhabitants—types that are the basis of a society in which commodity economy and capitalist production prevail. These types are the rural bourgeoisie (chiefly petty bourgeoisie) and the rural proletariat—a class of commodity producers in agriculture and a class of agricultural wage-workers. [1899: 175–77]

Lenin saw a process of transformation leading to the elimination of peasants; that is, the elimination of rural residents who produce much of their own subsistence and have some ability to withdraw from the larger system. In his vision, peasants differentiate into two classes with different relations to the land and the use of labor power. The commodity producers (rural bourgeoisie) control the land and produce things to sell in the market by buying the labor power of the rural proletariat. The rural proletariat has no control over land and must sell its labor to survive. Both labor power and agricultural products become commodities that must enter the market to produce livelihood for those who sell them.

It is worth wondering why ideas put forth in 1899 took so long to become central to studies in the United States. I see two main reasons. First, the great increase in economic interdependency after World War II made Lenin's ideas more relevant than they had been. Processes of agricultural change, like those described for Zinacantan, were widespread. Capitalist expansion in consumer goods and technology (for example, fertilizer), faster transportation and communications, and government expansion (like farm support prices and production programs) all increased connectedness. The second, and probably more important, reason for the delay is political. The Marxist framework used by Lenin and by most political economists is seen as politically loaded in the United States. In recent years some political economists have appropriately responded by pointing out the political loadings of other approaches to peasant studies. But earlier, in the 1950's, for example, the country was closed to broad discussion of such questions.[8]

In the last two decades many studies that elaborate and modify Lenin's framework and ideas have been done. Two ideas that characterize the political economy approach in general as well as Marxist analysis have been widely used in this period. They are the idea that the political economy beyond the village accounts for much local behavior, and the idea that peasants must be studied in terms of specific historical

[8] Because of this, Eric Wolf's use of the fundamental methodological tenets of the political economy approach (see the section above on "When and Why Do Closed Corporate Communities Appear?") in the 1950's was selectively accepted. His closed-corporate-community idea became the center of much of the homogeneity thinking used by anthropologists studying peasants, and thus he is described as a homogeneity theorist in this paper. In fact, he anticipated much of the political economy approach reviewed in this section. His recent comment on his early papers in the light of subsequent work by others makes his intent clear (Wolf 1986).

processes. As Carmen Diana Deere notes in a review of recent political economy studies in Latin America, there has been a "shift in the temporal and spatial focus of the field from the community studies of the 1960's, to the historical analyses of regional processes of capitalist development in the literature of the 1970's and 1980's" (1987: 2). In this volume, Chapter 14 introduces the basic ideas, and Roseberry's chapter on "Peasants and the World" (Chapter 5) discusses the methodological implications of these ideas.

How Does Lenin's Model Apply?

The core of differentiation theory is Lenin's idea that peasants will be replaced by other classes—that clear class opposition will develop as capitalism spreads into the countryside. This has not occurred: Peasants have not regularly and rapidly differentiated into capitalist and proletarian classes when they came into contact with capitalism. Deere says: "We have learned that the penetration of capital does not automatically lead to the spread of capitalist class relations" (ibid.). She also suggests that simple differentiation theory—the idea that there will be clear, sharp class opposition—represents an incorrect reading of Lenin. The insights that come from Lenin's vision require a more complex understanding of the interaction of capitalist forces and peasant communities. There are many different answers to the questions Lenin raised.

In some places rural economic life is characterized by clear class relations. That is, most people work for wages, and a few people control the means of production (the land, knowledge, and equipment, and the connections needed to market the product). For example, sugar production, where large-scale processing in a centralized mill provides a great advantage, is usually organized this way. This kind of situation lends the strongest support to simple differentiation theory. In many other activities, like those in Paso, household-centered peasant production continues. Peasant production sometimes seems to be more efficient than capitalist production, and peasants continue as "independent" producers. They are rarely really self-sufficient, for although they do not work for wages, what they plant and how they sell it are often controlled or greatly influenced by the private firms and government agencies on which they depend for the seed, fertilizer, and credit needed for production. In other situations it seems that peasants survive as peasants by self-exploitation; that is, by having many family members work in a way that yields low return per hour of work but permits the family to survive on its own land. Because all these different forms have appeared as peasants have adapted to increased con-

TABLE 6.2
Corn Production by Nachig Men, 1967 and 1983

1967			1983		
Field size*	Number of men	Percentage of men	Field size	Number of men	Percentage of men
none	9	4	none	130	40
1–3	107	52	1–3	123	38
4–6	61	29	4–6	61	19
7–10	31	15	7–10	7	2
TOTAL	208	100		321	99

SOURCE: Cancian 1987: 132.
  *Field size is in *tablones* (see Fig. 6.2). Since land quality varies greatly, field size is also measured by the volume of seed corn used (Cancian 1972: 183–88). About 15 liters of seed corn is used for a tablon.

tact with the larger economy, the issues Lenin raised cannot be settled quickly and clearly.[9]

Though the process has taken many different forms and has had many different results, I believe there has been an overall trend towards proletarianization. The general direction is clear: Populations that were farmers or peasants two or three decades ago have become heavily dependent on wage work in labor markets tied to the world economy. Those who have remained agriculturalists have become more and more dependent on buying manufactured inputs (like chemical fertilizers) and on selling their products in the fluctuating world market (Pearse 1978).

Zinacantan provides a good example of many of these trends. Although the Zinacantan of the 1960's displayed many features of a closed corporate community, the process of change between the 1960's and the 1980's has many features commonly found in the transformation of peasant communities. Great change in the production of corn is shown in figures from the hamlet of Nachig (Table 6.2). In 1967 virtually every Nachig man had cornfields on which his family could depend for its basic food; but by 1983 only about 60 percent had such fields, and the number growing a lot of corn for sale (that is, more than about 3 *tablones* in all) was down from 44 percent to 21 percent.

  [9] The political economy approach is complex and recent. It includes different schools of thought and many current debates. Thus I am not able to summarize and codify it here in a way parallel to the smaller, simpler, and older homogeneity and heterogeneity approaches. You can begin exploring the political economy literature on peasants through the *Journal of Peasant Studies*, various issues of *Latin American Perspectives* (especially numbers 18 and 19 in 1978 and number 27 in 1980), reviews and review articles by Harris (1978), Heynig (1982), Smith (1982), and Deere (1987), a collection by Harriss (1982) and, for Mexico, through Hewitt de Alcantara's book (1984). These sources (and Roseberry's chapter in this volume) cite many excellent case studies.

Zinacantecos abandoned their predominant commitment to corn farming for complex but commonplace reasons. In the 1960s roads were built in the area where Zinacantecos rented land (see Cancian 1972). The roads, in combination with a milk processing plant built by the Nestle company near the place where the new roads met the Panamerican Highway, made it attractive for landowners to shift to milk production, and many Zinacantecos were displaced from rented land they had been farming. Others were displaced by increasing beef cattle production (see Wasserstrom 1983), and still others had to leave when the dam built at Angostura caused the flooding of huge areas in the Grijalva valley. That dam and two other government hydroelectric projects in Chiapas increased the demand for construction labor in the 1970s; and private construction during the period of economic boom likewise offered opportunities to increase earnings outside of corn farming. At the same time government programs in the highlands encouraged production of fruit and vegetable crops and opened the way for Indian entrepreneurs in the expanding truck transportation system.

In sum, wages for construction labor increased, making such work a more attractive alternative to farming; and land became more difficult to find. At the same time, those who continued in farming faced a decline in the real price of corn and an increase in the wages they had to pay in order to recruit workers whose alternative employment was in construction. Thus, Zinacantecos were pushed and pulled out of corn farming. [Cancian 1987: 133]

Because of these changes and the additional demand for labor that followed the discovery of great petroleum reserves in Chiapas and nearby Tabasco in the late 1970's, the men of Nachig had a variety of occupations in 1983. Some old sidelines (like wage labor and trading) expanded, in some cases into full-time occupations; and new work appeared (including some full-time jobs as formal government employees with civil service security of employment).

The 130 men who devote themselves exclusively to non-farming occupations, and those who combine non-farming with farming activities, may be divided into three major groups: merchants, proletarians and truck owners. For the most part the merchants buy and sell the major products of Zinacanteco agriculture—corn, beans, fruit, and flowers—usually retailing them in the major urban markets of the state. They are full-time practitioners of a role that has long been part of the peasant repertoire in Zinacantan.

The proletarians, those who sell their labor, reflect the diversity of the changing regional economy and the roles of Indians in it. The unskilled laborers work mostly on construction outside of Zinacantan. They represent continuity with earlier labor roles, and, as before, they are predominantly young men. The government employees, truck drivers and artisans (mostly masons) are in new occupations. Most of the government employees work in new reforestation programs; many of the artisans learned their trades during the construction boom in the 1970s; and the truck drivers are part of the expanded Indian role in local transportation that resulted from new roads and subsidized gasoline prices. All of these new occupations are tied to state and/or capitalist development programs that blossomed in the last ten or 15 years.

The truck owners are the emerging economic elite in the local population.

They are different from the farmers, merchants and proletarians who are their neighbors, especially because they have complex connections inside and outside the municipality. On the one hand they depend on the patronage of fellow Zinacantecos, and on the other they are tied to the bankers, transportation bureaucrats and auto service facilities located outside of Zinacantan.

In sum, there has been a major shift away from the relatively autonomous peasant adaptation of Zinacanteco men that was dominant two decades ago. While agriculturalists still predominate in numbers, they are no longer clearly dominant in the economic life of the municipality. The non-agriculturalists, including both the proletarians and the transportation elite, are heavily dependent on trends in the regional and national economies. As a result, both internal relations and the role of external forces in internal relations have changed greatly in the last two decades. [Cancian 1987: 134]

It is hard to generalize about the details of parallel changes that took place in many parts of the world. Every community and every regional and national economy is different in some ways. Even local differences can be great. For example, as mentioned above, Zinacantan's neighbor, Chamula, has much less land per capita and is more distant from the lowland fields where Zinacantecos do most of their farming. For decades, great numbers of Chamula men have migrated to work on the coffee plantations on the Pacific coast of Chiapas. At home, Chamula men and women have concentrated on craft production much more than Zinacantecos. They have supplied Zinacantecos and others with cooking pots, wood products, including furniture and guitars, wool and woolen blankets, and rum.

Despite the great diversity within Chiapas and across the world, some generalizations are possible and worth making. We can generalize about three levels of analysis from which the peasants' situations can be seen: the labor process, the household, and the community. Much of what has been learned about the first two is relevant to the peasants' relation to the capitalist system. Less is known about the third level.

Study of the labor process lends support to Lenin's ideas. In their comparison of agriculture in California, Chile, Egypt, and India, deJanvry and Vandeman (1987) find some common features underlying the different labor practices and historical details that go with the diverse situations. In each place, over the period studied (all between 1960 and the early 1980's) more and more agricultural production was done with proletarian labor; that is, more of the total agricultural output was produced by people working for wages, and less by family farmers and peasants. Thus, looked at from the point of view of the labor process, the separation into capitalist and proletarian classes clearly increased.

On the other hand, workers who are proletarians in the labor process are often "semiproletarians" from the point of view of the household.

That is, they combine wage work in capitalist agriculture with peasant production on their own limited land (and other activities by various family members) to survive. For example, in the case of California agriculture, many of the proletarians involved come from and return to Mexican peasant households, where they work some land that is crucial to the family's survival. Thus the migrant who is a proletarian in California agriculture is a semiproletarian from the household point of view.

This household-level viewpoint clarifies the processes that led to modifications of simple differentiation theory. One of the most important involves the observation that "a class of full-time proletarians and a proletarian consciousness emerge only slowly from the rural labor households" (deJanvry and Vandeman 1987: 28). The path to sharp class divisions is muted by the complex economic adaptation of the peasant household.

Another modification of simple differentiation theory involves advantages that semiproletarian households give to capitalist development:

First, these households constitute a flexible labor reserve that is 'on call' to meet the requirements for seasonal labor in the capitalist sector. . . . Second, the semiproletarian status of the majority of wage workers cheapens the cost of labor power to capital because a portion of their subsistence is generated out of peasant production. Therefore, they are able to work for lower wages than can full proletarians. [deJanvry and Vandeman 1987: 67]

This interpretation of the role of semiproletarian labor in capitalist production means that coexistence of peasant and capitalist production is more advantageous to capitalists than is the elimination of the peasant way of life. Thus eliminating the peasantry does not follow as clearly as it does from simple differentiation theory.

Less is known about how community social and economic life is affected by the processes described above. Scholars working with the political economy approach have focused on the larger political economy (regional, national, and international systems) and on the household, and have done little at the community level of analysis; similarly, most scholars working in the older homogeneity and heterogeneity approaches, which are aimed at understanding the community and its internal relations, have not done the historical analysis needed to understand the recent transformations of peasant society. Attention to the community as an independent social form existing between the larger system and the household under contemporary conditions has increased in recent years (see Long and Roberts 1978 and the case studies cited in Wolf 1986), but generalizations are still hard to make.

In sum, Lenin envisioned an historical process leading to differentiation into capitalist and proletarian classes. That has not happened in many places: The process has been slow, at best, and there seem to be strong forces resisting simple differentiation of peasant communities. On the other hand, there have been great changes in the peasant situation, and they have been in the direction Lenin suggested. These changes have made the people in peasant communities more dependent on the capitalist world system. They can no longer easily withdraw into self-sufficient production of their own food; they must sell their labor. Thus it is reasonable to argue that many peasants have been eliminated, and it is reasonable to argue that many fundamental peasant adaptations have persisted. In this situation it is important to hold on to the insights that stem from differentiation theory, even if they are complex. Lenin's broad vision and the modifications developed recently by those who take the political economy approach are crucial additions to the picture provided by the homogeneity and heterogeneity approaches.

The New Meanings of "Peasant"

Before we look at the future, I want to generalize about the kinds of economic activities and economic relations (relations of production) now found in the countryside. Peasants have long been partly market dependent and partly subsistence producers, partially autonomous and partially controlled from outside. But today many of them produce little of their own food—especially in places where other activities offer a better living than working the little land they might have. Subsistence production is no longer the main activity of most of the people who are called peasants. So, we have a problem of definition: The term "peasant" is being used to identify the diverse people who began as peasants and underwent the transformation discussed above. New, rigid categories would make things worse in this dynamic situation, so I will discuss the overall trends and propose a tentative.set of labels for activities that, when properly mixed, constitute the economic activities of actual people.

The income-producing activities of peasants may be lumped into two categories on the basis of the economic relations involved. One is wage work. Broadly conceived, "wage work" covers all situations in which peasants sell their labor—from unskilled construction labor near home to long-distance migration to do agricultural work at piece rates. I will call the other category "petty commodity production." This covers production (and trading) that involves low capital investment and little, if any, hired labor. This category includes artisans producing items for local and regional markets like the Chamulas described above (see also Smith 1984, discussed below in Chapter 14), and even agricultural producers like those in Paso who produce coffee and tobacco for sale in national and international markets. Because they have little capital and hire little labor, I also include petty traders in this category of producers. Zinacantecos who buy flowers from various neighbors (who are also petty commodity producers) and take them to city markets to sell at retail are a good example of traders who fit this category. In the following list I have tried to sum up these ideas about the major kinds of economic activities and economic relations of peasants and other people who live in the countryside:

The elite: A capitalist class in Lenin's sense. People who depend on capital and connections with national and international capitalist classes. They hire labor and sell goods and services.

The proletariat: A proletarian class in Lenin's sense. People who have little choice except to sell their labor for wages.

The peasants: People who have some ability to produce their own food, or have a close kinship connection to people who have some ability to produce their own food, or interact in a local economy with people who have some ability to produce their own food. This category includes various loosely defined subtypes: *peasants* (people who currently produce a substantial part of their own food); *petty commodity producers* (people who currently produce things for sale or live by trading in local markets—with low capital investment and little if any hired labor); and *semiproletarians* (people who currently work for wages but who also depend on food production or petty commodity production by themselves or their kinsmen for survival).

Actual peasant households use different mixed strategies for survival, and the activities of any household may change with its growth and with shifts in the local and regional economy. For example, one family member (usually a young man) might work at a mine or construction project far from home, while other family members produce subsistence grains and agricultural commodities on their land. Some or all of those at home may run a small store, trade in local markets, engage in craft production, or do local wage labor from time to time. If working conditions are difficult, transport is cheap, and the family has quite a bit of land, the young man might come home during the peak seasons to help with agricultural work. Or he may stay away, sending home money, and perhaps saving for a wedding or the purchase of land as well. Eventually, he may return to the countryside to live for most of the year, establish a family away from the village, return to the village injured or exhausted by the work, or fall into a regular pattern of migrant labor. Meanwhile, the other members of his household will be changing their activities to match the opportunities available. Given the variation in the composition and the resources of peasant households, they will produce an endless variety of mixed strategies from the limited kinds of activities and relations described in the list above. In sum, "peasant" has many new meanings.

The Future of Peasant Communities

What will become of peasants and peasant communities? Will the transformation described above go on until they are completely eliminated? Or will they somehow remain as an important socioeconomic form for many decades to come?

Each alternative has its supporters. One approach sees long-run trends toward integration of all people into a single worldwide system —a system in which all peasant communities will be open and will eventually lose their distinctiveness. The other sees a cyclical pattern of opening and closing of peasant communities over past centuries of their interaction with the larger system, and expects the pattern to continue.

Both modernization theorists and Marxist theorists support the first position.[10] They expect historical change to continue in the direction it has recently taken. They agree that peasant communities will become more connected to the larger system in the future. Modernization theorists emphasize the spread of technology and the transformation of peasants into small farmers integrated into modern production systems; Marxist theorists emphasize the spread of capitalist economic relations, the proletarianization of individuals, and the differentiation of rural communities into powerful landed people and landless wage workers. In each case the partial autonomy that is characteristic of peasant communities is destroyed.

These interpretations of recent history have much to support them. Communications and transportation are ever faster and ever more wide reaching. As world population goes up, fewer people can support themselves on the land, and even those that can are less independent than they were. To compete in the world market for the products they produce, they must often purchase farm imputs like fertilizers and

[10] Modernization theorists are connected to homogeneity theory. They see economic development as a process that transforms Third World people into modern people. In the case of peasants, technological innovation in agriculture is crucial to the process. When peasants resist such change, modernization theorists often invoke ideas like those in homogeneity theory to explain the peasants' behavior. Marxist theorists are connected to the political economy approach.

pesticides. As noted above in the section on political economy, those without land often migrate to sell their labor in urban and international markets; once peasants, they are now proletarians. And millions more are semiproletarians who combine peasant farming and wage work to make a living. Thus, as both theories foresaw, people in rural communities are losing much of their ability to withdraw from the larger system.

It is hard to imagine that these trends will be reversed. Whether seen in terms of technological links or economic relations, peasant livelihood has become firmly entwined with the larger system. In Zinacantan, for example, the increase shows up in many details of everyday life—right down to the availability of firewood for cooking fuel. As in many parts of the world, increased population and crowding have ended simple access to this basic household necessity. In 1960 most Zinacanteco women collected their household supply of firewood from hillsides of communal or private land and carried it home. Collecting firewood was an important part of a woman's productive activity. By the mid-1980's many families in the crowded hamlets near the major road had to buy rights to cut wood on private lands in remote parts of the municipality. Men did the work at these distant sites, often with the help of power saws, and trucks were used to haul the wood to the buyer's house. One landless man I know tried to avoid these new expenses by buying a stove that uses bottled gas, but he found he was too poor to afford it. Over the last 30 years many Zinacantecos have become much more dependent on purchased firewood and tools, and an important economic contribution of Zinacanteco women has been greatly reduced. This change and many others involving peasant life in many parts of the world seem irreversible. In the case of firewood, the local environment is unlikely to produce new resources. In other cases, it seems unlikely that peasants will end their new dependency on purchased inputs and consumer goods.

Although these trends look unidirectional, they may not be. Some observers see cyclical processes that lead to closing of peasant communities after they have been through a long period of opening like that described above. For example, Wolf has argued that Indian communities in Mexico opened and closed in response to conditions in the world outside them:

When [Mexican] society is politically secure and opens its windows on the world in economic expansion and widening trade, the Indian communities retreat and often disintegrate in retreating. Such a process occurred during the economic prosperity of the 18th century and during the economic expansion under Porfirio Díaz in the second half of the 19th century; it is happening again at present.

When, however, the larger society disintegrates into an arena of gladitorial combat and people abandon their exposed positions in industry and commerce to seek security in the rural area, then the Indian communities again wax strong. This was what happened in the 17th century. . . . This was again the case during the first half of the 19th century, in the aftermath of the Mexican War for Independence; and yet again in the initial decades of the 20th century, during the great revolution which began in 1910 and the disorders which followed in its wake. [1960: 3–4]

During and after Cárdenas's presidency (1934–40), Mexico stabilized, and peasants became less concerned with local social relations and more concerned with economic opportunities in the larger system. When this happened, Wolf argues, conflict increased inside peasant communities. Wolf's observation and interpretation of the history of peasant communities in Mexico suggest an important conditional generalization: Interpersonal relations in peasant communities are better when the larger system is lacking in economic opportunity for peasants, and worse when things are better on the outside. These changes are independent of the unidirectional change envisioned in modernization and Marxist theory.

G. William Skinner found parallel patterns of opening and closing in Chinese peasant communities. He says:

In short, in the course of the dynastic cycle in China, the rural communities to which peasants belonged went through a characteristic cycle from an open structure during the dynastic heyday to closure during the period of interdynastic chaos. At the upper turning point of the cycle, communities were so open in all senses of the term . . . as to constitute an extreme in cross-societal perspective. The cycle's lower turning point brought examples of complete closure that approach the opposite extreme. I have argued that the progressive closure of villages and intervillage local systems in traditional China represented the cumulation of rational responses to an increasingly unstable and threatening external environment, and conversely that their progressive opening up represented the cumulation of rational responses to an increasingly stable and benign external environment. [1971: 280]

In sum, both the closed corporate community in Mexico and the open peasant community in China became more and less open and closed in response to the same kind of events in the world around them. And when the communities became more closed, interpersonal relations in the community were more carefully controlled and less openly conflictful.

During the Mexican prosperity and oil boom of the 1970's, Zinacantan changed in keeping with this pattern. Corn farming became less attractive as well-paid wage jobs in construction were opened to Indians. Many Zinacantecos came to depend on wage work outside the community. And at about the same time, political conflict in Zinacantan increased. Even the fiesta system, and for a time the cargo system, became politicized. Cargo holders would not serve with members of the opposing party. Each party hired its own band for fiestas. And people going before the municipal court insisted on judges from their own party—or took disputes to non-Zinacanteco authorities in San Cristóbal.

Then the outside world changed again. The Mexican economic crisis began in 1982. Government expenditures were immediately cut back, and many Zinacantecos lost the well-paid wage jobs that had become their main source of support. Soon the International Monetary Fund forced the Mexican government to raise gasoline prices that had been subsidized for many years—so corn farming in distant places, the profitable innovation of the 1960's, became a money-losing proposition for many Zinacantecos.

Zinacantecos responded to the new changes in many ways. Some used mixed strategies: They planted land near their homes that could be worked at low cost with traditional technology (plus purchased fertilizer), and they migrated greater distances in search of wage work. Others withdrew into locally based farming, despite the limited income it produced. The outside world was still safe, but it was no longer welcoming to Zinacantecos in search of work. It is not clear yet (in 1987) if these economic changes in the larger system will lead to changes in interpersonal relations within Zinacantan. There are signs of revitalization of the community—that is, signs that the inward-looking community will become stronger again. It is too soon to tell if these changes will quiet the troubles that began in the 1970's.

The cyclical interpretations just discussed are important for two reasons. First, they give peasants and peasant communities an active role in their relations with the larger system. Both modernization theory and Marxist theory usually have a "centralist bias" (Long and Roberts 1978: 304) that exaggerates the degree to which technological inputs and capitalist economic relations determine what goes on in the countryside. The closing of a peasant community (that is, defensive withdrawal from economic relations with the outside) is a peasant action, not a central initiative played out in the peasant community. Because peasants are subordinated people, their actions cannot be directly compared with those of the dominant sectors or classes in the national and international system. Withdrawal from a relation with the outside world may be the strongest weapon peasants have.

Second, as I suggested at the beginning of this chapter, expressions of ethnic or racial solidarity by subordinated urban people resemble in some ways the insularity shown by closed corporate communities. This makes me think that peasants, even if they lose some of their distinctive ability to withdraw that is based on subsistence food production, will not become completely open to urban influence and completely dependent on urban initiatives—especially if times are bad in the larger system.

In recent years, events have favored interpretations that stress the transformation of peasant society, and I find it hard to believe that a dramatic reversal of these trends will take place in the near future. But the transformation is not complete. There are many reasons to think that active peasants and their descendants will put their own stamp on the future.

7

Markets and Marketplaces

Stuart Plattner

Markets are essential to the integration of commercial societies.[1] Just as the great stock exchanges of New York and Chicago exemplify the industrial-capitalist structure of North American society, periodic marketplaces are the commercial life of agrarian or peasant societies. The markets usually meet once every few days; crowds come from the countryside to sell their farm products and buy manufactured goods and foodstuffs from other areas. Government officials often visit on market days, and local places of worship hold services so that farm families can combine economic, political, and religious activities at one time and place. Peasant markets are also lively arenas of social interaction. They have much of the excitement of a fair, with friendships made, love affairs begun, and marriages arranged. In many societies, the end of market day is often marked by drinking, dancing, and fighting.

I will give some basic elements of market theory in this chapter and will discuss the conditions necessary in an area for markets to develop through itinerant peddling or mobile retailing. Then I will describe regional systems of markets in two representative peasant societies, China and Guatemala. In the next chapter I will discuss individual behavior in market settings, focusing on the importance of information and risk. That chapter will show why people maintain long-term

---

I thank Peggy Barlett for her many helpful comments on a draft of this paper.

[1] I will use the term "market" to mean the social institution of exchanges where prices or exchange equivalencies exist. "Marketplace" refers to these interactions in a customary place and time. "Marketing" denotes buying and selling in a market. A market can exist without being localized in a marketplace, but it is hard to imagine a marketplace without some sort of institutions governing exchanges. Note that this is an inclusive definition of marketing, covering institutions that others would omit from the term. The most conventional alternative definition reserves "market" to mean a capitalist market where labor is traded as a commodity.

personalized economic relationships.[2] To introduce the issues, I will compare a Mexican urban marketplace and a U.S. shopping mall.

A Mexican Urban Marketplace and a U.S. Shopping Mall

The marketplace in the small Mexican city of San Cristóbal is typical of urban marketplaces in developing countries. The market exists in a brick and concrete structure built and administered by the local government. Inside the structure some 500 small concrete stalls are rented on a long-term basis by food, dry goods, and hardware sellers. Most of these sellers are Spanish-speaking, non-Indians (called Ladinos or Mestizos locally). Outside the market, almost a thousand vendors, many of them Mayan Indians, rent stalls or spaces on the ground, where they spread their wares.

The scale of business varies from the cloth seller in an enclosed store with a few thousand dollars in durable goods to the Indian farmer sitting on the ground with less than $10 of mixed vegetables spread on a cloth. The crowded excitement of the thousands of people who throng the market daily, the strong bright colors, powerful smells, sights, and sounds form a vibrant experience for everyone concerned. Many exotically clothed Mayan Indians have traveled hours for this shopping trip in the "big city." After selling their few goods (usually no more than can be carried by one or two adults), they shop in the market and the surrounding streets for everything from stationery to hardware to cigarettes and illegal rum.

The government has offices open nearby to serve the people who come into town from the surrounding region. Most of the Indians arrive early, having traveled by dark to sell their wares, do their shopping and legal business, and leave town by nightfall. People still remember when an Indian on the streets of San Cristóbal at night was fair game for gangs of Ladino toughs, who would beat the Indians under the careless eyes of the local police.

The colorful clothes and exotic Mayan languages may lead the observer to think that the market was traditional and unchanging. It is in many ways, yet the structure was built within the past fifteen years. At that time the city decided to lessen downtown congestion by moving the market from the center of town to the outskirts, which also facilitated market access to the growing number of motor vehicles. The Mayans in their colorful ribbons and embroideries own trucks

---

[2] The two sections are analogous to the division in economics between macroeconomics and microeconomics.

and buses, and aggressively seek new, often distant wholesale markets for their local products such as flowers. The surrounding streets have large, self-service supermarkets, variety stores, and hardware stores in addition to tiny shops formed out of the street-level room of a private house. There are rumors that the city wants to move the marketplace again, because of the congestion of the heavy diesel trucks that choke the roads near the market.

This sort of market is called a public marketplace, meaning that it is composed of small, owner-operated firms and owned and operated by a municipality. Public markets were the dominant urban form of market in developed societies as well until the early twentieth century. The food function of such markets was then replaced by chain stores, and later by supermarkets; the durable goods function was replaced by central shopping districts, and later by malls.

The shopping mall is the public marketplace of the wealthy industrialized societies. The typical mall is privately owned and operated, although often with significant government aid in the form of tax abatements. Malls are expensive to build and operate, and typically several gigantic chain department stores act as "anchors" for the mall. These department stores are connected by climate-controlled passageways lined with smaller stores offering everything from ice cream to specialty clothing to movie theaters. There are usually less than 100 stores in total, but one store can have hundreds of workers. Malls have the social excitement and public safety of marketplaces and are used for recreation as well as shopping. Teenagers use malls to meet and socialize with each other, and old people use them as safe places to be with other people or to exercise out of the weather.

The gigantic multi-item supermarket, where most families buy the bulk of their foods, is rarely placed as an anchor in this type of mall. Food shopping trips tend to be specialized because of the need to refrigerate food quickly for fear of spoilage.

Compare the experience of a city person shopping for food in a developing and in a developed country. The shopper in San Cristóbal is confronted by a seasonally changing variety of local and regional produce, fresh-killed meats, and live poultry. Most produce has been naturally ripened and is often of outstanding high quality, but spoils very quickly and is not available out of season. Refrigeration and packaging is barely existent (although plastic bags are everywhere), so the shopper must carry a basket and is usually accompanied by young children to help. Once at the market, the food shopper must choose whether to shop the many tiny vendors outside the market or the fewer, somewhat larger stalls inside. Shopping is laborious since products vary, prices are not usually displayed, and some bargaining is expected. Families shop the market frequently, sometimes daily. Most shoppers have personalized economic relationships with some vendors, who reserve special items for them and minimize the bargaining required to get a fair market price. The vendor is often the producer of the item as well.

The urban food shopper in a developed country like the United States usually drives to one, privately owned, often enormous store. The store provides shopping carts, bags, and packaging and loading services, as well as other services like cashing checks and paying bills. Most families try to shop infrequently, perhaps once a week. Supermarkets offer an incredible assortment of packaged, processed, chilled, frozen, and fresh foods drawn from every part of the nation and the world. Seasonal produce like tomatoes, grapes, and even peaches are available year-round. The food is standardized as much as possible, all prices are posted, and bargaining would be socially unacceptable and downright deviant. Personal relationships are usually anonymous because the "vendors" are employees of a large corporation. The typical supermarket is part of a vertically integrated firm that may own farms, trucks, warehouses, and food brokerage firms as well as retail stores. The range of diversity of foods offered is extraordinary (although lovers of fresh produce may complain that the out-of-season produce tastes like the plastic it is packaged in).

The marketplace in the developing area is run on some principles identical to those operating in the mall and supermarket, and some that are very different. The similarities concern the fact that in both places it is good to "buy cheap and sell dear" and involve physical constraints like the fact that fresh produce loses economic value very fast while dry goods are relatively stable in value in both situations. Most studies affirm that individuals and firms in both situations prefer more to less income and lower to higher costs.

Differences between the developing marketplace and the developed malls/supermarkets have to do with the poverty of the developing world, which implies cheap labor, expensive capital, and high risks, and the wealth of the developed world, which implies expensive labor, cheap capital, and insurance against risk. One obvious difference is that marketplace vendors in developing countries substitute labor for capital whenever possible, which explains why there are so many of them and why they provide personalized services that tie consumers to them and reduce risks. Developed market vendors offer lots of capital-intensive aids (expensive supermarket carts, for example) to cut down on their unionized, highly salaried, impersonal employees.

This brief sketch should convince the student of the need for an economic anthropology of markets and marketing. The following sections discuss the functions markets serve for individuals; then the institutional and societal conditions facilitating markets are analyzed. Before the discussion on markets, however, we must briefly introduce the subject of money.

Money

Shopping malls and peasant marketplaces are both commercialized, meaning that people use money to effect economic exchanges. Money is so fundamental to modern commercial life that it is hard to conceive of any societies without it. It seems like air to people or water for fish—so pervasive, ever present, and fundamental that it is hard to distinguish its separate functions. Anthropology's comparative perspective is especially useful in this sort of circumstance. By showing alternatives to familiar patterns of life, it illuminates every-day reality better. One of the major contributions of early economic anthropology was to describe the wide range of things used to accomplish money functions. The list is enormous, including salt, shells, stones, beads, feathers, fur, bones, and teeth, as well as agricultural crops, animals, and, of course, metals, from iron to gold and silver. This section will introduce money as a subject of study.[3] As is common with things that are critically important to societies, most analysts would disagree on a precise definition of money. However, most would agree that, whatever else it is, money is something used to make payments for other things as well as to measure their value.

Case Study: Tiv Spheres of Exchange

A case study of the uses of a primitive money will help the modern reader understand how these things function in a very different setting. The Tiv of Nigeria, as described by Bohannan in 1955, are a well-known example. Their precolonial subsistence economy had been structured into three "spheres of exchange": (1) a subsistence domain involving the trade of foodstuffs, household utensils, and raw materials for each other; (2) a prestige domain of slaves, cattle, a special type of cloth, and brass rods; and (3) a "supreme" domain involving rights in people other than slaves, mainly wives. Things were properly exchanged within categories, but not normally across them. Wives were exchanged between kinship groups, but the exchange was conceptualized as kinship reciprocity—the Tiv found the idea of buying and

---

[3] The best introduction to the subject is Walter C. Neale's brief, readable "Monies in Societies" (1976); the classic reference is Einzig (1948); and Dalton (1965) gives an influential, but biased perspective.

selling wives undignified. The Tiv had marketplaces for subsistence exchange and were enthusiastic traders. But trade and markets were not necessary for people to eat—a shortfall in one household's subsistence was made up for by gifts from relatives. Normally items in one sphere were not supposed to be traded in another, and the spheres of exchange were ranked morally. As Bohannan summarized it,

The moral basis of the hierarchy is evident in the fact that the ethics of kinship are more compelling than the ethics of mere prestige (and always take precedence—ideally one must always sacrifice prestige or hope of gain to aid a kinsman); the ethics of prestige are more compelling than the mores of markets and exchange of subsistence wealth—a man forgoes gain in subsistence wealth for the sake of prestige or to fulfil kinship obligations. [1955: 65]

The Tiv strategy for personal aggrandizement involved "trading up," however. This meant capitalizing on another's misfortune by trading subsistence goods for prestige goods and by trading one's cows and brass rods for a wife. The individual who was successful in this was said to have a "strong heart," while the unfortunate who needed food badly (for an important ritual feast, for example) and who had no dependents or kinsmen to help out, and so had to trade a prestige item for the food, was disparaged for weakness. The best exchange was to obtain a wife for bride wealth, subverting the normal procedure of exchanging a woman from one's "marriage-ward sharing group" for a wife. The bride obtained by wealth was not the concern of the wider group, and her property and children were controlled by the husband and his sons rather than by the wider group. This relative independence from normal social responsibilities was what the "strong heart" referred to.

The British colonial administration outlawed slaves and exchange marriages and introduced taxation payable in pounds, shillings, and pence as well as introducing attractive consumer goods. The Tiv were excellent long-distance traders, and the colonial peace allowed regional trade to flourish. Soon Tiv men were making good money on long-distance trade while other groups, such as Hausa and Ibo, entered Tiv subsistence markets to buy for export. The Tiv elders complained about the truckloads of food being driven out of their markets while food seemed more scarce to them. They would sometimes forbid their wives to sell any food in the market but were powerless when they were disobeyed since their own morality supported the exchange of food for valuables. They cursed the foreign money because it confounded their traditional system of values. Food-for-money was classified as a subsistence exchange, but money-for-cows, or cloth, or bride wealth was another issue. Because the administration policy favored bride wealth, the customary amounts of bride wealth inflated dramatically. To the Tiv, the idea was deplorable of having to "sell" their daughters for money obtained in exchange for food. There was no dignity in it since the possibility of converting a bride-wealth marriage into an exchange marriage was destroyed.

Functions of Money

When a Tiv gave a basket in exchange for a pile of vegetables, the basket was used as a means of payment, an object taken in free exchange for another object or service. When brass rods were taken in exchange for cattle, and then the rods were given for slaves, they were being used as a medium of exchange, where the money object holds the value of a good and is used to exchange for another good. The economic value of the cattle was converted into the rods and then reconverted into slaves, the rods being an intermediate stage in value conversion. When the value of cattle was discussed in terms of numbers of rods, the rods were being used as a standard of value, a metric that equates the values of different things. When the rods, cattle, cloths, slaves, and so on were held for future disposition, they were stores of value, or wealth. Many analysts also mention the idea that money things can be used to express a future obligation, serving as a standard of deferred payment, and that things can be used to record payments and serve as a unit of account. In addition, many analysts include the following critical attributes of money: fungibility, or the quality that any item of money can be used in place of, or substituted for, any other item of the same value (that is, four quarters are just as acceptable as one dollar bill or ten dimes); durability; portability; divisibility; and recognizability (Neale 1976: 8).

Primitive monies are special purpose, meaning they do not function in all of the ways mentioned above. Brass rods in Tivland were means of payment and mediums of exchange, as well as stores of and standards of value for some, but not all, things. It is not clear whether they were used as standards of deferred payment, and they were not used as units of account. They certainly were not fungible. In contrast, dollars, pesos, yen, pounds, and so on are general purpose (or multipurpose) monies. They possess all of the functions and attributes mentioned.

There is no clear division between special- and general-purpose monies—the terms are meant to refer to a continuum. Special-purpose monies usually have more moral restrictions on their use than do general-purpose monies. The idea of selling a brass rod for subsistence foods is repugnant to a Tiv. But remember that the idea of selling a daughter for brass rods is also repugnant to a Tiv, and the tragedy of someone pawning a family heirloom for cash in the United States reflects a similar equation of morals and money.

Even in an advanced capitalist society, it is not right to sell some things for money. For example, in most places it is illegal as well as immoral to exchange sexual favors for money, and it is always wrong to exchange political favors for money. Our general-purpose money is in fact quite hedged with moral, ethical, and legal constraints. Let me make this point clearer with a personal anecdote. I once did a favor for a friend: He had to leave town and asked me to get rid of trash from his rented apartment. When I went to clean it up, I found an envelope with a note from him thanking me. There was also some money "to buy myself a fancy meal" in payment for my favor. I was insulted, because although I would have been delighted to have been taken out for a meal, I resented getting money for my gift of work as if I were a stranger.

Other Topics in the Economic Anthropology of Money

Our general-purpose money is used for different kinds of payments. In the first place the basic value of the money is set by the state, the only legal issuer, in response to policy decisions. The common exchange of money for goods or services is at a ratio (price) set by competitive forces (albeit subject to political control). We also use money for payments to government in taxes and fees at rates determined by the political process (although subject to economic control). Finally, we give gifts (to friends, religious institutions, and other charities) at rates determined by each individual, acting as a social person.

In primitive chiefdoms the most valuable objects were used in reciprocal, noncommercial payments in political relations of war, peace, and marriage (see the discussion of salt money in New Guinea in Chapter 14, below). "Blood payment" was a major use, where the kin group of the murderer avoided hostilities by giving valuables to the kin group of the victim. In chiefdoms, the valuables were often produced under the direction of the chiefs, who used the food they received from dependents to pay for the valuables. The common experience under colonial domination was for some primitive valuables to become more plentiful since their use was supported by European traders. For example, cowrie shells were used as ballast by European ships on the trip out from Europe to many areas of the Pacific and to China, India, and Africa. These shells were to be used as payments for native goods. The massive influx of valuables inflated the price of local goods and, coupled with the decline in the power and status of local chiefs, allowed lower-status natives to own valuables they could not have had access to in precolonial times. Thus the Europeans often saw a distorted view of native uses of money, one much more like all-purpose money than the precolonial reality (cf. Dalton 1965).

Money and Markets

Multipurpose money facilitates exchanges. The more multipurpose the money, the easier and more convenient it is to buy and sell. Thus market-dominated societies have developed multipurpose moneys to fit their markets, and these moneys have facilitated the colonial domination of agrarian and tribal societies. Societies like the Tiv had markets also, in which several special-purpose moneys functioned. There also have been marketplaces without money of any sort. If the simplest definition of a marketplace is a space where people exchange goods along terms other than kinship or tribute, the famous "silent trade" qualifies. Herskovits describes several cases, where one group places its goods, for example, fish, on the ground and retires; individuals in the other group then take the fish and leave taro. If the terms of trade are acceptable, those of the first group take the taro and leave; if not, they retire again to await the increase (1952: 185–87).[4] Direct barter (that is, trade without money) occurs in commercial markets also (Orlove 1986). Because barter is a difficult way of conducting trade, it will occur only where there are strong institutional constraints on the use of money (see the following section on the preconditions for trade) or where the barter symbolically denotes a special social relationship and is used in well-defined conditions (Orlove describes a case from modern Peru). To sum up, multipurpose money in markets is like lubrication for machines—necessary for the most efficient function, but not necessary for the existence of the market itself.

In conclusion, the anthropological treatment of primitive money focuses on its special-purpose uses, where morality, politics, and social relations are important. As so often happens, the analysis of a function in a primitive society (for example, the morality of different means of payment) points us to analogous functions in industrialized nations. This perspective counterbalances the purely economic focus on financial values. With the nature of money clarified, we can continue our discussion of markets.

[4] Herskovits also cites descriptions of silent trade of commodities for special purpose moneys, for example, shells.

Preconditions for Market Trade in an Agrarian Region

The potential for trade in an agrarian region comes from the functional difference between the food-producing, merchandise-consuming, politically dependent farms of the outlands and the food-consuming, merchandise-distributing, politically dominant homes, shops, and offices of the towns. Farmers, like every other producer, can increase their income by specializing in a marketable product. If a peasant farm family focuses all its labor on growing, for example, beans for market, it must give up making its own clothing, rope, soap, and tools and raising animals, vegetables, grains, flowers, and all the other things the family members need to live their definition of a normal life.

This specialization is often forced by an urban-based class of elite leaders or dominators through the imposition of taxes or tribute upon the rural producers. The fifteenth-century Mexican Aztecs, for example, imposed tribute requirements (for example, thousands of bundles of cotton cloth or sacks of grain) on newly conquered kingdoms (see Chapter 4, this volume). In other situations, the dominant elites imposed restrictions or requirements on production or consumption. For example, the Spanish colonial government in Latin America demanded that Indians produce goods for Spanish consumption and required Indian families to purchase Spanish goods from royal monopolies.

The specialization that forms the basis for exchange can function on a regional level by integrating communities from different ecosystems into one regional market system. Many markets in the developing world present striking pictures of this, with members of different producing villages dressed in traditional costumes that vary from village to village. Individuals sell products that are practically identical within each village, but specialized across villages. The product becomes synonymous with the producing village. In Oaxaca, Mexico, for example, blankets come from Teotitlán del Valle, pottery from another village, stone grinders (metates) from a third, rope from a fourth, chile peppers from a fifth, and so on. Some have explained the origin of markets in evolving chiefdoms with reference to the integration of regional ecological diversity.[5] The argument is that market exchange allows people to settle in the full range of producing areas available to them.

If the farm family becomes more specialized, it must give up some independence and control over its well-being. The income from specialized production promises increased welfare from the ability to buy more and better products. This is the problem subsistence farmers face

[5] See Beals (1975) and Cook and Diskin (1976) for an example from Mexico.

if they have this choice: to increase, rather than decrease, their family's well-being by giving up food crops for commercial market production. What attributes does a market have to offer to get farmers to freely commit themselves to it?

Regularity. The market must be available and predictable for people to entrust their future to it. The supply of goods should be sufficient and appropriate, and the demand for farm goods must be predictable and steady for farm households to schedule their lives around it. Prices must be predictable and reasonable so that the majority of producers can afford to deal with the market.

Adequacy. The assortment of goods offered must be sufficient to satisfy the needs of the farm families; likewise, the transport and storage resources available must be adequate to handle all the farm product that farmers wish to sell.

Security. Activity in the market system must be protected by authorities so that people can trade without fear for their safety. This security includes the enforcement of contracts between strangers so that trade can extend beyond kinship or residential ties.

Markets become regular, adequate, and secure when regions are integrated economically, politically, and socially. Regional integration comes from investment in infrastructure, meaning the basic technology of transportation and communications. This includes:

Sufficient and reasonably priced transportation, which derives from investment in roads, vehicles, and support systems like travelers' rest houses and sources of food, as well as gasoline stations and spare parts suppliers for motorized transport, in addition to indirect investment in credit support to help buyers finance truck and bus purchases.

Sufficient and reasonably priced storage facilities, which implies that the interest rate for capital must be reasonable, or else people will not afford to save capital in the form of crops.

In contemporary societies, effective and available communications media, such as newspapers, telephone, and telegraph systems so that the availability of demand and supply can be made known at a distance; the lack of this sort of information supports local monopolies.

Political integration of regional societies so that traders are not subject to exploitation by local officials when they cross local borders and so that trade is not disrupted by violence. Warfare obviously makes normal trade difficult or impossible.

Individuals must be present who are knowledgeable about trade, have freedom of movement, and have sufficient capital to enter trade as middlemen. Local social or cultural restrictions on trade often allow resident "strangers," middleman minorities, or "trade diasporas" (Weber 1968; Bonacich 1973; Curtin 1984) to monopolize trade. Such groups can capitalize on their extended international or interregional kinship connections to reduce their costs and risks. This allows them to outcompete local traders who do not have access to comparable networks. The Jews in nineteenth-century Europe, Indians in East Africa, Arabs in West Africa, Armenians in Turkey, and Chinese in Southeast Asia are well-known examples of "diaspora" trading communities.[6]

Elements of Central Place Theory

The previous discussion focused on an individual level of concern about market functions. In this section the discussion deals with a regional or societal level of function. We would expect markets to exist in situations where the preconditions for marketing are satisfied. Where will the markets locate, and how will different markets relate to each other? Central place theory was proposed in the 1930's by the German geographers Walter Christaller and August Losch to answer these questions. The basic theory is built upon several formal simplifying assumptions that are so abstract that they seem entirely unrelated to the real world. Yet the final model has been shown to be strikingly appropriate to several real-world societies; more important, it brought a fresh understanding of how such systems work.

Imagine a featureless landscape, without such natural obstacles as mountains, but without such natural highways as rivers. Transport is equally easy in all directions and, at least initially, the population is evenly distributed among "lowest level" agricultural settlements without markets. This is the fundamental assumption of the basic central place model.

The theory also assumes that all the population's commercial activity is economically motivated, that the region is without social or political barriers to trade, and that traders are freely competitive so that markets can arise on the landscape in response to purely economic factors. The effect of these assumptions is to imagine a constant demand for goods and services evenly distributed across a featureless landscape. The assumptions also imply that every member of the population will shop at the nearest market; as a result, the markets that do arise in response to demand will be evenly spaced. The idea that demand can be treated as a variable distributed in space is fundamental to central place theory.

[6] Bonacich and Modell (1980: ch. 2) give an excellent introduction to the subject of middleman minorities.

The Spatial Demand Cone and Fixed Markets

The basic element of the spatial demand distribution is the "maximum range" of the consumers' demand for a good. This refers to the longest distance a consumer will travel to obtain a unit of the merchandise from the vendor. This range is constructed from the model of demand given in Fig. 7.1. Assume that all consumers have identical demand functions and that their consumption of the good is purely dependent upon its final real cost. This cost is composed of the price at the center plus the cost of transportation from the center to the consumer's

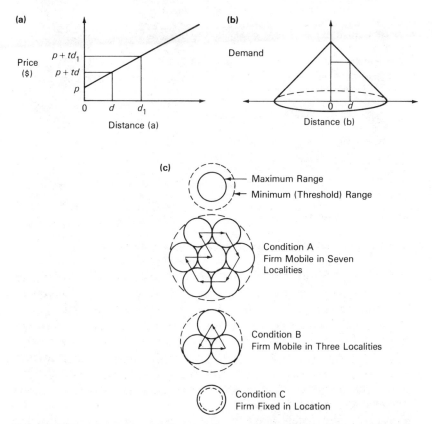

Fig. 7.1. Price, demand, and distance from a central point. (a) Price as a function of distance (t = transport rate). (b) Demand as a function of distance: the spatial demand cone. [Based on Brian J. L. Berry, *Geography of Market Centers and Retail Distribution* (1967), pp. 60–61. Redrawn by permission of Prentice-Hall, Inc., Englewood Cliffs, New Jersey.] (c) Maximum and minimum ranges and mobility of a firm. [Based on Stine 1962. Redrawn by permission of the University of Oregon Bureau of Business Research.]

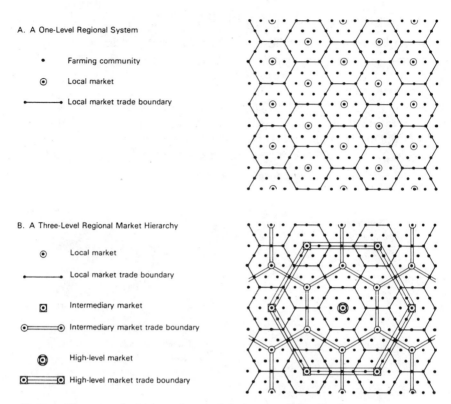

A. A One-Level Regional System

- • Farming community

- ⊙ Local market

- •————• Local market trade boundary

B. A Three-Level Regional Market Hierarchy

- ⊙ Local market

- •————• Local market trade boundary

- ▣ Intermediary market

- ⊙▬▬▬⊙ Intermediary market trade boundary

- ◉ High-level market

- ▣▬▬▬▣ High-level market trade boundary

Fig. 7.2. The central place market model of regional distribution.

home (see Fig. 7.1.a). Thus consumers with identical "demands" and opportunity costs will buy decreasing amounts of the same merchandise with increasing distance from the center, until sales drop to zero at some distance from the center.[7] Because population density is related in some determinate (usually decreasing) way to distance from the center, the total quantity demanded can be expressed in units of distance from the central point of supply, holding price at the center constant. This relationship is shown rotated around the center to form the "spatial demand cone" in Fig. 7.1.b.

Because of the spatial demand cone, another important concept can be defined: the minimum threshold of the trading firm. This refers to the volume of sales, corresponding to a definite spatial area, that creates the minimum income necesary for a firm selling a particular good to

[7] See the appendix at the end of this chapter for a discussion of some complexities involved in analyzing consumer costs.

come into full-time existence. For example, a tomato seller who needs to sell $100 worth of produce a day to stay in business needs one square kilometer demand area if families buy $1 a day and are distributed at a rate of 100 per square kilometer. The size of the threshold range is determined by the opportunity cost of the trader's time and money as well as the demand density in the area. The threshold range and the maximum demand range are both expressed in terms of area and are directly comparable.[8]

Figure 7.2.a shows a schematized model of a landscape with farming communities surrounding local market communities. There is only one level in this marketing system, with local markets selling goods like fresh produce and simple tools. When the marketing system increases in complexity to have several levels, the model looks like Figure 7.2.b. The intermediary level may offer goods such as cloth and heavier machinery, whereas the high-level market may offer motor vehicles, luxury goods, and legal services. The unrealistically regular distribution of central places in this model reflects the simplifying assumption of a "featureless" landscape and a regular distribution of income across the landscape. We will see below how real landscapes conform to this sort of schematized model.

The Theory of Mobile Retailing

If the minimum range of a good is smaller than its maximum range, a vendor can set up a shop and earn a living from a fixed setting. James H. Stine (1962) explored the implications of the case where minimum ranges are larger than maximum ranges. In this case, the firm cannot be fixed, full-time and survive. But if the firm becomes mobile, it increases its consumer population by relocating the point from which it offers goods. This has the same effect as an increase in the maximum range of the goods it offers. In condition A of Fig. 7.1.c, the firm must visit seven demand areas to survive, whereas in condition B the firm must relocate only three times, and in condition C the firm is able to remain fixed. Note that the consumer's willingness to travel has not changed—the radius of each local demand area (the maximum range) has remained the same. But the individual families in each place may buy more goods as a result of their increased income, the firm's sales may increase at each location because of more densely settled population, the firm's costs may decline, or its notion of an acceptable minimal income may decrease—any of these changes can affect the mobility of firms. Thus this model describes the conditions for the existence

[8] As is common in such models, time is held constant.

of trading firms that are able to stay in business full-time by offering part-time services to more than one local demand area.

Periodicity of Demand and the Mobile Vendor's Monopoly

The need for goods varies with time: The demand cycle for food is short, either daily or weekly; that for clothing is usually seasonal; and that for durables such as tools is annual or longer. In all cases, because fixed stores are usually open for much of the time (normally closing only overnight), little constraint is placed on the consumer's purchasing schedule. In periodic marketing, goods are *not* available in a place for most of the time, causing the demand to be accumulated. The *potential* demand per unit time (the quantity of goods that would be bought if they were offered continuously) is condensed into *actual* sales in a fraction of that time. As Stine put it, "The consumer, by submitting to the discipline of time, is able to escape the discipline of space" (1962: 70). From the vendor's point of view, his relative monopoly allows him to enforce this discipline and achieve an adequate sales volume. This allows the seller to travel to another selling area or earn an income in another occupation in the remaining time.

To sum up, both part-time and full-time periodic trading keep the trader's income above a threshold. Revenue is increased by the condensation of economic exchange into shorter periods. The ability to condense sales usually results from monopolistic competition, while periodism is a function of low demand densities.

Simple Agrarian Marketing Systems

The most primitive market system in an agrarian society exists where the region develops a central place that serves and controls certain economic and political functions. At its simplest, this refers to two types of settlements: rural farm villages and central manufacturing, distributing, or governing towns. Through manufacture or import, the town provides essential nonfarm goods. The town also consumes farm goods and provides the location and skilled services necessary for arbitrating differences in farm production. Therefore, a true functional integration exists in the region. Traveling specialists based in the center supply the hinterland with goods and services.[9]

The region itself may not be independent, but part of a larger social

[9] See Neumark (1957) for a description of the pivotal role of peddlers along the South African frontier; Dahl (1960) on traveling peddlers in nineteenth-century Sweden; Davis (1966) on peddlers in sixteenth-century England; and Helle (1964) for an analysis of mobile truck retailing in modern Finland.

system. The more complex system evolves when some of the rural villages become sites of periodic markets. This can occur as a consequence of economic development, which stimulates increases in demand density and decreases in the costs of transportation. The hinterland population comes to support fixed stores and marketplaces, and central-place suppliers become able to deliver supplies to the erstwhile hinterland at a regular schedule for reasonable costs.

The Development of Consumer Demand for Goods

Commercialization of rural families usually varies inversely with distance from the center. Families close to the town in an agrarian region consume relatively little of their own production and produce relatively little of their total consumption. At the other extreme, families in distant zones are more subsistence oriented, with little effective demand for a wide range of purchased goods.[10] In the middle zone of viable periodic trading are families who produce their basic subsistence food and some additional farm goods for sale, such as animals (poultry, pigs) or specialty crops (coffee, tobacco). These families buy items like cloth, clothing, hardware, pots, and pans. When peddling first penetrates an area, the list of items demanded by farm households is small and tends to be composed of hardware like tools and metal pots. But the loss of self-sufficiency and increase in market dependence of hinterland peoples in the world is universal and inexorable—it is reversed only briefly in times of disaster, when the market breaks down.

The demand of rural households for manufactured goods is income-elastic,[11] both seasonally and in the long run. The hungry, preharvest season is usually a time of minimal purchases, limited to necessary goods. The postharvest season is the time of expanded demand for goods. Thus the quantity of goods sold per week or month is not constant over the year but is a function of the agricultural cycle, which is usually allied to the ceremonial cycle. Over the long run, with increasing transport efficiency and commercialization in the region, money incomes rise, as does the total quantity of goods purchased per unit area.

Although the income elasticity of demand is elastic over annual and longer periods, the price elasticity of demand probably varies as the

[10] Hinterland people are fascinated by manufactured goods, but they do not have the income to pay for them.

[11] This term refers to the proportional change in goods bought with changes in income. If a 10 percent change in income produces more than a 10 percent change in goods bought, the relationship is termed "elastic." Conversely, if the percentage change in purchases is smaller than that of income, the relationship is called "inelastic."

income of consumers changes.[12] Poor families will defer purchases until the need is most pressing. Each purchase is then more critical than the case where buyers anticipate need in order to take advantage of bargains. In other words, the absolute price may be less important than the absolute need at that time. Such a family is a prisoner of its own poverty, paying more for goods because it is unable to delay purchases until more favorable terms are available.

Regional Development Around a Market Town

The traders in central market towns benefit from each other's presence. The maximum range for goods is increased close to a market center by the association of each good with other attractions that the center possesses. The cost of transporting a particular good to the buyer's home is spread across many goods on a multiple-objective trip, which makes the real cost of the good cheaper than if it were purchased alone (Webber and Symanski 1973). This principle explains why stores congregate in shopping centers.

This sort of centralized region can be visualized as a series of concentric demand zones surrounding the central town, as shown in Fig. 7.3. Here the central zone has the largest demand density because of the positive association of population density, commercialization, and transport efficiency with nearness to the center. Since each seller in the town offers, in effect, all of the goods and services of the town in addition to his or her own wares, the population of this zone will pass by any rural stores to buy and sell only at the center.[13] The minimum range of a trading firm is small because of the dense demand, whereas the maximum range coincides with the size of the zone itself by definition.

Zone B of Fig. 7.4 is defined by the interaction of several parameters: population density and commercialization, which decrease with distance from the center, and transport costs, which increase with distance from the center. Other parameters include the relative degree of monopolization of supply that a mobile firm possesses, which increases with distance, and the firm's threshold income (minimum range). Population density, commercialization, and transport costs can be combined into a single complex parameter of economic demand per unit area, which falls with distance from the center, as shown in

[12] Demand is price-elastic if a given percentage change in price elicits more than that percentage change in purchases. If a 10 percent increase in price decreases purchases by less than 10 percent, then the demand for that item is labeled inelastic.

[13] The normal ceteris paribus assumptions hold. When people have special needs or constraints, they may find it worthwhile to buy from itinerants. For example, peddlers may offer personalized credit plans or access to otherwise unavailable goods.

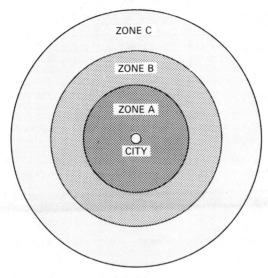

Fig. 7.3. Zones of demand density in an underdeveloped region. Shading indicates density of population and degree of commercialization. Source: Plattner 1975a.

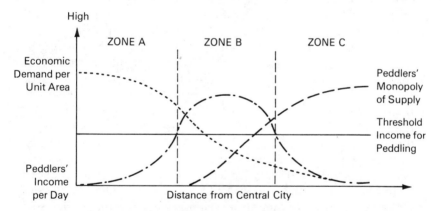

Fig. 7.4. Income of itinerant peddlers and distance from a central town. Source: Plattner 1975a.

Fig. 7.4. This means the minimum range of the trading firm increases with distance as the maximum range of consumers decreases.

These factors interact to produce a potential daily income from peddling, which is the significant variable from the trader's point of view. Zone B, which is the zone of viable commerce for periodic traders, is defined as the distance from the center where the daily income is above the threshold. Zone C is a hinterland where demand is too weak and transportation too difficult to support even itinerants. Over time, such zones expand outward from the center as the region develops.

Itinerant peddlers coordinate and unite centers with hinterlands. As a region develops, the zone of viable peddling radiates across the landscape. As income and demand increase in hinterland areas, the potential for fixed stores becomes actual. This allows the itinerants to settle down as fixed storekeepers in their old selling locations, to shift to wholesale functions to provision the new fixed stores, or to continuing as itinerant operators in the new frontier zones. As the expanding hinterlands of local systems begin to bump into each other, the potential areas for itinerants to serve decrease and vanish. Thus the success of these frontier operators in joining new areas to the expanding central market forces them to change their business or migrate. The following case study of itinerant peddlers shows one situation in southern Mexico.

Case Study: Itinerant Peddling in Southern Mexico

Plattner (1975a, 1980) studied a community of long-distance itinerant peddlers in Chiapas, Mexico, in the late 1960's. The trade area surrounding the home city of San Cristóbal is shown in Map 7.1. The long-distance traders worked in an area to the north and east of the city, since access to the south and west was impeded by a river valley some 900 to 1,520 m below the city. The far borders of the peddlers' trade zone were defined by the encroaching trade area of another city to the north and by dense, relatively uninhabited forest to the east.

The peddlers all came from Cuxtitali, a relatively endogamous neighborhood of the town where peddling and pig slaughter were the traditional occupations of the men. Cuxtitaleros bought cloth, clothing, and trinkets from stores in the city. Traders in the 1960's customarily loaded three or four pack animals and walked two to five days along well-worn mountain trails to get to their usual selling area. Once there, they sold goods from door to door to Mayan Indian peasant farmers. The rural Indians subsisted on corn and beans, and raised pigs, poultry, sugar cane, and coffee for sale.

The traditional basis of the San Cristóbal peddlers' trade was their access to a type of cloth used by hinterland Indian women for their skirts. Indian clothing styles were very traditional, and all the women in each community in this area wore identical dark blue skirts and white embroidered blouses. Indian women had to rely upon the peddlers as their sole source of this important piece of clothing. The cotton

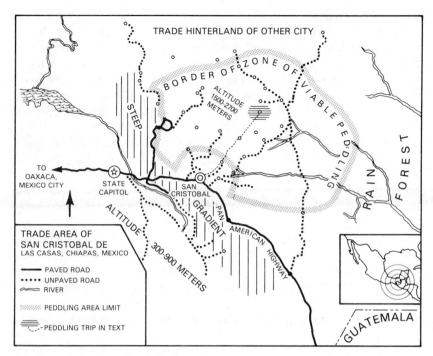

Map 7.1. Highland Chiapas.

cloth (*nagua negra*) was woven by Ladino craftsmen in the city, in a division of labor between Indians and Ladinos that dated from colonial times. The peddlers obtained the cloth from weavers in a neighboring section of the town where weaving was the traditional occupation of men. The cloth was scarce, and peddlers maintained personalized economic relationships with the weavers to assure themselves a reliable supply of high-quality cloth. Weaving and peddling, as well as other traditional occupations like candle making, were declining in importance because young men preferred more modern jobs in factory or construction work.

Peddlers also maintained personalized relationships with Indian families, as well as with the relatively few Ladino families in the hinterlands. This was necessary in order to get food and lodging, since there were no hotels or restaurants in these distant places. The hinterland settlements had no marketplaces, paved roads, electricity, or potable water systems, and had just received public schools in the previous twenty years.

Each sale in the selling area was intensively, sometimes excruciatingly, bargained over. Peddlers would set down their heavy bundles, unpack the merchandise, and display their wares with extraordinary patience to make sales that were often minuscule.[14] As they went along, the peddlers bought pigs and other farm produce like eggs or coffee to take back for resale. After staying in a remote hamlet for a few days, the peddlers would shift location to a nearby hamlet, in a pattern that would take them through an area where they knew the people well enough to assess their credit worthiness.

The peddlers spoke Mayan, since few rural Indians spoke Spanish. Many peddlers served as "culture brokers," interpreting the alien Ladino culture to the Indians and vice versa. The peddlers' daily lives while on a trip were matched to the farmers' schedules. To catch the men at home, peddlers woke early and made a round of nearby homes before breakfast. In many communities the peddlers could not approach farm homes while the men were away in the fields, because the women could not deal with them alone. During the middle of the day the peddlers would sell out of their borrowed space and would care for their animals and equipment. At the end of the trip, most peddlers had purchased a herd of pigs, which they drove to the city, a slower walk than their outward trip because the pigs could not travel in the heat of the sun.

This was truly "petty commerce," because the average net daily income of peddlers was about ten times the daily wage for an unskilled laborer. An unskilled day laborer's income was based on his labor time alone. The peddlers' income was caused by their labor time, entrepreneurial ability, capital, mules, and equipment, as well as their spouses' work in those families where they slaughtered pigs.

The conditions of sale for itinerant peddlers were unique. When they sold in the homes of their customers, in contrast to street selling, the customers could not witness other sales. This placed buyers in a weak position in bargaining, since they could not rely upon the experience of similar sales to help them evaluate prices. Customers of itinerants could discuss prices with friends and relatives, but their knowledge of current prices was always impaired in comparison with the knowledge available to a marketplace consumer. The convenience of being able to buy goods in one's own home brought with it a severe disadvantage in bargaining. This rewarded the peddlers for introducing new

[14] A representative peddling trip in 1968 included 3,730 items in 97 separate categories, with a total retail value of less than $1,000. The average sale was for $2.80 worth of goods, and about 10 percent of the sales were on credit, to be paid for on the peddler's next trip. About half of the sales were transacted on short-term credit, where the peddler made the sale on his outward-bound route but collected the cash a few days to two weeks later on his homeward-bound trip.

goods. Knowledge of the goods' standard price spread slowly in the hinterlands, and peddlers had a long period during which they could charge a high price for new articles. This was the economic base for the peddlers' role as cultural brokers between Ladino towns and Indian hinterlands.[15]

The peddlers' economic niche was caused by the general underdevelopment of the region. There were few markets to satisfy the economic needs of rural people. By the 1980's the federal government had built enough automobile roads to allow farm goods to be shipped out. This raised incomes enough to allow more fixed stores and coincidentally lowered travel times so that rural people could more easily shop in towns. The peddlers became economically extinct. The process of development was one that most regions of the world had gone through. The following section discusses the central place theory of market development.

The Central Place Theory Hierarchy of Markets

The concepts used to make up the minimum and maximum thresholds of the firm can also be used to build a theory of a hierarchy of markets. Obviously the ranges of some goods and services differ from the ranges of others by orders of magnitude. For example, an individual household will want commodities such as fresh vegetables quite often, yet the consumer may not be willing to travel very far to buy them. The vegetable supplier in turn can be satisfied by the demands of a relatively small number of households, because in the course of a year each consumer will buy a great deal of his produce even though each individual transaction will be small. Commodities of this kind are called low-order goods. The area of positive demand for them, meaning their maximum range, is small; at the same time the frequency of demand means that their minimum range is also small.

Higher-order goods and services are characterized by greater maximum and minimum ranges. Articles of furniture or the advice of an attorney have large maximum ranges because their cost is high and because consumers need to buy them infrequently. The consumer's cost of travel is trivial by comparison. The minimum range for such goods is also large. The purchases made by each household are infrequent; if the supplier is to carry out the number of transactions necessary to stay in business, his trade area must be an extended one.

Christaller's central place models predict that any center where high-

---

[15] Did the itinerant traders "exploit" their Indian customers? See the appendix for a discussion of this issue.

order goods are available will also offer low-order ones, but a center where low-order articles are available will not necessarily provide high-order ones (1966). Different kinds of central places will come into existence, dealing in goods with different ranges. The model must therefore account for systematically integrated hierarchies of markets. How do such regional networks arise?

Christaller imagined a population living in marketless, lowest-level settlements evenly distributed across a featureless plain. Given the stipulation that no part of the plain will be left unserved, the theory assumes that itinerant peddlers will traverse the plain on some route and schedule (Hay 1971; R. H. T. Smith 1971).

If we assume a process of economic development—whereby rural households increase their economic involvement with outsiders and become less subsistence-oriented and more market-oriented—then fixed periodic markets for these goods will arise. The markets will exist at a series of settlements spaced so that the circular trade area of each market slightly overlaps the trade area of the next. Packing efficiency demands that overlapping be eliminated by converting the circles into a grid of tangent hexagons that exactly fill the space and that minimize the disadvantage to consumers in the hinterland farthest removed from each central place. We shall call the market for the higher-order goods at each of these central places a regional market center.

The households all have a similar demand for lower-order goods with smaller maximum range. Where will the markets for these goods (call them standard centers) arise? Because of economies of scale, the first such markets will certainly be at the places where the regional markets are already established. Consumers are already visiting the regional markets. If they also buy lower-order goods at the same center, this splits the cost of transportation between the two classes of commodities, in effect reducing the real price of the lower-order goods and increasing their maximum range.

Because the maximum range of the goods offered at standard markets is smaller than the maximum range of the regional center goods, the regional center hinterlands will still include large regions of unsatisfied demand for lower-order articles. If the unserved areas equal the minimum range of the lower-order goods, then additional standard market centers will arise in these vacant areas. When the process is complete, the kind of market hierarchy the model displays will have one standard central place pattern. The market area lying inside a large regional market center hexagon is made up of the hinterlands of three standard market centers as follows. One of the three is the standard center hinterland, which lies entirely within the boundaries of the regional center hinterland. The other two are not entire standard center hinterlands; rather, they consist of a one-third share of each of the six surrounding standard center hinterlands that lie partly inside the regional center hexagon.

A hierarchy need not involve only two classes of markets. The same ordering process can be imagined for markets dealing in goods with any number of ranges. No matter how elaborate the hierarchy, in this pattern the market specializing in goods with the greatest range would have a total hinterland equivalent to three market areas of the next lower order. Each of the three would embrace three of a still lower order, for a total of nine. The number of markets in the order below that would be 27, the number below that would be 81, and so forth.

Christaller called this pattern a marketing structure, because it is most attuned to the needs of rural consumers. This is so because the ratio of high-level centers to low-level centers is at a maximum.[16] Each successive lower-order market is equidistant from three higher-order markets so that a standard center consumer or trader has a choice of three equally convenient places to shop for higher-order goods. At the same time, a regional center consumer or trader in search of lower-order goods can tap not only the resources of his "home" standard center market but also those of six adjacent centers.

By relaxing the constraint that travel on the model landscape be equally easy in all directions, Christaller formulated a second kind of market hierarchy. Applying what he called the transport principle, he connected the higher-order regional centers to one another by means of fully developed communications routes, such as rivers or roads. Because the developed routes lowered consumers' travel costs, the real cost of goods bought from places along those routes was also lower. This sort of model approximates real-world situations such as mountainous areas, where road construction is costly and where it is cheaper to travel greater distances on existing roads than to build more direct ones. Another real-world situation that is approximated by the transport principle model is one where travel by land is not particularly expensive, but where waterways allow freight to move at an exceptionally cheap cost per ton-mile.

Christaller proposed more models, which were all intellectually and graphically elegant, but which were not shown to be truly descriptive of real-world situations. Skinner's study of the Chinese marketing system (summarized below) was the first to show that these abstract models represented the complex ethnographic reality found in fieldwork.

---

[16] This is usually called a "K-3" pattern, where K denotes the standard market area.

Marketplaces in Traditional and Modern China

Skinner observed the traditional rural marketing system in Szechwan and found historical records for many parts of China covering over 300 years. He discovered that the match between the abstract model's predictions and the on-the-ground reality was impressive (1964, 1985). Fig. 7.5 shows an example: an area near Szechwan, represented as a map, as an abstraction indicating trade areas, and as a formalized abstraction matching Christaller's model. After the communist revolution, when the central government tried to "leap forward" in the countryside by restructuring the traditional hierarchy of rural markets,

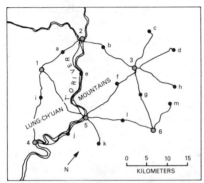

Second Szechwan Area surveyed by Skinner lay northwest of Chengtu; the landscape included part of a mountain range and a navigable stretch of the T'o River. Skinner found six larger market towns (*gray*), three of them on the river, and 13 smaller market towns (*black*), some of them in mountainous terrain. The two classes have been assigned numbers and letters respectively. Roads shown connect higher-level and lower-level towns.

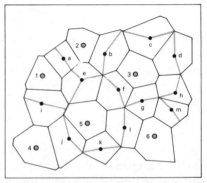

First Abstraction of the 19-center hierarchy ignores river and mountainous terrain and divides the landscape into small (*black*) and large (*grey*) polygons that represent the market areas of *B* centers and *A* centers respectively. Road network is also omitted.

Fig. 7.5. Chinese marketing system: From map to model. Source: Plattner 1975b. Copyright © 1975 by *Scientific American*, Inc. All rights reserved.

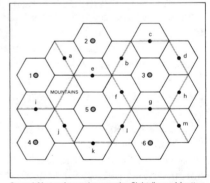

Second Abstraction produces another Christaller-model pattern of larger and smaller hexagons. Note, however, that one of the smaller hexagons (*left*) does not include a *B*-center market town but is a space filler that makes allowance for the rigors of mountain transport. The pattern that has emerged is that of the Christaller K-equals-four model.

the normal flow of trade was disastrously affected. The bureaucrats were able to restore the orderly flow of commodities from the rural communes to the urban populations only by reinstituting the old marketing structure.

The similarities between the model's predictions and Skinner's findings begin with a broad network of "standard markets" resembling the standard centers defined above. Neighboring rural households could satisfy virtually all their normal commercial needs at these markets. The standard market was the downward terminus for manufactured goods and the upward entry point for the farm produce that flowed through the regional marketing system.[17]

Given an even distribution of population, as in Christaller's model, such a standard center should be surrounded by concentric rings of marketless settlements, numbering 6 in the first ring, 12 in the next, 18 in the third, and so on. Skinner found that the usual Chinese pattern was a two-ring one, with an average of 18 villages surrounding each standard market, and a total population of villages and marketing town of about 8,000. This formed a "standard marketing community," which was the fundamental unit of traditional Chinese rural society. Skinner noted that an adult male in such a unit had a "nodding acquaintance with almost every adult in all parts of the . . . system" because he has traveled to the marketing center thousands of times, as have all the farmers from the other villages in the market community.

Skinner found that the standard markets, or standard centers, were geographically distributed with respect to higher-level markets, or regional centers, and that their trade boundaries could be rearranged into the pattern of tangent hexagons typical of the Christaller models. For example, fifteen market towns southeast of Chengtu could quite readily be "abstracted" into a K-equals-three model. Another group of market towns to the northeast of Chengtu, where a portion of a mountain range restricts travel and where a navigable stream provides an alternative to travel by road, could be abstracted into a K-equals-four model.

The spatial organization of the Szechwan markets was matched temporally by a complex interlocking system of alternate market days. If, for example, one regional center market met on the fourth, seventh, and tenth days of a ten-day cycle, the adjacent regional centers were likely to hold their markets on the third, sixth, and ninth days or on the second, fifth, and eighth days. The same nonconflicting periodicity

[17] There was a lower category of market based in the village where fresh vegetables were exchanged between households. These were omitted from the regional analysis since their exchange did not normally involve the upward movement of produce.

characterized the schedule of standard center market days with respect to the regional center schedule.

This served everyone's interests. If a farmer from a standard center satellite village happened to need some high-order article obtainable only at the regional center, his trip to acquire the item need not have cost him a lost standard center market day. Similarly, one of the local elite who resided in the standard center hinterland and needed regional center goods or services, such as books or medical attention, could obtain them and still not leave his place of work on a standard center market day. The itinerant traders who played important roles in the vertical flow of goods could make the rounds of the standard center markets on a schedule that enabled them to return to their regional center bases at regular intervals. They could dispose of the lower-order commodities they had acquired during their travels and replenish their stock of higher-order merchandise.

One of Skinner's most important findings is that the standard market community constitutes an endogamous unit. That means that people may choose their spouses within or without their home village but normally do not marry outside of their standard marketing community. Personal knowledge of the character of one's potential in-laws is an important factor in matchmaking, and information of this kind would be relatively available within one's standard marketing community. This finding is a powerful corrective to the anthropological tendency to regard the local village community as the most meaningful unit of study.

Skinner estimated that the average size of the standard marketing community varied with distance from the core areas of the geographic-political macroregions that he identified in traditional China. The sparsely settled peripheries contained about 120 square kilometers and included some 1,800 households, while the corresponding figures for the regional centers were 45 square kilometers and 2,200 households. He pointed out that a standard marketing system of 120 square km implied that the most disadvantaged farmer would have to travel about 7 km to market, a round trip that was easily managed in a day.

The average geographic size of the marketing areas decreased with nearness to the center, except when very efficient water transportation allowed the cost of travel to drop significantly. In these areas he found a curvilinear relation between distance from the center and size of marketing area: largest in the periphery, decreasing with increasing closeness to the more densely populated and commercialized core areas, then increasing again as the effects of the efficient water transport systems allowed people to travel greater distances in less time.

The Chinese communist government has cycled through several anti-

and pro-market policy changes. In the 1950's the new regime attempted to socialize rural trade. State trading companies and cooperatives were created with the aim to control all rural trade. But widespread criticism of inefficiencies—such as excessive travel by farmers to buy low-level goods, spoiled perishables, and gross inequalities in the distribution of goods—forced the government to relax its policies. After a crisis in 1958–1959, the government allowed the rural marketing system to function, although the Cultural Revolution of 1966 returned to strong anti-market policies. After 1977 the relative liberalization of China's economic policies allowed markets to flourish in a less restricted manner than any time since 1953.

The match between the abstract central place model and the on-the-ground reality of the Chinese marketing system is impressive. Skinner claims it is due to the many hundreds of years of noncolonial commercial development that Chinese society enjoyed up to the nineteenth century. Carol Smith showed how the basic central place model could be used to analyze a very different type of situation: the bi-ethnic colonial nation of Guatemala.

Marketplaces in Western Guatemala

Smith (1974, 1976, 1977) studied a system of rural periodic marketplaces surrounding higher-level urban market towns, as did Skinner. Her study is based on her own fieldwork, whereas Skinner's is mainly derived from historical records. Smith's analysis gives a more finely detailed picture than Skinner's. But in spite of the superficial similarities of the abstracted Central Place maps, the difference between the two systems is profound. Fig. 7.6 shows Smith's research area as a map, as an abstraction indicating trade areas, and as a formalized abstraction (cf. Fig. 7.5).

This does not reflect weakness in the basic central place model but is a warning that the model is built on specific assumptions that have to be examined for relevance to each empirical situation. The real-world situation in China is culturally homogeneous, although socially stratified. In Guatemala the effects of the Spanish conquest of the Mayan Indian kingdoms in the sixteenth century are pervasive. Modern Guatemala is divided into two quite different worlds: the Ladino and the Indian. In itself the difference may not be significant. What gives it meaning is the fact that the Ladino world controls the national economy.

Indians, whose first language is Mayan rather than Spanish, make up about half the Guatemalan population. Most have traditionally worked

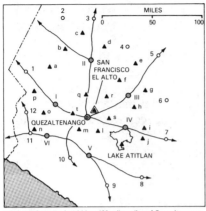

Western Guatemala within a 100-mile radius of Quezaltenango, the second-largest city in the nation, was surveyed in the 1960's by Carol A. Smith. She found a ring of six sizable Ladino market towns surrounding Quezaltenango (*Roman numerals*) and 12 lesser Ladino market towns (*Arabic numerals*) peripheral to them. An independent grid of markets dealing in Indian agricultural produce (*lettered black triangles*) was also present, but only a few of the 20 major bulking centers were located on the main highways. In the same way that Quezaltenango was central to the network of Ladino markets, a nearby major Indian market, San Francisco el Alto, was central to the network of rural bulking centers.

Fig. 7.6. Guatemalan marketing system: From map to model. Source: Plattner 1975b. Copyright © 1975 by *Scientific American*, Inc. All rights reserved.

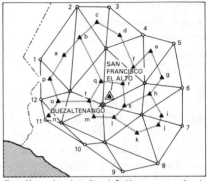

First Abstraction that allowed Smith to connect the six intermediate Ladino market towns to Quezaltenango and to one another with straight lines and similarly to connect the peripheral and the intermediate Ladino market towns produced a curious pattern. All 20 rural bulking centers (*black*) fell within one or another of the 24 triangles formed by lines connecting the Ladino markets. When the bulking centers were grouped into irregular but tangent hexagons (*grey lines*), each contained one of the higher-level Ladino markets.

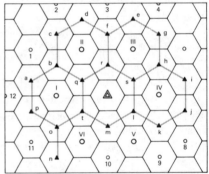

Second Abstraction of the Guatemala market hierarchy is arranged to approximate a Christaller K-equals-three model. The divergence of the real-life situation from the model is evident. *B*-center Ladino markets are not interspersed among the Ladino *A* centers but are peripheral to them. Only in the highest central place is a rural bulking center found along with a Ladino market. Moreover, the shares of bulking-center hinterland ''belonging'' to Ladino *A* centers actually represent not a two-way flow between higher and lower markets in a single integrated hierarchy but a one-way Ladino levy of Indian foodstuffs.

as semisubsistence farmers and live according to Mayan cultural patterns. Ladinos, whose first language is Spanish, are heirs to a tradition that is culturally (and often genetically) a mixture of Spanish and Indian. The Ladinos usually live in towns and are most often engaged in nonagricultural work. They are socially, politically, and economically the heirs of the conquistadors and are the dominant power in the nation.

Smith studied a market system surrounding the regional center of western Guatemala: Quetzaltenango, whose population was about 40,000 in the 1970's. Many commercial establishments are permanently located there, and manufactured goods of importance to the economy of the surrounding area are available in the city. The size of the resident nonagricultural population means that Quetzaltenango generates a strong demand for farm produce from the adjacent countryside. In the regional market hierarchy, Smith classifies Quetzaltenango as the pinnacle of the Ladino market-town system.

The city's major lines of communication lead radially outward to six intermediate-level Ladino market towns. For the sake of comparison, the six can be likened to the regional centers of the Christaller models. Beyond these regional centers, lying either on the same major branches or minor roads, are twelve lower-level Ladino market towns; these can be likened to the standard centers of the models. These nineteen central places, Quetzaltenango included, constitute the framework of Ladino economic control: The vertical distribution of goods manufactured outside of western Guatemala—fuel, machinery, tools, and factory-made cloth and clothing—begins in the city and moves downward to the regional centers and thence to the standard centers. Quetzaltenango and five of the six regional centers are also the administrative capitals of their districts and so control political disbursements as well.

The geographical distribution of the Ladino central places differs from that predicted by the classical central place models. When the demand for goods is distributed evenly over the landscape, the models predict that the regional centers will be widely spaced and that the lesser standard centers will be distributed between the regional centers. In western Guatemala, however, the standard centers are peripheral to the regional centers. Smith explains this deviation from the classical model's prediction by the uneven distribution of demand. Purchasing power decreases significantly in proportion to distance from the city. In addition, the number of Ladino households in the regional centers is greater than the number in the standard centers, and the Ladino population of Quetzaltenango is largest of all. The Indian population reflects the same gradient. It is most commercialized in the central zone, where relatively few Indian households engage in subsistence agriculture and where family income is highest. In response to these factors, the best roads are in the central zone and the worst ones are on the periphery.

The subsistence needs of the region's Ladino households are largely met by purchases of Indian-grown foods. The trade network that delivers the produce is composed of a grid of lower-level central places that Smith calls rural bulking centers. The predominance of wholesale over retail trade is what distinguishes the bulking centers from their

Ladino counterparts. They are situated in Indian communities, where large commercial establishments are rarely if ever found. The Indian markets meet periodically, primarily to collect produce for export to the Ladino market towns but also to meet the Indian demand for such products as salt and cloth.

Smith identified twenty major rural bulking centers in western Guatemala, excluding the largest one. This was situated near Quetzaltenango in the Indian market town of San Francisco el Alto, and it played a predominant role in the wholesaling of Indian produce. In effect, the San Francisco market occupied a position with respect to the rest of the rural bulking center network very much like the position of Quetzaltenango with respect to the network of Ladino market towns. Smith also found that when she connected the various Ladino market towns with abstract straight lines, most of the triangles so constructed contained a rural bulking center. Such a pattern, with lower-level markets enmeshed in a grid that connects higher-level markets, replicates the classical marketing pattern.

How does the Guatemalan marketing pattern differ from the traditional Chinese one, and what do the differences mean? Smith concluded that the clustering of major central places near Quetzaltenango, the economic center of the region, was not predicted by standard central place theory. She found that the spatial economy of Guatemala was strongly influenced by the distribution of political power and ethnic considerations. Ladino control over the political system translates into monopoly over the distribution of high-level goods and services and a skewing of the distribution of demand away from the central place assumption of even distribution. Ladinos live in the centers and consume more goods than Indians because they possess more income and wealth; therefore, the marketing system has adjusted to serve this demand.

How is Ladino dominance maintained? In addition to brute force, such as the use of military power to suppress revolts and kill Indian leaders, the structure of the marketing system facilitates Ladino control along the divide and conquer principle. Goods are not free to flow in any direction in the market structure, as the normal central place system assumes. There is a clear division of function in Guatemala between Indian rural bulking centers and Ladino market centers. The bulking of foodstuffs by Indian marketplaces and their shipment to the Ladino towns is a one-way process, not reciprocated by a downwards distribution of farm goods shipped to the Ladino market towns from other zones. When the foodstuffs reach the Ladino towns, they remain there to be consumed by the local Ladino population.

Smith has argued that the marketing system blocks development, instead of facilitating it. In the Chinese example the free flow of goods through the marketing system means that any local community can specialize in the production of a single commodity, secure in the knowledge that the staples the community does not produce will be forthcoming from the market. In Guatemala, because the Ladino market towns do not send foodstuffs back to Indians, the only exchange of agricultural goods between villages is at the level of the rural bulking centers. No bulking center is connected to any other center through a higher-level market.

The result is that the market system neither integrates the region nor assists in the development of regional economic specialization. The rural farmers engage mainly in subsistence agriculture or petty trading, limiting the Indian communities' ability to raise cash crops that would increase their incomes.

Integration and Underdevelopment

Do markets evolve on their own once demand density increases past some critical threshold? Or are markets imposed by a more developed, often exogenous economic system to facilitate extraction of rural goods in exchange for urban products? No matter how markets evolve, do they always serve to maximize productivity and therefore economic development? In many cases market systems have been imposed from above as part of a process of colonial domination. No matter what the origin of a system, the work of Skinner and Smith suggests that markets do not always stimulate economic development. The Chinese case can be taken as an example of an *integrating* market system while the Guatemalan case can be labeled an *underdevelopmental* system.

An integrating market system stimulates economic development by allowing different parts of the region to exchange horizontally as well as vertically. These terms refer to the central place order of the goods. For example, an Indian farming community in Latin America could specialize in its most productive product (such as peppers) since subsistence food (corn, beans, and other staples) will be available at a reasonable price from other similar farming communities in horizontal exchange. Manufactured urban goods may be available in vertical exchange (from towns to villages) for agricultural products, or goods from a craft-producing village may be available in horizontal (village-to-village) exchange. This process of regional economic integration stimulates economic development.

When the system of exchange is controlled by and for an urban elite population, then the horizontal links are minimized in order to stress the vertical ties. The elite is interested in supplying itself with food and in obtaining agricultural goods for export in exchange for the downward distribution of imported and urban-produced manufactured goods. Because the urban populations are wealthier and more powerful than farmers, the terms of trade are in their favor, and the exchange is unequal, meaning that a net flow of wealth leaves the rural areas for (and through) the towns. Thus this process is underdevelopmental.

Both processes have operated in all parts of the world, and both integration and underdevelopment can be analyzed as potentials of most marketing systems.

Andre Gunder Frank (1966) explained the lack of infrastructure and poverty of underdeveloped nations not as a result of their exclusion from world trade, but as a direct result of such involvement. The colonizing powers established marketing systems to facilitate the downward flow of manufactured goods and the upward flow of agricultural products for urban consumption or export. But there was no horizontal flow of farm produce to integrate the different agricultural districts of the region. Farmers in such a system cannot specialize fully lest they gamble their welfare on a market system that is not structured to deliver the food they need. Artisans cannot become manufacturers, because the goods imported from abroad are likely to be cheaper and better made than the local products. The low level of profits perpetuates this pattern of underdevelopment. In an independent system, such as China, the profits from commerce and agriculture are invested in support services such as education, communications, and transportation. Basic infrastructural resources of this kind increase the productivity of labor over the long run. In a dependent system such as Guatemala, the market facilitates the introduction of imported goods and impedes the development of local specialization. The profits tend to flow up and out of the system to the universities, highways, and commerce of the capital city or from there to the foreign nation. The gap widens between Ladinos and Indians within Guatemala, and also between countries like Guatemala and the developed nations. The formal shape of the marketing system is diagnostic of the political reality of the society. These issues of unequal exchange and inequality are discussed below, in the chapter on Marxism. The following chapter looks at economic behavior in the context of market exchange.

Appendix

Consumer Costs

The assumptions just mentioned imply that all consumers will be charged the same price for the same article at any particular market. But the real cost to consumers is more than that: The price of goods at the vendor's place is one component, the cost of transporting the goods from the vendor's location to the consumer's home is another, and the cost of transporting the consumer from his or her home to the vendor's place and back again is the third. The consumer's transport includes the indirect costs of the value of the activities foregone at home while on the purchasing trip (that is, the opportunity cost of the time), above the direct or out-of-pocket cost of transport.[18]

Costs can be shared among various goods. For example, your trip to the shopping center takes the same travel time and costs the same if you buy one thing or many. For any consumer, the more goods one buys on any trip, the cheaper the real cost of each item.[19]

The real value of a good offered for sale is a function of its environment. For example, consider a single parent who is at home with some sick children. What is the value of a normal grocery basket full of staple food? Clearly most people would pay some "reasonable" amount more than the in-store price to have the food selected and delivered to the home. The most important nonphysical element of an exchange is the transaction. A good is more attractive if it is made available at the precise place, time, form, and conditions of payment preferred by the consumer. In many cases, the merchandise is not purchasable if particular selling arrangements, especially credit, are not available.

Just as the physical characteristics of the good are not sufficient to ensure its sale, the actual need of the consumer for the good is not enough to ensure a purchase. Consumers obviously need the cash or

[18] It is easy to measure the monetary cost of wages to field hands for farmers who leave the farm or wages to baby-sitters for parents who leave the home. It is more difficult to measure the nonmonetary cost of a shopping trip, such as the Indian farmer in Latin America who goes to an alien town and risks harassment from locals, including the police. These latter sorts of costs can be equated with money in a rough and variable way, although the cost is rarely thought of as monetary. Thus, one may not walk through a hostile neighborhood to buy a $50 commodity for its price, but one may decide to run the risk if the price is $20.

[19] This is true only to a point, after which special costs and trouble increase from large quantities. Implicit cost sharing explains why itinerant sellers can offer cheaper prices at the consumer's door than those obtainable by the consumer himself at the central commercial place. Trade discounts, where the wholesaler lowers the unit price because bulk buyers save on transactions costs, and lower unit transport costs due to larger bulk would permit such economies.

the means of payment. In addition, the cost must meet people's notion of an "acceptable price." Some of the most exciting research in individual behavior is in the field of behavioral economic decision making. People "frame" prices and decide whether they are reasonable or not according to situational factors. An obvious example of this is the purchase of optional features of new cars or houses. People will spend many hundreds of dollars on a radio for a new car, when they would not spend that much to install the same radio in their used car. The difference is that the cost of the feature is cognized as a small fraction of the total cost instead of on its own (Thaler 1980). My point in introducing these details is to stress that a buyer's notion of the acceptable price for a commodity is tied to a particular place, time, and condition of payment. The basic theory abstracts from these particulars to give us a valuable outline, but when the model is applied to a particular case, these details become relevant. For example, the acceptability of more than one price for different bundles of retail services accounts for the ability of itinerant vendors to operate in the context of fixed stores. The itinerants usually select goods for their customers and provide services like credit that the fixed stores may not provide.

Exploitation

Did long-distance itinerant peddlers exploit their customers? The conditions existed for unfair dealing, because of the different knowledge of prices available to peddlers and Indians. I will discuss the question of exploitation in this section, keeping in mind the social class structure of the region. Both Indians and Ladinos are born into a culture that defines Ladinos as superior and Indians as inferior. This inequality is reinforced by a rural-urban discrimination, whereby urban people are superior to rurals.

All peddlers worked hard to earn a living and provided a service that was valued by their customers. Some were cruel, some kind; some were rapacious, some altruistic. Rural folk in most cultures usually are suspicious of urban traders ("city slickers") and accuse them of exploitation. But an objective analysis of exploitation is more complex than that.

Three types of relationships must be distinguished and considered separately in evaluating the equity of an economic exchange: the terms of trade as it relates to the relative wealth of each group, the opportunity costs of trade as an occupation, and the competitive status of each exchange. In the first place, the terms of trade of an exchange determine its fairness. The general level of income of one party to an exchange may be much higher than that of the other, and this difference may be supported by the exchange. The overall structure of the society may favor one party over another. In Chiapas, the peddlers, being Ladinos, enjoy higher incomes and access to more public services than Indians. Merely by virtue of Ladino birth they possess higher social, political, and economic standing. So Ladinos, as a class, have more of the society's wealth than Indians.

If a peddler were concerned about this difference in social status and decided to charge less than the "normal" price for his goods, he would in effect be transferring income from his family to his customers. Can the peddlers' families afford to lose this income? What is the relevant standard of comparison for the level of living of a peddler's family? This introduces the second relationship: the comparison of the peddlers' income with the income the peddlers could earn if they worked at their best alternative occupation—the "opportunity cost" of peddling. If the peddlers earned less than other people essentially similar to them—people of the same socioeconomic background, with the same level of training, possession of capital, and propensity to work—then even though the peddlers were earning more than their customers, they would not be doing well by their own standards.

The most relevant comparison groups for the peddlers are the petty artisans of San Cristóbal. These carpenters, potters, iron-workers, candle-makers, leather-workers, and fireworks specialists all lived at the same, or somewhat above, the life-style level of the peddlers. In 1970, practically no peddler lived in a home with piped water, and about half lived in dirt-floored homes; not one street in their neighborhood was paved, and the average incomes of a sample of peddlers for whom this sensitive data were obtained was about $825 annually. For comparison, the lowest level elementary school teacher in the area, with about the equivalent of a high school education, earned from about $865 to $1,120 dollars. School teachers also received valuable social services—such as health insurance and access to government price-supported retail stores—that significantly raised their real income.

Peddlers identified with Ladinos in contrast to Indians. There were Ladinos of enormous wealth in the area, who owned large ranches, drove expensive cars, and sent their children to European and North American schools. As far as the peddlers were concerned, they were at the bottom of their own social class.

In southern Mexico, the terms of trade were against the Indians, yet the peddlers lived no better than, and often worse than, their relevant peers. Why didn't the peddlers earn more profit? This brings up the third relationship, the state of competition in peddling. If the peddlers faced heavy competition, their yields would be similar to their costs.

For example, the peddlers used capital in their business that they could borrow at interest or loan out to others. If capital yielded more than it cost, this excess income would be profit. The analytical task is to estimate the yield of capital separate from the yield of labor and the other factors that produce income in peddling, and to compare that with the opportunity cost.

The average peddler used about $590 per trip in 1970 to buy merchandise (mainly on credit) and farm goods for resale, to pay expenses, and so on. Based on fairly complete statistical data for a sample of 47 itinerant peddling trips, I estimated the marginal product of capital on peddling trips to be about 0.25, while the opportunity cost of the peddler's capital was about 0.36. Given the small sample size, and the fact that the data are based on individual interviews rather than aggregate statistics, these two figures are not out of line. The statistical evidence supports the evidence from the comparison of life-styles to conclude that the peddlers were not making excess profits.

The evidence suggests that peddlers faced enough competition to ensure that their incomes were similar to their peers'. The basic structure of the society favored Ladinos over Indians, and the peddlers were the agents of exploitative Ladino-Indian exchanges, but they did not profit by it. Petty traders in developing countries are often accused of exploitation by local governments, but analysis usually shows that the middlemen do not profit by their trade, in the sense of earning "unfair" incomes (Babb 1985; Hollier 1985).

8

Economic Behavior in Markets

Stuart Plattner

The previous chapter deals with economic behavior in settlements, towns, and systems of markets but does not focus explicitly upon individuals. This chapter explores individual economic behavior in markets. It analyzes the conditions that lead people to establish personalized economic relationships, which seem as much "social" as "economic." Why does a buyer or a seller in a market sometimes search for the best short-run deal available at one time, and at other times establish a personalized, long-run reciprocal relationship with a customer?[1] The answer is that reciprocal economic relationships reduce risk in transactions that would otherwise be too uncertain or expensive to undertake.

The *transaction* is a key concept here. It refers to any change in the status of a good or service between persons, such as a sale. Transactions have costs. Some costs are obvious: If I use a credit card, I will probably pay interest on the amount; if the store I prefer is across town, I might spend hours accomplishing my purchase. Some costs are not obvious and relate to the risk of making a "bad" purchase. A well-known example in the used car market (to be analyzed below) is the risk of buying a "lemon." These risks will be analyzed here.

I will first define differences between personalized, long-run and impersonal, short-run economic relationships. The importance of information in economic relationships is then examined by analyzing problems in the separate elements of an exchange: the type of goods, the nature of the transaction, and the identity of the actors. Then the causes of informational problems are analyzed by looking at market infrastructure, consisting of systems of communications, political inte-

[1] The scientific strategy of analyzing social situations as caused by choice does not imply that every actor actively thinks about each strategy every day. But this approach forces the social scientist to consider the rationality of behavior that otherwise could be merely labeled as "habit," "custom," or "tradition."

gration, and transportation and storage. These causes are finally set in the context of the basic relationship between labor and capital in the society.

This abstract analysis can be set in a context by describing the problems in collecting a debt that two Mexican long-distance traders told me about in the 1970's. They had sold a horse to a resident of a distant town while on a peddling trip. (See the case study in Chapter 7.) The buyer paid them a small amount and said he would gather the rest of the money while they continued their peddling trip, and would deliver the cash to them when they passed through his town on their return. Ten days later they returned, traveling by horseback in this region of few paved roads, to find him not at home. They pastured their horses (for a fee) and put up in a hotel, "suffering," as they put it, "the cost of feeding ourselves in restaurants." There were no telephones, so they had to periodically visit his home to see if he was there. He finally arrived and said he would gather the money in a few days, since his own business was going poorly. They pleaded with him to pay them, but he refused. They finally appealed to the man's father for help. After another day they got their payment in the form of sacks of coffee. They considered themselves lucky to have gotten paid at all.

The peddlers' problems were typical and were caused in large part by faulty information due to a poor economic environment. This chapter will analyze the effects of such problems on economic transactions. The first step in the analysis is to define two opposite types, or modes, of exchange.

Modes of Exchange: Impersonal Versus Personal

There are basically two diametrically opposite ways to engage in transactions: They can be impersonal or *atomized*, or else personal or *embedded* (Granovetter 1985). Impersonal transactors have no relationship with each other beyond the short term of the exchange; thus in the aggregate they are *atomized*, or not organized into groups or social structures. Personalized transactions are between people who have a relationship that endures past the exchange; they are *embedded* in networks of social relations. The hypothetical "perfectly competitive market" of classical economic theory is built upon an assumption of atomized actors engaging in impersonal transactions. These buyers and sellers have no interest in a long-term relationship but consider only the specifics of each transaction with an eye toward maximal profit. In the real world, academics as well as businessmen have noted that people do not act that way. In most circumstances they establish long-run relationships with economic partners. Is this irrational? Are such trans-actors losing money, or trading off economic goals for social approval, status, or power? This chapter argues that a long-term personalized relationship is economically superior in certain environments.

The most important attribute of long-run exchanges is that they tend to be personalized, meaning that knowledge of the other's personality, family, history, church, and so on is relevant to the trust one has that the exchange will be satisfactorily completed. The riskier the economic environment, the more traders need additional information about a partner over and above the specific facts of the proposed deal. The Mexican peddlers in the story above might have known about their debtor's tendency to avoid paying his bills, but they needed to make the deal; and in any case they also knew enough to find and convince his father to help them.

The impersonal mode of exchange refers to short-run exchanges where each transaction has few implications for the future. These trans-actions can be said to be closed-ended, as opposed to the open-ended personal mode of exchange. The relationship between the buyer and seller in a department store is a good example. The transactions usually have no meaning aside from the specific things exchanged, and the dominant goal for each actor is to protect and maximize self-interest. The fact that the relationship is openly instrumental is appropriate, within the bounds of social norms. We understand that diners in road-side restaurants, where they do not expect to see the waiter again, feel free to leave little or no tip.[2] The relationship exists to support and facilitate the exchange, rather than the other way around.[3]

Economic exchanges within families are extreme examples of person-alized market exchange. Consider the hiring of dependent children by family firms. A parent who searches for the best worker to hand over the family business to, rather than encouraging a child to work in the firm, would be seen as odd. A family worker should not attempt to bargain with a family boss about working hours or vacation time in the same way that a nonrelative could. The work relationship is in the context of a long-term flow of resources and obligations. Continuing the relationship is the dominant goal. A child who attempted to de-compose the transactions and negotiate each element separately—for example, by asking for extra money for work to be done extra carefully and extra fast—would be morally criticized. In fact, the group (espe-

[2] Granovetter (1985) discusses why they would leave a tip at all in his consideration of "embeddedness" and the concepts of "oversocialized" and "undersocialized" actors.

[3] Frank Cancian (1966) discusses maximization as a behavioral norm in comparison with other uses of the maximization strategy.

cially the family) is often the basic actor whose interest governs those of each individual. If an extrafamilial authority is called in, it is usually a sign that the family structure has lost its integrity. We can categorize these relationships as long-term, open-ended, and generalized with a strong affective, noninstrumental component.

In reality, impersonal and personal market modes are not so neatly separated. Corporations often want their employees to feel a "family" loyalty toward the firm.[4] This normally means they should place the corporation's interests above their own in the short run, in return for the expectation of sharing the firm's long-run success. Family farmers often exchange services and goods in the name of "neighboring" and friendship, while they secretly record a count of the economic values exchanged "to keep things straight" (Bennett 1968).

Long-term trading partnerships, in which elements of impersonal and of personal modes intermingle, are often found in peasant market-places. The goal of each actor is his or her economic self-interest, yet the maintainance of the relationship is valued over an immediate short-run profit. Transactions are contracted in specific commercial terms, but a parallel relationship of generalized reciprocity seems to support the strictly commercial relationship.[5] The key element is that exchanges do not have to be balanced in the short run, since past or future short-falls are adjusted in the continuing stream of exchanges. In developed societies, these relationships have been reported for situations where the quality of the goods is hard to assess. For example, consider fisher-men and fish dealers. The cost of unloading a shipload of fish (or any variable, perishable, low central-place level good) is too great to do so without a commitment to buy, and the price fluctuates at the wholesale market. A price is usually negotiated before the ship is unloaded. If later events show that price to have been unfair to either party, future prices are adjusted to make up for these past imbalances (Wilson 1980). For example, an average price may have been negotiated at dockside, but the fish later resold for a very high price. The fisherman can expect the broker to share the windfall profits. In the same way, a dealer who

---

[4] One organizational theorist talks about "clan" industrial organization, where firms achieve high productivity through kinship-type role expectations (Ouchi 1980).

[5] Generalized reciprocity is defined as an exchange relationship balanced only in the long run, where the maintenance of the relationship is more important than any short-run gain and where the norm of the relationship is altruism (the parent-child relationship is exemplary). It is contrasted with balanced reciprocity, where the balance is calculated (but not too overtly) and where fair exchange is the norm (the relationship between business partners is an example). The other extreme is negative reciprocity, where selfishness with no attention to balance is the norm of the relationship. Exchanges between strangers —who will never meet again and whose behavior is not governed by altruistic goals— would be expected to fit in this category (Sahlins 1972).

pays a relatively high price at the shore but who can sell the fish for only very low prices will argue for a low price the next time to make up the shortfall. The possibilities for cheating and the need for trust in this situation are clear. (See Acheson 1985 for a case study of these issues in the Maine lobster market.)

I name this latter class of economic relationships "equilibrating" to call attention to these key features: the predominance of long- over short-run goals and the flexible, continuing process of reciprocating value in a relationship that is explicitly instrumental.[6] In some circumstances equilibrating relationships become so strong and regular (that is, formalized) that they are described as "trading partnerships." One of the most significant contributions of the economic anthropology of markets has been the analysis of such relationships in the markets of underdeveloped societies. Mintz provided the seminal description of these partnerships in Haiti, where they are known as *pratik*:[7]

A buying pratik who knows her selling pratik is coming will wait at the proper place and time, refusing to buy stock from others that she is sure her pratik is carrying. . . . [T]o the extent that her stock is committed in such arrangements a selling pratik will refuse to sell to others until she has met her pratik buyer. [Mintz 1961: 61]

This sort of behavior gives rise to the famous (probably apocryphal) story of the female market trader trudging to market on a dusty road with a heavy sack of produce on her head. A foreigner met her and offered a relatively enormous amount of money for the entire sack. She refused and continued on her way. Frustrated, the foreigner complained about the lack of economic sense in her behavior (and by extension, the behavior of all petty market traders): "They are more interested in socializing with their friends at market than they are in making a profit." The truth is that it would have been foolish for a trader to sacrifice a long-run business relationship (by disappointing a regular customer) for a one-time killing—assuming that in fact such a partner were waiting at the market.

Long-term trading partnerships are important mechanisms for reducing trading risks, and as such they are advantageous to both parties. Traders report many reasons for these relationships. The sellers' desire to stabilize and regularize their incomes and the buyers' wish to do the

---

[6] I use the term "equilibrating" rather than "reciprocal" for these intermediary modes to point to the balancing procedure that the back-and-forth transactions are aimed at. The term does not imply equilibrium in the conventional economic sense.

[7] Several economic anthropologists have studied similar trading relationships: of higglers in Jamaica (Katzin 1960), *Onibara* in Nigeria (Trager 1981), *Suki* in the Philippines (Szanton 1972; Davis 1973), and *clientes* in Guatemala (Swetnam 1978).

same for their value over the long run are fundamental. As Mintz concludes, "Those middlemen who make pratik state that they trade some part of their gain in return for long-range security, and some protection from the vagaries of the market" (1964: 262).

Elements of Exchange: Goods, Transactions, Actors

Why do some traders concentrate on security before income? Basically, because some exchanges are too risky to engage in without the extra security of personalized relationships. Risk exists because of faulty information in the three major components of exchanges: goods, meaning the things exchanged (including services for simplicity); transactions, referring to the rules, understandings, and procedures that pertain; and actors, meaning the people engaging in the exchange. The classic model of perfect competition is predicated on full information about goods, transactions, and actors. In the real world the information necessary for safe and sensible decisions is always imperfect and incomplete.

Goods

Goods possess multiple attributes, or qualities, about which a buyer must learn. It is important to distinguish two aspects of goods: "search" and "experience quality" (Nelson 1970). The former denotes obvious attributes—the style, size, or color in clothing, for example. The consumer's problem is to locate the preferred bundle of attributes in the market. "Experience quality" refers to those attributes revealed only through use, such as durability in clothing. The buyer's information problem is to find out any particular good's "experience quality" *before* purchase, when that quality is not apparent.

For example, a new car is high in "search" quality, since it is standardized. A buyer may assume that any given car of a particular make and model is the same as any other, and devote his or her time to searching out the best deal. But a used car is an "experience quality" good. It may be a normal specimen, or it may be a lemon. How is an average buyer to know?

Consider the plight of the seller of a used car in perfect condition. The seller knows that his car is worth more than most similar cars, but how does the buyer? Unless the seller can give accurate information about his unique automobile to the buyer, the latter will normally only offer an average price. (Because used cars are not standardized like new cars, the original equivalence of model and price no longer holds.)

The situation becomes worse as the used car market is flooded with lemons, or below-average cars, as Akerloff's influential work shows (1970). Because buyers cannot evaluate the cars as well as sellers, lemons can be sold as average cars for profit. The reasonable buyer who becomes familiar with the market will not offer more than the value of a lemon if he cannot evaluate each car. A seller of an average or superior car will be faced with accepting less than fair value or of not selling his car at all.

The problem is that the buyer and the vendor do not have the same information about the value of the good. Because the buyer cannot rely upon a standardized rule to assess value (as he can with new cars), he and the vendor must somehow agree upon a fair, accurate measure of the value of unique and variable goods.[8] Equilibrating relationships resolve this problem by extending the payment schedule (the quid pro quo) of each transaction in time so that problems can be adjusted. When the buyer discovers that the deal is not what he or she thought it was, the existence of the long-run relationship allows a renegotiation of the price. Others must rely on the seller's reputation in the community, spend the resources to evaluate the car on their own, take the risk of buying a lemon, or stay out of the market.

In more general terms, market performance is impaired; in fact, a market may cease to function without government intervention, in conditions of "asymmetrical imperfect information" (Spence 1976). This issue is relevant to the developing world, which much of economic anthropology studies, since most goods traded in traditional market systems are unstandardized and highly variable. Hence the problem of establishing value is crucial. Akerloff's contribution is to show that unequal information about variable goods is at the heart of the market problem. The solution chosen in most situations of cheap labor is to personalize the trade relationship so that equilibration can reduce the risks created by imperfect information.

Transactions

The information most relevant to a transaction is the price, the conditions of payment, and the probability that the transaction will be successfully completed. Knowledge of the price alone is not enough, since one must also know the context. Exchanges that occur under short-run profiteering conditions are obviously different from those where the terms of the transaction are in line with a long-run pattern. For example, the unreliable distribution of commodities to an underdevel-

---

[8] Note that the individual's problem of not having enough information to make a sensible decision translates into society's problem of the useless market, which brings sellers and buyers together who cannot agree upon a price.

oped area allows local monopolists to exploit the situation. When a delivery of sugar (or cooking oil, or some other good) fails to arrive at a hinterland town, the store owners may withdraw old stock from their shelves in order to mark it up or sell it "under the counter." Consumers with long-term relationships may buy at the normal price or may be assured of a supply in this circumstance. Automobile drivers in the United States learned this lesson in the gasoline shortages of the mid-1970's, when some drivers found it convenient to make off-hours appointments with their gasoline dealer to buy a tank of gas.

The rules that define payment include the specification of what things may be exchanged (cash, other valuables, services) and the time frame (immediate or deferred payment, credit charges, and so on). For example, long-distance itinerant traders I studied in Chiapas, Mexico, would sell their goods cheaply to hinterland Indian customers, from whom they would buy food and lodging. In the traders' minds, the lower income received for goods was worth the assurance of hospitality; for the Indians, the sowing of hospitality reaped cheaper manufactured goods and cultural brokerage (see the case study in Chapter 7).

These issues may seem irrelevant to transactions in the developed world. People in rich economies tend to assume that transactions will probably be completed as specified. Communities in the United States have small claims courts, Better Business Bureaus, and consumer protection agencies as support systems. Businessmen have all the legal protection they can buy. Compare that to the situation of the Mexican peddlers described above.

I found a similar example in a study of buyers of fresh produce on wholesale spot markets. The conditions under which they transact their business make it impossible to examine the entire lot of apples or oranges. They buy produce in the middle of the night, with strong social pressures to buy large quantities of boxed produce that cannot be inspected until unpacked at the point of retail sale. The best buyers are those who have efficient personal relationships with wholesalers. The wholesale vendors will not cheat them (or will cheat them less) because they know they will be relying upon each other for future deals (Plattner 1982, 1983).

In summary, problematic information about prices, payments, and probabilities increases risk in transactions. Some interpret this risk as a heavy cost to producers and assume that it is the major variable explaining the very existence of firms. This approach asks why firms choose to incorporate the production of intermediate goods rather than purchase them on a spot market. (Williamson 1981 has been very influential.) Consider the example of a restaurant deciding whether to bake its own bread or buy from a baker. The higher the cost of the transactions with the independent baker, the more attractive the employed baker becomes. Is the price of the bread seriously unpredictable? Will the baker sometimes insist upon cash payment and other times deliver on credit? (That is, are the conditions of payment not specifiable in advance?) And, perhaps worst of all, is the delivery not reliable? Imagine the problem of running a restaurant and not being sure of the price, quality, and quantity of bread available to you each day.[9]

Actors

Economists from Adam Smith to Milton Friedman have dreamed of a market where the smooth workings of competition ensure economic efficiency between faceless traders. But problems of information create incentives for people to know more than the nature of the goods and the transaction.

A well-known example of troublesome personal information concerns "adverse selection" in an insurance market. A vendor of dental insurance, for example, can set his rates by calculating the cost of fixing an average person's teeth. People with bad teeth will have incentives to sign up, since they expect heavy dental bills. The insurance, being predicated on the average need, will cost less than they expect to spend. People with good teeth may or may not sign up, depending upon their preference for insurance. But if the people with dental problems are overrepresented in the insurance company's clientele, then the insurer must raise the rates to cover the higher-than-average costs. The higher the rates, the less likely the healthy folks are to join, and the higher the proportion of expensive clients, bringing about even higher costs, and so on.

This is a problem of information, as Akerloff points out (1970: 493). The vendor of insurance does not know the likelihood that his insured population will claim benefits as well as the buyers do. Without accurate information about the personal characteristics of each client or some institutional support (like group rates or Medicare), the market will fail. This will leave people who want to buy insurance unable to deal with people who want to sell.

In circumstances of pervasive market ignorance, the most significant piece of information to know about a trader is what social category he

[9] Ouchi (1980) extends Williamson's analysis to discuss "clan" industrial organizations. His use of the term "clan" is loose, however. Oberschall and Leifer (1986) take a broad look at this sort of analysis, which they identify as the "new institutional economics." They doubt that "efficiency" is adequate as an explanation of social institutions, without analysis of power and goal ambiguities.

or she belongs to. In the extreme this may be a caste identity; otherwise, it may be a class, kinship, or social network affiliation. Knowing *who* a trader is may sometimes be the best way to know *what* he is buying or selling. Ben-Porath argues that specialization in identity can also create savings (1980). He generalizes Adam Smith's argument that specialization lowers costs because of returns to scale in production. The scale benefits exist when a significant part of the costs are "set-up" as opposed to production flow costs (the difference between a license to trade and a tax on sales). The Mexican peddlers' experience, described in Chapter 7, is an example of such costs. Once they learned who the trustworthy people were in that distant town, their next visits would be much more productive.

To summarize the argument so far, I have characterized economic exchanges on a continuum whose polar extremes are impersonal and personal modes of behavior. When information about important elements of exchanges is lacking, the impersonal mode of behavior (implying faceless traders and transactions without past or future) involves excessive risk and cost. Impersonality may not allow economic exchange if traders deal in goods high in experience quality, which can create a restricted, "lemons" market, if prices are variable and transactions are risky; or if traders are ignorant about important attributes of trading partners so that adverse selection is a problem. In such conditions, traders choose to invest their resources in establishing long-term relations with partners whose identity becomes a factor of economic value (if the government does not intervene to support the market).

The frequency of exchange (the Central Place order of the good, in terms defined in Chapter 7) is an important cause of equilibration. Exchanges that take place rarely may not be important enough to merit equilibration, whereas frequent exchanges allow the ongoing adjustment of values. The more significant the transaction costs, the larger the share of set-up over production flow costs; the more frequent the transaction, the more likely are traders to seek equilibrating relationships.[10]

In the next section I discuss how infrastructural poverty increases risks and costs.

---

[10] Oberschall and Leifer (1986) look at transactional efficiency as a cause of social institutions in general. They discuss the importance of *uncertainty*, meaning the costliness of knowledge about the goods; *frequency*, referring to the central place order of the goods (see Chapter 7), and *asset specificity*, meaning the investment necessary to engage in specialized transactions. High levels of uncertainty, frequency, and asset specificity motivate decision makers to invest in equilibrating relationships.

Market Infrastructure

One of the main differences between the developing and the developed world is in the wealth invested in the institutions that support economic exchange. Institutional poverty in communications, political control, transportation, and storage creates problems for buyers and sellers.

If there is no efficient communication network for news of the availability of goods to flow between producing, distributing, and consuming areas, then buyers and sellers must seek out those who have the relevant information and judge for themselves whether their sources are truthful or not. This process is obviously riskier the further one gets from a personal network.

If society is poorly integrated under one legal authority, so that contracts made between strangers in one area are not easily enforceable elsewhere, then anyone attempting to trade with someone outside his personal network will face some risk of loss.

For example, in 1968 I studied rural Ladino (non-Indian) traders in the Mayan Indian town of Bachajon, Chiapas, Mexico. They obtained their dry goods from the stores in the regional center of San Cristóbal, a three-day walk. The rural retailers were born in San Cristóbal, and the personal contacts that they had were the only reason they were provisioned from San Cristóbal rather than from other sources in the region. They knew that prices were lower in the state capital. But they could not afford to pay cash, and since they did not live in the capital, they had no credit with wholesalers there (Plattner 1975). Retailers also knew that factories in Mexico City sold merchandise more cheaply, but they could not afford the trip (by mule to the regional center and by bus to the capital, a one-way total of four travel days) and did not have the contacts needed to place their orders.[11]

If the state of roads, railways, and other avenues of transportation makes costs extraordinarily high, then poorer people will be priced out of the market. Likewise, if processing or storage facilities are not available to prolong the life of perishable items, then the variability of goods will be increased, as will the problems discussed above concerning being able to experience goods. The factors mentioned here heighten seasonal variation in agricultural goods and cause sporadic fluctuations in the supply of all goods not produced in a local area. Mintz describes the effects of this in Haiti, where

[11] By 1982, the economic development of the region had advanced such that goods were available by telegraph order from central Mexico or from large warehouses in the state capital.

distribution is likely to have a markedly irregular character. This unevenness is magnified when seasonal variation in the supply of various goods, and income, is often sharp. . . . Under such circumstances, pratik relationships stabilize sequences of dyadic economic transactions. Taken together, they afford greater order to the distributing system as a whole. [1961: 55]

Factors of Production: Cheap Labor and Scarce Capital

In markets where capital is expensive and labor cheap, the style of economic relationships requires a heavy input of time. Barbara Ward's seminal work has shown how the credit market in traditional societies is instituted on the need for personal relationships between creditors and debtors (1960). Ward shows that asymmetrical information about credit causes adverse selection, which is avoided by knowledge from personal relationships. Her work is important because she showed that a non-Western style of relationships was based upon familiar economic constraints.

In summary, the infrastructural problems that give rise to the need for equilibrating relationships also maintain a low value of labor and facilitate the process of specialization by identity. The "old-fashioned" style of business in many developing countries, where personal conversation and sociability circumscribe business relationships, has a clear basis in economic structure of (cf. Dannhaeuser 1979).

Conclusion

In socioeconomic environments rich in information, impersonal market relationships are suitable for goods high in "search" quality. The poorer the information, the higher the "experience" quality of the goods; the higher the transaction costs, the riskier the exchange and the more valuable an investment in personalized relationships.

This discussion has dealt with market societies, but the principles generalize to any economic exchange. A New Guinea tribesman seeking to barter feather plumes for shells must also be concerned with the risk that his transaction will fail. Healey (1984) studied exchanges among the Kundagai Maring of Papua New Guinea. This central highland tribe raised pigs and cultivated swidden gardens (see Chapter 3, this volume). They distinguished trade in material objects from "prestations" (Healey's term), which were explicitly concerned with human relationships. Bride wealth and death payments were the major forms of prestations. Trade took place between related or unrelated people and always took the form of barter, an exchange of object for object. How-

TABLE 8.1
Kundagai Maring Trading Patterns

	Relations between traders	
	Not related	Related
Exchange delayed	35	697
Exchange immediate	483	71
Total	518	768

SOURCE: Healey (1984).

ever, some trades were reciprocated immediately, while others were paid back later. Healey studied the trading histories of 58 adult men and hypothesized that whether the exchange was delayed or immediate was a function of the personal relationship between the traders. The data is reproduced in Table 8.1. Trade between nonrelatives was most often immediate, whereas the increased trust between relatives allowed trades to be delayed. The additional support of a kinship tie is relied upon to reduce the risk of default.

In many cases tribesmen seeking to exchange goods call unrelated persons by kin terms. This extension of kinship expectations to non-kin is built on relationships such as the fact that the traders' mothers were born in the same village. Healey notes that "the search for kinship ties between erstwhile strangers introduces moral principles that should obtain between the parties" (1984: 55). In other words, the lack of political integration between local communities increases the risk that traders will default, so individuals personalize their exchange relationships. Embedding such relationships in a kinship matrix lowers the risk because of the added moral sanction.

In this chapter I have shown how individuals struggle to get around problems of risky transactions by creating and using the personal networks available to them. The issues discussed here are part of a broad movement in social science called "socio-economics" (Etzioni 1988). Similar issues are discussed in legal studies, where the contract, instead of the transaction, is the focus (Macneil 1981). The approach taken here is to analyze the difference in economic behavior between societies as due to economic constraint and rational choice rather than to differences of cultural or economic values and goals. This is not meant to deny the importance of such differences, but to put them into perspective.

9

Marketing in Developing Urban Areas

Norbert Dannhaeuser

The Third World has changed dramatically since the concept of a "developing world" gained popularity after World War II. This is clear from the kinds of products people consume. Cigarettes and mass-produced textiles have been a worldwide phenomenon for a long time; carbonated soft drinks, though more recent, are today nearly as widespread; cassette players and radios can be found in many villages in countries as diverse as Brazil, India, and Nigeria; and the TV and VCR are becoming necessary status symbols to many peoples of the urban Third World. Imported and locally produced mass consumer goods are now an integral part of the consumption pattern of virtually all urban classes in developing countries.

Anthropologists are only beginning to study market institutions associated with mass consumerism in the Third World. This is partly because consumerism is a recent phenomenon in these societies and partly because it is a subject outside the traditional purview of their discipline. It is important for anthropologists to concern themselves with mass consumerism if they want to understand the cultural transformation Third World societies are currently undergoing. Another discipline, marketing, has since its beginning made consumerism its primary focus.

To economic anthropologists, marketing denotes the act of buying and selling commodities under competitive conditions in which relative value is determined by supply and demand. In the field of marketing, the concept has a more restricted meaning. According to the American Marketing Association, "marketing is the performance of business activities that direct the flow of goods and services from producer to consumer or user" (Kotler 1980: 9). Here, product distribution is emphasized.

A more normative definition states that "marketing is getting the right goods and services to the right people at the right place at the right time at the right price with the right communication and promotion" (ibid.). In this sense, marketing includes a conscious effort by the firm to package its products in such a way—through design, promotions, credit, special distribution channels—that it will perform effectively in a market. In addition to studying the subject, the field of marketing is also an applied discipline that for 70 years has argued that an active marketing orientation is necessary for firms to succeed in the mass consumer market.

The normative side of marketing is as removed from anthropology as the normative side of economics (see the discussion in Chapter 1). The discussion here will focus on the descriptive, analytical study of marketing.

Although much of the activity of the marketing discipline continues to be confined to developed economies, the application of marketing principles has also made its mark in the Third World. Hundreds of would-be and actual managers of consumer goods companies trading in developing countries pass through local and international marketing schools each year and later try to implement what they have learned. Market-oriented firms, often multinationals, force others, often local producers and distributors of industrial consumer goods, to adopt modern marketing methods to survive. The American-derived marketing credo has become an ideal in the corporate sector of the urban Third World.

The following discussion will cover four aspects of the marketing of industrial consumer goods in the urban Third World. First, the spread of consumer goods in these societies will be illustrated. Second, the structure of trade in Third World cities will be analyzed. Third, the market channel concept will be introduced to illuminate the process by which mass consumer goods find their way to consumers. Fourth, several detailed cases will be presented of aggressive marketing and of trade organizations engaged in consumer goods distribution.

The Diffusion of Industrial Mass Consumer Goods

In a recent study of mass markets in Malaysia, McGee (1985: 216) notes that during the 1970's "there has . . . been a sharp increase of motor vehicles which has become the leading edge of the growth of consumption of consumer durables." During this period, "a massive increase in advertising through television, newspapers and radio" took place "concentrating on the increase of purchase of products such as automobiles, houses, furniture, electronic products, clothing, cosmetics and food products such as fast foods often franchised by multinational companies" (ibid.). Malaysia is better off than many other developing countries because of its rubber, palm oil, and tin production, but mass consumer goods have also made significant inroads in less prosperous areas.

Walk the streets of any large city in the Third World and you will find almost the full range of mass consumer goods obtainable in Manchester, Hamburg, or Denver. Cars, motorcycles, polyester suits, canned goods, cameras, toothpaste, refrigerators, stereos, chewing gum, bicycles, watches—one can go on endlessly. They are all offered for the taking, provided one has the money. Who buys them?

Members of the wealthy upper class, of course, are important consumers of these items. But they are not the only ones. The middle class in India, for example, now numbers about 100 million mostly urban people, and it continues to grow. To members of this class, and to their counterparts in other less-developed countries, industrial consumer goods have become a necessity, convenience, and a status symbol. To continue with the Malaysian example, "status appears to be the name of the game in the rise of fast food popularity. In Malaysia, where a car sticker bearing the name of an overseas university can open doors, and where office workers plunk down a month's wages to buy a belt with a designer buckle, chomping American burgers and guzzling root beer helps prompt the wished for man about town image" (quoted in McGee 1985: 210).

The low-income sectors of urban populations are also involved. Even if they obtain fewer and cheaper items, they are also closely bound to the industrial consumer goods economy. Writing about São Paulo, Brazil, Roberts notes that "canned and other processed 'convenience' foods become an element in the diet of poor families when the wife or other female family members work outside the home" (1978: 113). In addition to necessity, convenience, enjoyment, and prestige also play a part, and a substantial proportion of the household budget of all but the very destitute is allocated to commodities from the industrial sector. In Lima, Peru, for instance, 75 percent of the factory workers' family spending is in industrial consumer products (including packaged foods), while studies in cities like São Paulo and Rio de Janeiro show how the urban working class uses available credit to purchase televisions, refrigerators, radios, and electrical or gas stoves (ibid.; cf. Cunningham et al. 1974). A study in Pakistan showed the penetration of VCRs:

At the Gulberg market in Lahore there is one place where the widest range of the city's social classes gather in the evening. Milkmen, unemployed youth, rich housewives, students, bureaucrats, and construction workers pour in and out of the some 20 video-cassette lending libraries. For just Rs 20 (U.S. $1.25) they can hire the very latest Hollywood thriller or Bombay musical. In Karachi, where there are thousands of video-cassette lending libraries, the price is often as little as Rs 10 for a night's viewing. [Rasheed 1986: 54]

The incorporation of urban households into the mass consumer market has been accompanied by a parallel development in local trading facilities. Most industrial consumer goods can be found alongside more traditional ones in marketplaces, bazaars, neighborhood stores, general merchandise stores, and similar outlets that have a long history in Third World societies. But new institutions, often specializing in mass consumer goods, are spreading. In medium-sized market towns throughout much of the Third World, wholesale and retail services have appeared that are very familiar to the Western eye. These include gasoline stations, appliance stores, boutiques, textile stores, small multistoried department stores, and small supermarkets. Finance companies secure installment purchases for consumers, stores are packed with promotional material, and a number of wholesale and retail outlets are branches or exclusive dealerships of large consumer goods companies.

All of these trappings of mass consumerism, and more, also exist in the large metropolitan centers of the Third World. In 1977, Kuala Lumpur, Malaysia, had 11 supermarkets, Manila 32, Bangkok 35, and Djarkarta, Indonesia, 10 (Kaynak 1982: 55–57). Full-fledged department stores with a wide selection of merchandise organized along product lines are common in most large cities. In 1969, credit cards entered on a large scale in São Paulo, and by 1972 consumers could choose from ten bank cards (Cunningham et al. 1974: 2). Shopping centers and malls have sprung up in response to suburbanization and to accommodate the rising middle class in cities such as Manila, Bangkok, Damascus, Jidda (Saudi Arabia), and Mexico City. Finally, there is advertising. By means of newsprint, radio, posters, point-of-sale displays, and commercial TV, Third World urban consumers are subjected to intense sales messages. By the mid-1980's at least $10 billion was being spent annually on consumer goods advertising in the Third World alone.[1]

Europe, America, and Japan saw the spread of industrial consumer goods and the rise of mass markets some time ago, and it is helpful to understand their experience. In England, for example, the mass market was encouraged in the late nineteenth century by the following developments: (1) growth in the number of customers, (2) increasing disposable income, (3) growing literacy rate, (4) improved transporta-

---

[1] This figure is based on an extrapolation of trends published in World Advertising Expenditures (1981), and it does not include Singapore, Hong Kong, Taiwan, and South Korea.

tion and communication, (5) innovations in consumer goods marketing (department stores, advertising), and (6) "growing differences between the bourgeoisie and the working classes that created an ideological environment in which advertising would utilize status as an important promotion style in creating demand for mass products" (McGee 1985: 211; cf, Dawson 1979: 154–66). Fundamental to all of this were the creation of a large class of urban wage workers, the separation of the family from the production process so that the family became mainly a consumption unit in which new wants could be constantly created, and the appearance of a manufacturing sector geared to mass production to reach economies of scale.

Similar changes are taking place in the Third World today. The urban population has recently increased dramatically; disposable income has grown, even if only haltingly in some areas; internal communication and links with the outside world have multiplied; and the status-giving character of industrial consumer goods is hardly questioned. In some cases—such as South Korea and Taiwan, and to a lesser degree in Brazil and Mexico—this has been accompanied by considerable industrialization. At the same time it must be noted that in many regions of the Third World, especially in Africa and Asia, the urban population, though increasing in absolute terms, still includes only a minority of people. In India, for example, only 23 percent of the population was urban in 1980; this compares with over 70 percent in much of Latin America. Furthermore, most of the industry that has appeared since World War II in the developing world is limited in that it mainly assembles imported components, surviving only because of protective tariff walls.

To simplify a complex situation, it is mainly with respect to industry that the West and Japan are different from the developing countries. In the former case, the foundation for mass consumerism was created through genuine industrialization, whereas in the latter case the mass market is based on the importation or local assembly of imported consumer goods rather than upon their production. In other words, most Third World countries differ from the Western model with respect to production, or industrialization, while they are becoming similar with respect to marketing and consumption services. A cultural uniformity is appearing in the Third World patterned largely on material consumption traditions first developed in the West. "The essential qualities of consumption and circulation are becoming similar throughout the Third World, a similarity most obvious in the built environments, transport and life styles of the cities, but also increasingly a feature of the countryside" (McGee 1985: 210).

Many people concerned with development consider the spread of industrial mass consumerism and aggressive marketing in the Third World a negative phenomenon. To them, it undermines the morally defined economic arrangements among subsistence producers; it re-inforces relations of dominance and dependence between those who produce and distribute and those who consume; it destroys local cultural autonomy and diversity; and it encourages those who can least afford to do so—peasants and the urban poor—to squander scarce resources on inessentials (Beals 1975: 281; Dholakia and Sherry 1987: 137; McGee 1985: 216–19; Scott 1976). We will not argue about the pros and cons of mass consumerism in the Third World. The task, instead, is to recognize the importance of this phenomenon and to understand the institutions and processes associated with it.

Third World Urban Commercial Structure

Describing conditions in market towns in India, one observer notes that

to the occasional visitor, middle-range cities contain a bewildering variety of economic activities. Often the first glimmering of the city's economic life is encountered at the railroad station or bus stand, typically congested with tea stalls, sweet shops and rickshaw drivers. Turning to the streets of the bazaar . . . one finds, for example, bicycle sales shops and bicycle mechanics, small-scale metal workers who manufacture trunks and agricultural implements, the shops of medical practitioners and dispensers of medicine, cloth shops and brass shops, tailors and dry cleaners, radio repair shops and shops labelled simply 'general merchandise,' gold merchants and grain merchants. . . . Both traditional consumer goods and luxury goods of more recent origin can be found. [Hazlehurst 1968: 540]

On a more general level, referring to "the teeming metropolises of lesser developed countries," Smith paints the following picture:

Streets are crowded with vehicles of all kinds carrying people and goods; vendors roam the sidewalks seeking customers for such items as cooked foods, ballpoint pens and wrist-watches; modest little speciality shops selling cloth, local handicraft products etc. stand cheek by jowl with large department stores and supermarkets more characteristic of western cities; and there are few cities without at least one large market or bazaar where locally grown fruit and vegetable products (as well as other local and imported goods) are offered for sale in a more traditional context. [1978: 113]

These descriptions, though rich in detail, picture only what is visible in urban trade. Wholesalers, commissioned agents, company salesmen, distributors, import firms, local factory producers, not to mention the channels that bind them all together, largely remain hidden from the visitor's view. Yet without this supply backup, urban retail trade would wither. These descriptions, however, do suggest that commerce in these communities has a particular structure. Two models have been constructed to summarize this structure.

The Dual Model

The most popular model of urban commerce in developing economies assumes that it is composed of two parts. When first suggested, the model distinguished between the "bazaar" type versus the "firm" type in a Javanese town (Geertz 1963). This dichotomy has since been refined into the concepts of "unorganized" versus "organized" sectors, "informal" versus "formal" sectors, and "lower" versus "upper" circuits (Santos 1979; Sethuraman 1976).[2] The terms used are not so important, but the notion that the Third World urban economies are divisible into two components is.

In the informal sector, enterprises operate on a small scale in unregulated and competitive markets, use labor-intensive and "adapted" (that is, old, remade, pieced-together) technologies. Entry into a market is comparatively easy since little capital is needed and the work force usually comes from the family. Workers are often household residents who work irregular hours, and the scale of operations is "microscopic" (Hackenberg 1980; Sethuraman 1976). Most important, the informal sector operates without any public or organized large-scale insurance protection.

The formal sector has the opposite characteristics. Formal training is often required to enter, enterprises are large and capital intensive, corporate kinds of organizations are typical, formal management techniques prevail, and connections with national and international institutions are profound. In a nutshell, "economic activities of the *upper circuit* are banking, export trade, modern industry, modern services, wholesaling, and some forms of transportation (shipping and airlines). The *lower circuit* consists of noncapital intensive industry, services, and trading" (McGee 1974: 5).

This classification uses two dimensions to group economic activities: wealth and size on the one hand, and the manner of operation on the other. These dimensions do not always coincide, but in most cases they do. The larger the enterprise and the more capital intensive it is, the more connections with public institutions it will have, and the

[2] Though these concepts have slightly different meanings, no distinctions will be made between them here. For convenience and because it is most popular, the "formal/informal" concept will be used throughout this chapter.

more bureaucratic its operations are likely to be (for example, department stores and supermarkets versus market stalls and neighborhood stores). This dual model points out the fact that enormous income disparities prevail in Third World cities and that large, capital-intensive and bureaucratically organized firms exist side by side with small, poor family firms.

The Tripartite Model

Another way to model urban commerce is to focus on enterprise types. We will define a tripartite division that recognizes an intermediary enterprise type that incorporates aspects of both the formal and informal sectors.

First, and most numerous, are the individual enterprises. They are comprised of craft workers active on their own account, street traders and service workers (peddlers, messengers, food vendors, public letter writers), casual construction workers, and underground occupations (professional beggars, prostitutes). Most of them work on the street, except for the handicraft workers, who labor at home. They account for about 25 to 40 percent of the labor force, of which 5 to 15 percent are "unemployed." Although some of these activities can give an adequate return (for example, hawking and craft production), most members of this enterprise sector are poor. Job specialization, temporary engagement, and hustling for jobs characterize individual enterprises. With constant immigration and ease of entry, "the available work is spread among the largest possible number of workers at the expense of income which is not only very low but frequently intermittent" (Friedmann and Sullivan 1974: 392–93; see also Fook 1983: 743; Nattrass 1987). This is an important part of the explanation for the large number of stationary and mobile petty traders gracing the urban Third World.

The second sector is defined as family enterprises. It is distinguished from the one above by a higher degree of organization, fixed abodes, and more capital per worker. Family enterprises are divided into trade/service establishments and manufacturing workshops, and 35 to 45 percent of the urban labor force is employed by them. Trade and service include small shop proprietors and market stall vendors, neighborhood store operators, salesmen in small businesses, barbers, restaurant workers, and garage mechanics (Friedmann and Sullivan 1974: 394). It also includes the fixed, family-owned street stores with two or three employees that under colonial conditions—less so today—were often operated by aliens (Chinese in Southeast Asia, Indians in East Africa). Today they continue to be an important intermediary institution, even in small towns (see, for example, O'Connor 1983: 155).

Capital-intensive businesses, the government, and the professions make up the final component, the corporate enterprise sector. Workers are found in bureaucratic organizations, tend to be legally protected, and manage highly capital-intensive equipment. This sector is made up of blue- and white-collar workers (for instance, sales personnel in supermarkets). About 10 to 30 percent of all workers belong to it. Topping corporate enterprises are the owner-entrepreneurs, middle-level professionals, and the elite, who make up 5 to 10 percent of the labor force (Friedmann and Sullivan 1974: 395–97).

Relations Between the Sectors

Aside from being useful as summaries of complex conditions, models have their dangers, one of which is reification—turning a mental abstraction into a real thing. In the case of the sectoral model, as the tripartite as well as the dual models will be called, the danger is that the commercial sectors are seen as closed and fixed, like so many layers of cake. If that is the image that this model conveys, then it distorts reality. Third World city economies are dynamic and ever changing, and the sectors that our model identifies are closely linked.

First, there are two different ways in which the informal and formal sectors relate to one another. On the one hand, the sectors can operate parallel to one another as systems that are at times in symbiosis, at other times in competition with one another. The important functional issue is whether capital accumulation and development are possible in the informal sector. The informal sector may be an essential but traditional element of the urban economy in which capital accumulation is possible. On the other hand, the relation can be less egalitarian. The informal sector may form a reserve labor pool for corporate enterprises or be composed of risk-bearing agents serving formal sector firms. Under this condition, wealth accumulation is difficult in the informal sector, which is subordinate to, shaped by, and dependent on the formal sector (Davies 1979; Hackenberg 1980).

This difference is nicely illustrated in Africa. In towns that had a vigorous commercial life predating the colonial imposition—for example, Ibadan (Nigeria), Khartoum (Sudan), and Addis Ababa (Ethiopia)—the first, development-oriented relationship between sectors dominates (O'Connor 1983; cf. Trager 1985). In colonial cities—such as Lusaka (Zambia) and Nairobi (Kenya)—the informal sector is indeed subservient to and dependent on the formal one. It is important to remember that elements of both relations coexist in most Third World cities.

Second, the components of Third World urban commerce interpenetrate one another. There is a constant exchange of personnel, products, and finance between them, not to mention of information in the form of advertising and other communication. The distributive trade of consumer goods shows this better than any other activity. Today's hawker may have been yesterday's sales clerk in a supermarket, today's marketplace vendor may be tomorrow's owner of a street store, and the contemporary giant drug store chain may have seen its origin 40 years ago in a humble family retail store. Many traders stay in the same enterprise sector for their lives, but others move from one sector to another.

Products pass over compartmental boundaries with ever increasing ease. Some time ago it was true that individual and family enterprises handled mainly nonstandardized traditional products. Today, with the exception of produce, inventory of most trade establishments is largely derived from industry. From what source does the neighborhood store trader obtain, for example, Carnation milk? Ultimately from a large import house or an assembly plant of a multinational corporation. The family enterprise usually serves as the connecting link between corporate and individual enterprises, although the product channel has become even more direct during recent years, as will be shown below. Channels of distribution are undermining the autonomy of the urban commercial sectors.

The same is true for finance. Money moves products and people throughout the urban economy, and credit facilitates the process in all sectors. For corporate enterprises, money and credit sources are institutional—banks and other formal financial enterprises. Much of the money and credit needs of family and individual enterprises is covered by local and personal sources, in the main by kin. However, here connections exist also. Intermediary family enterprises often use banking facilities to maintain checking accounts and to obtain short-term cash loans. The link is far more important in the case of product credit. Usually it runs downward along a product channel: Large corporate enterprises extend product credit to wholesalers, who finance sales to retailers, who may sell on consignment to street peddlers.

Third World urban commerce can be depicted by means of a sectoral model, but the borders between the sectors are porous to say the least, and market channels are one of the major institutions that provide a link between them, contributing to their survival and transformation.

Market Channels

"The set of all the firms and individuals that cooperate to produce, distribute, and consume the particular good or service of a particular producer" is a market channel (Kotler 1980: 47–48). Who is included in market channels? Producers, insofar that they are engaged in selling; merchant middlemen (traders who take title to goods); and agent middlemen (brokers and others who do not take title). Facilitators and marketing firms, such as warehouses, banks, and advertising agencies, are also part of the channel because they assist in the distribution of products. Finally, there are the consumers, the provisioning of whom is the central function of market channels.

Types of Channels

Channels have a structure, a system of internal domination, and strategies that members pursue. Channel structure refers to the number of trade levels that exist between the producer and consumer and to the size, number, and types of firms that exist on each level. Channels in which products pass through a large number of trade levels and in which each level contains a multiplicity of different firms are said to be complex and vertically fragmented.

Channel domination refers to the degree to which one firm or a set of firms dominates or influences other members along a channel. In vertically fragmented channels, also called conventional channels, power is typically spread throughout the trade hierarchy, and no member dominates the system. Structurally these channels tend to be complex. Coordinated or vertically integrated channels, by contrast, exhibit some power concentration. In their case, either manufacturers, middlemen, or consumers control the overall operation of the channel, and power to influence extends beyond the channel level of the dominant member.

The last dimension is the marketing strategy adopted by channel members (see Dannhaeuser 1983 for details). Because we are interested in distributive channels—institutions responsible for the movement of goods from producer to final consumer—and not in assembly channels, marketing strategies in this context involve the manner in which firms dispose of their products and what auxiliary tools, such as advertising, they employ to do so. Several types are distinguishable. There is first the passive strategy. In this case sellers, be they producers or traders, sit back and wait for customers. Beyond offering a certain range of goods at certain prices, suppliers make no overt or covert effort to reach out to customers. This strategy, fostered where a seller's market (or supply scarcity) prevails, is usually associated with conventional channels in which a low degree of power concentration exists.

A variant form of the passive strategy, one that may be difficult to document because it is also common in conventional channels, is the semipassive mode. Sellers seek to attract customers by means that go beyond price and product availability, and they do so by offering private deals based on personal relations and trust. They behave as if they were not actively seeking an outlet for their products, but covertly they do so by offering personal services confidentially. These services include special credit privileges, unannounced (unpublished) price discounts, "baker's dozen," availability of scarce products to preferred customers, and so on. Insecurity breeds this strategy, and it is often encountered among ethnic minorities that control trade along a channel.

Aggressive marketing can be pursued by traders in a more open manner. If they do so, they are said to engage in active marketing and to promote channel coordination. Hawkers that move from city ward to city ward in search of customers practice active marketing. So do market stall vendors in retail textile marketplaces who call out to passersby and offer soft drinks to promising customers who linger at their stalls and fondle the cloth. Also large retail outlets practice it when they arrange displays attractively, allow self-service, offer credit cards, and advertise in newspapers. Of special interest to us, however, are the active strategies followed by consumer goods suppliers further up the channel hierarchy—manufacturers, distributors, and large wholesalers.

There are three principal ways in which active marketing is organizationally realized. The first does not affect the channel structure directly; the other two do so by vertically integrating it. In "sales penetration," suppliers reach down the channel levels by sending itinerant salesmen to take orders from, and deliver to, wholesale and retail customers in a region. This allows the supply company to bypass lower trade levels and to establish direct contacts with smaller customers at little cost and with minimal disruption of the existing channel structure. "Contractual penetration" and "ownership penetration" affect the structure more. In the former strategy, members extend their control across trade levels through contractual means; in the latter strategy they do so by buying themselves into different levels. In contractual penetration, manufacturers and large trade companies appoint retail franchisees to handle their products, and retail branching is the most common organizational form that ownership penetration takes. Both strategies result in vertical channel integration and indicate a condition wherein power is concentrated in the hands of few members.

Channel Evolution

This typology is more than a classification. There is also a dynamic element involved, for it also reflects a progression in channel evolution as an economy expands and matures. In the industrial West, especially in America, there has been a trend toward channel coordination in many product lines. As large firms have sought to extend their influence over the distribution of their products, channel control has become prevalent. Nowadays channel dominance by retailers, manufacturers, or consumer groups is common; vertical integration is a widespread phenomenon spelling the decline of the wholesaler in many lines; and active marketing is the norm of virtually all large consumer goods companies.

What explains this shift toward active marketing? As the American industrial economy expanded and a market for mass consumer goods became a possibility, consumer goods firms faced a number of constraints that led them toward channel integration and active marketing: increasing capital requirements and high fixed costs; declining profits and rates of return on investments; growing complexity and insecurity of the distribution process; a need to rapidly relocate product availability regionally; and the growing economies of scale gained through integrated channels (McCammon and Bates 1967: 290–91). Add to this the demonstration effect, which leads firms to copy those successful in active marketing, and the trajectory toward channel coordination was given. The possibility of a mass market at the turn of the century initiated this development, but once it was on its way, the more aggressive sales behavior and new channel organizations made the mass consumer market a reality.

In the urban Third World, industrial consumer goods channels have changed in the same direction, although developments there have not gone as far as in the West. Although in America during recent decades marketing power has shifted in many cases from the upper channel levels (from manufacturers and wholesalers) to lower ones (for example, to retail chains), in developing countries large manufacturers and wholesalers continue to dominate distribution channels. Also Third World consumer goods manufacturers are only beginning to allow marketing to become the basic orientation around which their entire business revolves, a condition that U.S. companies reached some 30 years ago. Personal contacts between firms along channels continue to be very important in the Third World because of cultural preferences, limited availability of modern communication facilities, and less security. This makes the itinerant company field man a more important figure there than in the West. Finally, compared to developed economies, the spread of the active marketing mode in the Third World has been influenced even more by the demonstration effect. For some time local entrepreneurs have adopted sales methods that have worked in the Western consumer market, and they have applied what they have learned in local or overseas business schools. Through this, aggressive marketing that promotes mass consumerism has become part of the corporate culture in the urban Third World, and predictions about channel evolution have been turned into self-fulfilling prophecies.

Channel Congruence

Market channels change because of internal as well as environmental factors. The concept of congruence between trade levels helps make this clear. The concept also reminds us that consumer goods channels often traverse the formal/informal sectoral divide that characterizes Third World urban economies.

Market channels can be classified according to whether firms on different trade levels are organized in a similar manner. Are they all family concerns, or are some family and some individually operated units? Is their business organization arranged according to bureaucratic management principles, or is it the result of adjustments to family needs? Organizational noncongruence is common if the channel runs from the formal to the informal commercial sector. However, interlevel conflict and change need not result from this. Formal sector corporate suppliers may want to deal with informal sector small outlets; others, though, may want to change, substitute, or bypass them. Organizational noncongruence therefore can be complementary or contradictory. Only in the latter case is the channel likely to change.

The channel concept is important because it allows one to trace commercial connections that exist not only within any of the city economic sectors but, even more importantly, between them. This is necessary if one wants to understand the organizational means by which mass consumer goods of the corporate sector find their way into other sectors and to the ultimate consumer, whether rich or poor, urban or rural. The next section will flesh out this discussion by presenting several ethnographic examples of aggressive marketing and by analyzing some of the institutions associated with Third World urban commerce.

Cases

What does active marketing of industrial consumer goods in the Third World mean in practice? (See Dannhaeuser 1987a.) For one, it means that companies make an effort to adapt their products to local conditions. Take the case in the Philippines of *tengi*—that is, the buying of items in very small units by especially poor consumers. Colgate was one of the first companies to try marketing shampoo in *tengi* form by providing shops with containers and dispensers. Rural customers were then urged to keep a small Colgate bottle, and for 20–30 centavos they could fill it with a measure of concentrate that, diluted, gave them half a bottle of shampoo. The attempt succeeded, and "today, every shampoo in the Philippines is marketed in rural areas in 'tengi' form" (Blauvelt 1982: 58), a fact also true among retailers serving poor consumers in urban areas.

Promotions to consumers by large companies have increased, and some reach even into villages. In Thailand, for example, a manufacturer of dry cell batteries sends trucks into the countryside to supply small retailers. They are also "fitted for showing a free program of movies in the evening in those towns and villages which have no theatre. . . . Between reels in the film, flashlights or transistor batteries are sold at retail from the side of the truck to the spectators" (Anderson 1970: 76–77).

Just as important, but less visible, is that wholesalers and retailers on the lower channel levels are encouraged by large suppliers to pursue active marketing strategies themselves. For example, in South India during the 1960's a passive "take or leave it" attitude prevailed in chemical fertilizer distribution. This changed as supplies became more available. Today, fertilizer companies supply technical literature to dealers, and they offer training to the town-based sales representatives. Some companies even provide soil tests to customers through their dealers. Backed by companies, dealers increasingly offer a package of services that goes beyond just selling. They practice marketing acording to the definition of the American Marketing Association.

Some mass consumer concerns are extremely large affairs, and their sales network reaches far down the channel, covering a large proportion of potential customers. San Miguel Co. of the Philippines, the license holder of Coca-Cola, illustrates this. Maintaining sixteen bottling plants in the country, San Miguel uses its 1,000-plus trucks to deliver soft drinks to some 150,000 stores, most of them neighborhood stores. Pangasinan, a province north of Manila with a population of 1.6 million and with 12,000 stationary retail establishments, most of them urban, is served by twenty company trucks. Each covers 300 retail customers a week, and in larger towns retailers are visited even twice a week. All in all, through its 40 field men San Miguel contacts 4,000 to 6,000 retailers in Pangasinan every week, which is about half of all stores. Pepsi's marketing setup does not lag far behind.

The sales organization of these companies is combined with a promotional strategy in which those retailing Coke and Pepsi are encouraged to display the respective brand logo on company-financed billboards that also announce the store's name. These metropolitan companies —cigarette manufacturers are another example—have used the traditional individual enterprise type—the neighborhood store—for some time as a key outlet for their products, and by means of this they have spread the imagery of modern consumerism throughout the urban and much of the rural Philippines.

Trade Between a Metropolis and a Secondary City

To illustrate more systematically the kinds of marketing strategies that large consumer goods companies follow in the urban context, it is useful to look at a case of interurban trade between a metropolis and a secondary city. Nasik, an Indian market town with a population of 260,000 located 160 km northeast of Bombay, will serve as an example. This case also shows how marketing institutions responsible for mass consumer goods have penetrated into communities beyond Third World metropolitan centers (see Dannhaeuser 1987b for more details).

Until the early 1950's, companies handling provisions, drugs, and other packaged consumer goods relied on two channel organizations to reach into Nasik. In one of them, Nasik's merchant wholesalers traveled to Bombay to place orders while the supply side remained passive. This arrangement continues to be important in the textile and hardware trade today, and 20 to 30 percent of provisions still enter Nasik through this conventional channel.

The second method involved a more active participation of suppliers. Companies in large cities sent field men to Nasik who contacted those wholesalers and store retailers who could place sufficiently large orders. It was left up to the Nasik customers to dispose of the product any way they wished. An open market reigned supreme, while sales penetration gave suppliers some control over distribution.

Since then, a formally appointed wholesale level composed of what are locally called "stockists" appeared in Nasik. These are wholesale dealers who, in exchange for steady supply and a commission from the metropolitan principal firm, shoulder the cost of selling. Relations vary between Nasik stockists and the supply companies that appoint them. Some stockists handle the company goods only on commission, while others obtain title to the goods; some are not allowed to carry competing lines, others are permitted to do so. All of them, however, are expected to provide warehousing for the principal, to help finance sales by extending some credit to retailers in their area, and to assist in the marketing of the company products. The last expectation means that some stockists engage in their own sales penetration of Nasik down to the neighborhood store and vendor.

In the metropolis, the size of the supply companies corresponds to the size and complexity of the stockist system. Some of these are elaborate affairs. Large companies may have several thousand stockists and several depots from which to serve them throughout the country. Hindustan Lever, for example, the largest soap and toiletries company in India, has 4,000 stockists in as many urban areas in India (one of them in Nasik) through which it reaches some 700,000 retailers (out of some 2 million) in the country.

Such companies also have an elaborate in-house marketing organization supporting the stockist setup. Headed by a marketing manager, it consists of dozens of supervisors and hundreds of field men, who help stockists collect orders. To return to Hindustan Lever, each product line (toiletries, foods, animal feeds, detergents) is treated as a profit center, and general sales managers are assigned to them. Each of these divisions is also represented by area sales managers, who are attached to each of the company branches in Bombay, Delhi, Calcutta, and Madras. Together, they formulate promotional strategies and sales tactics. For any area sales manager there are one to two supervisors who coordinate the activities of field salesmen and watch their performance. There are about ten field men per supervisor so that some 600-plus company field men keep the company informed about the market and lubricate the relation between headquarters and the subwholesale and retail customers.

Retail franchising is a practical channel arrangement for those companies interested in active marketing. It assures company control over retailers by contractually specifying store layout, what retailers can sell, prices they can charge, and the business organization of the franchise holder. At the same time, the store trader is, from a legal standpoint, an independent merchant who is expected to shoulder the stocking and selling costs. He is similar to stockists, except that he caters to consumers rather than retailers. Franchise holders, in turn, find the managerial help provided by the principal of advantage, as well as the exclusive use of a nationally known brand name and steady supply.

Singer Sewing Machines, under the name of Merritt, appointed a franchise dealer in Nasik in the 1950's. Since then, appliance and motor vehicle manufacturers and several textile mills have entered the town in this fashion, and today about 60 franchised retail dealerships exist in Nasik. All are expected to provide modern display space for the company products. The management of the businesses is monitored by the principal, and in the case of appliances and motor vehicles, repair service has to be offered. A number of franchisors also insist that their dealers handle only products of the company, that is, to be product exclusive. Some dealers maintain subdealers in lower order towns in

Nasik's environs, thus in effect combining wholesaling and retailing and extending contractual penetration of the supply companies further into the hinterland.

Although sales and contractual penetration of Nasik by metropolitan companies is common today, retail branching is not. The gasoline trade is one of the few examples, although even in this case companies do not employ local personnel themselves. Instead, company-owned stations are leased to local interests, and the leaseholders (the retail dealers) do the hiring. During the 1950's and 1960's, intensive competition between the major oil companies in India led all of them to open full-line service stations in Nasik. Vertical channel integration was tight, with brand exclusivity strictly enforced and display and operations carefully defined by the companies. By the early 1970's, gasoline distribution into Nasik reached a standard not far removed from that existing in the West.

Since then, accompanied by the oil crisis in the 1970's, all oil companies in India were nationalized. This did not change the structure of the channel; however, what did change was the marketing strategy of the nationalized industry. It became passive. A monopoly over supply made this possible, with the result that no new stations have been added and that the existing ones have been allowed to decay. In this case active marketing, ample supplies, and the international example combined to create ownership penetration by the gasoline companies of Nasik. Once established, however, monopolistic interests prevented the channel structure from fragmenting after passive marketing became the mode—to the detriment of the consumer.

The Bata India Company (shoes) is an unusual case. Together with the Indian-owned Carona Sahu Company (also shoes), Bata maintains some of the very few genuine retail branches of consumer goods companies in Nasik. For a long time the Toronto-based multinational corporation has shown an inclination to be innovative in marketing throughout the world. In Nasik the Indian subsidiary opened a retail branch in 1956, later adding another one; Carona also has two stores in the town —this out of 1,100 branch stores Bata has in India and 300 operated by Carona.

These are completely company-owned establishments, with personnel, including the manager, employed by the company. Local autonomy is minimized as district managers keep a close look over the operations of the branches. One result is that kinship plays not even a hidden role in these enterprises, a fact rare in Nasik. Frequent inventory control, fixed prices, innovative store layout, and formal incentives and training for branch managers indicate that a progressive merchandising policy prevails.

However, there is more to the distributive setup of Bata and Carona than the branch system—backed by mass advertising and various promotions—suggests. Recognizing the considerable wealth differences of urban consumers in India, branches are designed to cater mainly to the upper- and middle-income brackets; the lower levels are served with a different and cheaper brand of shoes through company-appointed stockists who supply most of Nasik's 50-odd independent shoe retailers. Here the companies realize channel control and marketing flexibility by using two channel organizations, a strategy that maximizes the range of consumers they can cover.

The Supply Channel as Determinant of Urban Retail Structure

The structure of retailing in Third World cities is mainly caused by the economic characteristics of the consumers served, the underemployed individuals pressing into trade, the product types handled, and the competition between retailers. The structure of supply also plays a role. Channels of manufactured consumer goods leave their imprint on those urban retail establishments, whether part of the formal or informal sector, which are the main source of mass consumer products for the general population. This is made clear if Nasik is compared with a similar second-order town in the Philippines, Dagupan. This community has a population of 100,000 and is located 200 km north of Manila (see Dannhaeuser 1985).

How does the retail structure of Nasik and Dagupan compare? First, the proportionate importance of modern trade establishments is greater in Dagupan than in Nasik.[3] In Nasik, 140 modern street stores can be found (84 of them branches and franchises of companies), which is 9 percent of all stores in the town, and they are responsible for 30 percent of turnover of all street stores. In Dagupan there are 175 modern stores (80 branches and franchises), which is 35 percent of all stores, and 49 percent of the total turnover passes through them. Second, innovative retail organizations have made greater inroads in Dagupan than Nasik. In Dagupan a number of supermarkets, superettes, and small department stores are found, all of which are absent in Nasik. Moreover, dozens of itinerant salesmen and tipsters who search for orders in Dagupan and beyond are attached to the city's appliance, hardware, and motor vehicle dealers, whereas dealers of these product lines in Nasik rely less on this help.

The final difference refers to the informal sector. In both communities

[3] These are stores with modern physical features (air conditioning, display cases, glass windows, and so on) and ones that carry modern products. Many, but by no means all, are also operated according to modern management techniques.

a large proportion of provisions and other packaged household goods find their way to consumers by way of neighborhood stores—*sari-sari* stores in Dagupan and *kirana* stores in Nasik. In Nasik, though, they are less numerous in relation to the size of the trade community (30 percent of all stores) and less significant in turnover (8 percent of non-marketplace store sales) than in Dagupan, where the respective ratios are 68 and 13 percent. In other words, Dagupan's consumers are more exposed to retail outlets that are closely associated with mass consumer goods than those in Nasik.

What explains these differences? Channels penetrating the two communities from higher order cities constitute the most immediate factor. More removed, but no less real, is the wider socioeconomic context. Channels do not exist in isolation but are part of a particular social, economic, and political setting. They do influence this context, but more so, they are an expression of it. In the Philippines, the environment has encouraged consumer goods companies to enter into aggressive marketing and downward channel control, whereas in India circumstances have almost had the opposite effect.

First, the size and complexity of the two countries differ. Companies wanting to cover the urban markets nationally in India will find that they have to mobilize far more resources than if they would do the same in the Philippines. Also the cultural plurality is less extreme in the Philippines. In India, caste, religious, linguistic, class, and tribal identities make up a mosaic far more complex than in the Philippines. Compare Dagupan with Nasik. In Dagupan, Chinese are important in the wholesale and large retail trade, whereas Filipinos are found mainly in smaller establishments among neighborhood store operators and marketplace vendors. But there is a lot of overlap between the two. In Nasik, by contrast, Marwaris dominate provisions, Bohra Muslims specialize in hardware, Gujarati Jains are important in textiles, and Sardashis have a big say in auto supply. Moreover, although in virtually all Philippine cities the Chinese/Filipino divide is repeated, in India the ethnic, religious, and caste composition in trade varies from town to town.

Second, there is the colonial experience. The marketing concept received its first formal definition in America, and it was there that manufacturers first accepted it as an ideal. With Americans dominating the economy in the Philippines for decades after the turn of this century, it is no wonder that the marketing ideology, together with the notion of consumerism, was early introduced into that country. In India this took place only in the late 1950's, well after the British had left the country as a colonial power. Third, the higher literacy rate and per capita income in the Philippines than in India make a difference to firms trying to create a mass consumer market for their product.

Fourth, the two countries contrast in taxes and government regulations. The Indian bureaucracy has imposed territorial taxes on goods that enter towns to be sold there. Further, the central government has chosen to keep control over national development, and in doing so it has regulated the total amount of consumer goods that companies can produce. At times, it has also fixed the maximum prices they can charge. This has created a condition of chronic undersupply in some product lines. The Philippines does not have territorial taxes on the movement of goods, nor has it manipulated the production and pricing of consumer goods as vigorously as India—oversupply has typified its consumer market.

When all factors are put together, it is clear that mass consumer goods companies are likely to follow active marketing and channel coordination with greater vigor in the Philippines than in India. In the case of Nasik and Dagupan, this translates into the following. Packaged consumer goods find their way into Nasik through sales penetration and the stockist system described above. In Dagupan, companies like Colgate-Palmolive, Procter and Gamble, and Kimberly-Clark retain greater company control over the channel. First, quite a few metropolitan companies maintain warehouse branches in the town, and company field men fan out to collect orders from large and small traders. Warehouse branching into Nasik is hardly known. Second, many companies have appointed wholesale dealers among merchants in Dagupan to stock their goods. Similar to stockists in Nasik, these dealers are encouraged to sell. But unlike the setup in Nasik, most company field men buy back much of the stock from their Dagupan dealers to fill orders they had collected among retailers. Here, dealers serve mainly as passive warehouse points, while company agents see to sales and promotions. In the Indian stockist system, channel control is shallower because large companies leave much of the marketing responsibilities in the hands of their stockists.

Sales penetration is a very useful method for suppliers to adopt if they want to bridge the formal/informal gap in urban commerce. Although the large-scale supply and small-scale retail ends are organizationally noncongruent, sales penetration turns this into a complementary condition, and channel stability is assured. This is true in both communities, but in Dagupan, neighborhood store operators feel the company presence more than those in Nasik, who at times even have to visit stockists to be served at all. This has had two effects. First, it has encouraged a greater number of individuals in Dagupan than in Nasik to enter into neighborhood store operations. These individuals have little difficulty receiving credit help from company salesmen and from local wholesalers trying to maintain their competitive position. This is one reason why neighborhood stores are more common in Dagupan than in Nasik.

Second, the deeper sales penetration has also meant that novel ideas about products, display, store layout, management, and related matters have been introduced more effectively to the retail level, including neighborhood stores, in Dagupan than Nasik. The fact that some store operators in central locations have converted their establishments into superettes illustrates this. In Nasik, where company salesmen only seldom urge retail traders to adopt innovations, no such development has taken place.

There remains contractual and ownership penetration. These strategies have two consequences. First, retail franchises and branches of consumer goods companies are likely to be modern not only in appearance but also in substance; that is, they are likely to be run along formal management principles. Second, the existence of these dealerships and branches has a multiplier effect on the diffusion of retail practices associated with mass consumer goods because local independent retailers are likely to copy at least some of the innovations they introduce. These developments have taken place in both towns, but in Dagupan they have gone further; in this case they did so because conditions in the Philippines have led metropolitan companies to enter Dagupan through retail branching and franchising at an earlier date and on a more massive scale than in Nasik.

In sum, the spread of mass consumer goods in less-developed countries is related to the kinds of retail institutions through which consumers obtain them. This section has shown that in order to understand the retail structure of the urban Third World, we must examine the supply channels that serve it. Understanding these channels, in turn, requires that we see them in the context of the culture and political economy of the Third World city and of the wider society.

Channel Devolution

In recent decades, consumer goods channels in the urban Third World have evolved in the same general direction as similar channels have done in the West. However, the case for channel evolution under conditions of development in the Third World should not be overstated. Much of the distributive trade in these societies—even of industrial consumer goods—continues to pass through conventional channels. Moreover, even if a tightly coordinated channel based on aggressive marketing has come into being, there is no guarantee that it may not devolve into a more conventional form. Channel congruence through formal sector vertical integration is no guarantee for channel stability, especially in Third World societies, which have a long way to move along the development path and in which ethnic plurality remains important. Supply conditions and ethnic factors can undermine channel integration even if companies adhere to active marketing. A good example is the household appliance trade in the Philippines (see Dannhaeuser 1983: 122–60).

As many other Third World countries have done, in the 1950's and 1960's the Philippines enforced an import substitution policy. This meant that imports of industrial consumer goods were restricted in entering the country in the hope that this would stimulate factory production locally. Because of this policy, these decades saw the rapid expansion around Manila of industrial facilities that assembled imported components for the local market. Pseudo-industrialization was the outcome, with an emphasis on consumer goods. In the household appliance line, General Electric, Admiral, Fedders, and other American companies were represented by Filipino firms that held licenses to assemble and market company products. Urged on by their American principals, these companies moved aggressively into contractual and ownership penetration of Manila and other cities.

By the early 1970's, each of them had several score retail branches or dealerships in Manila and at least one in towns like Dagupan to serve consumers ranging from the lower to the upper classes. Each outlet was more glamorous than the next, offered installment sales, and brand exclusivity was complete. Channel control by the major suppliers could not have been more complete, but change was on its way.

During the 1970's the producers had an increasingly difficult time unloading their goods through their exclusive channels. For one, they had overproduced because they misjudged the size of the urban market. More seriously, tariff barriers against imports were lowered to force local manufacturers to become more efficient, and low-priced products from Japan began to flood the market.

At this point the role of the Chinese enters the picture. Up to the 1970's, they had hardly participated in the appliance trade. This was so partly because retail trade had been nationalized in the Philippines, which meant that only Filipino citizens could legally retail. In fact, virtually all appliance outlets were managed by Filipinos—in this case an integrated channel in the formal sector unexpectedly helped to indigenize retail trade. The other reason the Chinese did not participate was that they did not want to. American companies had appointed Filipino firms as assemblers and distributors, and when these proceeded to build integrated channels, the only way the Chinese could retail appliances was as dealers or branch managers of these companies. One cultural characteristic of overseas Chinese merchants is to avoid binding contractual obligations to a single supplier, especially if non-Chinese. This would restrict their freedom of action intolerably.

Conditions changed when the appliance market experienced oversupply and imports became available. Chinese import houses took advantage of the Japanese goods and retailed them at low margin through large Chinese-owned showrooms in Manila or via mostly Chinese subwholesale and retail stores in provincial towns. In contrast to the integrated channel that had become traditional in the appliance trade, the imports passed through a vertically fragmented channel in which retailers were independent and not required to be brand exclusive. An open market came into being in which anyone who had resources to place sufficiently large orders could buy from the Chinese supply firms in Manila. This development put a strain on the exclusive channels of the local assemblers. One assembler after another surreptitiously sold some of their output to the financially strong Chinese appliance traders to relieve their overstocked warehouses, and thereby they began to compete against their own exclusive retailers.

It was then only a matter of time for the vertically integrated channels to succumb. After hanging on to channel control as long as possible, some assemblers changed the costly branch system they had constructed to a franchise system; others permitted dealers to carry any brand they wished; and some suppliers ceased to be concerned with retail trade at all except through advertising and promotions. The result was that by the early 1980's a set of vertically integrated channels and exclusive retail outlets organized along lines laid down by company demand devolved into a vertically fragmented channel with urban retail outlets not only legally, but actually independent. Appliance retail stores remained modern in appearance, but now a far greater proportion were run on familistic principles than when only branches and franchises of metropolitan companies handled this product line.

Integrated market channels have their advantages: (1) they encourage the flow of information and products across trade levels; (2) they include only members actually needed for distribution, thereby reducing redundancy; (3) innovations readily diffuse throughout the channel; and (4) trade relations are routinized, minimizing time expenditure and disagreements. Channel integration, however, also entails costs, especially if ownership penetration is involved: (1) the dominant channel member not only reaps much of the profit but also bears the costs of the channel; (2) if one part of the channel is disturbed, it will have immediate repercussions in the rest of the system; (3) unless agreed to by the dominant members, basic innovations in channel organization are unlikely to be experimented with; and (4) the lack of redundant members can be a handicap because it reduces the channel's resilience to environmental perturbations.

The effectiveness of a channel is not determined by some absolute standard but is relative to the trade environment in which it exists. The costs of the integrated appliance channel in the Philippine urban context became particularly pronounced in the 1970's so that, in the absence of monopoly power of assemblers, the streamlined system broke down. The weak points of integrated channels and the strengths of the conventional trade mode turned out to be most important during this period.

There was also the cultural factor, the "Chinese way" of doing business. It consists of turning semipassive marketing into a fine art. To overseas Chinese, formal written contracts, impersonally enforced obligations, and disregard of kinship and ethnic ties are practices to be avoided. For them—and for ethnic minorities elsewhere in commerce —trade relations are based on personal trust reinforced by ethnic and kin identities. To extend personal favors, especially in the form of credit, lubricates the system, and favors that are not made public consolidate it. Secrecy, confidentiality, and personalism define the trade game (Bonacich 1973). Among the Chinese, this is combined with a preference to keep their legal independence as merchants, to be able to switch allegiances, and not to be told how to run their business. Channels dominated by Chinese, therefore, are vertically fragmented, with family enterprises typical on each level. Underlying this fragmentation, however, are long-term vertical trade links based on trust and the extension of personal favors. Marketing is aggressive but is acted out covertly through the semipassive strategy.

Under conditions prevailing in the 1970's the modern integrated appliance channel had no chance to survive the competition posed by the Chinese marketing organization. Changes in the supply side and the ethnically based trade preferences of the Chinese conspired to dismantle a highly congruent, integrated, and formal sector channel.

Urban Retail Types

Retail outlets are not only the most visible element of distribution channels, but they are also the most immediate source through which the Third World urban population obtains consumer goods. It is important, therefore, to take a closer look at some of these institutions. This section will discuss cases that are positioned in the informal sector, yet they are often involved in the trade of mass consumer goods: hawkers and neighborhood stores. Their characteristics and the role they play in Third World urban retail trade mirror the supply side they are attached to and the more general economic and social conditions of the population they serve.

Marketplace vendors, hawkers, and neighborhood store operators constitute the bulk of informal sector retailers in most Third World cities. Many are individual enterprises, although some involve the family. All three are in some respects surviving elements of the traditional, preindustrial urban trading pattern. More important, however, is the fact that their current characteristics reflect changes the urban Third World is undergoing today.

For instance, Singapore's night markets (*pasar malam*), which handle clothing, food, and household goods during the evening, emerged only in the 1960's. In the 1970's there were nearly 70 of these mobile markets, which vary from 10 to 200 stalls. The spread of new high-rise apartment buildings during these years resulted in a shortage of stationary shopping facilities, a shortage that the night markets filled (Smith 1978: 114–15). Also the numerous informal periodic markets (*tianguis*) in Mexico City arose to serve the "urban poor in areas of low population density especially on the fringe of Mexico City" (ibid.: 114). Although the Mexican government discourages these markets, they are tolerated because they are needed.

Such tolerance toward informal sector trade does not always exist. Hawkers—itinerant peddlers and street stall sellers—are the subject of restrictions imposed by Third World city governments and are even occasionally harassed by those governments. Hawkers are considered a nuisance at best and a public danger at worst. They clog roads and hinder traffic, pose health hazards, often compete with stationary retail stores, and evade license fees. They make it difficult for city officials to proceed with Westernizing city streets, which mainly means controlling trading activities and traffic. Hawkers are mobile and therefore elusive.

What this attitude overlooks is that under present economic conditions hawkers play an important role in Third World cities. Middle- and lower-income consumers find them convenient; for the urban poor, hawking is one way to help make ends meet; and hawkers are important to mass consumer goods companies as a means to dispose of products, often through cash or consignment sales from street stores.

Although it is a humble occupation, it has its own complexities, as a comparative study of hawkers in six Southeast Asian cities shows (McGee and Yeung 1977).[4] First, they differ in their locational needs. Unprocessed food sellers obtain customers from their immediate neighborhoods. Among prepared food sellers, two locational types can be identified: "(1) those who locate in centres of customer need, as represented by hawkers who wait outside office complexes at lunch-time, and (2) those who draw their customers from considerable distances as, for instance, in the case of the night markets in Malaysian cities" (ibid.: 108). Each hawker concentration, moreover, contains several types of hawkers. There are those selling from stalls along sides of streets, and groups of mobile hawkers who lay their goods on pavements, often at the edge of static concentrations. In Singapore, 80 percent of the hawkers are stationary; in other cities, perhaps reflecting their less-developed economies, 60 percent are mobile.

Hawkers also differ in their economic dimension. The majority (about 60 percent) have a marginal or submarginal income. About 20 to 25 percent earn minimum incomes, while nonfood sellers—they stock both imported and locally produced industrial consumer goods—have the highest earnings. This corresponds to the fact that they occupy larger selling units, usually are static, and the value of their stock is high. Surprisingly, it is the young, better educated, and not so long established operators who are the most successful. Hawking, therefore, is not as monolithic and economically depressed an urban occupation without connections to the formal sector as one may think.

Concerning personal features, finally, females predominate hawking only in the Philippines. Beyond this, hawkers are divisible into three subgroups: (1) long-established residents in the city with poor education who entered hawking because of lack of opportunities; (2) recent rural migrants with poor education who also entered hawking because of no alternatives; and (3) long-established residents "who entered hawking after the experience of previous urban occupations for perceived economic opportunities" (ibid.: 112).

Another visible retail institution found in much of the urban Third World is the neighborhood store (see Dannhaeuser 1980). They are small, stationary operations, usually located in the residence of the operator and designed to sell foods and nonfoods that nearby households may need at a moment's notice. These stores are typically managed by the housewife, and their products include soft drinks, chewing gum, starch, grains, cooking oil, canned goods, sewing material, and patent

[4] The cities studied are Jarkarta and Bandung (Indonesia), Kuala Lumpur and Melaka (Malaysia), and Manila and Baguio (Philippines).

medicine. Their smallness belies their importance. Third World cities in much of Africa, Latin America, and in South and Southeast Asia contain a large number of them, especially in lower- and middle-income residential areas. To turn to Dagupan again as an example, there is a neighborhood store for every twenty households, and 15 percent of nonproduce retail trade passes through them. They constitute an important outlet for suppliers of low-priced mass consumer goods because 70 to 80 percent of their turnover involves industrial sector products. Collectively, therefore, neighborhood stores play an important role in Third World city commerce.

In contrast to hawkers who usually sell only on cash, the extension of product credit is an important way for neighborhood store operators to attract and retain customers. Operators know their customers personally and therefore can judge whether or not to provide credit in an insecure environment. A more negative reason, however, also exists. As members of a neighborhood, they are often pressured into selling on credit even if it means potential loss.

Also in contrast to conditions prevailing among hawkers, price competition between neighborhood store operators tends to be muted. Instead, they "compete" more over location, with respect to which, once they have chosen a store site, they actually enjoy some monopoly; or in more formal terms, a condition of monopolistic competition prevails over location. This condition exists because the location of neighborhood stores is fixed and dispersed, and because customer outreach is limited. Patrons of neighborhood stores tend to buy frequently from them, although each transaction is very small. Given this buying pattern, and the fact that the physical mobility of especially the poor in Third World cities is limited, customers of neighborhood stores are willing to travel only short distances to buy that one cigarette, that cup of sugar, or that aspirin pill. Because of its locational advantage—and it is here that the monopoly enters—a neighborhood store has at least some business guaranteed to it, and price manipulation by it, or others, will have little effect on this.

Neighborhood stores exhibit a condition that typifies much of Third World commerce; that is, the existence of a multiplicity of trade units (Dannhaeuser 1977). A large percentage of the labor force in the urban Third World is active in the tertiary economic sector (services), and many in this sector are independent traders, especially retailers. Consequently, a large number of retailers exists in relation to the urban population.

What are the reasons for this multiplicity? Neighborhood stores illustrate some of them. First, there are the factors that encourage individuals to enter this trade: (1) it is easy to start a neighborhood store because it is home based; (2) housewives and other family members can operate it; (3) inventory and overhead requirements are small; and (4) some credit is usually available from suppliers. Also the opportunity cost is likely to be low—no other economic activity is open for the operator, especially if she is a housewife, that offers an equivalent or higher return. Finally, an entrepreneurial element is also present. Some enter into the trade because they hope eventually to shift into store retailing or wholesaling.

Second, there is the limited growth capacity of individual neighborhood stores. These institutions are designed to serve the frequent but tiny purchases of neighbors. This means they would need to service a very large number of transactions daily to attain a turnover that approaches that of grocery stores. This is unlikely to happen for three reasons. First, neighborhood stores are not organizationally equipped to do so unless they expand personnel and offer self-service. Second, even if they were able to do so, such establishments still would have only a limited ability to grow because of the relative immobility of customers and the presence of other neighborhood stores in the vicinity. A third factor limiting the size of neighborhood stores and encouraging their multiplicity is important where credit sales are customary. To keep the risk of credit sales low, store operators need to trust customers, and such trust can develop only if operators know their customers personally. For any one operator, however, such knowledge is by necessity confined to a limited number of customers, with the result that there will be a large number of stores in relation to any one customer pool (Ward 1960). The final factor explaining the multiplicity of neighborhood stores is the high demand for them. Urban consumers find in the neighborhood store a highly convenient institution. It allows them to obtain on credit small amounts of a wide range of products at minimal travel cost, a circumstance that nicely dovetails with the realities of household budgets of the urban poor. It is for this reason that consumer goods suppliers like them, and in so doing, directly or indirectly, help them to multiply.

Far from being a mere leftover of traditional times, the neighborhood store, as with the hawker and marketplace vendor, today reflects the contemporary condition prevailing in the urban Third World.

And the Future?

What developments are likely to take place in urban marketing in the Third World? As the cases of neighborhood stores and hawkers suggest, marketing in the urban Third World will for a long time show characteristics that differ from those encountered in the industrial West. But the persistence of these differences should not be overrated if recent developments are any guide for the future. Even if market vendors, hawkers, neighborhood stores, fragmented channels, passive marketing, and the informal/formal sector divide continue to play an important role in urban commerce in the future, industrial consumer goods will become available in ever increasing quantities in the Third World, and new and aggressive marketing methods together with novel, often imported, trade institutions will grow in importance. The pace of this development will be especially rapid in those areas of the Third World that will experience long-term improvements in living standards.

Why is this development significant? Humankind is in the midst of a fundamental transformation. A cultural revolution, albeit a silent one, is taking place. The world, including the Third World, is changing from being a place in which cultural plurality from region to region was the typical state of affairs, to one in which cultural similarity characterizes vast numbers of people over vast regions. Mass consumerism no doubt is playing an active role in this transformation.

The increasing availability of industrial consumer goods and the proliferation of marketing firms that promote them have an impact that goes beyond their immediate material use. Whether peasants learn about the outside world by means of their own TV or radio sets, or via hearsay from their landlords, makes a difference to their perception of the world. Whether urban households store perishables in refrigerators or consume them as fast as possible affects the daily routine of their members. Regular shopping in department stores, supermarkets, or malls encourages expectations about preferred forms of living by urban consumers different from those encouraged in the traditional public marketplace or bazaar. Mass consumer goods and institutions promoting them influence us more than we care to admit (which is not to say that the influence is not reciprocal), and an increasing proportion of people in the Third World are subject to this influence.

Is humankind heading toward a world culture? Over the long run probably yes, especially with respect to the material component of culture. True, a shared range of mass consumer goods and marketing institutions alone does not a single culture make. But it does encourage convergence. French people remain different from Swedes, and both continue to be culturally distinct from the Japanese—and this difference exists although all three societies have a common industrial base. But they are far more alike now than they were in 1900. Even though they do not share an industrial tradition, the same point can be made if the more advanced Third World countries—especially their urban populations—are compared with the industrial West. Today a greater degree of cultural similarity exists between them than at the beginning of this century. Marketing and the proliferation of standardized industrial consumer goods have been among the major factors responsible for this trend. For this reason alone, they are significant and deserve our close attention.

10

Industrial Agriculture

Peggy F. Barlett

The food-production system characteristic of industrial states is called industrial agriculture, because it uses the products of industry in its own production process. Industrial agriculture is capital-intensive, substituting machinery and purchased inputs such as processed fertilizers for human or animal labor. Anthropologists have shown increasing interest in industrial agriculture in recent years for two reasons: first, we have begun to do more research in the United States and other industrialized countries, where changing agricultural patterns are an important part of major societal changes. Second, aspects of industrial agriculture are spreading to nonindustrial, "developing" countries, where anthropologists encounter them in our field research there. This spread of technology and production methods is often promoted by ministries of agriculture and international agencies that adopt the industrial agriculture model as their national goal. Industrial agriculture is also spread by corporations that seek cheaper lands and labor in developing countries to produce crops and livestock for export. Corporations producing machinery and inputs seek to promote industrial agriculture to expand their markets. As a food-production system, then, industrial agriculture is spreading beyond its origin in the United States and Europe and is coming to have an impact across the globe. Its characteristics are of importance not only in the industrialized countries, but also in a wide range of countries with diverse political systems and ecological zones. The following chapter will deal primarily with research on U.S. and Canadian farms, not because the variants in Europe, Japan, or de-

Research for this chapter was partially supported by the National Science Foundation under Grant No. BNS-8121459. Any opinions, findings, conclusions, or recommendations expressed herein are those of the author and do not necessarily reflect the views of the National Science Foundation. I would also like to acknowledge the helpful comments and criticisms of Frederick Buttel, R. Edward Brown, Lawrence Busch, Elizabeth Cashdan, Ivery Clifton, Christina Gladwin, Luther Tweeten, and Miriam Wells.

veloping countries are not important or relevant, but because of space limitations.

The anthropological approach to the study of industrial agriculture is different from that of historians, sociologists, economists, or other agricultural scientists. Based in a tradition of cross-cultural research, economic anthropologists are more interested in approaches and measurements that look at long-term patterns of human settlement, community structure, resource use, ecological interactions, and bioenergetic efficiency. We are sometimes cautious in using culturally specific measures such as market values for units of land or labor, recognizing that these values reflect power relations and ideological issues. We have a bias toward the long-term, evolutionary perspective of human societies and are more likely to be troubled by the ways in which industrial agriculture is not sustainable or contributes to a loss of control over productive resources for an increasing segment of the population. Production methods that move from more egalitarian human relations, such as in areas made up of many family farms, to more stratified relations, such as on corporate "factories in the field," also tend to be seen more negatively by researchers in this area.

Anthropologists traditionally study non-state-level societies through participant observation and interviewing in small communities; these methods are often brought to the study of industrial societies as well. Such a focus on individuals, their behavior, and their decisions tends to recognize but not study the large-scale aspects of a hierarchically organized complex society that may control or constrain those actor-level decisions. Thus economic anthropologists have rarely studied the agricultural research institutions, the agricultural input industries, or the government policy processes that create the conditions under which U.S. and Canadian farmers adapt. Likewise, anthropologists are usually more interested in production issues than in the food-processing or marketing aspects of the total system.

The strength of anthropological work lies in the complexity of patterns studied on the local level and the linkage of micro and macro levels of analysis. The decisions of farm and family units are linked to long-term ethnic differences, community vitality, religious and secular values, family dynamics, and economic and ecological outcomes. Power structures and political processes on the local level illustrate the specific outcomes of control and influence exerted by national or regional groups. One of the tasks of economic anthropology over the next few decades will be to decide whether and how the field will expand to find new methodologies and approaches to improve our ability to research significant questions within a highly stratified and globally linked economic and political system.

The following discussion of industrial agriculture will review some of the most important aspects of the system, as outlined by anthropologists and researchers from other fields. Industrial agriculture is characterized by constant innovations (Barlett 1987b), unlike some tribal and peasant food-production systems that maintain stable economic and ecological adaptations for hundreds of years. The historical context of the last 150 years in the United States is therefore important to understand the aspects of industrial agriculture that are different from peasant or tribal production. Six general characteristics will be discussed:

1. Increased use of complex technology and the technology treadmill.
2. Increased substitution of capital for labor.
3. Increased energy use.
4. Increased influence of the state.
5. A tendency toward competition, specialization, and overproduction.
6. Increased interdependence between farm units and agribusinesses that control inputs, machinery, product sales, processing, and transport.

The dynamics of industrial agriculture will then be explored for two main organizational forms: family farms and corporate (or industrial-type) farms. Though there is great variation in the production units in industrial agriculture, discussion of these two simplified types will expand our picture of the U.S. farming system. Research on family farming has explored its internal dynamics, division of labor, management styles, and ethnic variability. The special forms of part-type farming and family farm partnerships will also be discussed. The contrasting characteristics of corporate farms will be linked to studies on farm workers, the state, and the community impacts of corporate farming. The chapter will conclude with a brief summary of the current issues of concern to anthropological researchers of industrial agriculture.

Characteristics of Industrial Agriculture

1. Increased Use of Complex Technology and the Technology Treadmill

Industrial agriculture today involves the use of machines, chemicals, and complex production techniques, many of which are new since

World War II. Genetic research has also developed new plant and animal varieties, leading to sharp gains in yields. The directions of technological change are determined by various agencies, institutions, and businesses and are usually outside of farmers' control. Some examples of complex technology from U.S. agriculture will illustrate the technological aspects of industrial agriculture.

Machinery. Mechanization of agricultural methods has greatly reduced farm labor and allows a higher standard of living to farmers who are now able to operate larger units. Mechanization also has helped keep food prices down as wages have generally risen in the United States (Madden 1980). Machinery is both the cause and consequence of the increased affluence of farmers today, though many other changes were necessary to make farm consumption levels approach nonfarm levels (Tweeten 1971: 8). Cotton production, for example, is one area of agricultural production that has seen rapid mechanical change over the last 50 years. In the Southeast during the 1930's, the use of mules and horses for plowing began to be replaced by tractors, whose efficiency allowed some landowners to evict sharecroppers and move toward larger operating units. After World War II, the perfection of the mechanical cotton picker replaced unskilled harvest labor and eliminated much of the drudgery of cotton harvest. Today, a mechanical cotton picker can cost as much as $80,000, an investment that limits ownership to only a few, larger producers. Smaller cotton producers can sometimes arrange to hire custom harvesting from machinery owners, but such arrangements can be sufficiently problematic to discourage some farmers from continuing cotton production.

The development of mechanical cotton pickers set off other technological changes. Further research led to improved varieties of cotton more amenable to machine harvest. Planting methods changed, and the chemical defoliation of plants before harvest became necessary. Mechanical pickers mix more stems, leaves, and dirt with the cotton, which forced cotton gins to experiment with new cleaning machines and methods. Thus, a change in one aspect of the cotton production process interacts with changes in processing techniques, planting methods, biological innovations, crop choice, land tenure, and rural population.

Another study of technical change focused on Wisconsin dairy farmers (Dorner 1983). The development of refrigerated bulk tanks in the early 1950's had a range of impacts on production and sale and made it more difficult for small farmers to stay in business. Previously, farmers stored milk in ten-gallon cans, held in a cooling tank, until a private trucker transported them each day to a processing plant. The new refrigerated bulk tanks were accompanied by pipeline milking systems that moved milk directly from the cow to the tank. The new tanks reduced possibilities of milk contamination and decreased farmers' workloads by eliminating maintenance of the ten-gallon cans. Bulk tanks came to be served by special milk tank trucks. "It soon became almost impossible for a dairy farmer to operate without this new equipment, which called for both a major investment and a larger dairy herd than many farmers had at the time. . . . New technology created major pressures for farm-size expansion in Wisconsin dairying" (Dorner 1983: 79). New sanitation laws passed about this time required the use of the new bulk tanks as well.

This case of dairy mechanization illustrates the working of an important aspect of industrial agriculture: the "technology treadmill" (Cochrane 1979). An innovation that increases production or lowers costs gives early adopters a competitive advantage and a period of higher profits. In this dairy example, reduced labor costs and ease of transport favored the shift to bulk tanks, though the costs of making the changeover in milking systems were considerable. In most cases of the technology treadmill, once the innovation is widely adopted, its benefits are reduced by increased production and lowered prices. Farmers who resist a change in its early stages are often hurt by these lowered prices and may be forced to adopt the innovation just to survive. In the Wisconsin case, farmers who wanted to stay small were forced onto the technology treadmill when dairies or trucking companies no longer accepted their ten-gallon cans or when sanitation laws required them to buy bulk tanks. Small herds cannot justify the expense of such new technology, and farmers were forced to get bigger or get out. The technology treadmill can be seen to operate in many aspects of capital intensification and mechanization.

Chemicals. Increasing use of fertilizers, insecticides, herbicides, and other chemicals is an important aspect of industrial agriculture. Fertilizer use in U.S. agriculture has increased by over 500 percent since 1950 (Schertz et al. 1979: 27). Chemicals are now essential to the production of many crops. As Table 10.1 shows, both machinery and chemical technology have increased greatly in U.S. agriculture since the 1920's.

Tobacco production, for instance, currently requires the application of three chemicals at planting: a fungicide to inhibit mold, a nematicide to control nematodes, and an herbicide to deter weeds. Insecticide is sprayed every month over the growing season, followed by several applications of a fifth chemical that inhibits sucker production. A sixth type of chemical that induces leaf ripening is also available to farmers. For each category, of course, competing brands are available.

TABLE 10.1
Indexes of Total Farm Inputs, United States,
1920–84 (1977 = 100)

Year	Labor	Mechanical power and machinery	Agricultural chemicals
1920	486	27	5
1925	482	28	5
1930	465	34	6
1935	427	28	5
1940	417	36	9
1945	386	50	13
1950	310	72	19
1955	264	83	26
1960	207	83	32
1965	156	80	49
1970	126	85	75
1975	107	96	83
1980	92	104	120
1984	80	88	120

SOURCE: USDA (1985a: 391, 1985b: 9–11).
NOTE: The farm crisis of the 1980's has led to a slowdown in levels of farm machinery and chemical investment as farm incomes have plummeted and debts have risen.

Chemical use allows greater productivity of some crops and may reduce the total land area needed for food production. It has raised the quality of some foods, such as the elimination of wormy apples, though chemical residues in food alarm some experts and consumers (Busch and Lacy 1984). Insecticides are important in reducing insect damage in stored crops, and herbicides are now commonly used in conservation tillage methods that reduce soil erosion in many parts of the United States (Swanson 1981). Chemical contamination of water sources and the destabilization of ecological systems are some of the disadvantages to this aspect of agricultural technology. Synthetic organic pesticide use has increased over 40 times since the 1940's (Paarlberg 1980), and heavy fertilizer and chemical use has suppressed or destroyed the ecosystem's ability to recycle nutrients naturally and to control weeds, diseases, and insects (Sampson 1984: 15).

The increasing use of chemicals has caused concern about dangers to farmers' health as well. Farming is a dangerous occupation—injuries from heavy machinery provide one of the highest accident rates among U.S. industries. Less well known are the long-term chronic health problems. The use of agricultural chemicals is linked to increased risk of a variety of cancers (Strange et al. 1984). Leukemia is one form of cancer that affects farmers more than nonfarmers. In Iowa and Nebraska, corn farmers exposed to agricultural chemicals through intensive production experienced 44 to 63 percent greater risk of leukemia. Health concerns about chemicals used in grape production have led to strikes by the United Farm Workers and litigation among workers and owners on California grape farms.

Health problems of industrial agriculture have spread beyond effects on farmers and farm families. The standard practice of feeding antibiotics to cattle and other livestock has produced antibiotic resistance in organisms such as salmonella. One such outbreak in Minnesota left several people seriously ill from drug-resistant salmonella in ground beef and resulted in the death of a man in South Dakota. If subtherapeutic antibiotic use in livestock production were to be banned, it would increase the disease problems inherent in animal confinement systems. Livestock raising in smaller units would be favored over larger units, an outcome resisted by powerful livestock farmers' organizations. This example shows how technological changes may serve different, conflicting interests in the industrial agricultural system.

Genetic technology. Industrial agriculture often makes use of hybrid varieties of plants or animals and relies on genetic improvement of seeds or breeds to increase output. The classic example is hybrid corn. Compared to an average yield in Georgia of under 20 bushels/acre in the 1920's, improved corn varieties now give average yields of 60–150 bushels per acre, depending on rainfall and irrigation. Corn production in Iowa and Illinois that tops 200 bushels per acre is not rare, demonstrating the power of plant-breeding efforts when combined with high fertilizer applications and good soil. Genetic changes can also lower costs, as in cases of animals bred to convert feed to meat more efficiently.

When geneticists select for certain features, other adaptive features are sometimes lost. Early hybrid corn was criticized by livestock feeders because it was lower in protein than traditional varieties. Though protein levels have improved somewhat, soybeans are currently added to animal feed to make up the protein deficiency. Corn varieties bred to avoid the costs of detasseling were later found to be more susceptible to corn-leaf blight than previous strains, and an outbreak in 1970 resulted in massive losses to farmers (Tatum 1971).

Changes in genetic technology can sometimes precipitate other changes in the production process. Many hybrid corn varieties today are planted close together, and in some types, their stalks are bred to be short and slender, putting more of the plant's energy into the grain. Slender stalks and heavier ears, however, can more easily be blown over, and farmers dependent upon mechanical combines cannot harvest corn fallen to the ground. Where such crop losses are a problem, farmers have learned to harvest the corn as soon as it is ripe, but before the grain has dried in the field. To keep the wet grain from spoilage after harvest, it must now be dried in a mechanical dryer, adding the expense of the dryer and energy inputs to the costs of corn production. Corn provides a good example of higher yields and lower costs per bushel, but accompanied by increased total farm costs and therefore higher risks through the use of more complex technology.

2. *Increased Use of Capital in Substitution for Labor*

Industrial agriculture uses more capital per unit of production than other farming systems. Capital can take the form of machinery, annual costs for purchased seeds and fertilizers, or long-term investments such as irrigation systems or barns. "In 1950, labor accounted for almost 40 percent of the value of all resources used in farming; by 1977, it had declined to 14 percent. In 1950, capital (machinery and chemicals) accounted for 25 percent of all resources used in farming; by 1977, it had increased to 43 percent" (Schertz et al. 1979: 27–28). This use of capital to replace labor has been an accelerating trend, as seen in Fig. 10.1. United States farmers have sought labor-replacing technology to lower costs and increase their competitive position. For farmers using con-

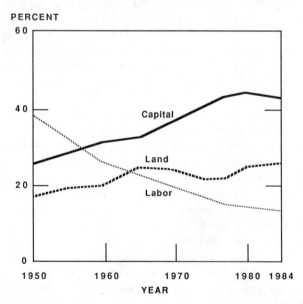

Fig. 10.1. Resources used in farming ("Other" category omitted). Source: Schertz et al. 1979: 28 (updated by USDA).

siderable amounts of hired labor, capital intensification can sometimes free production from the constraints of organized farm labor.

The costs of farming have increased both from inflation and also from more capital-intensive methods. United States farm-production expenses jumped from an average of $7,048 per farm in 1950 to $15,047 per farm in 1970 and to $59,911 in 1984 (USDA, 1970, 1985a). Part of the increasing use of capital in agriculture is the role of credit. Many farmers must finance these purchases with borrowed money, adding interest expenses to their other costs. Using Georgia as an example, in the eight-year period from 1977 to 1985, the number of farms declined from 56,000 to 50,000, but the level of total farm indebtedness rose from $2 billion to $4.35 billion (Georgia Crop Reporting Service, personal communication). High costs of farming reduce farmers' flexibility. Once $80,000 is invested in a cotton picker, even if prices drop and cotton is less profitable, the farmer must stay in cotton production to recoup the investment.

3. Increased Energy Use

Industrial agriculture has been called "subsidized agriculture" because it depends upon inputs of energy (such as gasoline for tractors) and materials (such as nitrates for fertilizers) from outside the local ecological system (Hardesty 1977: 99; Odum 1971). For each calorie of food the U.S. system harvests, it burns about 2½ calories of fossil fuel in machines, fertilizers, and other inputs (Perelman 1978: 11). Then, because our system is so specialized, most food must be transported to where it is consumed. Food packaging and processing industries are the fourth largest consumer of energy of all the industrial groupings of the Department of Commerce. One kilogram of breakfast cereal, for example, provides 3,600 kcal of food energy but requires 15,675 kcal to produce and transport (Pimentel and Pimentel 1979: 121). Often, more energy is used in packaging, processing, and transportation than in growing the food. A wooden berry box takes 69 kcal to produce, as compared to 1,006 kcal for a steel can and 2,159 for a plastic half-gallon milk container (ibid.: 122). In sum, "for each calorie of food produced in the U.S., more than six calories of fossil fuel are consumed" (Perelman 1977: 12).

A comparison between labor-intensive Japanese and capital-intensive Arkansas rice farmers shows the higher energy use in the U.S. system. Cottrell (1955) found that both systems produce rice with similar yields of 50 bushels per acre, but the Japanese use much more human effort: 90 human-days per acre as opposed to 14.1 in Arkansas. Hardesty calculated total horsepower-hours of energy used in each system,

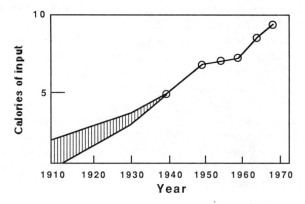

Fig. 10.2. Energy subsidy to the U.S. food system: calories of input per food calorie of output. Shaded area is the range of estimated values. Source: Steinhart and Steinhart 1974: 311.

including the energy from fossil fuel to run tractors and trucks and also from electricity used on the farm. The Japanese total of 90 horsepower-hours of energy used in rice production is shown to be more energy efficient when compared with the Arkansas total of 805 horsepower-hours for the same rice yield. Fig. 10.2 illustrates the trend of rising energy inputs to the U.S. food system over this century.

Industrial agriculture has responded to scarce and expensive labor by substituting machinery and chemicals; the resulting labor efficiency allows less than 4 percent of the U.S. population to farm in order to feed the rest (Cochrane 1979). But efficiency per unit of energy or capital is not characteristic of the system, because such large quantities are used per unit of output (DeWalt 1984).

4. Increased Influence of the State

The state (or the federal government, in the case of the United States) is an entity that affects many aspects of industrial food production. Government agencies determine what kinds of land can be used, recommend how farming is to be carried out, regulate contents of fertilizers and other inputs, and establish and certify the safety of chemicals. They also oversee marketing units, set prices for some crops, provide capital for various farm investments, certify the quality and grading of harvests, and influence the survival or dissolution of certain kinds of farms through special subsidies, tax laws, and production restrictions. Government plays a role in creating international markets and in breaking them off through shifting political alliances or even embargoes. The federal government also supports the development of agricultural technology in the land grant university research system and the Agricultural Research Service and encourages the dissemination of the results of that research by the agricultural extension service.

To take one example of government influence, tax laws affecting agriculture (especially estate taxes, tax shelters, and methods of accounting for income and expenses) have had an important effect over the last twenty years in raising the value of farmland, encouraging farm investments by nonfarmers, and fueling the rise of larger farms. Tax benefits to certain kinds of capital-intensive investments in farming can change regional production patterns and favor certain kinds of farms over others. The spread of irrigation in Nebraska has been encouraged by tax shelter provisions, turning large areas of pasture into wheatfields. Farm-management companies have provided opportunities for nonfarm investors to finance these irrigation systems. The increased wheat acreage contributes to the current glut of wheat in the United States, while medium-size family farms in Nebraska are disadvantaged in competition with the irrigated large farms (Center for Rural Affairs 1985).

In recent years, federal programs have provided a range of incentives, rewards, and restrictions to farmers. For some crops such as corn and wheat, target prices are set annually. If open market sales do not reach these prices, farmers may sell their crop to the government or hold it in warehouses and obtain a loan for the crop at the target price value. For other crops such as peanuts and tobacco, the government regulates the land in production or the amount of harvest that can be marketed at a special price. Direct payments to producers are another way in which farm incomes have been enhanced. The government provides a range of institutions (such as the Farmers Home Administration) that loan money to farmers for operating expenses. Certain investments such as terracing or tree planting to prevent soil erosion are eligible for government cost-sharing programs.

In each of these programs, regulations respond to competing political interests, and different kinds of farmers are favored. Survival depends on the producer's ability to "farm the programs" as well as the land. All eligible farms do not benefit equally from such government programs, however. The largest 1 percent of farmers receive 29 percent of all government payments (Paarlberg 1980). Government programs have been shown to contribute to the reduction in the number of farms in the United States and the increasing concentration of farmland in fewer hands (Carter and Johnston 1978; Coughenour 1984; Ford 1973).

One response to increased government involvement in agriculture is the rise of a range of organizations to defend farmers' interests. From the National Soybean Association to the American Farm Bureau Federation, these lobbying and support groups are part of the bureaucratic layers of organizational complexity that characterize industrial agriculture. As Rappaport suggests, in any complex system, subparts can become powerful in serving their own interests, to the detriment of the larger unit (1979: 163). The U.S. dairy lobby and its impact on federal milk supports over the last 30 years is an example of the state's response to such powerful interest groups.

The government also plays an important role in subsidizing and directing research. The University of California Agricultural Experiment Station was the primary research establishment responsible for the development of a mechanical tomato harvester and the appropriate tough-skinned varieties of tomato. By reducing dependence on harvest labor, this invention "saved the tomato industry for California" by keeping tomato processing companies from moving to Mexico (Friedland and Barton 1975: 51). Another effect of this research was to give an advantage to larger growers who specialized in tomato production and could afford to buy the machines. From 4,000 tomato growers in California in 1962, mechanization reduced that number to 597 in 1973 (Friedland and Barton 1975: 54).

5. Tendency Toward Competition, Specialization, and Overproduction

A brief overview of U.S. agricultural history will help explain the origins of the characteristics of industrial agriculture. The capital-intensive nature of this food-production system emerged because of a unique historical combination of abundant fertile land, scarce labor, competition with industry for that labor, cheap energy, abundant capital, and an economy that encouraged technological development (Cochrane 1979).

All the regions of the country were affected by the vast areas of prairies and forest available for food cultivation, once the native American populations were removed. An essential fact that makes U.S. agriculture so different from other parts of the world is the size and ecological richness of the continent that was colonized and purchased, and the sparse population that inhabited it. Food production in much of the continental United States began, therefore, in a context of labor scarcity that gave rise to wasteful and destructive land-use practices. Thomas Jefferson himself recognized the relative value of land and labor on his farm by refusing to fertilize his land since "we can buy an acre of new land cheaper than we can manure an old acre" (Gates 1960: 101).

The abundant land resources in North America financed more than cheap food; they financed the building of canals and railroads through land grants (and subsequent land sales) to development companies

(Cochrane 1979). They financed the federal government without burdensome taxation, because the proceeds from federal land auctions filled national coffers (Perelman 1978). Abundant land made many aspects of politics, nation building, and economic industrialization less costly. Resources were available to support trade, industry, agriculture, and an improving standard of living without the struggles that would have been necessary had the land and its soil fertility been unavailable. Our national optimism and expansionism were conditioned by this economic reality, and when the frontier finally closed after 1900, it took decades for readjustment to an age of limits to begin.

Good transportation and abundant land available through homestead acts fostered commercial agriculture and specialization. Families financed their settlement on the U.S. frontier with credit, and their debts had to be repaid through sales of crops and livestock. Though overproduction soon emerged as a problem affecting many regions, settlers in debt were unable to reduce production to subsistence levels. Where transportation linked farmers to national and international markets, specialization in a few crops was common, though it increased the risk of bad years. Such specialization was supported by commercial establishments that provided needed foodstuffs and manufactured goods. Land payments and consumption debts pushed further specialization, to maximize returns from the land. The Southeast after the Civil War is a good example. Farmers struggling to rebuild were squeezed by high transportation costs and falling cotton prices. Yet cotton produced the highest return per acre, leading to monocrop dependence on cotton and on imports of food staples from the Midwest. Cotton overproduction, of course, only drove prices even lower.

From the beginnings of European settlement in North America, labor costs were high, encouraging methods to cut labor inputs. "A British farm worker in 1830, for example, could purchase about 1/10 acre of land with his annual salary; an Illinois farm worker could afford 80 acres for a year's wages" (Gates 1960: 276). During the agricultural expansion in the 1800's, industry was also expanding, creating competition for labor. Labor scarcity, in part from the expanses of land being settled and in part from the availability of industrial alternatives, encouraged the substitution of capital for labor. Machinery, developed by industry to expand its market, served farmers who needed to expand production in the face of falling prices or rising labor costs. Capital intensification over the long run only exacerbated overproduction and raised the competitive stakes of the technology treadmill. As seen in several cases discussed so far, farmers are often faced with the choice to adopt expensive technology or to lose profitability and be squeezed out.

Specialization was increasingly necessary as technology and machinery use raised overall farm costs. The fertility of newly settled regions permitted specialization and even monocropping without immediate soil depletion. Cheap fertilizers and cheap forms of energy also played an important part in pushing capital-intensive specialization. In much of the United States, debts on land, low crop prices, fertile soils, and good transportation networks all worked together to foster commercial agriculture based on a relatively small number of crops. In the face of these economic pressures, sometimes only ecological disaster can force farmers to shift out of the dominant commercial crops (Buttel 1980). Cotton production, for instance, continued in some areas of the Southeast until the topsoil was completely eroded away, down to the barren red clay subsoil. Ultimately, boll weevil infestations were responsible for ending the reign of King Cotton and moving cotton production farther west.

As profit margins have declined from competition and the technology treadmill, regional specialization has sometimes emerged. The technological improvements in milking efficiency discussed above, together with new techniques of herd management and waste disposal, increased the optimum dairy herd size throughout the country. This change gave an advantage to Wisconsin over New England dairy farmers, because their flatter and more fertile terrain permits fields to be larger and closer to the dairy barns (Kramer 1980: 55). Farmers can thus produce more of their total feed needs and spend less on transportation, favoring the shift of dairy production out of New England. In a similar process, competition has forced midwestern farms toward heavy reliance on corn and soybeans, eliminating other soil-regenerating crop rotations that provide lower per-acre profits. Livestock production has also become increasingly specialized, replacing mixed livestock and grain farms. Specialization takes advantage of higher profits in certain commodities, but it also increases dependence on the market conditions of a narrow range of products.

Since World War II, the processes of capital intensification, specialization, and competition have led to fewer and larger farms. The total number of U.S. farms has dropped sharply—over 2,000 farms a week have been lost since the 1950's (Coughenour and Swanson 1983: 24). For every six farms that go out of business, it is estimated that one independent farm-related business is lost as well. Rural communities may see an erosion of their economic base as farm sizes increase (Goldschmidt 1978; Madden 1980). Rising off-farm incomes have put pressure on the farm sector to support a more affluent life-style in order to keep young couples on the land. Increased profits have come both through technological innovations and through increased farm size. By combining several small farms into one larger farm, a family not only can afford machinery and other investments that allow economies of scale but also can provide itself with a broader base on which to earn a middle-class income. The historical disparity between farm incomes and nonfarm incomes has declined sharply, and farmers' life-styles now have much in common with urban and suburban residents (Coughenour 1984). In this process, farm life has come to be a less distinctive subculture (Paarlberg 1980), and the values and aspirations of farm families have come to more closely resemble those found among families in other occupations in industrial society.

Thus, the favorable agricultural and industrial conditions in the United States have fostered a capital-intensive commercial agriculture. Characterized by competition, overproduction, and the technology treadmill, this system has in recent years combined increased production with declining farm numbers and increasing farm affluence.

6. Increased Interdependence Between Farm Units and Agribusinesses

Many components of on-farm production have moved to the industrial sector and are now provided as purchased inputs and services to farmers. The term "agribusiness" will be used here to refer to food- and fiber-related enterprises not engaged in actual production. Farmers' growing dependence on agribusinesses is another characteristic of industrial agriculture.

All aspects of the production process are affected. Beginning with the seeds grown, farmers no longer routinely select and save their seeds, but buy hybrid or improved varieties from seed corporations. With recent legislation allowing seeds to be patented and their reproduction restricted, seed stocks worldwide may be increasingly controlled by the seed supply industry (Busch and Lacy 1984). Fertilizers, once produced on-farm with composts and manures, are now manufactured from petroleum and other sources and purchased from fertilizer companies. Machinery and chemicals are also essential to the production process. Even the application of chemicals or fertilizers can now be purchased. Aerial spraying of crops or bulk applications of fertilizer are common in some areas. Specialty crops like nuts or fruits are sometimes harvested by specialized companies; other firms provide drying, processing, or storage services. Food producers also deal with a range of insurance companies, credit companies, bookkeepers, accountants, tax advisers, and investment counselors. All these services and products are provided to farmers at a profit, and the farm becomes increasingly tied to this wide range of companies. The parts of the production process that are under the farmers' control are thus narrower than in tribal or peasant economies. Farmers become "price takers" not only for the sale of their crops but also for the purchase of needed inputs. Often the riskiest aspects of production are left under the control of the individual farmer.

Some researchers point to concentration in these agribusinesses as an ongoing process that parallels the increasing concentration among farms and in the wider industrial economy as well. Harvesting machinery in the United States is now dominated by four top firms that control 79 percent of total sales; four tractor attachment companies account for 80 percent of all sales; and eight major agricultural chemical companies control 64 percent of this multimillion-dollar industry (Wessel 1983; U.S. Bureau of the Census 1977). Farmers selling grain deal directly or indirectly with the six major grain traders, which handle 85 percent of the world's grain (Morgan 1979). Concentration in these industries may reduce competition and further constrain farmers' control over the conditions of agricultural production.

Vertical integration and contracting provide ways for agribusinesses to be more closely linked to the production process. Vertical integration refers to the actions of a company that joins under its control two or more successive steps of production or distribution. A farmer who contracts with a corporate buyer benefits from a secure market and a guaranteed price but loses some degree of control over farming practices. Different commodities are more or less regulated, but the vertical integration process usually stipulates farming methods in order to achieve a uniform product. Broiler chicken production, for instance, is now 100 percent contracted in the United States. The agribusiness firm actually owns the chicks and pays growers a fee for raising them to a specified size.

Some aspects of the New England dairy industry show the links between technological change, capital expenses, agribusiness control, and farm size and operations. In the late 1800's, the invention of the cream separator and a simple test of butterfat level set off a chain of innovations and reactions (Kramer 1980). Once cream could be separated from the milk, farmers could ship cream for processing to a growing industry of creameries and cheese factories. The butterfat test allowed farmers to evaluate the quality of milk produced by each cow and led to rapid developments in breeding efforts.

Some farms began to specialize in cattle breeding, first of stud animals and later of refrigerated semen for artificial insemination. From 100 companies producing semen for 5 million head of cattle each year in 1953, today there are approximately 20 companies, able to inseminate 8 million head. Profits in dairy breeding are now concentrated in the hands of national organizations and large conglomerates that own these twenty companies. Before dairy herd improvements over the last 50 years, milk production per cow averaged 5,000 pounds per year. The national average yield per cow in the 1980's is 15,000 pounds. One exceptional cow has even broken the 50,000 pounds per year record, showing the potential for future dairy herd breeding efforts. Genetic material from her offspring is now sold to improve production throughout the nation. Future developments such as semen sexing and embryo transplants will increase the spread of certain genetic improvements in dairy cattle. The use of synthetic growth hormone to increase milk production is another innovation on the horizon, though some farm organizations fear its spread will only put more farmers out of business. The dairy industry already faces problems of massive overproduction, encouraged by artificially high government support prices. As each cow produces more milk, the number of cows needed to meet national demand will decline. The number of cows necessary to run a profitable dairy operation in New England has already increased from 10 a century ago, to between 50 and 100 today. The number of dairy farms has declined as well, and agriculturally based rural economies have suffered. Though the characteristics of each specialized commodity system are different, technological change, overproduction, competition, and concentration in farm producers and in agribusinesses are linked processes characteristic of industrial agriculture.

Two Forms: The Family Farm and the Corporate Farm

Industrial agriculture takes many organizational forms, but two major types dominate and will be called here the family farm and the corporate farm. They can be distinguished on the basis of their organization of the production process. Family farms are agricultural enterprises that are owned and operated by family units that combine their own labor with management of the farms. Most family farmers own some land, though many rent part of the land they operate. Family farmers may also hire labor, either on a part-time or a regular basis, but much of the work is still performed by the owner-operators.[1] Family farms are the most widespread production form in U.S. agriculture, both in numbers and in geographical extent.

[1] These definitions of family farm and corporate farm gloss over the complexities of U.S. agriculture and drastically simplify the agricultural reality. For research purposes, definitions would have to be altered, depending on the locale. For instance, in some areas the type and amount of labor hired on a family farm is significant; for others, hired hands are sufficiently rare as to obviate the need for such distinctions.

A second type of farm in industrial agriculture will be called here the corporate farm. Padfield and Martin (1965) refer to these units as "agricultural industries." Another term used in the literature is the "industrial-type farm" (Goss, Rodefeld, and Buttel 1980). Corporate farms are large-scale enterprises in which land, labor, capital, and management are linked to separate groups of people: owners, managers, and workers. Operated like a factory, corporate farms may hire dozens or even hundreds of agricultural workers. Corporate farms predominate in fruit and vegetable production; family farms predominate in grain farming and other mixed enterprises that include row crops.

These two forms of industrial agriculture are ideal types, and much variation is not included in such a typology. Some family farms are incorporated for tax and inheritance reasons, but they operate the same as their unincorporated neighbors. Some large-scale corporate farms are actually owned by families, who may provide management expertise. Their day-to-day operations will nevertheless resemble other corporate farms rather than family farms. The contract producer, such as the broiler chicken farm described above, is a special form that combines some aspects of family farms and corporate farms. Because research on industrial agriculture has concentrated on either family farms or corporate farms, the rest of this chapter will focus on these two groups.

The Family Farm: Internal Dynamics and Management Style

One puzzling aspect of the persistence of family farms within the capitalist context of industrial society has been the failure of pressures toward differentiation into an elite class of landowners and a larger, propertyless class of farm workers. Friedmann's analysis of family farms in a North Dakota county (1978) shows that wage labor was intrinsic to the success of independent farm households but that these hired hands were often the sons of other family farmers, not a separate class. Using census data from 1920, she showed that the average size farm needed 1.75 full-time agricultural workers to produce wheat successfully. Because the family cycle resulted in fluctuations in the number of sons available to help on the farm, the typical household hired labor during some phases of the life cycle and sent out sons to work in other phases. The wages earned by a son were used by his family to finance farm expansion, and when the son married, he was helped to establish an independent farm in his own right. Thus, involvement in a wage labor market was a phase in the reproduction of the family farm.

Not all hired hands were sons of farm owners, however; there was a group of permanent workers contributing about half of the hired labor in the county. This group did not live on family farms, could not accumulate wages because it needed them for daily consumption, and therefore faced difficulties in becoming independent farm operators. Friedmann's calculation of the quantity of capital necessary to begin farming in North Dakota in 1920 (over $12,000) led her to conclude "the 'agricultural ladder' by which proletarians achieve the position of entrepreneur was missing its lower rungs" (1978: 95). Family farms in industrial agriculture are thus embedded in markets for labor, land, inputs, and final products, but nevertheless they maintain a distint organization based on kinship. Friedmann's analysis suggests that the existence of a wage labor market may be necessary to redistribute labor resources from surplus to deficit households, allowing both the adequate functioning of the farm households and their reproduction. The relationship of family farms to the class of full-time farm workers has been studied in detail in England (Newby 1979).

One distinctive characteristic of the family farm is the way it must combine and coordinate the demands and resources of its two constituent units: the domestic group or family and the farm enterprise (Bennett and Kohl 1982). Each unit has its own process of formation, development, and decline. Social and economic roles of family members merge and conflict over the life cycle of both units. For example, "there is tension between the capital allocated to the household and the amount allocated to the farm. Constant trade-offs between these two are required. . . . Children may reach an expensive stage of growth at the very time when the enterprise is in need of capital" (Bennett 1982: 115). The diverse needs of the family farm unit are held together with an ideology of cooperation: "One for all and all for one." This cooperation sometimes conflicts with an ethic of independence and choice on many family farms. Labor, for example, is provided mostly by family members, but children are often reared with considerable freedom to choose farming or reject it. Children who wish to continue farming are permitted to choose their own mates, but there are consequences for the farm enterprise. If spouses are chosen from among nearby farm families, important neighborly ties and exchanges are possible.

Maintaining close family ties and strong cooperation in a family farm cannot be accomplished by strict attention to formal rationality or "the greatest financial return to a given input of resources" (Bennett 1982: 118). Farm management must adapt to the changing needs of family members over a long period of time in a way that promotes the continued link between the family and farm units over the developmental cycle. Family farm managers "must anticipate consequences, defer expenditures in favor of more pressing needs, and construct trade-offs between one set of demands and another" (Bennett and Kohl 1982: 147). This long-term management process contrasts with the kind of economic rationality possible in a corporate farm.

Responsibilities and tasks on family farms are usually divided by gender. The husband is generally seen as primarily responsible for the farm operation, both its daily and long-term management (Craig, Lambert, and Moore 1983). Wives vary in the extent to which they share decisions. Some are equal partners in running the farm, others are involved only in big decisions, and still others leave all farming decisions to their husbands (Rosenfeld 1985: Sachs 1983). In general, responsibility for the household and for the operation of the domestic unit is allocated primarily to the wife. Women manage family consumption, maintenance, child rearing, and ties to kin and neighbors. Each partner "helps out" the other in times of need: Women may drive trucks during harvest; men may help with childcare or gardening at times. Research suggests that women help men more than vice versa and that women's daily work loads are on the average 25 percent longer than men's (Craig, Lambert, and Moore 1983: 22). The gender division of labor on the family farm also varies by the commodity produced. In dairy farms, women often take a more central role in production activities, but in row crop and livestock farms, women are less involved with the daily farm activities (Sachs 1983). Regardless of the "all for one . . ." cooperative ideology and the important economic contributions of farm women, family farms participate in the larger national culture that expects and reinforces male dominance within the family.

The current gender division of labor has changed over time. Using archival and ethnographic data from family farms in Iowa, Fink (1986) shows that before World War II women had responsibility for poultry, eggs, dairy cattle, and gardens for home consumption. Men concentrated on row crop production for sale. As farming became more specialized and most Iowa farms abandoned their chicken, egg, and other sideline activities, women became more likely to see themselves as "just helping out" with the farm operation than was true in the past.

Either the husband or the wife can add a job off the farm without substantially changing the general division of labor by gender. If wives get jobs, they tend to do less farmwork but are still responsible for the domestic sphere. If husbands get jobs, they tend to cut back on the farm operations. Though some researchers have noted an increase in women's farmwork when the farm crisis of the 1980's forced husbands to take off-farm jobs (Gladwin 1982), women generally run farms only when divorced or widowed (Ehlers 1987; Rosenfeld 1985). A growing number of single women are inheriting and operating farms the same as their brothers might, but they are still a very small percentage of total farm operators.

Research on women farm operators in Iowa (Ehlers 1987) shows that some women are handicapped when they inherit or start a farm operation, especially from lack of familiarity with machinery repair—an essential skill in the farmer's repertoire. Women may also have different goals and may change the priorities and management style of the farm when they take over. In one case:

For years, Sophie's husband, Adam, had juggled the management of two separate dairy herds with custom harvesting (for cash) in three counties. They worked seven days and nights a week to improve their cash flow, but still, herd management was slipshod, costing them thousands in lost calves and unproductive cows. And the family never saw Adam. Her husband's accident forced Sophie to make some changes to allow them to stay in business. This she did gladly by refusing all custom jobs, selling weaker cows, concentrating the two herds into one, and rebuilding it. She recruited two of her high school-aged children as full-time hands. The results were impressive. In her initial ten months as a farm operator, Sophie brought their dairy business into the black for the first time in its 18-year history. [Ehlers 1987: 150–51]

The family farm operation involves the balancing of ecological resources and economic risk to achieve agricultural production over the family life cycle. In his study of Canadian farming and ranching units in the Jasper area, Bennett (1982) developed and refined the concept of *management style*. He found three such general styles, based on enterprise activity, productivity, efficiency, debt loads, and future stability. The first style—called "pushers" or "plungers" by local people—involves active management of resources aimed at high yield but also leads to rapid resource depletion. The second, more moderate style is called "conservative development," and local experts might say such a manager is "doing a good job." Care is shown to sustain resources while extracting a moderate profit from the land. The third style ("a sitter") is characterized by "underuse" of resources. Yields are low, but resource depletion is minimal. In a rare situation of long-term data availability, the results of these three management styles can be seen on farm yields (Table 10.2). Yields for all farms not using fertilizer drop in both active and moderately active categories, but the drop is half or less for the second group. An inactive management style does not seem to result in resource depletion. Though fertilizer use on farms is common in industrial agriculture, this case provides interesting documentation of land-use styles and soil fertility.

TABLE 10.2
Ecological Impact of Three Farm-Management
Styles in Jasper, Saskatchewan, Canada

Management style	Changes in yields over 10–25 years
Active	Wheat: yield dropped an average of 3.5 bu/acre Barley: yield dropped an average of 2 bu/acre
Moderately active	Wheat: yield dropped an average of 1 bu/acre Barley: no consistent pattern of drop or gain
Inactive	No perceptible or consistent changes

SOURCE: Adapted from Bennett 1982: 106.
   NOTE: To measure ecological impact, only farms not using fertilizer are included.

Bennett's work traced the changes in farmers' management styles over the period from 1960 to 1970 and found that enterprises using active styles increased, while those with inactive styles decreased. The conclusion that resource-depleting forms of management have gained ground and that less active farmers have been forced out of business is not correct, however, because management style fluctuates over the enterprise and family cycle. Many former "inactives" become active because of increased economic opportunity (abundant credit and good prices) but also because they were at the stage in which they wished to build up the enterprise in order to pass it on to a son or to sell it. The maturational cycle of the enterprise—not just economic conditions —thus affects the choice of appropriate management style.

Management style is also linked to variability in yield and income. Very active managers try risky experiments that are designed to bring large returns but that sometimes do not work. Their income and yields vary markedly from year to year, and there is more disparity between their expected and actual yields (Bennett 1982: 398). More moderately active managers experience some variation in yields, but the fluctuations are more moderate, on a two- or three-year cycle of investment or innovation and payoff. The inactive management style results in stable and predictable yields, year after year.

These findings from Canada illustrate an important aspect of industrial agriculture: Development of an enterprise and profit maximization are commonly linked to high risk, fluctuations in yield and income, and resource depletion. Farms subject to the pressures of the technology

treadmill often experiment with new techniques with unknown ecological consequences. Such risks can have high payoffs, but they can
also lead to disaster. The constantly changing technology of industrial
agriculture means that it is hard to assess the ecological and economic
results over the long term. For some farmers, the long term seems irrelevant, because techniques will change soon and short-term farm failure
is a more pressing concern (Barlett 1987a).

Family Farm Goals and Ethnic Variation

Family farms exist in an environment that allows many diverse economic choices; the range of crops, livestock, and production techniques
available is often much greater than for less volatile peasant economies.
Especially because off-farm work provides attractive alternatives, the
family's goals and values play a major role in determining how the farm
will be run and toward which ends. A wider range of life-styles and
consumption patterns is open to U.S. farmers, and these choices can
lead families to pick a low-budget daily life with rapid farm expansion
as the goal or an upper middle-class life-style with little reinvestment
in the farm. Families can ease their work load with hired labor but in
doing so will amass less capital and perhaps be more dependent on
loans for annual expenses.

Ethnic background plays an important role in influencing such
choices on family farms (Rogers 1985; Rogers and Salomon 1983; Salamon 1980, 1985; Salomon, Gengenbacher, and Penas 1985). In the Illinois cornbelt, Salomon found that German Catholics follow a yeoman
tradition of commitment to a diversified agriculture, with a goal of
family continuity on the land. At the other extreme of various ethnic
groups studied are the Yankee entrepreneurs of British Isles origin. For
over 100 years, they have followed a different tradition that emphasizes
farming as "a business, land as an investment, and operations . . . run
unsentimentally for profit" (Salomon 1985: 325). The yeoman family
feels a close connection to the land: "Your land is really part of you. To
sell it is like cutting off your arm" (ibid.: 329). Land is acquired through
careful use of family capital to enable as many children as possible to
stay on the land. In contrast, entrepreneur families are willing to buy
and resell land if a good profit can be made. Sons are sometimes discouraged from continuing in farming: "There isn't enough money in
it," said one farmer. "Sons can do better" (ibid.: 325). Independence
is highly valued, and entrepreneur parents are more likely to let their
children struggle financially than to support their entry into farming in
the yeoman cooperative tradition.

These ethnic traditions have implications for farming organization

TABLE 10.3

A Typology of Major Persistent and Parallel Illinois Farming Patterns

Farming types	
Yeoman	Entrepreneur

Goals

Reproduce a viable farm and at least one farmer in each generation	Manage a well-run business that optimizes short-run financial returns

Strategy

Ownership of land farmed preferred	Ownership plus rental land to best utilize equipment
Expansion limited to family capabilities	Ambitious expansion limited by available capital
Diversify to use land and family most creatively	Manage the most efficient operation possible

Farming organization

Smaller than average operations	Larger than average operations
Animals plus grain, crop variety	Monoculture cash grain
Land fragmentation	Land consolidation
Landowners often operators	Landowners frequently absentee
Expansion of community territory	Community territory stable

Family characteristics

Intergenerational cooperation	Intergenerational competition
Parents responsible for setting up son/ heir	Incumbent upon son/heir to set up self
Many children, nonfarmers, live nearby	Often all children leave farming
Parents responsible for intergenerational transfer	Heirs responsible for intergenerational transfer
Early retirement geared to succession by children	Retirement geared to personal desires

Community structure

Village central focus of community	Village declining
Community loyalty	Weak community attachment
Population relatively stable	Population diminishing
Strong church attachment	Church consolidations
Farmers involved in village	Farmers uninvolved in village

SOURCE: Salamon 1985: 326. Reprinted courtesy of *Rural Sociology*.

and community structure. Table 10.3 summarizes the contrasts between these two styles of farming. Entrepreneur farms are 50 percent larger, on the average, than yeoman farms, because the Yankees seek to expand their farms through land rentals (Salamon 1985: 332). The German Catholic yeoman families tend to operate mixed crop, livestock, and dairy operations, while entrepreneurs rely more on specialized corn and soybean grain farming. A commitment to land ownership has made land in the yeoman community more scarce, and land is rarely sold to noncommunity members. The community's boundaries are expanding, while the Yankee community has remained stable in size. Absentee landholders are much more common in the Yankee community: "A lot of land is owned by people for investment—they've got nothing to do with farming" (Salamon 1985: 336).

Each group expresses satisfaction with its success in reaching their goals. The yeoman group has maintained both farm continuity and an ethnically homogeneous community. They experience their prosperous town and its churches as a vital, integrated environment in which to live and work. The entrepreneurs have preserved "their independence and flexibility while permitting their children a similar latitude in career choice" (Salamon 1985: 337). Their communities and county show population decline, little religious integration, and little commercial or civic vitality. The large-acreage strategies of the entrepreneurs come with greater risks of farm loss, but since continuity in farming is not a high priority, their satisfactions in trying to run a successful and expanding business take precedence.

These two types show the most clear contrasts, and obviously the fertile soils of the Illinois plains have allowed both to survive. Ethnic variations in farm operation may have conferred stronger advantages in other regions for one group or another, leading to that group's dominance in the current farm scene.

Not all ethnic groups have been as successful in gaining control of farmland as the Germans, Irish, Swedes, Norwegians, and English in Illinois. Black farmers, in particular, have faced formal and informal restrictions on their ability to farm. A heritage of unequal access to resources makes farming for blacks more difficult and less profitable in many areas of the country. Among elderly black and white farmers in North Carolina, Groger (1983) found that blacks have smaller, less profitable farms that were most often bought from strangers or nonkin. Whites tend to buy or inherit their larger and more fertile farms from family members, especially parents. Black farmers are more likely to face poverty in their old age and to rely on help from their children who have migrated to work elsewhere. Blacks who have been able to hold on to their farms benefit from homeownership and higher quality housing. Farm owners tend to live close to kin and are helped by shared meals and other resources. Land ownership makes a large difference in standard of living, economic security, and the quality of ties to children.

Part-Time Farming

One way that many family farmers have responded to a desire for a higher standard of living in the postwar era is to combine off-farm income with the farm income. By 1979, 92 percent of farm families had some form of off-farm income, and in a fifth of the total, both husband and wife had jobs (Carlin and Ghelfi 1979: 272; U.S. Bureau of the Census 1979: 224). At first, the trend toward combining jobs and farming seemed to be a temporary response; farmers were either moving into or out of full-time farming. In recent decades, it is clear that part-time farming is a permanent adaptation. Between a third and a half of family farms depend on their regular jobs for most of their income and carry out farming tasks in the evenings and on weekends. As would be expected from the family division of labor discussed above, the scale of farming depends most heavily on whether the husband is employed. If not, the wife's off-farm income can be an important contribution to the household budget. Some full-time farmers say, "My wife makes the living," while the farm income goes to meet farm debts and expenses. When the husband has a full-time job, however, the acreage of the farm is likely to be much smaller.

Part-time farming families see themselves as getting "the best of both worlds" (Van Es et al. 1982). They enjoy a high standard of living and the security of a regular paycheck, with all the satisfactions of farm life as well. Part-time farmers interviewed in Dodge County, Georgia, talk of the meaning farm work holds for them: "We farm because we love it. I love the magic of growing things and the personal satisfaction of creating something" (Barlett 1986b). Farming is a form of recreation and provides a healthful contrast to the frustrations and tensions of off-farm jobs. The yearly gamble of prices, weather, and yields "gets in your blood," and farmers value the opportunity to "be your own boss." Part-time farmers sometimes talk of the farm as a hobby or form of recreation, though most operate smaller versions of full-time farms, producing several row crops and livestock on a median of 131 acres.

Dodge County part-time farmers stress economic reasons for farming as well. For many, it is a form of moonlighting, a second income that lets them buy "special things" or finance their children's education. The purchase of a farm early in married life is often part of a long-term plan for retirement. Many retired couples in the county carry out small-scale farming to pay the bills and keep themselves productive. The purchase of farmland is also considered a sound investment.

The Dodge County study found that most part-time farmers rejected full-time farming early in life and made a commitment to some kind of off-farm job. Later, in their twenties or thirties, they added a farm, often but not always with land previously in the family. A few use hired workers to help with farm tasks, but most do all the farmwork themselves. Part-time farmers hold a wide range of jobs. Some are white-collar professionals—lawyers, nurses, and administrators—while others are skilled blue-collar technicians, mechanics, or public safety officers. Business owners and janitors both share the commitment to farming "on the side." The average part-time farming family earns over $24,000 from salaries and lives a comfortable, middle-class life-style.

Part-time farming provides greater security in an agricultural slump. Such families can cut back their operations or use their off-farm income to subsidize the farm. In Dodge County, after successive years of drought and poor prices, only 20 percent of part-time farmers face serious or critical debt loads (Barlett 1986b). In contrast, almost double that proportion of full-time farmers face debilitating debts and the possibility of farm loss. A few part-time farmers have already faced an economic crisis—17 percent of the part-time farmers studied had recently taken off-farm work as a result of the adverse farm economy. Some of these transitional part-time farmers hoped to go back to full-time farming in the future, though others had given up and cut back their acreage to fit the constraints of after-hours farming.

The current slump in agriculture in the 1980's and the greater participation in the labor market have changed some families' attitudes. Loyalty to farming as a way of life, regardless of its cost, is less common nowadays. The hard times that farmers face combined with the sometimes higher status of other occupations led one father, when asked if he would encourage his sons to go into farming, to say: "I will try to learn 'em about farming, then they can make up their own minds. I can't encourage anybody to go into it, but there's no better life than farm life—I enjoy it" (Barlett 1986a).

The decision whether to combine farming and off-farm work is a complex one. In some areas of the country, rural jobs are plentiful; in others, farmers have few options for off-farm work. Time spent in jobs must be taken from other tasks, and family labor allocation can change as well. Craig, Lambert, and Moore (1983) found that only in families in which the wife was employed outside the farm were her work hours more parallel to her husband's.

The criteria involved in women's decisions regarding part-time farming were studied by Gladwin in Florida (1982). Fig. 10.3 illustrates the decision process, using a hierarchical decision model (Gladwin 1984). The first constraints in the decision whether to farm full-time or part-time or to take off-farm work are health and age. The infirm or elderly women (5 out of 48 interviewed) choose to mix part-time farming and housework. The second major constraint is the presence of young children or ill family members who require the woman to be at home. A

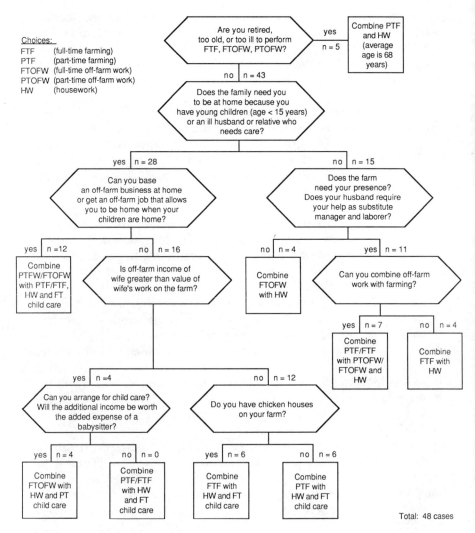

Fig. 10.3. Flowchart of farm women's decisions to farm or work off the farm.
Source: Adapted from Gladwin 1982: 12.

majority (58 percent) face this challenge, and some respond by taking a full-time or part-time job or running an in-home business that allows them to be home when children are there. Others work in full-time chicken production on the farm or hire a baby-sitter and work off the farm full-time. The women without childcare constraints choose among full-time off-farm work, full-time farming, and combinations of part-time farming and part-time jobs according to whether they are needed on the farm and can obtain suitable off-farm work. Hierarchical decision models have also been used to explore structural change in U.S. agriculture (Gladwin and Zabawa 1984; Zabawa 1987).

Family Farm Partnerships

A final issue in family farming is the importance of partnerships and the different forms they take. Family farms in the United States are most commonly run by one family, but father-son and sibling partnerships are important variants. In Washington and Idaho, Carlson and Dillman (1983) found that kinship ties among co-operators, especially in father-son operations, are linked to higher rates of adoption of new soil conservation techniques and other farm innovations. This greater innovativeness may be due to the long-term planning possible in such a two-generation farm, to the fact that these farms are often larger and more prosperous, or to some other way in which father-son interactions produce more dynamic decision making. Among Illinois Irish farming families (Salamon 1980), close cooperation of siblings is the cultural goal, and in fact such farms occur more than twice as often as among other ethnic groups. Sibling teams seem to provide certain advantages: larger farm acreage (two and a half times the size of father-son farms), sufficient farm labor to avoid the necessity for hired hands, pooling of capital for buildings and equipment, and specialization in tasks such as marketing or repair work. Sibling solidarity is encouraged among these Irish families at the expense of a closer father-son tie. The reverse is true for German families studied in Illinois (Salamon 1980), in which the father-son bond is stronger but sibling rivalry makes sibling cooperation on the farm less common.

Partnerships seem to be a way for family farms to cope with the rising costs and technological complexity of industrial agriculture. They also benefit from having closer ties between management and labor and provide the careful supervision of farm operations less common to corporate farms. The role of women may be crucial on partnership farms, because they provide needed capital via off-farm jobs. It also seems to be the case that women are less likely to have a central role in the farm operation when several male kin cooperate.

Corporate Farms

The family farm as a producer of food in industrial society is losing ground to the corporate farm. How rapidly this change is occurring depends on the data and the definitions used. Marxist theoreticians see such a transition to a completely capitalist industrial structure as inevitable. The logic of industrial society is expected to penetrate and overwhelm any small-scale or family-based economic unit, and family farms will go the way of independent family drugstores or gas stations. The problem of interest to many such researchers is why the transition has taken so long and why family farms are still viable in Western economies. They argue that the interests of the larger economic entities are served by leaving certain risky aspects of production in the hands of family farms. Neoclassical economists also assume the transition to corporate farming is inevitable, citing the greater efficiency of larger units as technology has developed in recent decades. "Modern farming" is seen to require a scale that leads to a separation of ownership, management, and labor. Both groups of researchers also point to the political influence and market power of large producers and argue that small- and medium-size producers are handicapped in this competition. A third group of researchers takes a populist perspective. They challenge the presumed efficiency of larger units and argue that a more diverse farm structure will foster democracy and healthy rural communities. Based on the trends in areas with concentrations of corporate farms, the populists argue that government programs that give advantages to such units work against the long-term national interest. Such government policies are susceptible to change, they argue, and the trend to corporate farming can be reversed.

Characteristics of Corporate Farming

Corporate farming has been most thoroughly studied in fruit and vegetable production in the Southwest. In these accounts, the themes of industrial agriculture discussed above emerge again: capital-intensive technology, the role of the state, links to agribusinesses, competition, and specialization. Corporate farming involves the complex coordination of workers and managers and often involves the use of highly mechanized production methods. Mark Kramer (1980) eloquently describes the harvest on a California corporate farm that grows tomatoes for processing:

This harvest happens nearly without people. A hundred million tomatoes grown up, irrigated, fed, sprayed, now taken, soon to be cooled, squashed, boiled, barreled and held at ready, then canned, shipped, sold, bought, and after being sold and bought a few more times, uncanned and dumped on pizza. . . .
     The six harvesting machines drift across the gray-green tomato-leaf sea. . . . The nearest harvester draws steadily closer, yawing and moving in at about the speed of a slow amble, roaring as it comes. Up close, it looks like the aftermath of a collison between a grandstand and a San Francisco tramcar. It's two stories high, rolls on wheels that don't seem large enough, astraddle a wide row of

jumbled and unstaked tomato vines. It is not streamlined. It resembles a Mars Lander. Gangways, catwalks, gates, conveyors, roofs and ladders are fastened on all over the lumbering rig. As it closes in, its front end snuffles up whole tomato plants as surely as a hungry pig loose in a farmer's garden. Its hind end excretes a steady stream of stems and rejects. Between the ingestion and the elimination, fourteen laborers face each other on long benches. They sit on either side of a conveyor that moves the new harvest rapidly past them. Their hands dart out and back as they sort through the red stream in front of them. . . . The folks aboard . . . are working hard for low wages, culling out what is not quite fit for pizza sauce—the "greens," "molds," "mechanicals," and the odd tomato-sized clod of dirt. . . . A half-full tractor trailer runs along next to the harvester, receiving its steady flume of tomatoes. . . .

As per cannery contract, each of the semi-trailer loads of tomatoes must contain no more than 4 percent green tomatoes, 3 percent tomatoes suffering mechanical damage from the harvestor, 1 percent tomatoes that have begun to mold, and 0.5 percent clods of dirt.

"The whole idea of this thing," a harvest executive had explained earlier in the day, "is to get as many tons as you can per hour. Now, the people culling on the machine strive to sort everything that's defective. But to us, that's as bad as picking out too little. . . . If we're allowed 7 or 8 percent defective tomatoes and we don't have 7 or 8 percent defective tomatoes in the load, we've given away money. And what's worse, we're paying these guys to make the load too good. It's a double loss. . . . So what you do is run the belt too fast, and sample the percentages in the output from each machine. If the load is too poor, we add another worker. If it's too good, we send someone home." . . .

The introduction of the harvester brought about other changes, too. Processors thought that tomatoes ought to have more solid material, ought to be less acid, ought to be smaller in size. Engineers called for tomatoes that had tougher shells and were oblong so they wouldn't climb up or roll back down tilted conveyor belts. Larger growers, more able to substitute capital for labor, wanted more tonnage per acre, resistance to cracking from sudden growth spurts that follow irrigation, leaf shade for the fruit, to prevent scalding from the hot sun, determinate plant varieties that grow only so high, to keep those vines in rows, out of the flood irrigation ditches.

As geneticists selectively bred for these characteristics, they lost control of others. They bred for thick-walledness, less acidity, more uniform ripening, oblongness, leafiness, and high yield—and they could not also select for flavor. And while the geneticists worked on tomato characteristics, chemists were perfecting an aid of their own. Called ethylene, it is in fact also manufactured by tomato plants themselves. All in good time, it promotes reddening. Sprayed on a field that has reached a certain stage of maturity . . . the substance . . . induces redness. . . . It assures the growers precision. [Kramer 1980: 197–213][2]

Corporate farming suffers from the disadvantages of any complex bureaucracy but also benefits from some of the advantages of its large scale. Management decisions and day-to-day operations are affected by the layers of responsibility that characterize the organization. Cen-

[2] Reprinted by permission of Georges Borchardt, Inc. Copyright © 1977, 1979, 1980 by Mark Kramer.

tral office personnel may seek to maximize yields while holding down costs, but day-to-day judgments that field supervisors must make are necessarily constrained by a desire to protect themselves and their jobs. For example, a field manager may order the immediate spraying of a field when its conditions only partially indicate spraying is desirable. In this way, if the harvest turns out to be lower than expected, he can say to his boss that he carried out all possible protective practices. A family farmer has responsibility for the whole operation and can weigh the likelihood of insect damage and decide to take the risk to delay spraying in order to save the money involved. The large farm manager doesn't know the whole picture but is vulnerable to criticism if there is crop loss as well as if too much money is spent. Decisions sometimes will be referred upwards to the boss, but that involves delays when time may be crucial. Another handicap to the corporate farm is the lack of direct connection between action and result. Workers who are in-attentive to planting depth or the clank of a combine may not have a way to learn of the lower harvest in that field or the subsequent break-down of the machine. The patient care of livestock is less likely to be rewarded or even noticed; staying up all night in calving or farrowing season is less likely to occur on a corporate farm.

On the other hand, corporate farms can hire and fire labor as needs dictate. Larger farms can deliver larger loads to canneries or proces-sors and thus squeeze smaller farmers out of contracts. Sophisticated accounting and money management may allow large farms to take better advantage of tax laws, futures markets, bulk purchases, and special leasing and consulting arrangements. Some researchers con-clude these advantages to corporate farms outweigh the family farmers' superior operational expertise. Some people lament the loss of craft, pride, stewardship, and concern about the quality of the product that corporate farming engenders. Others see such changes as typical of all aspects of industrial society and not unique to the changes in agricul-ture.

Corporate Farm Workers, Ethnicity, and the State

Corporate farming may involve even more capital intensification, more specialization, and more technological sophistication on larger acreages than family farms. Its primary difference with family farming, however, is that it depends on hired hands for its field labor. Thirty percent of all agricultural work in the United States is carried out by hired workers (Martin 1983: 54). Reliable, skilled labor at a price that does not threaten profits is the requirement for successful corporate farming. The nature of the crop being produced dictates the relation-

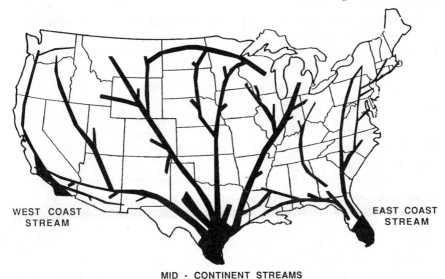

WEST COAST
STREAM

EAST COAST
STREAM

MID - CONTINENT STREAMS

Fig. 10.4. Travel patterns of seasonal migratory agricultural workers. Source: Vogeler 1981: 230.

ship between owners, managers, and workers. If workers are needed year-round for careful, skilled care of plants (as in strawberry production), relations among workers and with owners can be more personal and complex than on farms that need only temporary harvest labor. For example, says one lemon grower in Arizona: "In early fall, we need 500 workers. . . . It's 135 degrees in those groves and no movement of air at all. The gnats are unbelievable. This Yuma lemon grows 24 hours a day. When it gets to size you had better harvest it or it is out of size for commercial value" (Padfield and Martin 1965: 258). The challenge to these growers is to find large numbers of workers willing to accept some of the lowest paid jobs in the country. Migrant labor moves through fruit and vegetable areas of the country, providing harvest labor for a wide range of farm types. Fig. 10.4 illustrates the routes of travel followed by many seasonal farm workers in the United States.

Over the history of the United States, the government has cooperated with growers to assure that a variety of immigrant and temporary worker groups have been available for work in the fields (Majka and Majka 1982). The slaves brought from various parts of Africa were the first, followed by workers from China, the Philippines, Mexico, Japan, and various Caribbean nations. In the Southwest, farm labor relations have been a continuing struggle among owners, workers, unions, and the government. Often, the workers are divided among themselves, and ethnic differences are reinforced by farm owners, who create opportunities for some groups over others (Thomas 1985). In Arizona, researchers studied six ranks of farm workers (from the technological elite to the transient day laborers) in three kinds of crops (lettuce, cotton, and citrus). It was found that Anglos dominate the higher ranking jobs (except for the "Anglo-isolate" group of older and middle-aged men who have dropped out of other occupations). Mexican-Americans were found through all six ranks, but predominated in the middle, and blacks and Indians were concentrated near the bottom (Padfield and Martin 1965).

Mechanization and technological changes provide an opportunity for some worker groups to displace others. As field labor in Arizona cotton production was replaced by machines, Indians, blacks, and Mexican-Americans were squeezed out, and Anglos dominated skilled machine operator jobs (ibid.). In lettuce production, however, the introduction of vacuum-cooled packing displaced an elite, unionized group of Anglo and Mexican-American workers. The newer, less-skilled jobs then went primarily to Mexicans. As a result, the nearby communities of Anglo workers declined rapidly. Just as in manufacturing, agricultural industries can change their needs for workers and skills, causing disruptions of community and family ties. Ethnic differences among farmworkers have been shown to be linked to a range of life-style characteristics (Padfield and Martin 1965). Ethnic differences among corporate farm owners and managers have not been studied.

Farmworker unionization has been an important trend in the recent history of corporate farming. In this aspect of the lives of farmworkers, corporate agriculture bears many similarities to other industries, and agriculture can often be treated as any other industrial workplace. Unions have brought wage increases, improved working conditions, and greater security to farmworkers. In response, some farm owners have moved toward labor-replacing mechanization to hold down costs. Others have tried to control the unions or keep them from becoming established in the first place.

The case of strawberry production in California (Wells 1981; 1984) illustrates a number of aspects of corporate farming—high productivity, competition, reliance on wage labor, and changing government policies with regard to workers—in a particular commodity in which complete mechanization is not feasible. Strawberry production epitomizes the rapid change in productivity possible with industrial agricultural technology. Yields in California rose from 2.9 tons per acre in 1941 to over 20 tons per acre in 1978–81. Some growers have even reached harvests as high as 57 tons per acre (Wells 1981: 682). Strawberry production is heavily capital-intensive, using expensive land, plant varieties, chemicals, and fertilizers. Labor, however, is the largest single cost, and high-quality labor is critical to success in strawberries. The fragility of the crop and the need for constant care put a premium on the timing of tasks. Fluctuations and uncertainty in strawberry prices leave growers eager to keep labor costs as low as possible while assuring a reliable labor supply.

Before World War II, most strawberries were grown on small, Japanese family farms, but in the postwar period, Mexican nationals through the federal bracero program came to dominate the strawberry labor market. The termination of the bracero program and the rise of the United Farm Workers Union sharply threatened the available low-cost labor supply. Different sizes of growers adopted different strategies in response.

The small- and medium-size growers developed close, personalistic ties with their workers. These growers attempted to stabilize their labor supply by offering higher wages, longer periods of employment, better working conditions, and special benefits such as housing. Their workforce is primarily Mexican and often related to each other by kinship.

Larger farmers have adopted a sharecropping system that has successfully shut out the United Farm Workers Union and assured a low-cost, stable workforce. The landowners subdivide the property into small plots, for which legal Mexican immigrant workers sign annual contracts. Owners pay most production expenses and provide inputs and supervision. Sharecroppers carry out production tasks, recruiting and paying for necessary hired labor. Kin networks, including illegal Mexican immigrants, are utilized to generate a high-quality workforce at low prices. Because the UFW considers sharecroppers to be growers, they have not attempted to recruit them into the union. Laborers hired by the sharecroppers are tied to them by favors and family ties and have been resistant to union organizing efforts. Thus, on the larger strawberry farms, workers have been stratified into two groups, "with different prerogatives and somewhat conflicting interests" (Wells 1981: 698). On all sizes of farms, the pressure of unions toward higher wages has been met with diverse organizations of the production process.

Corporate farmers as well as family farmers see themselves as subject to pressures from buyers, processors, and other agribusiness industries. In the Arizona study, farm owners and managers hold low labor costs to be essential to their survival but assert: "We don't get the big bite. The big larceny is at the chain store level—whether one dollar or two dollars a carton, they sell lettuce $0.29 a head. . . . A guy that buys 100 [railroad] cars a day has more power and control than a guy who buys two" (Padfield and Martin 1965: 255). In some areas and crops, vertical integration has changed the traditionally competitive ties among growers, buyers, and processors. The Tenneco Corporation once boasted to its stockholders that it wants to develop a food system integrated "from seedling to supermarket." The recent slump in the farm economy, however, seems to have dampened the interest of many nonfarm corporations in expansion into agricultural production.

Community Impacts of Corporate Farming

Corporate farms generate a more class-stratified community in which wealthy owners and managers are distinct from farm workers. Community activities (civic, religious, educational) tend to be dominated by the owners and managers, while workers are less involved in such activities (Heffernan 1978:31). Fig. 10.5 contrasts the smaller number of farm operators in a corporate farm (large-scale farm) area. Farm laborers make up the majority of the population under such production systems. In a comparison of two California communities producing identical total values of farm products, Goldschmidt (1978) found that moderate-size family farms produce more vital and economically healthy rural communities. Smaller-scale agriculture generates a higher average family income and a higher average standard of living, because wealth is less concentrated in a few hands, as in the large-scale farming community. The corporate farming community is characterized by fewer schools, higher teacher turnover rates, fewer businesses, fewer social organizations, lower town participation rates, fewer churches, and less religious participation. The small-scale community exhibits more involvement in town activities and more civic pride. Merchants there do almost double the retail trade, and there are more than twice as

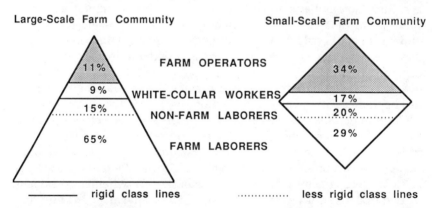

Fig. 10.5. Class structure of communities dominated by agribusiness and family farms. Source: Vogeler 1981: 256.

many businesses and shops. Though the agricultural systems generate the same amount of total revenue, the different distribution of wealth and land ownership leads to very different qualities of community life.

Goldschmidt's results have been criticized and his communities restudied with mixed results (California Small Farm Viability Project 1977; Hayes and Olmstead 1984; Heffernan 1978). No one, however, has carefully replicated the study in other parts of the country. Current national trends seem to support the conclusions that a decline in numbers of farms results in less vital communities and an overall lower quality of life for rural residents. The trend toward increasing corporate farm dominance in U.S. agriculture must be assessed with these consequences in mind.

Current Concerns and Trends in the Study of Industrial Agriculture

All through this chapter, topics have been discussed such as the welfare and working conditions of farm laborers, the safety of farm chemicals, and the declining numbers of farmers—that raise concerns among researchers, consumers, and producers. When we look toward the future of industrial agriculture, a few other issues must also be raised. Primary among these is a concern about the sustainability of industrial agriculture. Can it survive with its heavy use of nonrenewable resources, its tendency to erode and deplete the soils it uses, and the contamination of the soil, water, and food products with possibly harmful chemicals? Efforts have been made by environmental groups and government organizations to push for changes in traditional practices to address these concerns. Ways have been sought to cut energy costs, encourage soil conservation, and find alternatives to heavy chemical use.

Another response has been the organic agriculture movement. Organic farming avoids chemical fertilizers, pesticides, hormones, and the prophylactic use of antibiotics. It places emphasis on soil quality by applying compost and other natural materials and seeks a balance of organisms and nutrients. Although studies show such practices can result in lower yields per acre, costs are lowered as well (Lockeretz and Wernick 1980). Farmers in a range of farm sizes and commodities —even midwestern corn farmers—have found they come out ahead in financial terms and are able to reduce health risks to themselves and their families. Organic farming is but one group within a larger alternative agricultural movement that seeks support for nonconventional agricultural techniques. Their goals are a more nutritious food product, a healthier production process, and a more sustainable, less energy-intensive overall food system.

Another concern arises from the quality of food produced in industrial agriculture. Monocropping on soils with declining levels of organic matter can produce less nutritious crops. A carrot is a carrot is a carrot, maintains the U.S. Department of Agriculture, responding to the pressures of corporate farming. But research suggests that nutrient levels can vary widely. Other invisible changes in products such as chemical residues or bacterial contamination force consumers to rely on government agencies to monitor and test the food supply. The look, smell, or taste of food is no longer a safe guide.

Our current food system is highly vulnerable to ecological disturbance. The reduction in the number of crop varieties and greater fragility in hybrid varieties in some cases make sudden fluctuations in yields more likely in industrial agriculture. Extremes of weather can bring about wider global repercussions than ever before. Industrial agriculture now uses heavy doses of fossil energy to maintain productivity. When the era of cheap and abundant petroleum is over, some predict that farming will have to return to more labor-intensive and energy-conserving methods. Other commentators expect that the commitment to industrial agriculture will be so strong that such a retrenchment will be politically unacceptable. New breakthroughs in energy development or genetic engineering may lead to new phases of these predictions.

Another concern stems from the context of agricultural production. Though anthropologists tend to focus more on local-level production units, these units are being integrated ever more tightly into a global agricultural system. It is now commonplace for governmental policies in one country to create new cropping patterns in a second country, with disastrous consequences to the agriculture of a third. Global grain trade remains virtually unregulated, and concentration in grain dealers has been succeeded by concentration in machinery companies, input suppliers, meat packers, and food processors. Predictions abound that biotechnology will further stimulate the growth of complex agribusiness multinational corporations. The consequences in an ever more closely connected world food market are unclear. Whether family farms continue as a viable form of food production or are replaced by corporate agriculture is, in large part, dependent on this larger agricultural context.

This chapter has focused on the United States and Canada, but the international trends of industrial agriculture are an important area of current research. When looking at our own industrial society, we can see that food production is a negotiated process, as farm owners and workers, family farms and corporate farms, producers and agribusinesses each seek to further their own interests in the marketplace and through government concessions and rewards. Efficiency or productivity may be less important than legislative lobbying efforts, campaign contributions, and political influence. In the context of overproduction, the question remains, Who will be allowed to produce? And with what consequences to communities, the nation, and the world as a whole? Industrial agriculture, the newest human subsistence system, has changed rapidly over the last 100 years, and its current rate of change is more rapid still. Only time will tell if it will spread throughout the world, adapt to changing conditions, and become dominant, or whether it will be a temporary aberration in the history of human food production.

11

The Informal Economy

M. Estellie Smith

In the years following World War II, a new topic of economic concern emerged. Terms such as "black market," "moonlighting," "off the books," and—the one preferred here—"the informal economy" became increasingly common as a growing mountain of evidence revealed an extraordinarily productive system that engaged people in the labor, circulation, and consumption of goods and services, largely outside the ken of the government. Somehow these activities escaped being fully illuminated by or totally captured in official statistics. Spain exported far more footware than could be accounted for in factory production figures; squatter settlements in Latin American cities mushroomed overnight, peopled by former rural peasants who, while officially constituting a vast army of urban "unemployed," managed to earn wages to maintain their households—and, in addition, to provide their own sewer systems, trash collection, electricity, and even schools. An army of illegal immigrants—running the gamut from college-educated Irish working as computer experts and actuaries in Boston to unskilled workers from Pakistan doing menial service jobs in Tokyo—gave tantalizing hints to their presence, while whole villages in the tribal hill region of Southeast Asia's Golden Triangle participated in the international drug trade. In every major city in the world, street hawkers peddled their wares, women did piece work at home, children worked urban trash heaps, the elderly ran "garage sales," and men worked two jobs—one officially tracked, the other "after hours" and unrecorded. As Tanzi (1980: 2) noted, "[L]ike the wind, the underground economy may still be hidden to the eye, but its presence is, now, very much felt."

The range of activities ran the spectrum from the ordinary, everyday activities of the poor—things that had always been done to "make ends meet" but had never seemed worthy of official notice—through the questionably, even quasi-legal activities of expense-account padding or "creative bookkeeping" of large firms, to the opposite end of untold billions being circulated through international crime networks.

Interestingly, officialdom began to concentrate on the low end of the spectrum. They realized that, despite the minimal sums involved per individual or household, the numbers added up cumulatively. They had, in short, discovered the truth of the old adage that if one "takes care of the pennies, the dollars will take care of themselves."

Yet it was exactly those "ordinary, everyday kinds of activities" and the lives of those who engaged in them that were well known to anthropologists, especially those studying peasant and complex, urban societies.[1] We had for many years been concerned with learning about the day-to-day informal routines of people, meaning household-based and family-based private activities. This was in contrast to the formal economy, meaning that related sequence of production-distribution-consumption activities regulated and tracked by the official record-keeping system of a polity's governing sector.

Informal economy activities preclude most if not all of the protection offered by the umbrella of national caretaking programs; worse, labor laws protecting employee rights to fair wages, safe working conditions, negotiating rights, and so on are usually denied informal sector employees under their conditions of employment. Portes and Walton (1981: 87) focused on this when they defined the informal economy as the sphere that includes "all income-producing activities outside formal sector wages and social security payments." The definition is flawed, however, in that it limits the formal sector to those whose national system provides for social security payments (using the term in a generic rather than specific sense) and who earn wages rather than take income from their profits. Because, say in the United States, such coverage has emerged only recently (primarily in the 1930's), these criteria are too confining.

Many definitions are based on the assumption that the informal sector is a product of recent times. But historians, especially European historians, have provided us with a long history of the attempts of states to identify, monitor, regulate, prohibit, and, most important, derive revenues from the production, circulation, and consumption of goods and services (see, for example, the laws against smuggling, poaching, prostitution,[2] and economic activities prohibited to such groups as Jews and

[1] See, for example, Bohannan and Bohannan 1968; Bohannan and Dalton 1962; Brookfield 1969; Dewey 1962; Edel 1967; Firth 1946; Firth and Yamey 1963; Forde 1949; Foster 1942, 1948; Geertz 1963; Herskovits 1937; Herskovits and Harwitz 1964; Hill 1969, 1970; Honigmann 1949; Isaac 1965; Katzin 1959, 1960, 1964; Little 1951; Mayer 1961, 1980; Mintz 1955, 1959, 1967; Miracle 1962a, 1962b; Nash 1961; Orans 1968; Plattner 1975a; Powdermaker 1962; Richards 1932; Tax 1953; Udy 1959; Ward 1967; Waterbury 1970; Wolf 1966.

[2] Rossiaud (1988) has done an excellent study of the way in which the French government between the fourteenth and fifteenth centuries legalized prostitution—certainly not to control it, since in one town of 10,000 there were over 100 prostitutes, but to control the economics of it.

Gypsies). Long before the centrally planned economies of twentieth-century communist countries, states established monopolies as the sole producer or seller (for example, of timber, salt, or alcoholic beverages) or monopsonies (for example, the government of Japan still maintains such a buyer's monopoly over the rice produced by its farmers). Indeed, black markets have existed from ancient times, usually appearing in time of scarcity or intense government restrictions, as during wars. As Uzzell notes, informal sector activities exist "where the dominant mode of production is inadequate to meet the perceived needs of the population, whatever that mode of production may be" (1980: 43).

Finally, Mattera's definition (1985: 1) identifies the activities in this sector as all having in common that they are "transactions that . . . do not conform with the rules set down by the state in its role as overseer of the economy." This is intuitively attractive because it emphasizes the close relationship between the economic and the political spheres. It also directs our attention to the rules imposed by some public authority that acts to implement and audit (in order to ensure conformity to) some public set of rules governing production, distribution, and consumption.

For these reasons, this review will define the informal sector as consisting of those activities that capture resources by (1) increasing private access to community resources beyond the normative allocation; and (2) partially or totally evading public monitoring or entry into the general accounts as well as any obligatory or reciprocal corporate assessment (that is, tax). In short, the primary participants in this sector are producers of goods and services who provide some marketable commodity that for various reasons escapes enumeration, regulation, or other type of public monitoring or auditing. The category includes any economic activity—production, distribution, and even consumption, as when there are sumptuary laws or, say, tabooed substances such as alcohol or drugs—that eludes, is discounted, or is ignored by the state's national accounting system.[3]

---

[3] The national account consists of the gross national product (GNP) and national income. National income is tallied by tracking (1) the total earnings of labor and property that arise from the production of goods and services in the nation's economy during a given year; (2) direct taxes, involuntary exactions of local, state/provincial, or national governments (for example, personal income, inheritance, and social insurance assessments) that are deemed to be the specific outcome of the employment of labor. Based on market prices the GNP reckons the distribution of goods and services—gross private domestic investments, private consumer and government purchases, and goods/services exported, including so-called indirect taxes (such as excise, sales, and value-added taxes, customs duties, business property taxes), the burden of which the person required to pay the tax to the government can pass on to others. To balance GNP and national income, we then deduct various indirect taxes, transfer payments, depreciation on capital goods,

This is not a simple definition, but the issue addressed is not simple —as is always the case when human behavior and sociocultural issues are being discussed. Further, it raises the issue of nonstate societies.

Can There Be Informal Economies in Nonstate Societies?

Although the definition just presented is framed in terms of structures and processes prevalent in the current world system of nation-states, its essentials could easily be adapted to apply to nonstate societies, hunting and gathering groups, autonomous village units, multisettlement chiefdoms, and, of course, city-states. A brief restatement would be: The informal sector consists of any production, distribution, or consumption activities that occur outside of the constraints/ opportunities accepted by the members of an inclusive social unit as proper, right, publicly accountable, and legitimately subject to assessment. This thesis is grounded in the assumption that the formal economy, no less than the informal, has its roots in such nonstate sociocultural structures as household, family, neighborly, and pan-associational contexts—contexts that impose duties and obligations as well as grant rights and privileges.[4]

It may be argued that any accounting process requires, at the least, literacy and numeracy as well as a double entry system of bookkeeping in which debits are weighed against credits. However, though literacy and numeracy are indeed critical for records in states (the first tallies of trade and tribute, as well as legal prescriptions for and violations of such trade and tribute, appear as early as ancient Sumer and Egypt), members of smaller, nonliterate aggregates are also capable of monitoring and "keeping account" of each other's performances. See, for example, McGuire and Netting (1982: 284) for a cautionary tale of supernatural monitoring and punishment of cheaters in a Swiss peasant community.

The members of all sociocultures take care to inculcate new members with the rules, chief among which are those relating to subsistence activities—for example, obligations to share, to consume appropriately, and restrictions or prohibitions on using resources. There are no societies known in which rules relating to right and wrong use of resources do not exist, especially as related to corporate (held in common by the

---

etc., from the GNP while adding to it such figures as subsidies (less the government's current surpluses) (Sloan and Zurcher 1970).

[4] Halperin and Sturdevant (1988) have also explored this wider application.

unit's members) subsistence resources. Given that such rules exist and that people are expected to follow them, one would expect to find some institutionalized way of making sure they are obeyed. And this means that there has to be some kind of auditing mechanism.

A chief and his assistants, a headman, the elders of multicephalous village councils, and community members at large all participate in ensuring there is a proper "minding of the rules."

The techniques by which people audit other people are often quite ingenious. For example, among the Andamanese, a hunting and gathering society, especially valued foods are considered dangerous to eat. It is believed that consuming such foods causes the body to give off odors specific to each item (as when we can tell the difference between the person who has just eaten garlic or had a beer). If, however, one is careful to observe the rules that require one to paint one's body with distinctive designs—each specific to the food eaten—the odor is eliminated and malevolent spirits, attracted by the odor, are foiled (Radcliffe-Brown 1964). Decorating one's body with particular colors and patterns linked to the specific product may have guaranteed that the spirits ignored one's feasts, but it also made it impossible to eat these foods without the other humans learning about it. Only the most exceptionally defiant individual would attempt both to break the rules against sharing and to try to hide the act (though risk losing oneself to the gods) by not using the protective paint. These are techniques of auditing individual behavior and making it difficult if not impossible to engage in any informal activities.

Similarly, among the Amerindian pueblos of the U.S. Southwest, the water-scarce environment requires that community members commonly maintain the irrigation ditches and obey council rules for using the water in their fields, especially during times of scarcity. In addition to ditch riders who patrol the fields, neighbors do more visiting during dry times, "casually" checking the state of one another's crops. Should someone's fields look suspiciously green or sturdy relative to those of other village members, rumors fly, the ditch bosses keep a closer eye on the comings and goings of the farmer, and a member of the governing council might stop by for a chat—which will include such remarks as how "some people in the village are talking about some others who, though I really cannot believe this to be true, are taking more than their allotted share of water." Here we have an example of (1) the statement of the formal perimeters of community participation, (2) monitoring to guard against a breach of the rules, (3) a crossing of the boundaries into the informal sector, where private goals take precedence over civic law, and (4) the way in which a representative of the formal system moves to reinforce conformity with the formal sector.

In short, in small, even preliterate communities, accounts are kept and payment is exacted.

The Discovery of the Informal Sector

If the informal sector is not a recent invention, why has the topic waited so long to emerge with its own group of researchers? Why did the crystallization occur only during the 1970's and not sooner or later? This is discussed in more detail in the last section of this chapter, but certainly two factors were the "growth industry" in Third World development planning and the rise of socialist societies in Europe after World War II. Studies of centrally planned economies by scholars like Berliner (1957) revealed that, despite sophisticated efforts in stringent control and rigorous oversight, even the most formalized operations were ridden with informal structures and processes. And, if anything, the operations detected bore the distinct odor of entrepreneurial capitalism. Thus some of the earliest writings on this newly discovered underground economy dealt with the way it intermeshed or articulated with the "state capitalism" of eastern Europe (see, for example, Cassel and Cichy 1968 on the growing "shadow economy" of East and West).

Urban research in the United States showed that, despite the apparent differences between East and West, there was the same interplay between formal programs that delivered goods and services from the top down versus informal and ad hoc "programs" that intended recipients worked out at the grass-roots level. For example, the Fermans (1973) focused on Detroit to study what they labeled "the irregular economy" of the urban poor, who mobilized self-help networks to produce, trade, swap, and barter goods and services among the members. "Goods and services did not have to be produced and consumed in officially recognized and registered enterprises" (Ferman, Henry, and Hoyman 1987: 14).

In one industrial mill town in New England, for example, most in the flood of new Portuguese immigrants in the period 1955–75 could not have survived without the informal economy. Arriving without funds and handicapped by their lack of English, industrial skills, or knowledge of the system in general, many initially earned nothing but their room and board, doing household maintenance or remodeling, housekeeping, and child care to free their hosts to do outside work. News of possible employment came not through any official agency but through the neighborhood grapevine; a popular saying in the community was, "It's not what you know, it's who you know—and who they know." While staying at home to care for children (their own or others), women also did piece work "off the books" for the town's dominant garment industry. Men worked, usually irregularly, as night watchmen, maintenance workers, car washers, delivery men, or any job where English or some level of industrial experience was not necessary. Until the new arrival got settled—that is, became permanently employed or was able to get an independent entrepreneurial venture established on a paying basis—those kin who had promised assistance before the immigrants even left home, plus the neighbors of those kin, helped out by providing food, lodging, clothes, and information.

One couple with whom I worked was able to buy a home within a few years of arriving because the wife had learned English by working as a civilian employee at a U.S. military base in Portugal; she tutored immigrants for cash or barter (exchanging her services for anything the family could use, such as house furnishings, home preserves, clothes, and the care of her children when she went out to give lessons). The husband dug up "free" bushes and trees—in isolated wooded areas and along country roads, even using greenery along state highways or in public parks—and replanted them as part of a landscaping service he offered in new home developments. He also often bartered his services, exchanging landscaping in return, say, for a used car for his wife, construction supplies to remodel the run-down house they bought, or a second-hand freezer and about 100 pounds of venison. All of this was off the books. So, even though the family was self-sufficient within four months of its arrival, so far as any official records showed this couple lived in the United States for more than five years seemingly dependent on the woman's cousin, who had sponsored them.

Though this pattern could be repeated in every city in the world, in most locales those who barely manage are far more frequent than the success stories that keep hope alive. It is important to note, however, that the process leaves little if any trace in the official records. In Peru, for example, people who sell in the markets or on the streets are supposed to be licensed, or they must pay a flat sales tax plus an annual fee for a health certificate. Most vendors comply with one or the other condition, but in neither case is there an official quantitative record of goods and services exchanged or income derived. The extent to which these vendors contribute to national productivity can only be guesstimated. However, as Benedict pointed out in discussing the role of itinerant marketeers, "It is precisely because of market imperfections . . . that marketeers can profit by engaging in arbitrage as a stratagem" (1972: 91).[5] In short, such people both reflect a response to current needs and serve as agents for creating new demand, assisting both producer and consumer.

As more research emerged, observers of the informal sector's functioning and functions rather quickly divided into two camps. Those in the one emphasized the techniques employed by the poor, the elderly, the disadvantaged, and those who fell between the cracks of governmental and privately available caretaking systems—who, in the face of difficulty as well as over-rigid and tight-fisted bureaucratic bumbling, struggled to make ends meet.

Others—whether in centrally planned or mixed (that is, a combination of private and public sector) economies—saw it in dramatically different perspective. For them, these were the tactics of greedy and irresponsible cheats, subversive to the total fabric of society and doubling the burden of honest responsible citizens. The crux of the matter for mixed economies was the extent to which such underground operations evaded taxation. Taxes, proponents held, provide the wherewithal for all the services that serve society: education; caretaking of the sick, elderly, mentally ill, and unemployed; highways; public parks; housing; defense; environmental protection; scientific research; support for the arts, and so on. As the tax base declines, the government is less capable of providing these services at an adequate level, and in the long run the socioculture and its individual members must suffer for it. Individuals and even families might benefit from the extra resources they attracted, but only at the cost of the larger public good (Tanzi 1980: 35). Not the least of the cost would be the contaminating effect that such enterprises would have on the willingness of others, albeit more able, to contribute to the commonwealth. As a Gloucester fisherman explained to me why he broke the rules:

I'd see some bum cheating and I'd say, "What the hell am I being honest for?" I felt like I had horns [that is, a husband whose wife is having affairs with other men] when other guys flashed the big bucks and bragged about how they got 'em cause they were smart—which hadda mean the guy who didn't bend a few things, who didn't land illegal fish, or sell under the counter, and don't cook the books—he's gotta be some kind of clown. I don't like it; I worry about getting caught and making my family ashamed. But if I don't do it, maybe I lose my boat or my house even. So I don't stop unless they stop. A guy with a family gotta make out, right?

[5] He also stressed that such market systems "appear to be a response to an involuntary shift of labor from . . . agriculture to services" (1972: 83). Plattner (1975b) also studied the itinerant peddler as entrepreneur, a solitary decision maker who does not have to contend with bureaucratic or other organizational constraints.

The Dual Economy Approach

Another dimension was added to the picture when, in 1971, Keith Hart, an anthropologist working on development projects in Ghana, suggested that most Third World countries had not one but dual economies (meaning formal and informal, rather than the more familiar traditional and modern economies; see Hart 1973). To understand the significance of Hart's contribution, one must go back to the years immediately after World War II. Following the success in rebuilding Europe, similar programs were initiated in the less-developed countries; these programs also emphasized the goal of technology transfer—in industry, agriculture, and national health and education services. Specific projects would start the national machinery of general economic growth. The "poor and backward natives" would be trained to produce and, with their newly found spending power, would buy more goods, which would create a demand for more new jobs, which would create more demand . . . all in a never-ceasing upward spiral of growth. With the new prosperity, countries would have the wherewithal to improve social welfare programs as well as develop transportation networks to tie rural and urban regions together, improving circulation of goods and services and helping to integrate the newly independent nations.

Such programs, of course, were capital-intensive, requiring high initial investments in machinery, buildings, and so on. Using the old adage that "You need to spend money to make money," governments and business were encouraged to obtain foreign aid loans; otherwise, officials in these newly independent countries were told, they could not leap forward into the twentieth century.

Time passed and the results were not encouraging. There were few examples of the significant economic changes that had been expected. Some anthropologists, such as the Banfields (1958), Geertz (1963), and Swift (1965), maintained that "take-off"—the leap from small- to large-scale production for economic development—could not take place until those bottlenecks to large-scale structures, the so-called traditional individualistic and familial organizations that predated the colonial period, were bypassed or eliminated.[6] Press (1966: 285) concluded that, "where applied change succeeds, it is more often in spite of, rather than because of, the innovators and the plan of action."

It seemed such societies were trapped in a vicious circle: The econ-

[6] Adams and Woltemade presented a model of the pre-British Indian village community and its economy and concluded that "religious values, the joint family, the caste system, and the social welfare aspects of the *jajmani* economy work against mobility and flexibility and stifle experimental, innovative, and accumulative undertakings" (1970: 54).

omy could not change so long as precapitalist modes of production existed and sustained the sociocultural life-styles derived from these modes; the earlier modes, however, were necessary to sustain the folk until "take-off" occurred.

Hart argued that the majority, if not all, of such countries had "dual economies"—formal and informal, the distinction "based essentially on that between wage-earning and self-employment" (1973: 68). Small-scale, informal production of goods and services did not conflict with large-scale, modern production; the two parts of the economy complemented each other.

In the formal economy (which included the public sector of government), foreign aid programs and monies were developing enterprises that would grow through their access to credit resources for capital development. This sphere included officially licensed businesses, with fixed physical plants, and which employed regularly salaried workers with particular job skills to produce goods and services that were regulated, statistically tracked, and taxed by the government.

The informal sector was characterized by self-employed individuals entering into enterprises that were small scale, tended to focus on less profitable activities, had little access to credit for expansion, and, as such, were marked by greater risk and uncertainty. They frequently substitute for what many see as more desirable wage work that provides more income on a predictable basis.

In their analyses of the economic status of one or another country, economists measured economic activity by tabulating income and the GNP. But, said Hart,

Price inflation, inadequate wages, and an increasing surplus to the requirements of the urban labor market have led to a high degree of informality in the income-generating activities of the sub-proletariat [the urban under- and unemployed]. Consequently income and expenditure patterns are more complex than is normally allowed for in the economic analysis of poor countries. [1973: 61]

He added:

The informal sector has . . . been assumed to depend on demand created by current levels of activity in the formal sector, as measured by movements in [GNP] or total formal wage expenditure. Such a picture leaves many questions unresolved, *although it allows economists to equate significant economic activity with what is measured.* [1973: 84, emphasis added]

In short, economists were not doing a good job of measuring the *total* economy, and this resulted in badly skewed pictures of what was happening productively. Except for the residual category of, say, "under-

or unemployed," economists failed to include the nonwage income of those in this category. Yet, unable to find full-time jobs, the irregularly employed were required to improvise; any venture that offered ease of entry was acceptable. Such improvisations, ignored in the economic tabulations, contributed significantly to the wealth and economic health of the society.

Having only marginal access to the formal section led those in this "reserve army of the unemployed," these urban subproletariat, to participate in the small manufacturing and trading section and to supplement wages through income acquired via petty commodity enterprises. The enterprises encompassed anything and everything: market gardening, making or selling beer and spirits, doing repair or construction work, begging, tailoring, street hawking, performing ritual services, lending money, dealing drugs, picking pockets, and gambling, to mention some of those Hart listed.

The links maintained with extended kin groups are both a blessing and a curse for the urban migrant in developing countries. The indigenous, obligatory social ties that involve "the continuous exchange of personnel, goods, and services within an extended kin-group resident in both urban and rural areas" (Hart 1973: 65) can lend support when income disappears, but these same people make comparable demands on income resources.[7]

Other studies complemented these ideas. Brush examined the "myth of the idle peasant" and argued that "unemployment" was measured by poorly defined units and, more important, derived from the cultural assumptions of outside development personnel as to "what peasants should and should not be doing with their time" (1977: 77). He maintained that 97.6 percent of the labor days available were used in productive labor but that observers, assigning specific occupations (such as "field work") to peasants, ignored other work useful or even necessary to household maintenance. Thus the observers might ignore repairing items in the house or gathering firewood and not include either (including a trip to town to sell that wood) as labor contributing to the necessary income of the household.

It is probable that Hart's words were heeded, because what historians call "the climate of opinion" had already altered enough to provide a receptive environment for his argument. During the late 1960's there had been a rising chorus of voices following the lead of such noted theorists as E. F. Schumacher (*Small Is Beautiful: Economics As If People Mattered*,

---

[7] Isaac (1971), for example, analyzed business failures in a West African town and challenged previous studies that linked obligations and constraints imposed by the extended family system to the lack of success in entrepreneurial ventures.

1973), who argued against wholesale exportation of Euroamerican industrialism and capitalist economics, and who urged consideration of the many benefits of what some were calling "microtechnology."

As early as 1972 the International Labor Office (ILO) adopted the model provided by Hart and began to differentiate formal from informal by contrasting characteristics of easy versus difficult entry, small versus large scale, family versus corporate ownership, and unregulated versus protected (Trager 1985: 260–61). The World Bank quickly followed and within a few years was referring to the urban labor market as consisting of a formal "protected" sector as well as an informal, "unprotected" sector, enterprises in the former having (1) access to various forms of credit both to expand and to underwrite the risks of new business and (2) employees who were protected by regulated working conditions and entitlement rights to certain private as well as public benefits and protections.

Hart's provocative study stimulated an enormous amount of new thinking and a great many questions: Were there growing numbers in the informal sector, or were procedures for monitoring the work force improving? How many who worked in the one sector also worked in the other? Was one sector more, or less, vulnerable to external variables?

Underrecording of Women's Work

At the same time there were indications that the number of working females in both sectors seemed to be growing. Various theses were suggested to explain this: (1) women workers, even those in certain factory positions, had not been counted in earlier enumerations;[8] (2) much of what women did was casual, part-time labor and thus fell below some arbitrary, statistically counterproductive cutoff point;[9] (3) income was deliberately concealed in order not to jeopardize other income or increase income costs, as in Italy, where women reported themselves unemployed so as not to lose a family allowance paid to households with a "full-time mother" at home; (4) studies ignored paid work done

[8] Trager (1987: 240) comments that, even after large-scale investigations on the informal economy had taken place, "the sampling frame used and the types of enterprises focused on have nearly eliminated informal sector activities carried out by women," and it is this that may have led to the surprise expressed by Sethuraman (1981: 190) at the small amount of informal sector activity by females. Trager further notes that "The ILO Lagos study achieved skewed results . . . because the sample was selected to include a larger proportion of manufacturing and service activities than of trade activities; women, of course, predominate in trade."

[9] An economist with whom I worked on a fishery project decided, for reasons that were never made clear, that we should not count as "commercial fishermen" those who worked at it less than 15 hours per week or fewer than 90 days a year.

at home as a cottage industry or as piece work; or (5) studies discounted unpaid but productive labor done by women in their home, including for the households of others (see, for example, the popular response from nonsalaried women to the question, "What do you do?"—"Oh, I don't work; I'm only a housewife").[10] Thus, for example, Saunders and Mehenna (1986) studied women's farmwork in an Egyptian village and concluded that women made a far greater contribution to agricultural production than either national statistics or their menfolk allowed. They concluded that, among the factors for underreporting were that women's labor was seasonal, considered a secondary aspect of their primary roles as wives and daughters, and a sign of low prestige among women themselves. It is becoming increasingly clear, however, that in addition to having a circular effect on the value of women's work, ignoring the contribution of these types of invisible and "free" contributions greatly skews cost calculations.

This last point is important because estimating future costs and benefits without including replacement costs of currently "free" informal sector labor is unrealistic. The uncounted labor may be unavailable at the time of budget implementation. For example, the famous nineteenth-century American philosopher Thoreau extolled the virtues of the "isolated and primitive" life of Walden Pond. There, "in solitary commune with nature," he lived a free, unfettered life and, as a general guide for others, urged that all humans follow his maxim that life was too dear to be wasted making a living. He failed to mention that, during the brief two years he enjoyed his "wilderness apart," his mother regularly traveled the two miles from his family home in Concord, Massachusetts, to wash and mend his clothes, as well as bring food baskets from her kitchen. His accounting technique ignored these contributions in the same way it also overlooked the contribution made by his good friend Ralph Waldo Emerson, who owned and paid the taxes on the land where Thoreau had built his log cabin. One wonders what he might have done had his mother adopted his slogan!

All of these and more are part of the productive work that makes life possible and, for managers, it is becoming increasingly important to determine the extent to which such work lends itself to system maintenance. Yet so many activities in "the little economy" are so common-

---

[10] Or the not untypical male comment that, "My wife doesn't work; she just stays at home." For example, a study by Maher (1977) of rural women near Marrakech reports that the consensus of males interviewed was that the woman's contribution to the household consisted of cooking. Yet 80 percent of the women surveyed regularly did field work or went to the mountains for wood, and 14 percent worked for wages. For an interesting examination of this whole issue see Bose, Feldberg, and Sokoloff 1987.

place, so taken for granted, that we trivialize them—or, like Thoreau, take no account of them. Thus, in certain areas of the world (India, for example), wood is a scarce and costly commodity; providing a valuable and necessary service are the street vendors who cook and sell cheap "fast food" to the poor. The latter may lack homes, access to cooking facilities, or, given that fuel costs for some amount to one-third their monthly income, funds to buy wood. One can imagine what might happen in the cities if a governmental campaign to eliminate such hawkers of food were a success.

Such needs are not limited to the Third World. Yvonne Jones (1988) discussed several varieties of vendors in an American city. One peddled food from a small van, servicing residents in a high-crime area of urban blight. Not only did this area lack even one grocery store, but the residents had no convenient access to stores outside the area because less than 25 percent owned automobiles and because public transit service had been curtailed due to the unwillingness of bus drivers to work runs in the area. One such vendor had originally operated in the informal sector but, "to protect himself from being mistaken as a mobile drug dealer by police during their frequent sweeps of the area," ultimately registered for a peddler's license.[11] The in-depth, participant-observation style of research favored by anthropologists gives strong support to the argument that the majority of such "penny capitalists" provide useful goods and services in the areas they service.

Hart concluded his original study by commenting:

Socialists may argue that foreign capitalist dominance of these economies determines the scope for informal (and formal) development, and condemns the majority of the urban population to deprivation and exploitation. More optimistic liberals may see in informal activities, as described here, the possibility of a dramatic "bootstrap" operation, lifting the underdeveloped economies through their own indigenous enterprise. Before either view—or a middle course stressing both external constraint and autonomous effort—may be espoused, much more empirical research is required. [1973: 88–89]

His prediction was correct; those who listened interpreted his finds in two ways. One of the richest debates of the decade that followed, a debate still under way and highly productive of that empirical research for which Hart called, centers around the distinction between the analytical power of the construct of the "informal economy" versus that which is labeled "petty commodity production" (PCP).

[11] A classic study called "The Role of the Middleman in the Internal Distribution System of a Caribbean Peasant Economy" was done by Sidney Mintz (1957).

Petty Commodity Production Versus the
Informal Economy

Hart was only one anthropologist forced to rethink his position as a result of Third World development projects and the plethora of quick-fix solutions that came to hand so easily in the years immediately after World War II. Eric Wolf labeled such programs "a new form of unilineal social Darwinism, created to justify the advance of the enlightened at the expense of the wretched of the earth" (1972: 411). He argued that development projects suffered particularly from their inability "to explain the mutual interdependence of 'advanced' and 'backward' features of the same system, or of dominant and dependent systems" (ibid.: 410–11). His reappraisal provoked some of the most difficult and searching questions in economic analysis, not the least of which concerned the last mentioned.

The debate that emerged was grounded in a basic theoretical schism separating "non-Marxists" from those who relied on one or another of the models derived from the Marxian paradigm.[12] The latter position was put most succinctly by Long and Richardson (1978), who argued that Hart's differentiation attempted to deal with the necessarily tripartite labor force required by capitalism: the employed, the temporarily unemployed, and the permanently unemployed. The latter were not truly nonworking but were, instead, unpaid household and voluntary workers, as well as others involved in what the state defined as "illegal" work. Similarly, the temporarily unemployed were more likely to be forced into whatever jobs they could obtain in order to survive until able (or willing) to rejoin those listed in the formal system's "employed" category. Those in the "surplus" labor force (the two latter categories) were necessary for a capitalistic economy, which needed to have such flexibility and recourse to free labor in order to rationalize costs and maximize profits.

The issue, as Long and Richardson saw it, was straightforward. The informal sector did exist, but Hart's model disguised that sector's true functioning and function. It was not that there were dual economies that operated side by side or parallel to each other. Rather, the two articulated with each other so as to encourage the conservation of such noncapitalist modes as petty commodity production "since the relationship allows capitalism to accumulate capital" (Long and Richard-

[12] Marx (1967: 1:761) defines petty commodity production as a situation "where the laborer is the private owner of his own means of labor set in action by himself." For a general discussion, see Kahn 1975 and Friedmann 1980.

son 1978: 183). So, the argument goes, goods and services turned into market commodities were functional to capitalism because when those who labor can satisfy their needs more cheaply, the wages required for survival can be lowered and thus the rate of surplus value to the owner of capital is increased. Goods and services were usually cheaper —and, equally important, available—in the informal sector (as in South Africa, where prostitutes in the informal sector provide sexual services for urban male workers who are legally required to leave spouses and children behind in the home territories).

As Trager (1987: 244) has pointed out, on the one hand, the heart of this critique of the dual economy model was "a failure to see how the informal sector is dependent on and subordinate to the formal sector." On the other hand, the petty commodity production model (derived from the Marxian paradigm) allowed analysts to appreciate that "the linkages are exploitative and the informal sector has emerged in large part as a response to conditions in the formal sector and is in general subordinate to it" (ibid.).

The debate continues unresolved—not the least because ideological positions held by those on both sides make any real dialogue difficult. In the meantime, the data and insights furnished provide a wealth of cross-cultural data on both the actors and the complex tapestry of economic activities portrayed.[13]

The Chicken or the Egg Problem

One of the most hotly debated issues of the informal economy is the question of whether the activities in this realm are (1) innovative responses to increasing governmental taxation, regulation, and "interference" in people's lives, or (2) traditional patterns, now being "criminalized" in optative attempts by the state to extract additional surplus. It seems best to take the middle ground, as we did in the debate on petty commodity production, and argue that circumstances condition cases. Indeed, in the following example it would seem that both are at work simultaneously.

In central Asia, pastoral tribespeople have for millennia moved their herds from one grazing area to another. Among other things, sound stock-breeding practices and the need to rebuild flocks (sometimes

[13] In addition to those cited, for more on this extremely rich debate see the following sampling: Arizpe 1977; Barker and Smith 1986; Bremen 1976; Bromley 1982; Bromley and Gerry 1979; Clammer 1987; Davies 1979; Ditton and Brown 1981; Gerry 1978, 1987; Gerry and Birkbeck 1981; Kriedte, Medick, and Schlumbohm 1981; Littlefield 1978; Long and Roberts 1978; Mars and Nicod 1981, 1983; Moser 1978; Peattie 1982; Santos 1979.

badly depleted by a hard winter) decreed that groups try to avoid feuds and work to maintain cordial relations with other groups through visiting, celebrating festive events together, and arranging marriage ties. All of these were enhanced through the exchange of gifts, barter, and trade.

In this century, however, the political tension among China, India, and Russia led to the tightening of borders, preventing the transhumant movement of pastoralists and interfering with cross-group network maintenance. A traditional move from summer to winter pasturage became an illegal border crossing; gifts and other exchange items became contraband. As the respective governments grew more repressive, groups became more resentful and more adept at evasion. They also became more sophisticated about the utility of smuggling as a way of compensating for the economic problems they were facing because of the constraints on pastoralism. Thus, on the one hand, the state defined the informal sector into existence by criminalizing legitimate activities of a subordinated and captive group; on the other hand, in response to the hardships caused by the closing of borders, the group —which did have such other options as becoming part of a sedentary cooperative or moving down into a nearby valley and becoming farm wage laborers—chose to add the enterprise of trader *cum* smuggler.

Similarly, in an illustration closer to home, European farm folk and peasants have long produced commodities for barter or sale. Women, especially, have used their "spare" time to produce goods that could be sold at fairs and markets. Sometimes fees were charged for the right to sell in markets or fairs, but it was a fixed amount and no account was taken of what or how much was sold. The sale of a length of cloth, a woodcarving, or some foodstuffs to passersby who stopped at the farmstead was rarely of concern to officialdom. It was rare (as is still true in many parts of the world) for any official to audit the 75 or 100 pounds of fish that the small-scale fishermen landed. The men pulled their boats up on the beach and peddled their catches to buyers who selected their dinner from the variety of marine species that lay in the bottom of the boats. That was all there was to it. Such people find it difficult to understand why the government now requires them to purchase licenses, permits, warrants, and special stamps to formalize such transactions, or why they may be viewed as doing something shady if they engage in them. This is particularly true when rural migrants to the city must attempt to market what skills they have and find jobs where they can.

The Minotaur and Labyrinth: Only a Myth?

In ancient Greek mythology it was told how, in Crete, during the time when Greece was subject to it, there was a monster, sometimes described as giant and slow-moving but crafty, since it had the body of a bull and the head of a man or, alternately, a bull-headed man. The creature lived in a special temple whose structure consisted of a complex network of winding passages with many dead ends, impossible for any but the priests to travel without becoming lost. Yearly, Athens was forced to contribute seven young men and seven young women to feed the creature.[14]

For many, but not all, this story serves as a metaphor for government involvement in the economic sector. Supported by much research, people claim that the informal sector is a last resort, to which they turn only because it is impossible to negotiate the maze to operate legitimately. It encourages the growth of big, rather than small, business because only the former has the resources (financial, legal, and social) that make feasible passage through and existence within the system.

In Lima, Peru, the Institute for Liberty and Democracy was organized by Hernando de Soto[15] with, as one of its primary foci, the study of informal economy. De Soto became convinced that much of what generated the steam behind Peru's informal system was the nearly impenetrable bureaucratic thicket—given that the number of laws, executive orders, decrees ad infinitum exceed 500,000, most of which are issued by the president and the various government ministries (with only about 1 percent coming from Parliament even though it is the designated legislative body). Those in the Institute decided to test the process by going through the motions of officially registering a business whose workshop consisted of nothing more than two sewing machines. The process took 289 working days, the equivalent of 32 months' income at the minimal wage (Llosa 1987: 46).

In such a system, one with which even the most sophisticated have difficulty coping, it is not surprising that the penny capitalist, whether of generations born to the city or newly arrived from the hinterland,

---

[14] The cunning hero, Theseus, was finally able to slay the creature. Volunteering to be one of those sent for sacrifice, he was artful enough to unravel his cloak as he and his companions were led into the maze, and after his victory he was able to lead the way out and return triumphantly to Athens.

[15] De Soto, a leading figure in Peruvian life, obtained his degrees in economics and international law from the Swiss Institut Universitaire des Hautes Etudes Internationales and worked for a time in the world body overseeing trade (GATT) located in Geneva. Though labeled a right-wing thinker by Marxist viewers, "he likes the bipartisan 'rightist Marxist' label Mexican intellectuals have given him" (Germani 1988: 7).

should be forced or chose to bypass the bureaucratic gatekeepers. What is more poignant, however, is that the same regulatory maze baffles those who are in the wage sector and aids those "rotten eggs" who use it to misdirect and frighten the many illiterate and legally naive workers in the informal sector from the exercise of any legitimate rights they might have.

The European Community (that integrative network designed to free the flow of goods and people across borders) is beginning to grasp how informal-minded individuals can use the regulatory economic efforts to evade the intent of the law while engaging in legal (though, in Hart's sense, not legitimate) activities. One man bought a truck, loaded it with butter, and traveled around Europe for six weeks, simply making a point of crossing the right borders at the right time, given fluctuating currency and market rates (Grout-Smith, n.d.). Not one pound of butter changed hands, and after returning the butter to cold storage for another go-around later, the designer of the venture pocketed a $5,000 profit. Another example is that of several large companies exporting butter to Yugoslavia, where butter receives a large subsidy in order to be sold to Yugoslavians at affordable prices. In that country, however, the butter goes to a factory that creates a "diet mayonnaise" by adding eggs, water, salt, and pepper to the butter, which it then ships to West Germany for a factory there to extract the butter—and start the process all over again.

Long observed but now being being officially confirmed by socialist countries everywhere—and particularly the Soviet Union as a result of the new policies being pushed by Soviet leader Gorbachev—the formal and informal sectors articulate in centrally planned economies as elsewhere in the world.[16] The informal adds to and maintains the formal by creating jobs in the bureaucracy (and occasionally adding substantially to their income through the opportunities such positions offer for various forms of corruption) while the shortages created by bumbling inefficiency and lackadaisical performances of those in the formal economy encourage people to obtain scarce goods through the black markets. As the Russian economist A. Antonov estimated in an article that appeared in the Soviet labor newspaper *Trud* (Labor), "The loss of potatoes and other vegetables that rotted before they ever reached stores cost the Soviet Union at least one billion rubles annually" (Wilson-Smith 1988: 25).

[16] See, for example, Sampson (1987) as well as Gregory Grossman's extensive bibliography, *The Second Economy in the USSR and Eastern Europe* (1987), which permits entry into the issue on a wider geographic scale. Wedel (1986) has produced an excellent study on Poland's informal economy that provides a basis for comparing similarities and differences in Eastern Europe.

Sampson has emphasized the extent to which the Soviet bureaucrats, especially factory managers, "are constrained by central planning decisions, central allocations of supplies, and limitations on wages and labor discipline. Plan fulfillment is every manager's prime concern" (1987: 128). Constant fiddling and manipulation, shortcuts, and under-the-counter deals are required to circumvent bottlenecks and obtain necessary goods and services. Bribery, misreporting, creating "family circles" (informal networks of managers who help each other), and an almost institutionalized position of the "fixer" (someone whose primary job consists of acting as a procurement broker in tracking down and obtaining necessary resources) all seem necessary if the system is to function even at its currently flawed and inadequate level of supply.

Necessity is the mother of invention, however, and Sampson (drawing also on similar research done by Simis 1982: 147) describes how "tens of thousands" of underground factories encapsulated within the official state structures specialize in the daily production of "small, simply manufactured, easily transportable and marketable consumer items." These goods include clothing, jewelry, food, and household items, and these factories usurp funds, supplies, labor, packaging, shipping, and even distribution outlets of the official system. Profits from the underground factory can be only partially invested. These second economy entrepreneurs may spend their profits as conspicuous consumption on big houses, vacations, cars, and feasts, and to help offspring or godchildren pay their bribes to get good job placements or enter medical school.[17]

Some anthropologists have pointed out that people can become involved in the informal economy in order to resist effectively or symbolically what appears to them to be counter-cultural behavior on the part of those controlling the government or economic sector. Just as the Boston Tea Party was a symbolic gesture of defiance by American colonists, producers and consumers often engage in acts that make them part of the informal economy in order to express their opposition (or so they say). Noguchi has an insightful analysis of "law, custom and morality in Japan" as seen through "the culture of cheating on fares on the Japanese national railways" (1979). He gives as one rationale for trying to avoid paying the few cents involved as resistance to official rules seen as intrusive in areas traditionally subject to self-regulation. Others have analyzed such activities as employee pilfering and income tax evasion

---

[17] In a footnote (p. 129) Sampson cites Simis (1982:166) as saying that one " 'black' millionaire Laziashvili had an annual income of R10–12 million and paid out R1 million yearly to [Russian] Georgian party officials."

as "acts of rebellion by a proletariat deprived of control over its own means of production."[18]

Finally, as touched on earlier, the decision to operate wholly or in part in the informal sector may be based on the accepted patterns (read "traditions") and normative thinking of individuals who simply do what has always been done, unaware that some or all of their activities have come under censure. Neither the subteen entrepreneur who sold worms nor his parents were aware that they were required to register the business, obtain a sales tax number, and file as well as pay an amount that reflected the tax on sales. Similarly, in a cultural analysis of Greek-American small businesses and their owners, Chock (1981) notes that business is seen by Greeks as a domestic matter: Initial funding should be obtained from those within the extended family network, not come from an outside agency; the organization of labor in the business should rely as much as possible on the use of kin; and, unlike "the help" (outsiders hired only as a last resort because it is believed non-kin lack a sense of responsibility toward their work), family workers are viewed as co-investors who, preferably, share profits rather than receive wages. Thus, despite the various hardships that are imposed and the familial stress that can result, Greek-Americans continue to strive to be "their own boss" and initiate the process within the domestic context.

The Bucks Stop Here

As we have just seen—somewhat paradoxically, given the charges of inefficiency—some of the most adept actors in the informal arena are in government itself.[19]

Big or small, officials can use government positions as a way of improving their life-style via the informal economy. Civil servants (as well as politicians) frequently find it difficult to stretch their salaries to maintain a standard of living consonant with cultural norms for their professional status. Some are not above requiring that those expecting their services, formal or informal, pay something extra if the work is to be expedited or even done at all. And, indeed, in some countries such salaries are low, considering the training of those filling the positions. This could have several historical causes: the positions were

[18] For example, in The Contentious French (1986), noted historian Charles Tilly presents the thesis that ordinary people resist the collaborative exploitation of state and capitalism with what those in authority label "disorder."

[19] Bennett and Di Lorenzo (1983) have argued that budgets constitute a major way in which government spending and borrowing is concealed from general public scrutiny. Lomnitz (1971) reviews the interplay between that system of reciprocity called in Latin America "compadrazgo" and getting things done in the Chilean bureaucracy.

considered honorary or part of one's public duty; such positions were "political plums," given by leaders to reward loyalty and expected to generate whatever resources the holder could milk from those administered (so long as it did not cause unrest and diminish whatever royal income was expected to be achieved from the performance); and, in general, the theory of the ruling elite seemed to be that the royal treasury, held to belong to the crown rather than the public, should not be drained to serve the folk.[20] Further, government personnel are not exempt from the desire to see their own immediate "domains" grow: more duties require more people and bigger budgets, all of which increases the prestige of those who head such units—as well as their potential to increase demands in the next go-around. However, every government occasionally calls for economy drives. Thus, another factor that fuels bureaucracy and red tape is the aim to protect oneself by being as indispensable as possible.

Remember that "parallel" was one of the terms for the informal economy, and note that France was rocked in the summer of 1986 by a scandal involving "parallel financing" and "parallel diplomacy." An investigation into corruption of the previous government's foreign aid ministry revealed that a semipublic organization called Carrefour du Développement (Development Crossroads) acted as a channel for public money that was siphoned off to African leaders under the guise of development funds. French officials acknowledged that to maintain smooth relations with former colonies, money designated for aid projects really went to the leaders of those countries. To make matters worse (but in the traditional spirit of reciprocity), some of the leaders then contributed funds (returning the same money?) to French leaders to use in their political campaigns (Lewis 1986).

Rich Man, Poor Man, Beggar Man, Thief

There appear to be no limits to the variety of social types that engage in the informal economy. Although the lines between legal, quasi-legal, and illegal are blurred, there are some activities that, in an ideal world, few would accept as legitimate. Blackmail, extortion, drug dealing, and political corruption are all income-generating activities that most people, most of the time, would negatively sanction—even those who argue that most of what is defined as illegal is, on the one hand, catalogued as such only by the repressive ruling class and, on the other hand, consists of attempts by the underclass to defy their oppressors.

[20] See my comments on the concept of "dominion" rule in Smith 1985, esp. pp. 110–14.

The enterprises of those who participate in this subterranean arena are so far removed from the activities of the majority in the informal economy that any substantive discussion would unduly complicate the other themes reviewed here. This said, however, there are some aspects that bear looking at.

Gambling in most places is a legal way of turning a profit—so long as one is willing to pay taxes on the earnings. However, gamblers, along with organized crime rings and major drug dealers, have at least one problem in common with some participants in the formal sector, such as the largest corporations and the very rich: how to pay just enough taxes on large profits to avoid investigation and prosecution for tax evasion while concealing the full extent of the gains so as to preserve the lion's share for themselves. The former have the additional difficulty of having to convert illicit dollars to seemingly legal wealth despite it being almost impossible these days to avoid some sort of paper trail that government personnel can use to look for suspiciously large cash deposits.

Otherwise legitimate concerns and honest individuals become involved in the informal economy to facilitate such a laundering process. In May 1988, E. F. Hutton & Co. pleaded guilty and paid $1 million in fines in response to Justice Department charges that the major financial house had conspired "with business people trying to hide income from the Internal Revenue Service and for organized-crime figures" (*Wall Street Journal* 1988: 8). In Detroit, a number of retirees cooperated with professional gamblers by collecting the bettors' winnings and declaring themselves as the winners. The gamblers avoided possible investigation for race fixing and the retirees were rewarded with sufficient money to cover their additional tax plus a bonus (*U.S. News and World Report* 1979: 50–51). And in a reverse switch, major lottery winners have been found selling their tickets for a 10 percent premium to criminals who can then deposit the "winnings" and provide the ticket stub for the required explanation as to the origin of the otherwise suspiciously large cash deposit. Further, when this scam was finally uncovered, those who received convictions included two bank vice presidents and several branch managers. Their collusion was necessary since bank personnel could hardly be persuaded that the same depositor could win big on the lottery week after week (ibid.).

Conclusion

The informal sector is the label for all those activities in which people engage to augment deficiencies in income or consumption opportunities available in the formal sector. It is likely that governments every-where will increase efforts to capture this economic sector. Two factors combine to lend support to this prediction. The first derives from the explosive population growth in the world's urban centers. The second is grounded in the development of sophisticated electronic gear that has a great potential for storing, retrieving, and, most of all, manipulating data.[21]

Two other significant developments occurring in the last few years are critically linked with the response of central governments to infor-mation on the informal economy. Governments everywhere are putting an increasing emphasis on privatization—moving what were state ac-tivities into the private sector or encouraging expansion of private asso-ciations or firms in these areas—and decentralization—transferring the right (and the responsibility) of decision making to regional or local bodies. Both developments derive from attempts by central govern-ments to save or make more efficient use of revenues, and thus are two sides of the same coin. Whether large or small, socialist or capi-talist, First or Third World, and despite sociocultural differences, we see a high degree of cross-cultural and temporal commonality (Japan appears to be the one outstanding exception). The explanation will un-doubtedly emerge as complex and situationally varied, but there can be no question that the emphasis on implementation of these two pro-cesses is linked to the detrimental effects of central government "over-load" and the growing national and international fiscal crises. Clearly, such moves are linked to the growing body of information concerning the informal sector.

The last decade of this century is bound to see other kinds of activities resulting from the informal sector. The range of actors and strategies is wide, as has been shown by this review. The informal economy pro-vides alternative income but cheats the government of needed revenue for broad programs. It fills a gap when people "fall through the cracks" or get blocked by the bureaucracy, but by that very fact removes pres-sure on the public system to be more effective and responsive. It is flexible and situationally adaptive, but its elusiveness leaves dangerous gaps and generates erroneous calculations that affect long-range plan-ning. It is a form of self-help and encourages entrepreneurialism, but it allows unscrupulous individuals to exploit workers by paying substan-dard wages to people often employed in less than optimum working conditions (and may offer inferior or unsafe products to the consumer). It is grounded in networks supportive of ties of family and friend-

[21] For an expanded discussion of these projections, as well as privatization and decen-tralization, see Smith 1988.

ship, but it encourages nepotism, cronyism, and trivialization of unpaid labor, as well as those who perform it. It contributes to maintaining what is the best, and worst, of varying economic and political systems. But it is important to realize a similar checklist could be produced by the formal sector.

What special contribution does the economic anthropologist make to studies of the informal economy? First, because that sector includes activities taken for granted, activities grounded in what many view as the private area of personal economics, and activities that are marginally if not blatantly illegal, it is unlikely that its rich complexity would be illuminated using the techniques usually employed by economists. Further, anthropologists are aware of the extraordinary diversity that sociocultural systems demonstrate; while subject to their own biases and vulnerable to the blinders of ethnocentrism, they are at least trained to consider the extent to which their research may be tainted by these. They are sensitive to the extent to which we can overemphasize, trivialize, or be blind to the different behavior of others, misjudging as well as misinterpreting, or, worse, arrogantly dismissing others as simply "wrong-headed" and in need of the benefit of our wisdom. At the same time, the imperative for comparative cross-cultural analysis also requires us to see beyond what may be only surface differences and attempt to find what commonalities exist in the problems addressed, the strategies selected to resolve them, and the goals for which people strive. Along these same lines, our perspective leads us to give greater weight and considerable depth to the roles played by such diverse factors as history, environment, biology, cognition, technology, and values.

Next, few if any anthropologists ignore the ethical dilemmas involved in researching behavior that is at the least disdained and, maximally, criminalized. We are continually aware of the dual responsibilities imposed by being both scientific researcher—with the responsibility to search out as well as disseminate information upon which others may build—and trusted confidant. Last, anthropologists are aware that people live their day-to-day lives incapsulated in a holistic sociocultural matrix. Our many in-depth and detailed studies have over the decades provided a wealth of data proving that decisions about production, distribution, and consumption are not made in an antiseptic economic "black box." Rather, they are based on the totality of past experiences, present knowledge, and future goals; they are embedded in self and in ties or conflicts with others, the product of individuals, families, classes, and all the varied social groups that make up the larger system. At the same time, the informal sector illustrates both the range of alternatives and the extent to which people are constrained in their choices.

It is in this area of the informal that we find many of the locally generated and specifically responsive techniques for survival that particular populations have developed (see, for example, a study of squatter settlements and government self-help projects, Stepick and Murphy 1980). Not all of these are sound, whether in the short or long term, but they cannot and should not be dismissed out of hand. Government planners and other agents of change would be well served to note them; they can make plans go awry and might even offer ways to improve on or provide alternatives to them.

What significance do our findings on the informal economy hold for economic anthropology specifically and anthropology generally? First and foremost, the data are especially apt for illustrating how people yield to or escape from the matrix of "nonrational" sociocultural custom. They reveal the degree to which individual actors can stretch or compress the normative system, while still believing themselves "just to be doing what everybody does." They also indicate the extent to which many of the concepts of formal economics need to be refined and given the more robust dimensions that cross-cultural analysis demands.

Although there is little doubt concerning the strength of the formal/ informal articulation, the structural character and processual dynamics of that relationship are only beginning to emerge. Because all individuals in all societies engage in economic decision making, investigation of this particular arena for the conflict between private and public directives provides anthropologists with a wealth of material for sociocultural analysis.

12

Women and Economic Institutions

Laurel Bossen

Early descriptions of economic activities in other cultures largely ignored women. When women's work was recognized, individual women were rarely described making decisions about production, investment, distribution, and consumption. Women were viewed as wards of male household heads who controlled their labor. The serious study of women's economic behavior and strategies by anthropologists is still relatively new.

In this chapter, I analyze women's relationships to economic institutions. The first section discusses the sexual division of labor and the significance of shifting gender patterns as societies evolved from foraging to farming and toward more complex forms of economic organization. In the second section, I examine the topic of women and development, and how changes associated with industrial market economies impinge on traditional gender systems and tend to squeeze women into a narrow range of economic opportunities and a weak institutional position.

The Sexual Division of Labor

All societies practice at least some division of labor by sex and age. If traditional Western models were correct in assuming that men were always the economic providers whose role was variable and dynamic, and women were always domestic consumers whose role was essentially static, it would make good sense to concentrate on *homo economicus*, the rational *man*—in the narrow masculine sense. But women's economic behavior in our own and other cultures is not as uniform and

I would like to thank Carol Smith for suggesting that I write this chapter, as well as the numerous friends who read and commented on drafts of it. These include Rebecca Aiken, Don Attwood, Nathan Bossen, Stuart Plattner, Gloria Rudolf, Philip Salzman, Richard Salisbury, Colin Scott, Louise Sperling, and Jaci Winters. I would also like to thank Linda Figsby for her help in word processing.

dependent as once assumed. What anthropologists, along with others in the social sciences, have been discovering in recent years is that men are only *partial* economic providers. Male contributions to the support of women and children vary considerably cross-culturally and also depend on variations in women's work. Women often make vital economic decisions and contributions not only for their own support but also for the support of children, men, the aged, and larger social institutions. Thus fundamental concerns in analyzing any economic system are the division of labor and the ways that the burdens and fruits of labor are shared, negotiated, and exchanged between the sexes inside and outside the household, and also between members of the same sex.

Foraging Societies

Models of foraging societies and theories about the early bases for the sexual division of labor have been continually modified and debated as more complete studies have been carried out and challenged earlier assumptions and interpretations.

The early model of man-the-hunter implicitly and explicitly presented men as the chief providers and decision makers for foraging populations. As the basic blueprint for the sexual division of labor among foragers and in early human evolution, this model has been widely criticized. Originally, it was assumed that foragers consumed a diet that was predominantly meat and that men always and exclusively performed the hunting, while women stayed in camp with the children and waited for men to bring back their next meal. This speculative model was challenged when economic and ecological anthropologists began to study the actual diets and work contributions of contemporary foragers more thoroughly, paying attention to what women were doing. Recent research suggests at least four important modifications to the hunter-provider model:

1. In many foraging societies, meat does not provide the dietary staple, nor even close to half the total food intake.

2. When meat is less important in the diet than plant foods, men may still devote much of their time to hunting, and women may actually be the principal food providers for the group through their foraging activities.

3. Even the male-hunting and female-gathering model overstates sexual dichotomy in food contributions, particularly between animal and vegetable foods. Sexual divisions of labor are often flexible and overlapping in both individual and cooperative efforts.

4. In evaluations of subsistence contributions, a heavy concentration on food tends to oversimplify the complexity of sexual divisions of labor.

The first point is based on cross-cultural samples which show that a large proportion of foragers rely primarily on gathered plant foods for their diet (Lee 1968; Martin and Voorhies 1975). Detailed ethnographic research on foragers in the Kalahari Desert, discussed in Chapter 2, demonstrates the importance of dietary plants. Lee (1979) and Tanaka (1980: 74), who studied different groups of Kalahari San in Botswana, concur that vegetables provide 60 to 80 percent of the diet, with meat representing as little as 15 percent of the caloric value in one estimate (Tanaka 1980: 70). There are also foraging economies where fishing or hunting provides the bulk of the food. However, current research suggests that hunting itself represents a dietary staple for 25 percent or less of the foraging societies sampled cross-culturally (Ember 1978; Lee 1968; Martin and Voorhies 1975). Gathering and fishing have been seriously underrated by the man-the-hunter model of foragers.

The second revision addresses the economic prominence of men and suggests that the presumed universal role of men as primary providers for the family is a myth, as is women's presumed dependency. Detailed observations show that women generally do the bulk of the food gathering. When plant foods predominate in the diet, women are often providers in quantities sufficient to feed not only themselves and their children but also the hunters when they return empty-handed. Berndt (1981: 164) claims that for the Australian aborigines, "Women valued men's contribution of large red-meat animals but did not depend on men for economic support. Men, however, did depend on women in that regard." Lee's research on the !Kung San shows that although men dedicated more of their hours to subsistence activities than women (see Chapter 2), their combined hunting and gathering activities produced only about 44 percent of the total weight and calories of food brought into camp, whereas women provided about 56 percent of the food (including plant foods that are high in protein). Considering that women are generally slightly smaller than men and that their caloric intake as estimated by Lee is only 78 percent that of men (excluding women who are directly supporting the young through pregnancy and lactation), it appears that women's food contributions to other members of the family or camp are more substantial than men's. In dietary terms, !Kung women provide 27 percent more food and consume 22 percent less than the men in the study.

The revised view of men as partial providers does not support generalizations about the relative contributions and productivity of men and women foragers. It does suggest, however, that even if women invest less time in the food quest than men, they may be more efficient both in terms of time and caloric expenditure than men who go out hunting. The effort spent in getting food does not necessarily correspond to yields. Cashdan, in Chapter 2, points out that foragers may not be exclusively concerned with high caloric yields, but that dietary diversity and security enter into their decisions. Current views on the sexual division of labor among foragers emphasize the advantages of systematic diversification and the complementarity of male and female foraging strategies. Spreading risks appears to be an important consideration in male-female collaboration.

Lee views the division of labor between hunters and gatherers as a crucial basis for exchange and risk taking: "Differentiation of tasks allowed a most important step in human affairs—risk taking—whereby an individual could attempt a difficult subsistence task such as hunting, which has a potentially great return but a rather small chance of success" (1979: 49). The risk of unsuccessful hunting can mean hunger and exhaustion unless there is a partner simultaneously obtaining reliable foods (Lee's research found that !Kung hunters were successful in only about 25 percent of their trips). The supporting partner is similarly a risk taker in that extra food gathering to feed a hunter day after day may not be reciprocated if the hunter is unsuccessful or if the hunter decides not to return a fair share of the meat. Strong cultural norms of meat sharing ensure that gatherers are rewarded for their risks, or else fights and fission of foraging camps may follow. Clearly the economic division between hunters and gatherers, or between female and male subsistence activities, rests upon a planned reciprocity and shared risk taking.

The third critique of the hunting model concerns the stereotyping of foraging sex roles into male hunters and female gatherers. Despite considerable evidence that this pattern is neither absolute nor inflexible (and ignores the male and female occupation of fishing), such convenient stereotyping is difficult to overcome and often lends itself to biological determinist theories about economic capabilities. Hunting, defined as obtaining undomesticated animal food, frequently has little to do with the pursuit of dangerous big game. The urban world's romantic image of masculine sport hunting ignores the possibility that most meat in the forager's diet may come from small animals and birds that are beaten with a stick, club, or stone, trapped in logs, caught in snares, or slain by some other animal. The techniques of capturing many small mammals as well as less glamorous menu items such as frogs, turtles, snails, eggs, grubs, and insects are used by women and even children on occasion. Hunting parties, as among the Mbuti of Zaire, can also be formed by groups of men and women who cooperate in surrounding game, and in various societies individual women have become known as capable hunters. Moreover, hunting success is often dependent on the skills of dogs, as opposed to those of men or women. This is true for Tiwi women, who hunt land mammals in Australia, for Agta men and women in the Philippines, as well as for the !Kung San men in Botswana (Goodale 1971; Estioko-Griffin and Griffin 1981; Lee 1979).[1]

It is also important that gathering should not be construed as an exclusively female activity, nor as one that lacks skills. Men frequently gather plant foods, sometimes in the course of their hunting and other times side by side with women. Gathering requires extensive knowledge of plant species, their growth cycles, locations, and processing techniques. Both gatherers and hunters profit from sharing information about the activities of plants and animals. Finally, fish are a major source of food to many foragers and, using a variety of techniques, may be provided by either sex (Halperin 1980).

Although substantial versatility is found in food resources and food-getting techniques, clearly men more often focus on hunting while women concentrate on gathering. In Chapter 2, several ideas were suggested concerning the nature of the subsistence task and its compatibility with childcare—particularly with respect to mobility, task duration, and danger. Because small children are biologically fragile and, among foragers, dependent on mother's milk for several years, women assume the greater proportion of direct care for small children. In assessing food-getting strategies, foraging women must consider their capacity to carry small children for long distances, the limited endurance of older children, and the weight and distance they must carry food and water supplies before they reach camp. In comparison to gathering, hunting involves traveling light for longer distances; when silence is required, children would be a big handicap. Although hunting is less compatible with childcare than gathering, Lee has suggested that even gathering is fairly incompatible, and that foragers tend to have low fertility rates, spacing their children widely to avoid having to breast-feed or carry more than one child at a time (1979).

---

[1] Lee's table of hunting output over four weeks shows that hunting with dogs was by far the most common (73 percent) while none of the kills employed the bow and arrow, the technique associated with masculinity. Although Lee suggests that large game provide up to 50 percent of the meat, the largest kill in that four-week period was a warthog —77 kg (1979: 230, 271). Agta men and women both hunt with dogs, and in some areas women are successful hunters and experts with the bow and arrow (Estioko-Griffin and Griffin 1981).

The fourth critique concerns the tendency to allow food to overshadow all other essential economic contributions. According to the environment, sources of fresh water, winter clothing and bedding, warm shelter, firewood, a variety of tools, bags, baskets, and pots may be needed in the quest, retrieval, processing, and storage of food. The concept of economic provider cannot be reduced to a single set of factors such as the weight of food collected, its caloric value, its protein value, or the number of hours spent in procuring it (Halperin 1980).

Theories about economic dominance and dependence of one sex toward the other, as well as theories of economic equality, are often based on the idea that those who provide food have power over those who accept it, with various modifications concerning the possible priority of certain kinds of foods (protein-rich, calorie-rich, sweet) that are supposed to bestow greater power or prestige on the provider. This food-getter theory underwrote the man-the-hunter model of male economic dominance and the revised woman-the-gatherer model of economic reciprocity. The problem with the food-getter emphasis is that both sexes tend to have specialized skills, knowledge, and spheres of activity that increase food security and survival chances. The observation that one sex may specialize in, or monopolize, a certain activity means that they also forgo other activities. Specialization is not enough to demonstrate that there is the leverage to establish a relationship of systematic economic dominance. Given the nomadism, lack of accumulated property, and loose group structure reported for many foragers, it seems that systematic domination would be difficult and costly to enforce; fission and regroupment are options to those who are disaffected. Research on dominance and conflict between the sexes in foraging societies remains inconclusive.

Horticultural Societies

In Chapter 3, Johnson discussed some difficulties of sharply separating horticultural societies from agricultural societies. One of the key differences is the intensity of farming, a feature with major implications for the sexual division of labor. Horticulturalists use land extensively and invest less labor in cultivation than agriculturalists. Periodically they clear new fields, but generally they do not invest their labor in leveling, terracing, or fertilizing the land. Horticulture is mainly associated with the use of hand tools, whereas agriculturalists often use plows and draft animals, if not tractors, to farm their permanent fields.

In general, horticultural practices such as shifting cultivation strongly correlate with major female contributions to cultivation. Men are found to increase their work time in the more intensive, densely populated farming systems such as those using plow or irrigation techniques on permanent fields (Martin and Voorhies 1975). Boserup (1970) emphasized this sexual contrast by broadly labeling farming systems "female" or "male," depending on which sex put more time into cultivation. She also observed regional patterns in the distribution of female and male responsibility for farming. In Africa south of the Sahara, she found that "female" systems using horticultural techniques were more common, whereas in Europe and Asia, particularly in the areas of Old World agricultural civilizations, "male" farming prevailed.

Cross-cultural research confirms the central importance of women farmers in most horticultural systems.[2] It also illustrates a gender shift in responsibility as dependence on cultivated food increases. Where cultigens account for less than 55 percent of the diet, women are almost always the principal cultivators. In the middle range, where 55 to 75 percent of the diet comes from cultivation, responsibility is more often about equal. When dependence on cultivated foods surpasses 75 percent of the diet, equal responsibility is still the main pattern, but the percentage of societies with men as principal cultivators increases (Martin and Voorhies 1975). In other words, as societies become more dependent on farming for food, men transfer more labor into farming, and when dependence becomes very high, men may surpass women's direct contribution to farmwork.

Given the usual cultural assumption that farming is a male activity, the importance of women as horticultural farmers is curious. How does farming relate to other economic activities, and how do societies determine which sex does what? By looking at cross-cultural data, anthropologists have identified four factors that seem to shape the choices that men and women make about farming and other work:

1. Compatibility with childcare: the locational model.
2. The productive sequence: economies of effort.
3. The daily work schedule: time and intensity.
4. Complementary activities and risks.

These factors will first be discussed for horticultural societies, and later in the context of the shift in the sexual division of labor in societies practicing intensive agriculture.

The first factor concerns childcare and work site. As in foraging societies, the compatibility of tasks with the care of unweaned and un-

---

[2] Within the horticultural category, a cross-cultural sample of 515 societies showed that women were the main farmers in 41 percent of the cases and that both sexes participated equally in 37 percent. In only 22 percent of the horticultural cases were men the principal cultivators (Martin and Voorhies 1975).

trained children remains an important consideration for women. In areas where food gathering and hunting continue to provide significant amounts of food alongside horticulture, women's farming may be seen as a gradual transition and intensification of their use of reliable plant resources. Cultivation reduces the time and distance they will have to spend in searching out and transporting foods along with their children. As women become more sedentary by cultivating food, they enhance the compatibility of their work with childcare.[3]

In societies that practice shifting cultivation, there may still be a demand to seek wild game or gourmet foods, as well as raw materials to make tools, clothing, and housing. When horticulture can provide reliable staple foods, considerable time can still be invested in other wants and needs without putting children at risk. As with foraging, the considerations of distance, danger, and task duration apply, and men can be expected to concentrate on those tasks that would be too strenuous or risky to accomplish with a child in tow: hunting and searching for resources located farthest from camp (Brown 1970; Burton et al. 1977; Ember 1983). In sum, the sexual division of labor remains strongly influenced by choices involving work location and the needs of children.

The sedentarization associated with horticultural communities leads to diminishing returns from local wild game and environmental resources. In response, men can choose between more distant and time-consuming foraging expeditions that risk competition with other groups, or they can invest more time in local horticulture and intensify their use of local resources. The choice depends on the environmental resource constellation and the possibilities for fulfilling diverse nutritional and material needs through local intensification or through trade and expansion. According to the locational model, women—particularly women with children—would choose intensification in either case. Thus, among the Iroquois at the time of white contact, women practiced horticulture in stable villages while men specialized in long-distance hunting, trading, raiding, and territorial defense (Trigger 1985). Among the South American Machiguenga, however, men devote a large part of their time to farming staple crops since neither hunting nor trade brings substantial returns (Johnson, see Chapter 3).

The second major factor is the production sequence and its relationship to economies of effort. The production sequence refers to the fact that production can often be divided into a series of distinct, separable

---

[3] Reduced requirements for long-distance carrying and changes toward a diet of domesticated plants can lessen the economic constraints on reproduction that seem to affect mobile foragers, and decrease the effective child spacing interval as women become sedentary (see Draper 1975; Lee 1979).

tasks en route from raw material to consumable product. Burton et al. (1977) used cross-cultural data to study sequences of productive tasks. According to their model, the similarity of adjacent tasks favors a minimization of switching from one sex to another in a production sequence since switching involves extra effort. Also, locational factors rather than the particular techniques used may be critical in determining which sex begins the sequence. Combining the locational model with the production sequence, they predict that men will be more likely than women to begin production sequences where distance and danger are factors. They reason that raw materials and natural resources are often obtained "from nature," or away from the homestead. Accordingly, if men begin a sequence (far from home), it may be finished by men alone, women alone, or both together; whereas if women begin a sequence (closer to home), they rarely transfer it to men for completion.

This model fits the data for production sequences involving cultivation: clearing land, preparing soil, planting, tending and harvesting crops, preparing vegetables, and cooking. When women start the sequence in any particular culture, they usually participate in all succeeding stages without transferring tasks to men; whereas when men start the sequence, they may either proceed to the next task by themselves, or the work may be shared and finally pass entirely into women's hands. The model of production sequences seems relevant for shifting horticultural societies where men claim and clear new land (which may be dangerous if other groups contest them), but when the village moves to the new site, women do all subsequent farming operations such as planting, weeding, and harvesting. If work location is not a factor, however, as in the case of domestic crafts, this model does not predict which sex will start and finish a production sequence.

An extension of the locational model may also fit distribution sequences that begin in or near home. Using the locational assumption again, either sex might start the sequence, but if it terminates far from home, a switch to male hands is predicted. This would apply to household industries or agricultural products destined for a market (near or far). Boserup (1970) suggested such a pattern when she observed that around the world, women and men were apt to sell their own products in local markets, but long-distance trade, or trade into foreign markets (presumably more dangerous), was more likely to be carried out by men.

A third factor to consider is the daily work schedule. Horticulture and shifting cultivation are commonly associated with tropical regions and root crops. In these regions, where there are smaller seasonal variations in temperature and rainfall as compared to temperate zones, root

TABLE 12.1
Productive Activities of Machiguenga
(percentage of daylight hours, 6 A.M. to 7 P.M.)

	Married men	Married women
Food production	34.1%	13.2%
Manufacture	10.4	15.9
Food preparation	1.5	18.1
Child rearing	.1	8.8
Total	46.1%	56.2%
Total hours per day (percentage × 13 hours)	6.0	7.3

SOURCE: Johnson and Johnson 1975: 639: Table 2. Reproduced by permission of the American Anthropological Association from *American Ethnologist* 2, no. 4 (November 1975). Not for further reproduction.

crops can be grown with relatively low labor inputs and can be left in the ground and harvested as needed. The work schedule in cultivating and harvesting does not require massive labor inputs concentrated during a short growing season, and can be handled by women alone or by both sexes together without working a long day. Similarly, the processing of most root crops does not require long hours of sustained effort each day. Ember estimates that the average work day for men is 5.15 hours and for women is 6.7 hours in "simple agricultural" (horticultural) societies (1983: 288).[4] Data from several cases show that women's time is divided between an average of 4.68 hours of outside work and 2.9 hours of inside work, compared to men, who showed 5.08 hours in outside work and 0.8 in inside work. Ember suggests that such a work schedule is compatible with women's obligations to feed and care for children and others on a daily basis.

Research on the Machiguenga (Johnson and Johnson 1975; see also Chapter 3) provides a specific example of the work schedule of a tropical horticultural society where wild game is scarce and where men contribute more labor to gardening than women (see Table 12.1).

In this case, men work more in garden labor and wild food collection, but women's total labor time in manufacture, food preparation, and childcare surpasses male labor time.[5] However, the comparison of male and female work contributions is complex. Men are found to work "harder" (expend one-third more caloric energy) and with more sustained effort than women in almost all activities, while women's work is intermittent. This gender difference in work styles—the latter one

---

[4] Ember's estimates are based on Minge-Klevana's (1980) time allocation data.

[5] This study measured only daylight working hours. It seems likely that the two activities, childcare and cooking, might often extend into the evening and predawn hours and extend married women's labor time.

being more compatible with the interruptions of children—means that it is difficult to compare women's and men's work efforts since they differ on measures of length and intensity. Perhaps it is reasonable to conclude that if one sex measures higher on intensity but lower on total time or vice versa, then the overall distribution of physical work effort is probably not very unbalanced.[6] This case also fits the production sequence prediction in that field clearance is a male responsibility, field work is performed by both sexes, and food preparation (close to home and handy for hungry children) is predominantly female work.

The fourth factor concerns complementary activities and risks. The sexual division of labor can vary from complementarity between completely separate activities to cooperation and joint performance in the same general occupational categories. In societies where women specialize in horticulture, the fulfillment of other compelling needs may require men to enter different spheres of activity. When men concentrate on nonhorticultural activities in distant or dangerous locations (that is, the activities incompatible with childcare), they are absent from the home and gardens and less available for close cooperation.

Two activities that keep men away from horticultural work are hunting (discussed earlier) and warfare. In Chapter 3, Johnson discussed warfare and competition over scarce natural resources. Although variations are great, most horticultural societies experience frequent warfare unless they have come under the control of an overriding government. Ember (1983) has shown that warfare in horticultural societies tends to be conducted by all able-bodied men rather than by specialized armies, and tends to compete with crop production for male labor. Horticulture is usually practiced in tropical zones and is often a year-round activity. Therefore, warfare in any season removes men from regular farming contributions. Regular food supplies are maintained by women while men fight.

Pastoralism and trade are two other occupational activities that may complement horticulture and engage male labor. These two specialties can increase the reliability and accessibility of animal products and other raw and manufactured materials. Compared to horticulture, both pastoralism and trade can involve longer distance travel and danger by attracting thieves. Unlike bulky root crops, livestock and luxury trade goods offer greater value per volume and therefore greater payoffs to mobile raiders. Although women often play significant roles in pastoralism and trade (Cloud 1986: 34; Henderson 1986: 138), these

---

[6] A good part of men's greater energy expenditure may be due to their higher basal metabolism, since men are on average slightly larger than women. Energy and time use are only rough measures of work; they do not measure skill and efficiency. As far as I know, no one has tried to measure and compare intellectual work effort.

activities tend to be absorbed into the men's domain if distance and danger are involved. Ironically, some societies, traditionally regarded as pastoral because men's economic interest centers on cattle, turn out to depend primarily upon horticulture once subsistence and the work of women are examined. Such is the case of the famous Nuer cattle herders studied by Evans-Pritchard (1940).[7] As with hunting, anthropologists often assume that pastoralism, and particularly herding large livestock, is men's work; but recent research on East African pastoralists demonstrates that women also herd both large and small animals (Wienpahl 1984). Generally, women care for livestock kept close to the campsite, where their tasks include bringing water and fodder, caring for sick and very young stock, milking, and processing milk products and hides (Dahl 1987: 250).

Strategies of specialization and diversification help reduce risk for any group willing and able to establish conventions of trust and exchange. The advantage of sexual specialization and complementarity is that it builds on the institutions of family attachment: parent-child, sibling, and conjugal bonds. Such ties, based on shared relations and knowledge of people, appear to be more reliable than those between strangers who belong to different groups specializing in different foods or resources. The transition from simple sex and age divisions of labor to more complex systems of regional and tribal specialization and interdependence is fraught with possibilities for mistrust, betrayal, and conflict, yet can convey vital benefits when population pressure and territorial competition for resources are high. Although the prestige economy of generosity and feasting is one way of building alliances that offer greater economic security, the practice of exogamy, or intermarriage between groups, is an extremely important strategy for enhancing economic cooperation and complementarity.

As with foragers, discussions of gender in farming economies usually focus on comparative work contributions and attempt to determine the value of each sex's contribution. Although research on the division of labor again confirms that women are an essential part of the labor force, efforts to determine the relative value of male or female activity are hampered by the lack of a single standard of measurement. Some anthropologists suggest that the quantity of work or subsistence contributions does not have any consistent relationship to women's status (Johnson and Johnson 1975; Sanday 1974). Or, they propose that the

---

[7] Turton (1980: 78–79) analyzed the ratios of cattle to people and concluded that at most 20 percent of Nuer dietary requirements were met by their herds, with 80 to 90 percent coming from cultivation and fishing. However, since rainfall and crops can be highly erratic in this region, men devote extraordinary attention to cattle, which are an essential emergency resource that can be sold for grain in years of crop failure.

social organization of work groups can establish a social basis for power and can influence the degree of sexual antagonism. In situations where women work together with each other or with men of their households, sex antagonisms will be low. In contrast, where women's work is solitary and men join together in economic (including warfare) activities, women will have low status. In part, what is suggested is that concepts of value are influenced more by group power than by work effort alone. A group has a better ability to define, publicize, and negotiate its worth than a solitary individual. This, of course, has a bearing on questions of gender and economic value when corporate descent groups are present and unified by bonds between one sex only, as in patrilineal or matrilineal descent groups.

Agricultural Societies: Men Take to the Fields

In societies with greater reliance on cultivated foods and intensive agriculture, men's farmwork also increases, both absolutely and relatively. A general shift from female to male predominance in farming operations seems to occur. This shift has often been interpreted to mean that women drop out or are pushed out of agriculture because men "take over." However, a more detailed look at work patterns in agricultural societies suggests that this is a misconception. Although women's participation declines relative to men's, there is usually no absolute decline. Women's contributions to outdoor farmwork remain roughly constant with intensification, but men go from a minimal or irregular input to a much more substantial contribution.[8] Together, the total labor time in farming increases.

How do we account for this shift in the division of labor? There is no single all-purpose explanation, but various theories consider the diverse factors affecting the male and female supply and demand for labor as well as their mutual interaction. On the demand side, agricultural systems, particularly with dense populations, generally require more labor than horticultural ones, and labor needs may be highly concentrated in a short planting or harvesting season. When land becomes scarce, people invest more time in farming what land they have, and men are under pressure to increase their input. On the supply side, there are two main considerations. One is that the availability of male labor increases, and the other is that women's time for field operations reaches a limit that is generally below that for men.

[8] See Boserup (1970) and Ember (1983). Ember shows that women's average contribution to outside work is about 4.7 hours per day in simple (extensive) agriculture, and 4.5 hours per day in intensive agriculture, whereas men's outside work contribution jumps from 5.1 to 7.3 hours per day.

Why is male labor released for cultivation activities in intensive agricultural regimes? Several reasons are proposed: (1) hunting declines; (2) military recruitment changes; and (3) extensive livestock herding by men declines. First, with intensive, permanent and densely settled agricultural regimes, game is depleted and most men give up hunting to undertake more productive pursuits. Second, intensive cultivation is associated with a change in military organization and a greater probability of having specialized fighting forces or a standing army (Ember 1983: 288–89). Specialized military units can release the remaining men for field work. The implication of such specialization is, of course, the development of socioeconomic stratification and the military-administrative apparatus of the state, which are characteristics of intensive agricultural societies. The third reason is that with intensive farming, most of the land is permanently cultivated, and little land is available for extensive pasturing. Extensive pastoralism becomes a specialty of distinct groups that use peripheral or marginal lands, while the livestock retained in intensive farming zones are increasingly confined and controlled for use as draft animals or intensive domestic exploitation in dairying or poultry, pig, or rabbit raising. Thus more men can respond to the increased demand for field labor.

Turning to women's work, we find a contrasting pattern of increasing demands on their time, both competing with field labor and increasing their overall labor time. Here, the main considerations regarding women's economic activity point to the following changes:

1. Food preservation and processing times increase substantially.
2. Fertility and hence childcare requirements increase.
3. Domestic animal care and related food processing increase.
4. Less hunting and fewer animal pelts entail shifts of labor to growing and processing plant and animal fibers into clothing, bedding, and sacking.

The added time needed for food preservation and processing occurs because intensive cultivation is largely associated with cereal crops rather than root crops. Cereal crops must be harvested at once and dried for year-round storage. This makes their transformation into edible food much more time-consuming than that of root crops. Threshing, drying, grinding, milling, soaking, and longer cooking times are typical requirements that increase the daily workload of farm women considerably.[9] Consistent with the locational and production sequence

[9] Ember (1983: 289) uses a sample of simple and intensive agriculturalists to show that the inside work of women is only 2.9 hours per day for simple agriculturalists, but doubles to 5.9 hours per day for intensive agriculturalists.

models discussed earlier, these tasks tend to become women's work. The time scheduling of food processing activities is more compatible with childcare than activities such as plowing, which, because of the effort to harness and continuously maintain control over animals on the way to and from the fields as well as during plowing, is very hard to manage in conjunction with childcare.

Greater fertility has also been associated with intensive agriculture (Ember 1983). Complex factors may account for this indirectly (for instance, changes in diet and cultural practices such as postpartum sex taboos may affect infant survival rates and child spacing) and directly through the explicit desire for more children to help with farm chores or to serve in military or religious institutions. Even if children become a net addition to family labor, in the short run they clearly create heavier demands and constraints on an adult woman's time and limit her availability for field work.

Many societies with intensive cultivation also have added tasks in domestic animal care. This is particularly true for those that grow cereal crops (White et al. 1981: 829). Cross-cultural studies suggest that for intensive agriculturalists, increased use of domestic animals is linked to decreased participation of women in agriculture per se. Care of domestic livestock usually means far more than simple maintenance of draft animals for field work. It includes keeping animals close to home and fencing them away from fields where they might eat the crops. Domestic livestock are kept for a variety of purposes: high-protein foods, diversified food reserves and savings, useful animal by-products and fertilizer. Domestic animals entail additional food processing activities (milking, making cheese and butter, collecting eggs, curing meat, making sausages), fodder collection and processing (chopping and cooking pig feed, for example), collecting and processing animal by-products for clothing (hides, down feathers, wool), and recycling their manure for fertilizing the gardens and fields.[10] These add up to substantial additional farm labor demands that may be vital to farming success and yet compete with the time available for field work. If a large portion of livestock maintenance and processing takes place close to the house, location and time scheduling would favor increased female labor.

The fourth consideration is that the decreased game around densely settled farmers translates into a scarcity of pelts in the face of increased demand for clothing. Although hides can still be used, denser popula-

[10] Sheridan (1984) provides a fascinating description of women's heavy labor in preparing pig feed in the People's Republic of China, where the value of pigs in producing manure for fertilizer exceeds their value as food.

tions require more rapidly renewable sources of plant and animal fibers to produce enough clothing. Shearing, carding, spinning, and weaving wool is one labor-intensive solution. Others are to use tree bark or to plant and process vegetable fibers such as sisal, cotton, and hemp. In intensive agricultural societies, producing clothing and textiles (for bedding, carpets, grain sacks, and so on) is labor-intensive and requires time, training, knowledge, and skill. Although both sexes may contribute in various ways, women generally contribute a very large proportion of the total labor in household textile production (Schneider and Weiner 1986: 181). Taking these competing labor demands into account, clearly women have little extra time to increase field labor as well.

Research among the Maya of highland Guatemala illustrates the limitations on the availability of female labor for increased field work (Bossen 1984). The Maya of T'oj Nam practice permanent hoe cultivation near their village and medium-term slash-and-burn farming on the more distant hillsides. Men are primarily responsible for maize, the main crop, although they are assisted by women in planting potatoes, beans, and subsidiary crops, as well as in weeding, watering, and harvesting. Women's time, however, is already heavily committed to processing food and manufacturing clothing. Unless they live in the vicinity of power mills, women may spend up to five hours per day boiling and grinding grains, and shaping and baking tortillas for their families. Most women also spend three to five hours daily hand weaving cotton cloth. It takes about a month and a half to weave the cloth for a man's shirt. When trousers, women's blouses, skirts, belts, shawls, and carrying cloths are considered, it is clearly difficult for one adult woman to make one full set of clothing for each family member annually. With their limited cash incomes, people of T'oj Nam now purchase some factory-made clothing. Yet the secondary role of women in the fields can still be explained by the high daily labor requirements in preindustrial food processing and cloth production. In addition, women wash the family's clothes and often assume full responsibility for farmyard animals such as chickens, pigs, ducks, rabbits, and dogs. One reason women perform most of these activities is that they do not involve carrying or coaxing children to walk long distances or leaving children poorly supervised for long periods. Further, whenever a woman has an unweaned child depending on her, economies of scale mean that older children will remain under her care as well.

The Maya case illustrates that settled farming involves a great many concomitant developments in resource use that are labor-intensive. Some activities are more compatible with childcare than plowing or other types of field work. The variety and importance of these related activities that diversify food production and processing, expand food storage, intensify and expand production of textiles, and increase the production of fertilizer indicate that a single-minded emphasis on agricultural field work as the primary economic base seriously distorts the complexity of economic development in intensive farming societies. Some anthropologists are beginning to make the case, for example, that textile traditions are "as central as agricultural production for social and evolutionary theory" (Schneider and Weiner 1986).

Several other theories have received attention as possible explanations for the sexual division of labor in agricultural households, and particularly the tendency for men to predominate in farming where plow technology is used. One argument is that men tend to monopolize the plow because of their physical strength and ability to control draft animals so that women lose their pivotal position in farmwork and retire to second place in the domestic sphere (Maclachlan 1983). This "plow thesis" has been criticized on the grounds that women are also physically capable of plowing and do so in some societies (Ember 1983). An alternate view points again to the characteristics of plowing that makes it less compatible with childcare: duration, distance, and danger. Taking small children to the fields risks that they may get underfoot (not only of mother, but also of oxen). They cannot safely be left underattended (in the field) or unattended at home while the mother drives draft animals for a full workday. Although using the plow is an important technological change, there is no reason to assume that women by not plowing are somehow doing less work overall.

Although plow use correlates with male participation in farming, cross-cultural analysis suggests that length of dry seasons and degree of dependence on domesticated animals may be even more strongly linked to male farm labor (Burton and White 1984). Curiously, the dry season hypothesis proposes that long dry seasons are associated with short, sharply defined planting and harvesting periods when demand for labor is extraordinarily high. Because of competing daily work commitments, women are not as free as men to devote their hours over long workdays during such periods of peak demand. They experience scheduling conflicts (and their average workdays are generally longer than men's anyway). Therefore, men are required to contribute more sustained labor to cultivation over a short time period. Although the dry season/peak labor demand theory and other theories of competing labor requirements need further exploration and testing, they represent advances in the perception of farming households as institutions facing, among other complex decisions, the scheduling of male and female labor to multiple economic activities.

The question of gender and family farm management remains to be considered. It is difficult to discuss changes in the sexual division of labor without making assumptions about the division of economic power and about who is controlling whom and what. The question of which sex does more farming is often thought to determine who commands the farm economy (Maclachlan 1983). Yet some anthropologists maintain that the theory that primary subsistence contributions confer economic control is not well supported (Johnson and Johnson 1975). It is not fully clear why long hours behind a plow should permit men to acquire more economic influence than women, whose total work time in field, farmyard, and farmhouse is often greater (Ember 1983; Nag, White, and Peet 1978).

Viewing the sexual division of farm labor as a basis for family farm management and control rests either on an implicit theory of labor exchange whereby the sexes obtain economic influence on the basis of the quantity or quality of labor they provide, or on a theory of skill or special experience whereby performance of some critical task is a necessary qualification for managerial authority.[11] Similar approaches are frequently seen in theories of the division of labor and economic power in pastoral societies. Dahl (1987: 258) points out that many authors, following Engels, see "male domination over livestock ownership as a direct result of the typical division of labor in pastoral societies. Men herd animals, thus they own them." Aside from the fact that women often do contribute substantially to herding and pastoral production,[12] Dahl argues that "the relation between herding as a task and ownership of livestock is in reality not so simple. In fact, the men who own stock are frequently not the same men who herd the stock" (ibid.).

These theories are difficult enough to apply in situations where crucial subsistence resources are freely accessible and where land and livestock are not privately owned or threatened by competitors. They are even less useful when private, clan, or village ownership of land and other forms of capital are important economic institutions defended by armed forces or the state. In these latter cases, private, feudal, or patriarchal monopolies over capital and resources can completely skew

[11] Following Maclachlan (1983) in his study of a South Indian farming system, Burton and White recently argued that the physical strength of young men makes them "the best candidates for farm labor" during peak periods of demand, and "because critical agricultural decisions are made during these times, men gain farm management experience that women do not have" (1984: 570). From this, they argue that older men end up being the managers of family farms.

[12] Based on "objective" assessments of work contributions alone, Dahl (1987: 253) notes that one might expect pastoral women and men to have equal economic power in a "balanced symbiosis," but cautions that such a conclusion would be premature when "emic" cultural assessments may devalue women's work.

the bargaining position between the sexes and devalue the labor of all those who lack property and means of coercion. By looking solely at the household or community-level sexual divisions of labor as the basis for economic control, anthropologists risk ignoring the extent to which larger political and economic institutions have shaped rural life (see Roseberry, Chapter 5).

Stacey (1983) argues that the relationship of the state to peasant farming households can bolster male authority and economic control in ways that have little to do with the respective labor contributions of the sexes. Why the state so often chooses to support male authority and control over peasant households is a challenging question. The reason may be that the state must offer rewards for military and labor drafts of men. By drafting and rewarding only men for state undertakings that are distant and dangerous (for example, military service), there is less chance that agricultural production and human reproductive levels will be disrupted. The exemption (or exclusion) of women from such service means they can continue to produce food and children to support future state undertakings and corvées. The rewarding of men with control over family land and labor promotes their loyalty to the state and maintains their incentive to serve as its soldiers. As experienced soldiers, men would have more leverage in negotiating with the state than the women who have stayed at home maintaining subsistence production and reproduction.

As with farming and military activities, market activities are also characterized by sexual divisions of labor. Some anthropologists suggest that women more often produce for family subsistence than for exchange and thus are handicapped relative to men in the larger economy. Although women frequently have highly visible roles in public markets, particularly in Africa, Southeast Asia, and highland Central and South America, their participation is regionally and culturally quite variable (Boserup 1970). The locational and production sequence model predicts that women would tend to sell the products that they produce or finish themselves unless the markets are distant and dangerous. Men would similarly tend to sell what they produce or finish but would also be more likely to become the long-distance traders or the ethnic merchant enclave residing in a foreign (and potentially hostile) environment.[13]

In some cases, one sex sells the other's product because the work

[13] For example, the Tuareg of North Africa sometimes had servant women organize donkey caravans to obtain palm reeds, but Saharan and trans-Saharan camel caravans carrying more valuable commodities such as salt, and engaging in raiding en route, were organized by men (Bourgeot 1987; Oxby 1987).

site and market site are incompatible. For instance, in Ghana, men spend their days at sea fishing; and when they return, women buy their catch and sell it in local markets or preserve it and sell it in more distant markets (Gladwin 1975). In rural Yucatan, Mexico, indigenous Maya women produce cotton hammocks in home industries, but the distribution to distant urban markets is generally undertaken by men (Littlefield 1978). Similarly, in highland Guatemala, Maya women sell their own handwoven cotton textiles in their homes and in local markets but often rely on male intermediaries to get their products to urban tourist markets. Few women, unless they have grown children, are able to set aside domestic responsibilities to travel regularly to urban tourist shops (a round-trip that can take two to three days). In contrast, one Quiché Maya community, Tecpanaco, has a family cottage industry where women first card and spin wool, and then men weave it into blankets (Bossen 1975; Carmack 1979). Both local and long-distance marketing of their joint product are almost exclusively in the hands of men. These men are the archetypal long-distance traders in Guatemala, similar to the Otaveleño men of Ecuador. In both cases, male merchants from these indigenous communities travel widely, not only beyond their ethnic communities in their own countries but throughout Central America and Panama, establishing permanent shops and returning seasonally to their homes for visits and more textiles.

Examination of the sexual divisions of labor in food production, military service, and marketing shows how households and society at large allocate labor between competing ends, one of which is the continued reproduction of human life and which has special constraints for women. I have argued that this does not necessarily reveal the relationship between labor and economic power. In complex, stratified societies, control over property and resources and the right to own, manage, mortgage, or sell land, livestock, or other forms of productive property tend to bear little immediate relationship to the performance of productive labor. More often, differences in control derive from institutionalized advantages and disadvantages based on social categories of race, class, ethnicity, and gender. Studies of the sexual division of labor are useful for identifying the points at which men or women can create leverage on the basis of the tasks they perform to secure a greater measure of influence, if not formal control, for themselves. A deeper understanding of women's variable economic power and influence cross-culturally requires historical examination of gender in political and economic institutions.

Institutionalized advantages are perpetuated through systems of marriage and social reproduction, which affect occupation and inheritance. The creation of new households and kin ties based on a sexual division of labor and long-term investment in a new generation involves major economic shifts for individual women and men, and for society as a whole. These shifts often involve explicit family and group investment decisions and negotiations regarding claims to people and property. Male and female choice may be constrained by the institutionalized authority vested in the state, church, kin group, or family patriarch. In stratified agrarian societies, marriage as an economic institution governing landed property as well as parenthood tends to be much more rigidly controlled than in foraging and horticultural societies. With respect to women, the cross-cultural study and interpretation of marriage payments and of practices such as bride service, bride wealth, and dowry (controversial concepts in themselves) have generated much debate.[14]

Part of the controversy stems from the tendency to focus on the perspectives of men in negotiating, among themselves, the disposition of marriageable women as if women were inanimate and inarticulate rather than active participants with a distinct, definable set of interests. Although analysis of the cultural economics of marriage institutions lies beyond the scope of this chapter, a critical discussion of this literature, distinguishing women's and men's perspectives and economic interests in marriage transactions, is presented elsewhere (Bossen 1988).

In agrarian and urban societies, the distribution of property rights and marriage rights between men and women is deeply affected by the development of larger political or economic institutions that often override the interests of individuals as they negotiate the division of labor and benefits within household units of production. One criticism of economic development policies regarding women in recent years concerns the widespread practice of issuing titles to public or communal lands to poor or landless men on behalf of the household (discussed further in the next section). Legally, this makes women economic dependents (or junior partners at best) of the assumed household head no matter how much productive labor they contribute. If enforced, the widespread assumption that household heads exist and are male can thus transform myth into reality.

The changes in the sexual division of labor in production and distribution as societies evolve suggest that the question of which sex is economic provider and which is economic dependent may have little to do with the performance of productive work. The evident lack of female economic power in most intensive agricultural regimes seems to

[14] See, for example, Grey (1968), Goody (1973), Rubin (1975), and Comaroff (1980).

have other causes. My view is that the weakness of women's economic position is at least partly due to the shift in military organization toward more specialized and permanent fighting forces. Military forces can redefine the system of economic negotiation between men and women, and between classes and strata. Men who serve in armies learn not the value of labor, but the value of power. In horticultural societies, a successful warrior may win captives who can be put to death or to work. In agricultural societies, successful soldiers and military careerists are often rewarded with landed estates and administrative posts as well as booty and other privileges. The state and its military forces can redefine property relations and impose authoritarian family structures that override local norms and negotiations between men and women in their communities and kin groups. Because military institutions are generally restricted to males, the conversion of soldiers into landowning household heads can be a crucial factor in decreasing women's economic bargaining power, regardless of their labor contributions.[15]

Women and Development

The subject of women in development was not widely recognized until Boserup's landmark book, *Women's Role in Economic Development*, appeared in 1970. It outlined serious neglect and negative consequences of development for women on a global scale. Since then, many more anthropologists and development specialists have begun to examine what happens to traditional economic institutions and sexual divisions of labor when preindustrial economies are influenced by more powerful industrialized economies.

The economic development of preindustrial societies and the introduction of capitalist processes of market exchange, private property, capital accumulation, and wage-labor competition seem to be associated with a widening gap between male and female economic positions. This issue of equity in development is a complicated one because there are so many different dimensions along which economic benefits might be measured. Moreover, there is rarely a single standard of value that can be examined throughout the transition from a subsistence to cash economy, or from an agrarian to urban-industrial economy.

Whether women's position improves or declines relative to men in their society, there is considerable evidence that both women's and men's economic benefits have generally improved in an absolute sense

[15] This may be mitigated for some women, however, by their role in the social reproduction of stratified societies. As mothers, sisters, or wives of powerful men, some women can acquire political and economic privileges denied to lower strata or classes.

over the last century. Some of the benefits of development have been channeled into improved health and population growth, wider access to primary and higher education, and accumulation of material goods. This observation does not imply uninterrupted progress, nor does it ignore disastrous wars, famines, and endemic poverty that persist in many parts of the world.

Numerous measures of male and female economic status show that the developed capitalist economies, for all their successes, have not achieved full sexual equality in access to occupations, in wages and salaries, or in domestic responsibilities. Similarly, socialist countries with more explicit commitments to economic equality, and with state control over large parts of their economy, have not been successful in eliminating sex-based wage gaps, job discrimination, and the double work load of women in domestic and public spheres. In both types of system, women's input into major state, industrial, and military policies remains low (Lapidus 1978; Stacey 1983; Wolf 1985; Croll 1986). In the Third World, capitalist development is also very uneven by sex, region, and class (Nash and Safa 1986). In specific cases, women may be experiencing relative gains or losses compared to men, but there is a growing consensus that whether under the auspices of colonial or market economies, development has not generally been conducive to equal participation and reward for women (Boserup 1970; Bossen 1984; Charlton 1984; Creevey 1986).

Methodological Issues

In the past decade, many anthropologists have begun to examine the multiple effects of economic change on women in developing countries and to analyze the methodological problems that have permitted this topic to go unnoticed for so long. Much of the work that women do has not been effectively counted in national economic surveys. One reason for this undercounting and the resulting "invisibility" of women is that women are disproportionately involved in domestic and informal sector work, where participation and productivity are not as easily measured as in the formal sector. Informal sector employment (see Dannhaeuser, Chapter 9) is often intermittent, seasonal, mobile, small-scale family or individual economic activity that may be intermingled with other family responsibilities. It includes the production of commodities in the home, selling food at temporary locations on the street or in markets, service work in private homes, and seasonal wage labor in agriculture. Formal census takers find it time-consuming and difficult to categorize and record reliable data on this very fluid, dispersed sector of the economy. For instance, if census takers record "occupation" only on the day or week of the census, widespread seasonal wage labor by women could be completely ignored unless the census were carried out at the peak of the busy harvest. There would remain the problem of categorizing seasonal workers as "unemployed" or "employed," as "full time" or "part time," or as having one occupation or several. For men, as presumed economic household "heads" and economic providers, informal occupations have generally been viewed as employment, whereas for women, the reverse has been the case. By using alternate methods of long-term, first-hand observation of women's roles, anthropologists have identified much higher degrees of economic activity and occupational multiplicity than is recorded for women in national censuses.

Some anthropologists have vociferously criticized development economists for neglecting to collect data on the full range of economic pursuits and for naively assuming that census and statistical data in developing countries have an acceptable level of accuracy (Hill 1986). For women, a reevaluation of concepts and methods has begun. The validity of such widely accepted concepts as "head" of household— a convenient shortcut for collecting internationally comparable data on family production—has been challenged as fostering inappropriate economic assumptions about gender and family systems, and as misrepresenting women's roles in work, consumption, and property organization for many non-Western societies (Aguiar 1986: 25; Bossen 1981).

The use of this "head" concept implicitly diminishes the economic roles of women, placing them in the category of economic dependents (often labeled "housewives") and ignoring any independent productive, managerial, or commercial activities they carry out in other cultures. As a result, development programs intending to work with what is erroneously and ethnocentrically believed to be the status quo tend to deliver training, technology, and resources to men. In the process, these programs can revolutionize systems of gender relations by putting men in charge of all major material resources. At the same time, benefits to the assumed household head are often falsely perceived as equally benefiting the household members.

Even such progressive-sounding development institutions as cooperatives can be organized so that they reduce cooperation and establish more authoritarian relations between men and women. Venema (1986: 88–90) describes the creation in Senegal of village agricultural cooperatives where membership was 99 percent male "heads of household." Although women continued to cultivate their own fields, they became dependent on male cooperative members for access to seed, fertilizer (often at higher interest rates), and mechanical farm implements, while the women's crop deliveries to the cooperative were credited to and paid to male members as "household heads." Venema remarks that "when it is payday, it is the man who cashes the slips. Because all the women were illiterate . . . the rumors I heard of heads of household giving their wives only part of the money owed to them were probably not groundless" (1986: 90).

Because of these criticisms, demands for disaggregation of social and economic data by sex have increased. In terms of actual field methods, Hill made the following observation:

Three-cornered conversations, involving the conjugal pair and the statistical investigator, are no more likely to yield reliable information about the wife's economic affairs than are enquiries made of the male householders who, as we have seen, are commonly biased or ignorant, partly because of female secretiveness. If may be of some assistance to employ female investigators, but not if the male householder insists on obtruding himself. In general, the occupational statistics in population censuses greatly understate the numbers of women who work on the household farmland. [1986: 143]

Anthropologists recognize that the conditions under which data are collected have a great deal to do with the reliability of those data. If trust and security regarding the individuals who collect economic data and the use to which those data will be put are lacking, the quality of the data suffers. Willingness to disclose economic activities is affected by a number of cultural and power differentials that foster distrust and that tend to be particularly magnified for women. These include separations (1) between male and female spheres of action, (2) between male and female socially acceptable modes of communication, (3) between outsiders and "known" individuals, (4) between those empowered with literacy and those who cannot read, and (5) between those who command the national language and those who understand only the local dialect. Women commonly have less experience with strangers, literacy, and speakers of the national language than men. Community-based studies of women have demonstrated that much of the macrolevel census data on women is erroneous, or at best incomplete (Rogers 1980: 164; Bossen 1981, 1984; Aguiar 1986; Charlton 1984: 42).

In recent years, research illuminating women's economic participation and the continuing problems of gender discrimination in developing countries has greatly expanded. Anthropologists now explore women's changing economic contributions in agriculture, high-technology industries, cottage industries, markets and informal employment, migrant labor, domestic service, and in many other situations where women of different cultural traditions are encountering the world market economy.[16] These studies demonstrate a wide range of female economic activities that previously went unnoticed and unanalyzed. They also identify a host of new problems concerning the cultural and institutional tendencies to exclude women from key aspects of economic development. I will now address several development issues that affect rural women's economic roles profoundly: the increasing scarcity of land, the growing access to industrial commodities, and the shift to urban extrafamilial employment.

Rural Development: Land and Commodities

The expansion of international trade and commercial agricultural production has produced increasing competition for land that can be commercially developed. In many areas, land that is not permanently settled or individually owned is being converted into legally titled property by which named individuals or groups have more exclusively defined rights to exploitation. This process of establishing private written land claims, often begun under colonial rule, has been shown to result in an exclusion of women as individual owners in many areas, even where they had traditional usufruct claims upon land (Ifeka-Muller 1975). Citing the work of anthropologists Edith Clarke, Polly Hill, Mary Douglas, and others, Rogers (1980) notes that colonial powers have often transformed matrilineal and bilateral inheritance systems into ones that favored male ownership rights. This process continues with contemporary land reforms, national development, and resettlement projects, which continue to assign land titles to men on behalf of their families (Rogers 1980: 122–47; Brain 1976; Llanos Albornoz 1985). A similar pattern of male entitlement has occurred with certain government livestock replacement programs. For instance, after the Sahelian drought destroyed herds, new livestock were issued to men only, ignoring traditions whereby women owned their own livestock (Cloud 1986: 33–35).

Beyond cases of direct, legalized sexual discrimination, the operation of the commercial economy itself may favor men over women in terms of the accumulation of productive assets. A Guatemalan example illustrates how commercialization of traditional responsibilities can contribute to a growing gender gap (Bossen 1984). In T'oj Nam, a rugged mountain district with relatively few urban consumer goods, Mayans still rely considerably on subsistence farming and domestic manufac-

[16] See Babb (1986), Benería (1983), Bossen (1984), Buechler (1986), Cook (1986), Creevey (1986), Dahl (1987), Fernandez-Kelly (1983), Leacock and Safa (1986), Nash and Safa (1986), and Rothstein (1983).

ture. Most of the land is currently held by men through patrilineal in-heritance.[17] Over the past 40 years, population has grown rapidly, and T'oj Nam has roughly doubled its population, simultaneously halving the amount of land per capita. Plots have been fragmented, and most dropped well below the amount needed for the family food supply. Yet as the primary owners and users of farmland, any men who still con-trol land and its products experience an increase in the value of their landed property.

At the same time, a trickle of cheap consumer goods and labor-saving household technology has become a steadier stream, including dyed thread, ready-made cloth, ready-made clothing, sewing machines, mo-torized corn mills, neighborhood water pipes, and electricity. Purchas-ing these items requires scarce cash. Their availability, however, has lowered the labor cost of goods and services traditionally provided by women. Access to cash income thus becomes an increasingly important determinant of economic values, including those exchanged between the sexes. Unlike land, however, women's assets are not in rising de-mand.

Extreme regional poverty means that both men and women migrate to perform low-paid agricultural piecework. When paid strictly by piece rates and permitted to work at the same jobs, harvesting coffee or cot-ton, women are able to earn as much as men. However, the serious health risks to small children when mothers migrate are a deterrent so that women less frequently take such work. Only a few opportunities for formal employment at much higher pay rates have become available to Maya men, but there has not yet been a single opportunity, and none on the horizon, that has opened for Maya women in the formal sector. In this situation, wider market participation can be predicted to affect the value of men and women in several different ways (see Table 12.2).

Although these four types of market change are relatively recent and have not affected all households equally, taken together they point toward a growing imbalance between men as preferential owners of landed capital and holders of most formal wage jobs, and women as a growing surplus of domestic laborers whose manual skills cannot com-pete with cheap industrial products and who lack personal access to productive capital. This sketch suggests that economic inequality be-tween the sexes is increasing. Although both men and women experi-ence landlessness, the process is less systematic for men; overall, men have better access to formal jobs and agricultural wage labor, which

[17] This statement refers to lands within the municipal district. In the nation as a whole, it can be said that most of the cultivable land (about two-thirds) is controlled by a small but powerful class of landowners—roughly 2 percent of the population (Bossen 1984).

TABLE 12.2
Consequences of Market Participation

Wider market participation	Consequences
Increased scarcity of land due to population growth locally, and expansion of large-scale capitalist agriculture for export nationally	Value of male assets in land increases, demand for subsistence crops is sustained
Increased flow of cheap consumer goods and domestic labor substitutes	Value of female assets and domestic labor decreases, domestic cash costs rise
Accessibility of abundant low-wage, temporary piece-rate jobs to both sexes	Value of labor is equal but female participation is lower due to children
Creation of few, modern wage jobs with government or development projects, or as plantation agents	Value of men's labor (and education) increases since women not selected

improves their chances of acquiring capital assets. Moreover, family members can pool wages to buy land, but the title itself is effectively assigned to the man. In this rural community, as in many others, the extension of modern legal and economic institutions tends to generate a pattern whereby men get de jure custody of land and material resources, and women get de facto custody of children.

Various characteristics of development—the increasing scarcity of land, the increasing replacement of domestic subsistence goods by commercial goods, and the differential access by men and women to formal employment—are associated with changes in male and female economic value. The impact of these changes can, in turn, be linked to changes in the economics of marriage transactions. For instance, in India a widespread shift from bride wealth to dowry and from low dowry to high dowry demands has been observed. Bride wealth requires the groom's family to transfer wealth to the bride's family, and dowry requires the bride's family to contribute to the groom's. It is widely held that the direction of payments is at least partly a cultural reflection of economic contributions by sex: where women do farmwork, bride wealth is paid; where men are farmers (and especially if they own land), they may be able to demand a wife who brings dowry (see Bossen 1988).

In rural areas, landed men hold assets that undoubtedly have gone up in value, given the population growth India has experienced. In urban areas, men's higher educational levels and superior access to salaried jobs maintain their advantage over women. Women's labor most likely has gone down in value relative to the new industrial products and appliances that are available. Yet women's participation in the market economy is highly restricted and, if the census measures have any validity, may even have decreased from 44 to 41 percent between 1960 and 1980 (Sivard 1985: 29). Culturally, women belonging to families that have the means are expected to stay out of the public sector and remain in *purdah* (domestic seclusion). Thus it is difficult for women themselves to generate the income to buy the vast array of new consumer goods that have become attractive to households. Their economic dependence on male capital and cash incomes means their own kinsmen have to compensate for their weak market position by supplying ever increasing amounts of consumer durables and cash dowries to them as they enter the marriage market. If high dowries are any indication (*India Today* 1986), women's dependency on men seems to be spreading regionally and increasing in intensity.

If Indian women can make greater inroads into the urban salaried occupations or gain equal rights to inherit land or other productive assets, this devaluation may reverse itself. Yet some groups seem to have resorted to female infanticide and fatal neglect of daughters in order to avoid paying dowry, resulting in a real demographic scarcity of women in parts of India (Miller 1981). The national sex ratio decreased from 972 females per 1,000 males in 1901 to 935 in 1981 (*India Today* 1986). Even so, families of girls who have to pay dowry "speak as though marrying their daughters was the hardest of tasks, and decent husbands were dearer than gold" (Sharma 1980: 142). Because men are anything but scarce in India, this strong preference for sons persists because women are so severely handicapped in India's developing economy.

Increased access to the market economy may stimulate demand for manufactured commodities, but it can also stimulate commodity production in the countryside. Cook's research in the valley of Oaxaca, Mexico (1986, forthcoming) describes women who perform intensive handicraft work in rural cottage industries. The women work for low wages or contribute unpaid labor to capital accumulation in family enterprises managed by men. In general, local returns are not attractive enough in these sideline occupations for women to perform them full time in preference to other subsistence tasks. In the few instances in which an international tourist market offers higher prices for crafts, Cook (forthcoming) found that men switch into some of women's traditional crafts such as weaving, work full time, and take their products to more distant urban markets that offer higher prices. The combined responsibilities for childcare and family maintenance apparently tie women down and prevent them from weaving continuously and traveling regularly to the better markets. Perhaps the women have also been less exposed to the national language, education, foreign styles, and big-city ways than the men, and are therefore less equipped to undertake their own marketing.

Migration and Urban Development

Another consequence of economic development for women in rural areas is the tendency for men to commute or migrate to work in extra-domestic commercial agriculture or industrial employment. When families are separated by the push and pull of national and international labor markets, it is typically men who migrate to the types of mining, plantation, and industrial jobs that are least compatible with childcare, while women are left with growing children and must continually dig into their savings or earnings to feed them from day to day. Migrant men thus have a greater capacity to save their wages to invest either in land or in new forms of urban enterprises.

The withdrawal of men from subsistence production, along with the increasing withdrawal of children for formal education, may mean that married women (mothers) are left with heavier responsibilities for maintaining farm, livestock, or craft production along with household management.[18] Although male formal employment may improve total household cash income, women's claims to this income are weak compared to the individual who was directly paid and has the cash in hand.

In some instances, women seem to be preferred for industrial wage employment. However, the wages paid in female-labor-intensive industries are generally lower than those men will accept. Studies of Mexican women employed in the strawberry export industry and in border electronics industries (Arizpe and Aranda 1986; Fernandez-Kelly 1983) show many similarities to the early women textile workers in nineteenth-century New England (Dublin 1979). The women are overwhelmingly young (age 16 to 21), single, and earning too little to support themselves independently. These Mexican workers tend to live with their parents until they marry and quit work, whereas in nineteenth-century New England young women workers were housed in dormitories where their moral behavior was closely supervised. The fact that many young country women are willing to commute or migrate to work for meager wages indicates that the commercial substitutes for female activities have created rural underemployment. Over the long run, however, these women are generally forced to choose between

---

[18] See Creevey (1986), Venema (1986), Minge-Klevana (1980), and Rothstein (1983).

a commitment to industrial work or a commitment to marriage and family.

The development of modern urban economies is associated with a narrow range of "new" occupational choices for women in modern sector employment and the ongoing but altered constraints of childcare and socialization. In developing economies there is generally an extensive demand for female labor in urban service-sector jobs. These range from informal domestic services and marketing as major sources of employment for uneducated urban women to more formal white-collar jobs—teaching, nursing, and secretarial—which are commonly occupations for educated women in both developing and developed countries. Although women have been breaking out of some female occupational ghettos as their educational levels rise, their access to the full range of modern occupations remains limited, and their earning capacity is lower than men's.

Most studies of employment in the developing world show that men have a distinct advantage in obtaining a variety of formal, higher paying jobs, while women are concentrated in the less profitable informal service sectors, where the competition is intense (Babb 1985; Nelson 1979). When women are young and single, they may obtain work as domestic servants or, more rarely, as factory workers in labor-intensive industries if slightly better educated. Women experience particular disadvantages if they have small children, for relatively few urban jobs are compatible with childcare. Women thus crowd into self-employed activities such as vegetable retailing in urban markets where they can look after their children while at work (Babb 1985).

In urban Guatemala, as in most of Latin America, there is a surfeit of women who have been displaced from the rural household economy and have migrated to the city to get work. These women are very vulnerable, having almost no means to accumulate capital and savings on their own. When they are encumbered with dependent children, they have strong incentives to participate in subversion of property, private or public, when they join in squatter "invasions" to gain access to land or housing, and when they "squat" on city streets to sell their wares without paying rent or taxes. Of course, their poverty is never strictly a matter of gender, for each new generation includes children of both sexes who start out with no inheritance. But because women lack legal titles to real estate, they have a harder time raising cash or credit for new urban business ventures, and they are more limited than men in their capacity to expand their informal self-employment into regular, if not major, enterprises.

In modern industrial economies, childcare responsibilities and associated domestic work continue to be a major constraint for women, although the dimensions of this are changing (Minge 1986). Families have fewer children but are investing far more time and money in their education. There are more nonmaternal feeding and childcare alternatives; day-care centers and public school systems make it possible for more women to hold regular full-time jobs with fewer and shorter interruptions for childcare. But given the current retention of traditional gender values and gendered job opportunities, women's mobility is more constrained by parenthood, and men are still preferred for jobs that demand mobility and uninterrupted work. For women, general nurturing obligations still affect the length of the workday they can accept. Along with the development of labor-saving domestic technology, standards for domestic services have increased, and time-consuming domestic work is still largely women's responsibility (Luxton 1980). In fact, as Minge (1986) and Rothstein (1985) point out, during the transition to industrial society, women's share of domestic work may even increase as other family members shift to formal employment and educational activities outside the home.

The organizational requirements for large-scale and efficient modern industries and bureaucracies have had a profound impact on family systems. The weakening of the family as a productive unit and the transition to individual cash wages have enabled divorce rates in modern economies to rise. Changes in marital and parental obligations, support, and claims upon conjugal assets have led women to try to improve their position in the market economy since they cannot always count on the family for economic support and security. Compared to landowning peasants, the easier divorce or separation of urban, industrial societies reflects the privatization of monetary income that makes it both possible and necessary for women to strive for economic independence.

As anthropologists have responded to demands for more information on women's economic roles in other cultures, they have shown that the development of world markets and economic institutions have complex effects that often differ for men and women. In particular, women's access to employment, resources, education, and technology is still constrained by childcare obligations as well as the cultural expectation that children will interfere with women's performance. These conflicts are real. As women succeed in gaining more formal jobs and greater economic independence, they often elect to have fewer children. The economic disadvantages women experience from the combination of poor employment opportunities and unilateral or imbalanced childcare responsibilities ultimately affect the formation of the next generation. The changing relationships between generations and gender in the process of economic development require greater attention if effective planning for sustainable development and demographic stability is ever to occur. Although some economists, anthropologists, and development experts may continue to ignore gender differences, the customary exclusion of women from economic analysis and economic planning is increasingly hard to justify.

13

Management of Common-Property Resources

James M. Acheson

During the past two decades, the modern world has become painfully aware of the damage humans have done to their natural environment. In the United States, scarcely a week goes by without a major news story about loss of agricultural land, pollution, fishery failures, acid rain, toxic wastes, degeneration of forests, and so on. In underdeveloped countries, another set of problems has come to the fore: soil erosion, deforestation, overgrazing, and the loss of wildlife. Once the environment is damaged, drought or other natural disasters can quickly lead to massive starvation, social disorganization, and usually social unrest. This has occurred in Bangladesh, Haiti, and the entire Sahel region of Africa within the living memory of most American college students. We have only begun to try to calculate all the costs of these problems.

One of the most popular and controversial explanations for these problems is the "theory of common-property resources," which has become one of the most influential theories guiding resource management policy in the world today. In recent years the debate concerning common-property problems has gained vitality as traditional ways of handling resource problems have proven inadequate. It has gained attention not only in academic circles but in government agencies, corporations, and foundations as well.

Essentially the common-property issue is concerned with ways in which resources shared by all the people in the society can best be protected. According to this theory, all resources held in common such as oceans, rivers, parks, air, publicly owned forests and grazing lands will inevitably be overexploited. Such "common-property resources" are owned by no one, and thus it is not in anyone's interest to protect them. Even worse, people exploiting common-property resources are caught in a situation in which it is only logical that they increase their exploitive effort without limit. Why should a fisherman, for example, control his own fishing practices to conserve the fish stocks? The fish he does not take may be caught by another fisherman within a matter of hours. Under these conditions, a fisherman is only being rational and sensible to catch all the fish that he can as quickly as possible. As a result, resources in the public domain are likely to be stripped bare by an uncaring public.

Privately owned resources ostensibly will not be overexploited. After all, they have an owner to protect them, and it is not in his best interests to irrevocably damage his own property.

The Tragedy of the Commons

The idea that the commons are subject to problems is an old idea in Western thought (McCay and Acheson 1987: 2). The idea gained widespread attention with the publication of Garrett Hardin's paper "The Tragedy of the Commons," which was published in 1968 at the height of the ecology movement in the United States. Hardin developed the theory to put forth his view that untrammeled freedom to produce children would result in disaster for the world. The parable he used, however, was that of a pasture used in common by a group of herdsmen. The first herdsmen who use the pasture do no damage to it, but as they add more animals overgrazing occurs. Even then, Hardin points out that it is only rational for herdsmen to continue to add additional sheep to their herds. The reason is that each herdsman gains the full benefit of each sheep he adds, while the costs of his action are shared by all herdsmen jointly. To be precise, the gain in meat, wool, or milk belongs to the individual herd owner, who deducts the out-of-pocket costs from this gain to get net income. The gain is due (in part) to the pasture eaten by each animal, but the owner does not pay for the pasture eaten by his or her sheep. In other words, each sheep the herdsman brings to the pasture brings him a gain of almost $+1$; his loss is only a small fraction of -1. Thus it is only sensible for each herdsman to increase the number of sheep without limit. The result is depletion of the pasture, erosion, and a sharp decline in carrying capacity, which harms everyone. Nevertheless, when resources are limited and publicly owned, it is rational for each individual to overexploit them even though this behavior ultimately results in tragedy for the group. For Hardin, "Therein lies the tragedy. Each man is locked into a system that compels him to increase his (share) without limit—in a world that is limited. Ruin is the destination toward which all men rush, each pursuing his own best interest in a society that believes in the freedom of the commons. Freedom in a commons brings ruin to all" (1968: 1244). Hardin's solution is repressive governmental action. He concludes that we cannot ask people to voluntarily restrain their use of any commons with any hope of success; "coercion" is necessary. The coercion should be "mutually agreed upon" (ibid.: 1247), but it need not be just (1977: 275). "The alternative of the commons is too horrifying to contemplate. Injustice is preferable to total ruin."

Hardin is particularly interested in the world population problem, which he sees as a common-property issue. The costs of breeding do not fall on those who have additional children, but are passed on to the society as a whole (1968: 1246). Hardin is not sanguine about the prospects for Third World countries because he does not believe their governments can develop effective population controls. The future he sees for such countries is the same one Tertullian saw for them in the third century: devastated by the "scourges of pestilence, famine, wars" (Hardin 1977: 263).

The solution to all "tragedies of the commons," from Hardin's point of view, is mutually agreed on "coercion" (Hardin 1968: 1247), by which he means some sort of management by the government enforceable by law, and perhaps not very democratically imposed.

Hardin's article created a minor furor when it was published in 1968, and another book by Hardin and his followers added fuel to the fire (see Hardin and Baden 1977). My darkest side suspects that the interest in Hardin's work stemmed from the fact that he articulated problems others had thought about and that he gave a rationalization to radical solutions they had considered. His theory attempted to explain many things, such as water pollution, acid rain, and resource depletion of concern to U.S. society.

Hardin's theory and concepts have been soundly criticized by a number of scholars on a variety of grounds.[1] But none of these critiques attack what I see as some of the most obvious weaknesses in the theory; namely, the fact that it rests upon questionable assumptions and that it is highly culture bound. The theory's assertions do not hold true cross-culturally and are not even applicable to all situations in the United States.

---

[1] Estellie Smith (1984) deplores Hardin's willingness to use draconian governmental action and his insistence that welfare and the green revolution are simply exacerbating the population problem. Daniel Fife points out that freedom in a commons means disaster for the commons—not necessarily for those who exploit them (1977: 76). Beryl Crowe argues that government action is not apt to be an effective solution to the commons dilemma in today's anarchic world (1977: 55–67).

The Economic Assumptions of
Common-Property Resources

Though the "tragedy of the commons" is most often linked with Hardin, economists were the first to suggest that resources with no private owner were prone to serious problems. The most important conclusion of these economists is that private property results in more efficient use and conservation of resources and greater increases in wealth than do less exclusive forms of property (Johnson 1972: 259). These benefits stem from the fact that property rights do away with what economists call "externalities." An externality is a factor of production or a good not under the direct control of the producer or consumer (see Cheung 1970). For example, to produce skis, the owner of a firm must pay costs such as labor, interest, insurance, and so on; and when the skis are sold, the owner receives all the benefits in the form of revenues. These costs are internal to the firm in that the firm must pay them all; the revenues are internal as well in that no one outside the firm will get them. Some firms produce not only internal costs and benefits but external costs and benefits as well. A beehive owner produces an internal benefit (honey for sale) and also external benefits for the owner of a nearby apple orchard, whose trees are pollinated by the hive owner's bees. By the same token, some firms that pollute rivers and the air are creating external costs. By definition, firms cannot capture external benefits they produce, nor must they pay for the external costs that result from their operations. The owner of the beehive cannot collect a pollination fee from the owner of the apple orchard because he could not stop his bees from pollinating the farmers' trees if the farmer refused to pay. Likewise, a firm that pollutes is also creating external costs, passing off some of its costs of production onto people downwind or downstream and the larger society. Those who pay are people downstream or downwind who are deprived of all the benefits of living in a clean environment. These external costs range from loss of recreational opportunities for people who own riverfront property to costs of repainting houses and health for people who live downwind from the smokestack of a mill.

Property rights mean that the internal benefits and costs accrue to the owner (Demsetz 1967). A person who owns a piece of land has the right to everything produced on that land, and he alone loses if the land is degraded. In contrast, a person who does not own property cannot benefit from any improvements he makes on that property nor will he lose by any damage he does to it. From this point of view, gaining property rights, as a number of economists have defined it, is a process of internalization of benefits and costs.

Transactions Costs

Establishing property rights confers several benefits. First, private property makes it possible to enter into contracts easily, which in turn makes it possible to solve many problems with a minimum loss of time and effort (that is, transactions costs). If property rights are established and clear-cut, there is little difficulty in finding out who can lay claim to the income produced by that property and who must be compensated if that resource or asset is damaged. If the Penobscot River is polluted, private property rights make it possible to locate all owners of the lands on the river, including the polluter, at relatively low cost. The polluter can then buy up the property of people who are damaged or compensate them for their loss and use the river as an open sewer. Conversely, the landowners can get together to buy out the polluter and return the river to its pristine state. In either case, private ownership allows exchanges to be made at low transactions costs. Common property makes such exchanges prohibitively costly. The problem of coping with acid rain is going to be very expensive for just this reason. How can all the people whose trees have been damaged by acid rain or who have been denied recreational opportunities on lakes devoid of fish possibly stop the pollution or be compensated easily? Because the air is not owned, the polluters can and do use it to carry off their factory emissions free of charge and unhampered. How can they be forced to cease their polluting activities? Who is going to pay for the damage? How can manufacturers make arrangements to use the air and water? In the absence of property rights, answers to these questions will come only when legislation is developed after years of negotiations and lobbying in the political arena. In the meantime, the public will go on suffering the effects of air pollution, and the industries that have expropriated the use of air will do so in the future at increased risk and cost.

Maldistribution

So far, we have seen that private property rights lower the cost of economic transactions. In addition, the theory of private ownership argues that resources are used more efficiently because the owner is free to seize on those options that will grant him the greatest wealth and to reject less productive uses. The owner of land is free to lease it, rent it, give it to sharecroppers, or use it for a variety of purposes—whichever option is to his or her advantage. In this sense, efficiency comes from the freedom to enter into contracts of various sorts in which the market is free to operate. The efficiency of private property also stems from the fact that the owner of a resource must pay all costs of using that resource—including the cost of the land itself (that is, "rent" on the land or resources) and take this into account in his decision making. If privately owned resources are squandered, only he will experience the repercussions. For this reason, private property is said to result in the best use of resources for the society as a whole (Scott 1955). Owners have no incentive to waste resources or misallocate them (Bromley 1973: 385–87). With common property there is a divergence between the interests of the individual and the interests of society. It is rational for individuals to overexploit resources that are communally owned— even though it is not in the long-run best interests of the society to do so.

Overcapitalization

Perhaps most important, users of common-property resources do not pay for them. The "rents" are not being collected. This results in great inefficiency because the users of common-property resources have incomplete incentives to use them at maximum efficiency. Overcapitalization is the rule in industries exploiting common-property resources (Gordon 1954). Entry into an industry will occur as long as there are profits to be made; and where common property is concerned, abnormally high profits are the rule because the full costs of production are not paid. Timber companies using unowned forests in the Amazon Basin do not pay the costs of growing the trees; fishermen do not pay the costs of growing the fish. Consequently, there are typically far more firms and capital equipment employed in the exploitation of common-property resources than are needed to harvest them efficiently. In the Maine lobster industry, for example, it has been estimated that the entire annual catch could be harvested by 1,000 well-equipped boats (Huq and Hasey 1972: 1); yet there are approximately 2,300 boats employed full-time and another 5,000 part-time. Such overcapitalized industries are capable of harvesting these commonly owned resources very quickly. Given the competition among firms in such industries, they usually do just that.

In conclusion, according to economic theory, common property is less efficient than private property in terms of high transactions costs, maldistribution, and overcapitalization. Common property also results in escalating abuse of resources. According to economists interested in the theory of property rights, the solution is relatively simple: Establish more exclusive property rights. If the property cannot be made truly private, then society should establish rights that have the same effect. The solutions typically include requiring licenses, setting quotas, charging rent, issuing stock certificates, or levying taxes. Just as private ownership reserves the use of property for a set of people (the owners), policies such as setting quotas and charging rent reserve common property for a select set of people—those who have paid to rent land or have bought the right to catch a certain quota of fish. These policy options theoretically force the users of common-property resources to pay the entire cost of using these resources, which should lower exploitation rates and increase efficiency. In this sense, they mimic the effect of private property. The solution these economists offer is different from that of Hardin, who emphasizes the importance of forceful governmental action in solving the common-property dilemma. But the underlying model is the same: common property causes overexploitation and abuse of resources.

Tragedies of the commons certainly exist. Particularly in modern, industrialized countries, there are innumerable cases where "open access resources" have been badly overexploited. One of the most publicized recent cases concerns the fisheries of the Gulf of Maine, which were badly overfished by fleets of factory ships from Europe, the United States, and Canada in the late 1960's. Even though the European ships largely left the area in the early 1970's, some stocks of herring, haddock, and cod have not recovered (Acheson 1984: 320). Another case is afforded by the Alaska salmon fishery, which was severely damaged early this century by overfishing (Crutchfield and Pontecorvo 1969: 70–71). And every schoolchild has heard of the extermination of the massive buffalo herds in the 1870's and 1880's. In all of these cases, there were no institutions in effect to protect the fish and animal resources, or those institutions were singularly ineffective. However, as we shall see, the conditions that produce such tragedies are not universal by any means.

The Assumptions of the Common-Property Model

Behind this theory of common-property resources developed by both the economists and Hardin are the following assumptions:

1. The users of common-property resources are individualistic profit maximizers driven by economic goals to overexploit the resources on which their livelihood depends despite the best interests of the society as a whole.

2. The users of these resources have the technical capacity to exceed the biological maximum rate of renewal of the resource. (Any resource has a natural rate at which it renews itself, and the definition of the

problem implies that the users of these resources can and will exceed that renewal rate.)

3. Those using common-property resources and the local-level communities they live in cannot or will not erect effective institutions to protect the resources they live on.

4. The exploitation of collectively owned resources can be halted only by either instituting private property or the government taking action.

The primary contribution of anthropologists and other social scientists to the body of theory on common-property resources has been to show that these presuppositions hold true only under certain circumstances or are wrong.

Institutions and Resources

An important contribution anthropologists have made to the study of property rights is to point out that in society after society people have effectively generated institutions and rules that limit exploitation rates.

Anthropologists have discovered a wide variety of such institutions. Some involve the imposition of property rights of one kind or another; others limit exploitive effort by such means as gear and seasonal restrictions, restrictions on size and sex of animals sought, and so on. In many societies, there are institutions and rules controlling access to resources. In other societies, access may be relatively open, but there are rules and customs in place that limit exploitation rates. In many societies, both limits on access and controls on exploitive rates exist (Acheson 1981: 280–81). Most important, the near universality of such institutions needs to be stressed: Few societies or even local-level communities have no restrictions at all on the use of resources. In talking about fisheries, Fikret Berkes says, "These assets are almost never truly open-access" (Berkes 1985: 204). The same point can be made for communally owned pasturage, farmland, forest, and so on.

Contrary to what the common-property theorists assert, privitization and government control are not the only mechanisms to affect the use of natural resources. There is a middle way: rules developed at the community level.

Communal Property as Open-Access or Controlled-Access Resource

The first and perhaps one of the most important critiques of the common-property resources theory was made by social scientists, who pointed out that communally owned property is not automatically subject to overexploitation. Only property that can be exploited by everyone without charge is subject to problems. Communally owned property can be effectively and efficiently managed. Ciriacy-Wantrup and Bishop (1975), for example, point out that the forests of Germany have been well managed for centuries, even though they are indisputably communally owned. Access to those forests is strictly controlled, however. Thus it is critical to distinguish between "open-access resources" and "communally owned resources." They are not the same. Property owned communally does have an owner after all. We will be careful to make this distinction through the remainder of this article. The term "common property" confuses these two different kinds of ownership, whose effects on exploitation rates are quite different.

There are a wide variety of communal property arrangements in the world. Communally owned property is particularly common in tribal societies in which there is little personal property and productive goods are largely in the form of land held under group tenure (Erasmus 1977: 79). In such societies, wealth was accumulated in the form of surplus food and exchanged for prestige—not with further production in mind.

In many tribal societies, land was owned by kinship groups. Among the Ibo, a double-descent society, some land was held by patrilineages, but most was in the hands of the matrilineages. No individual owned land or had permanent rights to any land; rather, each person was allocated land by the leaders of these kinship groupings (Ottenberg 1966: 8). In Sri Lanka, estates were held as jointly owned property by kinship groups, and genealogies were used to allocate shares of the estate. Periodically the land shares were redistributed (Obeyesekere 1967). A somewhat similar system was used by the Swat Pathans (horticultural tribe) of Afghanistan (Barth 1959: 23–30).

In Europe, where some grazing areas and forests have been communally owned for centuries, a different system was in use. Here the co-owners of the commons were the people from particular villages or municipalities. They were allowed to graze usually only during daylight hours and for a set season. No person was allowed to graze more animals than he could feed during the winter; if a shortage of space or forage threatened, each co-owner was assigned a quota, which was called "stinting" (McCay and Acheson 1987: 28–29).

In some societies, land is held either privately or communally. In others, people prefer to keep some land in communal ownership even in societies where most things are held in private property. This is true in peasant communities in the Andes (Godoy 1984); Japan (Ostrom 1987: 254); and the Swiss Alps (Netting 1972). In all these cases, access to communally owned land was strictly controlled.

Which parcels of land were apt to be kept as communal property?

Netting argues that resources whose productivity is low or unproductive and which are diffuse are apt to be kept as commons. "Smaller, easier divisible, and more highly productive areas may be owned and inherited by individuals" (Netting 1982: 471).

In some societies, land alternates back and forth between communal and private ownership over long periods of time. Among the Tigray of Ethiopia, a tribal horticultural and pastoral society, land is switched by decision of the village council from private tenure to communally owned property in order to attract additional population. (People are attracted to live in the community to share in the community's land.) Whenever overpopulation threatens, the land is switched back to private ownership to deter migration (Bauer 1987: 219–224). In one peasant agricultural village in Borneo, land is treated as "private property in the dry, rice growing season and as common property in the rainy season when the land is covered by water" (Vondal 1987). During the wet season the fields are used by duck farmers.

In many fishing societies in the world, rights to fish are controlled by the establishment of ownership rights over "fishing space." These territorial or sea-tenure systems exist in such a wide variety that it is difficult to generalize about them. In some societies, fishing rights are held by individuals. This is true among many tribal Indian groups of the northwest coast of North America such as the Salish (Suttles 1974); among present-day herring fishermen in Sweden (Lofgren 1979); among the peasant lobster fishermen of the Yucatan Peninsula in Mexico (Miller 1982); among inshore fishermen of Japan (Asada 1973); and in the fixed-gear fisheries of the Canadian Great Lakes, where certain families have held "traditional . . . fishing rights for generations" (Berkes 1985: 202).

In even more cases, fishing rights are owned communally, and access to ocean area and fish resources are reserved for community members. This is true in such diverse fisheries as the Maine lobster fishery, where the lobster fishermen from each harbor jointly own the lobster fishing rights in the waters adjacent to their own harbors (Acheson 1972, 1979); the inshore cod fishery of Newfoundland (Andersen and Stiles 1973: 48); the inland sea of Japan, where peasant fishing villages either possess exclusive fishing rights or share it with neighboring communities (Ruddle 1985: 164) as well as among the Miskito, a tribal group of coastal Nicaragua (Neitschman 1974); among raft fishermen of Brazil (Forman 1970); and among Sri Lankan peasantry, where beach seining rights are held by members of one kinship group (Alexander 1980: 102–3). In the Ponam area of New Guinea (a tribal society), rights to reef and ocean fishing areas were "the property of patrilineal descent groups" (Carrier 1987); the same was true in the Torres Islands area (Nietschman 1985:

145) and among the tribal Yolngu of northern Australia (Davis 1985: 110). Throughout Oceania, which contains hundreds of different tribal and peasant societies, ocean areas and fish resources were commonly owned by various kinds of kinship and local groupings (Johannes 1978: 350–51).[2] In summary, the idea that ocean resources are generally open-access resources—unowned and unprotected—is not borne out by the ethnography.

Other Institutions: Quotas, Technology Restrictions, and Secrecy

Communal or individual property rights are not the only means of controlling access to ocean resources. Other local-level institutions accomplished these goals within both modern and traditional communities. Such institutions include quotas, restrictions on technology and areas that can be used, restrictions on the ages and sexes of the animals that can be taken, and secrecy.

In many societies, fishermen have established informal quotas. In one industrialized fishery in New Jersey, the cooperative established a quota on whiting—the most important species. Each day, the cooperative manager set a quota depending on the amount of fish he could sell at a reasonable price. The catches of all boats that had fished that day were pooled, and the proceeds from the day's catch were shared jointly by all boats—regardless of what they actually caught. This reduced the incentive to overfish and to invest in the newest and most efficient equipment (McCay 1980). In the Lake Erie trawl fishery, a similar quota system was set up by a processor—based on the amount he could process and sell. In the Cornish oyster fishery, which had been overfished, fishermen voluntarily used a simple technology and put pressure on each other not to overfish. "Newcomers were warned by older fishermen not to overwork" (Cove 1973). In a similar fashion in the Maine lobster industry, a good deal of pressure is put on "hogs"— men who take more than their share of the catch (Acheson 1977: 118).

Moreover, in many fishing societies, fishermen have conserved resources by preventing the adoption of more effective technology, which would put greater exploitive pressure on the fish resources. In some cases, fishermen lobby to have restrictions put on the kinds of technology that can be employed. In the Chesapeake oyster fishery, boats must be propelled by sail, and only hand tongs can be used. In other cases, the fishermen resort to violence and more extreme means to pre-

[2] Although the ownership of ocean, river, and fish resources is common in both traditional and modern societies, they are not universal. "There was no concept of individual or group ownership of marine resources" in Indonesia (Sya'rani and Willoughby 1985: 255), and the same appears to be true for the aboriginal coastal societies of West Africa.

vent new boats and gear from entering overcrowded fisheries. One of the best examples is provided by Gersuny and Poggie (1974), who discuss all of the ways fishermen in Rhode Island have sought to erect barriers to the adoption of bigger boats and better technology. It should be noted that fishermen are not objecting to new technology out of altruism, but rather because they do not want to be outclassed by other fishermen or put out of business by newer boats. Fisheries economists point out that controls on more effective gear may be adaptive from the point of view of those in the industry, but it results in inefficiency (Crutchfield and Pontecorvo 1969: 34).

Nor are fishermen in the developed world alone in generating mechanisms to protect marine resources. Such institutions are apparently common in many traditional societies. In Oceania, where such institutions have been most thoroughly studied, a wide variety of techniques have been used for centuries to manage marine resources. R. E. Johannes, a biologist, has stated that Pacific islanders "devised and practiced almost every basic form of modern marine fisheries conservation measure centuries ago, long before the need for marine conservation was even recognized in Western countries" (1982: 259). In some societies there were bans on taking small fish (size limitations). In others, access to marine resources was limited, and seasonal restrictions to protect species during spawning were invoked along with quotas and closed areas. In other societies, there were limitations on numbers and amount of gear that could be used. In some societies, there were bans on destroying eggs or spawning animals, while in other societies species were owned. In addition, some proportion of the fish or turtles were allowed to escape to maintain the breeding stock (Johannes 1978: 352–54; Klee 1980: 253–55).

Another common mechanism that effectively limits access to fish stocks is secrecy. Knowledge or skill is vital for success in fishing, yet both are difficult to acquire. Fish are rarely evenly spread over the bottom; rather, they are concentrated in specific locations, which can change relatively fast as fish migrate. It is always more difficult for fishermen to learn as much about desirable species than it is for hunters or farmers, who can observe the species they are after. Under these conditions, those with knowledge of fishing locations often have much to gain by keeping that knowledge secret or by sharing it only with other fishermen who can be counted on to reciprocate. Raoul Andersen points out that in the Newfoundland trawler fishery, the name of the fishing game is "hunt and deceive." Andersen does a particularly effective job of describing the radio strategies skippers use to give as little information as possible to others while maximizing the information they obtain about others' fishing success and while still supplying the managers onshore with necessary information (Andersen 1972). At times the effort to keep one's activities secret "reaches comical extremes: men were known to mask their oil lamps on arising, tiptoe down to the wharf in their 'worsteds' (wool socks) and slip the lines before anyone knew they were gone!" (Andersen and Stiles 1973: 49). The ocean is a huge place, and sometimes it pays handsomely to pool information with a few select boats to increase the likelihood of finding fish concentrations. In the San Diego tuna fleet, secret information is passed between boats by an elaborate secret code, which is jealously guarded (Orbach 1977: 114–32). In this fishery, words indicating location, species found, water conditions, and so on are indicated by number sequences. Originally messages are generally of the form "I'm at 4378 . . . got 4568 on board . . . going 2343 . . . may stop at 0789 for a while" (ibid.: 115). A similar code is used in the West Coast inshore fleet (Stuster 1978).

Secrecy also plays an important role in many traditional fisheries, from Brazil (Forman 1980: 20–21) to New Guinea (Carrier 1987: 147). Forman points out that secrecy "minimizes competition by affording temporary property rights to individual fishermen" (1980: 22).

Other institutions also give temporary property rights. In some societies, temporary rights to choice fishing spots are allocated to the boat that reaches the fishing grounds first, as is the case in Newfoundland (Britan 1979). In other cases, fishermen are organized in ways that allow different crews to take turns exploiting choice fishing spots. In one peasant Sri Lankan village, beach seine crews must alternate placing their nets on the "harbor side" and the "rock side" according to a complicated set of rules (Alexander 1980: 100). In an Irish salmon fishery, boats are expected to set their nets sequentially in a prime river location. Each boat is allowed to set its nets in the prime spot and then is expected to move on to allow another boat to take its place (Taylor 1987: 296–97). In an industrialized fishery in Newfoundland, fishermen devised a system for drawing named "berths" that would give them rights to fish in that location for the entire season (Faris 1966: 226).

Fishing is one of the most uncertain and riskiest occupations humans undertake. All of the institutions discussed so far help to lower uncertainty. If one cannot do anything about the weather and the vagaries of fish migrations, one can make arrangements with other people to reserve what fish there are for one's self.

Private Property Rights and Conservation

How effective are private property rights in conserving resources? A key tenet of the theory of common-property resources is that private property rights conserve. Is this true? On this point, there is much disagreement and even less hard evidence. There is no simple answer. In some societies operating under certain conditions, property rights do seem to aid conservation. We have reviewed a number of such cases in the previous section. In other societies, property rights do not appear to conserve. (Students should note that this is an open or undecided issue in the study of common-property resources. There is nothing unusual in this situation. On the frontier of any field, scholars are always engaged in debate and argument. Social scientists interested in the common-property problem are no exception.) Given the importance of this question, it is useful to go over some of the conflicting cases and evidence.

Do property rights conserve resources? The answer at this point appears to depend on which case one looks at. The problem is exemplified by what has happened in our own society. It might seem only a matter of common sense that landowners would want to conserve their own property in their own best interests. However, the literature on pastoralists, farmers, and loggers shows that even in our own society "resource conservation is not always ensured by the private property status of resources" (Gilles and Jamtgaard 1982, quoted in McCay and Acheson 1987: 9). My own state of Maine is a case in point. In Aroostook County, Maine, potato farmers make no pretense of contour plowing or other strategies to conserve the soil. In other parts of Maine, the forestry practices of some of the big paper companies are dominated more by the need to make a profit in the short run than by conservation of the forests for the long term. Maine is not alone, of course. The dust bowl conditions of the 1930's were caused by irresponsible soil-management practices. These cases underline the fact that at times private landowners are no more responsible than users of open-access resources. Nor are these anomalous cases. Several social scientists have pointed out that under certain conditions it is rational for the owners of resources to use them up very rapidly and to disregard future benefits. This occurs when the growth rate of the resource is less than the interest rate. It makes no sense to borrow money from the bank at 10 percent interest to invest in forests that increase in value at only 5 percent a year. This would not be a rational investment. If one owns a resource whose growth rate is less than the interest rate, it is rational to use it up as fast as possible (Clark 1973).

In some circumstances, private owners can be less responsible than those managing communally owned property. For example, German forests in private hands were managed far less efficiently than municipally owned forests, which have become models of forest management (Ciriacy-Wantrup and Bishop 1975: 720–21).

The same kinds of arguments exist in other ethnographic areas. Johannes argues that property rights over reefs and lagoons control access and lower fishing pressure. In this regard, he says: "Marine tenure systems in Oceania are designed to enable the islanders to control the types and degrees of exploitation of their waters and thereby protect them against impoverishment. The mechanism is simple. Where fishing rights exist it is clearly to the advantage of those who control them to fish in moderation, for this ensures the future productivity of their fishing grounds. In the absence of such controls it would be to the advantage of a fisherman to catch all he could and to use destructive methods in doing so if they simplified his task. If he didn't, someone else would. Moderation would be pointless and the resources would therefore dwindle" (Johannes 1977: 122). In short, Johannes believes that the theory of common-property resources applies in this case.

Other anthropologists find the model less relevant. James Carrier, who worked in the Ponam area of New Guinea, argues that private property rights over reef and lagoon areas did nothing to conserve the fish resources and probably increased exploitive effort. Here fish resources are owned by clans, and people in this society are more than willing to exchange fishing privileges for prestige. "The point of ownership on Ponam, then, was not to accumulate fish—this could be done in ways that did not involve ownership—but to be as generous as possible with one's own and one's lineage's property . . . echoing Malinowski's much earlier statement (1918: 90) that, among Trobriand fishermen 'the privilege of giving is highly valued'" (Carrier 1987: 159). One owns property here to give it away with prestige and power in mind—not to conserve it or hoard for one's own use. Here private property rights do not conserve resources, in stark contrast to the theory.

The same kind of controversy exists with regard to hunters. Several anthropologists who have worked with Indian hunting groups in northern Canada argue that these societies have generated a set of practices, including territorial rights, that conserve resources. In these societies, one of the most important institutions affecting access to fur-bearing animals is the trap line system. These are essentially traditional family hunting territories, which are now registered with the government (Berkes 1981: 169, 1987: 4–5). Berkes argues that the "trap line system is good management" because families that conserve the animals on their lines and leave an adequate breeding stock gain in the future in increased catches (1981: 169).

In addition, northern Indians are said to practice conservation of other species in the absence of any property system. The Waswanipi Cree are careful to kill only a limited number of moose in any area to leave a sufficient breeding stock (Feit 1973). In addition, Canada geese, which have very predictable migration routes, are hunted on a territorial basis. To limit kills, there are rules about not firing into the center of a flock (Berkes 1987: 70). All these arguments reinforce the idea that hunters have intentionally developed institutions to conserve game.

Other anthropologists who have worked with hunters describe conservation as an unintended consequence of other activities. Hames argues convincingly that if Amazonian tribal hunters conserve game, it may only be an accidental by-product of their attempt to be as efficient hunters as possible. These hunters avoid areas where game has been depleted and focus their efforts on areas where larger concentrations of animals are located. His data suggest that they do this for the sake of efficiency and that conservation is not their goal. He points out that "Ye'kwana and Yanomamo hunters take game in near zones if they encounter it, even when they are passing through those zones in order to reach more distant hunting zones" (Hames 1987). If conservation were their goal, they would leave animals alone in those overdepleted areas. It is true that in avoiding overexploited areas, they are helping to conserve game, but this is not a purposeful, conscious strategy.

However, it should be noted that in all these debates, there is little solid evidence linking ownership of property or territoriality to conservation of resources. Anthropologists have made competing claims, but they present few facts to back them up. The same is true with Hardin and the economists. They have made many statements about property rights causing "tragedies of the commons," but have appealed more to logic than data. There is at least one case where hard quantitative data exist to demonstrate that enforcing property rights not only conserves the resource but also has many of the favorable economic effects predicted by the economists interested in the common-property question. This is the case of the Maine lobster industry.

Lobstermen from each harbor all along the coast of central Maine claim inshore fishing rights to particular ocean areas. These territories are held jointly, and all of the men from each harbor are allowed to go fishing throughout the entire range of the area "owned" by the men of each harbor. Although their claims are unrecognized by the state or federal governments, they are defended by surreptitious violence. That is, if anyone who is not a member of the gang places traps in the gang's area, the offending traps, sooner or later, will be destroyed—usually by having the buoy and rope cut off and the trap pushed overboard in deep water.

There are two kinds of fishing territories: nucleated and perimeter-defended areas. In nucleated areas, the sense of ownership is very strong close to the mouth of the harbor but grows progressively weaker the farther from the harbor one goes. On the periphery, there is almost no sense of territoriality, and a good deal of mixed fishing takes place (that is, boats from two or more harbors place traps in the same area). Men fishing in perimeter-defended areas have a strong sense of ownership out to the boundaries. Here, boundaries are sharply drawn and defended to the yard; there is no mixed fishing here (Acheson 1988: 156).

Ownership rights are maintained in both types of territoriality; access is far more controlled in perimeter-defended areas than in nucleated areas. The perimeter-defended areas are found generally around islands that have been in the hands of one or more of the old established families for generations, who generally reserve all fishing rights for themselves. In contrast, it is far easier for a newcomer to join the gangs of "harbors" where nucleated territories are found (Acheson 1975: 189–90).[3]

Exploitive effort is substantially less in perimeter-defended areas than in nucleated areas. Because it is more difficult to join these island harbor gangs, the men fishing perimeter-defended areas have more fishing area per boat than men from nucleated areas. In addition, the fishermen in some perimeter-defended areas practice some conservation measures. The fishermen on two islands voluntarily limited the number of traps each man can fish. This cuts expenses and also alleviates the "ghost trap problem." A man with fewer traps tends them more frequently and loses fewer. This lowers mortality on the lobsters because lobsters in lost traps ("ghost traps") are likely to die in those traps. Moreover, when traps are pulled often, molting lobsters that would otherwise have been eaten by their fellows are released and have a better chance of survival.

There are both economic and biological benefits from perimeter-defended areas. There are fewer men fishing in these areas and thus fewer to share the catch. In addition, because they are not putting as much exploitive effort on the lobsters, lobsters have a greater chance to survive to larger sizes. As a result, men in perimeter-defended areas catch more and bigger lobsters, and they catch them with less effort. In every season, the number of lobsters caught per trap is larger in perimeter-defended areas than in nucleated areas, and the mean size of those lobsters is bigger as well (Acheson 1988: 156). As a result, fishermen in perimeter-defended areas earn significantly more money

[3] At the turn of the century, all areas along the coast were apparently perimeter-defended areas. Along the mainland, these perimeter-defended areas have been amalgamated into larger nucleated areas primarily because of political pressure from fishermen from harbors up the estuaries. This process has been described in some detail in another publication (see Acheson 1979).

than those from nucleated areas (ibid.). In addition, a larger number of lobsters in perimeter-defended areas are capable of extruding eggs, which means that more eggs are released in the water in perimeter-defended areas than in nucleated areas. Thus the territorial norms of the perimeter-defended areas not only raise incomes of fishermen in those areas but also increase the long-run prospects of the industry itself. Lobsters that are conserved because of the efforts of fishermen in these areas extrude eggs that float through the current to all areas of the Gulf of Maine, enhancing the yield of small lobsters.

There is no reason to believe that the areas around perimeter-defended islands are inherently richer in lobsters. The differences in catches and lobster sizes are due to the practices of fishermen. Because perimeter-defended areas restrict access more than nucleated territoriality, the lobster fishery case appears to substantiate the idea that property rights help conserve resources at least under certain conditions. It also underlines the fact that communally owned resources are not automatically doomed to overexploitation at the hands of the people using them.

Management of Resources:
Local Level and the Government

Although local-level management systems certainly exist and can effectively curb exploitive effort, it is important to note that all societies in the world exist within national states and have been influenced by those states. Although anthropologists sometimes talk about traditional societies as if they existed in isolation, they are really encapsulated political systems (Bailey 1969). They are systems within systems, and to one extent or another they have had to adapt to the larger society even if they are not fully integrated into it.

The relationships between local-level communities, with their resource-management devices, and national governments are complicated and highly variable. Fig. 13.1, which charts the relationships between different amounts of management of various kinds, is useful for this discussion. I will discuss the societies in each cell, give information on the prevalence of such situations, and briefly discuss the conditions under which each comes into being.

When there is little management either by the government or the local-level community, the resource is an open-access resource and subject to all the problems Hardin and the common-property economists foresaw (cell 3). Such situations are so rare as to be almost nonexistent.

Far more common are various kinds of local-level management systems, which we have seen exist in greatest numbers and in a lot of dif-

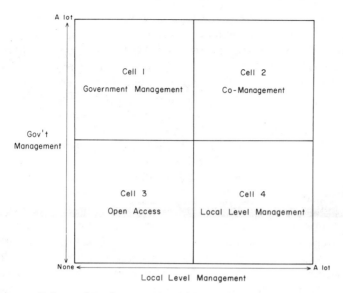

Fig. 13.1. Relationships between local-level communities and national governments.

ferent variations (cell 4). We might classify some out-of-the-way places in the Third World, where the power of the government rarely is felt and where local people are allowed to make most of their decisions unimpeded by government officers, as belonging in cell 4. But these situations are rare and are becoming even rarer as communications and development affect even the world's most isolated areas. More often, these local-level management systems are influenced to one degree or another by the government. They are not truly independent indigenous management systems. For example, the Cree trappers in northern Quebec have exclusive fishing rights through the James Bay Treaty with the Canadian government (Berkes 1981: 168), and in the peasant agricultural villages of the town in Indonesian Borneo studied by Vondal, "use-rights required the payment of land taxes in rice and coin to the sultan and rice to the local religious leader" (1987: 235).

Sometimes it is difficult to say whether a society should be classified as having a little or a lot of government management. The lobster fishing territories of Maine are a case in point. The rules concerning territoriality are generated and enforced completely by fishermen in secret; the government does not officially know about the system. Yet that system would cease to exist if Maine decided to strenuously enforce the law concerning trap cutting. This management system exists only because of the benign neglect of the state.

Management is sometimes practiced by the national government with little or no local involvement (cell 1). Often, anthropologists have discovered, this government intervention into resource management is far less effective than Hardin would have us believe. In West Malaya, the rules the government set up, which were not enforced adequately, contributed to massive overfishing by a modernized trawler fleet, with subsequent hardship for small inshore vessels (Anderson 1987: 329–30). A small war resulted in which owners of small inshore boats attempted to drive out more efficient, large trawlers by burning them. In the United States in the late 1970's, the federal government enforced quota regulations on the groundfishing industry in New England. The result was a "quota race," which resulted in massive investment. That is, when quotas are enforced, the largest and best equipped boats catch a disproportionate share of the fish. If others are going to remain in business, they have little choice but to get bigger and better equipped vessels as well. The result of these "conservation rules" was a fleet that was far more capable of overfishing than the one that had existed previously (Acheson 1984: 325–27).

With fisheries, the failures of government action may be due to the fact that management by government typically attempts to simulate property rights through such management schemes as quotas, licenses, and gear and seasonal regulations. The problem is that such simulated property rights set up "disharmonious incentives" (Townsend and Wilson 1987: 319). That is, there is no incentive to maintain the rule and all the incentive in the world to cheat or get around the rule. Rules limiting the length of a boat can be circumvented by building fatter boats or putting bigger engines in them. Quotas can be avoided by selling fish caught over the limit to other boats or by misreporting. Townsend and Wilson believe that fisheries management would be furthered if managers abandoned the property model, which does not have the beneficial effects envisioned by the common-property economists, and imposed "expensive and basically pointless regulations on the fishery." They recommend trying to develop policies that would reinforce the "normal tendency of fishermen to switch away from declining stocks" (1987: 323).

In recent years, anthropologists have realized that in a surprising number of cases, government and local-level units have mutually adapted themselves to each other in what Evelyn Pinkerton (1987) calls "co-management results" (Fig 13.1, cell 2). The fisheries of Iceland, for example, are managed exclusively by the Icelandic government, but government policy is strongly influenced by the fishermen and others in the fishing industry. Iceland is a small country, one where even the most humble can influence government policy. In the fishing industry—the largest and most important industry in the nation—the influence the industry has over regulations governing it is enormous (Durrenberger and Palsson 1987: 372). Another example is afforded by the salmon fishing communities of British Columbia, where fishing is regulated both by provincial and local rules. The province has many regulations on salmon fishing, including a limitation on licenses. Local communities, however, successfully lobbied the provincial government for regulations they believed in the best interests of the stocks and enforced their own. One Indian community pressured the provincial government to close an area to fishing to protect an endangered local stock. This community then policed a voluntary closure in its own local area for a number of years (Pinkerton 1987: 364–65). In the Maine lobster industry, fishermen are involved in two kinds of management efforts. The first is the territorial system, which is kept entirely secret from the state and its officials. Fishermen are also reasonably effective in lobbying the state legislature for rules they believe would benefit the industry. In the past few years they have had passed a "venting bill," which makes it mandatory for all traps to be equipped with holes to allow undersized lobsters to escape unharmed from traps. At this writing, the Maine Lobsterman's Association is lobbying to retain several laws to protect proven breeding stock. If the association succeeds, it will be another example of users of a resource jointly managing it with the government (Acheson and Bayer, forthcoming).

In some instances, local communities and governments exist in an antagonistic relationship—one in which they are ceaselessly trying to wrest control of a resource from each other. But in others, local groupings not only have accommodated to the government but have been able to use the power of the central government for their own purpose. When one Irish community was offered control over its own salmon fishery, it refused, reasoning that it could not develop its own management and enforcement system without undue conflict. "The river would run red with blood," they said. Instead, community members preferred to fish for salmon illegally and forced the government officers to do the onerous job of enforcing the conservation laws. The Irish solution is not unique (Taylor 1987). Enforcement of norms is always difficult. It is not an accident that in most advanced societies, norms are enforced by paid moral guardians: the police.

Despite the problems, local-level management has proved so effective, and management by the government has proved so costly that there are increasing calls for community-level management of natural resources. To begin to get the benefit of local-level management means

that governmental managers are going to have to stop thinking that resource users are bent on putting themselves out of business (they are
well indoctrinated with the tragedy of the commons model) and start
thinking of mechanisms to buttress community-level rule structures
concerning resources if they are effective (Berkes 1987: 22).

The Political Economy of Resource Depletion

The tragedy of the commons sees the overexploitation of natural resources as rooted in the system of property rights. Some anthropologists and other social scientists see this as an oversimplification, one
that ignores the role of other factors in the socioeconomic system. They
believe the problems blamed on open-access property rights are more
closely related to political economy—issues of population growth, industrialization, and the expansion of the capitalist system and markets.

Any given area on earth has a maximum amount of renewable
resources that can be harvested without damaging the reproductive
capacity of the animals and plants that inhabit the land. That amount is
variously called "carrying capacity," or "maximum sustainable yield."
Small populations operating with a low level of technology and local
markets will rarely overexploit resources. They do not need large
amounts of food and resources to support their populations, and they
have no need to extract large amounts to sell to international markets.
Even if they wanted to produce more, they could not because of technological limitations. If populations are increased, the rate of output
rises and can exceed the replacement rate—even if the technology remains at a low level. If markets expand, perhaps because it becomes
possible to sell goods on the international market, and the technology
increases as well, it may also be possible to exceed the natural replacement rate of resources—even if populations remain small. If populations expand, along with markets and technology, a tragedy may be
inevitable despite the property rights system involved. Many social
scientists are convinced that this combination of factors has led to many
resource problems worldwide. For example, the problems in the Sahel
areas of Africa have been blamed on irresponsible expansion of cattle
herds, which have damaged the range. This is due to an expansion
of the human population in combination with increased markets for
cattle (Franke and Chasin 1980). Another example is afforded by Central America, where the number of cattle has increased 80 percent in
twenty years because of high profits that can be gained raising cattle for
the U.S. market (Dewalt 1983: 19). The vast expansion of pastureland
led to a destruction of both tropical forests and agricultural land, which
has led to unemployment, malnutrition, and may eventually lead to far

more serious long-term consequences for the world's ecosystem (ibid.: 21–22).

Expansion of markets has led to problems for other resources as well. In the past twenty years, Panamanian shrimp stocks have begun to be overfished because of the opening of the U.S. market, which has stimulated inefficient big vessels and modern packing technology. In nearby Nicaragua, the Miskito Indians, who had previously hunted only for their own subsistence needs, began to overexploit the local turtle population with the opening of a modern turtle-meat packing plant (Neitschman 1972: 60–61). In Micronesia, commercialization of fisheries led not only to overexploitation but, even worse, to the decline in traditional resource-management systems. The importation of the profit motive, combined with increased markets, means that a "fisherman finds himself competing for money and therefore for fish. In order to compete effectively he must buy better equipment and fish harder. . . . Under these conditions a conservation ethic cannot thrive. Conservation customs practiced by the individual erode first. Pressure is put on traditional leaders . . . to relax or abandon traditional conservation laws in the name of increased profits" (Johannes 1978: 356–57).

With both the Miskito Indians and the societies of Micronesia, population increase also was a contributing factor in resource decline.

If this viewpoint is accurate, poverty, underdevelopment, and overpopulation are primary causes of resource depletion in the Third World. Perhaps a more important cause is the opening of markets in the United States and the rest of the developed world, which makes it profitable for tribal people and peasants to overexploit natural resources.

Generating Institutions to Manage Resources

Under some circumstances, local-level communities can generate institutions to manage their resources. Under other circumstances, they do not or cannot and tragedies occur. The key question is under what conditions are these institutions generated. Although there has been a considerable amount of work on the generation of institutions, there is little consensus on the circumstances under which institutions of various sorts are produced. When people generate rules or institutions to manage a resource, they are creating what Mancur Olson calls a "public or collective good" (1965: 15). They are creating a good that helps a community or collectivity achieve a goal. In most cases, the goal cannot be provided by an individual working alone. It might seem obvious that individuals will work together to provide public goods, such as rules to protect communal resources, when those goods benefit everyone in the community and cannot be provided by individuals. Olson points out that this is not the case. Rational individuals will join a collective effort only when there are what he calls "selective incentives" that do away with the so-called free rider problem. For example, everyone admits that there are too many lobster traps in Maine and that the fishery would be better off if the number of traps were limited. If all fishermen had 300 traps instead of the 400 to 650 they currently fish, they would catch the same number of lobsters over the course of the year, and they would not have to maintain as many traps or pay for so much bait and fuel. Yet no single fisherman will lower the number of traps he fishes unless others are forced to do likewise. As one fisherman told me, "I'd be a fool to cut down to 300 (traps) while everyone else had 500. They would catch a lot more than I would." Under these circumstances, a trap limit will come into being only when an enforceable rule is generated—one that would allow selective incentives to be imposed on those who have more than the permitted number.

Although it is difficult to predict when institutions are created, for our purposes, the most important institution is that of property rights. "The importance of territoriality is that it can be the basis for the development of more restrictive common property institutions: rules and regulations about the distribution, use and transfer of rights in the commons. If we can keep others out, it makes sense for us to do something about our own behavior" (McCay and Acheson 1987: 11). Because of the importance of territoriality, a key question is under what circumstances property rights and territoriality arise.

Some economists see the genesis of territoriality and property rights in terms of externalities. Property confers many benefits (efficiency, allocation of resources, and so on) because it does away with externalities. Demsetz has hypothesized that property rights are instituted when the costs associated with a lack of property are smaller than the gains to be had from establishing property rights (Demsetz 1967: 350). When the fur trade began, the value of furs went up and the losses due to overhunting and trapping were far more extensive and serious. Hunting and trapping territories were established, Demsetz says, to allow Indians to do away with these harmful externalities (overtrapping) and gain the benefits of property (conservation of fur-bearing animals) (ibid.: 352).

Anthropologists Dyson-Hudson and Smith have proposed a similar hypothesis to account for establishment of property rights. They say that territoriality comes about when "critical resources are sufficiently abundant and predictable in space and time, so that costs of exclusive use and defense of an area are outweighed by the benefits gained from resource control" (1978: 21). They note that the Objibwa did not establish territories when they were primarily dependent on caribou and moose, which roam widely and are thus highly unpredictable. When the Ojibwa became dependent on small animals, which do not migrate so far, it became worthwhile to establish and defend territories (ibid.: 35).

Wilson and Acheson (1980) link the establishment of property rights in fishing societies to the problem of acquiring skill and knowledge. To find concentrations of fish in the ocean requires a lot of knowledge of the species and the environment. Success is largely a matter of skill, not luck. With relatively sedentary species, the duration of knowledge is long. If one discovers a concentration of clams or lobsters, one can come back for days to harvest them—unless other fishermen get them first. The knowledge of where to find these species lasts a long time. Under these conditions, it becomes worthwhile to establish territories and to be secretive. Lobster fishermen have territories, and clammers are so secretive that a day spent clamming resembles a CIA operation. When one is pursuing highly mobile species such as tuna and herring, the duration of knowledge is very short. When one finds a school of these fish, one does not know whether they will be in the same place the next day or even the next hour. Under these conditions, it is not worthwhile to go to the trouble of establishing territories. Secrecy is also not worthwhile. In such fisheries, men share information about fish locations to broaden out the area that the fleet can effectively search.

These three theories about the establishment of territories share several features. All assume that establishing territories results in costs (such as the costs of defense of boundaries) as well as benefits (primarily reserving the game, land, and so on for oneself). Territories are established when the benefits outweigh the costs. In addition, all of these theories assume that the costs of establishing territories are strongly influenced by ecological factors.

Summary and Conclusion

Because of the work of anthropologists, the theory of common-property resources needs to be extended and modified in several ways. Virtually all of the basic axioms on which the model is based are flawed. Let us examine those axioms in view of what anthropologists have learned about resource use in other cultures.

First, the common-property model assumes that in the absence of private property rights, individuals are driven to achieve economic goals to overexploit resources on which their livelihood depends. In reality, individual rights are subordinate to community rights. In virtually all societies, there are controls on access to resources and various kinds of rules and institutional arrangements to limit exploitive activities. Individuals are not allowed to seek their short-term goals at the expense of the society. In many industrialized or overpopulated societies, tragedies of the commons do exist, but this is not due to the fact that societies generally abandon their resources to anyone who wants to exploit them. Perhaps this axiom can be restated as follows: In most societies, individual rights to resources are subordinate to those of the community. In a minority of instances, individuals are free to overexploit essential resources.

The second axiom of the common-property theorists is that those using such resources have the technical capacity to overexploit them. In fact, in many technologically backward societies—particularly those with small populations and no access to large-scale markets—people do not have either the ability or the motive to overexploit natural resources. It is difficult, for example, for a small hunting-and-gathering band to wipe out a clam population digging them with their bare hands; and they would have little reason to do so because they cannot sell the clams and can eat only so many themselves. This axiom might be rephrased: Natural resources are more likely to be overexploited in technologically advanced societies, with large populations where resources are sold in large international markets.

The third presupposition of the common-property theorists is that individuals using common-property resources and the communities in which they live cannot and will not erect effective institutions to protect those resources. As we have seen, most societies have generated some institutions to control exploitive efforts, ranging from various kinds of controls on access to limits of types of exploitive gear that can be used. In some societies, both primitive and modern, many such mechanisms have been developed. Private property is one mechanism; but another that is commonly used is community or joint-ownership arrangements. (Again, this is different from open access.) Once some kind of property rights are established, other rules restricting the use of resources may be established. Although there is some debate on the effectiveness of property rights in conserving natural resources, there is evidence from a few studies that they do conserve resources (for example, the Maine lobster industry).

Fourth, the common-property theorists assumed that collectively owned resources can be managed only by either the institution of private property (the economist's solution) or government action (Hardin's solution). Both private property and the government can conserve resources under some conditions, but private property does not always result in conservation (as in Ponam), and government action is not always effective. More important, this axiom ignores the existence of a wide range of mechanisms that can conserve resources—including a large number of norms and institutions erected at the local level. In addition, many cases of co-management exist, in which local level and governmental forces are at work in limiting access to resources. This presupposition can be restated: Resources can be managed by privitization, government action, a wide variety of local-level institutions, or co-management. None of these solutions is necessarily effective in every case.

There are strong managerial implications in some of these findings, especially the fourth axiom. In the words of Gilles, "For years people were saying that you essentially had to choose between this public or private approach to resources; otherwise you'd go to hell in a hand basket. There's a middle ground that has been overlooked" (Jarmul 1987: 3). One intermediate solution is local-level management, which hundreds of societies have used for centuries. Does this mean that the solution to the world's resource problems is to hand over control of resources to the grass roots or small communities (Fig. 13.1, cell 4)? In some cases, that might work. But the power of national states and multinational corporations is such that many local communities could not maintain their own management regimes for long. A better solution in most cases would be co-management in which the traditional norms and strategies of local communities are reinforced or taken into account by officials of national states in management plans.

Behind these questions concerning resource management is a far larger theoretical issue concerning the relationship between institutions and economic choices. Economic anthropologists have long known that the decisions of individuals are influenced by the institutions and norms of society. For example, in our own society, the Federal Deposit Insurance Corporation insures deposits in banks, lowering the risk to investors and influencing the decisions of people to save. Laws enforcing contracts make exchanges and deals possible that people would otherwise hesitate to undertake.

The opposite can also occur. The decisions of hundreds of individuals in a society can change the institution or the rule structure. As F. G. Bailey has pointed out, if a rule is broken enough by some individuals, a new rule will come into being (1969: 13). The way that institutions are generated are less well understood, although much work has been done on this issue (see Heath 1976).

The institutional perspective puts the theory of common-property resources in a different perspective. First, the common-property theory assumes a set of institutions that motivate all humans to overexploit their environment. The result is ostensibly a tragic downward spiral that can only end in disaster. As we have seen, such institutions are not universal, and people are not universally motivated to overexploit.

Moreover, the theory ignores the possibility that groups and local-level communities can generate institutions to control or prevent over-exploitation. Yet people in some societies have been able to erect a variety of such institutions, including communal and private property arrangements. They are not universal, and their generation appears to be sporadic. Under these circumstances, the key question is, What circumstances foster overexploitation? Under what circumstances do people foster organizations to conserve resources? Can a large number of societies create such institutions? Given the escalating problems of resource abuse, the answers to these questions may well determine whether human societies, as we know them, can survive on this planet.

These questions must be answered if the theory of common-property resources is to be advanced. This can be done if we increase our understanding of the generation of institutions and the ways in which institutions constrain and open economic opportunities for people. This is a major task for economic anthropology, a challenge the discipline cannot ignore. Extending our understanding of the relationship between the choices of individuals and institutions would help to further our understanding not only of the common-property issue but also of other issues such as social change, modernization and development, and the area of decision making and strategic choice. Coase, Williamson, Commons, and various institutional economists have pioneered one approach to institutions and choice (Acheson 1982: 327–28). Some cultural anthropologists have suggested another. Ortner, for example, points out that one of the most pressing questions for anthropology is to determine how individual practices or choices determine structure or institutions (1984: 141–49). Economic anthropologists should extend and synthesize this work.

14

Marxism

Stuart Plattner

Marxism, meaning the theory derived from the writings of Karl Marx
(1818–83), is the dominant social science paradigm in much of the world
outside the United States. In fact, Hart (1983) calls Marx "the greatest
economic anthropologist of all time." In this chapter I will introduce the
basic concepts of a modern Marxist, or historical materialist, approach
to economic anthropology.[1] I will describe three types of *modes of production*, or fundamental organization of society: capitalist, tributary, and
kinship (after Wolf 1982). The approach will be illustrated with several
case studies: the production and distribution of salt by a highland New
Guinea tribe, the Hindu prohibition on eating cattle, and the economics
of weaving by Indians in highland western Guatemala.

Marxism grew out of a time in the nineteenth century of explosive change in European history. European nations such as England,
France, and Germany were spreading their power over the globe while
much of their laboring populations worked and lived in abject misery.
The mainstream intellectual climate of the time explained the power
and dynamism of these nations as the result of natural, immutable economic law. European writers saw Europe's domination as the logical
culmination of world history. Economists like Adam Smith and sociologists like Herbert Spencer accounted for the misery of the poor by
a natural selection theory, attributing poverty to an innate lack of economic ability of the poor and justifying wealth by the adaptive powers
of the rich. Economic science thus gave a theoretical justification for
(and a moral legitimization of) low wage policies and a lack of social
responsibility on the part of employers.

This chapter was originally to have been written by Carol Smith, who had to decline
because of other commitments. I thank Smith, Laurel Bossen, and Donald Donham for
commenting on a draft of the chapter.

[1] Some basic concepts of neoclassical economics were given in the Introduction to this
volume.

Marx formed his theories in response to this situation. He objected to the theories that explained poverty by the attributes of the poor, his grounds being that these theories in effect accused the poor of causing their own misery. Marx was outraged at explanations that interpreted poor people's behavior as irrational or stupid. He assumed that these explanations were "cover stories" put out by those in power to hide their exploitation of the poor. Marx interpreted social life as a constant struggle between economic classes for control over wealth, and he insisted on the intellectual value of simply looking at the division of material resources. The dominant nineteenth-century explanation of differentials in wealth and power was evolutionary. The differences in the wealth of nations were explained by their status on an evolutionary ladder, with Western Europe on the top; and similarly the wealth of economic classes was explained by reference to moral development and ability. Marx's goal was to make a theory that would explain differences in wealth as due to the capture of income by some groups at the expense of others, a theory that would explain capitalism as a specific historical social system, not an inexorable culmination of world history.

Modern Marxist studies are sometimes called "neo-Marxism." They are based on Marx's interests and concepts and incorporate his sense of outrage and moral fervor, but use modern social scientific knowledge. The basic approach of Marxist social science is *holistic*, *historical*, and *production-oriented*. It is holistic because a society's institutions are analyzed by examining the interaction of economic, social, ideational, and political forces. Marx analyzed the family system, morality, religion, jurisprudence, education, and other institutions of society as if they were designed to support the economically productive institutions of society. For example, Marx analyzed the nuclear family as uniquely suited to the needs of nineteenth-century capitalism. Parents and children lived separately from relatives who could help out with economic needs, which made workers dependent upon the wage relation and forced labor to flow wherever industry demanded it. Ideas about the value of personal independence and freedom of independent movement, which supported the nuclear family, were seen by Marx as directly supporting capitalism.

The paradigm is historical because Marxists believe that historical explanations of social institutions are the most satisfying. Other explanations, such as functional analyses, are criticized as dealing with the maintenance of, rather than the causes of, societies. Only historical explanations show how a society's institutions developed into the particular relationships that are observed. Because human behavior is shaped by the particular institutional configuration of society at that point in history, any explanation of behavior must begin by under-standing the corresponding historical "moment." For example, a Marx-ist answer to the question, Why are Guatemalan Indians poor? lies in the history of exploitative interactions between Spaniards and Indians that began with the conquest in the sixteenth century. A functionalist might point to the lack of education and skills available to Indians, to which the Marxist would respond with a discussion of infrastructure and superstructure, arguing that education alone might not be enough to make up for a lack of access to productive capital.

Marxism is production-oriented because it assumes that the fun-damental human activity is "social labor," or the socially patterned way humans relate to the environment to obtain energy to reproduce society. The importance of labor in Marxism is crucial. Human social productive labor, culturally defined and organized, is seen as the su-premely creative part of human existence. Marxists criticize modern economics, sociology, and political science because the dominant para-digms in these disciplines are interaction-oriented, based on a theory of individual rational choice (distribution in economics, social relations in sociology, and political relations in political science). Marxists argue that the focus on interaction orients the analyses toward individual, rather than social, realities, and ignores the critically important class relations.

The focus on holism, historicism, and productive labor leads Marx-ism to be concerned with *dialectics* (the creative engagement of oppo-sites) as an analytical method. People's lives are shaped by material conditions of production and the social arrangements they live in. The reciprocal interplay of material production and social arrangements, as interpreted through cultural categories and values, is like a dialog be-tween the physical and the nonphysical, or the social and ideological.[2] The term serves to focus attention on the social, interactive, ideological nature of production.

The Capitalist Mode of Production

The basic concepts of Marxist theory will be presented via Marx's en-during contribution, the model of capitalism as a mode of production. Consider a producer in an industrial capitalist society—a computer fac-tory, for example—as compared with a producer in a kin-based society —say, a canoe maker. The computer producer is actually a social orga-

[2] Marx borrowed the term dialectic from Hegel, but his use of it is different. Bloch (1983: 29) gives a brief discussion of the differences.

nization known as a *firm*, a legal entity based on contractual financial relationships. The firm buys materials that are brought to a physical location where workers transform and assemble them into computers. The owners of the *means of production* (the building, machinery, raw materials and subcomponents, techniques, and plans) are *capitalists* because their ownership is attained through their possession of capital (money, wealth, and productive resources) rather than through political status or kinship links. The owners may work quite hard (or they may loaf—for example, they may rent land to the firm), but their income is assured because of their investment of money rather than because of their work.

The tribal canoe maker inherited his skill or else received a supernatural mandate to learn the skill from an expert.[3] He is a part-time specialist who also produces food by his own labor from land (or water resources) whose access is controlled by kinship, not by capital. He works in or near his home, with no machines, using raw materials obtained directly from nature or given to him by people who have a moral (kinship-based) obligation to supply him with materials. If other people work with him, they are usually kinsmen; and if his activity is subject to administration by others, the basis for his submission to their will is moral (usually kinship). He receives no commercial payment for the finished product, but people may give him gifts. Again, the "meaning" of the gifts is the satisfaction of moral, usually kinship, obligations. The idea of paying someone for a product outside of a kinship relationship is known, but reserved for extracommunity relations that are as much political as economic.

Consider the way workers in these two situations get subsistence items—food, shelter, clothing, and services (medical, transportation, and so on). The factory workers earn cash, which they use to buy goods and services. If they lose their job, they lose their ability to feed, clothe, and house themselves. In Marxian terms, they are "free wage labor," or a *proletariat*. They are "free" in the sense that they contract with an employer on an individual basis. They are also "free" to go hungry, wear cheap clothing, and become homeless if they have no income. The state may set a lower limit of consumption and allocate public funds to ensure that households live above that level, but this is out of the hands of the workers—they are dependent on wages or welfare. In Marxian terms, they have lost ownership of the *means of production*, or the tools and techniques that create products. The first fundamental attribute of a capitalist mode of production is that the workers do not

[3] Canoe makers, weapon makers, or tool makers tend to be male. Female specialist producers tend to make valuables like woven goods.

control (are "alienated" from) the means of production. They cannot by themselves produce the things they need to live. The canoe maker, by comparison, can grow or obtain his own food, clothing, and housing like every able-bodied person in his society. His ability to care for himself and his family, and reproduce (meaning endure over time as a type of producer) is not contingent upon his labor in canoe manufacture.

The second diagnostic attribute of capitalism is that the workers can gain access to the means of production, and thereby earn their livelihood, only through a wage relation (ignoring welfare for now). Thus the society can be understood as being composed of two great classes —capitalists, who by virtue of owning capital control the means of production, and workers, who by virtue of lacking capital *must* contract with capital in a wage relation. The important point is that workers are forced to hire their labor out or suffer the negative consequences to their level of living—which are social and cultural as well as economic.

The capitalist class is more prestigious, more admired, better-educated, healthier, and happier than the worker class. Further, the workers usually agree with and support the value system that ranks the wealthier higher than the poorer. The reason for the workers' self-depreciating agreement with the capitalists' value system (which Marxist theoreticians call "ideological hegemony" because it is a form of control over workers by capitalists) is that the capitalist class controls the educational system (defined broadly to include the public media), which teaches (and interprets) basic concepts and values. Marxists point out that these concepts and definitions are historically produced to function with the mode of production and are not (as the capitalists would prefer to see it) logically true.

Marxists note that things, mainly money, are seen in capitalist ideology to have a life and dynamic of their own. The cause of profit, for example, is analyzed by neoclassical economic theory as lying in capital (in various forms, including money, machinery, land) and labor. Thus economists analyze the product of a firm into shares contributed by capital and labor. Marxists see this as reifying capital and label the analytical procedure as "*commodity fetishism*." Marxists claim this denigrates labor in order to oppress laborers and enrich capitalists. In the Marxist view, the only theoretically justifiable cause of a product is labor.[4]

The third attribute of capitalism comes about because the wage paid to workers is less than the product of their labor. The "surplus" produced by workers over their wage is retained by the owners of capital and, in conventional economic theory, represents reimbursement for

---

[4] See Bloch (1983) or any standard reference on Marxist theory for a discussion of the labor theory of value.

various contributions to production by capital (cost of machinery, administration, rent) as well as profit. The capitalist's goal is to increase profit, which is attained by decreasing wages or by increasing the product of labor. This accounts for the basic "dynamic" of capitalism, which is a constant pressure to increase the scale of production, to invest more capital in more productive machinery, to encompass more production within the scope of the enterprise. This dynamism explains why the capitalist mode of production has extended its hegemony over so much of the modern world. In Marxist theory, the shares of the product over and above wages are exploited from the workers because of the political strength of the capitalist class. The dynamism of capitalism is seen as exploitation caused by unequal exchange.

Merchant Capitalism

Marxists disagree whether there can be such a thing as merchant capitalism, meaning a capitalist mode of production based on exchange and distribution rather than on production. In the history of the world, merchants (who used wealth to buy goods from artisans or nonwage producers, goods they transported and transformed for resale in order to create profit) predated production capitalists. Did mercantile wealth function like capital? Merchants in the Middle Ages hired labor (but not in a free labor market), transformed products (by moving them from place to place and sometimes by "putting out" raw materials to be processed by workers), and made profits. The historical merchant economies of the Middle Ages evolved into the capitalist economies in the industrial revolution of the eighteenth century. The prevailing opinion seems to be that mercantilism is ancestral to, but distinct from, capitalism. "Wealth . . . is not capital until it controls the means of production, buys labor power and puts it to work, expands and begins to raise surpluses by intensifying productivity through an ever-increasing curve of technical inputs" (Wolf 1981: 49). The key difference is the existence of "free" labor and the ideological "fetishization" of capital. The point of the definition is not mere hairsplitting, but is meant to highlight the dynamism of capitalist production, which has certainly transformed the world in the past 300 years.

The Tributary Mode of Production

Marx discussed many modes of production, including capitalism, feudalism, communitarianism, slaveholding, and a "Germanic" as well as a "Slavonic" mode of production. Nineteenth-century writers did not use terms as precisely as we are used to, and this discussion follows Eric Wolf (1982) in grouping these various concepts into three general types: capitalist, tributary, and kinship.[5] Workers in tributary modes of production have direct access to the means of production, but their activities are directed through political domination. The threat of violent force underlies the control by overlord-elites of serf-peasants.

Wolf defines two types of tributary modes of production: a centralized and a fragmented (or dispersed) system. In the centralized mode of production (which Marx called "Asiatic"), the ruling elite is all-powerful. The ultimate source of power is control over some important resource in production, such as large-scale waterworks, or command over a uniquely powerful force, such as the largest army. This domination limits the power of local overlords as well as the development of local political organizations such as guilds. The dispersed, or fragmented, mode of production (called "feudal" by Marx) denotes a relatively weak central power and correspondingly strong local overlords. Here, local alliances are important, factional struggles endemic, and the strategy of the highest-level elite is to foment discord in the provinces, to "divide and conquer" the local lords.

Wealth in a tributary mode of production is generated by direct coercion or tribute. Producers owe a part of their product to their lords because heaven ordained it and because the lords have the moral as well as legal right to kill or enslave them if they violate the heaven-inspired order of things. The social system is supported by an ideology that justifies domination on earth by heavenly approval. The cosmos is seen as hierarchical, where God in heaven works through the overlords on earth to subject unruly humanity to an orderly society. This "ideological model displaces the real relation between power-wielding surplus takers and dominated producers onto the imagined relation between superior deity and inferior 'subject'" (Wolf 1982: 83). The effect of this ideology is to transform the problem of public power into one of private morality, and to equate the maintenance of public order with the continuation of heavenly order. The fact that the dominated, often miserably poor underdogs, accept the rulers' definition of (and rationalization for) their low position is termed "false consciousness" in Marxist studies, and is an example of the "ideological hegemony" of modes of production. Clearly modes of production are not simple relations between people, things, and environment but include coordinated belief systems as well.[6]

The overlords use their wealth to generate more wealth through

---

[5] The tributary mode of production (after Amin 1973) includes the feudal and asiatic modes of production.

[6] The idea that Marxism consists of a simplistic relation of causality from the material world through social institutions to ideology is often called "vulgar Marxism."

long-distance trade, usually in elite goods. Possession of such luxuries validates their elite status and gives them a valuable symbol to use in control of lesser lords. Long-distance merchants in historical tributary societies were often political emissaries as well, and their possession of wealth and knowledge of the world gave them a status that could compete with that of the rulers. The societies usually had norms and beliefs that denigrated mercantile wealth and that relegated such activities to outsider groups such as the Jews in Europe or the *tlatelolcans* in the Aztec empire (see Chapter 4, this volume). In some societies relatively weak central rulers made deals with merchants to bolster their power. This sort of fragmentary, complex situation in Western Europe ultimately gave rise to the industrial revolution. The capitalist mode of production did not originally develop in most parts of Asia because the centralized tributary modes of production characteristic of the region did not allow merchants the same opportunities.

The Kinship Mode of Production

In societies ordinarily known as tribal or foraging societies, the most important thing to know about someone is what family he or she "comes from." Kinship is absolutely fundamental in these societies, because one's kinship identity controls access to all of the necessities of life—the means of production, legal protection, social and religious support, and so on (see Chapters 2 and 3, this volume). Kinship can be seen as a way of identifying people with particular groups. Through the use of symbolic analogues to biological relations, such as marriage, lineal descent (consanguinity), and affinal descent (through marriage), individual activities are organized into group behavior. Kin groups such as extended families, lineages, and clans define the organization of production. The major inequalities that exist in such societies can be basic, as between seniors and juniors or men and women, or more abstract, such as whether one is related more or less closely to a mythical ancestor.

Wolf distinguishes two types of kinship modes of production: a simpler one where resources are widely available to anyone with the necessary skills (for example, foraging bands) and a more complex one where access to resources is structured by organized kinship groups. Chiefdoms—where kinship groups are ranked in prestige and authority and where aristocratic leaders can organize fairly large labor, trade, or fighting parties—are really intermediary between kinship and tributary modes of production. The important issues are whether economic classes exist, in the sense of clearly defined groups who have significantly different access to the means of production, which cause corresponding differences in their level of living.

Inequalities in capitalist societies are supported and reproduced by an ideology of class whereby commodities are made into measures of the worth of people. Those who have less are thought to deserve less. The inequalities in kinship societies are defined by age seniority, male domination over women, and geneological closeness to a "founder" patri- or matriline. How are inequalities "reproduced" in kinship societies? Donham argues that it is through a "fetishization of fertility" in his analysis of the Maale of Ethiopia:

Whereas in reality the success of men and women in bearing children and in accumulating wealth depended upon their own procreative and productive powers, the way that labor was structured in nineteenth-century Maale made it *appear* as if that success was dependent upon other people's fertility: that of the king and chiefs in the first place, that of descent group elders in the second, and finally that of husband-fathers. Correspondingly, failures and misfortunes seemed to be the result of these other persons withholding their fertilizing and beneficent powers. [Forthcoming]

For example, the Maale king prayed to the ancestors for rain and planted first in the agricultural season. After the king planted, the chiefs planted, then the subchiefs, and finally the household heads, in strict order of kinship seniority (closeness to the founding patriline) as well as seniority (elders before juniors). Any violation of the order of things was considered to be a serious crime against society in that it would bring the wrath of the ancestors down upon the living. When natural disasters did occur, they were widely interpreted as proof that past infractions against the natural order were causal (Donham, forthcoming).

Case Study: New Guinea Tribal Salt Producers

Production and distribution in a kinship mode of production can be illustrated with a case study of salt manufacture among the Baruya, a highland tribal group of New Guinea. Baruya society consisted of about 1,500 people in the 1960's, when they were studied by Godelier (1971). They lived in a dozen villages and hamlets of the rugged New Guinea mountains in a political organization of independent villages without a paramount chief. Each settlement was composed of patrilineal clans, eight of whom were descended from the first settlers in the region and seven from later settlers. These kin groups were "corporate," in the sense that they held collective (traditional) title to the land.

The basic social organization of the society was composed of kinship categories combined with a hierarchical division of the population into four age groups. These age divisions crosscut the lineages and clans and linked all the villages, unifying the society ideologically (through a cycle of initiations) and militarily as a fighting group (ibid.: 55).

The economy was based on sweet potato agriculture, pig husbandry, and salt manufacture, with hunting and gathering economically insignificant but symbolically important. The Baruya were involved in complex channels of intertribal trade, exchanging salt for a wide range of goods, including European steel axes and knives. Salt was used as a condiment, as a means of exchange and store of value, and also as a necessary element in religious ceremonies. Normally salt was produced from sea water by coastal villages, but the rough landscape, high level of intertribal warfare, and large distances made salt acquisition difficult for tribes deep in the interior. The Baruya were one of a few highland tribes who produced salt from plants.

Salt Production

The Baruya harvested salt grass from irrigated areas ranging from 0.8 to 12 hectares in size, which were divided into marked plots. Each area was owned by specific kinship groups, but in fact no one was refused access to the salt grass if he first asked the owners' permission. Salt production was organized by individuals who coordinated the labor of their relatives. The grass was cut every year during the dry period and grew back naturally. After a week or two of drying, the grass was heaped and burned, and then the ashes were roofed over and left to settle for several months. In the next phase of production, the ashes were packed into filters made of gourds with plant burrs on the bottom, and pure water was slowly poured through. As it passed through the gourds, the water became saturated with minerals and dripped out into a gutter of leaves leading to long bamboo tubes.

The full tubes were taken to a salt workshop, owned by a salt production specialist. It contained an oven with a row of twelve to fifteen oblong molds, 80 cm long and 12 cm wide. Each mold was lined with a form made of banana leaves and filled with the salt solution. The salt specialist maintained a constant temperature in the oven for about five days to allow the salt solution to evaporate and crystallize. In addition to regulating the heat to prevent the solution from boiling and skimming off the impurities, the salt specialist performed ritual salt magic. After five or six days the crystallized salt, in the form of very hard bars 60 to 72 cm long and 10 to 13 cm wide, were removed, scraped to take more regular form, and wrapped carefully in banana leaves and bark to form watertight packages. Each bar weighed about 2 kilograms, and bars were classified by size as small, medium, or large.

Both men and women participated in salt production. Godelier calculated that the various production tasks took about 21 days of "social labor," involving one to ten men and women. The tasks included cutting the grass, gathering firewood, burning, gathering and transporting the ashes to the oven, and salt evaporation and wrapping. The production run created fifteen bars of salt, at a cost of about 1½ days of labor per bar. The salt production was terminated by a collective ceremonial meal prepared by the individual who orchestrated the procedure and therefore owned the salt.

Salt Distribution

The owner of the salt customarily gave one or two bars to the salt specialist, and five to ten bars to his in-laws, cousins, and friends who helped out in the production of the salt or who deserved reciprocal gifts. The rest was kept as wealth to be used for barter and for religious ceremonies. Some bars of salt assumed heirloom or relic status. Godelier describes "bars of salt almost a generation old, desiccated and black with soot, . . . hanging over the hearth" (1971: 71). Having once been received as gifts intended to validate agreements or relationships, the bars are symbols of past achievements. The barter uses of salt make it a special-purpose money, since it was exchanged (at set rates) for axes, knives, bows and arrows, stone clubs, various shell, feather, and bead valuables, pigs, dogs, and sorcerer/curer services. Salt was never exchanged for basic subsistence goods such as yams or taro. Trade took place over long distances and could incur serious risks, as the following story told by Godelier illustrates:

[A]bout 1942, the Youwarrounatche, at war with the Baruya, cut the route to the Tairora villages, located one to two days' walk to the north along the Lamari River. Since axes, bushknives, and a much-appreciated variety of large cowrie shells came through the Tairora, some Baruya men decided to contact the Watchakes, a "kukukuku" [linguistic] group living to the northeast, beyond the Kratke Range (Mount Piora, 3720 m). Three men left, accompanied by a woman to prove their peaceful intentions. They received a warm welcome which put them at ease except for one who stood on his guard. This saved him, because a few hours later the three men were rudely attacked by their hosts; he succeeded in escaping, but his two companions were wounded and later ritually killed and eaten. The woman was married to one of the murderers. The Baruya organized a punitive expedition which failed because the Watchakes had posted watch in the forest. Nevertheless, some time later, the Baruya made a second attempt to create commercial ties with the Watchakes and this time they succeeded. [1971: 62]

Exchange rates were set by custom, bargaining, and precedence. Godelier mentions a dramatic price change between the Baruya and the group mentioned above, the Watchakes:

When the Baruya contacted the Watchakes in order to obtain steel axes, they offered one salt bar for one axe and this rate was accepted until the day when a Baruya man, not having spoken to those who had come before him, and being terrified by the Watchakes who were known to be cannibals, threw three salt bars onto the ground and fled with the axe which was given to him. He had applied the rate which the Baruya used with the Yoyue. After that, the Watchakes refused to exchange an axe for less than three salt bars and the man at fault was insulted for his stupidity and cowardice. [1971: 67]

This brief sketch shows several basic themes. First, Baruya society had inequalities. Social ranking was based on kinship and residence, and distinguished early from late settlers in a manner reminiscent of the Daughters of the American Revolution. The salt grounds were "owned" by specific groups, but this inequality did not translate into differentials in access to the means of production, since anyone could harvest salt grass upon request. Thus anyone could create wealth, in the form of salt, by recruiting family labor.

Second, the individual decisions being made were fully rational in the sense of preferring more over less of a valued good. The fact that the frightened trader was insulted means that the tribe was fully aware of its privileged position and enjoyed the unequal exchange as long as it could. And, finally, the multiple functions of salt in Baruya life show the importance of noncommercial (religious, political, symbolic) functions of commodities in kinship modes of production.

Case Study: The Indian Sacred Cow

In 1966 Harris published an influential article claiming that the well-known Hindu aversion to eating beef could be explained better as an adaptive economic strategy than as an ideological rule. Harris felt he was following Marx's precept that social life is eminently rational if one looks at material conditions. Previous scholars had pointed out that the Hindu ideology, which considered cattle as sacred beings, prevented poor individuals from consuming this available resource. Indian society was desperately poor and could have used the cattle to ameliorate poverty, but the religious considerations were more important than the economic ones. The case had been put forward as an example of the dominance of ideological over economic forces.

Harris analyzed the economic and ecological conditions of agriculture in India and pointed out that the cows performed many positive functions, including the provision of traction for plowing, dung for fires, leather for industry, and finally meat for those low castes not proscribed from eating meat. He showed that the consumption of beef would lower the efficiency of the total economic system and that therefore the religious prohibition could be explained as having positive economic and ecological effects. Further, he showed that Hindu farmers selectively culled their cattle to produce favorable sex ratios, in spite of the religious prohibition against cattle slaughter. Harris created a picture of a social system where people said one thing (that cattle were sacred, were not ever killed, and were revered for their religious status), but did something quite different (used cattle in practical ways to run the economic system and adjusted the death rate of male animals to wind up with two cows for each bull).

This article was criticized from left and right. More orthodox Marxists criticized it as "vulgar economic determinism" and tautology, since the positive functions of the cattle slaughter prohibition were simply defined as causal; idealists pointed out that the positive functions could have been attained without the elaborate ideological structure. The work was criticized as functionalist, because it explained social facts by looking at their positive contributions to society. The argument was quite productive (see Harris 1979 for a summary), and while experts differ on the validity of details of his interpretation, the overall point seems accepted. This example of a religious institution controverting economic rationality in a situation of economic duress was shown to be open to serious question. The value of the Marxian approach of searching for practical rationality in strange or exotic institutions on the assumption that *someone* must be benefiting from the manipulation of productive assets was supported.

The Relevance of Marxism to Kin-Based Societies

Marx's concepts and theories were developed to explain how nineteenth-century capitalism worked and are not directly relevant to such different societies as bands and tribes. Anthropologists interested in the basic Marxist approach but who wanted to study kinship-dominated societies found themselves frustrated by this mismatch between theory and empirical reality. They debated whether elders could be said to "exploit" juniors because elders disposed of the labor products of the juniors, when all juniors had the potential to become elders.

The typical hierarchy of authority in such societies goes, in the abstract, from male lineage elders > mature married men > young men > married women > young women. However, women often produce most of the food in these societies. A major preoccupation of senior adults in lineage societies is the disposition of the unmarried females belonging to their lineage (see Chapter 12, this volume). Thus the situation of young but economically critical females controlled by senior males should make gender relations a fruitful area for Marxist analysis. The problem is that gender crosscuts everything else in the society. The abstract hierarchy of authority is one thing, but the mother or senior wife of a senior male is usually an extremely important person, someone in control of far more resources than a junior male. In these situations, the concept of class-based exploitation becomes difficult to apply. Marxists, as part of their nineteenth-century ideological heritage, have often assumed that females were always dependent rather than empirically identifying their changing authority with age and parenthood (see Chapter 12).

To conclude, the Marxist approach is most relevant to studies of capitalist modes of production and sometimes may seem like a theory looking for a home in studies of kinship modes of production. The most exciting work is in the area of development, where developed industrial capitalist societies interact with developing, agrarian societies whose modes of production are mixed blends of capitalism and tribute.

A case study from Guatemala illustrates the approach. Most people on earth are called "peasants," meaning they live in rural communities in independent households and earn their living by farming small plots of land, supplementing their income with "petty" (small-scale, nonindustrialized, household-based) manufacture and wage labor. Peasants do not fit neatly into Marx's conceptual scheme when they own their own land, sell their produce on a capitalist market, and hire labor to work on their farm as well as hire household members out as wage laborers to capitalist firms. Because they own land, hire laborers, and engage in manufacture where they own the means of production (that is, crafts production), they look like capitalists. But since they are often desperately poor, household-based, subject to the whim of prices set by large-scale heavily capitalized firms (such as fertilizer companies), and at times work for wages, they look like proletariat.

After much discussion and debate in the literature, the concept of a *petty commodity form of production* crystallized.[7] This refers to a production situation within a capitalist mode of production where competitive markets exist, and where specialized producers (who control their own

---

[7] One ongoing debate is whether this is a real mode of production, with the ability to reproduce itself, or merely a "petty commodity *form* of production" within the capitalist mode of production. Interested readers should look through the journal *Peasant Studies* for examples of the argument.

means of production) compete with each other to sell products and are able to hire free labor, but do not extract "significant" surplus value from wage labor. (See the discussion in Chapter 6, this volume.)

The small-scale cloth weavers of Totonicapán, Guatemala, are a good example (Smith 1983, 1984a, 1984b). These Mayan Indians use relatively simple technology, comprised of wooden footlooms made by local craftsmen and which cost about one-third of an average craftsman's annual net income. They buy cotton thread (either locally made or imported from industrialized countries) and sell commodities. Weavers hire laborers, often in an apprenticeship mode, meaning the apprentices live in their households and receive room and board as well as wages while they "learn the trade." The product is a length of heavy, tightly woven, brightly colored cloth of traditional design used for skirts by local Indian women. Non-Indians do not wear this cloth, and some Indians have given it up in favor of industrial-factory skirts and dresses that cost considerably less but that convey no Indian or traditional identity.

The largest producers are typically male householders and use (roughly) from $400 to $1,300 worth of capital in the form of looms, sewing machines, and other tools.[8] The average producer hires from none to ten wage workers to work along with from two to six family workers and from none to three apprentices to produce (very roughly) from $6,000 to $26,000 worth of cloth a year, which is the equivalent of from $800 to $7,000 net income. This translates into an average income of from $1.60 to $5.25 per day per household member in an area where the average daily wage is $3.00 per day.[9] The reason for the term "petty" in this sort of commodity production should now be clear.

Most weavers have plots of agricultural land that they use to grow subsistence crops, mainly corn and beans. A criterion of peasant culture is that households make every attempt to grow part, if not all, of their staple subsistence food. This is only partly a "rational" economic strategy in the face of unstable market systems; more importantly, the definition of a mature, adult life includes direct farming activity to grow one's own food. People are not happy if they do not have access to at least a small parcel of land for subsistence crops.

People learn their weaving trade by growing up in a household where weaving takes place. Most often this occurs by birth; fairly often it

[8] Maya women traditionally lacked access to the capital and skill needed for independent footloom weaving. In such households they formed the necessary auxiliary labor force by spinning thread to supply the male weavers (Bossen 1975).

[9] All figures are Guatemalan Quetzals, which were valued at par with the U.S. dollar in the mid-1970's, when these data were collected.

occurs by apprenticeship. After two to five years apprentices know enough about weaving to think of working independently. Given the relatively low cost of the basic means of production in weaving, a young man can rather easily set himself up as an independent weaver. This ability keeps wages high and limits the ability of entrepreneurial weavers to expand. No sooner do they hire and train an expert worker than the worker leaves to set up his own business. This produces an industry where the average business is small and with a lot of direct competition by producers for market niches. This in turn keeps prices rather low, which limits capital accumulation, which constrains an entrepreneur's ability to raise wages, expand his scale of production, and so on.

Smith (1984a) analyzed this case study in light of a crucial issue in Marxist studies: the causes of the development of socioeconomic classes. Lenin (cited in Smith 1984a and discussed in Chapter 6, this volume) theorized that "the prevalence of commodity economy . . . gives rise to competition among producers, and, while ruining the mass, enriches the few." Because of the existence of a capitalist commodity economy, the essential dynamic of the capitalist mode of production should lead capitalists to become larger in scale and richer, while workers gradually lose more control over the means of production and become poorer. Why has this not happened over the past 100 years in western Guatemala?

An economic analysis of costs and incomes provides the answer. The difficulty in amassing capital caused by easy access into the craft and high wage rates limits the potential for capital accumulation. Why has a wealthy merchant from outside the region not moved into the area and used previously accumulated capital to set up a large-scale manufactory that would outcompete the local household-based manufacturers? This has happened in many areas of the world, as relatively expensive machines replaced high-priced labor with unskilled, cheaper laborers, and allowed large-scale producers to compete with skilled craftsmen and put them out of business.

In other areas of production in this area, pottery, tanning, shoemaking, soap making, and other crafts have declined or disappeared in the face of an onslaught of mass-produced goods (see Chapter 9, this volume, for a discussion of this trend in the world economy). Certainly this has happened with the weaving industry in Guatemala at large, since textiles imported from Mexico and other more industrialized countries have put local industries out of business. However, the potential for income from the sale of Indian skirt cloth is just too limited to attract this sort of capitalist. Essentially the local demand is too restricted to support large-scale capital investment.

This case (and many others in the anthropological literature) is intriguing because it represents a puzzle to Marxist theory. Petty commodity producers are bound to markets—they buy and sell commodities on the market just like any other capitalist. But they extract surplus from no labor but their own (including their family members). Being embedded in a market, they face the standard capitalist market forces to expand production. But lack of labor keeps them small because they do not have the social power to expropriate the labor of other Indians. For example, labor is cheaper in nearby Indian villages. Why have Totonicapán weavers not hired laborers from Nahuala (a nearby community with a lower wage rate)? Smith argues that the corporate community mentality of Indian communities prevents them from hiring outside their own community (see Chapter 6 for a discussion of the closed corporate community). This mentality was established during the early days of the colonial era, when the dominant mode of production was tributary. The division of the national society into "Indian" and "Ladino" (meaning non-Indian) castes maintained the lack of solidarity between Indian communities. The operation of a caste-like social system and attendant intercaste suspicions in the present capitalist mode of production is a "contradiction" in Marxist terms. It is problematic for capitalists and is a sort of "fault line" along which the society can experience conflict.

These issues are causes of debate and change in Marxist theory. The term "peasant" has a clear meaning in traditional Marxist theory, relative to the tribute mode of production. The attempt to apply the best of this theory to a new, changing, and complex reality produces lots of intellectual ferment. Are cases such as the Guatemala cloth producers to be analyzed as articulation of a tributary and a capitalist mode of production, or as a case of an incomplete transition from one to the other? Where is the causality coming from, the external demands of "international capital" or the internal dynamic of the social system?

The case just mentioned is a challenge to Marxist theory. The rising wealth of workers in West European and North American capitalism is an even stronger challenge. Marxist theory predicted an ever worsening condition for workers, while history reveals an improving situation. Does this mean the theory is irrelevant? Marxist scholars argue that the increasing wealth of industrial capitalism is at the cost of increasing poverty in the non-Western world. Scholars like Wallerstein (1974), Frank (1966), and Wolf (1982) argue that the unit of analysis has changed and that the world system gives evidence of worsening class relations that supports Marxist theory.

The existence of glaring inequalities in the distribution of wealth, power, and prestige in the world make Marxist theory attractive to many scholars. The ethnographic method is most conveniently practiced with poor people, who have low opportunity costs for the time they spend with the ethnographer. Familiarity with economic oppression leads researchers to want to understand the causes of inequality. Neoclassical economics does not usually attempt to deal with such large-scale questions. As Donham says, "Neoclassical theory trains an exceptionally bright light on a very small area. It is possible both to appreciate the brightness and to regret the smallness." Referring to Marxism as "macro-anthropology," he concludes: "History, power and ideology furnish, then, grand questions for macro-anthropology" (1981: 538).

15

On the Division of Labor Between Economics and Economic Anthropology

Christina H. Gladwin

Fifty years ago it was easy to distinguish an economist from an anthropologist. Anthropologists like Mead and Malinowski studied Third World peoples and cultures by actually living with exotic peoples in faraway places; economists like Keynes and Adam Smith confined themselves to their offices to think up theories and analyze statistics about the economic behavior of First World peoples. For the most part, the differences between the two disciplines are still enormous. However, some economists—especially development and agricultural economists—are now found studying the economic behavior of indigenous peoples all over the world: in Africa (Eicher 1982, 1986; Johnston 1986); in Asia (Falcon 1970; Johnston 1966; Timmer 1974); and in Latin America (de Janvry 1981; Deere 1983). At the same time, more anthropologists are studying First World economic phenomena (Barlett 1984; Gladwin 1983b; Gladwin and Zabawa 1984; Harris and Ross 1978; Hoben 1980; Margolis 1984; Spradley 1970).

As the world becomes smaller, the division of labor between development economists and economic anthropologists becomes fuzzier, and it is now hard to distinguish some economists from some economic anthropologists. When one meets a development specialist at the Norfolk Bar in Nairobi or at a plaza cafe in Oaxaca, one can no longer guess whether the person will be an anthropologist, an economist, a political scientist, or even a sociologist. By dress and by jargon, they are often undifferentiated. When one picks up a "hot" text in African development (for example, Bates 1981; Hart 1982; Hyden 1980; Sacks 1979), it is difficult to say a priori what the discipline of the author will be. In fact, I

I am grateful for the aid, helpful comments, and critiques of Robert Zabawa, Peggy Barlett, Hugh Gladwin, and Stuart Plattner, as well as of farmers interviewed in Mexico, Guatemala, and Florida. Thanks also to the *American Journal of Agricultural Economics* and *Human Organization* for allowing me to reprint published figures.

have often wondered about myself: Am I an anthropological economist or an economic anthropologist?[1]

Partly to answer this personal question, I address the question of what distinguishes an economist from an economic anthropologist. Today, how are the two disciplines different? To answer this question, I will examine the following more or less conventional assertions about features that distinguish economic anthropologists from economists:

1. The anthropologist is more concerned with the study of micro-level economic phenomena in a village, whereas the economist is more concerned with macrolevel phenomena in a region or country.

2. The economist is preoccupied with formal methods, often to the exclusion of substance, whereas anthropologists are naive when it comes to quantitative methods and deal only with qualitative data.

3. The anthropologist is eclectic and aims for a holistic, almost ge-stalt impression of a culture; the economist looks only at economic phenomena.

3a. (corollary of 3) Economic anthropologists switch back and forth from the neoclassical economic paradigm to the Marxist paradigm, taking what they need from either paradigm to explain observed behavior. Economists, on the other hand, are clearer about what paradigm they're in: They are either neoclassicists or Marxists, but not both.

4. The anthropologist uses the ethnographic discovery process to base ethnographic observations on and to build ethnographic models. This is a totally different approach from the linear sequence of hypothesis testing used in both neoclassical and Marxist economics.

The weight of evidence from the works of both economists and economic anthropologists, as well as my own work, is brought to bear on each of these assertions in the following pages.

Anthropology at the Village Level
or the Regional Level?

Examples of village-level studies abound in economic anthropology (Barlett 1977; Bennett 1969; Brush 1976; Cancian 1972; Chibnik 1980;

---

[1] The reason that I am confused about myself is that I started off with a B.A. in physics, married an anthropologist, went to Ghana and was trained in fieldwork, and then spent two years in the multidisciplinary School of Social Science at the University of California at Irvine. After learning how to be a social scientist, I then got a Ph.D. in agricultural economics at the Food Research Institute, Stanford. Now I pass myself off as an anthropologist to agricultural economists, but to anthropologists I am an agricultural economist.

Plattner 1975); while examples of macrolevel studies by economists are too numerous to mention but a few (Adelman and Morris 1973; Boserup 1970; deJanvry 1981; Johnston 1958; Jones 1972; Timmer, Falcon, and Pearson 1983). It is just as easy, however, to cite village-level studies by development or agricultural economists (Deere 1977; Hill 1963, 1970, 1972; Hayami 1978; Norman, Simmons, and Hays 1982; Jones 1983). It is a little more difficult to cite regional-level or country-level works by economic anthropologists, because they are often unhappy using poor-quality secondary data. Lately, however, anthropologists have themselves collected regional data; their works appear under the rubric of "regional analysis" (Smith 1976), or "macro-micro linkages in development" (Cohen 1985; DeWalt 1984), or "political economy" (Hart 1982; Smith 1978) or even "women in development" (Croll 1979; Spring 1983). And ecological anthropologists have tended to aim their analyses at the regional or macro level to show that development is really only an extension of the process of human adaptation (Adams 1975; Bennett 1976; DeWalt 1984; Geertz 1966; Moran 1979; Sahlins and Service 1960). Finally, anthropologists doing cross-cultural work with the Human Area Relations File data, in which the unit of analysis is an entire society or culture, of course do macrolevel analysis (Burton and White 1984; Ember 1982; Murdock 1967; Murdock and White 1969). Are these the exceptions that prove the rule? I think not.

In my own work, I have used ethnographic methods and decision tree analysis to model farmers' decision processes at the village level and the regional level in order to inform agricultural researchers why farmers are not adopting the new improved technologies coming out of their experiment stations. In both studies, summarized below, I used the same methodology; was I an anthropologist at the village level and an economist at the regional level?

A Case Study: Decision Models at the Village Level

In 1973–74, a study was conducted of farmers' adoption or non-adoption of the agronomic recommendations of the Puebla Project, which aimed to increase yields of rain-fed maize in Puebla, Mexico. The project, started by CIMMYT (Centro Internacional de Majoramiento de Maiz y Trigo), focused on deriving recommendations about fertilizer use and timing and plant population for the local variety of maize. The aim of the study was to view the Plan Puebla through the eyes of the proposed adopters of the new technology—farmers in one representative village—and explain why so few (less than 20 percent) farmers were adopting the Plan Puebla technologies. The methodology used was the development of decision tree models for each of four farmers' decisions: to get credit for fertilizer, to increase plant population, to increase the number of fertilizer applications, and to use a recommended level of fertilizer per hectare. Previous studies of the Puebla Project had lumped all these four decisions together to describe why the farmers did not adopt the package of recommendations (Benito 1976; Moscardi 1979; Moscardi and deJanvry 1977; Villa Issa 1976). This study, however, assumed farmers could decide to adopt one agronomic recommendation without adopting the others. The decision models were developed after intensive interviews with twenty or more farmers in the village to discover their reasoning and elicit their perceived alternatives and decision criteria. They were then tested in interviews with another, separate set of 34 decision makers. The method can be understood via the following example.

The Decision to Fertilize Twice Instead of Once

Traditionally, farmers in Puebla fertilize once, at the first weeding, which occurs when the plants are 10 to 20 cm high, or about 20 days after planting. The Plan Puebla, however, recommends fertilizing twice, at planting and at the second weeding, which occurs when the plants are 50 cm high or about 40 days after planting. Nevertheless, no farmer in the village in 1973–74 fertilized at planting in all his fields, and few farmers fertilized at planting in one field.

Why didn't the farmers follow the economic experts' advice? Was it unthinking conservatism, or was there an economic cause? Ethnographic research can answer this sort of question. After interviews with twenty farmers, the decision tree model in Fig. 15.1 was put together. It is read from top to bottom, and asks each decision maker a set of questions in the diamonds (denoted by < >) about the alternatives he or she has to choose between in order to reach an outcome (denoted by []) at the end of a branch.[2]

The model in Fig. 15.1 states that farmers will try to fertilize twice, at

[2] Decision models are treelike or "hierarchical" rather than linear additive as in a multiple regression analysis because it is assumed that people compare alternatives on a piecemeal basis, that is, one dimension at a time, when making real-life decisions. The decision model is specified after personal interviews with a representative sample of farmers; it is then tested against actual choice data collected from a second, independent sample of decision makers. The use of elicitation procedures to generate the specific decision criteria (and their logical order in the tree) also distinguishes decision tree models from more conventional decision models used in economic analysis. In a linear programming model, for example, the objective function and constraints are usually assumed to be correctly specified but are in fact always untested against choice data collected from a sample of decision makers. Decision tree models, in contrast, are quite easily tested during personal or phone interviews with a survey instrument applied to a sample of decision makers.

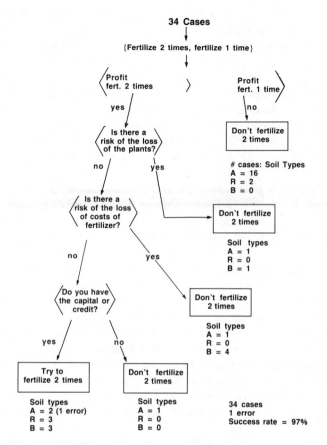

Fig. 15.1. The decision to fertilize twice, at planting and at the second weeding. Source: Gladwin 1976: 885.

planting and the second weeding, if they think fertilizing at planting is profitable and if they can pass constraints, including the risk of loss of plants and input costs, as well as a capital or credit constraint.[3]

These profitability criteria are different for the different types of fields in the village: type R, fields with irrigation; type A, fields without irrigation but with volcanic ash in the soil, which gives it enough moisture if plowed correctly after the preceding harvest so that the farmer can plant early in April; and type B, fields with sodiclike soils and without irrigation or moisture in April so that the farmer must wait for the

---

[3] The model is a bit more complicated than shown, because the profitability criterion is itself a set of criteria or logical statements of the form: if you do X in a field of type Y, then fertilizing at planting is profitable.

first regular rain to plant, which may occur in April or May but often as late as June. The profitability criteria for type A soils state that it is not profitable to fertilize at planting if a farmer plants early in April "in dryness" (en seco)—as he should—and does the first weeding before the first regular rains come. In that case, the soil is too dry at planting to let the fertilizer (applied by hand above the ground) dissolve, so that it just sits there until the first regular rains come and does nothing. There is no head start for the plants with fertilizer at planting for a good farmer with type A soils. Most demonstrations of the Plan Puebla were in April on type A soils; they used fertilizer at planting and lost credibility with village farmers.

The opposite is true for type R and B fields, however. It is profitable to fertilize at planting in fields that are moist at planting (soils wet by irrigation or by a previous regular rain) because the fertilizer will dissolve at planting and give the plants a head start. Plants in type B soils, because of later planting, can really use a fast start if they are to withstand too much water from the heavy rains that come in the middle to end of June.

Thus the main factor limiting adoption of this recommendation was nonprofitability on type A soils: 16 out of 21 farmers with type A soils did not think it was worth their while to fertilize at planting. On type R soils, three out of five farmers tried fertilizer at planting. On type B soils, the factor limiting adoption was risk of loss of plants or input costs. The model successfully predicts 97 percent of village farmers' decisions about fertilizing at planting. Unfortunately, data at the regional level were not available to test this model in the Puebla region as a whole.

This ethnographic model gives a satisfying explanation of the farmers' behavior, because their decisions are shown to "make sense." In this case the purely economic recommendation about fertilizers was not useful to farmers because it did not distinguish the relevant local factors —soil types and time of rainfall—which farmers needed to take into account. This is common in most cases when anthropologists are critical of other scientists' analyses and recommendations about situations the anthropologists have studied. The ethnographer's knowledge and sensitivity about local factors make them aware of the most relevant factors from the natives' point of view.

Decision Models at the Regional Level

Policy makers in Guatemala face a problem: Indian peasant farmers in the Highlands devote too much land to corn in areas where there is too little rain and where the growing season is too long for corn. The price of corn is too low. How can policy makers or project planners get them to grow and sell higher valued cash crops and buy corn in the marketplace? My study, done with the Guatemalan farming systems research and extension program at the Institute of Agricultural Science and Technology (ICTA) in 1978–79, attempted to answer this question (Gladwin 1982, 1983a). My goal was to build one decision model of farmers' cropping patterns that would be generalizable to all the different agroclimatic, socioeconomic subregions or zones in the Highlands. A model of the farmer's cropping decision was developed via interviews with twenty farmers in one location or zone with homogeneous agroclimatic, socioeconomic conditions. It was then tested and revised based on interviews with another 60 farmers in the six different agroclimatic, socioeconomic zones shown in Table 15.1. These include: (1) Totonicapán, which is the geographical and indigenous commercial center of the Highlands (Smith 1975, 1976); (2) Tecpán in Chimaltenango, the department nearest the capital city; (3) San Carlos Sija, a high-altitude region of large farmers with strong Ladino (that is, Spanish) heritage; (4) the Xela Valley near Quezaltenango, the Ladino commercial center of the highlands (Smith 1975); (5) Almolonga, an irrigated valley in Quezaltenango; and (6) Llanos de Pinal, an area of rain-fed vegetables, also in Quezaltenango. Some of the features that distinguish the zones one from another are shown in Table 15.1 and include altitude, average cultivated farm size, crop mix, type of off-farm labor available, socioeconomic features of inhabitants, and percentage of the population that is rural, indigenous, and in agriculture.

The study tested the hypothesis first proposed by Gladwin and Murtaugh (1984) that some decision rules are shared by decision makers in a wide geographical region so that one decision model can be built for the region. If farmers in different agroclimatic, socioeconomic zones within the region make different choices (for example, plant different sets of crops), the diversity may be due to differences in initial agroclimatic, socioeconomic conditions rather than differences in farmers' decision rules. In short, farmers in a region may think the same but end up growing different sets of crops in different locations in the region because the agroclimatic, socioeconomic conditions within the region are so location-specific.

The main subroutine of the cropping decision model, described in more detail elsewhere (Gladwin 1980, 1983a), is shown in Fig. 15.2 along with the results of testing it on cropping choice data gathered from another 118 farmers in the six zones. As in the previous example, the model tests or processes data from each farmer independently.

The farmer's cropping decision is a two-stage choice process. In

TABLE 15.1
Features of the Zones

Zones	Altitude	Average amount of cultivated land	Crop Mix	Type of off-farm labor available, socioeconomic features	% population rural (1973)	% population indigenous (1973)	% population in agriculture (1973)	% farmers for whom model predicts *every* crop in crop mix	% crops for which model predicts correctly
1. Totonicapán	8,100–8,800 ft	0.50 ha (0.77 mz) (12.3 cdas^a)	Corn^c, wheat, some fruit trees	Indigenous weaving, furniture making, trading in center of indigenous marketing system	83.7%	95.32%	22.43%	95%	97.5%
2. Tecpán, Patzun Patzicia, Santa Cruz Balanya, Chimaltenango	6,500–7,800 ft	2.47 ha (3.63 mz) (21.79 cdas^b)	Corn, wheat, cabbage, peas, cauliflower, potatoes	Full-time farmers, female artisans; good access to export vegetable market	n.a.	n.a.	n.a.	69.2	94.2
3. a) San Carlos Sija b) S. Francisco Quezaltenango	8,700–9,100 ft	2.23 ha (3.17 mz) (50.68 cdas^a)	Corn, wheat, potatoes	a) Mostly full-time Ladino farmers, female farmers, some seasonal migration to coastal plantations b) Indigenous farmers also traders	89.2 / 77.9	31.3 / 99.5	88.2 / 41.3	85	94.1 / —

4. Valle de Xela (Olintepeque, Cajolá, S. Miguel Siguilá, San Juan Ostuncalco, La Esperanza)	7,500–8,100 ft	1.82 ha (2.58 mz) (41.34 cdas[a])	Corn, wheat, some fruit trees	Some commerce; good access to off-farm labor markets in city of Quezaltenango	72.7	87.2	74.15	83	96.3
5. Almolonga, Quezaltenango	7,100–8,100 ft	0.36 ha (0.52 mz) (8.26 cdas[a])	Corn, irrigated potatoes, irrigated vegetables	Distribution of vegetables to both home and export markets, highly developed by Almolongenans	13.4	98.5	66.8	90	97.0
6. Llanos de Pinal, Quezaltenango	7,500–8,100 ft	1.10 ha (1.56 mz) (25.01 cdas[a])	Corn, wheat, *rainfed* vegetables	Male construction work and female trading of vegetables in Quezaltenango	n.a.	n.a.	n.a.	95	99.3

[a] 16 cuerdas (cdas) = 1 manzana (mz); 1 manzana = 0.69 hectares (ha)
[b] 6 cuerdas = 1 manzana.
[c] Corn in all the zones means corn and beans interplanted.

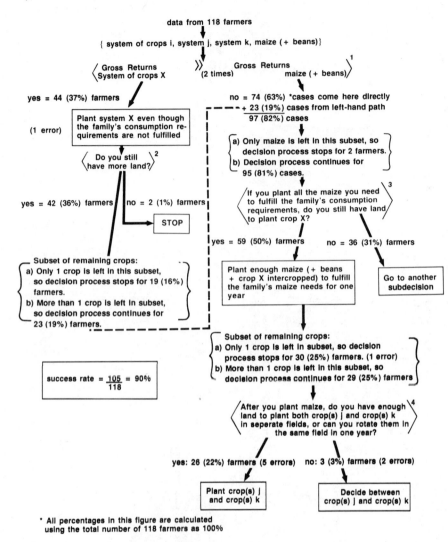

Fig. 15.2. Stage 2 results in six zones of the Altiplano, Guatemala. Source: Gladwin 1983a: 153.

stage 1, he or she first narrows down the complete set of possible crops to a feasible subset that satisfies minimal conditions. For example, given eight to ten different crops, a farmer may rapidly, often unconsciously, not consider (or eliminate) vegetables because of a lack of irrigation. He or she might not consider planting potatoes because he or she does not know how to plant them or apply pesticides. Or he or she might not even think of growing coffee because the land is at too high an altitude to grow coffee. In addition to constraints of altitude, water, and knowledge, stage 1 criteria also include time, capital, and market demand constraints. With the smaller subset of feasible crops that emerges from this stage (called "elimination-by-aspects" by Tversky 1972), the farmer proceeds to stage 2, the hard-core part of the decision process.

Stage 2 models the process by which the farmer chooses to plant the crops that pass stage 1 constraints. If the farmer has a lot of land, stage 2 is a simple decision process; all the crops that pass stage 1 will be planted. If, however, the farmer does not own or operate much land, the crops that pass stage 1 constraints compete for the little land there is, and the decision process and model become more complicated.

Criterion 1 proposes that farmers give first priority to crops or systems of crops that are at least two times as profitable as maize, the main consumption crop. Each alternative cropping system is compared with maize because, as the farmers testify, "maize is first." (In the Highlands, people do not feel comfortable sleeping without at least a six-month supply of maize stored above their heads on rafters.) Usually, maize is intercropped with beans; for brevity, hereafter I will refer only to maize. A system of crops is also defined here as a set of crops that is harvested on the same field in one year (for example, a first harvest of wheat and a second harvest of peas, or two harvests per year of potatoes, or three harvests per year of vegetables).

The very profitable crops, which may be up to five times as profitable as maize, are then "sent down" the left-hand branch of the tree. Of the 118 test farmers, only 44 (37 percent) have a crop (or system of crops) that is twice as profitable as maize. Data from these farmers pass to the outcome "Plant that crop even though you may not fulfill the family's consumption needs for maize." Farmers thus consider only a handful of cash crops so profitable that they will be planted before maize. These cash crops require irrigation, which exists in Almolonga, or special soil/climate conditions marked by sandy soils and an afternoon cloud cover, such as occurs in Llanos de Pinal. The results show that one crop per year of rain-fed vegetables, potatoes, or wheat is not profitable enough to be planted first, before maize; they are therefore sent down the right-hand path to criterion 3. If the farmer still operates more land after planting the very profitable crop 1 (criterion 2), the model sends him or her to the consumption criterion 3 on the right-hand branch of the tree. Here the farmer is asked if he or she has enough land to plant the not-so-profitable cash crop(s) after enough maize has been planted to meet the family's consumption requirements. If there is enough land, the outcome below criterion 3 predicts that maize will be planted first, before the decision of how many cash crops will be planted.

Ninety-seven farmers proceed to the decision process on the right-hand branch; 74 go directly to criterion 3 because they do not have a crop that passes stage 1 constraints and is twice as profitable as maize. Twenty-three cases come from the left-hand path because they have more land left after planting the twice-as-profitable-as-maize crop, and have two or more crops left in their feasible subset from stage 1. At this point the decision process stops for two farmers because maize is the only crop left in the feasible subset.

Of the 95 remaining farmers, 59 (50 percent) pass the consumption constraint. They have the land to plant enough maize to fulfill their family's consumption requirement and one or more cash crops. After planting enough maize to satisfy their consumption needs between harvests, these farmers allocate their remaining fields to the cash crops that remain in their feasible subsets. For 30 of the 59 farmers, only one cash crop is left in the feasible subset at this point. The remaining farmers have two or more cash crops still in the feasible subset, so their decision process continues on to the diversification criterion 4.

The latter diversification decision between two or more cash crops is simple if the farmer has enough land to plant both crops. If there is not enough land and the farmer cannot rotate the crops within the year, then he or she must decide between them by trading off the profitability and risk of the cash crops, the model of which is presented elsewhere (Gladwin 1980). Results show that 26 of the 29 farmers with two feasible cash crops manage to squeeze out the land required to grow both crops; or the climate and altitude is such that they can rotate the two crops on the same field within the year, as occurs in Llanos de Pinal and Tecpán.

Thirty-six of the 95 farmers on the right-hand branch of the tree fail the consumption criterion: they do not have enough land to be self-sufficient in maize and plant a cash crop. Their data are therefore sent to another subroutine presented elsewhere (Gladwin 1983a), which tells them to plant only maize unless certain conditions are met: if cash crops can be interplanted or multicropped with maize, if land can be rented for the cash crop, if special agroclimatic conditions limit the production of maize on all farmers' fields, and if the farmer needs cash badly. In those cases, the farmer will plant the cash crop, even though he or she will then not be self-sufficient in maize, unless some other conditions are met: he or she cannot risk depending on the marketplace to buy maize, he or she does not have the capital to buy maize in the marketplace when it is needed, or it is unprofitable to grow and sell a cash crop and buy maize in the marketplace. Three-quarters of these test cases end up planting a cash crop, even though it means sacrificing self-sufficiency in maize.

The decision model in Fig. 15.2 has a 90 percent success rate; that is, the model successfully predicts what crops 105 of 118 farmers in the test sample plant across the region as a whole. The results in each of the six zones are shown in the last two columns of Table 15.1. They show that the success rate ranges from 69 to 95 percent in the different zones; that is, the model predicts every crop in the crop mix for 69 percent of the farmers in Tecpán, but for 95 percent of the farmers in Totonicapán and Llanos de Pinal. A chi-square test shows that these differences are not significant so that the assumption of one decision model for the region is not rejected.

Implications

Because the results consist of data collected over a region rather than only a village, they have policy implications. Politicians and advisers who just look at simple, short-run profit ratios to conclude that "maize is not the right crop for the Highlands" do not acknowledge that farmers are the real experts at what they should do. Farmers know all the reasons why they should plant maize. In the subregions sampled, 60 percent of the farmers plant a cash crop only if they can first meet their consumption needs for maize, because dependence on the marketplace for a subsistence crop is a very risky thing (for reasons shown in the chapter above on markets), especially since maize in the Guatemalan Highlands is eaten three times a day, often alone.

The anthropological approach is to recognize that farmers are the real experts in making cropping decisions. Their own "expert systems" (which is another name for decision trees in the field of artificial intelligence) can be used by policy planners to help farmers diversify their cropping strategies. Because we know they will plant maize first, one diversification strategy is to increase maize yields so that more cash crops can be planted after maize. This should prove to be the most effective diversification strategy. Another strategy is to introduce irrigation into more subregions so that more twice-as-profitable-as-maize crops can be planted. Another diversification strategy taken from this model is intercropping or multiple cropping with maize. All these diversification strategies can be encouraged as workable improvements to the farmers' situation because they are based on results from the model of the farmers' decision process.

Quantitative and Qualitative Data in Economics and Anthropology

The conventional wisdom is that anthropology is a qualitative, inductive field and that economics is a quantitative, deductive field of study. Certainly economists and especially econometricians are concerned with model building via the deductive method, as well as model testing via econometric (statistical) methods. A quick glance at an economics or agricultural economics journal (for example, *American Economic Review*, or *American Journal of Agricultural Economics*) will convince the reader of this point. On the other hand, top anthropological journals like *American Ethnologist* rarely contain mathematical formulas or statistical tests but do contain plenty of what anthropologists call "ethnographic observations," that is, a report of the ethnographer's observations and intuitions about the society observed—qualitative data.

However, we can point to anthropological studies using formal methods (for example, Plattner 1975). These are of two types. Some use the usual statistical techniques applicable to quantitative data, such as standard statistical tests (Gladwin and Zabawa 1984, 1986) and multiple regression analysis (Burton and White 1984; C. Gladwin 1975, 1979; Plattner 1975). Others use more sophisticated (and more interesting) techniques designed especially for the qualitative data that are easier to gather and often more reliable in Third World settings. These techniques include triads tests, nonparametric statistics (Ember 1982); Guttman scaling (Shapiro 1975); multidimensional scaling and cluster analysis (Shepard, Romney, and Nerlove 1972); entailment analysis (Burton and Romney 1975; Burton, Brudner, and White 1977; D'Andrade 1976); computer simulations (H. Gladwin 1975, Plattner 1984); and of course decision trees, tables, and rules (Gladwin 1975, 1980; Lave, Stepick, and Sailer 1977; Mukhopadhyay 1984; Schoepfle, Burton, and Morgan 1984; Young 1980, 1981).

At the same time that many anthropologists are using more quantitative models and testing procedures, economists—especially those in the fields of rural and agricultural development—are finding that sophisticated, aesthetically pleasing models and quantitative tests do not allow them to represent the complexities of the development (or underdevelopment) process. These economists fall into two camps. In one camp are those who provide powerful logical arguments to the literature, but no more rigorous tests than descriptive statistics allow (Eicher 1982, 1986; Johnston 1966, 1986; Johnston and Kilby 1975; deJanvry 1981). These development economists are among the most read and cited in the field of agricultural economics (D. Adams 1985). Johnston's "unimodal strategy" of economic development, for example, is being read and cited more and more (Johnston and Kilby 1975). His argument for a broad-based, small-holder strategy of development rests, however, only on straightforward, sensible propositions about demographics, linkages between the agricultural and nonagricultural sectors (manufacturing, service), and the scarcity of capital and foreign exchange typical of Third World countries. Aside from simple calculations about the growth in labor demand in the nonagricultural sectors needed to offset population increases in the agricultural sector, there is no mathematical sophistication to his powerful analysis.

In the other camp are those who argue for a return to simple methods and interdisciplinary studies that would erase the boundaries between social and biological disciplines (Hildebrand 1981). This camp would train a social scientist who would rely more on untested "ethnographic observation" than on statistical results or fancy mathematical models. The diffusion of enthusiasm for the "farming systems" approach to agricultural research and extension and its applicability to Third World development shows how forceful such a "back to the basics" approach can be.

Once again I ask, Are these the exceptions that prove the rule? Obviously, I think not.

Theoretical Eclecticism in Economics and Anthropology

Anthropology is well known as a discipline that respects no boundaries and borrows from every theoretical field. Economics is equally well known, in the United States, as a discipline with a rigidly defined (and powerful) theoretical paradigm. That anthropologists are eclectic is verified by the works of the famous ethnographers like Margaret Mead and Malinowski: Their goals are to describe the culture in its entirety and predict its impact on individual behavior within the culture. The training of a cultural anthropologist is also broader than that of an economist, since in many departments he or she must take courses in archeology, linguistics, and biological anthropology in addition to cultural anthropology. Further, cultural anthropologists are encouraged to train in the other social sciences: psychology, linguistics, economics, and sociology. An economist, on the other hand, is rarely encouraged and usually discouraged from taking courses outside of the economics department and sticks to micro- and macroeconomics.

Recently, however, more economists are using economic tools to look at nonmarket phenomena; for example, Becker (1981) has used utility and demand theory to study marriage in the United States. The new household economics school has used standard price theory to study the extent of women's participation in the labor force (Mincer 1962), the supply of farm women's labor both on and off the U.S. farm (Huffman and Lange 1983), the value of U.S. farm women's unpaid work (Huffman 1976), time allocation decisions within the Third World household (Evenson 1978), and fertility decisions and the demand for children in the U.S. and Third World family (Nerlove 1974).

Economic anthropologists, on the other hand, have more recently begun to drop the standard ethnography filled with all kinds of facts (for example, Cohen 1967) in order to focus more on market phenomena and economic issues (Cancian 1972; Barlett 1982). In doing so, they bring to bear on these economic topics some traditional anthropological tools, such as the ethnographic in-depth interview (Spradley 1979) and participant observation, as well as some traditional anthropological concepts, such as social stratification and adaptive strategies (Barlett 1980).

One result of being an eclectic scholar who values synthesis of research findings is that anthropologists can see the insights that both the neoclassical and Marxist paradigms shed on development problems and issues. Thus, for example, anthropologist Hart (1982) and political economist Hyden (1980), both from a Marxist perspective, can urge African governments to get the engine of the capitalist mode of agricultural production fired up and encourage large-scale commercial agriculture to solve the food crisis. Other economic anthropologists can talk about the effect of policies and new technology on social stratification in a peasant community without seeing (or acknowledging) the links to the Marxist paradigm, which contrasts with the neoclassical paradigm in focusing on the differentiation rate and social stratification process within a homogeneous community.

On the other hand, economists—especially U.S. economists—have been for a long time very protective of "their" paradigm. If they're in the neoclassical paradigm, they do not tolerate even the jargon used by the "other" paradigm, never mind the presence of courses or faculty members of that persuasion in their departments. In the good economic departments (in the United States), therefore, the greatest debate of our time—that is, between the two paradigms in economics—does not go on.[4] One must give them some credit, however: They at least recognize the theoretical differences between the labor theory of value and the market theory of value, and they argue over the importance of equity versus efficiency considerations.

Lately, however, economic anthropologists have focused some of their work on this great debate between neoclassical and Marxist interpretations of economic development. In doing so, they shed light on

[4] I confine my remarks to U.S. departments because Latin American universities teach the viewpoints of both paradigms, and even Chinese universities are more tolerant of the neoclassical paradigm than are U.S. universities tolerant of the Marxist paradigm.

the theoretical differences between the paradigms, rather than unconsciously switch back and forth between them or ignore one paradigm entirely. Thus, for example, Smith (1978) distinguishes between the different dependency schools in an analysis of regional dependency in highland Guatemala; Barkin and DeWalt (1984) describe the increased production of sorghum in Mexico in light of the new internationalization of capital; Meillassoux (1978) relates kinship relations and the relations of production; Haugarud (1984) contrasts the Chayanovian and Marxist theories of the differentiation process (Chayanov 1966); and Harris (1979) rewrites anthropological theory in what he calls a "materialist" (that is, Marxist) perspective.

Example: Explaining the U.S. Farm Crisis

Some of the theoretical differences between the Marxist and neoclassical paradigms can also be seen in a study of the present U.S. farm crisis in one north Florida county, Gadsden County. The study was conducted by Robert Zabawa and myself (Gladwin and Zabawa 1984, 1986, 1987; Zabawa 1984, 1987). It traces the historical events that result in the fewer but larger farms that is the typical pattern of "industrial agriculture," as described by Barlett in an earlier chapter. This pattern is indeed the result of the processes of capital intensification, specialization, and competition described by Barlett; these changes are also called "structural change in agriculture" at the macro or national level.

As a result of these changes, only 284,000 full-time farms are now left operating in the United States as a whole, as compared to 6 million in 1935 (Cochrane 1986); and 17 percent of them were at risk of going out of business in 1986 (Gladwin and Zulauf 1989). About half of the nation's net farm income now goes to corporate "superfarms" with gross sales over $500,000; while family farms with gross sales under $40,000 are no longer making any net income from farming. And farms averaging $40,000 to $100,000 sales are now, on average, part-time farms (Zulauf 1986).

As Barlett claims in this volume, the distinguishing features of industrial agricultures are quite different from those of peasant agricultures and include increased use of complex technology, increased substitution of capital for labor, increased energy use, a tendency toward specialization and overproduction, and so on. But how did industrial agriculture evolve from peasant agriculture? How did structural change in U.S. agriculture occur?

Explanations of structural change, and the farm crisis of the 1980's, come from both the neoclassical and Marxist paradigms; understandably, they are quite different explanations. Let's review them both, for purposes of comparison. The theory behind the neoclassical paradigm focuses on consumer preferences and their aggregation into a demand function, producer preferences and their aggregation into a supply function, and the "invisible hand" of the market, which arbitrates both sets of preferences. In the 1950's and 1960's, economists Schultz (1953) and Houthakker (1967) applied these concepts to explain the presence of too many producers in U.S. agriculture, at the time called "a farm problem." They postulated that it is really economic growth that causes the problem because growth itself results in an "inelastic" demand for farm products, since people tend to spend a smaller proportion of their incomes on necessities like food as incomes rise (Engel's Law). When coupled with technological change that increases the supply of food, there is an oversupply of farm products. Prices and thus farm incomes fall, and some producers have to leave agriculture, get off-farm work, or produce exports to an expanded world market. This export-outlet strategy was pushed by U.S. policy makers starting in the 1950's and worked beautifully in the 1970's to slow the rate at which U.S. farmers were leaving agriculture, until the too-strong dollar and "export bust" of the early 1980's brought the farm crisis back in full force.

The Marxist Explanation

To explain the farm crisis, proponents of the Marxist paradigm do not talk only about oversupply, inelastic demand, and technological change, although they do mention these causal factors (deJanvry 1982). But they also focus their analysis on the resulting "unequal development" and conflict that results when some producers manage to marshal these market forces but others do not, as happens with the "technology treadmill" effect described earlier (Cochrane 1986) by Barlett. They describe what happens to a homogeneous community when some producers are able to realize their goals of maximizing profits while others are not. This unequal development, they claim, characterizes the historical development of capitalism and the accumulation of capital (deJanvry 1981). As capitalism penetrates agriculture, it transforms existing social relations in ways that result in different class and land tenure patterns. One way this is done is what deJanvry (1981: 107) calls the "farmer" or "American" road to capitalist development, whereby some peasants or small farmers are able to take advantage of market conditions, maximize their profits, and become bigger capitalist farmers, while others are forced to leave the farm and become wage laborers in industry. The result is

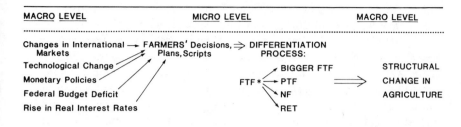

* FTF = a full-time farmer, PTF = a part-time farmer, NF = a non-farmer,
  RET = a retired farmer.

Fig. 15.3. Complementarity of ethnoscientific, structural, and materialist models of structural change in agriculture. Source: Gladwin and Zabawa 1987.

a far-reaching social differentiation among rural producers as the most enterprising and fortunate peasants . . . with more favorable endowments accumulate land and capital and hire labor power, while the majority suffer losses and are eventually converted into proletarians. The end point of this process of differentiation is that "an insignificant minority of small producers wax rich, get on in the world, turn into bourgeois, while the over-whelming majority are either utterly ruined and become wage workers or paupers, or eternally eke out an almost proletarian existence." [deJanvry 1981: 108, quoting Lenin]

How does this process occur? Marxists propose that it starts with macrolevel changes in the mode of production that cause the macrolevel changes or concentration forces seen at the left-hand side of Fig. 15.3: changes in international markets, technological change, capital intensification, changes in monetary and fiscal policies, increases in the real interest rate. These in turn affect the decision-making individual farmer in the center of the figure, who is not just a passive bystander but a reactive actor. By making plans and decisions in response to these macrolevel forces, farmers at the microlevel then go through a "differentiation process" and become either bigger farmers, smaller part-time farmers, or nonfarmers (that is, "proletarians"). In the aggregate and at the macrolevel again (at the right-hand side of the diagram), this differentiation process results in change in the structure of the agricultural sector as a whole. This change can occur slowly (as in the 1960's and 1970's) or rapidly, as it is now doing in the farm crisis of the 1980's.

A Case Study: Farmers in North Florida

An illustration of the process outlined in Fig. 15.3 is provided via an analysis of detailed farm history, decision data, and financial data over time from a homogeneous set of farmers in Gadsden County, Florida.

This farm region lost its major money crop, shade tobacco, during the mid-1970's because of changes in international markets coupled with technological change. The events that followed, and the farmers' decision processes in reaction to those changes, forced some full-time farmers to go out of business entirely and others to cut back production substantially. The farmers who remained in business either were or became larger operators, or they gradually got transformed into part-time farmers. Evidence to support this comes from a tested model of farmers' decisions to cut back production after the demise of the market for shade tobacco, and a comparison of farmers' financial positions before and after the market demise of shade tobacco.

Since 1935, Gadsden County has exhibited the usual symptoms of concentration. These include a declining number of farms and increasing average size of farm, a decreasing amount of land in farms and harvested cropland and an increasing proportion of part owners of farmland, and a highly skewed distribution of land in farms and gross sales (Zabawa 1984). The uniqueness of Gadsden was due to the presence, since 1890, of shade—or cigar-wrapper—tobacco, which accounted for 65 percent of the value of all the county's agricultural products in 1969. From 1969 to 1977, however, "shade" as a money crop disappeared because of increasing costs of production, competition from Central America, and the decline in demand for cigars. In addition, the development of a synthetic "homogenized" wrapper for cigars and the use of a plastic tip meant that a full leaf was no longer necessary to bind the cigar together. With the market decline of shade tobacco, farmers who used to have the tobacco companies as regular buyers of their product now found they had to look for new cropping strategies and in some cases completely new ways of making a living.

Individual Farmers' Responses to the Loss of Shade Tobacco

The first decision most farmers made was to cut back farm production and increase off-farm employment, shown in Fig. 15.4. Interrelated logically with this decision are subdecisions, for brevity presented elsewhere, that include the change of crop decision, the decision of how to cut back, the decision to sell land, and the decision to lease out land (Gladwin and Zabawa 1986, 1987; Zabawa 1984). In Gadsden County, data from 30 farmers were used to build the model in 1982; while data from 72 farmers (51 ex-shade producers and 21 nonshade producers) were used to test the model in 1982–83.

The model in Fig. 15.4 posits that the Gadsden County farmer, faced with the decision of whether or not to cut back production, must have at least one of the reasons to cut back specified in the decision criteria.

These include the sudden appearance of a buyer with an offer too good to refuse (criterion 1); a reason for not being able to farm all of one's land on one's own, for example, bad health, old age, or off-farm work (criterion 2); an inability to make money farming or subsidize the farm with off-farm income (criterion 3); a reason and ability to change the present cropping strategy (criteria 4 and 5); a large debt-to-asset ratio and negative feedback from a lender (criteria 7, 9, 10, 11, 12); and the decision by one or more family members to increase their off-farm work involvement (criterion 8).

Given a farmer's presence at any "cut back" command, he or she (that is, his or her data) proceed to the decision model of how to cut back, shown elsewhere. Alternative methods, ranked by the degree to which the farmer relinquishes control over the land, include: hire a manager, get a partner, cut back land usually rented in, lease (out) land, or sell land. After elimination of the first three easy ways to cut back, a farmer decides whether to sell or lease (out) land. Reasons to sell rather than lease include an inability to pay the mortgage from farm income, an immediate need for a sizable amount of capital, or a need for a change in life-style. Given any of the above reasons, farmers sell land if they consider the reasons to sell more important than the reasons to lease, and they pass constraints including clear title to land, presence of an interested buyer, and a good price offer. Farmers quit farming altogether if they sell most or all of their land. Failing one constraint, farmers pass to the subdecision to lease, which includes criteria such as presence of a renter at a good price, presence of the motivating pull of profit or push of possible loss of the tax exemption, and risk criteria. Farmers' failing to pass criteria in both subdecisions continue to search for a solution and farm the land themselves.

The models were tested on 230 cases of possible cutbacks by 72 farmers because farmers could decide to cut back more than once in the farm's history. Test cases included every time farmers actually cut back production or land use or reported that they thought about cutting back. The results are shown, for brevity, on the trees themselves; the model, including all subdecisions, correctly describes 95 percent of the choices made.

Some results show support for the neoclassical explanation of the farm crisis. Cases in which farmers cut back due to low farm incomes could be separated from cases in which other factors such as old age or bad health were important. Results in Fig. 15.4 show that 30.4 percent of the cases—some of whom are shade tobacco producers (denoted by st) and some of whom are nonshade (ns) producers—were cutback decisions because farmers could no longer farm all their land themselves

N = 230 cases of 72 farmers
{Cut Back Production, Don't Cut Back}

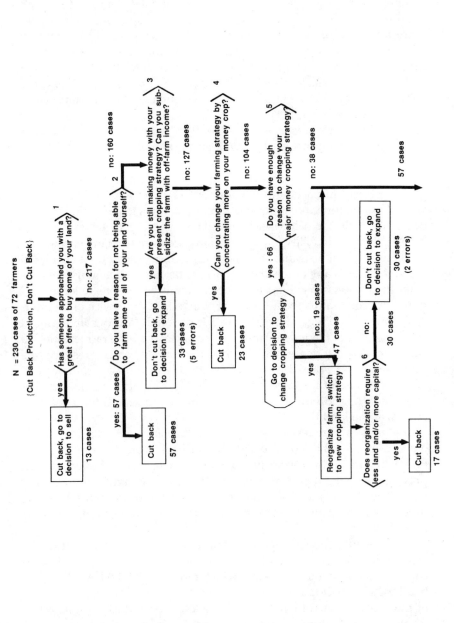

Has someone approached you with a great offer to buy some of your land? 1

yes → Cut back, go to decision to sell — 13 cases

no: 217 cases

Do you have a reason for not being able to farm some or all of your land yourself? 2

yes: 57 cases → Cut back — 57 cases

no: 160 cases

Are you still making money with your present cropping strategy? Can you subsidize the farm with off-farm income? 3

yes → Don't cut back, go to decision to expand — 33 cases (5 errors)

no: 127 cases

Can you change your farming strategy by concentrating more on your money crop? 4

yes → Cut back — 23 cases

no: 104 cases

Do you have enough reason to change your major money cropping strategy? 5

yes : 66 → Go to decision to change cropping strategy

no: 38 cases

no: 19 cases

yes — 47 cases → Reorganize farm, switch to new cropping strategy

Does reorganization require less land and/or more capital? 6

yes → Cut back — 17 cases

no: 30 cases → Don't cut back, go to decision to expand — 30 cases (2 errors)

57 cases

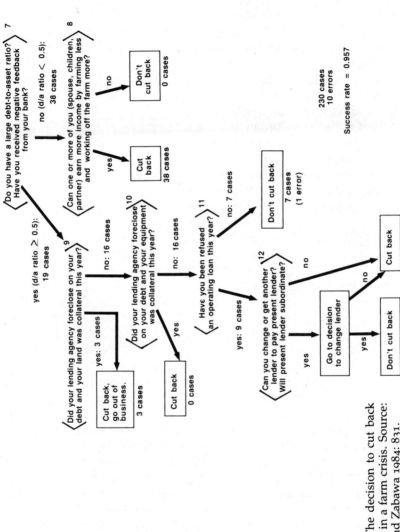

Fig. 15.4. The decision to cut back production in a farm crisis. Source: Gladwin and Zabawa 1984: 831.

because of time demands of off-farm work, old age, or bad health; or they had received a good offer from a buyer (criteria 1, 2). In more than half the cases (55 percent), however, farmers were no longer making money farming (criterion 3). To remedy this situation, farmers in 37.8 percent of the cases had to cut back as a result of change of crops or lender, or an increase in off-farm work. In another 31.8 percent of the cases, farmers chose not to cut back. Of those who did, however, more farmers were pushed out of farming by low farm incomes than by other conditions.

Although these results lend support for the Schultz and Houthakker argument (in the neoclassical paradigm) that low farm incomes are the main reason farmers quit farming, the data as a whole lend more support to the Marxist paradigm, which focuses on the differentiation process as being an inevitable by-product of the process of capitalist development or economic growth. Clearly, one result of farmers' going through the decision process described above is that the previously homogeneous set of shade producers is differentiated into four subsets of bigger full-time farmers, smaller part-time farmers, even smaller nonfarmers, and retired farmers. Supporting data are summarized in Table 15.2, which shows the change in financial position of the full-time shade producers in the period from the last year of shade production in the mid-1970's to 1982 (Gladwin and Zabawa 1984: Table 1).

As a result of their decisions to cut back production, lease (out) or sell land, 19 of the 51 shade producers became larger full-time farmers by 1982 in terms of gross sales and assets; 11 became smaller part-time farmers; 9 quit farming altogether; and 12 retired from farming. Tests of the differences between subgroup means in the mid-1970's show that farmers who remained full-time were younger than the part-timers and retired farmers; farmers who quit farming had less wealth (assets, owned acreage) than the full-timers but no differences in age, education, or debts; and part-timers had no less assets but were older than the full-timers and had smaller debts and debt-to-asset ratios. Clearly, the older farmers who became part-timers were not used (or willing) to incur the heavy debt load of the full-timers with similar assets.

Results in Table 15.2 show that the differences between the subgroups of ex-shade producers became magnified over time, as expected by proponents of the Marxist paradigm. Gross sales, net farm income, and assets of the full-time ex-shade producers were significantly greater in 1982; whereas assets and owned acreage of the part-timers did not change significantly; and assets and owned acreage of the nonfarmers (that is, the quitters and the retired farmers) decreased significantly. Debt and debt-to-asset ratios of the full-timers, however, also increased

TABLE 15.2
The Transformation of Full-Time Shade Farmers to Full-Time,
Part-Time, Nonfarm, and Retired Farmers

Shade sample (N = 51 full-timers in last year of shade)	Full-time[a] in 1982 (N = 19)	Part-time in 1982 (N = 11)	Nonfarmer in 1982 (N = 9)	Retired in 1982 (N = 12)
Gross sales in last year of shade ($)	110,868	105,818	89,374	73,667
Gross sales in 1982 ($)	295,469**[b]	31,404***	1,130***	1,395***
Net farm income, last year of shade ($)	−10,342	14,000	0	9,167
Net farm income in 1982 ($)	71,574***	2,676**	1,064	658
Total family income, last year shade ($)	−7,237	20,200	5,875	11,333
Total family income in 1982 ($)	82,606***	50,743	27,508*	658[c]
Debts in last year of shade ($)	61,741	10,909	48,333	28,583
Debts in 1982 ($)	182,921**	12,273	10,000*	22,917
Assets in last year of shade ($)	385,169	387,727	166,263	182,687
Assets in 1982 ($)	681,781*	516,727	99,000	146,713
Debt-to-asset ratio, last year shade (%)	17.9	5.2	31.9	15.0
Debt-to-asset ratio in 1982 (%)	33.6*	4.5	3.5**	7.2
Owned acreage in last year shade (ac.)	509.7	442.1	172.7	267.0
Owned acreage in 1982 (ac.)	436.7	480.5	81.9*	164.9*

SOURCE: Gladwin and Zabawa 1984: 834.

[a] We define a full-time farmer to be one who farms at least 40 hours per week year-round, a part-time farmer to be one who farms between 8 and 40 hours per week year-round, and a nonfarmer to be one who farms less than 8 hours per week year-round.

[b] T-value tests difference between means of previous rows. Significance levels of the one-sided T-test are: * > 0.05 and < 0.10, ** < 0.05, *** < 0.01.

[c] This value does not include Social Security or other retirement or health benefits.

significantly; whereas debts of the part-timers and retired farmers did not change, and those of the nonfarmers decreased significantly. These results suggest that part-time farmers' conservative credit policies were allowing them to hold onto their assets. Although full-time farmers are now larger, their debts have tripled and their debt-to-asset ratios have doubled in approximately seven years! Clearly, these results do not paint a promising picture for the survival of full-time family farmers. Rather than focus structure debates on whether small farms are more beautiful, satisfying, and soil- and energy-efficient than larger farms (Tweeten 1983), our results suggest that structure debates should focus on alternative policy prescriptions aimed at dealing with the transformation of the medium-size and large full-time farmer into a small, part-time farmer.

The case of Gadsden County, north Florida, thus sheds some light on the theoretical differences between the neoclassical and Marxist paradigms. The case study lends some support to the Schultz-Houthakker argument in the neoclassical paradigm because the decision tree results show farmers cutting back farming because of low farm incomes. These results do not disagree with those of the Marxist paradigm, however. Farmers try to maximize profit but cannot—and so the majority are differentiated out of production and the means of production. In Gadsden, the result of farmers' cutting back production is that they undergo this differentiation process, whereby a minority of the farmers remain full-time on a larger scale than before, while the majority become either part-time farmers or nonfarmers. In the aggregate and over time, this transformation of full-time farmers results in either a slow "structural change" in agriculture or a more rapid "farm crisis." In my judgment, the case of the farm crisis of the 1980's—and the gradual disappearance of U.S. full-time family farms over the last 50 years— lends more support to the Marxist than neoclassical paradigm, because only the Marxist paradigm focuses on social differentiation as a central part of the theory. Only the Marxist paradigm asks what happens to the people who try to maximize profit but cannot make it.

Research Design: Field Versus Office Research in Economics and Anthropology

In a classic monograph in economic anthropology (called *Penny Capitalism*), Sol Tax reported his conversation with an economist. Tax had just published his study after more than ten years of research on the economic behavior of a small village of Guatemalan Indians, and wanted to know what his economist friend would have done differently with this sort of data. "The considered reply was unexpected to me, yet wholly obvious. As an economist, she would not have spent years in a community of 800 people" (1953: iv). This anecdote points to a major difference between the two disciplines. Anthropologists, being fieldworkers, feel that one cannot say anything really meaningful about a society until one has lived in it and studied it for at least a year. The scale of the study is often, by necessity, small if not intimate. Economists, being "office workers," use data sets that are usually collected by others, for diverse purposes, and do not often have the intimate firsthand knowledge of the social systems they study. Some are uncomfortable with small-scale or local studies because their goal is often to deal with society-wide industries or sectors.

This difference used to be simply characterized as that between inductive (meaning fact-driven) and deductive (meaning theory-driven) research strategies (Herskovits 1952: 507). Anthropologists, with their long investment of research time in specific societies, take the "facts" as primary and look for theories to explain them. Economists, with their powerful theoretical paradigm, take the theory as given and look for facts to test it with. The saying is that, given a discrepancy between theory and facts, the anthropologists would throw out the theory and the economists would throw out the facts. This difference is exaggerated here for didactic effect. Most researchers in each field make data interact with theory in an iterative process of analysis. New theories demand new kinds of data, and new data and unexpected results call for different kinds of theory.

The real difference between the disciplines is that ethnographers go through more cycles of adapting theory to data and data to theory, since they spend more time in contact with the reality they are studying, and their goal is to approximate an insider's understanding. Economists go through fewer cycles between data and theory, are not concerned with learning how to think like a native, and pretend to attain the ideal goal of a linear research strategy. Here, in a straight-line fashion, the researcher defines a research problem, formulates a model or hypotheses to be tested in accordance to some theory, makes operational definitions to specify the model, designs a research instrument (for example, decides on a sampling strategy and designs a survey or experiment), gathers the data to test the hypotheses, analyzes the data, and draws conclusions and writes a report.

Anthropologists usually strive to understand the native's (or insider's) way of life from the native's (or insider's) point of view. Ethnography means learning from people as much as studying people (Spradley 1979). For the ethnographer, the trick is to get informants to become teachers of their "native expressions" and cultural rules so that the student ethnographer can internalize their indigenous knowledge systems (Brokensha, Warren, and Werner 1980; Brush 1980; Johnson 1974).

The ethnographic style of research critically distinguishes anthropologists from economists. Discovering the insider's view is a different species of knowledge from one that rests primarily on the outsider's view. Recently, however, for the new, modern economic anthropologist, use of the ethnographic research method is not enough; it is

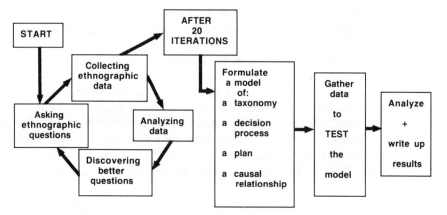

Fig. 15.5. Combining the ethnographic research cycle and the linear hypothesis-testing process.

merely a necessary but not sufficient condition for good research. These days, good research design is summarized by Fig. 15.5, in which the ethnographer cycles through the ethnographic discovery process for several iterations and then goes on to the linear research plan of formulating a model, gathering data to test the model while still in the field, analyzing the data, and writing up the results. Decision tree models, for example, are usually built after interviews with 25-plus informants during nine or more months; they are put together in the field and then tested via a special questionnaire during interviews with another sample of 30 or more informants. Combining both the ethnographic research cycle and the linear hypothesis-testing sequence takes time, of course; and usually the ethnographic part of the process takes nine months to two years, while the model-testing part takes three to six months. The new economic anthropologist thus needs more fieldwork time than before; quick-and-dirty research methods such as the rapid reconnaissance survey often used in farming systems projects (Hildebrand 1981) will not suffice! He or she also needs theory courses in economics and statistics before going to the field, because both models and survey instruments to test the models must be formulated in the field, not back home at the university. Data analysis and write-up may be done back home; but as microcomputers become smaller and cheaper, it will not be long before these two steps will also be done under fieldwork conditions. Naturally, the new economic anthropologist is both numerate and literate on the microcomputer.

To the reader, it may seem as if quite a bit is expected from the new economic anthropologist. He or she should know economics, statistics, and computers, as well as anthropological theory, and then spend years in fieldwork combining ethnographic research with the linear hypothesis-testing process. Not only should the new economic anthropologist know and do all these things, but so should the new anthropological economist. And who is that individual? He or she is the new economist who is tired of the unrealistic behavioral assumptions that abound in the economics literature, who is wary of the value judgments that underlie the neoclassical paradigm, and who is ready for a socioeconomic paradigm (McCloskey 1985) that can offer an alternative to both neoclassical and Marxist paradigms for the study of economic behavior.[5] In addition, the new anthropological economist is willing to spend one to two years in fieldwork, using the ethnographic research cycle before modeling economic behavior. As a result, when this individual meets the new economic anthropologist at the Norfolk Bar in Nairobi, they are indistinguishable.

[5] "Socioeconomics" seeks to draw on a variety of social sciences to formulate alternate paradigms for the study of economic behavior to that of neoclassical economics. Socioeconomics propositions contain at least one independent variable of economics and one of another social science. It assumes that competition is an embedded subsystem, part of society, polity, and culture, and not a self-contained system. It assumes that individual choices are shaped by people's values, emotions, social bonds, and knowledge. For a copy of "Socio-Economic Notes," write Arvil V. Adams, George Washington University, 2020 K Street, NW, Suite 240, Washington, D.C., 20006.

Reference Matter

References Cited

Preface

Belshaw, Cyril
  1965 *Traditional Exchange and Modern Markets*. Englewood Cliffs, N.J.: Prentice-Hall.
Bennett, John, & John Bowen (eds.)
  1988 *Power and Autonomy: Anthropological Studies and Critiques of Development*. Monographs in Economic Anthropology, no. 5. Lanham, Md.: University Press of America, for the Society for Economic Anthropology.
Cancian, Frank
  1965 *Economics and Prestige in a Maya Community*. Stanford, Calif.: Stanford University Press.
Dalton, George
  1967 *Tribal and Peasant Economies: Readings in Economic Anthropology*. Garden City, N.Y.: Natural History Press.
Greenfield, Sidney, & Arnold Strickon (eds.)
  1986 *Entrepreneurship and Social Change*. Monographs in Economic Anthropology, no. 2. Lanham, Md.: University Press of America, for the Society for Economic Anthropology.
Herskovits, Melville
  1952 *Economic Anthropology*. New York: Knopf.
LeClair, Edward, & Harold K. Schneider
  1968 *Economic Anthropology: Readings in Theory and Analysis*. New York: Holt, Rinehart & Winston.
Maclachlan, Morgan
  1987 *Household Economies and Their Transformations*. Monographs in Economic Anthropology, no. 3. Lanham, Md.: University Press of America, for the Society for Economic Anthropology.
Nash, Manning
  1966 *Primitive and Peasant Economic Systems*. San Francisco: Chandler.
Ortiz, Sutti
  1983 *Economic Anthropology: Topics and Theories*. Monographs in Economic Anthropology, no. 1. Lanham, Md.: University Press of America, for the Society for Economic Anthropology.
Plattner, Stuart
  1975 "Rural Market Networks." *Scientific American* 232: 66–79.

1985   *Markets and Marketing*. Monographs in Economic Anthropology, no. 4. Lanham, Md.: University Press of America, for the Society for Economic Anthropology.

Sahlins, Marshall
1972   *Stone-Age Economics*. Chicago: Aldine.
1968   *Tribesmen*. Englewood Cliffs, N.J.: Prentice-Hall.

Schneider, Harold
1974   *Economic Man*. New York: Free Press.

Service, Elman
1966   *The Hunters*. Englewood Cliffs, N.J.: Prentice-Hall.

Tax, Sol
1953   *Penny Capitalism*. Smithsonian Institute of Social Anthropology Publication, no. 16. Washington, D.C.: U.S. Government Printing Office.

Wolf, Eric
1966   *Peasants*. Englewood Cliffs, N.J.: Prentice-Hall.

Plattner: Introduction

Barlett, Peggy (ed.)
1980   *Agricultural Decision Making*. New York: Academic Press.

Bernard, H. Russell
1988   *Research Methods in Cultural Anthropology*. New York: Sage.

Cancian, Frank
1966   "Maximization: Norm, Strategy, and Theory." *American Anthropologist* 68: 465–70.

Dalton, George
1961   "Economic Theory and Primitive Society." *American Anthropologist* 63: 1–25.
1968   *Primitive, Archaic, and Modern Economies: Essays of Karl Polanyi*, edited by G. Dalton. New York: Anchor.

Donham, Donald
Forthcoming *History, Power, Ideology: Central Issues in Marxism and Anthropology*. Cambridge: Cambridge University Press.

Frank, Andre Gunder
1968   *Capitalism and Underdevelopment in Latin America*. New York: Monthly Review Press.

Friedman, Milton
1953   *Essays in Positive Economics*. Chicago: University of Chicago Press.

Geertz, Clifford
1984   "Distinguished Lecture: Anti Anti-Relativism." *American Anthropologist* 66: 263–78.

Granovetter, Mark
1985   "Economic Action and Social Structure: The Problem of Embeddedness." *American Journal of Sociology* 91: 481–510.

Gudeman, Stephen
1986   *Economics as Culture: Models and Metaphors of Livelihood*. New York: Methuen.

Healey, Christopher
1984   "Trade and Sociability: Balanced Reciprocity as Generosity in the New Guinea Highlands." *American Ethnologist* 11: 42–60.

LaBarre, Weston
  1962 *They Shall Take Up Serpents*. Minneapolis: University of Minnesota Press.
LeClair, Edward, & Harold K. Schneider
  1968 *Economic Anthropology: Readings in Theory and Analysis*. New York: Holt, Rinehart & Winston.
Marx, Karl
  1976 *Capital*. Middlesex, England: Penguin.
Myerhoff, Barbara
  1978 *Number Our Days*. New York: Simon & Schuster.
Plattner, Stuart
  1974 "Formal Models and Formalist Economic Anthropology: The Problem of Maximization." *Reviews in Anthropology* 1: 572–82.
Polanyi, Karl
  1957 "The Economy as Instituted Process." In *Trade and Market in the Early Empires*, edited by K. Polanyi, C. W. Arensberg, and H. W. Pearson. New York: Free Press.
Robbins, Lionel
  1932 "The Subject Matter of Economics." In *An Essay on the Nature and Significance of Economic Science*. London: Macmillan. (Reprinted in LeClair & Schneider 1968.)
Sahlins, Marshall
  1972 *Stone-age Economics*. Chicago: Aldine.
Samuelson, Paul
  1963 "Comment to 'Assumptions in Economic Theory.'" *American Economic Association Papers and Proceedings* 53: 231–36.
Samuelson, Paul, & William Nordhaus
  1985 *Economics*. 12th Edition. New York: McGraw-Hill.
Spiro, Melford
  1986 "Cultural Relativism and the Future of Anthropology." *Cultural Anthropology* 1: 259–86.
Stack, Carol
  1974 *All Our Kin*. New York: Harper & Row.
Wallerstein, Immanuel
  1974 *The Modern World System*. New York: Academic Press.
Wolf, Eric
  1982 *Europe and the People Without History*. Berkeley: University of California Press.

Cashdan: Hunters and Gatherers

Bahuchet, S., & H. Guillaume
  1982 "Aka-Farmer Relations in the Northwest Congo Basin." In *Politics and History in Band Societies*, edited by E. Leacock and R. B. Lee. Cambridge: Cambridge University Press.
Binford, L. R.
  1978 *Nunamiut Ethnoarcheology*. New York: Academic Press.
  1980 "Willow Smoke and Dogs' Tails: Hunter-Gatherer Settlement Systems and Archaeological Site Formation." *American Antiquity* 45: 4–20.
Birdsell, J. B.
  1953 "Some Environmental and Cultural Factors Influencing the Structuring of Australian Aboriginal Populations." *American Naturalist* 87: 169–207.

432   *References Cited*

Brown, J.
  1970   "A Note on the Division of Labor by Sex." *American Anthropologist* 72:
          1074–78.
Cashdan, E.
  1980   "Egalitarianism Among Hunters and Gatherers." *American Anthropolo-
          gist* 82: 116–20.
  1984   "G//ana Territorial Organization." *Human Ecology* 12: 443–63.
  1986   "Competition Between Foragers and Food Producers on the Botletli
          River, Botswana." *Africa* 56: 299–317.
Coombs, H. C., B. Dexter, & L. Hiatt
  1982   "The Outstation Movement in Aboriginal Australia." In *Politics and His-
          tory in Band Societies,* edited by E. Leacock and R. B. Lee, Cambridge:
          Cambridge University Press.
Denbow, J. R.
  1984   "Prehistoric Herders and Foragers of the Kalahari: The Evidence for
          1500 Years of Interaction." In *Past and Present in Hunter Gatherer Studies,*
          edited by C. Schrire, 175–93. Orlando, Fla.: Academic Press.
Draper, P.
  Forthcoming   "!Kung Work: A Southern Perspective."
Dyson-Hudson, R., & E. A. Smith
  1978   "Human Territoriality: An Ecological Reassessment." *American Anthro-
          pologist* 80: 21–41.
Ember, C.
  1978   "Myths About Hunter-Gatherers." *Ethnology* 17: 439–48.
Feit, H. A.
  1982   "The Future of Hunters Within Nation-States: Anthropology and the
          James Bay Cree." In *Politics and History in Band Societies,* edited by
          E. Leacock and R. B. Lee. Cambridge: Cambridge University Press.
Gould, R.
  1981   "Comparative Ecology of Food-Sharing in Australia and Northwest
          California." In *Omnivorous Primates: Gathering and Hunting in Human
          Evolution,* edited by R. Harding and G. Teleki. New York: Columbia
          University Press.
Harako, R.
  1981   "The Cultural Ecology of Hunting Behavior Among Mbuti Pygmies in
          the Ituri Forest, Zaire." In *Omnivorous Primates: Gathering and Hunting
          in Human Evolution,* edited by R. Harding and G. Teleki. New York:
          Columbia University Press.
Harpending, H., & B. Davis
  1977   "Some Implications for Hunter-Gatherer Ecology Derived from the
          Spatial Structure of Resources." *World Archaeology* 8: 275–86.
Hart, J. A.
  1978   "From Subsistence to Market: A Case Study of the Mbuti Net Hunters."
          Human Ecology 6: 325–53.
Hart, T. B., & J. A. Hart
  1986   "The Ecological Basis of Hunter-Gatherer Subsistence in African Rain
          Forests: The Mbuti of Eastern Zaire." *Human Ecology* 14: 29–55.
Hawkes, K., K. Hill, & J. O'Connell
  1982   "Why Hunters Gather: Optimal Foraging and the Aché of Eastern Para-
          guay." *American Ethnologist* 9: 379–98.

Heinz, H. J.
1972 "Territoriality Among the Bushmen in General and the !Ko in Particular." *Anthropos* 67: 405–16.
Helm, J.
1972 "The Dogrib Indians." In *Hunters and Gatherers Today*, edited by M. G. Bicchieri. New York: Holt, Rinehart & Winston.
Hill, K., H. Kaplan, K. Hawkes, & A. M. Hurtado.
1985 "Men's Time Allocation to Subsistence Work Among the Aché of Eastern Paraguay." *Human Ecology* 13: 29–48.
Hitchcock, R. K.
1982 "Patterns of Sedentism Among the Basarwa of Eastern Botswana." In *Politics and History in Band Societies*, edited by E. Leacock and R. B. Lee. Cambridge: Cambridge University Press.
Hurtado, A. M., K. Hawkes, K. Hill, & H. Kaplan
1985 "Female Subsistence Strategies Among Aché Hunter-Gatherers of Eastern Paraguay." *Human Ecology* 13: 1–28.
Jochim, M. A.
1981 *Strategies for Survival: Cultural Behavior in an Ecological Context*. New York: Academic Press.
Kaplan, H., & K. Hill
1985 "Food Sharing Among Aché Foragers: Tests of Explanatory Hypotheses." *Current Anthropology* 26: 223–46.
Keene, A. S.
1981 "Optimal Foraging in a Nonmarginal Environment: A Model of Prehistoric Subsistence Strategies in Michigan." In *Hunter-Gatherer Foraging Strategies*, edited by B. Winterhalder and E. A. Smith. Chicago: University of Chicago Press.
Lee, R. B.
1968 "What Hunters Do for a Living, Or How to Make Out on Scarce Resources." In *Man the Hunter*, edited by R. B. Lee and I. DeVore. Chicago: Aldine.
1979 *The !Kung San: Men, Women, and Work in a Foraging Society*. Cambridge: Cambridge University Press.
Lee, R. B., & I. DeVore (eds.)
1968 *Man the Hunter*. Chicago: Aldine.
MacArthur, R. H., & E. R. Pianka
1966 "On the Optimal Use of a Patchy Environment." *American Naturalist* 100: 603–09.
Marshall, L.
1961 "Sharing, Talking and Giving: Relief of Social Tensions Among !Kung Bushmen." *Africa* 31: 231–49.
Martin, M. K., & B. Voorhies
1975 *Female of the Species*. New York: Columbia University Press.
Meggitt, M. J.
1962 *Desert People: A Study of the Walbiri Aborigines of Central Australia*. Chicago: University of Chicago Press.
Miller, S.
1969 "Contacts Between the Later Stone Age and the Early Iron Age in Southern Central Africa." *Azania* 4: 81–90.

O'Connell, J., & K. Hawkes
  1981 "Alyawara Plant Use and Optimal Foraging Theory." In *Hunter-Gatherer Foraging Strategies: Ethnographic and Archaeological Analyses*, edited by B. Winterhalder and E. A. Smith. Chicago: University of Chicago Press.
Peterson, J. T.
  1978 "Hunter-Gatherer Farmer Exchange." *American Anthropologist* 80: 335–51.
  1984 "Cash, Consumerism, and Savings: Economic Change Among the Agta Foragers of Luzon, Philippines." *Research in Economic Anthropology* 6: 53–73.
Peterson, N.
  1972 "Totemism Yesterday: Sentiment and Local Organization Among the Australian Aborigines." *Man* 7: 12–32.
  1982 "Aboriginal Land Rights in the Northern Territory of Australia." In *Politics and History in Band Societies*, edited by E. Leacock and R. B. Lee. Cambridge: Cambridge University Press.
Reidhead, Van A.
  1980 "The Economics of Subsistence Change: Test of an Optimization Model." In *Modeling Change in Prehistoric Subsistence Economies*, edited by T. Earle and A. Christenson. New York: Academic Press.
Rogers, E. S.
  1969 "Band Organization Among the Indians of Eastern Subarctic Canada." In *Contributions to Anthropology: Band Societies*, edited by D. Damas. Ottawa: Queen's Printer.
Seligmann, C. C., & B. Z. Seligmann
  1911 *The Veddas*. Cambridge: Cambridge University Press.
Sharp, L.
  1952 "Steel Axes for Stone Age Australians." *Human Organization* 11: 17–22.
Silberbauer, G. B.
  1981 *Hunter and Habitat in the Central Kalahari Desert*. Cambridge: Cambridge University Press.
Smith, E. A.
  1979 "Human Adaptation and Energetic Efficiency." *Human Ecology* 7: 53–74.
Steward, J.
  1938 *Basin-Plateau Aboriginal Sociopolitical Groups*. Washington, D.C.: Smithsonian Institute, BAE Bull. 120.
Tanaka, J.
  1980 *The San Hunter-Gatherers of the Kalahari: A Study in Ecological Anthropology*. (Trans. by D. Hughes.) Tokyo: University of Tokyo Press.
Truswell, A. S., & J. Hansen
  1976 "Medical Research Among the !Kung." In *Kalahari Hunter Gatherers*, edited by R. B. Lee and I. DeVore. Cambridge, Mass.: Harvard University Press.
Turnbull, C. M.
  1961 *The Forest People*. New York: Simon and Schuster.
Wiessner, P.
  1982 "Risk, Reciprocity and Social Influences on !Kung San Economics." In *Politics and History in Band Societies*, edited by E. Leacock and R. B. Lee. Cambridge: Cambridge University Press.

Wilmsen, E. N.
   1979 "Diet and Fertility Among Kalahari Bushmen." Boston University, African Studies Center. Working papers, no. 14.
Winterhalder, B.
   1981 "Foraging Strategies in the Boreal Forest: An Analysis of Cree Hunting and Gathering." In *Hunter-Gatherer Foraging Strategies*, edited by B. Winterhalder and E. A. Smith. Chicago: University of Chicago Press.
Woodburn, J.
   1968 "Stability and Flexibility in Hadza Residential Groupings." In *Man the Hunter*, edited by R. B. Lee and I. DeVore. Chicago: Aldine.
Yellen, J. E., & H. Harpending
   1972 "Hunter-Gatherer Populations and Archaeological Inference." *World Archaeology* 4: 244–53.

Johnson: Horticulturalists

Anderson, Edgar
   1954 *Plants, Man, and Life*. London: Andrew Melrose.
Arvelo-Jimenez, N.
   1984 "The Political Feasibility of Tribal Autonomy in Amazonia." Ms. Caracas: Instituto Venezolano de Investigaciones Cientificas.
Austen, L.
   1945 "Cultural Changes on Kiriwina." *Oceania* 16: 15–60.
Baksh, M.
   1985 "Faunal Food as a 'Limiting Factor' on Amazonian Cultural Behavior: A Machiguenga Example." *Research in Economic Anthropology* 7: 145–75.
Berlin, E., & E. Markell
   1977 "An Assessment of the Nutritional and Health Status of an Aguaruna Jivaro Community, Amazonas, Peru." *Ecology of Food and Nutrition* 6: 69–81.
Biocca, E.
   1971 *Yanoama: The Narrative of a White Girl Kidnapped by Amazon Indians*. New York: Dutton.
Bohannan, P.
   1955 "Some Principles of Exchange and Investment Among the Tiv." *American Anthropologist* 57: 60–70.
Burton, R.
   1975 "Why Do the Trobriands Have Chiefs?" *Man* 10: 544–58.
Carneiro, R.
   1960 "Slash-and-Burn Agriculture: A Closer Look at its Implications for Settlement Patterns." In *Men and Culture*, edited by A. Wallace. Philadelphia: University of Pennsylvania Press.
Chagnon, N.
   1980 "Highland New Guinea Models in the South American Lowlands." In *Studies in Hunting and Fishing in the Neotropics, Working Papers on South American Indians*, no. 2, edited by R. Hames. Bennington, Vt.: Bennington College.
   1983 *Yanomamo: The Fierce People*. 3d Edition. New York: Holt, Rinehart & Winston.

Clarke, W.
  1982 "Comment on 'Individual or Group Advantage?' J. Peoples." *Current Anthropology* 23: 301.
Cohen, M.
  1977 *The Food Crisis in Prehistory.* New Haven: Yale University Press.
Conklin, H.
  1957 "Hanunoo Agriculture." FAO Forestry Development Paper No. 12. Rome: Food and Agriculture Organization of the United Nations.
Geertz, C.
  1963 *Agricultural Involution.* Berkeley: University of California Press.
Gubser, N.
  1965 *The Nunamiut Eskimos.* New Haven: Yale University Press.
Gulliver, P.
  1951 *A Preliminary Survey of the Turkana.* Kenya: Colonial Social Science Research Council.
Hardesty, Donald L.
  1977 *Ecological Anthropology.* New York: John Wiley & Sons.
Harris, M.
  1977 *Cannibals and Kings.* New York: Random House.
Herskovits, M.
  1952 *Economic Anthropology.* New York: Norton.
Holmberg, A.
  1969 *Nomads of the Long Bow.* New York: Natural History Press.
Johnson, A.
  1983 "Machiguenga Gardens." In *Adaptive Responses of Native Amazonians,* edited by R. Hames and W. Vickers. New York: Academic Press.
Johnson, A., & M. Baksh
  1987 "Ecological and Structural Influences on the Proportions of Wild Foods in the Diets of Two Machiguenga Communities." In *Food and Evolution,* edited by M. Harris and E. Ross. Philadelphia: Temple University Press.
Johnson, A., & C. Behrens
  1982 "Nutritional Criteria in Machiguenga Food Production Decisions: A Linear Programming Analysis." *Human Ecology* 10: 167–89.
Johnson, A., & T. Earle
  1987 *The Evolution of Human Societies: From Forager Group to Agrarian State.* Stanford: Stanford University Press.
Keesing, Roger
  1983 *'Elota's Story: The Life and Times of a Solomon Islands Big Man.* New York: Holt, Rinehart & Winston.
Lee, R.
  1979 *The !Kung San.* Cambridge: Cambridge University Press.
  1984 *The Dobe !Kung.* New York: Holt, Rinehart & Winston.
Lewis, Oscar
  1951 *Life in a Mexican Village: Tepoztlán Restudied.* Urbana: University of Illinois Press.
Lowman, C.
  1980 "Environment, Society and Health: Ecological Bases of Community Growth and Decline in the Maring Regions of Papua New Guinea."

Unpublished Ph.D. dissertation, Anthropology Dept., Columbia University.

Malinowski, Bronislaw
1922 *Argonauts of the Western Pacific*. New York: Dutton.
1935 *Coral Gardens and Their Magic*. London: Allen and Unwin.

Maybury-Lewis, D.
1974 *Akwe-Shavante Society*. New York: Oxford University Press.

Meggers, B.
1954 "Environmental Limitation of the Development of Culture." *American Anthropologist* 56: 801–24.

Meggitt, M.
1977 *Blood Is Their Argument*. Palo Alto, Calif.: Mayfield.

Moseley, M., & K. Day
1982 *Chan Chan: Andean Desert City*. Albuquerque: University of New Mexico Press.

Newman, P.
1957 "An Intergroup Collectivity Among the Nootka." M.A. thesis, Department of Anthropology. Seattle: University of Washington.

Ongka
1974 "The Kawelka: Ongka's Big Moka." Grenada Television: Disappearing World Series. (Distributed by Thomas Howe Assoc.)

Peoples, J.
1982 "Individual or Group Advantage? A Reinterpretation of the Maring Ritual Cycle." *Current Anthropology* 23: 291–310.

Powell, H.
1960 "Competitive Leadership in Trobriand Political Organization." *Journal of the Royal Anthropological Institute* 90: 118–45.
1969 "Territoriality, Hierarchy and Kinship in Kiriwina." *Man* 4: 580–604.

Rappaport, R.
1967 *Pigs for the Ancestors*. New Haven: Yale University Press.

Sackschewsky, M.
1970 "The Clan Meeting in Enga Society." In *Exploring Enga Culture*, edited by P. Brennan. Wapenamanda, New Guinea: Kristen Press.

Smole, W.
1976 *The Yanoama Indians: A Cultural Geography*. Austin: University of Texas Press.

Spencer, R.
1959 *The North Alaskan Eskimo*. Washington, D.C.: Smithsonian Institute.

Uberoi, J.
1962 *Politics of the Kula Ring*. Manchester: Manchester University Press.

Waddell, E.
1972 *The Mound Builders*. Seattle: University of Washington Press.

Weiner, A.
1976 *Women of Value, Men of Renown*. Austin: University of Texas Press.
1983 "A World of Made Is Not a World of Born: Doing Kula in Kiriwina." In *The Kula: New Perspectives on Massim Exchange*, edited by J. Leach and E. Leach. Cambridge: Cambridge University Press.

White, L.
1959 *The Evolution of Culture*. New York: McGraw-Hill.

Berdan: Trade and Markets

Adams, Robert McC.
  1966 *The Evolution of Urban Society: Early Mesopotamia and Prehispanic Mexico.*
        Chicago: Aldine.
  1974 "Anthropological Perspectives on Ancient Trade." *Current Anthropology*
        15(3): 239–58.
Berdan, Frances F.
  1978 "Ports of Trade in Mesoamerica: A Reappraisal." In *Cultural Continuity
        in Mesoamerica,* edited by D. Browman. World Anthropology Series.
        The Hague: Mouton Publishers.
  1982 *The Aztecs of Central Mexico: An Imperial Society.* New York: Holt, Rine-
        hart & Winston.
  1983 "The Reconstruction of Ancient Economies: Perspectives from Archae-
        ology and Ethnohistory." In *Economic Anthropology: Topics and Theories,*
        edited by Sutti Ortiz. SEA Volume 1. Lanham, Md.: University Press
        of America.
  1985 "Markets in the Economy of Aztec Mexico." In *Markets and Marketing,*
        edited by Stuart Plattner. SEA Volume 4. Lanham, Md.: University
        Press of America.
Blanton, Richard
  1976 "Anthropological Studies of Cities." *Annual Review of Anthropology* 5:
        249–64.
  1978 *Monte Alban: Settlement Patterns at the Ancient Zapotec Capital.* New York:
        Academic Press.
Blanton, Richard, Stephen A. Kowalewski, Gary Feinman, & Jill Appel
  1981 *Ancient Mesoamerica: A Comparison of Change in Three Regions.* Cam-
        bridge: Cambridge University Press.
Blom, Franz
  1932 "Commerce, Trade and Monetary Units of the Maya." Middle Ameri-
        can Research Series Publication no. 4: 531–52.
Brumfiel, Elizabeth
  1983 "Aztec State Making: Ecology, Structure, and the Origin of the State."
        American Anthropologist 85(2): 261–84.
Burford, Alison
  1972 *Craftsmen in Greek and Roman Society.* London: Thames and Hudson.
Carneiro, Robert
  1970 "A Theory of the Origin of the State." *Science* 169: 733–38.
Carrasco, Pedro
  1978 "La Economía del México Prehispánico." In *Economía Política e Ideología
        en el México Prehispánico,* edited by Pedro Carrasco and Johanna Broda.
        Mexico: Editorial Nueva Imagen.
Casson, Lionel
  1984 *Ancient Trade and Society.* Detroit: Wayne State University Press.
Chapman, Anne
  1957 "Port of Trade Enclaves in Aztec and Maya Civilization." In *Trade and
        Market in the Early Empires,* edited by Karl Polanyi et al. New York: The
        Free Press.
Claessen, Henry J. J., & Peter Skalnik (eds.)
  1978 *The Early State.* The Hague: Mouton Publishers.

Cohen, Ronald, & Elman R. Service (eds.)
  1978 *Origins of the State: The Anthropology of Political Evolution.* Philadelphia: Institute for the Study of Human Issues.
Curtin, Philip D.
  1984 *Cross-Cultural Trade in World History.* Cambridge: Cambridge University Press.
Earle, Timothy
  1982 "Storage Facilities and State Finance in the Upper Mantaro Valley, Peru." In *Contexts for Prehistoric Exchange,* edited by Jonathon E. Ericson and Timothy K. Earle. New York: Academic Press.
Gibson, Charles
  1964 *The Aztecs Under Spanish Rule.* Stanford, Calif.: Stanford University Press.
Grierson, Philip
  1977 *The Origins of Money.* The Creighton Lecture in History, 1970. London: The Athlone Press.
Heichelheim, Fritz M.
  1958 *An Ancient Economic History, Volume I.* Leiden, The Netherlands: A.W. Sijthoff's Uitgeversmaatschappij N.V.
Hodge, Mary
  1984 *The Aztec City-States.* Ann Arbor: Memoirs of the Museum of Anthropology, University of Michigan, no. 18. Studies in Latin American Ethnohistory and Archaeology, volume 3.
Kemp, Barry J.
  1972 "Temple and Town in Ancient Egypt." In *Man, Settlement and Urbanism,* edited by Peter J. Ucko, Ruth Tringham, and G.W. Dimbleby. Cambridge, Mass.: Schenkman.
Kohl, Philip
  1978 "The Balance of Trade in Southwestern Asia in the Mid-Third Millennium B.C." *Current Anthropology* 19(3): 463–92.
La Lone, Darrell E.
  1982 "The Inca as a Nonmarket Economy: Supply on Command Versus Supply and Demand." In *Contexts for Prehistoric Exchange,* edited by Jonathon E. Ericson and Timothy K. Earle. New York: Academic Press.
Lamberg-Karlovsky, C. C.
  1975 "Third Millennium Modes of Exchange and Modes of Production." In *Ancient Civilization and Trade,* edited by Jeremy A. Sabloff and C.C. Lamberg-Korlovsky. Albuquerque: University of New Mexico Press.
Luttwak, Edward N.
  1976 *The Grand Strategy of the Roman Empire.* Baltimore: Johns Hopkins University Press.
Marcus, Joyce
  1983 "On the Nature of the Mesoamerican City." In *Prehistoric Settlement Patterns: Essays in Honor of Gordon R. Willey,* edited by Evon Z. Vogt and Richard Leventhal. Albuquerque: University of New Mexico Press.
Millon, René
  1976 "Social Relations in Ancient Teotihuacan." In *The Valley of Mexico: Studies in Pre-Hispanic Ecology and Society,* edited by Eric Wolf. Albuquerque: University of New Mexico Press.
  1981 "Teotihuacan: City, State, and Civilization." In *Supplement to the Hand-*

book of Middle American Indians, Volume 1: Archaeology. Austin: University of Texas Press.

Oppenheim, A. Leo
1977   *Ancient Mesopotamia: Portrait of a Dead Civilization*. Chicago & London: The University of Chicago Press.

Ozguc, Nimet
1969   "Assyrian Trade Colonies in Anatolia." *Archaeology* 22(4): 250–55.

Ozguc, Tahsin
1973   "Ancient Ararat." In *Cities: Their Origin, Growth and Human Impact*. San Francisco: W.H. Freeman & Company.

Polanyi, Karl
1957   "The Economy as Instituted Process." In *Trade and Market in the Early Empires*, edited by Karl Polanyi et al. New York: The Free Press.

Polanyi, Karl, Conrad M. Arensberg, & Harry W. Pearson (eds.)
1957   *Trade and Market in the Early Empires*. New York: The Free Press.

Postgate, J. N.
1972   "The Role of the Temple in the Mesopotamian Secular Community." In *Man, Settlement and Urbanism*, edited by Peter Ucko, Ruth Tringham, and G. W. Dimbleby. Cambridge, Mass.: Schenkman.

Sahagún, Bernardino de
1950–1982   *Florentine Codex: General History of the Things of New Spain*. (Trans. by Arthur J.O. Anderson and Charles E. Dibble.) Salt Lake City, Utah, and Santa Fe, N.M.: University of Utah Press and School of American Research, Santa Fe (originally written by 1569).

Sanders, William
1956   "The Central Mexican Symbiotic Region: A Study in Pre-Historic Settlement Patterns." In *Prehistoric Settlement Patterns in the New World*, edited by Gordon R. Willey. Viking Fund Publications in Anthropology, no. 23. New York: Wenner-Gren Foundation for Anthropological Research.

Service, Elman
1975   *Origins of the State and Civilization*. New York: Norton.

Silver, Morris
1983   "Karl Polanyi and Markets in the Ancient Near East: The Challenge of the Evidence." *Journal of Economic History* XLIII, no. 4: 795–829.
1985   *Economic Structures of the Ancient Near East*. Totowa, N.J.: Barnes and Noble Books.

Simkin, C. G. F.
1968   *The Traditional Trade of Asia*. London: Oxford University Press.

Sjoberg, Gideon
1960   *The Preindustrial City, Past and Present*. Glencoe, Ill.: The Free Press.

Skinner, G. William
1977   "Cities and the Hierarchy of Local Systems." In *The City in Late Imperial China*, edited by G. William Skinner. Stanford: Stanford University Press.

Trigger, Bruce
1972   "Determinants of Urban Growth in Pre-Industrial Societies." In *Man, Settlement and Urbanism*, edited by Peter J. Ucko, Ruth Tringham, and G. W. Dimbleby. Cambridge, Mass.: Schenkman.

Wenke, Robert J.
1980   *Patterns in Prehistory*. New York: Oxford University Press.

Wheatley, Paul
  1971   *The Pivot of the Four Quarters: A Preliminary Enquiry into the Origins and Character of the Ancient Chinese City.* Chicago: Aldine.
  1972   "The Concept of Urbanism." In *Man, Settlement and Urbanism*, edited by Peter J. Ucko, Ruth Tringham, and G. W. Dimbleby. Cambridge, Mass.: Schenkman.
Wittfogel, Karl
  1957   *Oriental Despotism.* New Haven: Yale University Press.
Wright, Henry T.
  1977   "Recent Research on the Origin of the State." *Annual Review of Anthropology*: 379–97. Palo Alto, Calif.: Annual Reviews, Inc.
Wright, Henry T., & Gregory A. Johnson
  1975   "Population, Exchange, and Early State Formation in Southwestern Iran." *American Anthropologist* 77(2): 267–89.

Roseberry: Peasants and the World

Bernstein, Henry
  1979   "African Peasantries: A Theoretical Framework." *Journal of Peasant Studies* 6(4): 421–44.
Chance, John, & William Taylor
  1985   "Cofradias and Cargos: An Historical Perspective on the Mesoamerican Civil-Religious Hierarchy." *American Ethnologist* 12(1): 1–26.
Chevalier, Jacques
  1983   "There Is Nothing Simple About Simple Commodity Production." *Journal of Peasant Studies* 10(4): 153–86."
Cook, Scott
  1976   "Value, Price and Simple Commodity Production: The Case of the Zapotec Stoneworkers." *Journal of Peasant Studies* 3(4): 395–427.
  1982   *Zapotec Stoneworkers.* Lanham, Md.: University Press of America.
  1984a   *Peasant Capitalist Industry.* Lanham, Md.: University Press of America.
  1984b   "Rural Industry, Social Differentiation, and the Contradictions of Provincial Mexican Capitalism." *Latin American Perspectives* 11(4): 60–85.
  1984c   "Peasant Economy, Rural Industry, and Capitalist Development in the Oaxaca Valley, Mexico." *Journal of Peasant Studies* 12(1): 3–40.
Deere, Carmen Diana, & Alain de Janvry
  1981   "Demographic and Social Differentiation Among Northern Peruvian Peasants." *Journal of Peasant Studies* 8(3): 335–67.
Ennew, Judith, et al.
  1977   " 'Peasantry' as an Economic Category." *Journal of Peasant Studies* 4(4): 295–322.
Frank, Andre Gunder
  1967   *Capitalism and Underdevelopment in Latin America.* New York: Monthly Review Press.
  1969   *Latin America: Underdevelopment or Revolution?* New York: Monthly Review Press.
Friedmann, Harriet
  1980   "Household Production and the National Economy: Concepts for the Analysis of Agrarian Formations." *Journal of Peasant Studies* 7(2): 158–84.

442   *References Cited*

Geertz, Clifford
  1973   *The Interpretation of Cultures*. New York: Basic Books.
Gjording, Chris
  Forthcoming. *The Cerro Colorado Copper Project: Panama, Multinational Corporations, and the Guaymi Indians*. Washington, D.C.: Smithsonian Institution Press.
Kahn, Joel
  1980   *Minangkabau Social Formations*. Cambridge: Cambridge University Press.
Kroeber, Alfred
  1948   *Anthropology*. New York: Harcourt Brace.
Lesser, Alexander
  1985   "Social Fields and the Evolution of Society." In *History, Evolution and the Concept of Culture*, edited by Sidney Mintz. New York: Cambridge University Press.
Lewis, Oscar
  1951   *Life in a Mexican Village: Tepoztlán Restudied*. Urbana: University of Illinois Press.
Littlejohn, Gary
  1977   "Peasant Economy and Society." In *Sociological Theories of the Economy*, edited by Barry Hindess. London: Macmillan and Co.
Mintz, Sidney
  1953   "The Culture History of a Puerto Rican Sugar-Cane Plantation, 1876–1949." *Hispanic American Historical Review* 33(2): 224–51.
  1959   "Labor and Sugar in Puerto Rico and in Jamaica, 1800–1850." *Comparative Studies in Society and History* 1(3): 273–81.
  1974a "The Rural Proletariat and the Problem of Rural Proletarian Consciousness." *Journal of Peasant Studies* 1(3): 291–325.
  1974b *Worker in the Cane*. New York: Norton. [Originally published in 1960 by Yale University Press.]
Redfield, Robert
  1930   *Tepoztlan, A Mexican Village: A Study of Folk Life*. Chicago: University of Chicago Press.
Roseberry, William
  1983   *Coffee and Capitalism in the Venezuelan Andes*. Austin: University of Texas Press.
  1985   "Something About Peasants, History and Capitalism." *Critique of Anthropology* 5(3): 69–76.
Rus, Jan, & Robert Wasserstrom
  1980   "Civil-Religious Hierarchies in Central Chiapas: A Critical Perspective." *American Ethnologist* 7: 466–78.
Silverman, Sydel
  1979   "The Peasant Concept in Anthropology." *Journal of Peasant Studies* 7(1): 49–69.
Smith, Carol
  1976   *Regional Analysis*, vol. 2. New York: Academic Press.
  1984a "Does a Commodity Economy Enrich the Few While Ruining the Masses? Differentiation Among Petty Commodity Producers in Guatemala." *Journal of Peasant Studies* 11(3): 60–95.

1984b "Forms of Production in Practice: Fresh Approaches to Simple Commodity Production." *Journal of Peasant Studies* 11(4): 201–21.

1984c "Local History in Global Context: Social and Economic Transitions in Western Guatemala." *Comparative Studies in Society and History* 26(2): 193–228.

1985 "Anthropology and History Look at Peasants and Capitalism." *Critique of Anthropology* 5(2): 87–94.

Smith, Gavin

1979 "Socio-Economic Differentiation and Relations of Production Among Petty Producers in Central Peru, 1880 to 1970." *Journal of Peasant Studies* 6(3): 286–310.

1985 "Reflections on the Social Relations of Simple Commodity Production." *Journal of Peasant Studies* 13(1): 99–108.

Steward, Julian

1950 *Area Research: Theory and Practice.* New York: Social Science Research Council, Bulletin 63.

1955 "Levels of Sociocultural Integration: An Operational Concept." In *Theory of Culture Change.* Urbana: University of Illinois Press.

Steward, Julian, et al.

1956 *The People of Puerto Rico.* Urbana: University of Illinois Press.

Stoler, Ann

1985 *Capitalism and Confrontation in Sumatra's Plantation Belt.* New Haven, Conn.: Yale University Press.

Wallerstein, Immanuel

1974 *The Modern World-System.* New York: Academic Press.

1979 *The Capitalist World Economy.* New York: Cambridge University Press.

Wasserstrom, Robert

1983 *Class and Society in Central Chiapas.* Berkeley: University of California Press.

Wolf, Eric

1955 "Types of Latin American Peasantry: A Preliminary Discussion." *American Anthropologist* 57: 452–71.

1982 *Europe and the People Without History.* Berkeley: University of California Press.

Cancian: Economic Behavior

Barlett, Peggy F.

1977 "The Structure of Decision Making in Paso." *American Ethnologist* 4: 285–307.

1982 *Agricultural Choice and Change: Decision Making in a Costa Rican Community.* New Brunswick, N.J.: Rutgers University Press.

Bossen, Laurel H.

1984 *The Redivision of Labor: Women and Economic Choice in Four Guatemalan Communities.* Albany: State University of New York Press.

Cancian, Frank

1965 *Economics and Prestige in a Maya Community.* Stanford, Calif.: Stanford University Press.

1972 *Change and Uncertainty in a Peasant Economy.* Stanford, Calif.: Stanford University Press.

1974 "New Patterns of Stratification in the Zinacantan Cargo System." *Journal of Anthropological Research* 30: 164–73.
1979 *The Innovator's Situation: Upper Middle Class Conservatism in Agricultural Communities.* Stanford, Calif.: Stanford University Press.
1981 "Community of Reference in Rural Stratification Research." *Rural Sociology* 46: 626–45.
1987 "Proletarianization in Zinacantan, 1960 to 1983." In *Household Economies and Their Transformations,* edited by Morgan D. Maclachlan. Lanham, Md.: University Press of America.

Chayanov, A. V.
1966 "Peasant Farm Organization." In *A. V. Chayanov on the Theory of Peasant Economy,* edited by Daniel Thorner, Basile Kerblay, and R. E. F. Smith. Homewood, Ill.: Richard D. Irwin for the American Economic Association.

Collier, George A.
1975 *The Fields of the Tzotzil: The Ecological Basis of Tradition in Highland Chiapas.* Austin: University of Texas Press.

Deere, Carmen Diana
1987 "The Peasantry in Political Economy: Trends of the 1980s." Occasional Papers Series no. 19, Program in Latin American Studies, University of Massachusetts at Amherst.

deJanvry, Alain, & Ann Vandeman
1987 "Patterns of Proletarianization in Agriculture: An International Comparison." In *Household Economies and Their Transformations,* edited by Morgan D. Maclachlan. Lanham, Md.: University Press of America.

DeWalt, Billie R.
1979 *Modernization in a Mexican Ejido: A Study in Economic Adaptation.* New York: Cambridge University Press.

Foster, George M.
1960–61 "Interpersonal Relations in Peasant Society." *Human Organization* 19: 174–78.
1964 "Treasure Tales, and the Image of the Static Economy in a Mexican Peasant Community." *Journal of American Folklore* 77: 39–44.
1965 "Peasant Society and the Image of Limited Good." *American Anthropologist* 67: 293–314.
1967 *Tzintzuntzan: Mexican Peasants in a Changing World.* Boston: Little, Brown.

Harris, Richard L.
1978 "Marxism and the Agrarian Question in Latin America." *Latin American Perspectives* 19: 2–26.

Harriss, John (ed.)
1982 *Rural Development: Theories of Peasant Economy and Agrarian Change.* London: Hutchinson University Library.

Hewitt de Alcantara, Cynthia
1984 *Anthropological Perspectives on Rural Mexico.* London: Routledge & Kegan Paul.

Heynig, Klaus
1982 "The Principal Schools of Thought on the Peasant Economy." *CEPAL Review* 16: 113–39.

Kroeber, Alfred
  1948 *Anthropology*. New York: Harcourt Brace.
Lenin, V. I.
  1899 *The Development of Capitalism in Russia*. Citations from second revised edition, Moscow: Progress Publishers, 1964.
Lewis, Oscar
  1960–61 "Some of My Best Friends Are Peasants." *Human Organization* 19: 179–80.
Long, Norman, & Bryan R. Roberts (eds.)
  1978 *Peasant Cooperation and Capitalist Expansion in Central Peru*. Austin: Institute of Latin American Studies, University of Texas.
Ortiz, Sutti R. de
  1973 *Uncertainties in Peasant Farming: A Colombian Case*. New York: Humanities Press.
Pearse, Andrew
  1978 "Technology and Peasant Production: Reflections on a Global Study." In *International Perspectives in Rural Sociology*, edited by Howard Newby. New York: John Wiley & Sons.
Pelto, Pertti J., & Gretel H. Pelto
  1975 "Intra-cultural Diversity: Some Theoretical Issues." *American Ethnologist* 2: 1–18.
Pitt-Rivers, Julian
  1960–61 " 'Interpersonal Relations in Peasant Society': A Comment." *Human Organization* 19: 180–83.
Rogers, Everett M.
  1983 *Diffusion of Innovations*, Third Edition. New York: The Free Press.
Shanin, Theodor
  1972 *The Awkward Class*. Oxford: Clarendon Press.
  1973 "The Nature and Logic of the Peasant Economy 1: A Generalization." *Journal of Peasant Studies* 1: 63–80.
  1987 *Peasants and Peasant Societies*. New York: Basil Blackwell.
Silverman, Sydel
  1979 "The Peasant Concept in Anthropology." *Journal of Peasant Studies* 7: 49–69.
Skinner, G. William
  1971 "Chinese Peasants and the Closed Community: An Open and Shut Case." *Comparative Studies in Society and History* 13: 270–81.
Smith, Carol A.
  1982 "Is There a 'New Economic Anthropology'?" *Reviews in Anthropology* 9: 63–75.
  1984 "Does a Commodity Economy Enrich the Few While Ruining the Masses? Differentiation Among Petty Commodity Producers in Guatemala." *Journal of Peasant Studies* 11: 60–95.
Vogt, Evon Z.
  1969 *Zinacantan: A Maya Community in the Highlands of Chiapas*. Cambridge, Mass.: Harvard University Press.
  1978 *Bibliography of the Harvard Chiapas Project: The First Twenty Years, 1957–1977*. Cambridge, Mass.: The Peabody Museum of Archaeology and Ethnology, Harvard University.

Wasserstrom, Robert
1983   *Class and Society in Central Chiapas.* Berkeley: University of California Press.
Wolf, Eric R.
1955   "Types of Latin American Peasantry." *American Anthropologist* 57: 452–71.
1957   "Closed Corporate Peasant Communities in Mesoamerica and Central Java." *Southwestern Journal of Anthropology* 13: 1–18.
1960   "The Indian in Mexican Society." *Alpha Kappa Deltan* 30: 3–6.
1986   "The Vicissitudes of the Closed Corporate Peasant Community." *American Ethnologist* 13: 325–29.

Plattner: Markets and Marketplaces

Babb, Florence
1985   "Middlemen and Marginal Women: Marketers and Dependency in Peru's Informal Sector." In *Markets and Marketing,* edited by Stuart Plattner. Lanham, Md.: University Press of America for the Society for Economic Anthropology.
Beals, Ralph
1975   *The Peasant Marketing System of Oaxaca, Mexico.* Berkeley: University of California Press.
Bohannan, Paul
1955   "Some Principles of Exchange and Investment Among the Tiv." *American Anthropologist* 57: 60–69.
Bonacich, Edna
1973   "A Theory of Middleman Minorities." *American Sociological Review* 38: 583–94.
Bonacich, Edna, & John Modell
1980   "Middleman Minorities." Ch. 2 in *The Economic Basic of Ethnic Solidarity: Small Business in the Japanese American Community.* Berkeley: University of California Press.
Christaller, Walter
1966   *Central Places in Southern Germany.* Englewood Cliffs, N.J.: Prentice-Hall (trans. of 1933 German original).
Cook, Scott, & Martin Diskin
1976   *Markets in Oaxaca.* Austin: University of Texas Press.
Curtin, Philip
1984   "Trade Diasporas and Cross-Cultural Trade." Ch. 1 in *Cross-Cultural Trade in World History.* Cambridge: Cambridge University Press.
Dahl, Svan
1960   "Travelling Pedlars in Nineteenth Century Sweden." *Scandinavian Economic History Review* 7: 167–78.
Dalton, George
1965   "Primitive Money." *American Anthropologist* 67: 44–65.
Davis, Dorothy
1966   "The Man With a Pack." Ch. 11 in *A History of Shopping.* London: Routledge & Kegan Paul.
Einzig, Paul
1948   *Primitive Money.* London: Eyre & Spottiswoode.

Frank, Andre Gunder
  1966 "The Development of Underdevelopment." *Monthly Review* 18: 17–31.
Hay, Alan
  1971 "Notes on the Economic Basis for Periodic Marketing in Developing
     Countries." *Geographical Analysis* 3: 393–401.
Helle, Reijo
  1964 "Retailing in Northern Finland, Particularly in Mobile Shops." *Fennia*
     91(3): 89–91.
Herskovits, Melville
  1952 *Economic Anthropology*. New York: Knopf.
Hollier, Graham
  1985 "Examining Allegations of Exploitation and Inefficiency in Rural Mar-
     keting Systems: Some Evidence from West Cameroon." *Journal of De-
     veloping Areas* 19: 393–416.
Neale, Walter C.
  1976 *Monies in Societies*. San Francisco: Chandler & Sharp.
Neumark, S. D.
  1957 *Economic Influences on the South African Frontier, 1652–1836*. Stanford,
     Calif.: Food Research Institute Misc. Pub. 12.
Orlove, Benjamin
  1986 "Barter and Cash Sale on Lake Titicaca: A Test of Competing Ap-
     proaches." *Current Anthropology* 27: 85–106.
Plattner, Stuart
  1975a "The Economics of Peddling." In *Formal Methods in Economic Anthro-
     pology*, edited by Stuart Plattner. Washington, D.C.: American Anthro-
     pological Association.
  1975b "Rural Market Networks." *Scientific American* 232: 66–79.
  1980 "Economic Development and Occupational Change in a Developing
     Area of Mexico." *Journal of Developing Areas* 14: 469–82.
Skinner, G. William
  1964 "Marketing and Social Structure in Rural China." *Journal of Asian Studies*
     24: 3–43; 195–228; 363–99.
  1985 "Rural Marketing in China: Revival and Reappraisal." In *Markets and
     Marketing*, edited by Stuart Plattner. Lanham, Md.: University Press of
     America for the Society for Economic Anthropology.
Smith, Carol A.
  1974 "Economics of Marketing Systems: Models From Economic Geogra-
     phy." *Annual Review of Anthropology* 3: 167–201.
  1976 *Regional Analysis*, Volumes 1 and 2. New York: Academic Press.
  1977 "How Marketing Systems Affect Economic Opportunity in Agrarian
     Societies." In *Peasant Livelihood*, edited by R. Halperin and J. Dow. New
     York: St. Martin's Press.
Smith, R. H. T.
  1971 "West African Marketplaces: Temporal Periodicity and Locational
     Spacing." In *The Development of Indigenous Trade and Markets in West
     Africa*, edited by Claude Meillassoux. London: Oxford University
     Press.
Stine, James
  1962 "Temporal Aspects of Tertiary Production Elements in Korea." In *Urban*

Systems and Economic Development, edited by F. Pitts. Eugene, Ore.: School of Business Administration.

Thaler, Richard
1980 "Toward a Positive Theory of Consumer Choice." *Journal of Economic Behavior and Organization* 1: 39–60.

Webber, M. J., & Richard Symanski
1973 "Periodic Markets: An Economic Location Analysis." *Economic Geography* 3: 213–27.

Weber, Max
1968 *Economy and Society.* New York: Bedminster Press.

Plattner: Economic Behavior in Markets

Acheson, James
1985 "Social Organization of the Maine Lobster Market." In *Markets and Marketing,* edited by S. Plattner. Lanham, Md.: University Press of America for the Society for Economic Anthropology.

Akerloff, George
1970 "The Market for 'Lemons': Quality Uncertainty and the Market Mechanism." *Quarterly Journal of Economics* 84: 488–500.

Bennett, John
1968 "Reciprocal Economic Exchanges Among North American Agricultural Operators." *Southwestern Journal of Anthropology* 24: 276–309.

Ben-Porath, Yoram
1980 "The F-Connection: Families, Friends, and Firms and the Organization of Exchange." *Population and Development Review* 6: 1–30.

Cancian, Frank
1966 "Maximization as Norm, Strategy and Theory." *American Anthropologist* 68: 465–70.

Dannhaeuser, Norbert
1979 "Development of a Distribution Channel in the Philippines: From Channel Integration to Channel Fragmentation." *Human Organization* 38: 74–78.

Davis, William
1973 *Social Relations in a Philippine Market.* Berkeley: University of California Press.

Etzioni, Amitai
1988 *The Moral Dimension.* New York: Free Press.

Granovetter, Mark
1985 "Economic Action and Social Structure: The Problem of Embeddedness." *American Journal of Sociology* 91: 481–510.

Healey, Christopher
1984 "Trade and Sociability: Balanced Reciprocity as Generosity in the New Guinea Highlands." *American Ethnologist* 11: 42–60.

Katzin, Margret
1960 "The Business of Higglering in Jamaica." *Social and Economic Studies* 9: 297–331.

Macneil, Ian
1981 "Economic Analysis of Contractual Relations: Its Shortfalls and the

Need for a 'Rich Classificatory Apparatus.'" *Northwestern University Law Review* 75: 1018–63.

Mintz, Sidney
1961 "Pratik: Haitian Personal Economic Relationships." *Proceedings of the 1961 Annual Spring Meeting of the American Ethnological Society.*
1964 "The Employment of Capital by Market Women in Haiti." In *Capital, Saving and Credit*, edited by R. Firth and B. Yamey. Chicago: Aldine.

Nelson, Paul
1970 "Information and Consumer Behavior." *Journal of Political Economy* 78: 311–29.

Oberschall, Anthony, & Eric Leifer
1986 "Efficiency and Social Institutions: Uses and Misuses of Economic Reasoning in Sociology." *Annual Review of Sociology* 12: 233–53.

Ouchi, William
1980 "Markets, Bureaucracies and Clans." *Administrative Science Quarterly* 25: 129–42.

Plattner, Stuart
1975 "The Economics of Peddling." In *Formal Methods in Economic Anthropology*, edited by S. Plattner. Washington, D.C.: American Anthropological Association.
1980 "Economic Development and Occupational Change in a Developing Area of Mexico." *Journal of Developing Areas* 14: 469–82.
1982 "Economic Custom in a Public Marketplace." *American Ethnologist* 9: 399–420.
1983 "Economic Custom in a Competitive Marketplace." *American Anthropologist* 85: 848–58.

Sahlins, Marshall
1972 "On the Sociology of Primitive Exchange." *Stone Age Economics*. Chicago: Aldine.

Spence, Michael
1976 "Information Aspects of Market Structure: An Introduction." *Quarterly Journal of Economics* 90: 591–97.

Swetnam, John
1978 "Interaction Between Urban and Rural Residents in a Guatemalan Marketplace." *Urban Anthropology* 7: 137–53.

Szanton, Maria
1972 *Right to Survive*. University Park: Pennsylvania State University Press.

Trager, Lillian
1981 "Customers and Creditors: Variations in Economic Personalism in a Nigerian Marketing System." *Ethnology* 20: 133–46.

Ward, Barbara
1960 "Cash or Credit Crops?" *Economic Development and Cultural Change* 8: 148–63.

Williamson, Oliver
1981 "The Economics of Organization: The Transaction Cost Approach." *American Journal of Sociology* 87: 548–77.

Wilson, James
1980 "Adaptation to Uncertainty and Small Numbers Exchange: The New England Fish Market." *Bell Journal of Economics* 11: 491–504.

Dannhaeuser: Developing Urban Areas

Anderson, Dole
  1970 *Marketing and Development: The Thailand Experience.* East Lansing: Institute of International Business and Economic Development Studies, Michigan State University.
Beals, Ralph
  1975 *The Peasant Marketing System of Oaxaca, Mexico.* Los Angeles: University of California Press.
Blauvelt, Euan
  1982 "The Philippines. Consumer Market Developments." In *Marketing Trends in the Asia Pacific Region: Economic Forecasts and Consumer Development,* edited by the Asia Pacific Center. Aldershot, England: Cover Publication Company.
Bonacich, Edna
  1973 "A Theory of Middleman Minorities." *American Sociological Review* 38: 583–95.
Cunningham, W. H., R. M. Moore, & I. C. M. Cunningham
  1974 "Urban Markets in Industrializing Countries: The São Paulo Experience." *Journal of Marketing* 38: 2–12.
Dannhaeuser, Norbert
  1977 "Distribution and the Structure of Retail Trade in a Philippine Commercial Town." *Economic Development and Cultural Change* 25: 471–503.
  1980 "The Role of the Neighborhood Store in Developing Economies: The Case of Dagupan City, Philippines." *Journal of Developing Areas* 14: 157–74.
  1983 *Contemporary Trade Strategies in the Philippines: A Study in Marketing Anthropology.* New Brunswick, N.J.: Rutgers University Press.
  1985 "Urban Market Channels Under Conditions of Development: The Case of India and the Philippines." In *Markets and Marketing,* edited by S. Plattner. Boston: University Press of America.
  1987a "Marketing Systems and Rural Development: A Review of Consumer Goods Distribution." *Human Organization* 46: 177–85.
  1987b "From the Metropolis Into the Up-Country: The Stockist System in India's Developing Mass Consumer Market." *The Journal of Developing Areas* 21: 259–76.
Davies, Rob
  1979 "Informal Sector or Subordinate Mode of Production? A Model." In *Casual Work and Poverty in Third World Cities,* edited by Ray Bromley and Chris Gerry. London: John Wiley & Sons.
Dawson, John A.
  1979 *The Marketing Environment.* New York: St. Martin's Press.
Dholakia, N., and John F. Sherry, Jr.
  1987 "Marketing and Development. A Resynthesis of Knowledge." In *Research in Marketing,* edited by J. N. Sheth. London: JAI Press.
Fook, Timothy L.
  1983 "Hawkers and Vendors in Melaka Town." In *Melaka: The Transformation of a Malay Capital, c. 1400–1980,* edited by K. S. Sandhu and P. Wheatly. New York: Oxford University Press.

Friedmann, John, & Flora Sullivan
   1974   "The Absorption of Labor in the Urban Economy: The Case of Develop-
          ing Countries." *Economic Development and Cultural Change* 22: 385–414.
Geertz, Clifford
   1963   *Peddlers and Princes: Social Development and Economic Change in Two Indo-
          nesian Towns*. Chicago: University of Chicago Press.
Hackenberg, R.
   1980   "New Patterns of Urbanization in Southeast Asia: An Assessment."
          Population and Development Review 6: 391–419.
Hazlehurst, Leighton W.
   1968   "The Middle Range City in India." *Asian Survey* 8: 539–52.
Kaynak, E.
   1982   "The Introduction of a Modern Food Retailing Institution to Less-
          Developed Economies: Problems and Opportunities." In *Marketing
          Channels: Domestic and International Perspectives*, edited by M. G. Harvey
          and R. F. Lusch. Norman: Center for Economic and Management
          Research School of Business Administration, the University of Okla-
          homa.
Kotler, Philip
   1980   *Principles of Marketing*. Englewood Cliffs, N.J.: Prentice-Hall.
McCammon, Bert C., Jr., & A. D. Bates
   1967   "The Emergence and Growth of Contractually Integrated Channels in
          the American Economy." In *The Marketing Channel: A Conceptual View-
          point*, edited by B. Mallen. New York: John Wiley & Sons.
McGee, T. G.
   1973   *Hawkers in Hong Kong: A Study of Planning and Policy in a Third World
          City*. Hong Kong: Centre of Asian Studies, University of Hong Kong.
   1985   "Mass Markets-Little Markets. Some Preliminary Thoughts on the
          Growth of Consumption and its Relationship to Urbanization: A Case
          Study of Malaysia." In *Markets and Marketing*, edited by S. Plattner.
          New York: University Press of America.
McGee, T. G., & Y. M. Yeung
   1977   *Hawkers in Southeast Asian Cities: Planning for the Bazaar Economy*. Ot-
          tawa: International Development Centre.
Nattrass, N. J.
   1987   "Street Trading in Transkei—A Struggle Against Poverty and Prosecu-
          tion." *World Development* 15: 861–76.
O'Connor, Anthony
   1983   *The African City*. New York: Africana Publishing Co.
Rasheed, Jamal
   1986   "Video-Cassette Boom Stalks Creative Culture." *Far Eastern Economic
          Review* (March 6): 54–55.
Roberts, Bryan
   1978   *Cities of Peasants: The Political Economy of Urbanization in the Third World*.
          London: Sage.
Santos, Milton
   1979   *The Shared Space: The Two Circuits of the Urban Economy in Underdeveloped
          Countries*. London: Methuen.
Scott, James C.
   1976   *The Moral Economy of the Peasant: Rebellion and Subsistence in Southeast
          Asia*. London: Yale University Press.

Sethuraman, S.
  1976 "The Urban Informal Sector: Concept, Measurement and Policy." *International Labour Review* 114: 69–81.
Smith, Robert H. T.
  1978 "Urban Market-Place Systems and Mobile Vendors." In *Periodic Markets, Hawkers, and Traders in Africa, Asia, and Latin America*, edited by Robert H. T. Smith. Vancouver: The Centre for Transportation Studies.
Trager, Lillian
  1985 "From Yams to Beer in a Nigerian City: Expansion and Change in Informal Sector Trade Activity." In *Markets and Marketing*, edited by S. Plattner. New York: University Press of America.
Ward, Barbara E.
  1960 "Cash or Credit Crops? An Examination of the Implication of Peasant Commercial Production with Special Reference to the Multiplicity of Traders and Middlemen." *Economic Development and Cultural Change* 8: 148–63.
World Advertising Expenditures
  1981 *World Advertising Expenditures in 1980*. New York: Starch Inra Hooper Group of Co.

Barlett: Industrial Agriculture

Barlett, Peggy F.
  1986a "Profile of Full-Time Farm Workers in a Georgia County." *Rural Sociology* 51(1): 78–96.
  1986b "Part-Time Farming: Saving the Farm or Saving the Lifestyle?" *Rural Sociology* 51(3): 290–314.
  1987a "The Crisis in Family Farming: Who Will Survive?" In *Farm Work and Fieldwork: Anthropological Studies of North American Agriculture*, edited by Michael Chibnik. New York: Cornell University Press.
  1987b "Industrial Agriculture in Evolutionary Perspective." *Cultural Anthropology* 2(1): 137–54.
Bennett, John W.
  1982 *Of Time and the Enterprise*. Minneapolis: University of Minnesota Press.
Bennett, John W., & Seena B. Kohl
  1982 "The Agrifamily System." In *Of Time and the Enterprise*, edited by John W. Bennett. Minneapolis: University of Minnesota Press.
Busch, Lawrence, & William B. Lacy (eds.)
  1984 *Food Security in the United States*. Boulder, Colo.: Westview Press.
Buttel, Frederick H., & Howard Newby (eds.)
  1980 *The Rural Sociology of the Advanced Societies*. Montclair, N.J.: Allanheld Osmun.
California Small Farm Viability Project
  1977 "The Family Farm in California." California Department of Agriculture. November.
Carlin, Thomas A., & Linda M. Ghelfi
  1979 "Off-Farm Employment and the Farm Sector." In *Structure Issues in American Agriculture*. USDA Agricultural Economics Report 438. Washington, D.C.

Carlson, John E., & Don A. Dillman
  1983 "Influence of Kin Arrangements on Farmer Innovativeness." *Rural Sociology* 48(2): 183–200.
Carter, Harold O., & Warren E. Johnston
  1978 "Some Forces Affecting the Changing Structure, Organization, and Control of American Agriculture." *American Journal of Agricultural Economics* 60: 738–48.
Center for Rural Affairs
  1985 *Newsletter*. Walthill, Nebraska.
Cochrane, Willard W.
  1979 *The Development of American Agriculture: A Historical Analysis*. Minneapolis: University of Minnesota Press.
Cottrell, Fred
  1955 *Energy and Society*. New York: McGraw-Hill.
Coughenour, C. Milton
  1984 "Farmers and Farm Workers: Perspectives on Occupational Change and Complexity." In *Research in Rural Sociology and Development*, edited by Harry K. Schwarzweller. Greenwich, Conn.: JAI Press.
Coughenour, C. Milton, & Louis Swanson
  1983 "Work Statuses and Occupations of Men and Women in Farm Families and the Structure of Farms." *Rural Sociology* 48(1): 24–43.
Craig, Russell, Virginia Lambert, & Keith M. Moore
  1983 "Domestic Labor on Family Farms: The Sexual Division of Labor and Reproduction." Paper presented at the Rural Sociological Society meetings, Lexington, Ky., August.
DeWalt, Billie R.
  1984 "International Development Paths and Policies: The Cultural Ecology of Development." *The Rural Sociologist* 4(4): 255–68.
Dorner, Peter
  1983 "Technology and U.S. Agriculture." In *Technology and Social Changes in Rural Areas*, edited by Gene F. Summers. Boulder, Colo.: Westview Press.
Ehlers, Tracy Bachrach
  1987 "The Matrifocal Farm." In *Farm Work and Fieldwork: Anthropological Studies of American Agriculture*, edited by Michael Chibnik. Ithaca, New York: Cornell University Press.
Fink, Deborah
  1986 *Open Country, Iowa: Rural Women, Tradition, and Change*. Albany, N.Y.: SUNY Press.
Ford, Arthur M.
  1973 *Political Economics of Rural Poverty in the South*. Cambridge, Mass.: Ballinger.
Friedland, William H., & Amy Barton
  1975 "Destalking the Wily Tomato: A Case Study in Social Consequences in California Agricultural Research." *Applied Behavioral Sciences*. College of Agricultural and Environmental Science. University of California, Davis.
Friedmann, Harriet
  1978 Simple Commodity Production and Wage Labour in the American Plains. *Journal of Peasant Studies* 6(1): 71–100.

Gates, Paul W.
  1960 *The Farmer's Age: Agriculture 1815–1860.* New York: Holt, Rinehart & Winston.
Gladwin, Christina
  1982 "Off-Farm Work and Its Effect on Florida Farm Wives' Contribution to the Family Farm." In *World Development and Women,* Vol. II, edited by M. Rojas. Blacksburg, Va.: The Virginia Tech Title XII Women in International Development Office.
  1984 "Frontiers in Hierarchical Decision Models." *Human Organization* 43(3): 198–276.
Gladwin, Christina, & Robert Zabawa
  1984 "Microdynamics of Contraction Decisions: A Cognitive Approach to Structural Change." *American Journal of Agricultural Economics* 66(5): 829–35.
Goldschmidt, Walter
  1978 *As You Sow: Three Studies in the Social Consequences of Agribusiness.* Montclair, N.J.: Allanheld Osmun.
Goss, Kevin F., Richard D. Rodefeld, & Frederick H. Buttel
  1980 "The Political Economy of Class Structure in U.S. Agriculture: A Theoretical Outline." In *The Rural Sociology of the Advanced Societies,* edited by Frederick H. Buttel and Howard Newby. Montclair, N.J.: Allanheld Osmun.
Groger, B. Lisa
  1983 "Growing Old With or Without It: The Meaning of Land in a Southern Rural Community." *Research on Aging* 5(4): 511–26.
Hardesty, Donald L.
  1977 *Ecological Anthropology.* New York: John Wiley & Sons.
Hayes, Michael N., & Alan L. Olmstead
  1984 "Farm Size and Community Quality: Arvin and Dinuba Revisited." *American Journal of Agricultural Economics* 66(4): 430–36.
Heffernan, William D.
  1978 "Agricultural Structure and the Community." In *Can the Family Farm Survive?* Special Report 219, Agricultural Experiment Station. University of Missouri-Columbia.
Kramer, Mark
  1980 *Three Farms: Making Milk, Meat, and Money from the American Soil.* New York: Bantam.
Lockeretz, William, & Sarah Wernick
  1980 "Commercial Organic Farming in the Corn Belt in Comparison to Conventional Practices." *Rural Sociology* 45(4): 708–22.
Madden, J. Patrick, Delworth B. Gardner, Diane S. Branch, David Holland, & Howard A. Osborn.
  1980 "Production Efficiency and Technology for Small Farms." Paper VII of the National Rural Center Small Farms Project. Washington, D.C.
Majka, Linda, & Theo Majka
  1982 *Farm Workers, Agribusiness, and the State.* Philadelphia: Temple University Press.
Martin, Philip L.
  1983 "Labor-Intensive Agriculture." *Scientific American* 249(4): 54–59.

Morgan, Daniel
  1979 *Merchants of Grain*. New York: Viking.
Newby, Howard
  1979 *The Deferential Worker*. Madison: University of Wisconsin Press.
Odum, Howard T.
  1971 *Environment, Power, and Society*. New York: Wiley-Interscience.
Paarlberg, Don
  1980 *Farm and Food Policy: Issues of the 1980s*. Lincoln: University of Nebraska Press.
Padfield, Harland, & William E. Martin
  1965 *Farmers, Workers, and Machines: Technological Social Change in Farm Industries of Arizona*. Tucson: University of Arizona Press.
Perelman, Michael
  1977 *Farming for Profit in a Hungry World: Capital and the Crisis in Agriculture*. Totowa, N.J.: Allanheld Osmun.
Pimentel, David, & Marcia Pimentel
  1979 *Food, Energy and Society*. New York: Halsted Press.
Rappaport, Roy A.
  1979 *Ecology, Meaning, and Religion*. Richmond, Calif.: North Atlantic Books.
Rogers, Susan Carol
  1985 "Owners and Operators of Farmland: Structural Changes in U.S. Agriculture." *Human Organization* 44(3): 206–14.
Rogers, Susan C., & Sonya Salamon
  1983 "Inheritance and Social Organization Among Family Farmers." *American Ethnologist* 10(3): 529–50.
Rosenfeld, Rachel
  1985 *Farm Women: Work, Farm, and Family in the United States*. Chapel Hill: University of North Carolina Press.
Sachs, Carolyn E.
  1983 *The Invisible Farmers: Women in Agricultural Production*. Totowa, N.J.: Allanheld Osmun.
Salamon, Sonya
  1980 "Ethnic Differences in Farm Family Land Transfers." *Rural Sociology* 45(2): 290–308.
  1985 "Ethnic Communities and the Structure of Agriculture." *Rural Sociology* 50(3): 323–40.
Salamon, Sonya, Kathleen M. Gengenbacher, & Dwight J. Penas
  1986 "Family Factors Affecting the Intergenerational Succession to Farming." *Human Organization* 45(1): 24–33.
Sampson, Neil
  1984 "America's Agricultural Land: Basis for Food Security?" In *Food Security in the United States*, edited by Lawrence Busch and William B. Lacy. Boulder, Colo.: Westview.
Schertz, Lyle P., et al.
  1979 "Another Revolution in U.S. Farming?" USDA Agricultural Economic Report 441. Washington, D.C.: U.S. Government Printing Office.
Steinhart, John S., & Carol E. Steinhart
  1974 "Energy Use in the U.S. Food System." *Science* 184: 307–16.

Strange, Marty (ed.)
  1984   *It's Not All Sunshine and Fresh Air: Chronic Health Effects of Modern Farming Practices.* Walthill, Nebr.: Center for Rural Affairs.
Swanson, Lou
  1981   "Reduced Tillage Technology and Kentucky Small Farmers." *Culture and Agriculture,* no. 12.
Tatum, L. A.
  1971   "The Southern Corn Leaf Blight Epidemic." *Science* 171: 1113–16.
Thomas, Robert J.
  1985   *Citizenship, Gender, and Work: Social Organization of Industrial Agriculture.* Berkeley: University of California Press.
Tweeten, Luther
  1981   "Agriculture at a Crucial Evolutionary Crossroads." *Research in Domestic and International Agribusiness Management* 2: 1–15.
United States Bureau of the Census
  1979   *Census of Agriculture.* Vol. 5, Part 6. Washington, D.C.: USGPO.
  1977   *Census of Manufacturing, 1977.* Washington, D.C.: USGPO.
United States Department of Agriculture
  1970   *Agricultural Statistics.* Washington, D.C.: USGPO.
  1985a   *Agricultural Statistics.* Washington, D.C.: USGPO.
  1985b   *Fact Book on U.S. Agriculture.* Washington, D.C.: USGPO.
Van Es, J. C., F. C. Fliegel, C. Erickson, H. Backus, & E. Harper
  1982   "Choosing the Best of Two Worlds: Small, Part-Time Farms in Illinois." Agricultural Economic Research Report 185. Urbana: University of Illinois, College of Agriculture.
Vogeler, Ingolf
  1981   *The Myth of the Family Farm: Agribusiness Dominance of U.S. Agriculture.* Boulder, Colo.: Westview.
Wells, Miriam J.
  1981   "Social Conflict, Commodity Constraints, and Labor Market Structure in Agriculture." *Comparative Studies in Society and History* 23(4): 679–704.
  1984   "What is a Worker? The Role of Sharecroppers in Contemporary Class Structure." *Politics and Society* 13(3): 295–320.
Wessel, James
  1983   *Trading the Future: Farm Exports and the Concentration of Economic Power in Our Food System.* San Francisco: Institute for Food and Development Policy.
Zabawa, Robert
  1987   "Macro-Micro Linkages and Structural Transformation: The Move from Full-Time to Part-Time Farming in a North Florida Agricultural Community." *American Anthropologist* 89: 366–82.

Smith: The Informal Economy

Adams, John, & Uwe J. Woltemade
  1970   "Village Economy in Traditional India: A Simplified Model." *Human Organization* 29: 49–56.
Arizpe, Lourdes
  1977   "Women in the Informal Sector: The Case of Mexico City." *Signs: Journal of Women in Culture and Society* (Fall): 45–59.

Banfield, E. C., & L. F. Banfield
1958 *The Moral Basis of a Backward Society*. Glencoe, Ill.: Free Press.

Barker, J., and G. Smith (eds.)
1986 *Rethinking Petty Commodity Production*, special issue of *Labor, Capital and Society* 19. Center for Developing-Area Studies. Montreal: McGill University.

Benedict, Peter
1972 "Itinerant Marketing: An Alternative Strategy." In *Social Exchange and Interaction*, edited by E. N. Wilmsen. Anthropological Papers no. 46, Museum of Anthropology. Ann Arbor: University of Michigan.

Bennett, James T., & Thomas J. DiLorenzo
1983 *Underground Government: The Off-Budget Public Sector*. Washington, D.C.: The Cato Institute.

Berliner, Joseph
1957 *Factory and Manager in the USSR*. Cambridge, Mass.: Harvard University Press.

Bohannan, Paul, & Laura Bohannan
1968 *Tiv Economy*. London: Longmans.

Bohannan, Paul, & George Dalton
1962 *Markets in Africa*. Evanston, Ill.: Northwestern University Press.

Bose, Christine, Roslyn Feldberg, & Natalie Sokoloff (eds.) (with the Women and Work Research Group)
1987 *Hidden Aspects of Women's Work*. New York: Praeger.

Bremen, J.
1976 "A Dualistic Labor System: A Critique of the Informal Sector Concept." *Economic and Political Weekly* 11: 1870–76.

Bromley, Ray
1982 "Working in the Streets: Survival Strategy, Necessity or Unavoidable Evil?" In *Urbanization in Contemporary Latin America*, edited by A. Gilbert, J. Hardy, and R. Ramirez. New York: John Wiley & Sons.

Bromley, Ray, & Chris Gerry (eds.)
1979 *Casual Work and Poverty in Third World Cities*. New York: John Wiley & Sons.

Brookfield, H. C. (ed.)
1969 *Pacific Market Places: A Collection of Essays*. Canberra: Australia National University Press.

Brush, Stephen
1977 "The Myth of the Idle Peasant: Employment in a Subsistence Economy." In *Peasant Livelihood*, edited by R. Halperin and J. Row. New York: St. Martin's Press.

Cassel, Dieter, & E. Ulrich Cichy
1968 "Explaining the Growing Shadow Economy in East and West: A Comparative Systems Approach." *Comparative Economic Studies* 28: 34–47.

Chock, Phyllis Pease
1981 "The Greek-American Small Businessman: A Cultural Analysis." *Journal of Anthropological Research* 37: 46–60.

Clammer, John
1987 "Peripheral Capitalism and Urban Order: 'Informal Sector' Theories in the Light of Singapore's Experience." In *Beyond the New Economic Anthropology*, edited by J. Clammer. New York: Macmillan.

Davies, R.
  1979 "Informal Sector or Subordinate Mode of Production? A Model." In
        Casual Work and Poverty in Third World Cities, edited by R. Bromley and
        C. Gerry. New York: John Wiley & Sons.
Dewey, Alice
  1962 *Peasant Marketing in Java*. New York: Free Press.
Ditton, Jason, & R. Brown
  1981 "Why Don't They Revolt? Invisible Income as a Neglected Dimension
        of Runciman's Relative Deprivation Thesis." *British Journal of Sociology*
        32: 30–52.
Edel, Matthew
  1967 "Jamaican Fishermen: Two Approaches in Economic Anthropology."
        Social and Economic Studies 16: 432–39.
Ferman, Louis A., Stuart Henry, & Michele Hoyman (eds.)
  1987 *The Informal Economy*. Special issue of *The Annals of the American Academy
        of Political and Social Science*. Newbury Park, Calif.: Sage Publications.
Ferman, Patricia R., and Louis A. Ferman
  1973 "The Structural Underpinning of the Irregular Economy." *Poverty and
        Human Resources Abstracts* 8: 3–17.
Firth, Raymond
  1946 *Malay Fishermen*. London: Kegan Paul.
Firth, Raymond, & B. S. Yamey (eds.)
  1963 *Capital, Saving and Credit in Peasant Societies: Studies from Asia, Oceania,
        the Caribbean and Middle America*. Chicago: Aldine.
Forde, C. D.
  1949 *Habitat, Society and Economy*. New York: Dutton (7th ed., orig. pub.
        London 1934).
Foster, George
  1942 *A Primitive Mexican Economy*. American Ethnological Society Mono-
        graphs, no. 5. Seattle: University of Washington Press.
  1948 "The Folk Economy of Rural Mexico with Special Reference to Market-
        ing." *Journal of Marketing* 13: 153–62.
Friedmann, Harriet
  1980 "Household Production and the National Economy: Concepts for the
        Analysis of Agrarian Formations." *The Journal of Peasant Studies* 7: 158–
        84.
Geertz, Clifford
  1963 *Peddlers and Princes*. Chicago: University of Chicago Press.
Germani, Clara
  1988 "A Path for Revitalizing Latin Democracies." *The Christian Science Moni-
        tor*, May 25, pp. 7–8.
Gerry, Chris
  1978 "Petty Production and Capitalist Production in Dakar: The Crisis of the
        Self-Employed." *World Development* 6: 1147–60.
  1987 "Developing Economies and the Informal Sector in Historical Perspec-
        tive." In *The Informal Economy*, edited by L. A. Ferman, S. Henry, and
        M. Hoyman. Special issue of *The Annals of the American Academy of
        Political and Social Science*. Newbury Park, Calif.: Sage Publications.
Gerry, Chris, & Chris Birkbeck
  1981 "The Petty Commodity Producer in Third World Cities: Petit Bourgeois

or Disguised Proletarian?" In *The Petite Bourgeoisie: Comparative Studies of the Uneasy Stratum*, edited by F. Bechhofer and B. Elliott. New York: Macmillan.

Grossman, Gregory
  1987 *The Second Economy in the USSR and Eastern Europe: A Bibliography.* Berkeley-Duke Occasional Papers on the Second Economy in the USSR, no. 1, University of California, Berkeley, and Duke University (updated).

Grout-Smith, Tim
  n.d. *Assignment: Eurofraud.* Produced for the BBC World Service.

Halperin, Rhoda, & Sara Sturdevant
  1988 "A Cross-Cultural Treatment of the Informal Economy." Paper presented at the Society for Economic Anthropology, annual meeting.

Hart, Keith
  1973 "Informal Income Opportunities and Urban Employment in Ghana." *Journal of Modern African Studies* 11(1): 61–89.

Herskovits, M. J.
  1937 *Life in a Haitian Valley.* New York: Harper and Brothers.

Herskovits, M. J., & M. Harwitz (eds.)
  1964 *Economic Transition in Africa.* Evanston, Ill.: Northwestern University Press.

Hill, Polly
  1969 "Hidden Trade in Hausaland." *Man* 4: 393–409.
  1970 *Studies in Rural Capitalism in West Africa.* Cambridge: Cambridge University Press.

Honigmann, John J.
  1949 "Incentives to Work in a Canadian Indian Community." *Human Organization* 8: 23–28.

Hoyman, Michele
  1987 "Female Participation in the Informal Economy: A Neglected Issue." In *The Informal Economy*, edited by L. A. Ferman, S. Henry, and M. Hoyman. Special issue of *The Annals of the American Academy of Political and Social Science.* Newbury Park, Calif.: Sage Publications.

Isaac, Barry L.
  1965 " 'Rational' and 'Irrational' Factors in Southern Mexican Indian 'Capitalism.' " *América Indígena* 25: 427–36.
  1971 "Business Failure in a Developing Town: Pendembu, Sierra Leone." *Human Organization* 30: 289–94.

Jones, Yvonne V.
  1988 "Street Peddlers as Entrepreneurs: Economic Adaptation to an Urban Area." *Urban Anthropology* 17: 143–70.

Kahn, Joel
  1975 "Economic Scale and the Cycle of Petty Commodity Production in West Sumatra." In *Marxist Analyses and Social Anthropology*, edited by M. Bloch. New York: John Wiley & Sons.

Katzin, Margaret
  1959 "The Jamaican Country Higgler." *Social and Economic Studies* 8: 35–42.
  1960 "The Business of Higglering in Jamaica." *Social and Economic Studies* 9: 297–331.
  1964 "The Role of the Small Entrepreneur." In *Economic Transition in Africa*,

edited by M. J. Herskovits and M. Harwitz. Evanston, Ill.: Northwestern University Press.

Kriedte, Peter, Hans Medick, & Jürgen Schlumbohm
1981 *Industrialization Before Industrialization*. Transl. Beate Schempp. New York: Cambridge University Press; Paris: Editions de la Maison des Sciences de l'Homme [first published in German as *Industrialisierung vor der Industrialisierung*, Vol. 53 of Veröffentlichungen des Max-Planc-Instituts für Geschichte. Göttingen: Vandenhoeck & Ruprecht, 1977].

Lewis, Flora
1986 "The Hidden French 'Parallels.'" *New York Times*, August 16, p. 10.

Little, Kenneth L.
1951 "The Mende Rice Farm and Its Cost." *Zaïre* 5: 227–73.

Littlefield, A.
1978 "Exploitation and the Expansion of Capitalism: The Case of the Hammock Industry of Yucatan." *American Ethnologist* 5: 495–508.

Llosa, Mario Vargas
1987 "In Defense of the Black Market." *New York Times Magazine*, February 22 (adapted from the preface to the book by Hernando de Soto, *El Otro Sendero* [The other path]).

Lomnitz, Larissa Adler
1971 "Reciprocity of Favors in the Urban Middle Class of Chile." In *Studies in Economic Anthropology*, Anthropological Studies no. 7, edited by G. Dalton. Washington, D.C.: American Anthropological Association.

Long, Norman, & Paul Richardson
1978 "Informal Sector, Petty Commodity Production, and the Social Relations of Small-Scale Enterprise." In *The New Economic Anthropology*, edited by John Clammer. New York: St. Martin's Press.

Long, Norman, & Bryan R. Roberts (eds.)
1978 *Peasant Cooperation and Capitalist Expansion in Central Peru*. Austin: University of Texas Press.

Maher, Vanessa
1977 "Women and Social Change in Morocco." In *Women in the Muslim World*, edited by L. Beck and N. Keddie. Cambridge, Mass.: Harvard University Press.

Mars, Gerald, & Michael Nicod
1981 "Hidden Rewards at Work: The Implications from a Study of British Hotels." In *Informal Institutions*, edited by S. Henry. New York: St. Martin's Press.
1983 *The World of Waiters*. London: George Allen & Unwin.

Marx, Karl
1967 *Capital*, vols. 1–3. New York: International Publishers.

Mattera, Philip
1985 *Off the Books: The Rise of the Underground Economy*. New York: St. Martin's Press.

Mayer, Philip (ed.)
1961 *Xhosa in Town: Studies of the Bantu-Speaking Population of East London, Cape Province*, vol. 2. Institute of Social and Economic Research, Rhodes University, Cape Town: Oxford University Press (2d ed., rev., 1971, *Townsmen or Tribesmen*. Cape Town: Oxford University Press).
1980 *Black Villagers in an Industrial Society: Anthropological Perspectives on Labor Migration in South Africa*. Cape Town: Oxford University Press.

McGuire, Randall, & Robert McC. Netting
1982 "Leveling Peasants? The Maintenance of Equality in a Swiss Alpine Community." In *Economic and Ecological Processes in Society and Culture*, edited by S. Gudeman, H. Schneider, V. Kerns, and N. Whitten, Jr. Special issue *American Ethnologist* 9(2): 269–90.
Mintz, Sidney
1955 "The Jamaican Internal Marketing Pattern: Some Notes and Hypotheses." *Social and Economic Studies* 4: 95–103.
1957 "The Role of the Middleman in the Internal Distribution System of a Caribbean Peasant Economy." *Human Organization* 15: 18–23.
1959 "Internal Market Systems as Mechanisms of Social Articulation." In *Proceedings* of the Annual Spring Meetings of the American Ethnological Society. Seattle: University of Washington Press.
1967 "Pratik: Haitian Personal Economic Relations." In *Peasant Society: A Reader*, edited by J. M. Potter et al. Boston: Little, Brown.
Miracle, Marvin P.
1962a "African Markets and Trade in the Copperbelt." In *Markets in Africa*, edited by P. Bohannan and G. Dalton. Evanston, Ill.: Northwestern University Press.
1962b "Apparent Changes in the Structure of African Commerce, Lusaka 1954–59." *Northern Rhodesia Journal* 5(2): 170–75.
Moser, Caroline
1978 "The Informal Sector or Petty Commodity Production: Dualism or Dependence in Urban Development?" *World Development* 6: 1041–64.
Nash, Manning
1961 "The Social Context of Economic Choice in a Small Society." *Man* 91: 186–91.
Noguchi, Paul
1979 "Law, Custom and Morality in Japan: The Culture of Cheating on the Japanese National Railways." *Anthropological Quarterly* 52: 165–77.
Orans, Martin
1968 "Maximizing in Jajmaniland: A Model of Caste Relations." *American Anthropologist* 70: 875–97.
Peattie, Lisa R.
1982 "What Is to Be Done with the 'Informal Sector'? A Case Study of Shoe Manufacturers in Colombia." In *Towards Political Economy of Urbanization in Third World Countries*, edited by Helen I. Safa. Delhi, India: Oxford University Press.
Plattner, Stuart
1975a "The Economics of Peddling." In *Formal Methods in Economic Anthropology*, edited by S. Plattner. Special publication no. 4. Washington, D.C.: American Anthropological Association.
1975b *Formal Methods in Economic Anthropology*. Special publication no. 4. Washington, D.C.: American Anthropological Association.
Portes, Alejandro, & John Walton
1981 *Labor, Class and the International System*. New York: Academic Press.
Powdermaker, Hortense
1962 *Copper Town: Changing Africa: The Human Situation on the Rhodesian Copperbelt*. New York: Harper & Row.

Press, Irwin
    1966 "Innovation in Spite of: A Lamp Factory for Maya Peasants." *Human Organization* 25: 284–94.
Radcliffe-Brown, A. R.
    1964 *The Andaman Islanders*. Glencoe, Ill.: Free Press.
Rossiaud, Jacques
    1988 *Medieval Prostitution*. Transl. L. G. Cochrane. New York: Basil Blackwell.
Sampson, Steven
    1987 "The Second Economy of the Soviet Union and Eastern Europe." In *The Informal Economy*, edited by L. A. Ferman, S. Henry, and M. Hoyman. Special issue of *The Annals of the American Academy of Political and Social Science*. Newbury Park, Calif.: Sage Publications.
Santos, Milton
    1979 *The Shared Space: The Two Circuits of the Urban Economy in Underdeveloped Countries*. London: Methuen.
Saunders, Lucie, & Sohair Mehenna
    1986 "Unseen Hands: Women's Farm Work in an Egyptian Village." *Anthropological Quarterly* 59: 105–14.
Schumacher, E. F.
    1973 *Small Is Beautiful: Economics As If People Mattered*. New York: Harper & Row.
Sethuraman, S. V.
    1981 "The Role of the Urban Informal Sector." In *The Urban Informal Sector in Developing Countries: Employment, Poverty and Environment*, edited by S. V. Sethuraman. Geneva: International Labor Office.
Simis, Konstantin
    1982 *USSR: The Corrupt Society—The Secret World of Soviet Capitalism*. New York: Simon & Schuster.
Sloan, Harold S., & Arnold J. Zurcher
    1970 *Dictionary of Economics*. New York: Barnes and Noble.
Smith, M. Estellie
    1985 "An Aspectual Analysis of Polity Formations." In *Development and Decline: The Evolution of Sociopolitical Organization*, edited by H. J. M. Claessen, P. van de Velde, and M. E. Smith. South Hadley, Mass.: Bergin & Garvey.
    1988 "Overview: The Informal Economy and the State." In *Traders Versus the State*, edited by G. Clark. Boulder, Colo.: Westview.
Stepick, Alex, & Arthur D. Murphy
    1980 "Comparing Squatter Settlements and Government Self-Help Projects as Housing Solutions in Oaxaca, Mexico." *Human Organization* 39: 339–43.
Swift, M. G.
    1965 *Malay Peasant Society in Jelebu*. LSE Monographs on Social Anthropology. London: Athlone Press.
Tanzi, Vito
    1980 "Underground Economy and Tax Evasion in the United States: Estimates and Implications." Paper presented at the 1980 meeting of the American Economic Association.

Tax, Sol
    1953 *Penny Capitalism: A Guatemalan Indian Economy.* Institute of Social An-
        thropology no. 16. Washington, D.C.: Smithsonian Institution.
Tilly, Charles
    1986 *The Contentious French.* Cambridge, Mass.: The Belknap Press of Har-
        vard University Press.
Trager, Lillian
    1985 "From Yams to Beer in a Nigerian City: Expansion and Change in
        Informal Sector Trade Activity." In *Markets and Marketing,* edited by
        S. Plattner. Monographs in Economic Anthropology no. 4. New York:
        University Press of America.
    1987 "The Urban Informal Sector in West Africa." *Canadian Journal of African
        Studies* 21: 238–55.
Udy, Stanley H., Jr.
    1959 *Organization of Work: A Comparative Analysis of Production Among Non-
        industrial Peoples.* New Haven, Conn.: HRAF Press.
U.S. News and World Report
    1979a "The Underground Economy: How 20 Million Americans Cheat Uncle
        Sam out of Billions in Taxes." October 22, pp. 49–52.
    1979b "Cheat on Taxes: A World Wide Pursuit." October 22, pp. 52–56.
Uzzell, J. Douglas
    1980 "Mixed Strategies and the Informal Sector: Three Faces of Reserve
        Labor." *Human Organization* 39: 40–49.
Wall Street Journal
    1988 "E. F. Hutton Admits Laundering Money, Pays $1 Million Fine." May
        17, p. 8.
Ward, Barbara E.
    1967 "Cash or Credit Crops? An Examination of Some Implications of Peas-
        ant Commercial Production with Special Reference to the Multiplicity
        of Traders and Middlemen." In *Peasant Society: A Reader,* edited by J. M.
        Potter et al. Boston: Little, Brown (reprinted from *Economic Development
        and Cultural Change* 8 [1960]: 148–68).
Waterbury, Ronald
    1970 "Urbanization and a Traditional Market System." In *The Social Anthro-
        pology of Latin America: Essays in Honor of Ralph Leon Beals,* edited by
        W. Goldschmidt and H. Hoijer. Los Angeles: Latin American Center,
        University of California.
Wedel, Janine
    1986 *The Private Poland.* New York: Facts on File.
Wilson-Smith, Anthony
    1988 "Springtime in Moscow." *Maclean's,* May 30, pp. 22–25.
Wolf, Eric
    1966 *Peasants.* Englewood Cliffs, N.J.: Prentice-Hall.
    1972 "Comment on Dalton's 'Peasantries in Anthropology and History.'"
        Current Anthropology 13: 410–11.

Bossen: Women and Economic Institutions

Aguiar, Neuma
    1986 "Research Guidelines: How to Study Women's Work in Latin America."

In *Women and Change in Latin America,* edited by June Nash and Helen Safa. South Hadley, Mass.: Bergin and Garvey.

Arizpe, Lourdes, & Josefina Aranda
  1986 "Women Workers in the Strawberry Agribusiness in Mexico." In *Women's Work,* edited by Eleanor Leacock and Helen Safa. South Hadley, Mass.: Bergin and Garvey.

Babb, Florence
  1985 "Middlemen and 'Marginal' Women: Marketers and Dependency in Peru's Informal Sector." In *Markets and Marketing,* edited by S. Plattner. Monographs in Economic Anthropology no. 4. Lanham, Md.: University Press of America for the Society for Economic Anthropology.
  1986 "Producers and Reproducers: Andean Marketwomen in the Economy." In *Women and Change in Latin America,* edited by June Nash and Helen Safa. South Hadley, Mass.: Bergin and Garvey.

Benería, Lourdes (ed.)
  1982 *Women and Development: The Sexual Division of Labor in Rural Economies.* Geneva: International Labor Organization.

Berndt, Catherine
  1981 "Interpretations and 'Facts' About Aboriginal Australia." In *Woman the Gatherer,* edited by F. Dahlberg. New Haven, Conn.: Yale University Press.

Boserup, Ester
  1970 *Woman's Role in Economic Development.* New York: St. Martin's Press.

Bossen, Laurel
  1975 "Women in Modernizing Societies." *American Ethnologist* 2(4): 587–601.
  1981 "The Household as Economic Agent." *Urban Anthropology* 10(3): 287–303.
  1984 *The Redivision of Labor: Women and Economic Choice in Four Guatemalan Communities.* Albany: State University of New York Press.
  1988 "Toward a Theory of Marriage: The Economic Anthropology of Marriage Transactions." *Ethnology* 28(2).

Bourgeot, André
  1987 "The Twareg Women of Ahaggar and the Creation of Value." *Ethnos* 52(1–2): 103–18.

Brain, James
  1976 "Less than Second-Class: Women in Rural Settlement Schemes in Tanzania." In *Women in Africa,* edited by N. Hafkin and E. Bay. Stanford: Stanford University Press.

Brown, Judith K.
  1970 "A Note on the Division of Labor by Sex." *American Anthropologist* 72(5): 1074–78.

Buechler, Judith-Maria
  1986 "Women in Petty Commodity Production in La Paz, Bolivia." In *Women and Change in Latin America,* edited by June Nash and Helen Safa. South Hadley, Mass.: Bergin and Garvey.

Burton, M. L., L. Brudner, & D. White
  1977 "A Model for the Sexual Division of Labor." *American Ethnologist* 4(2): 227–51.

Burton, M. L., & D. White
  1984 "Sexual Division of Labor in Agriculture." *American Anthropologist* 86(3): 568–83.

Carmack, Robert
　1979 *Historia Social de los Quichés*. Guatemala: Ministerio de Educación. Seminario de Integración Social Guatemalteca, no. 38.
Charlton, Sue-Ellen
　1984 *Women in Third World Development*. Boulder, Colo.: Westview.
Cloud, Kathleen
　1986 "Sex Roles in Food Production and Distribution Systems in the Sahel." In *Women Farmers in Africa*, edited by Lucy Creevey. Syracuse, N.Y.: Syracuse University Press.
Comaroff, John (ed.)
　1980 *The Meaning of Marriage Payments*. London: Academic Press.
Cook, Scott
　1986 "The 'Managerial' vs. the 'Labor' Function, Capital Accumulation and the Dynamics of Simple Commodity Production in Rural Oaxaca, Mexico." In *Entrepreneurship and Social Change*, edited by S. Greenfield and A. Strickon. Lanham, Md.: University Press of America for the Society for Economic Anthropology.
　Forthcoming "Female Labor, Commodity Production, and Ideology in Mexican Peasant-Artisan Households." In *Work Without Wages: Domestic Labor and Self-Employment Within Capitalism*, edited by Jane Collins and Martha E. Gimenez. Albany: SUNY Press.
Creevey, Lucy (ed.)
　1986 *Women Farmers in Africa: Rural Development in Mali and the Sahel*. Syracuse, N.Y.: Syracuse University Press.
Croll, Elizabeth
　1986 "Rural Production and Reproduction: Socialist Development Experiences." In *Women's Work*, edited by Eleanor Leacock and Helen Safa. South Hadley, Mass.: Bergin and Garvey.
Dahl, Gudrun
　1987 "Women in Pastoral Production: Some Theoretical Notes on Roles and Resources." *Ethnos* (Stockholm: The Ethnographical Museum of Sweden) 52(1–2): 246–79.
Draper, Pat
　1975 "!Kung Women: Contrasts in Sexual Egalitarianism in the Foraging and Sedentary Contexts." In *Toward an Anthropology of Women*, edited by R. Rapp Reiter. New York: Monthly Review Press.
Dublin, Thomas
　1979 *Women at Work*. New York: Columbia University Press.
Ember, Carol
　1978 "Myths about Hunter-Gatherers." *Ethnology* 17: 439–48.
　1983 "The Relative Decline in Women's Contribution to Agriculture with Intensification." *American Anthropologist* 85(2): 285–304.
Estioko-Griffin, A., & P. Bion-Griffin
　1981 "Woman the Hunter: The Agta." In *Woman the Gatherer*, edited by Frances Dahlberg. New Haven, Conn.: Yale University Press.
Evans-Pritchard, E. E.
　1940 *The Nuer*. Oxford: Clarendon Press.
Fernandez-Kelly, Maria
　1983 *For We Are Sold, I and My People: Women and Industry in Mexico's Frontier*. Albany, N.Y.: State University Press.

Gladwin, Christina
  1975 "A Model of the Supply of Smoked Fish from Cape Coast to Kumasi."
    In *Formal Methods in Anthropology*, edited by Stuart Plattner. Washing-
    ton, D.C.: American Anthropological Association.
Goodale, Jane
  1971 *Tiwi Wives*. Seattle: University of Washington Press.
Goody, Jack
  1973 "Bridewealth and Dowry in Africa and Eurasia." In *Bridewealth and
    Dowry*, edited by J. Goody and S. J. Tambiah. Cambridge: Cambridge
    University Press.
Grey, Robert
  1968 "Sonjo Brideprice and the Question of African 'Wife Purchase.'" In
    Economic Anthropology, edited by E. LeClair and H. Schneider. New
    York: Holt, Rinehart & Winston.
Halperin, Rhoda
  1980 "Ecology and Mode of Production: Seasonal Variation and the Division
    of Labor by Sex Among Hunter-Gatherers." *Journal of Anthropological
    Research* 36(3): 379–99.
Henderson, Helen
  1986 "The Grassroots Women's Committee as a Development Strategy in
    an Upper Volta Village." In *Women Farmers in Africa*, edited by Lucy
    Creevey. Syracuse, N.Y.: Syracuse University Press.
Hill, Polly
  1986 *Development Economics on Trial: The Anthropological Case for a Prosecution*.
    Cambridge: Cambridge University Press.
Ifeka-Muller, Caroline
  1975 "Female Militancy and Colonial Revolt: The Women's War of 1929,
    Eastern Nigeria." In *Perceiving Women*, edited by S. Ardener. New York:
    John Wiley & Sons.
India Today
  1986 "Female Infanticide: Born to Die." June 15, 1986, pp. 26–33.
Johnson, Orna, & Allen Johnson
  1975 "Male/Female Relations in the Organization of Work in a Machiguenga
    Community." *American Ethnologist* 2: 634–49.
Lapidus, Gail W.
  1978 *Women in Soviet Society: Equality, Development and Social Change*. Berke-
    ley: University of California Press.
Leacock, Eleanor, & Helen Safa (eds.)
  1986 *Women's Work: Development and the Division of Labor by Gender*. South
    Hadley, Mass.: Bergin and Garvey.
Lee, Richard B.
  1968 "What Hunters Do for a Living, or How to Make Out on Scarce Re-
    sources." In *Man the Hunter*, edited by Richard Lee and I. DeVore.
    Chicago: Aldine.
  1979 *The !Kung San: Men, Women and Work in a Foraging Society*. Cambridge:
    Cambridge University Press.
Littlefield, Alice
  1978 "Exploitation and the Expansion of Capitalism: The Case of the Ham-
    mock Industry of Yucatan." *American Ethnologist* 5(3): 494–508.

Llanos Albornóz, Martha
   1985 *Observations on the Role of Women in the San Julian Colonization Project.* Development Anthropology Network. Binghamton, N.Y.: Institute for Development Anthropology.
Luxton, Meg
   1980 *More than a Labour of Love: Three Generations of Work in the Home.* Toronto: The Women's Press.
Maclachlan, Morgan
   1983 "Why They Did Not Starve: Biocultural Adaptation in a South Indian Village." Philadelphia: Institute for the Study of Human Issues.
Martin, Kay, & Barbara Voorhies
   1975 *Female of the Species.* New York: Columbia University Press.
Miller, Barbara
   1981 *The Endangered Sex: Neglect of Female Children in Rural North India.* Ithaca, N.Y.: Cornell University Press.
Minge, Wanda
   1986 "The Industrial Revolution and the European Family: 'Childhood' as a Market for Family Labor." In *Women's Work*, edited by Eleanor Leacock and Helen Safa. South Hadley, Mass.: Bergin and Garvey.
Minge-Klevana, Wanda
   1980 "Does Labor Time Decrease with Industrialization: A Survey of Time Allocation Studies." *Current Anthropology* 21: 279–87.
Nag, Moni, B. White, & R. Peet
   1978 "An Anthropological Approach to the Study of the Economic Value of Children in Java and Nepal." *Current Anthropology* 19: 293–306.
Nash, June, & Helen Safa (eds.)
   1986 *Women and Change in Latin America.* South Hadley, Mass.: Bergin and Garvey.
Nelson, Nici
   1979 "How Women and Men Get By: The Sexual Division of Labour in the Informal Sector of a Nairobi Squatter Settlement." In *Casual Work and Poverty in Third World Cities*, edited by Ray Bromley and Chris Gerry. New York: John Wiley & Sons.
Oxby, Clare
   1987 "Women Unveiled: Class and Gender Among Kel Ferwan Twareg (Niger)." *Ethnos* 52(1–2): 119–35.
Rogers, Barbara
   1980 *The Domestication of Women.* New York: Tavistock.
Rothstein, Frances
   1983 *Three Different Worlds: Women, Men, and Children in an Industrializing Community.* Westport, Conn.: Greenwood.
   1985 "Capitalist Industrialization and the Increasing Cost of Children." In *Women and Change in Latin America*, edited by June Nash and Helen Safa. South Hadley, Mass.: Bergin and Garvey.
Rubin, Gayle
   1975 "The Traffic in Women: Notes on the Political Economy of Sex." In *Toward an Anthropology of Women*, edited by Rayna Rapp. New York: Monthly Review Press.
Sanday, Peggy
   1974 "Female Status in the Public Domain." In *Woman, Culture and Society,*

edited by M. Rosaldo and L. Lamphere. Stanford: Stanford University Press.

Schneider, Jane, & Annette Weiner
1986 "Cloth and the Organization of Human Experience." *Current Anthropology* 27(2): 178–84.

Sharma, Ursula
1980 *Women, Work and Property in North-West India.* New York: Tavistock.

Sheridan, Mary
1984 "Contemporary Generations: Zhao Xiuyin: Lady of the Sties." In *Lives: Chinese Working Women,* edited by M. Sheridan and J. Salaff. Bloomington: Indiana University Press.

Sivard, Ruth L.
1985 *Women: A World Survey.* Washington, D.C.: World Priorities.

Stacey, Judith
1983 *Patriarchy and Socialist Revolution in China.* Berkeley: University of California Press.

Tanaka, Jiro
1980 *The San: Hunter-Gatherers of the Kalahari.* Tokyo: University of Tokyo.

Tanner, Nancy M.
1983 "Hunters, Gatherers, and Sex Roles in Space and Time." *American Anthropologist* 85(2): 335–41.

Trigger, Bruce
1985 *Natives and Newcomers.* Montreal: McGill University Press.

Turton, David
1980 "The Economics of Mursi Bridewealth: A Comparative Perspective." In *The Meaning of Marriage Payments,* edited by J. Comaroff. London: Academic Press.

Venema, Barnhard
1986 "The Changing Role of Women in Sahelian Agriculture." In *Women Farmers in Africa,* edited by Lucy Creevey. Syracuse, N.Y.: Syracuse University Press.

White, D., M. L. Burton, & M. M. Dow
1981 "Sexual Division of Labor in African Agriculture: A Network Autocorrelation Analysis." *American Anthropologist* 83(4): 824–49.

Wienpahl, Jan
1984 "Women's Roles in Livestock Production Among the Turkana of Kenya." In *Research in Economic Anthropology,* edited by Barry Isaac. London: JAI Press.

Wolf, Marjorie
1985 *Revolution Postponed: Women in Contemporary China.* Stanford: Stanford University Press.

Acheson: Management of Common-Property Resources

Acheson, James
1972 "The Territories of the Lobstermen." *Natural History* 81: 60–69.
1975 "The Lobster Fiefs: Economic and Ecological Effects of Territoriality in the Maine Lobster Industry." *Human Ecology* 3(3): 183–207.
1977 "Technical Skills and Fishing Success in the Maine Lobster Industry." In *Material Culture: Styles, Organization and Dynamics of Technology,*

edited by H. Lechtman and R. Merrill. St. Paul, Minn.: West Publishing.

1979 "Variations in Traditional Inshore Fishing Rights in Maine Lobstering Communities." In *North Atlantic Maritime Cultures*, edited by Raoul Andersen. The Hague: Mouton.

1981 "Anthropology of Fishing." *Annual Review of Anthropology* 10: 275–316.

1982 "Limitations on Farm Size in a Tarascan Pueblo." *Human Organization* 41: 323–29.

1984 "Government Regulation and Exploitive Capacity: The Case of the New England Groundfishery." *Human Organization* 43(4): 319–29.

1988 *The Lobster Gangs of Maine.* Hanover, N.H.: University Press of New England.

Acheson, James M., and Robert Bayer
Forthcoming *The Political Use of Scientific Information in the Maine Lobster Industry.*

Alexander, Paul
1980 "Sea Tenure in Southern Sri Lanka." In *Maritime Adaptations: Essays on Contemporary Fishing Communities.* Pittsburgh: University of Pittsburgh Press.

Andersen, Raoul
1972 "Hunt and Deceive: Information Management in Newfoundland Deep-Sea Trawler Fishing." In *North Atlantic Fishermen*, edited by Raoul Andersen and Cato Wadel. St. Johns, Newfoundland: Memorial University of Newfoundland Institute for Social and Economic Research.

1973 "Resource Management and Spatial Competition in Newfoundland Fishing: An Exploratory Essay." In *Seafare and Community*, edited by Peter H. Fricke. London: Croom Helm.

Andersen, Raoul, and Jeffrey Stiles
1973 "Resource Management and Spatial Competition in Newfoundland Fishing: An Exploratory Essay." In *Seafarer and Community: Towards an Understanding of Seafaring.* London: Croom-Helm.

Anderson, Eugene N.
1987 "A Malaysian Tragedy of the Commons." In *The Question of the Commons*, edited by Bonnie McCay and James Acheson. Tucson: University of Arizona Press.

Asada, Y.
1973 "License Limitation Regulations: The Japanese System." *Journal of the Fisheries Research Board of Canada* 30: 2085–95.

Bailey, F. G.
1969 *Stratagems and Spoils: The Social Anthropology of Politics.* New York: Schocken.

Barth, Fredrik
1959 *Political Leadership Among Swat Pathans.* London: The Athlone Press.

Bauer, Dan
1988 "The Dynamics of Communal and Hereditary Land Tenure Among the Tigray of Ethiopia." In *The Question of the Commons*, edited by Bonnie McCay and James Acheson. Tucson: University of Arizona Press.

Berkes, Fikret
1981 "The Role of Self-Regulation in Living Resource Management in the

North." In *Renewable Resources and the Economy of the North*, edited by M. M. R. Freeman. Ottawa: ACUNS/MAB.

1985   "Fishermen and the 'Tragedy of the Commons.'" *Environmental Conservation* 12(5): 199–205.

1987   "Common Property Resource Management and Cree Indian Fisheries in Subarctic Canada." In *The Question of the Commons*, edited by Bonnie McCay and James Acheson. Tucson: University of Arizona Press.

Britan, Gerald

1979   "Modernization on the North Atlantic Coast: The Transformation of a Traditional Newfoundland Village." In *North Atlantic Maritime Cultures*, edited by Raoul Andersen. The Hague: Mouton.

Bromley, Richard C.

1973   "Limitation of Entry in the United States Fishing Industry: An Economic Appraisal of a Proposed Policy." *Land Economics* 49(4): 381–90.

Carrier, James

1987   "Marine Tenure and Conservation in Papua New Guinea." In *The Question of the Commons*, edited by Bonnie McCay and James Acheson. Tucson: University of Arizona Press.

Cheung, Stevens N. S.

1970   "The Structure of a Contract and the Theory of a Non-Exclusive Resource." *Journal of Law and Economics* 13(1): 45–70.

Ciriacy-Wantrup, S. V., & Richard C. Bishop

1975   "Common Property as a Concept." *Natural Resources Journal* 15: 713–27.

Clark, Colin W.

1973   "The Economics of Over-Exploitation." *Science* 181: 630–34.

Cove, J. J.

1973   "Hunters, Trappers and Gatherers of the Sea: A Comparative Study of Fishing Strategies." *Journal of the Fisheries Research Board of Canada* 30: 249–59.

Crowe, Beryl

1977   "The Tragedy of the Commons Revisited." In *Managing the Commons*, edited by Garrett Hardin and John Baden. San Francisco: W. H. Freeman.

Crutchfield, James A., & Giulio Pontecorvo

1969   *The Pacific Salmon Fisheries: A Study in Irrational Conservation*. Baltimore: The Johns Hopkins Press.

Davis, Stephen

1985   "Traditional Management of the Littoral Zone Among the Yolmgu of North Australia." In *The Traditional Knowledge and Management of Coastal Systems in Asia and the Pacific*, edited by Kenneth Ruddle and R. E. Johannes. Jakarta: UNESCO.

Demsetz, Harold

1967   "Toward a Theory of Property Rights." *American Economic Review* 62: 347–59.

DeWalt, Billie R.

1983   "The Cattle Are Eating the Forest." *Bulletin of the Atomic Scientists* 39(1): 18–23.

Durrenberger, Paul, & Gisli Palsson

1987   "'The Grassroots' and the State: Resource Management in Icelandic Fishing." In *The Question of the Commons*, edited by Bonnie McCay and James Acheson. Tucson: University of Arizona Press.

Dyson-Hudson, Rada, & Eric Smith
  1978 "Human Territoriality: An Ecological Reassessment." *American Anthropologist* 80(1): 21–41.
Erasmus, Charles J.
  1977 *In Search of the Common Good: Utopian Experiments Past and Future*. London: Collier Macmillian.
Farris, James
  1966 *Cat Harbor: A Newfoundland Fishing Settlement*. St. John's, Newfoundland: Memorial University of Newfoundland.
Feit, Harvey A.
  1973 "The Ethno-Ecology of the Waswanipi Cree: Or How Hunters Can Manage Their Resources." In *Cultural Ecology*, edited by B. Cox. Toronto: McClelland and Stewart.
Fife, Daniel
  1977 "Killing the Goose." In *Managing the Commons*, edited by Garrett Hardin and John Baden. San Francisco: W. H. Freeman.
Forman, Shepard
  1970 *The Raft Fishermen*. Bloomington: Indiana University Press.
  1980 "Cognition and the Catch: The Location of Fishing Spots in a Brazilian Coastal Village." In *Maritime Adaptations*, edited by Alexander Spoehr. Pittsburgh: University of Pittsburgh Press.
Franke, Richard W., & Barbara H. Chasin
  1980 *Seeds of Famine: Ecological Destruction and the Development Dilemma in the West African Sahel*. Montclair, N.J.: Allenheld Osmun.
Gersuny, C., & John Poggie
  1974 "Luddites and Fishermen: A Note on Response to Technological Change." *Marine Studies Management* 2: 38–47.
Gilles, Jere Lee, & Keith Jamtgaard
  1982 "Overgrazing in Pastoral Areas: The Commons Reconsidered." *Nomadic Peoples* 10: 1–10.
Godoy, Ricardo A.
  1984 "Andean Common Field Agriculture." Unpublished ms. Harvard Institute for International Development.
Gordon, H. Scott
  1954 "The Economic Theory of a Common Property Resource: The Fishery." *Journal of Political Economy* 62: 124–42.
Hames, Raymond
  1987 "Game Conservation or Efficient Hunting?" In *The Question of the Commons*, edited by Bonnie McCay and James Acheson. Tucson: University of Arizona Press.
Hardin, Garrett
  1968 "The Tragedy of the Commons." *Science* 162: 1243–48.
  1977 "Living on a Lifeboat." In *Managing the Commons*, edited by Garrett Hardin and John Baden. San Francisco: W. H. Freeman.
Hardin, Garrett, & John Baden (eds.)
  1977 *Managing the Commons*. San Francisco: W. H. Freeman.
Heath, Anthony
  1976 *Rational Choice and Exchange Theory*. Cambridge: Cambridge University Press.
Huq, Abdul, & Harland Hasey
  1972 "Socio-Economic Impact of Changes in the Harvesting Labor Force in

the Maine Lobster Industry." *Final Report: Manpower Research Project*. Orono: University of Maine.

Jarmul, David
1987 "Common Property Resources in the Developing World." *National Research Council News Report*, March issue. pp. 2–5.

Johannes, R. E.
1977 "Traditional Law of the Sea in Micronesia." *Micronesia* 13: 121–27.
1978 "Traditional Marine Conservation Methods in Oceania and Their Demise." *Annual Review of Ecology and Systematics* 9: 349–64.
1982 "Traditional Conservation Methods and Protected Marine Areas in Oceania." *Ambio* 11(5): 258–61.

Johnson, Omotunde E. G.
1972 "Economic Analysis, the Legal Framework and Land Tenure Systems." *Law and Economics* (15): 259–76.

Klee, Gary
1980 "Oceania." In *World Systems of Traditional Resource Management*, edited by Gary Klee. New York: John Wiley & Sons.

Lofgren, O.
1979 "Marine Ecotypes in Preindustrial Sweden: A Comparative Discussion of Swedish Peasant Fishermen." In *North Atlantic Maritime Cultures*, edited by Raoul Andersen. The Hague: Mouton.

McCay, Bonnie
1980 "A Fishermen's Cooperative: Limited Indigenous Resource Management in a Complex Society." *Anthropological Quarterly* 53: 29–38.

McCay, Bonnie, & James Acheson
1987 "Capturing the Commons: An Introduction." In *The Question of the Commons*, edited by Bonnie McCay and James Acheson. Tucson: University of Arizona Press.

McCay, Bonnie, and James Acheson (eds.)
1987 *The Question of the Commons*. Tucson: University of Arizona Press.

Miller, D. L.
1982 "Construction of Shallow-Water Habitat to Increase Lobster Production in Mexico." *Proceedings of the Gulf and Caribbean Fisheries Institute* 34: 168–79.

Neitschman, Bernard
1972 "Hunting and Fishing Forms Among the Miskito Indians, Eastern Nicaragua." *Human Ecology* 1: 41–67.
1974 "When the Turtle Collapses, The World Ends." *Natural History* 83: 34–43.
1985 "Torres Straight Islander Sea Resource Management and Sea Rights." In *Traditional Knowledge and Management of Coastal Systems in Asia and the Pacific*, edited by Kenneth Ruddle and R. E. Johannes. Jakarta: UNESCO.

Netting, Robert McC.
1972 "Of Mice and Meadows: Strategies of Alpine Land Use." *Anthropological Quarterly* 45(3): 132–44.
1982 "Territory, Property and Tenure." In *Behavioral and Social Science Research: A National Resource*, edited by Robert McC. Adams, N. J. Smelser, and D. J. Treiman. Washington, D.C.: National Academy Press.

Obeyesekere, G.
1967 *Land Tenure in Village Ceylon*. London.

Olson, Mancur
   1965   *The Logic of Collective Action: Public Goods and the Theory of Groups.* Cambridge, Mass: Harvard University Press.
Orbach, Michael J.
   1977   *Hunters, Seamen and Entrepreneurs.* Berkeley: University of California Press.
Ortner, Sherry
   1984   "Theory in Anthropology Since the Sixties." *Comparative Studies in Society and History* 26: 126–66.
Ostrom, Elinor
   1988   "Institutional Arrangement for Resolving the Commons Dilemma: Some Contending Approaches." In *The Question of the Commons,* edited by Bonnie McCay and James Acheson. Tucson: University of Arizona Press.
Ottenberg, Phoebe
   1966   "The Afikpo Ibo of Eastern Nigeria." In *Peoples of Africa,* edited by James L. Gibbs. New York: Holt, Rinehart & Winston.
Pinkerton, Evelyn
   1987   "Intercepting the State: Dramatic Processes in the Assertion of Local Co-Management Rights." In *The Question of the Commons,* edited by Bonnie McCay and James Acheson. Tucson: University of Arizona Press.
Ruddle, Kenneth
   1985   "The Continuity of Traditional Management Practices: The Case of Japanese Coastal Fisheries." In *The Traditional Knowledge and Management of Coastal Systems in Asia and the Pacific,* edited by Kenneth Ruddle and R. E. Johannes. Jakarta: UNESCO.
Scott, Anthony
   1955   "The Fishery: Objectives of Sole Ownership." *Journal of Political Economy* 63: 116–34.
Smith, M. Estellie
   1984   "The Triage of the Commons." Paper presented to the Annual Meeting of the Society for Applied Anthropology. March 14–18, Toronto, Canada.
Stuster, Jack
   1978   "Where Mabel May Mean Sea Bass." *Natural History* 87(9): 65–71.
Suttles, Wayne
   1974   *The Economic Life of the Coast Salish of Haro and Rosario Straights.* New York: Garland.
Sya'rani L., & N. C. Willoughby
   1985   "The Traditional Management of Marine Resources In Indonesia with Particular Reference to Central Java." In *The Traditional Knowledge and Management of Coastal Systems in Asia and the Pacific,* edited by Kenneth Ruddle and R. E. Johannes. Jakarta: UNESCO.
Taylor, Lawrence
   1987   " 'The River Would Run Red with Blood': Community and Common Property in an Irish Fishing Settlement." In *The Question of the Commons,* edited by Bonnie McCay and James Acheson. Tucson: University of Arizona Press.
Townsend, Ralph, & James Wilson
   1987   "An Economic View of the 'Tragedy of the Commons': From Priviti-

zation to Switching." In *The Question of the Commons,* edited by Bonnie McCay and James Acheson. Tucson: University of Arizona Press.

Vondal, Patricia J.

1987 "The Common Swamplands of Southeastern Borneo: Multiple Use, Management and Conflict." In *The Question of the Commons,* edited by Bonnie McCay and James Acheson. Tucson: University of Arizona Press.

Wilson, James A., & James Acheson

1980 "A Model of Adaptive Behavior in the New England Fishing Industry." In Vol. III of the *Final Report to the National Science Foundation of the University of Rhode Island, University of Maine Study of Social and Cultural Aspects of Fisheries Management in New England Under Extended Jurisdiction* (Ms.).

Plattner: Marxism

Amin, Samir

1973 *Neo-Colonialism in West Africa.* Harmondsworth: Penguin.

Bloch, Maurice

1983 *Marxism and Anthropology.* Oxford: Clarendon Press.

Bossen, Laurel

1975 "Women in Modernizing Societies." *American Ethnologist* 2(4): 587–601.

Donham, Donald

1981 "Beyond the Domestic Mode of Production." *Man* 16: 515–41.

Forthcoming "History, Power and Ideology: Essays on Marxism and Social Anthropology."

Frank, Andre Gunder

1966 "The Development of Underdevelopment." *Monthly Review* 18: 17–31.

Godelier, Maurice

1971 " 'Salt Currency' and the Circulation of Commodities Among the Baruya of New Guinea." In *Studies in Economic Anthropology,* edited by George Dalton. Washington, D.C.: American Anthropological Association.

Harris, Marvin

1966 "The Cultural Ecology of India's Sacred Cattle." *Current Anthropology* 7: 51–59.

1979 *Cultural Materialism.* New York: Random House.

Hart, Keith

1983 "The Contribution of Marxism to Economic Anthropology." In *Economic Anthropology: Topics and Theories,* edited by Sutti Ortiz. Lanham, Md.: University Press of America.

Smith, Carol

1983 "Regional Analysis in World-System Perspective: A Critique of Three Structural Theories of Uneven Development." In *Economic Anthropology: Topics and Theories,* edited by Sutti Ortiz. Lanham, Md.: University Press of America.

1984a "Does a Commodity Economy Enrich the Few While Ruining the Masses? Differentiation Among Petty Commodity Producers in Guatemala." *Journal of Peasant Studies* 11: 60–95.

1984b "Local History to Global Context: Social and Economic Transitions in Western Guatemala." *Comparative Studies in Society and History* 26: 193–228.

Wallerstein, Immanuel
1974 *The Modern World-System: Capitalist Agriculture and the Origins of the European World-Economy in the Sixteenth Century.* New York: Academic Press.

Wolf, Eric
1981 "The Mills of Inequality: A Marxian Approach." In *Social Inequality,* edited by Gerald Berreman. New York: Academic Press.
1982 *Europe and the People Without History.* Berkeley: University of California Press.

Gladwin: The Division of Labor

Adams, Dale
1985 "Assessing the Usefulness of Publications by Agricultural Economists Through Citations." Columbus: Ohio State University Economics and Sociology Occasional Paper 1215.

Adams, Richard N.
1975 *Energy and Structure.* Austin: University of Texas Press.

Adelman, Irma, & Cynthia Taft Morris
1973 *Economic Growth and Social Equity in Developing Countries.* Stanford: Stanford University Press.

Barkin, David, & Billie DeWalt
1984 "Sorgham, the Internationalization of Capital, and the Mexican Food Crisis." Mimeo, University of Kentucky Intsormil Project.

Barlett, Peggy F.
1977 "The Structure of Decision Making in Paso." *American Ethnologist* 4(2): 285–307.
1980 "Adaptive Strategies in Peasant Agricultural Production." *Annual Review of Anthropology* 9: 545–73.
1982 *Agricultural Choice and Change.* New Brunswick, N.J.: Rutgers University Press.
1984 "Microdynamics of Debt, Drought, and Default in South Georgia." *American Journal of Agricultural Economics* 66(5): 836–43.

Bates, Robert H.
1981 *Markets and States in Tropical Africa.* Berkeley: University of California Press.

Becker, Gary S.
1981 *A Treatise on the Family.* Cambridge, Mass.: Harvard University Press.

Benito, Carlos A.
1976 "Peasants' Response to Modernization Projects in Minifundia Economies." *American Journal of Agricultural Economics* 58(2): 143–51.

Bennett, John W.
1969 *Northern Plainsmen: Adaptive Strategy and Agrarian Life.* Chicago: Aldine.
1976 *The Ecological Transition: Cultural Anthropology and Human Adaptation.* New York: Pergamon Press.

Boserup, Ester
1970 *Women's Role in Economic Development.* New York: St. Martin's Press.

476 References Cited

Brokensha, David, D. M. Warren, & Oswald Werner
  1980 Indigenous Knowledge Systems. Lantham, Md.: University Press of America.
Brush, Stephen B.
  1976 "Introduction to Cultural Adaptations in Mountain Ecosystems." Human Ecology 4(2): 125–33.
  1980 "Potato Taxonomies in Andean Agriculture." In Indigenous Knowledge Systems, edited by D. Brokensha, D. Warren, and O. Werner. Lantham, Md.: University Press of America.
Burton, Michael, Lilyan Brudner, & Douglas White
  1977 "A Model of the Sexual Division of Labor." American Ethnologist 4: 227–51.
Burton, Michael, & Kim Romney
  1975 "A Multidimensional Representation of Role Terms." American Ethnologist 4(2): 227–51.
Burton, Michael, & Douglas White
  1984 "The Sexual Division of Labor in Agriculture." American Anthropologist 86(3): 568–83.
Cancian, Frank
  1972 Change and Uncertainty in a Peasant Economy: The Maya Corn Farmers of Zinacantan. Stanford: Stanford University Press.
Chayanov, A. V.
  1966 The Theory of Peasant Economy, edited by D. Thorner, B. Kerblay, and R. E. F. Smith. Chicago, Ill.: The American Economics Association.
Chibnik, Michael
  1980 "The Statistical Behavior Approach: The Choice Between Wage Labor and Cash Cropping in Rural Belize." In Agricultural Decision Making, edited by P. Barlett. New York: Academic Press.
Cochrane, Willard W.
  1986 "The Need to Rethink Agricultural Policy in General and to Perform Some Radical Surgery on Commodity Programs in Particular." In Agricultural Change: Consequences for Southern Farms and Rural Communities, edited by J. Molnar. Boulder, Colo.: Westview.
Cohen, Ronald
  1967 The Kanuri of Bornu. New York: Holt, Rinehart & Winston.
  1985 "Agricultural Transformation in Northern Nigeria: A Macro-micro Analysis." Mimeo. Gainesville: University of Florida.
Croll, Elizabeth
  1979 "Socialist Development Experience: Women in Rural Production and Reproduction in the Soviet Union, China, Cuba, and Tanzania." Discussion Paper (Institute of Development Studies, University of Sussex.) September.
D'Andrade, Roy
  1976 "A Propositional Analysis of American Beliefs About Illness." In Meaning in Anthropology, edited by K. Basso and H. Selby. Albuquerque: University of New Mexico Press.
Deere, Carmen Diana
  1977 "Changing Social Relations of Production and Peruvian Peasant Women's Work." Latin American Perspectives 4(1–2).
  1983 "Cooperative Development and Women's Participation in the Nicara-

guan Agrarian Reform." *American Journal of Agricultural Economics* 65(5): 1043–48.

deJanvry, Alain
1981 *The Agrarian Question and Reformism in Latin America.* Baltimore: Johns Hopkins University Press.
1982 "Historical Forces That Have Shaped World Agriculture." In *Agriculture, Change, and Human Values,* edited by R. Haines and R. Lanier. Gainesville: University of Florida.

DeWalt, Billie
1984 "International Development Paths and Policies: The Cultural Ecology of Development." *Rural Sociologist* 4(4): 255–68.

Eicher, Carl K.
1982 "Facing Up to Africa's Food Crisis." *Foreign Affairs* 61(1): 151–74.
1986 *Transforming African Agriculture.* San Francisco, Calif.: The Hunger Project, no. 4.

Ember, Carol R.
1982 "The Relative Decline in Women's Contribution to Agriculture with Intensification." *American Anthropologist* 85: 285–304.

Evenson, Robert
1978 "Time Allocation in Rural Philippine Households." *American Journal of Agricultural Economics* 60: 322–30.

Falcon, Walter
1970 "The Green Revolution: Generations of Problems." *American Journal of Agricultural Economics* 52 (Dec.): 698–710.

Geertz, Clifford
1966 *Agricultural Involution.* Berkeley: University of California Press.

Gladwin, Christina
1975 "A Model of the Supply of Smoked Fish from Cape Coast to Kumasi." In *Formal Methods in Economic Anthropology,* edited by S. Plattner. Washington, D.C.: A Special Publication of the American Anthropological Association, no. 4.
1976 "A View of the Plan Puebla: An Application of Hierarchical Decision Models." *American Journal of Agricultural Economics* 58(5): 881–87.
1979 "Production Functions and Decision Models: Complementary Models." *American Ethnologist* 6(4): 653–74.
1980 "A Theory of Real-Life Choice: Applications to Agricultural Decisions." In *Agricultural Decision Making: Anthropological Contributions to Rural Development,* edited by P. Barlett. New York: Academic Press.
1982 "The Role of a Cognitive Anthropologist in a Farming Systems Program Which Has Everything." In *The Role of Anthropologists and Other Social Scientists in Interdisciplinary Teams Developing Improved Food Production Technology.* Los Banos, Laguna, the Philippines: The International Rice Research Institute.
1983a "Contributions of Decision-Tree Methodology to a Farming Systems Program." *Human Organization* 42: 146–57.
1983b "Structural Change and Survival Strategies in Florida Agriculture." *Culture and Agriculture* 21 (fall): 1–7.

Gladwin, Christina, & Robert Zabawa
1984 "Microdynamics of Contraction Decisions: A Cognitive Approach to Structural Change." *American Journal of Agricultural Economics* 66(5): 829–35.

1986 "After Structural Change: Are Part-Time or Full-Time Farmers Better Off?" In *Agricultural Change: Consequences for Southern Farms and Rural Communities*, edited by Joseph Molnar. Boulder, Colo.: Westview.

1987 "Transformations of Full-Time Farms in the U.S.: Can They Survive?" In *Household Economies and Their Transformations*, edited by M. Maclachlan. Lantham, Md.: University Press of America.

Gladwin, Christina, & Carl Zulauf

1989 "The Case for the Disappearing Mid-Size Farm." In *Food and Farm: Current Debates and Policies*, edited by G. Gladwin and K. Truman. Lantham, Md.: University Press of America.

Gladwin, Hugh

1975 "Looking for an Aggregate Additive Model in Data from a Hierarchical Decision Process." In *Formal Methods in Economic Anthropology*, edited by S. Plattner. Washington, D.C.: A Special Publication of the American Anthropological Association, no. 4.

Gladwin, Hugh, & Michael Murtaugh

1984 "Test of a Hierarchical Model of Auto Choice on Data from the National Transportation Survey." *Human Organization* 43(3): 217–26.

Harris, Marvin

1979 *Cultural Materialism*. New York: Vintage Books.

Harris, Marvin, & Eric Ross

1978 "The Origins of the U.S. Preference for Beef." *Psychology Today*, October, pp. 88–94.

Hart, Keith

1982 *The Political Economy of West African Agriculture*. Cambridge: Cambridge University Press.

Haugerud, Angelique

1984 "Household Dynamics and Rural Political Economy Among Embu Farmers in the Kenya Highlands." Ph.D. dissertation, Northwestern University.

Hayami, Yujiro

1978 *Anatomy of a Peasant Economy: A Rice Village in the Philippines*. Los Banos, Laguna, the Philippines: The International Rice Research Institute.

Herskovits, Melville

1952 *Economic Anthropology: The Economic Life of Primitive Peoples*. New York: Norton.

Hildebrand, Peter E.

1981 "Combining Disciplines in Rapid Appraisal: The Sondeo Approach." *Agricultural Administration* 8: 423–32.

Hill, Polly

1963 *Migrant Cocoa-Farmers of Southern Ghana*. Cambridge: Cambridge University Press.

1970 *Studies in Rural Capitalism in West Africa*. Cambridge: Cambridge University Press.

1972 *Rural Hausa—A Village and a Setting*. London: Cambridge University Press.

Hoben, Allen

1980 "Agricultural Decision Making in Foreign Assistance: An Anthropological Analysis." In *Agricultural Decision Making*, edited by Peggy Barlett. New York: Academic Press.

Houthakker, Hendrick S.
1967 *Economic Policy for the Farm Sector*. Washington, D.C.: American Enterprise Institute for Public Policy Research.
Huffman, Wallace
1976 "The Value of Productive Time of Farm Wives: Iowa, N. Carolina and Oklahoma." *American Journal of Agricultural Economics* 58.
Huffman, Wallace, & Mark Lange
1983 *Off-Farm and Farm Work Decisions of Married Farm Males and Females*. Mimeo. Ames: Iowa State University.
Hyden, Goran
1980 *Beyond Ujamaa in Tanzania: Underdevelopment and an Uncaptured Peasantry*. Berkeley: University of California Press.
Johnson, Allen W.
1974 "Ethnoecology and Planting Practices in a Swidden Agricultural System." *American Ethnologist* 1: 87–101.
Johnston, Bruce F.
1958 *The Staple Food Economies of Western Tropical Africa*. Stanford: Stanford University Press.
1966 "Agriculture and Economic Development: The Relevance of the Japanese Experience." *Food Research Institute Studies* 6(3): 283–303.
1986 "Agricultural Development in Tropical Africa: The Search for Viable Strategies." In *Strategies for African Development*, edited by Robert J. Berg and Jennifer Whitaker. Berkeley: University of California Press.
Johnston, Bruce, & Peter Kilby
1975 *Agriculture and Structural Transformation*. New York: Oxford University Press.
Jones, Christine
1983 "The Mobilization of Women's Labor for Cash Crop Production: A Game Theoretic Approach." *American Journal of Agricultural Economics* 65(5): 1049–54.
Jones, William O.
1972 *Marketing Staple Food Crops in Tropical Africa*. Ithaca, N.Y.: Cornell University Press.
Lave, Jean, Alex Stepick, & Lee Sailor
1977 "Extending the Scope of Formal Analysis: A Technique For Integrating Analysis of Kinship Relations with Analysis of Other Dyadic Relations." *American Ethnologist* 4(2): 321–38.
Margolis, Maxine
1984 *Mothers and Such*. Berkeley: University of California Press.
McCloskey, Donald
1985 *The Rhetoric of Economics*. Madison: University of Wisconsin Press.
Meillassoux, Claude
1978 "Kinship Relations and Relations of Production." In *Relations of Production: Marxist Approaches to Economic Anthropology*, edited by D. Seddon. London: Frank Cass and Co.
Mincer, Jacob
1962 "Labor Force Participation of Married Women." In *Aspects of Labor Economics*, edited by National Bureau Committee for Economic Research. Princeton: Princeton University Press.

Moran, Emilio F.
  1979 *Human Adaptability: An Introduction to Ecological Anthropology.* North Scituate, R.I.: Duxbury.
Moscardi, Edgardo R.
  1979 "Methodology to Study Attitudes Toward Risk: The Puebla Project." In *Economics and the Design of Small-Farmer Technology,* edited by A. Valdes, G. Scobie, and J. Dillon. Ames: Iowa State University Press.
Moscardi, Edgardo, & Alain deJanvry
  1977 "Attitudes Toward Risk Among Peasants: An Econometric Approach." *American Journal of Agricultural Economics* 59(4): 710–16.
Mukhopadhyay, Carol
  1984 "Testing a Decision Process Model of the Sexual Division of Labor in the Family." *Human Organization* 43: 227–42.
Murdock, George
  1967 "Ethnographic Atlas." *Ethnology* 9: 122–225.
Murdock, George, & Douglas White
  1969 "Standard Cross-Cultural Sample." *Ethnology* 8: 329–69.
Nerlove, Mark
  1974 "Household and Economy: Toward a New Theory of Population and Economic Growth." *Journal of Political Economy* 82: 200–218.
Norman, David, Emmy Simmons, & Henry Hays
  1982 *Farming Systems in the Nigerian Savanna.* Boulder, Colo.: Westview.
Plattner, Stuart
  1975 "The Economics of Peddling." In *Formal Methods in Economic Anthropology,* edited by S. Plattner. Washington, D.C.: American Anthropological Association.
  1984 "Economic Decision Making of Marketplace Merchants: An Ethnographic Model." *Human Organization* 43(3): 252–64.
Sacks, Karen
  1979 *Sisters and Wives.* Urbana: University of Illinois Press.
Sahlins, Marshall, & Elman Service
  1960 *Evolution and Culture.* Ann Arbor: University of Michigan Press.
Schoepfle, Mark, Michael Burton, & Frank Morgan
  1984 "Navajos and Energy Development: Economic Decision Making Under Political Uncertainty." *Human Organization* 43(3): 265–76.
Schultz, Theodore W.
  1953 *Economic Organization of Agriculture.* New York: McGraw-Hill.
Shapiro, Kenneth H.
  1975 "Measuring Modernization Among Tanzanian Farmers: A New Methodology and an Illustration." In *Formal Methods in Economic Anthropology,* edited by S. Plattner. Washington, D.C.: American Anthropological Association.
Shepard, R. N., A. K. Romney, & S. Nerlove
  1972 *Multidimensional Scaling: Theory and Applications in the Behavioral Sciences.* New York: Seminar Press.
Smith, Carol
  1975 "Production in Western Guatemala: A Test of Von Thunen and Boserup." In *Formal Methods in Economic Anthropology,* edited by S. Plattner. Washington, D.C.: American Anthropological Association.
  1976 "Causes and Consequences of Central-Place Types in Western Guate-

mala." In *Regional Analysis: Economic Systems*, vol. 1, edited by C. A. Smith. New York: Academic Press.

1978 "Beyond Dependency Theory: National and Regional Patterns of Underdevelopment in Guatemala." *American Ethnologist* 5(3): 574–617.

Spradley, James P.
1970 *You Owe Yourself a Drunk*. Boston: Little, Brown.
1979 *The Ethnographic Interview*. New York: Holt, Rinehart & Winston.

Spring, Anita
1983 "Women and Agricultural Development in Malawi." Paper prepared for the International Congress of Anthropological and Ethnological Sciences, Vancouver, B.C., Aug. 20.

Tax, Sol
1953 *Penny Capitalism: A Guatemalan Indian Community*. Washington, D.C.: Smithsonian Institute of Social Anthropology, no. 16.

Timmer, C. Peter
1974 "A Model of Rice Marketing Margins in Indonesia." *Food Research Institute Studies* 13(2): 145–67.

Timmer, C. Peter, Walter Falcon, & Scott Pearson
1983 *Food Policy Analysis*. Washington, D.C.: World Bank.

Tversky, Amos
1972 "Elimination by Aspects: A Theory of Choice." *Psychological Review* 79: 281–99.

Tweeten, Luther
1983 "The Economics of Small Farms." *Science* 219: 1037–41.

Villa Issa, Manuel
1976 "The Effect of the Labor Market in the Adoption of New Production Technology in a Rural Development Project. The Case of Plan Puebla, Mexico." Ph.D. thesis. W. Lafayette, Ind.: Purdue University.

Young, James C.
1980 "A Model of Illness Treatment Decisions in a Tarascan Town." *American Ethnologist* 7(1): 106–31.
1981 *Medical Choice in a Mexican Village*. New Brunswick, N.J.: Rutgers University Press.

Zabawa, Robert
1984 "The Transformation of Farming in Gadsden County, North Florida." Ph.D. dissertation, Northwestern University.
1987 "Macro-Micro Linkages and Structural Transformation: The Move From Full-Time to Part-Time Farming in a North Florida Agricultural Community." *American Anthropologist* 89(2): 366–82.

Zulauf, Carl R.
1986 "Changes in Selected Characteristics of U.S. Farms During the 1970s and Early 1980s: An Investigation Based on Current and Constant Dollar Sales Categories." *Southern Journal of Agricultural Economics* 18(1): 113–22.

Index

Library of Congress Cataloging-in-Publication Data

Economic anthropology / edited, with an introduction, by Stuart Plattner.
p.   cm.
Bibliography: p.
Includes index.
ISBN 0-8047-1645-5 (alk. paper) — ISBN 0-8047-1752-4 (pbk.)
1. Economic anthropology.   I. Plattner, Stuart.
GN448.E26   1989
306.3—dc 20   89-4547
                                                         CIP